# CONTENT AREA READING AND WRITING

## *Fostering Literacies in Middle and High School Cultures*

## Norman Unrau

*California State University, Los Angeles*

PEARSON

Merrill
Prentice Hall

Upper Saddle River, New Jersey
Columbus, Ohio

**Library of Congress Cataloging-in-Publication Data**

Unrau, Norman.
    Content area reading and writing: fostering literacies in middle and high school cultures/
Norman Unrau.
      p. cm.
    Includes bibliographical references and index.
    ISBN 0-13-018455-1
    1. Language arts (Secondary)—United States. 2. Language arts—Correlation with content
subjects—United States. I. Title.

LB1631.U57 2004
428' .0071' 2—dc21

2002044469

**Vice President and Executive Publisher:** Jeffery W. Johnston
**Editor:** Linda Ashe Montgomery
**Development Editor:** Hope Madden
**Production Editor:** Mary M. Irvin
**Design Coordinator:** Diane C. Lorenzo
**Text Design and Production Coordination:** Amy Gehl, Carlisle Publishers Services
**Cover Designer:** Rod Harris
**Cover Photo:** SuperStock
**Production Manager:** Pamela D. Bennett
**Photo Coordinator:** Cynthia Cassidy
**Director of Marketing:** Ann Castel Davis
**Marketing Manager:** Darcy Betts Prybella
**Marketing Coordinator:** Tyra Poole

This book was set in Garamond by Carlisle Communications, Ltd., and was printed and bound by Courier
Kendallville, Inc. The cover was printed by Phoenix Color Corp.

**Photo Credits:** Barbara Schwartz/Merrill, p. 2; Tom Watson/Merrill, pp. 30, 361, 416; Terry Fincher/Getty Images
Inc.–Hulton Archive Photos, p. 36; Anne Vega/Merrill, pp. 56, 132, 233, 302, 380; Scott Cunningham/Merrill, pp. 80,
147, 170, 204; Anthony Magnacca/Merrill, pp. 110, 178, 248, 266, 327, 346, 435; Rob Gage/Getty Images, Inc.–Taxi,
p. 274; David Young-Wolff/PhotoEdit, p. 310; Daemmrich/Stock Boston, p. 401.

10 9 8 7 6 5 4 3 2
ISBN 0-13-018455-1

# PREFACE

## HOW CAN TODAY'S CONTENT AREA TEACHERS FACILITATE THEIR STUDENTS' LEARNING, LITERACY DEVELOPMENT, AND ENGAGEMENT IN LEARNING?

At the beginning of the school year, Ms. Wakefield asked her tenth-grade world history class to read a section of their textbook about classical Greek art and draw a diagram representing its content. Carlos, always drawing something, read the section with fascination, understood it in detail, and did a splendid job of representing it graphically. He knew a lot about art and could use what he knew to construct further knowledge. In contrast, Jaime struggled from sentence to sentence, making little sense of the three pages he read, paid little attention to his confusion, and wrote a few unconnected words in a circle. Knowing little about art, Jaime found the section "full of hard words." *Discovering Jaime's struggles, Ms. Wakefield knew she would have to learn more about her struggling student and find ways to support his literacy and learning.*

Teachers, like those you know and others you will meet in this book, work in middle and high schools every day to help their students acquire literacy strategies that make text materials accessible and promote learning in their content area classrooms. Some teachers approach this task with a strong understanding of reading and writing processes. Others know how to discover their students' literacy strengths and needs. Many have a multitude of strategies to teach their students at all levels to become more effective readers, writers, and learners. Some have discovered ways to heighten their students' engagement in learning. Yet others collaborate with colleagues and reflect on their practice so that content area instruction and literacy both improve. *When more teachers in our middle and high schools engage their students in learning with literacy's tools, more students will gain content knowledge and skills while acquiring strategies for lifelong learning.*

# What Are This Book's Purposes?

## Understanding Culture's Effects

Helping beginning teachers understand how cultures shape language, literacy, and learning is one main purpose for this book. Every community, whether family, ethnicity, school, or peer group-related, has a culture. This culture shares traditions, rules, ethics, values, and a social order, through which it shapes minds. When teachers understand how cultures merge and emerge in school settings, they can better understand how cultures contribute to students' literacy development. Teachers can also grasp how they contribute to culture creation and literacy growth in their own classrooms.

## Understanding the Reading Process

Reading is fundamental to every student's learning in the content areas, and helping teachers understand the reading process forms a fundamental purpose for this book. The model of reading presented shows teachers how their students read, what contributes to good reading, and how reading for learning may falter. Knowing where reading may break down and how to detect those breakdowns enables teachers to see what steps they can take to improve reading and learning for all students.

## Developing Literacy Strategies

To develop student reading, writing, and learning skills, content area teachers can apply research-based strategies. Another purpose for this book is to present literacy-enhancing strategies to integrate with daily instruction and to use with small groups and whole classrooms. These strategies will promote literacy and learning when teachers work with an entire class, provide opportunities for cooperative learning in small groups, or arrange for pairs of students to collaborate. While critical reading strategies explained in this book develop students' reasoning and thinking skills, writing strategies help teachers observe, evaluate, and promote their students' learning.

## Exploring Student Engagement and Motivation

Disengaged, unmotivated students who rarely complete reading or any other homework assignment often puzzle beginning teachers in every content area. They are not only perplexed but also dismayed by the disengagement. Thus, another purpose for this book is to help you understand what factors affect literacy engagement and what you can do to heighten it.

## Fitting It All In

New teachers often wonder how they can possibly fit all they have learned about teaching, including strategies to enhance literacy for all students, into their instructional day. Addressing state standards, where they apply, has contributed to many beginning teachers' bewilderment. This book was designed to help you align state standards with instruction and assessment practices in your content area classrooms.

## Reflecting and Collaborating for Professional Growth

Finally, teachers must help each other teach and learn to reflect on teaching. Those goals for teacher collaboration and reflection guided this book's creation. Several methods for growing collaborative, reflective cultures in your classrooms and schools appear in this book along with examples of teachers who have taken that path.

## HOW IS THIS BOOK ORGANIZED?

Chapter 1 shows how cultures shape the minds of middle and high school students; explores the influence of culture on students' school, community, and personal literacies; identifies the challenges of literacy development and learning in classroom communities; and reviews research-based practices and resources for teachers to meet those challenges, especially in schools and classrooms with struggling readers and disengaged learners.

Chapter 2 looks inside a reader's meaning construction zone to gain a better understanding of how a student reads and negotiates meanings in classroom contexts. In fact, the model of reading may serve as a model for cognition, skill acquisition, and problem solving in general. What follows as instructional recommendations in subsequent chapters is rooted in that model of reading.

Chapter 3 provides a step-by-step approach to diagnostic teaching. Building on the model of reading presented in Chapter 2, this chapter introduces you to a range of formal and informal methods to assess students' reading as represented in the model, shows you how to assess your own content area students, and provides methods for evaluating texts used in your instructional program.

Chapter 4 focuses on vocabulary, its connection with word recognition in the model of reading, and methods you can use to help your students learn unfamiliar words, including those that help them build a bridge to competence in your instructional field and those related to it.

Chapters 5, 6, and 7 offer a wide range of strategies you can teach students to develop their reading comprehension, methods to link collaborative classroom activity with literacy growth, and procedures to enhance your students' critical reading of texts and the cultures from which they arise.

Chapter 8 explores how you can use writing to assess, promote, and observe your students' learning. It includes methods for examining student work so that you can make decisions to improve student performance. You can then extend their understanding of concepts and their application to your field.

Chapter 9 addresses instructional programs and strategies for struggling readers and English learners.

Chapter 10 focuses on student engagement with reading and learning, examining dimensions of motivation that affect engagement and providing you with suggestions for deepening student engagement in your classrooms.

Chapter 11 shows you how literacy-enhancing strategies presented in earlier chapters can be integrated into lesson, unit, and yearlong planning for differentiated instruction. It demonstrates how state standards or learning goals, integrated strategy instruction, and assessment can be aligned. The chapter also presents ways to identify central concepts you want all students, even in highly diverse classrooms, to master and methods to develop criteria and rubrics with students to measure the degree to which they have mastered those concepts. These methods are designed to help students grasp how they are progressing and to see clearly what next steps they need to take to approach targets demonstrating mastery.

Finally, Chapter 12 focuses on teacher-to-teacher connections that foster literacy and reflective practice. It presents several approaches for teachers to look deeper into classroom teaching and learning and to move toward more collaborative cultures within schools that, through teachers' growth, contribute to students' literacies and learning.

## WHAT SPECIAL FEATURES FACILITATE THIS TEXT'S EFFECTIVENESS?

- *Purpose-setting Questions* at the beginning of each chapter to guide reading and frame inquiry.
- *Double-Entry Journal* prompt at the beginning and end of each chapter to heighten reader's engagement and to encourage the integration of new knowledge.
- *Graphic Summaries* at the end of each chapter to capture essential features and interconnections.
- *Step-by-Step "How To"* format with hints to execute strategies to effectively facilitate learning.
- Some chapters include *Activity Boxes, Teacher Tips,* and *Diagnostic Peepholes* to help teachers envision how well their students are reading by using formal or informal assessment instruments.

## ACKNOWLEDGMENTS

Many people contributed to the emergence of this book. First, I taught high school for 25 years and discovered by degrees enormous ranges in my students' capacities to read, write, and learn. Those discoveries drove me to provide support and invent tools that would help students at all levels, especially those striving to improve their chances to get into college and do well there. These high school students also sharpened my appreciation for the meaning and pleasure of a vital classroom and for the tools of literacy in building classroom communities. Second, I've taught hundreds of credential candidates in a course focused on literacy and learning at California State University, Los Angeles. Those candidates also taught me. From them I learned how deep and wide the struggle to address literacy while covering content was and how much they needed tools to engage in the struggle. Third, I worked for four years as a University Coach at Nightingale Middle School in Los Angeles, a school with over

2,000 students. I focused my coaching on literacy. Classrooms of energetic, inquisitive students, too many of whom struggled to understand texts of any kind, focused my attention on literacy development. Fourth, I served as editor of the *Journal of Adolescent and Adult Literacy* and saw how hundreds of teachers and researchers in the United States and in countries all over the world worked to help people young and old acquire literacy and a better life. From all these forces, I absorbed and guided energy into this book's creation. To all these students and teachers, my thanks.

As if that weren't enough, I also had the good fortune of working for several years with Dr. Robert Ruddell, now Professor Emeritus from the University of California, Berkeley, who, as an exceptionally influential teacher, offered advice on countless issues and opportunities to grow as a teacher and writer. In addition, I work with dedicated colleagues in the Charter College of Education at California State University, Los Angeles, who want to improve teaching and learning in every way and who provided me with ideas, encouragement, resources, and responses to chapters. I'd like to especially recognize Bob Land, Cheri Hawley, Judy Washburn, Julie Quinn, Carolyn Frank, Al Crawford, Nancy Hunt, Martin Brodwin, Diane Haager, Lupe Cadenas, and Andrea Maxie.

As for the publication of this book, I want to applaud the initiating powers of Linda Montgomery at Merrill/Prentice Hall and the text-shaping guidance of my development editor, Hope Madden, who mused me from chapter to chapter, deadline to deadline. The responses and recommendations of many manuscript reviewers contributed much to the mill of mulling over what to cover and how to cover it well. For their insights and comments, my thanks to each of the following reviewers: Priscilla Kurchinski, Colorado Christian University; Candace Poindexter, Loyola Marymount University; Kouider Mokhtari, Oklahoma State University; Dennise Bartelo, Plymouth State College; Edith Norris, West Texas A&M University; Nancy Bailey, Metropolitan State College of Denver; Janis M. Harmon, University of Texas at San Antonio; James E. McGlinn, University of North Carolina at Asheville; and Hazel Brauer, University of San Francisco. Many others provided guidance and support during production, including Mary Irvin, Becky Savage, Cynthia Cassidy, and at Carlisle Communications, Amy Gehl and Keri Miksza.

In closing, I dedicate this book to my wife Cherene and daughter Amy, who went through high school while I wrote. Cherene listened and responded to years of progress reports on chapter development, setbacks, and rewrites. If I am the ink, she is the paper.

*Norman Unrau*

# THE EASIEST WAY TO ENHANCE YOUR COURSE
## Proven Journals • Proven Strategies • Proven Media

## www.EducatorLearningCenter.com

Merrill Education is pleased to announce a new partnership with ASCD. The result of this partnership is a joint website, www.EducatorLearningCenter.com, with recent articles and cutting-edge teaching strategies. The Educator Learning Center combines the resources of the Association for Supervision and Curriculum Development (ASCD) and Merrill Education. At www.EducatorLearningCenter.com you will find resources that will enhance your students' understanding of course topics and of current educational issues, in addition to being invaluable for further research.

## How will Educator Learning Center help your students become better teachers?

- 600+ articles from the ASCD journal *Educational Leadership* discuss everyday issues faced by practicing teachers.
- Hundreds of lesson plans and teaching strategies are categorized by content area and age range.
- Excerpts from Merrill Education texts give your students insight on important topics of instructional methods, diverse populations, assessment, classroom management, technology, and refining practice.
- Case studies, classroom video, electronic tools, and computer simulations keep your students abreast of today's classrooms and current technologies.
- A direct link on the site to Research Navigator™, where your students will have access to many of the leading education journals as well as extensive content detailing the research process.

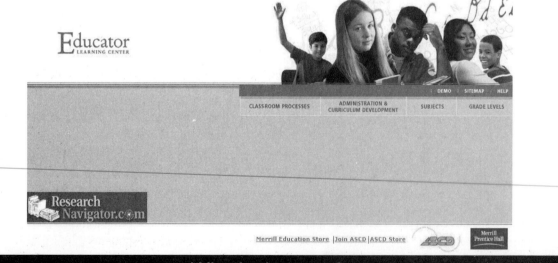

## What's the cost?

A four-month subscription to Educator Learning Center is $25 but is **FREE** when used in conjunction with this text. To obtain free passcodes for your students, simply contact your local Merrill/Prentice Hall sales representative, and your representative will give you a special ISBN to give your bookstore when ordering your textbooks. To preview the value of this website to you and your students, please go to www.EducatorLearningCenter.com and click on "Demo."

# Discover the Companion Website Accompanying This Book

## The Prentice Hall Companion Website: A Virtual Learning Environment

Technology is a constantly growing and changing aspect of our field that is creating a need for content and resources. To address this emerging need, Prentice Hall has developed an online learning environment for students and professors alike—Companion Websites—to support our textbooks.

In creating a Companion Website, our goal is to build on and enhance what the textbook already offers. For this reason, the content for each user-friendly website is organized by chapter and provides the professor and student with a variety of meaningful resources.

## For the Professor—

Every Companion Website integrates **Syllabus Manager**™, an online syllabus creation and management utility.

- **Syllabus Manager**™ provides you, the instructor, with an easy, step-by-step process to create and revise syllabi, with direct links into Companion Website and other online content without having to learn HTML.
- Students may logon to your syllabus during any study session. All they need to know is the web address for the Companion Website and the password you've assigned to your syllabus.
- After you have created a syllabus using **Syllabus Manager**™, students may enter the syllabus for their course section from any point in the Companion Website.
- Clicking on a date, the student is shown the list of activities for the assignment. The activities for each assignment are linked directly to actual content, saving time for students.
- Adding assignments consists of clicking on the desired due date, then filling in the details of the assignment—name of the assignment, instructions, and whether or not it is a one-time or repeating assignment.
- In addition, links to other activities can be created easily. If the activity is online, a URL can be entered in the space provided, and it will be linked automatically in the final syllabus.

♦ Your completed syllabus is hosted on our servers, allowing convenient updates from any computer on the Internet. Changes you make to your syllabus are immediately available to your students at their next logon.

## For the Student—

Common Companion Website features for students include:

♦ **Chapter Objectives**—Outline key concepts from the text.
♦ **Interactive Self-quizzes**—Complete with hints and automatic grading that provide immediate feedback for students. After students submit their answers for the interactive self-quizzes, the Companion Website **Results Reporter** computes a percentage grade, provides a graphic representation of how many questions were answered correctly and incorrectly, and gives a question-by-question analysis of the quiz. Students are given the option to send their quiz to up to four email addresses (professor, teaching assistant, study partner, etc.).
♦ **Web Destinations**—Links to www sites that relate to chapter content.
♦ **Message Board**—Virtual bulletin board to post or respond to questions or comments from a national audience.

To take advantage of the many available resources, please visit the *Content Area Reading and Writing* Companion Website at

**www.prenhall.com/unrau**

# CONTENTS

# 4 VOCABULARY AND CONCEPT DEVELOPMENT IN THE CONTENT AREAS  132

## 5   STRATEGIES TO ENHANCE COMPREHENSION   170

# 8 WRITING TO ASSESS, PROMOTE, AND OBSERVE LEARNING    274

# 9 STRUGGLING READERS AND ENGLISH LEARNERS: ADDRESSING THEIR COGNITIVE AND CULTURAL NEEDS    310

## 10  FOCUSING ON MOTIVATION TO READ CONTENT AREA TEXTS  346

## 11  DESIGNING LITERACY INTO ACADEMICALLY DIVERSE CONTENT AREA CLASSES: ALIGNING STANDARDS WITH STRATEGIES AND ASSESSMENTS  380

# 12 TEACHER TO TEACHER: FOSTERING LITERACY AND REFLECTIVE PRACTICE    416

**Note:** Every effort has been made to provide accurate and current Internet information in this book. However, the Internet and information posted on it are constantly changing, so it is inevitable that some of the Internet addresses listed in this textbook will change.

# About the Author

Norman Unrau is a Professor at California State University, Los Angeles, in the Division of Curriculum and Instruction, where he teaches a course to beginning teachers that addresses literacy and learning in content classrooms. He also serves as Coordinator of the MA in Education with a focus on middle and high school curriculum and instruction and facilitates MA candidates' pursuit of certification by the National Board for Professional Teaching Standards. He served as editor of the *Journal of Adolescent and Adult Literacy,* a publication of the International Reading Association for educators interested in the development of students' reading and writing. He is also co-editing the fifth edition of *Theoretical Models and Processes of Reading,* a text widely used to help educators understand the scope and depth of research on reading. For several years he served as a University Coach to develop literacy and learning in a large urban middle school in the Los Angeles Unified School District.

Dr. Unrau completed his master's degree at Columbia University's Teachers College. After teaching in Brooklyn and Vermont, he taught English and psychology in a San Francisco Bay area high school district. His teaching engagement in that district continued fruitfully for about 25 years, toward the end of which he began a doctoral program in education at the University of California, Berkeley. His work at Berkeley focused on cognition in reading and writing, an area that has long fascinated him.

Dr. Unrau previously wrote *Thoughtful Teachers, Thoughtful Learners: A Guide to Helping Adolescents Think Critically* (1997). That book, also translated into Russian, has been used in the Reading and Writing for Critical Thinking project in countries formerly part of the Soviet Union. He has also published several articles on reading, writing, critical thinking, assessment, motivation, and models of literacy processes that have appeared in the *Journal of Adolescent and Adult Literacy, Teacher Education Quarterly,* and other professional journals.

# 1 ENGAGING CULTURES AND LITERACIES FOR LEARNING

After reading Chapter 1, you should be able to answer the following questions:

1. How do cultures shape minds?
2. What cultures affect middle and high school students?
3. What literacies influence students' thinking and behavior in and out of school?
4. Where is our adolescent literacy crisis rooted?
5. How can teachers respond to literacy and learning challenges in their content area classrooms?

**DOUBLE-ENTRY JOURNAL:**
Before Reading

Now go to the Double-Entry Journal for Chapter 1 on our Companion Website at www.prenhall.com/unrau to fill out your journal entry.

*Before beginning to read this chapter, I would like you to try a comprehension strategy. You can complete the first phase of a strategy called the Double-Entry Journal (DEJ) by writing about 200 words in response to the "Before Reading" prompt just below. After reading the chapter, I'll ask you to complete a second journal entry to complement your first entry.*

To what cultures did you belong while in high school? For cultures, you could consider but not limit yourself to these: family, community, ethnic, school, classroom, teen, and any other sub-cultures. Looking back, which culture(s) seemed to influence you most? Why do you think that was the case? Create headings for each of the cultures of which you were a part and list the kinds of influences they had on you and your behavior. Put a star next to those cultures that had the strongest effects. After creating this matrix of cultures and their effects, write about the kinds of effects those cultures had on your use of language both in school and out.

## BEGINNING TEACHERS REMEMBER THEIR HIGH SCHOOL CULTURES AND LITERACIES

To help beginning teachers connect with the power and complexity of cultures and literacies that shape our schools, communities, and selves, I ask teachers in my credential program course to reflect on their past high school days and to write a brief memoir about those days. I ask them to describe the cultures to which they belonged and the literacies they practiced during high school. Through these memoirs I get to know my students, and they get in touch with aspects of their past that may influence their future as teachers. The range of response varies dramatically. I've selected three of these very brief memoirs to give you an idea of how beginning middle or high school teachers remember the cultures and literacies that affected them. The first, Yvette Bess, was a head cheerleader while attending a public high school. The second, Paul Perez, attended a Catholic boarding school and seminary. The third, Cindy Thai, came to America from China as a young girl but was fluent in English when she began high school. As you have guessed, I selected them because they each had very different cultural and literacy experiences.

### Looking Back (*by Yvette Bess*)

Looking back to my high school days seems almost like another life now, a life where finding out where the parties were going to be that weekend, who was dating who, and what I should wear tomorrow seemed to be my biggest dilemmas. Don't get me wrong. Academics were important, especially since I was head of the cheerleading squad and, if you did not maintain a certain GPA, you would be expelled from the squad. High school was a time in my life when I did not think for myself. My friends told me what to do, when to do it, and how. I was always trying to fit in with them.

The problem was that I was not the real me. . . . I did my own homework, unlike my friends who would just ask others wishing to be popular to do their homework for them. They would tease me and call me "bookworm," but I took it as a compliment. . . . There was a lot of pressure to fit in and be popular. We reigned for almost two and a half years as the "in crowd," and I can say it was pretty cool!

All of my friends were Hispanic, but none of us knew how to speak Spanish. Most of our language context consisted of: "Like I totally hate him" or "Oh–My–God! Did you see what she is wearing?" The words "like" and "totally" were essential in every other sentence. Since all my friends were in regular education classes and I was in college prep classes, I was able to escape in the classroom and be someone different than I was on campus. I loved speech and debate class, chemistry, and literature. Teachers never seem to expect much from cheerleaders and jocks, so it was easy to just use my friend the thesaurus and a few deep thoughts to impress my teachers. I definitely was not challenged in high school nor did I ask to be. I did "A" and "B" work knowing that I could do better. . . . I look back at the few teachers who challenged me, and I really thank them now. I was a total bookworm in junior high, but during high school, I no longer had time to read for fun. I limited myself to the required reading and would skim through it at best.

High school was filled with good memories. I really enjoyed the social aspect. . . . It made me more outgoing and companionable. As for my academic endeavors, well, high school did not prepare me for college.

## A Very Brief Memoir (*by Paul Perez*)

My high school was part of a unique culture in that it was a boarding school and a Catholic seminary. The influence of the Latino family culture was minor during that time because I lived at school, but seminarians with a similar background did engage in playful insults and jokes in Spanish. Being that St. Vincent's Seminary was a boarding school, I was more influenced culturally by the Catholic lifestyle imposed by the faculty and by the culture of my peers. Among my peers, class year, music, fashion, sports, hobbies, and popularity divided the cultures that existed. Since I did not play sports or belong to any clubs during my first year, I belonged to the "class year" culture and these were freshmen.

During the middle of my sophomore year, I began to fall into a culture where music played a dominant role. I used to listen to a style of music that was called New Wave. This music was played with synthesized instruments, and many of the bands were from England. I also enjoyed rock 'n' roll music from the 1960s and 1970s. It was also during this time that I began playing bass guitar in the band that played for our chapel services and masses. These influences caused a shift in my culture. I began dressing in a mixture of trendy and eccentric clothes, and my close friends were the musicians and those students that had similar interests. I remained in this "artsy and weird" type of culture until I graduated.

The community literacy that existed at St. Vincent's was a spiritual one. The seminarians had several blocks in our daily schedule where we would engage in spiritual exercises, religious celebrations, and retreats. During this time the students interacted with the priests and the religious, and this fostered a community where Christian brotherhood was important.

This time of my life definitely influenced how I've lived the ensuing years. The Christian teachings allowed me to retain a lifestyle that emphasizes fairness, acceptance, and spirituality. Even though I am not so religious, I've tried to maintain a

Christian lifestyle. The musical side has remained in me since I've pursued music as a career. It also played a role in my personality. I believe that my love of the music of the late 1960s and its messages of love of nature and individuality have remained with me even though some of my musical tastes have changed.

## Moving Between Two Cultures (*by Cindy Thai*)

High school was an interesting four-year experience. . . . As first generation Americans in our family, my brother and I adapted fairly well in high school. My family and I immigrated to the United States from China. I was two years old then. I attended public school and assimilated into an American. However, our family dinners did not consist of discussions about current affairs in the newspaper or how my day was at school. My parents talked mostly about their business. Looking back now, I wish I were more involved with the events of the nation at the time. I was, however, very Americanized and thus made it through high school without experiencing any culture shock. I was an average student in high school. But, thinking back now, I feel I was an underachiever with regards to my grades. My parents did not have the time or the capabilities to assist me with my schoolwork. My mother stressed the importance of continuing on to college but did not demand it of me. My father wanted my brother and me to skip college altogether. My father never saw the importance of an education. He wished for us to learn his trade and take over the family business after high school. My family culture was most influential during my high school years.

The school literacy I practiced in high school was English. I was already fluent in English by the time I reached high school. My social skills were fairly good, and I had my share of friends. When I was in high school, computers were not as abundant as they are now. Therefore, my computer literacy was not very good. As for my community literacy, I spoke English at school as well as to my friends. However, I spoke both English and Cantonese when I was at home. I saw myself as an American during my high school years. The Chinese culture that my parents practiced was overwhelmed by the powers of our assimilation into this country. In hindsight, I have come to realize that it was somewhat of a struggle for me to accommodate both cultures.

My perspectives on life now are quite different than they were then. And besides the age factor, I do acknowledge that I was fighting the two different cultures that were thrust upon me. The cultures and literacies of my high school years are a big part of who I am today. I have grown and matured as a result of my experiences during high school.

Cindy's being caught between cultures demonstrates struggles that almost all American teenagers experience as they progress through middle and high school on their way to adulthood. While her struggle may have been more intense because of the differences between her family's culture and that of her new country, teenagers are frequently pulled and pushed in different cultural directions as they struggle to define themselves, their values, and their purposes. Because cultures and languages are intimately related, Cindy's shifting from Chinese to English as her dominant language made up a significant element in her assimilation and emerging identity. But both Yvette in her persona as cheerleader and Paul as an emerging musician display in their memories of high school many of the cultural tensions that all students experience in our classrooms, school corridors, and communities.

In this chapter, we are going to explore the nature of culture and especially its connections with literacy. We'll begin by exploring the meaning of culture and how cultures shape minds, especially our students' minds and especially in our own classrooms. We'll explore various literacies, including those of the school students attend, the community in which they live, and the identities they have evolved. We'll then examine evidence to see if we're in the midst of an adolescent literacy crisis or a crisis of a different, perhaps more troubling kind. Finally, after looking at the literacy fostering practices of "beating the odds" teachers, we'll confront what is to be done to address the literacy and learning challenges we all find in our classrooms.

## How Do Cultures Shape Minds?

Cultures thrive everywhere. In concentration camps and battlefields, in equatorial jungles and arctic villages, cultures sustain. Get a group of people together, and they're going to start a culture. In Los Angeles, there's South Central's hip-hop culture; in Miami, a Cuban-American scene; in New York . . . well, in New York there's a cultural salad. We have mass culture, pop culture, youth culture, and culture wars. In his conception of culture, the renowned journalist Walter Lippmann (1913/1962) included "what people are interested in, . . . the books they read and the speeches they hear, their table-talk, gossip, controversies, . . . the quality of life they admire. All communities have a culture. It is the climate of their civilization." In schools and classrooms, the lives of teachers are inevitably immersed in cultures. But how well do we read and comprehend them?

## What Is Culture?

When we enter a culture, primitive or complex, we face a system, a "vast apparatus," noted anthropologist Bronislaw Malinowski (1944) called it, that is part material, part human, and part spiritual. That culture enables people to cope with a multitude of problems they must face to survive in an environment sometimes friendly, sometimes dangerous.

We might also view culture as a pattern or system of symbols and meanings that a group of people share. Through these shared meanings people communicate and perpetuate their knowledge of life and the attitudes they hold toward life (Geertz, 1973). Individuals holding these shared meanings and symbol systems interpret life experience through their own subjectivity. This notion of a cultural lens shaping experience is not a trivial one for teachers. Who our students take themselves to be and how they make meaning from their experiences are both shaped by culture. As teachers we, of course, try to interpret and make sense of them through our own cultural subjectivity.

## How Cultures Shape Minds

The influence of cultures on minds is by no means a new area of investigation. In the golden age of Greek civilization, Plato in his *Republic* expressed deep concern about how society shaped minds. In his description of the philosopher king for a utopian state, Plato focused on the influence of certain aspects of culture, such as an appropriate education for his philosopher king and even of the appropriateness of poetry in that educational program. But few people have paid as close attention to the ways in which culture becomes a part of each person's mind as did Lev Vygotsky, a Russian psychologist and author of *Mind in Society* (1978).

Among Vygotsky's (1978, 1986) many ideas, three will be of particular value in our efforts to understand the connections between culture and the development of minds. First, Vygotsky embraced the idea that only through understanding the historical and cultural contexts of each child's experiences can we ever understand an individual's intellectual or cognitive development. Relating back to the memoirs, only through knowing the context of Yvette's life, the communities in which she grew up, and the schools she attended, could we appreciate her mind's evolution. She developed in a specific historical and cultural context that shaped her mind in unique ways.

Second, Vygotsky believed that our individual development depends on signs that allow each of us to interact with others in our culture and to strive for self mastery. Signs, like those that make up language or our writing system, enable us to develop skills and higher mental functions. As children, Yvette, Paul, and Cindy all learned to speak English and applied their growing knowledge of language to the challenge of learning to read.

Third, Vygotsky believed that every step in a child's cultural development appeared twice: once on the social level as a process between people and secondly on the individual level as a process within each child. Interpersonal processes, like our use of language to communicate with each other, are transformed into intrapersonal ones, like our use of inner speech when we talk our way through to the solution of a complex problem. For example, I am explaining some of Vygotsky's key ideas to you (interpersonal process between you and me). You will internalize the language I've used and transform it into your own understanding of the ideas I've explained here. You could then carry on your own internal dialogue about Vygotsky's ideas, question them, look for evidence to confirm or challenge them, and perhaps even teach them to your students in language they would grasp. If you read about this two-stage concept of development but only experience the first stage and do not internalize it for your individual use, then it has not and cannot contribute to your development as a teacher.

What should be apparent to us is the great importance these notions of culture, language, and development have upon us as teachers attempting to understand the influence of culture. In sum, Vygotsky (1978, 1986) expressed the belief that we internalize our culture's sign systems. As we internalize these "sign systems," such as our culture's language, they function as a bridge that enables us to transform our behavior and our mental life. We become, as Elinor Ochs and Bambi Schieffelin (1984) have pointed out, competent members of our society largely through language and its acquisition.

On our way to competence, we often interact with and learn from others. To understand how that learning progresses, we should explore another of Vygotsky's ideas, the zone of proximal development (ZPD), which emphasizes the importance of the interactive, socially based nature of learning. The ZPD is the difference between what one can achieve alone and what one can achieve with the help of a more knowledgeable or capable person. Interactions between more and less able learners in the ZPD can enable the less knowledgeable partners to acquire information or skills to solve problems on their own that they could only have solved before with the help of their more able partners. As a result of educationally successful interactions between children and more able adults in the ZPD, children internalize culturally appropriate knowledge and behaviors that they can eventually demonstrate independent of their teachers. Cindy, who arrived in America from China, could not have learned English independently. She had to interact with those knowing more English than she knew. In Vygotsky's words, "An essential feature of learning is that it creates the zone of proximal development" (1978, p. 90). If we, as teachers, are not within that zone, our students are not learning those things that will awaken them to further development. If we are below that zone, students are likely to be bored because we are trying to teach what they already know. If we are above that zone, students are apt to be so frustrated they can't learn. The ZPD is where we as teachers must be for optimum learning to progress but where students who want to dodge engagement may not always want us.

Besides helping us understand culture's influence on learning, Vygotsky's ideas have had extensive influence on educators that will be reflected in many recommendations for literacy development throughout this textbook. Examples are everywhere, from effective student assessment practices to appropriate strategy instruction that enhances comprehension and understanding.

## SCHOOL CULTURES SHAPING STUDENTS' MINDS

While many cultural forces (a "dominant" American culture; a "pop" culture of film, television, and music; gender culture; and peer culture) shape our students' minds, school cultures are among the most powerful and problematic. School cultures are among the most powerful because of their effect on both students' knowledge base and their attitudes. School cultures are among the most problematic because they present students with many conflicts, including those between a growing personal identity and the pressures of conformity to a school's standards for conduct and learning.

### School Cultures

Teachers create an organizational culture in their schools after responding to their school environment in similar patterns over many years (Gruenert, 2000). The culture sets up expectations for teachers' behaviors and problem solving. While this culture doesn't affect student performance directly, it does so indirectly—somewhat like how a parent's personality affects a child's achievement—by providing a context for learning and a foundation for growth. Whether or not a school improves is dependent on its culture (Deal & Peterson, 1999).

School cultures have been categorized and labeled with terms that should tell us something about a school's readiness to support learning and embrace change. Vast differences accompany schools that are tense, fragmented, toxic, or contrived versus those that are collaborative, moving, organic, or responsive.

As first-year teachers reflect on their schools' cultures, we can learn a great deal about what they and each beginning teacher may experience. During their first year of teaching, five teachers who graduated from Harvard's Graduate School of Education met, discussed, and wrote about their experiences (Van der Bogert, Donaldson, & Poon, 1999). They responded to two questions: (a) How have you affected your school? (b) How has your school affected you? Summarized in the following section are their perceptions of the school cultures they found and tried to affect.

## Beginning Teachers Discover School Cultures

Kelly Klinefelter-Lee taught at a middle school in Chelsea, Massachusetts, about a mile or two north of downtown Boston. The student population was diverse with about a third of her students having English as a second language. Social issues of poverty surrounded her, but most difficult for her to digest was the school's response to its students. The school sought to standardize students with rules and test scores. While she believed in the importance of rules, she perceived "a culture of unwritten rules" that forced teachers to demand obedience through control. Her conflict with the school's ethos of control was exacerbated because she advocated student-centered instruction, such as cooperative learning, discussion, and student-led projects. Accustomed to authoritarian rule in the classroom, her students could not behave appropriately and took advantage of her methods. By not being able to have her students obey her commands, she felt that she had failed as a teacher and became isolated from her colleagues. In sum, the culture at the school exhausted her "spirit."

Brian Poon taught at Brookline High School in a middle class neighborhood a couple miles east of Boston. He approached his first year of teaching excited but scared. He strove to create classroom communities but found himself feeling that students took advantage of him at times. Although exhausted physically and mentally by November, he decided to bring change to the school community. His first target was the school cafeteria. Chunks of food and debris that littered the cafeteria after lunch and failed efforts to get students to patrol their own mess disgusted him. He started a "Change the Culture of the School Club" to get students interested in improving their environment. His plans for change were dashed by an overabundance of no-shows at every meeting. He, too, succumbed to the "culture of apathy" at the school. He, like Kelly Klinefelter-Lee, became isolated from his colleagues in a culture that sanctified the autonomy of the classroom. Following episodes of disrespect for teachers when they attempted to control the bullying of others at a basketball game or criticized inappropriate drinking on a bus bringing students to a prom, Brian retrenched to territory he could control: his classroom. There, as he put it, "the abstractions of book learning were steeped in the reality of everyday life." His ideal of teaching was "diverse folk learning from one another and taking a vested interest in their vital role in a community," but he never expected anything to touch that ideal. However, his ideal was touched when he pulled together a mock trial team that competed effectively. He discovered that, although he couldn't change the "big picture" at the high school, he could "carve out a piece and work with it." He modeled care where he could to "change the institution."

Allyson Mizoguchi, while teaching at a suburban high school in Wayland, Massachusetts, discovered that her students were obsessed with documented achievements that would pave the way to elite colleges. Grade grubbing talk drowned out questioning and learning. What she witnessed in her students she had herself pursued while a student in a suburban high school. Voiceless in high school, she found that her first year of teaching was her opportunity to find her voice. Being in the teacher seat gave her a perspective of education she had missed before, the determination to drop multiple-choice tests in favor of rubrics and portfolios, and the opportunity to discover that she didn't know how to teach her students to learn. While she was learning to learn, she was discovering how to teach her students to do the same. She found that questioning was at the center of learning. Driven from her comfort zone of right answers, she mustered the courage to move gradually into the zone of questioning. She began to take on a new self-image, that of advocate, debater, negotiator, and mediator, all labels she would have never used earlier to describe herself as a teacher. Still seeing her students shackled to SAT scores, GPAs, and multiple-choice exams, she strove to help them find a voice. Although she wondered if her emerging voice for change would ever be heard beyond her classroom walls, she found that teaching was about change within, change driven through self-discovery. And, while finding her own voice, she hoped to reach silent students and give them speech.

These first-year teachers made major discoveries about the school cultures they entered and about the effects they could have on those cultures. All experienced some degree of isolation. However, reflecting on their teaching with other teachers and writing about their dilemmas enabled them and us to see more clearly their challenges and responses to them. For these beginning teachers, collaboration held out hope for change. Collaborative school cultures that enable effective student and teacher learning can be nurtured through the study of a school's culture, the creation of structures for collaboration, the collection of data to assess school progress, and incentives for teacher cooperation (Gruenert, 2000).

## LINKS BETWEEN CULTURES AND LITERACIES

As Susanne Langer (1942) put it more than half a century ago when she described a new key to understanding how our minds work within cultures, "the edifice of human knowledge stands before us, not as a vast collection of sense reports, but as a structure of *facts that are symbols*." Our minds construct symbolic forms, like the words you are reading on this page. We communicate with them, and we build and maintain our cultures through them. These symbols contain both meaning and feeling, but neither the meanings they express nor the feelings they transmit are always obvious. The meaning and feelings of Beethoven's *Fifth Symphony* are ours to interpret, as is a Picasso painting, a Martha Graham dance, or a novel by Henry James.

As I demonstrate the connections between culture and literacy, as I ask you to shift your focus from one to the other, I want you to understand an assumption that I hope will permeate your reading of this entire book. That assumption is that we and our students read all kinds of texts, all manner of signs and symbols. As symbol makers and users, we are engulfed in them. They include not only the words you are now reading but all the signs and symbols that our minds interpret and generate, that make our world and make it meaningful. All these symbolic forms fostered by our cultures constitute a reservoir from which we can draw content for teaching. Whether words on a page, images on a screen, music in the air, or gestures on a stage, symbolic expression rings us round. One symbolic form, like a movie or singer's CD, may inform our understanding of another symbolic form, like a printed story in a student's anthology, an explanation of DNA replication, or a pattern in human history. We can draw upon and apply these symbolic representations of our cultures and literacies to promote our students' understanding and growth.

## What Is Literacy?

Words gain meanings through the ways we use them. When we ask ourselves what literacy means, we can turn to the ways we usually use the word. The primary meaning of literacy used to be *the ability to read*. Today the word literacy gets used in other ways to mean other things. Some of us use literacy as a term referring to our ability to read and to write as forms of cultural transmission. That's the common foundation for school-based concepts of literacy. However, it may be time to move beyond the false dichotomy of a person being literate or illiterate in terms of reading and writing and toward viewing individuals presenting a "literacy profile" composed on many literacies used in a variety of social contexts, including our classrooms.

Acknowledging that literacy and culture are inseparable, Judith Langer (1987) suggested broadening our conception of literacy to include ways of thinking and doing in cultural contexts. Literacies then are tools for getting things done in various cultures and contexts. When viewing literacy as a way of thinking, reasoning, and doing, math literacy becomes a special symbol system that enables a teacher and students to communicate in math classrooms, to address math problems, and to discover ways to solve them. The conventional notion of literacy, that of reading and writing to communicate, also gets morphed. The tools of reading and writing become ways of thinking that teachers can use to engage students in learning across all domains. But teachers may not always be experts in all school-used literacies. For instance, with years of exposure to the culture of the Internet, some students may be far more computer literate than their teachers. Viewing literacy as culturally based ways of thinking and acting takes us significantly beyond former conceptions of literacy limited to reading and writing. It opens our view of literacy to include how students think and function in their classrooms, schools, and in the communities where they live. Moreover, it opens our view of literacy to include who they are as individuals.

Three main literacies: School, community, and personal.   Some of the literacies we have mentioned, like reading and writing, play a larger role in middle and high schools than others. Having thought through what counts as literacy in and out of school, Margaret Gallego and Sandra Hollingsworth (2000) created three categories of literacies:

- ◆ school literacies,
- ◆ community literacies, and
- ◆ personal literacies.

*School literacies.   School literacies* encompass not only cognitive processes, like reading, but also social, cultural, and political processes. But standard English is the prime literacy, probably the most valued cultural capital in content classrooms (unless they're speaking French, German, or Spanish). Getting students to read,

*"I thought it was pretty good, for a book."*

*Source:* © 2002 The New Yorker Collection from cartoonbank.com. All rights reserved.

write, speak, and listen to standard, school-based English consumes an enormous amount of our time and energy as teachers. However, students also acquire content area literacies in math, science, and history. They often work toward mastering whole bodies of culture-based knowledge to gain, at least to some degree, what Hirsch (1987) referred to as cultural literacy. In some classrooms, students develop visual literacy through studying film, photographs, and paintings or diagrams, graphs, timelines, and maps (Moline, 1995). By building computer literacy, teachers help students become more conversant with Internet resources, our growing Webworld, and Netspeak, the new language of chat rooms and e-mail (Crystal, 2001). With teachers promoting critical literacy (Freire, 1993/1970), students develop a "critical consciousness," a form of awareness enabling them to examine the power structure operating within their community and how that structure influences their behavior. Critical literacy and its application in classrooms to enable students to gain a deeper understanding of how cultures define them will be addressed in a later chapter on critical reading.

***Community literacies.*** ***Community literacies*** include out-of-school cultures and literacies, such as that of a student fluent in Russian who speaks the language with his newly immigrated family. Sometimes these out-of-school literacies are accommodated in school, sometimes not. Knowing how children learn to communicate in their culture helps us understand the potential for mismatches between their communication styles and those in the classroom. Among the Warm Springs Indians living on their reservation in Oregon and carefully described in Philips (1983) classic study, regulation of turn taking during conversations differed from that of the Anglo rules that governed talk in classrooms. While Indian organization of interaction focused upon maximizing each individual's control over turn taking, Anglo interaction that dominated school discourse involved significantly greater control over turn-taking opportunities. Philips found three mechanisms contributing to the regulation of social interaction among the Indians:

1. Rather than focusing on a particular person during conversation in a group, speakers addressed the group in general.
2. A speaker's talk didn't always necessitate a response, certainly not an immediate one. Long pauses between turn taking were common.
3. Speakers were not interrupted. They stopped talking when they wanted.

Although we might think that a system of that kind could be exploited by a speaker who wouldn't stop talking, Philips observed that talk was usually equally distributed among participants who wished to take part in a conversation.

In school classrooms, however, a different set of guidelines for interaction prevailed because a teacher regulated turn taking and interaction. Getting or giving up the floor was under a teacher's control. Indian children were not accustomed to these conditions of social interaction. Furthermore, they were not accustomed to a single adult being in authority because, in their community, socialization of children was widely distributed. Unlike attention seeking that Philips observed in Anglo communities, Indian children did not compete for parental attention. These cultural factors within the Indian community contributed to Indian children withdrawing from classroom interaction, avoiding teacher-controlled responses, and failing to participate in show-and-tell opportunities. Teachers unaware of cultural differences between their own cultural styles and those of children from the Warm Springs Reservation may not see how culture contributes to conflicts or breakdowns in classroom communication.

*Personal literacies.* **Personal literacies** are reflected in students' critical awareness of themselves that arises from their examination of their backgrounds and histories in their schools and communities. From reading the brief memories that Yvette, Paul, and Cindy wrote, we gain significant insights into their personal literacies. Personal literacies also influence students' interpretations of texts in school contexts. How much a student knows about her own inner life or about the impact of her community on her thinking influences the depth of response to and understanding of texts. The richness of that capacity is particularly apparent when a student with an acute critical consciousness analyzes current political events. Furthermore, students familiar and comfortable with their personal knowledge more readily access and express their own "voices." We saw the importance of acquiring "voice" in the teaching of Allyson Mizoguchi, one of several beginning teachers hoping to influence their school's culture.

Tension can arise between school literacies and personal literacies. Evidence of these conflicts appears in the development of both girls and African-Americans. Researchers (Gilligan, Lyons, & Hammer, 1990) have found that girls may be at risk for losing their personal ways of speaking, their "voices," if they become too competent in school-approved literacies and seek approval only through that expressive mode. In addition, the identities of African-Americans who rush to embrace standard English put themselves at risk of abandoning their community literacy and a dialect that enables them to connect with their culture (Fecho, 1999).

If, like Cottle (2001), you believe adolescents are growing up in a "culture of distraction" that diverts them from reflection on their personal and social selves, then

### "Only the Shadow Knows"

Learning how students utilize and make sense of school is critical to every beginning teacher's understanding of students' engagement and the development of students' literacies. While new teachers sometimes assume that they know what "doing school" means because they did it, shadowing a student can lead to assumption-shedding discoveries that allow more accurate readings of students' lives and learning experiences in school classrooms.

The purpose of shadowing a student is to provide opportunities to witness schooling and school culture through students' eyes. As you glide through a student's schedule of classes like a silent shadow, you learn how a student responds to teachers, peers, and classroom instruction. Playing the shadow, you'll get to know the degree to which a student flows with teacher expectations and improvises on the themes of daily classroom and school life.

### The Assignment

I have adapted the work of Bullough and Gitlin (1995) for this walking shadow assignment:

For this activity, you are to "shadow" a student for a full school day (or as much of the day as possible). You can arrange for shadowing by talking with your cooperating or master teacher or school site administrator. You should select a student whom you find intriguing and who comes from a background different from yours. It's important that you explain to the student what you are going to be doing and that you have the student's consent to shadow. Otherwise shadowing may look more like stalking. Like any ethnographer, take "field notes" based on your observations. Describe what you witness in as much detail as you can capture. Save interpretation for later, but note insights as they come to mind so they aren't lost.

You want to learn as much as possible about this student's way of life in classrooms and school cultures. These questions may guide your note taking and later analysis:

- How is the student's time structured? How does he/she fit into those structures? How does the student "wiggle" within the boundaries set for them?

- What engages the student during the day? When is he/she most "alive"? What topics or activities does he/she engage or avoid engaging?

- What are the characteristics that describe relationships with teachers and peers? What are sources of excitement, satisfaction, or irritation?

- How does the student's language and literacy skills influence, reflect, or enable participation in classrooms and groups?

- What roles do teachers play and how does your student respond to teachers?

In writing your shadow paper, describe summarily your observations class by class, analyze and interpret your observations (with particular attention to how your student experiences school and how teachers shape that experience), and finally reflect on the significance of what you've discovered about your role as an emerging teacher and observer of students' cultural lives.

FIGURE 1.1   Ethnography in Classrooms: "Only the Shadow Knows."

personal literacies and any sense that students have found their identities or voices will make only rare appearances in our classroom. However, our classrooms could provide havens from the "mind fields" of popular culture so that students can find the time and space to reflect on themselves as learners and individuals.

To discover more about school culture and literacies, you can engage in some descriptive anthropology (or ethnography) by arranging to shadow a student at school. The ethnographic procedure, "Only The Shadow Knows," is explained in Figure 1.1 on page 14.

## IS THERE AN ADOLESCENT LITERACY CRISIS?

Crises are relative conditions and come in many sizes. There's a crisis, and then there's a **CRISIS!** We can identify emergencies which require our attention so they do not become worse, and we can identify a "zero hour" during which attention must be paid immediately or we're "toast." How we define the degree of urgency will influence how we come to decide whether or not we are in a crisis.

We would not find it difficult to build a pretty strong case for their being an adolescent literacy crisis. We could point out that, during the transition to middle and high school, students at risk become increasingly vulnerable to leaving school either psychologically or by actually dropping out. We could add that the numbers of students leaving school in fact or through disengagement are most staggering in our urban centers where learning and literacy in school are often devalued as children approach adulthood and their identities coalesce on the streets rather than in the classrooms. Teachers in inner-city schools all too often report that few of their students complete—or even start—homework assignments that entail reading and writing. Such disaffiliation from literacy and learning has contributed to problems not only in our schools but also in our communities and in the workplace. Lacking literacy skills young people are more subject to unemployment, crime, and gang affiliations.

However, is literacy on a national scale in more of a crisis than it was 30 years ago? Have the reading scores of students in middle and high schools plummeted over the past 30 years? This question we can address quite well.

In fact, the National Assessment of Educational Progress (NAEP) reading scores for 17- and 13-year-old students tell a story of minor improvements over 30 years (Campbell, Hombo, & Mazzeo, 2000). NAEP tests have been given to samples of students in sampled schools to measure national achievement trends over time and not to measure individual, school, or district performance. In 1971, the average reading proficiency of 17-year-old students was 285 (on a 500 point scale) and 288 in 1999, an increase of three points that is not statistically significant. Meanwhile, the reading scores of 13-year-old students are significantly higher even though the total point gain is small, moving from 255 in 1971 to 259 in 1999. (See Figure 1.2.) With these small changes in scores, we would have a difficult time arguing that a crisis had arisen over the past 30 years.

However, we might argue that these average reading proficiency scores are not sufficient for a nation whose economy is as large as that of the United States and whose political influence is as extensive worldwide. NAEP data show that in grades 8 and 12 fewer than 5% of students performed at an advanced level by examining, extending, and elaborating on the meaning of literary and informative texts (Campbell, Voelkl, & Donahue, 1997). If we believe that we must have far more than one out of twenty

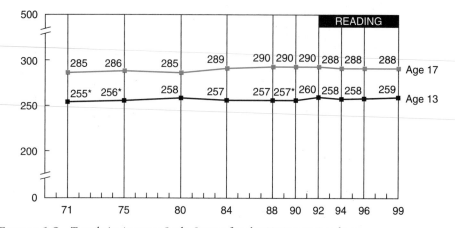

**FIGURE 1.2**    Trends in Average Scale Scores for the Nation in Reading.
*Significantly different from 1999.
*Source:* U.S. Department of Education. Office of Educational Research and Improvement. National Center for Education Statistics. *NAEP 1999 Trends in Academic Progress: Three Decades of Student Performace,* NCES 2000-469, by J.R. Campbell, C.M. Hombo, and J. Mazzeo. Washington, DC: 2000.

students functioning at an "advanced" literacy level when they are 13 or 17, then we could argue that these findings confirm a staggering adolescent literacy crisis.

In summary, the average reading scores of American students have not plunged in the last few years. Given this information, we would find it difficult to argue that recent downturns in reading assessment enable us to claim that a crisis exists in American adolescent literacy.

## Some Groups Struggle with School Literacy

However, it is important to keep in mind that reading proficiency among students in America is not evenly distributed. Segments of our student population struggle with reading and writing. A close look at reading data categorized by social, economic, racial, and ethnic groups or by parents' level of education shows quite clearly that some students are at a distinct disadvantage in terms of literacy.

Looking at trends in average NAEP reading scale scores by race and ethnicity reveals just the pattern to which I've referred (Campbell, Hombo, & Mazzeo, 2000). While the average reading scale score for whites aged 17 in 1999 was 295, the average score for Hispanic students aged 17 was 271, and for blacks, 264. These are dramatically significant differences. The good news is that the average for 17-year-old Hispanics has risen from 252 in 1975, while the average for African-Americans has risen from 239 in 1971. A similar pattern of average reading scores for white, Hispanic, and African-American students appears among 13-year-olds. In short, the gaps are shrinking but still large. (See Figure 1.3.)

Although some improvement in reading has occurred over the past few years in some groups, our efforts to increase the literacy levels of all students have not met with uniform success. From this point of view, we could argue solidly that our country has pockets of adolescent literacy crises. Many of those pockets are in our large cities where continuing disadvantages lead to students being underprepared for successful progression through middle and high school and on into the workforce or into college.

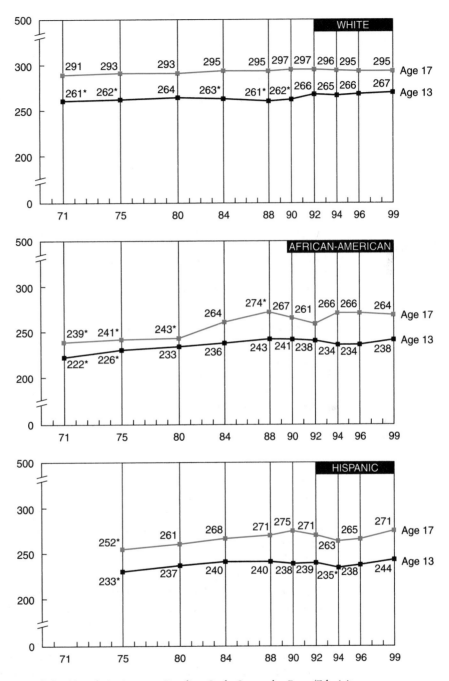

**FIGURE 1.3** Trends in Average Reading Scale Scores by Race/Ethnicity.

*Significantly different from 1999.

*Source:* U.S. Department of Education. Office of Educational Research and Improvement. National Center for Education Statistics. *NAEP 1999 Trends in Academic Progress: Three Decades of Student Performace,* NCES 2000-469, by J. R. Campbell, C. M. Hombo, and J. Mazzeo. Washington, DC: 2000.

## Is There a Crisis of Engagement with Learning at the Core of Middle and High School Cultures?

Perhaps the "literacy crisis" is a symptom of a more troubling trend in many of our schools. Some educators have observed and documented the deterioration of engagement with learning in many communities as children progress from elementary to middle and on to high schools. In her study entitled *Literacies Lost,* Cyrene Wells (1996) describes what happened to students as they moved from a progressive middle school to a traditional high school. She makes four assumptions about schooling that will help us understand her discoveries.

- ◆ First, she believes that schools are "agents of cultural transmission," and that what is transmitted is a reflection of those having the power to run the school, including community members and school faculty. Students attending different schools will have different experiences because each school has its unique culture.
- ◆ Second, she believes that culture is learned, that students acquire a set of customs from their cultural environment.
- ◆ Third, students, as they become enculturated, come to know what skills and knowledge are valued and how to acquire both.
- ◆ Fourth, she thinks that students also acquire attitudes toward learning that persist as an aspect of their sense of self even as they move from one learning environment or school to another.

In summary, the entire school culture with its structure, organization, values, and traditions affects student learning.

In Meadowbrook, the progressive middle school that Wells studied, students valued caring teachers, multiple approaches to learning content, choice in activities, and a welcoming classroom. They also felt that community was integral to learning and that they learned from each other as well as from the teacher. Talking was part of enjoyable learning. Grades were only one form of evaluation; they sometimes evaluated their own work. Importantly for us, they saw reading and writing as "integral to learning."

## Disconnects Between Students, Their Teachers, and the Curriculum

However, students found a different set of traditions, expectations, and beliefs about learning at the high school. According to Wells (1996), order predominated, even in meetings of the school's faculty. Little time was given to articulating a shared vision, in part, because teachers were not encouraged to voice their educational philosophy or encouraged to develop innovations. Control dominated creativity in classrooms and curriculum. Grades and the punitive consequences of poor ones were more important than students' understanding of course content. While the school functioned smoothly, the community gave it little support. The old heart of the city in which the school was located had once been a thriving mill town, but the factories had been all but forgotten even though the factory model of instruction still dominated in the high school.

A short time after beginning their acculturation at the high school, students were disappointed that teachers showed much less care than their middle school teachers, with some of their new teachers not even making an effort to learn their names. With some assignments amounting to no more than filling in worksheets or writing seemingly senseless essays to which teachers responded by commenting about grammar problems, these freshmen reoriented themselves. Some did what was demanded in order to get good grades. Some began to manifest behavior problems, like showing up late for class, not completing worksheets, and talking back to teachers. Others, who felt the work meaningless, "psyched out the system" and did only what was essential to get by.

As for literacy and its development, the place of writing and reading at the high school was quite different. At their middle school, writing had been integral to learning, but at the high school, instruction was driven by textbooks with very few opportunities to write about what was studied. Memorization replaced understanding. Reading became a search for answers to worksheet questions or questions at the end of a textbook chapter. Showing mastery of vocabulary words on tests was paramount for good grades. Wells, pointing out how boredom oppressed students, cites one student who said, "I have so much to learn, and I'm stuck here in this class." Few students felt any sense of connection with their teachers or sense of enthusiasm about learning. What sustained students was their social life and the pleasures of talking with friends.

Focusing on her theme of literacies lost, Wells noted that the middle school students at Meadowbrook wrote in many genres. They composed many types of fiction and non-fiction, including journals of many types, reflections, summaries, reports, self-evaluations, interpretations, and arguments. Teachers treated writing as a process over which students could confer as they composed. Students also did independent research using multiple methods of inquiry from library searches to personal interviews. With respect to reading, students at Meadowbrook read a wide variety of texts, both fiction and non-fiction. They learned to read for different purposes (scanning versus reading for detail), and they were encouraged to demonstrate their understanding of the texts they read in many modes from written and oral reports to debates, skits, and group discussions. Integrating—not segmenting—subject areas was encouraged.

In the high school, students were frequently told to read text chapters and respond by preparing for quizzes, writing outlines, completing textbook publisher's worksheets, and answering questions at the end of chapters. Little was asked of students by way of inquiry, exploration, integration, or reflection. Unfortunately, an absence of authentic, meaningful, or significant work inhibits student engagement. While few former Meadowbrook students complained about learning with textbooks, they did complain about not doing more. Although the students adapted to the high school teachers' expectations, their range of literacy development contracted to more routine and controlled patterns of response.

## Can We Generalize?

Wells (1996) looked carefully at one middle school and one high school. Each was unique, as all schools are unique in terms of culture, leadership, community, and individual students and teachers. Can we use her specific findings about these two schools to say anything worthwhile about middle and high schools in general?

Although measures of engagement among high school students are not abundant, the results of several studies echo findings that Wells (1996) reported. According to one researcher (Steinberg, 1996), about 40% of the students were "just going through the motions" of high school. These findings were based on student self-reports regarding their levels of effort in four main subject areas (English, math, social science, and science), time spent on homework, academic expectation levels, and class attendance. Well over a third of the students said that when they are in class they are either not paying attention to instruction or not trying very hard. According to Steinberg (1996), more than one out of three students are disengaged because they do not feel challenged or held accountable.

If Wells' study were among the few finding school conditions limiting engagement with learning and literacy growth, we could dismiss it more swiftly. However, several studies of high schools (Boyer, 1983; Goodlad, 1984; Marks, 2000; McNeil, 1988; Newmann, 1992; Sizer, 1992; Steinberg, 1996; Wagner, 1994) have drawn rather similar pictures. Levels of engagement with the content area curriculum or with the minds of teachers tend to be low, while levels of boredom and peer socializing tend to be high.

What researchers portray time and time again are schools demonstrating what Eisner (1988) terms "structured fragmentation." The traditional middle and high school typically breaks the day into six or seven periods with a break for nutrition after two periods and a break for lunch after four periods. At the ringing of a computerized bell-system, students move through the day from classroom to classroom where teachers present lessons in English, math, social studies, science, and a range of other "electives" that include art, music, and foreign languages. Connections between the subject areas are rare, and teachers infrequently discuss curriculum development or its integration with other teachers.

In most large middle and high schools, opportunities for the development of caring relationships between teachers and students are few. Students move through their scheduled day, often spending about 50 minutes in a classroom with 25 to 30 other students. They are controlled by the teachers' need to get through a required curriculum so that students will be prepared for their next instructional level—a higher course in an academic subject or perhaps college.

Perhaps Wells (1996) is correct when she concludes that "The system is not set up for caring teachers" (p. 174) who might use a multitude of means, including those that integrate and promote literacy in the content areas, to develop relationships and rapport with their students. While this story of transition into the freshman year in high school may be repeated in communities all too often, there are schools that continue to engage students in their efforts to understand, to acquire a range of literacies, and to grow as learners.

We know, too, that students are deeply affected by their school and classroom cultures. As Newmann put it in his study of student engagement and achievement in American secondary schools, "the effects of any specific school activity are best understood as cultural phenomena; that is, as outcomes that evolve through complex webs of institutionally sanctioned meanings, values, and incentives or disincentives for particular kinds of behavior" (1992, p. 182). An important part of what we do as teachers is to foster communities and classroom cultures that will engage students in what they perceive to be meaningful learning. That is far from a trivial challenge. But, it is one that teachers must engage to make a genuine difference in students' lives.

## WHAT IS TO BE DONE?

Given the cultures and literacies students bring with them, the central challenge we face as teachers is to engage them in meaningful learning that integrates literacy growth with standards-guided instruction in our content areas. We can use our understanding of how cultures shape minds to help ourselves manage that challenge. We have seen the importance of understanding our students' cultural heritage and history. We discovered that our students' development depends upon the mediating power of languages to acquire knowledge and skills that enable them to become masters of how they think and act. We found how central social interaction was to our students' cultural development because what students first experience socially becomes internalized as languages capable of transforming the way students think and behave. We also saw how important our being within our students' zones of proximal development is to their engagement and growth. Vygotsky's concept of ZPD (1978) helps us see how we can foster learning environments in the context of our classrooms. However, our challenge is to also create classrooms and learning environments where students are engaged and where literacies flourish.

## Cultures and Literacies as Resources for Engagement

I suspect that by now you are fairly well convinced that our students bring cultures and literacies of many kinds into our classrooms. These multiple cultures and literacies are priceless resources with which we can and must build the knowledge and skills that accompany our content area specialization. We can weave the threads of cultures and literacies that students bring to us into the fabric of our instruction.

First, we can use these threads of cultures and literacies to help us know and understand our students. We can draw upon these threads to discover how their cultures have shaped them and what personal literacies compel each student to speak with a unique voice. In describing how his school's culture affected him, Paul wrote that his friends embodied and reflected several types of school literacies.

Among these were conversational English, formal English, *Spanglish*, and musical jargon. Conversational English was spoken most of the time, and being that I was a teenager the normal mix of slang and profanity was part of this literacy. I can recall many times when during normal conversation, my classmates and I would play a sort of game by purposefully using formal English words that we learned in our vocabulary and English classes. Many of my schoolmates would use words that we found amusing or ones that had a certain rhythmic quality that we enjoyed. . . . *Spanglish* (a free flowing conversation using a mixture of English and Spanish) was practiced by the Latino seminarians. This literacy was used for fun, but during sporting events the Latino athletes would shout out strategies to each other in Spanglish so that our opponents wouldn't understand. The musicians would engage in a technically musical jargon where we would discuss songs for our services, and we also used it to talk about the music we enjoyed.

By being attuned to the cultures and literacies shaping Paul's identity, his teachers could deepen their understanding of him and his interests.

Second, we can use the cultural resources and literacies of our students and their community to inform the design and enrich the content of our curriculum. We can draw upon the funds of knowledge that are embedded in a school's surrounding community and that our students have acquired from interacting with various cultures to build our own instructional programs. For example, William Brozo, Paul Valerio, and Minerva Salazar (1996) integrated reading and writing strategies into a unit on Hispanic American culture that engaged eighth graders, made them more aware of their heritage, and improved their literacy. In Corpus Christi, Texas, these educators enabled students to walk through a Mexican American faith healer's garden and learn from her about the healing properties of plants. Students read Anaya's *Bless Me, Ultima* (1972), a novel rich in curanderismo (traditional Mexican American faith healing), and discovered how they could work cooperatively to construct meanings for the book. By using their community as a cultural resource, these students and their teachers enriched their understanding of the novel and of the heritage that surrounded them.

Third, if we so desire, we can use the cultures and literacies students bring with them as cornerstones for building a curriculum that enables students to explore and grasp the influence their cultures and literacies have had upon them. We can examine the cultures in which students are enmeshed to help them discover ways to understand the structure and power base that formed and perpetuated the culture's practices and principles. For example, Cindy Thai might have read Amy Tan's *Joy Luck Club* to explore aspects of Chinese culture and their influence on families and relationships.

Finally, all the cultural experiences and literacies that students bring to class with them can be called upon to interpret and understand the texts they read. Those texts include not only their current classroom textbooks, but also the multiple texts which make up our cultural lives. The background knowledge that students carry with them provides intertextual or between-text resources to make sense of new texts. That occurs when knowledge of a Biblical story or a Disney movie enables a student to interpret a new poem or when knowledge of the American revolution helps a student understand revolutions elsewhere.

## Addressing Teachers' Nightmares

Even with these cultural and literacy resources at hand, some teachers find the literacy challenges overwhelming. William Bintz (1997), a middle and high school teacher for many years, didn't know how to deal with students who rarely read his assignments or who wanted to read them but struggled and asked for assistance he didn't know how to give. Although he wanted to help his students, his teacher education program did not include any courses in reading. Having instructional nightmares of his own, Bintz spent several years collecting the reading nightmares of middle and high school teachers. He asked them to describe the nightmare in their reading closet, questions they had about reading they couldn't answer, and a wish that would help them get rid of their nightmare once and for all if it came true. He collected over a hundred nightmares of teachers in all the content areas, including science, math, social studies, English, home economics, and art. Several appear in Figure 1.4.

Questions these teachers asked frequently related to their classroom teaching dilemmas: "How do I make factual reading more interesting?" "How do I get more involved in reading when I don't read much myself?" "How am I able to help students comprehend what they are reading when no one else has?" "How do I have

**FIGURE 1.4** Teachers Across the Curriculum Sharing Their Reading Nightmares.

*Source:* Adapted from "Exploring Reading Nightmares of Middle and Secondary School Teachers," by W.P. Bintz, (1997), *Journal of Adolescent and Adult Literacy, 41*(1), pp. 12–24.

time to work on reading when I don't have time to present the subject matter I teach?" "How do I make sure that students grasp the important concepts in reading?"

The hopes these teachers had for a reading solution are reflected in their wishes: "I wish I knew how to teach reading and math together." "I wish that every teacher regardless of the content area would recognize the importance of reading." "I wish I could stop time so I could catch all kids up in reading."

Bintz proposes a number of solutions that include making sure new and apprenticing teachers gain a deeper understanding of reading and experience teaching it than he did during his university training. He also acknowledges that perceptions of the value and importance of reading need to be changed. Rather than viewing reading as a nagging problem, teachers could establish a climate that says, "We value reading in our school." Schools can focus on reading in their professional development programs that include asking teachers from across the curriculum to share reading strategies and the effects of those strategies on their students' reading and learning. Rather than viewing reading as a fanged ghoul dragging its reluctant victim beneath the black river, Bintz would like to see all schools, teachers, and students experience reading as a "tool for learning and thinking."

## Lessons from "Beating the Odds" Classrooms

How can teachers promote meaningful learning while developing literacy? Because literacy coupled with learning is our focus, I have drawn on the work of Judith Langer (2001) who found teachers using practices that led to their school's students "beating the odds" when it came to performance on standards-based state assessments. Langer identified educational practices that enabled students, mostly from schools in culturally diverse and poorer communities, to perform significantly better than students in comparable schools. Although her study focused on teachers of English in middle and high schools, her findings directly address literacy development across the curriculum while providing direction for meaningful learning. Active and meaningful engagement marked and facilitated the superior performance of students in "beating the odds" classrooms. Students were on task most of the time in academically rich instructional environments that promoted learning. Characteristics of literacy instruction that set these higher performing middle and high school classrooms and teachers apart from comparable but lower performing schools can inform decisions about what needs to be done in classrooms to address literacy growth while promoting meaningful learning across the content areas.

Langer (2001) focused on six issues at the center of the current education debate in literacy: (a) Enabling strategies, (b) approaches to skills instruction, (c) connected instruction, (d) conceptions of learning, (e) classroom organization, and (f) test preparation. Each of these six issues were reflected in differences observed in typical classrooms and practices in "beating the odds" classroom that are summarized in Figure 1.5.

Meaningful and successful learning in "beating the odds" classrooms and schools arose from (or was associated with) teachers whose instructional practice was based upon:

1. *The overt teaching of enabling strategies to carry out reading, writing, and thinking tasks.* This accomplishment echoes Langer's (1987) conception of literacy as a way of thinking and doing within a content domain. "Beating the odds" teachers taught their students strategic procedures, such as the use of graphic organizers, techniques of reciprocal teaching, or a process approach to writing, that they could use to address learning tasks and that resulted in enhanced performance. These strategies (all of which will be covered in later chapters in this book) helped students plan, organize, complete, and reflect upon their work. "Beating the odds" teachers often modeled and discussed procedures that would guide students toward successful task completion by breaking down complex tasks into parts and providing rubrics for the evaluation of their performance. "Typical" teachers in "typical" schools taught content and skills but gave very little attention to strategies for planning, organizing, or thinking about the tasks.

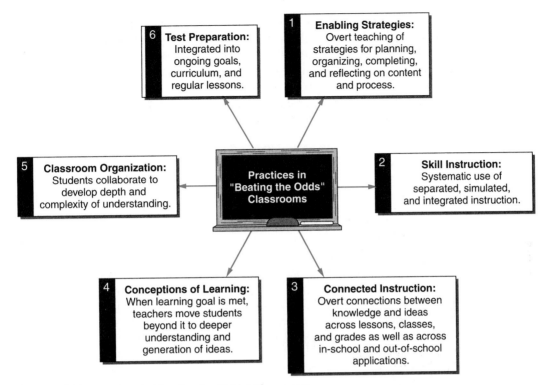

**FIGURE 1.5** Practices in "Beating the Odds" Classrooms.

2. *The systematic use of separated, simulated, and integrated skill instruction.* "Beating the odds" teachers did not allow their teaching of skills to be dominated by any one approach, such as the direct instruction of an isolated skill. Most used all three methods to introduce and teach literacy skills. For example, in teaching vocabulary, one "beating the odds" teacher selected unfamiliar words from a text her students were reading, showed them how they could apply the new words to classroom discussions, and found ways for them to incorporate those words in their writing assignments. In this way she made systematic use of separated, simulated, and integrated skill instruction. She used separated instruction when she presented vocabulary she believed to be challenging, simulated instruction when she asked students to apply their knowledge of these words to texts they were reading, and integrated instruction when she urged her students to use newly acquired words in their class discussions and essay writing. In contrast, a "typical" teacher used a vocabulary workbook from which words were periodically assigned, a form of separated instruction that left few opportunities for students to apply new knowledge in new domains of learning.

3. *The creation of overt connections between new knowledge across lessons, classes, grades, and even communities.* Ample research (Bransford, Brown, & Cocking, 1999) demonstrates that students are more likely to learn and remember concepts if they are connected to prior knowledge acquired both in and outside of school. "Beating the odds" teachers overtly made webs of inter-connections among multiple forms of student learning: Within lessons; across lessons, classes, and grades; and between in- and out-of-school knowledge. "Typical" teachers made few connections between what they were teaching and any other form of student learning. For example, during self-study at one "beating the odds" high school, teachers sought ways

to foster connected learning both within the school and between the school and the community it served. They focused on ways students could become more effective communicators in all grades across the curriculum. In the more "typical" schools Langer studied, teachers did little web spinning to show students how newly acquired knowledge was connected to earlier learning episodes or to other content areas or out-of-school communities. Lessons tended to stand on their own as isolated moments of unconnected instruction.

4. *The belief that achieving a learning goal is not an end point but an opportunity to extend and deepen understanding.*   What is it to know something, to understand it? With only about 1 in 20 middle and high school students able to deal analytically with challenging reading material, to examine, extend, and elaborate on the meanings of either literary or informative texts (Campbell, Voelkl, & Donahue, 1997), going beyond a command of facts to engage in thoughtful learning should gain priority. In "beating the odds" classrooms, teachers encourage their students to think and use knowledge—not acquire and bury facts or concepts in memory's cemetery. One "beating the odds" middle school teacher moved her students from learning to use the World Wide Web as a tool for research to discovering information about their surnames and genealogies to engaging in research on African–Americans, their history, and their lives in present-day America. In these classrooms, learning a concept or skill isn't an end state but a signal to begin to use it for thinking critically, for gaining deeper understanding.

5. *The notion that students collaborate in classrooms to gain depth and complexity of understanding.*   In many typical classrooms, students work alone, sometimes in groups, sometimes with their teacher; however, they rarely engage in rich discussion about ideas. In "beating the odds" classrooms, students collaborate in a community of interactive learners to develop deep levels of understanding. Students bring their cultural histories and the voices of multiple literacies into the classroom conversation. Learning is interactive. Literacy is a socially grounded activity. Classroom cultures thrive on sharing knowledge, interpretations, and discoveries. Students share ideas, respond to each other's interpretations, test out the soundness of their reasoning, and through cognitive collaboration build unique learning cultures. A "beating the odds" teacher, Myna LeBendig, favors discussions and fosters classroom collaboration for discovery. One of the first National Board Certified teachers in America, she said to her students at the beginning of the school year, "Fight to teach me." She wanted them to challenge her and their classmates, to engage in vigorous thinking, to ask the probing questions, and to explore her and their understanding of meanings they formed from books they read.

6. *Integrating test preparation into current learning goals, regular lessons, and units.*   With the spread of standards-based instruction and accountability programs to assess progress toward the achievement of standards, some schools across the nation, hoping to improve their performance, have adopted stand-alone test preparation modules. In short, they teach to the test. In efforts to get students test-ready, teachers have been asked to teach test-taking skills. In the "typical" schools that Langer studied, test preparation stood alone with the intent of increasing students' scores, not on improving their literacy skills, knowledge, and strategies. In "beating the odds" schools, teachers work on the assumption that integrating literacy skills into the year-round curriculum will improve both learning and student performance on state and local tests. After learning what they could about assessment programs and examining the structure and content of the accountability system, teachers in higher performing schools revised and restructured their literacy curriculum. Teach-

ers and administrators in some "beating the odds" schools analyzed samples of items usually included in test batteries, discovered what specific literacy skills, strategies, and knowledge would benefit their students, and revised the instructional program to promote mastery of those skills, strategies, and knowledge domains. Instruction related to the testing program was infused and integrated. It was not set up as a separate intervention to address students' testing program needs, as took place in more typical schools.

These "beating the odds" teachers, many serving in high-poverty communities, appear to operate on a common principle: We learn best while engaged in activities that are personally and socially meaningful. While more "typical" teaching may share that principle, teachers in higher achieving classrooms integrate the practices reviewed and weave them together into a tapestry of instruction. That tapestry shows what these teachers believe students should encounter in classrooms, what counts as learning, and how communities of students can interact to create broader, deeper understandings while mastering skills and strategies for lifelong learning. They helped their students internalize knowledge and strategies that would transfer to future classrooms, future learning challenges, and future tasks both in school and in outside communities. This is the kind of tapestry of teaching and learning that this textbook promotes. The perspectives, principles, and practices presented here are intended to equip and guide emerging teachers as they create classroom tapestries of their own with features like those woven by these master teachers.

To move toward the creation of these tapestries, to realize literacies as ways of thinking and doing in classroom communities across the content areas, and to realize these visions of student and teacher engagement across the curriculum, we must face challenges that may test the limits of our understanding and creativity. Viewed as apprentices, emerging teachers will enter new workshops to discover new materials and perhaps unfamiliar tools. Many of these reading, writing, and discussion practices will need to be learned and integrated with skills and strategies for instruction in fields that apprentice teachers already know, such as math, science, history, health, art, or physical education. Once apprenticing teachers have mastered strategic tools for fostering literacy development, the next critical learning goal is to integrate them into a curriculum that is personally and socially meaningful to students. These literacy and learning enhancing strategies are tools for engaging students in constructing deeper understandings. Teachers must show their students how these tools deepen engagement and learning in classroom communities.

## Meeting the Challenges of Literacy and Learning

Features found in "beating the odds" classrooms and schools point to knowledge, skills, and strategies that apprenticing teachers can acquire, cultivate, and integrate into their classroom instruction. However, no teacher with knowledge of separated skills, strategies, and content concepts can magically create classroom communities where students engage in meaningful learning. Also essential are a desire and disposition to know students, to discover how they learn, to understand what they need to master to progress, to formulate and achieve literacy and learning goals, and to reflect on what's working and what needs reworking. Acknowledging that there is no formula, no magic potion of procedures for creating engaged instruction in every

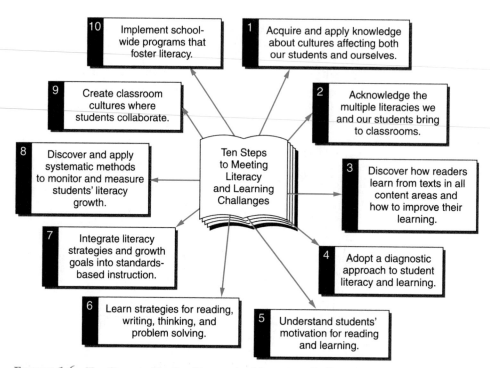

**FIGURE 1.6**   Ten Steps to Meeting Literacy and Learning Challenges.

classroom, there are several steps informed by research and best practices and summarized in Figure 1.6 that new and growing teachers can take to address the literacy and learning challenges they will meet in today's classrooms:

1. *Acquire and apply knowledge about cultures affecting both our students and ourselves.*   As we have seen in this chapter, cultures play big parts in the drama of classroom instruction. In a sense, they compose the settings for instructional episodes that we and our students write or improvise. Knowing what values, assumptions, beliefs, background knowledge, and expectations students bring into our classrooms enables us to make better judgments about what will engage them, what resources to use, what tools we need to put into their hands so they will be successful learners.

2. *Acknowledge the multiple literacies we and our students bring to classrooms.* Closely related to the cultures brought to our classrooms are the literacies participants bring. What literacies affect their thinking and acting in our classroom? How do our students express knowledge of literacies in the way they think and act?

3. *Discover how readers learn from texts in all content areas and how to improve their learning.*   In the past 30 years, we have learned what good readers do when they read, what may not be working well in weak readers, and what might be done to help struggling readers overcome frustrating obstacles to learning. To appreciate what can be done to help readers improve performance, we need first to know in more detail what happens in the mind of a reader. This textbook presents a model of the reading process based on extensive reading process research and implications of that model both for day-to-day instruction in classrooms and for struggling readers.

4. *Adopt a diagnostic approach to student literacy and learning.*   We can acquire assessment skills and strategies to look more closely at our students' work,

appreciate their strengths, and discover their frustrations so that we can envision instruction to improve reading and learning in all content areas. These tools for assessment enable teachers to make informed decisions about how best to approach students in academic trouble and improve the learning of those already successful in our classrooms. In the past, few teachers examined obstacles rooted in reading and writing that stood in the way of their students' learning. With significant numbers of students entering our classrooms with literacy problems, teachers need more tools to analyze their students' difficulties and make suggestions for improved performance.

5. *Understand students' motivation for reading and learning.* Teachers, especially those new to classrooms, are sometimes baffled by their students' disengagement with learning, a disconnect often revealed in not reading assigned texts. There are reasons for the disconnect, and there are ways to heighten motivation both internal and external. If teachers discover and appropriately apply these motive-methods, they can enhance their students' engagement in classrooms, school cultures, and in lifelong literacy growth.

6. *Learn strategies for reading, writing, thinking, and problem solving.* When apprenticing teachers master literacy strategies that influence both thinking and problem solving, they can help their own students overcome obstacles to productive learning, acquire vocabulary, improve comprehension, and deepen understandings across the disciplines. Many of these strategies enable teachers to activate their students' background knowledge, help them engage texts with purpose-guiding questions, and teach them tools to represent, organize, and reflect upon knowledge constructed from interacting with texts. Strategies for conducting whole class and small group instruction enable teachers to pave the way toward classroom learning communities and to help all students collaborate, including English learners.

7. *Integrate literacy strategies and growth goals into standards-guided instruction.* Standards-based instruction has spread nationwide. Some teachers believe they have no time to do anything but address standards, no time to teach strategically, no time to teach for thinking. However, as we saw in the classrooms of "beating the odds" teachers who work in states with standards and accountability programs, thinking and strategy instruction are among their highest priorities. Once content is acquired, that's a signal for deeper understandings to be pursued. They integrate literacy enhancing strategies throughout their instructional programs and help students internalize those strategies for use in other learning contexts. Through step-by-step explanations, apprenticing teachers can discover how they can accomplish these learning goals and design instruction so that standards, strategies, and assessment practices align.

8. *Discover and apply systematic methods to monitor and measure students' literacy growth.* With periodic progress measurements, teachers can determine the effectiveness of intervention programs they have put in place. The feedback from students provides teachers with information about students' reading, writing, and learning that inform decisions about future instructional improvements. Some schools collect period curriculum based measurements (or CBMs) to discover students' progress in reading and in other knowledge or skill domains, like math or social studies. Instructional programs may require modifications to show more substantial gains.

9. *Create classroom cultures where students collaborate.* Classrooms in "beating the odds" schools were usually organized to encourage collaboration between students and

the interactive exploration of concepts and ideas through discussion or the completion of projects. Apprentice teachers can learn techniques to pursue literacy development through whole class discussions, cooperative learning teams, or tutorials arranged within a class or across age groups. These forms of group interaction can help students learn content knowledge and skills while acquiring literacy and learning strategies.

10. *Implement school-wide programs that foster literacy.*   Entire schools can create literacy programs that improve reading for all students at all grade levels. Some of these programs, like Sustained Silent Reading, engage students and faculty in several minutes of daily reading. Other programs that are focused on teaching all students vocabulary and comprehension techniques may require a full period or more every day. Still others begin with extensive literacy training for teachers who then integrate techniques like reciprocal teaching into their curriculum and daily lesson plans to promote content learning and literacy growth.

You may wonder how you can learn to integrate these literacy and learning techniques into your content area teaching. As you may have guessed, this series of steps echoes the content and structure of the textbook you are now reading.

## Cycles of Inquiry

Mastering all the knowledge and skills presented in the following chapters, while it may be necessary, will not be sufficient. The implementation of that knowledge and those strategies needs an important added element: a sensible procedure for monitored implementation. We need to pursue a diagnostic, goal-driven, and results-oriented approach that focuses initially on individual students and expands to encompass whole classrooms. That same approach should inform the work of teacher teams, content area departments, schools, and districts. We can best deepen students' understanding of content, promote the development of literacy, and reach standards articulated by state or local educational agencies by engaging in an inquiry cycle practiced by many educators (Hopfenberg et al., 1993; Langer, 2001; Marzano, Pickering, & Pollock, 2001; Schmoker, 2001). A sensible procedure for monitoring implementation would look like the following cycle of events in which teachers, with administrative support, engage:

1. Begin by discovering the strengths and weaknesses in academic performance of individual students, whole classes, and even entire grade levels. We gather student data from multiple sources, including standardized tests and informal measures. Students "falling between the cracks" are identified during this process.
2. Target weaknesses or "challenge areas" and state explicit learning goals for classes as well as individual students. For example, if only 40% of tenth-grade world history students successfully comprehend their text, a teacher could set a growth target that would increase the percentage of successful comprehenders to 75% of the class for the academic year.
3. Brainstorm, talk with knowledgeable colleagues in the professional community to learn about promising strategies and programs to reach our targets (such as those implemented in Langers' (2001) "beating the odds" schools), and identify strategies with practical and research-based promise of addressing and improving students' performance in target areas.
4. Implement selected and synthesized strategies or a plan of action.
5. Monitor and measure progress and provide feedback to students on their performance. Look at student work. Gather data. Measure impact. Use rubrics. Tie feedback to the criteria that students know will be used in evaluation, and make specific recommendations for students about how to improve what is incorrect while commending them for what they have done well with respect to criteria.
6. Share and celebrate growth as victories—small and large. Meet with colleagues in teams, support groups, and departments to share strategic interventions and their impact on student work.
7. Engage periodically in repeating the above cycle.

In short, this textbook will explore and discover ways to work with students that will:

- enhance our capacity to understand how they read and learn,
- identify sources of trouble in struggling readers,
- decide what steps we can take to strengthen comprehension and learning of all our students,
- evaluate students' progress in literacy growth, and
- build richer, more caring teacher-student relationships and cultures.

By empowering ourselves with knowledge, strategies, and skills, we can provide more meaningful and productive schooling for all our students.

## DOUBLE-ENTRY JOURNAL: After Reading

Go to the Double-Entry Journal for Chapter 1 on our Companion Website at www.prenhall.com/unrau to complete your journal entry.

*Now that you have read Chapter 1, you are ready to complete the post-reading Double-Entry Journal (DEJ). To do that, write about 150 words in response to the directions below. Your instructor may collect and respond to your DEJs or ask you to submit them over the Internet.*

Having read this chapter, review what you wrote about the cultures that influenced you during high school. Which literacies did you practice while a student in high school? You could address these three: school, community, personal. Do you think cultures and literacies from your high school years shaped or influenced your development and your perspectives as an adult? If not, why not? If they did, how did they? How would you draw upon your own students' cultures and literacies to enhance teaching and learning in your content area?

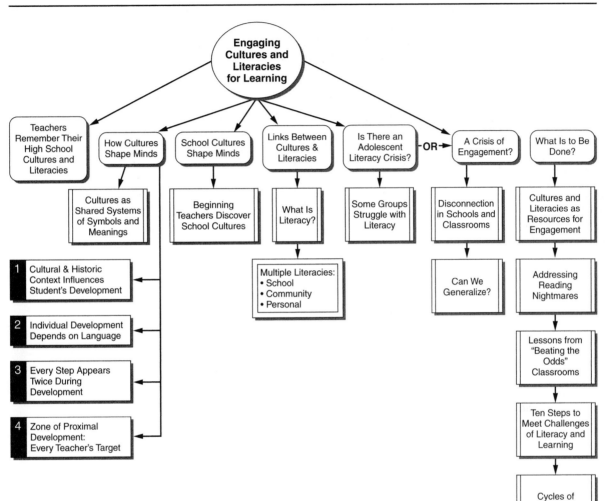

For exercises to clarify your understanding of chapter content, visit the self-assessments for Chapter 1 on our Companion Website at www.prenhall.com/unrau

# References

Anaya, R. (1972). *Bless me, Ultima.* New York: Warner.

Bintz, W. P. (1997). Exploring reading nightmares of middle and secondary school teachers. *Journal of Adolescent and Adult Literacy, 41*(1), 12–24.

Boyer, E. L. (1983). *High school: A report on secondary education in America.* New York: Harper & Row.

Bransford, J. D., Brown, A. L., & Cocking, R. R. (Eds.). (1999). *How people learn: Brain, mind, experience, and school.* Washington, DC: National Academy Press.

Brozo, W., Valerio, P., & Salazar, M. (1996). A walk through Gracie's garden: Literacy and cultural explorations in a Mexican American junior high school. *Journal of Adolescent and Adult Literacy, 40*(3), 164–170.

Bullough, R., Jr., & Gitlin, A. (1995). *Becoming a student of teaching: Methodologies for exploring self and school context.* New York: Garland Publishing.

Campbell, J., Hombo, C., & Mazzeo, J. (2000). *NAEP trends in academic progress: Three decades of student performance.* Jesup, MD: U.S. Department of Education.

Campbell, J., Voelkl, K., & Donahue, P. (1997). *NAEP 1996 trends in academic progress.* Washington, DC: National Center for Educational Statistics.

Cottle, T. J. (2001). *Mind fields: Adolescent consciousness in a culture of distraction.* New York: Peter Lang.

Crystal, D. (2001). *Language and the Internet.* Cambridge: Cambridge University Press.

Deal, T., & Peterson, K. (1999). *Shaping school culture: The heart of leadership.* San Francisco: Jossey-Bass.

Eisner, E. W. (1988). The ecology of school improvement. *Educational Leadership, 45*(5), 24–29.

Fecho, B. (1999). Crossing boundaries of race in a critical literacy classroom. In Alvermann, D. E., Hinchman, K. A., Moore, S. F., Phelps, S. F., & Waff, D. R. (Eds.), *Reconceptualizing the literacies in adolescents' lives* (pp. 75–101). Mahwah, NJ: Erlbaum.

Frank, C. (1999). *Ethnographic eyes: A teacher's guide to classroom observation.* Portsmouth, NH: Heinemann.

Freire, P. (1993/1970). *Pedagogy of the oppressed* (M.B. Ramos, Trans.). New York: Continuum.

Gallego, M., & Hollingsworth, S. (2000). Introduction: The idea of multiple literacies. In M. Gallego & S. Hollingsworth (Eds.), *What counts as literacy: Challenging the school standard* (pp. 1–23). New York: Teachers College Press.

Geertz, C. (1973). *Interpretation of cultures.* New York: Basic Books.

Gilligan, C., Lyons, N., & Hammer, T. (1990). *Making connections: The relational worlds of adolescent girls at Emma Willard School.* Cambridge, MA: Harvard University Press.

Goodlad, J. I. (1984). *A place called school: Prospects for the future.* New York: McGraw-Hill.

Gruenert, S. (2000). Shaping a new school culture. *Contemporary Education, 71*(2), 14–18.

Hirsch, E. D. (1987). *Cultural literacy: What every American needs to know.* Boston, MA: Houghton Mifflin.

Hopfenberg, W., Levin, H., Chase, C., Christensen, S. G., Moore, M., Soler, P., et al. (1993). *The Accelerated Schools resource guide.* San Francisco: Jossey-Bass.

Langer, J. (1987). A sociocognitive perspective on literacy. In J. Langer (Ed.), *Language, literacy, and culture: Issues of society and schooling* (pp. 1–20). Norwood, NJ: Ablex.

Langer, J. (2001). Beating the odds: Teaching middle and high school students to read and write well. *American Educational Research Journal, 38*(4), 837–880.

Langer, S. (1942). *Philosophy in a new key.* New York: Mentor Books.

Lippmann, W. (1913/1962). *A preface to politics.* Ann Arbor. MI: University of Michigan Press.

Malinowski, B. (1944). *A scientific theory of culture and other essays.* New York: Oxford University Press.

Marks, H. M. (2000). Student engagement in instructional activity: Patterns in the elementary, middle, and high school years. *American Educational Research Journal, 37*(1), 153–184.

Marzano, R., Pickering, D., & Pollock, J. (2001). *Classroom instruction that works: Research-based strategies for increasing student achievement*. Alexandria, VA: Association for Supervision and Curriculum Development.

McNeil, L. M. (1988). *Contradictions of control: School structure and school knowledge*. New York: Routledge.

Moline, S. (1995). *I see what you mean*. Portland, ME: Stenhouse Publishers.

Newmann, F. (1992). Conclusion. In F. Newmann (Ed.), *Student engagement and achievement in American secondary schools* (pp. 182–217). New York: Teachers College Press.

Ochs, E., & Schieffelin, B. (1984). Language acquisition and socialization: Three developmental stories and their implications. In R. A. Shweder & R. A. Levine (Eds.), *Culture theory: Essays on mind, self, and emotion* (pp. 276–320). Cambridge: Cambridge University Press.

Philips, S. (1983). *The invisible culture: Communication in classroom and community on the Warm Springs Indian Reservation*. New York: Longman.

Schmoker, M. (2001). *The results fieldbook: Practical strategies from dramatically improved schools*. Alexandria, VA: Association for Supervision and Curriculum Development.

Sizer, T. (1992). *Horace's school: Redesigning the American high school*. Boston: Houghton Mifflin.

Steinberg, L. (1996). *Beyond the classroom: Why school reform has failed and what parents need to do*. New York: Simon & Schuster.

Van der Bogert, R., Donaldson, M., & Poon, B. (1999). *Reflections of first-year teachers on school culture: Questions, hopes, and challenges*. San Francisco: Jossey-Bass.

Vygotsky, L. S. (1978). *Mind in society: The development of higher psychological processes*. Cambridge, MA: Harvard.

Vygotsky, L. S. (1986). *Thought and language*. Cambridge, MA: MIT Press.

Wagner, T. (1994). *How schools change: Lessons from three communities*. Boston: Beacon Press.

Wells, M. C. (1996). *Literacies lost: When students move from a progressive middle school to a traditional high school*. New York: Teacher College Press.

# 2 READERS READING: INSIDE THE MEANING CONSTRUCTION ZONE

After reading Chapter 2, you should be able to answer the following questions:

1. What do good readers do when they read?
2. What are some myths about how good readers read?
3. How would a model of the reading process help me to teach?
4. What does a peek into the meaning construction zone during reading reveal?
5. What are the implications of the model for my teaching?

| DOUBLE-ENTRY JOURNAL: Before Reading | Draw a picture, diagram, or map of the reading process as you think it works. After rendering the process, describe in writing how the process works. Or, if you prefer, describe the process in words first and then draw it. |
| --- | --- |

 Now go to the Double-Entry Journal for Chapter 2 on our Companion Website at www.prenhall.com/ unrau to fill out your journal entry.

## STUDENTS CONSTRUCT AND NEGOTIATE MEANINGS

When I was teaching American literature to eleventh graders, I enjoyed engaging them in discussions of J. D. Salinger's short stories. While grappling with the meaning of these stories, students contributed to the building of an interpretive classroom community in which they made significant discoveries about both the stories and themselves as readers. Here's a glimpse of that process.

After my students read Salinger's "The Laughing Man" and wrote their summaries or interpretations of it in their logs, they gathered in groups of three to read and discuss each others' summaries and interpretations. Each team selected a recorder to write down ideas and a reporter to communicate those ideas to the entire class after the small group discussions. The remaining group member was asked to be a prompter, to keep the group on task, to ask questions that would keep the conversation moving toward the goal of collecting ideas about the meaning of the story.

During the talk between students in small groups, meanings for the story often changed significantly as a result of reading—and then discussing—what others had written. For example, Kirk, whose initial response in his log was "I can not figure out what the story means, and its significance, so I will summarize it," commented that Susan "brought all my thoughts and understanding together" during small group discussion. In her journal, Susan had written, "I think the story is about a broken heart. The story inside the story was parallel. . . . When the Chief and Mary broke up, the Laughing Man died over the death of his wolf. He died of a broken heart, at the same time of the death of the love of Mary and the Chief." Several students said that reading such commentary and discussing various interpretations made them think in new ways about the story's significance.

After students in small groups read and discussed their reactions, the reporters presented ideas to the whole class. As groups reported, I encouraged the expression and elaboration of meanings—not only group meanings but also individual meanings within those groups and not only meanings for the entire story but also meanings for specific events or objects in the story. For example, during the discussion several students expressed different interpretations of the vial of eagle's blood that the Laughing Man crushes before he dies.

"We thought it represented his love for Mary Hudson," said Erica.

"How would that work out?" I asked.

"When their relationship was going well, the Laughing Man survived by drinking the blood," said Erica. "But, when Mary and the Chief broke up, the Laughing Man crushed the vial, and he died along with his love for Mary."

"Sort of his life blood being crushed?" I echoed in a question.

"Yeah," said Erica. "Something like that."

"What other explanations for the crushed vial came up in your small group discussions?" I asked the class.

"I thought it stood for the children in the Comanche Club," said Mark.

"How does that work?" I asked.

"I don't know. Just seems that way," answered Mark.

"But we need to tie the meaning to something. Events in the story. Ideas you had when reading it. Something so it makes sense," I said.

"Seemed to me that the children of the Comanche tribe were keeping the Laughing Man alive," Mark said.

"I thought it was the baseball game," said Alison.

"Someone in our group said it stood for a false lifestyle," said Katie.

"Does anyone want to explain how those meanings would make sense in the context of the story?" I asked.

"I don't know about baseball," added Katie, "but I thought there was something false about how the Chief was living or about his relationship with Mary and that when the truth was out, the relationship died."

"I'm not absolutely sure what the vial is," said John, "but, if it has a deep meaning, I'm sure it isn't baseball or the kids because they are not really deep issues. I can see the false lifestyle but there are inconsistencies in the story because the Chief doesn't have a false life but a different life than the kids see. The mask would be more appropriate."

"So what do you think the vial represents?" I asked John.

"I'd have to agree with Erica," he said. "The vial would be Mary and the Chief's love."

I explored these and other meanings with students. I frequently asked them to explain how an interpretation could be grounded in the text and how it made sense in relation to the whole story. But I tried not to impose my own "reading" of the story on the students—favoring interaction among them and with the text. Although I mentioned that the story might be saying some important things about the creative process and the unconscious mind, no students picked up or expanded upon that idea even though I pointed out the relationship between real life experience and its transformation into our dream life.

Nevertheless, the whole class discussion gave students an opportunity to create a class meaning for the story or parts of it. One student wrote that "The discussion changed my view of the story completely. I never saw any link between the Coach's life and his bizarre stories. I didn't understand that the Laughing Man's death meant anything."

This classroom discussion of Salinger's short story provides us with a glimpse of readers reading. It serves as a view into the meaning construction zone where readers make meaning for texts through several cognitive and social processes that will be examined in the rest of this chapter.

# CHARACTERISTICS OF GOOD READERS

In the first part of this chapter, we are going to explore what goes on in the minds of good readers. A number of researchers (Brown, Palincsar, & Armbruster, 1984; Duke & Pearson, 2002; Pearson, Roehler, Dole, & Duffy, 1992; Pressley, El-Kinary, & Brown, 1992,) have investigated the way good readers read and have identified several skills that contribute to their fluent reading. Although highly skilled readers may not engage in all of these comprehension-fostering activities all of the time, they are likely to use several of them, especially if they begin to have problems with comprehension.

1. Good readers activate and connect with the knowledge base related to the subject of the reading. We will see later in this chapter how this mental activity that fosters comprehension is connected with schema theory and the function of our long-term memory.
2. Good readers monitor their comprehension process while reading and recognize those moments of mental blackout and misunderstandings that lead us into confusion. Later, we will see how this activity is related to metacognition.
3. Good readers pay attention to the spectrum of information they are reading and categorize it from important to unimportant, giving priority to major content and secondary attention to trivia.
4. Good readers both make inferences and test them while reading. These inferences include hypotheses, interpretations, predictions, and conclusions.
5. Good readers periodically review what they have read and ask themselves questions about the reading. As we will discover, summarizing and questioning are powerful comprehension fostering processes.
6. Good readers do not ignore comprehension breakdowns or lapses. They take steps to correct comprehension once problems are recognized.
7. Good readers also clarify for themselves why they are reading and try to understand what is expected of them as readers and learners.
8. Good readers make sure the meanings they are constructing while reading are internally consistent and compatible with what they know and what makes sense. This constitutes part of their internalized standards of text evaluation.
9. Good readers identify key concepts or major propositions (aka macropropositions) when reading expository texts and use them as knowledge organizers.
10. Good readers also make good use of their working memory so they can hold alternative interpretations of a text in mind, compare them, and evaluate them to determine which interpretation should be granted greater credibility.

Of course good readers do not engage in all of these praiseworthy mental activities whenever they read, but many good readers have access to these skills and use them automatically or selectively to help themselves comprehend text. As we build a mental model of the reading process, we will want to be able to take account of all of these activities (as well as several others) and their contributions to the construction of meaning during the reading process.

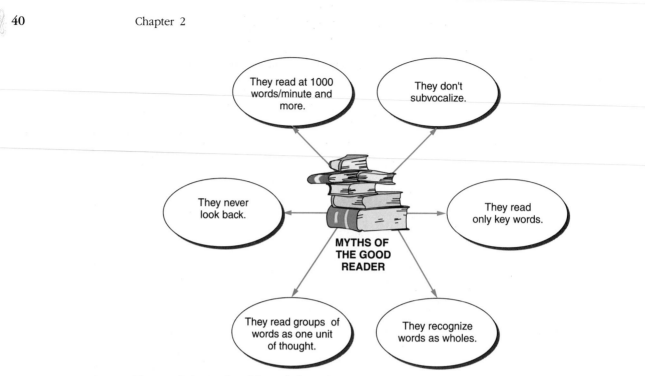

FIGURE 2.1    Myths of the Good Reader.

## MYTHS OF THE GOOD READER

Along with the previous ten documented mental activities in which good readers engage when reading, several other allegations about the qualities of good readers need to be presented and examined. We can look at these statements, which are summarized in Figure 2.1, and ask ourselves how much evidence supports them. Some educators (Whimbey & Lochhead, 1999) view these as myths of reading proficiency. Other educators (Adams, 1990) have used research to scrutinize widely held assumptions about reading.

### First Good Reader Myth: *They can read at 1,000 words a minute and more with improved comprehension*

Many speed reading courses proclaim that students can accelerate their reading rate and get more homework done more efficiently. In our time-driven lives, such accelerated reading sounds quite appealing. But, have you ever tried to read a college or high school physics text at 1,000 words a minute? How about a chemistry text? Or consider reading Shakespeare, Emily Dickinson, or Wallace Stevens at that rate. How about *The Federalist Papers* or Wittgenstein's *Philosophical Investigations?*

After taking a speed reading course and reading Tolstoy's voluminous Russian novel *War and Peace* in 20 minutes, Woody Allen summarized the book: "It's about Russia." When we look more carefully at the rate of eye fixations as able readers read, we'll see why average reading rates of 1,000 words per minute and more are mythic. Speed reading enables readers to cover more words per minute, but they pay a price: comprehension drops (Just & Carpenter, 1987).

**Angela loses control, spins out and hits the wall
in the final stretch of the National
Speed-Reading Championship.**

*Source:* In the Bleachers © Steve Moore. Reprinted with permission of UNIVERSAL PRESS SYNDICATE.
All rights reserved.

Obviously, we need to think of reading at different rates for different purposes. Although studies have shown repeatedly that, if readers push faster than about 300 words a minute, they sacrifice comprehension, some texts require even a more plodding speed—with several rereadings! Perhaps we could think about having various reading gears: a skim gear, a pleasure reading gear, a newspaper gear, a cognitive challenge gear, and a low-speed, frustration-management gear. And, by the way, remember that some readers really enjoy savoring the sounds of words and phrases, the images words may evoke, and the pleasures of reflecting on an insight about life's meanings or its ironic twists.

A reviewer of books for the *New York Times* (Volk, 1999) wrote that she read *Faster: The Acceleration of Just About Everything* by James Gleick in 412 minutes. I did a little calculation. The book runs 324 pages; approximate number of words per page came to about 400; that means the book has about 130,000 words. At 412 minutes, that means the book reviewer, who is also a novelist and essayist, was cruising along at about 315 words per minute. In a book critical of our accelerating just about everything, including reading, this reviewer was maintaining a pretty sensible—and predictable—speed.

## Second Good Reader Myth: *They don't subvocalize*

Subvocalization occurs when you hear the words you read in your mind or when your lips or tongue muscles move as you read. Some "experts" advise visual reading only without subvocalization of any kind. However, subvocalization appears to be a very important part of learning to read, and the inner echo in our mind of words on the page may enable us to improve our comprehension—especially of more difficult texts. Suppressing subvocalization is also likely to suppress comprehension (Waters, Caplan, & Hildebrandt, 1987). We will discover more about subvocalization and its connection with the role of phonological processing later in this chapter.

## Third Good Reader Myth: *They read only the key words*

As Whimbey and Lochhead (1999) point out, how will we know in advance of reading a text what the key words are that we must make sure we read to comprehend a passage? Trying to read only key words frequently results in readers' misinterpreting the text. Marilyn Adams (1990) points out that readers probably process every word they come upon in a text to gain an understanding of a text's meaning. Skipping even one word, like a word that negates a statement, in the hunt for only the key words may result in a complete misreading of the text. Good readers are frequently word-by-word readers, a phenomenon that will make more sense when we see how the mind processes print a little later on.

## Fourth Good Reader Myth: *They recognize words as wholes*

While good readers appear to recognize words as wholes, they also process virtually every letter of each word they read (Adams, 1994). Undoubtedly, good readers recognize many words at a glance. However, less frequently read words, words that may bear an enormous amount of importance for the meaning of a passage, are far more likely to be processed letter by letter (Ehri, 1991).

## Fifth Good Reader Myth: *They read groups of words as a unit of thought*

We may form units of thought, what we will call propositions, as we read. However, trying to take in a group of three or four words in one fixation and transform it into a proposition or part of a gist is unlikely to work. A cluster of words may not form a coherent or useful thought. Texts are more complex in the arrangement of their units of meaning, especially as we begin to construct an internal text representation in our minds. As mentioned above, Adams (1990) found evidence that readers usually read each word, one at a time. Nevertheless, some words may appear so frequently that we take them in as "sight words," words like *the* or *and,* that could be tied to other less frequently sighted words in a text. We might, on occasion, combine these words so rapidly that it appears as though we were taking in units of thought. However, pushing a reader to read in word groups, as is often done with a device called a *tachistiscope* that briefly flashes words or phrases on a screen, may increase the overall reading rate for certain kinds of texts but add nothing noteworthy to comprehension.

## Sixth Good Reader Myth: *They never look back*

Speed reading experts may urge readers to push their eyes forward, to grasp groups of words as units of thought, to practice by increasing the speed at which a tachistiscope or computer program flashes words or groups of words from a text. In forcing themselves to push forward, readers may miss important monitoring messages their minds are sending, messages like "I don't follow what's going on here. I need to reread this to understand." The reread strategy is one of the most basic solutions to the problem of misunderstanding or losing the thread of a text. Remember that good readers summarize and ask themselves questions about their levels of understanding. If good readers don't understand a text, they have strategies like looking back to help them comprehend successfully.

## WHAT ARE THE BENEFITS OF A READING PROCESS MODEL?

Like most teachers, you probably have an implicit "model" of the reading process even though that model may not be explicitly described—unless you're asked to picture and explain your understanding of the process, as you were at the beginning of this chapter. Nevertheless, your implicit understanding of reading may influence your instructional strategies in the classroom. Understanding the reading process more fully and explicitly will contribute to deeper knowledge of your students' learning and improvements in instructional practice for your students (Beck, 1989). The benefits of a reading model are summarized in Figure 2.2 and described in the following paragraphs.

First, a model integrates research findings, makes theory graphic, and provides us with an explanation of how reading takes place in accord with what we currently know (Tierney, 1994). Taking a car's engine apart helps us see how it works and how to repair it. But dismantling the reading process presents us with a very different problem. Reading is a highly complex and hidden process with no pistons, valves, or crankshafts to pull out for observation. However, we do have a substantial amount of research and theoretical knowledge about reading. Millions learn how to read even though we may not know all the details about how reading happens. What we do know from research and theory enables us to construct a model to visualize this mysterious, invisible, and very complex process. Having a model will reduce some of the mystery surrounding reading, and you could then explain the process to others so that they might understand more about a very important skill that is very hard to see. We might view the model as a metaphor or analogy that helps us visualize and understand research and theories that explain aspects of the reading process.

Second, knowing something about how the reading process works and having a model to render that knowledge enables us to make predictions about the reading process. For example, the model can help you to understand how the activities of good readers contribute to their high levels of comprehension.

Third, a model of reading will help you detect where points of breakdown in comprehension occur. Glitches happen. Perplexities arise. Things don't make sense. A model can help you visualize what components are vulnerable or fail to contribute to smooth meaning made while reading. In short, a model will help you understand what's going on when diagnosing a student's struggle with reading.

Lastly, a model will give you clues about intervention strategies that may help struggling readers at different points in the reading process. While viewing the model as a sure resource for formulating prescriptions that we can administer to the ailing reader may be dangerous, we can use it as a resource for good hints. There may be no clear, direct path from the model to classroom curriculum or tutoring strategies, but a model creates more opportunity for instructional interventions.

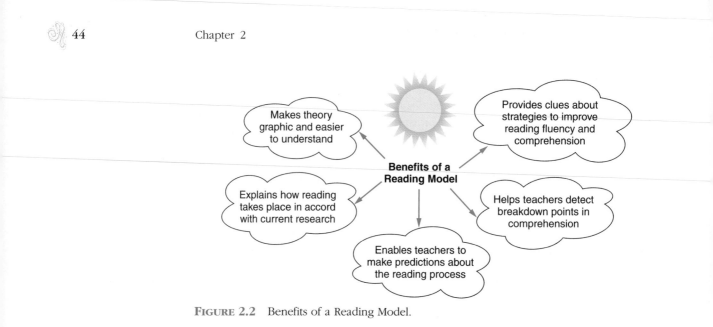

**FIGURE 2.2**    Benefits of a Reading Model.

## A PEEK INTO THE CONSTRUCTION ZONE

What we are going to go through in order to appreciate reading's complexity is a type of reading program or cognitive flow chart that replicates the reading process of a good reader. We cannot possibly replicate or even describe the mind's many parallel activities while we read. However, we can begin to see how the reading process works by breaking it down into components and sub-processes. In that way, we can begin to appreciate the knowledge, skills, and processing speed of good readers. Like almost any tour guide, I'll insert commentary about important landmarks as we pass them. Along the way, I'll point out factors that contribute to the trouble that some readers—both expert and struggling readers—may have when they read texts that are challenging for them. I'll also provide "Diagnostic Peepholes," points at which teachers can peek into the meaning construction zone to assess readers and gain information about their reading processes that could inform instruction.

### An Overview of the Reading Model

The reading model that I will present consists of several components and processes that contribute to our making sense of print as we read. To understand these components and processes, we are going to begin with an overview of the whole system. (See Figure 2.3.) After the overview, we'll examine its parts in more detail to help you gain a deeper understanding of reading in school contexts.

The model consists of four major components, as shown in Figure 2.3:

1. Our *sensory system* that is stimulated by an external text we see or hear,
2. Our *cognitive processes* that include orthographic and phonological processing, word recognition, long-term and working memory, construction of phrase and sentence sense, text building, and an internal text representation,
3. Our *metacognitive processes* that include both monitoring and control of our cognitive processes, and

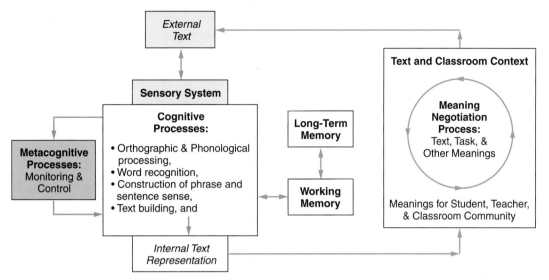

**FIGURE 2.3**  Overview of Socio-Cognitive Reading Model.

4. A *text and classroom context* in which we read, interpret, comprehend, discuss, analyze, and evaluate texts.

After viewing this big picture of the model of reading, I will magnify the sensory system, the cognitive and metacognitive processes, and the classroom context so that you can look much more closely at how each contributes to the reading process. All the components with details included will appear later in Figure 2.4.

## The Sensory System

For the purposes of reading, we use two primary modes of sensation: visual and auditory. Visually, we perceive images of letters and words from the external text assumed to be in a classroom context. Text can be printed on a page or electronically transmitted. These visual images initiate the processing of letters and words as symbols, also called orthographic processing. When a reader reads aloud, we hear sounds as speech symbols that we process as syllables, phonemes, and words, also called phonological processing. (We will not consider those using their fingers to read Braille.)

Both print and sounds that communicate language are symbolic systems that we learn to decode. That decoding process begins with either orthographic processing when print stimulates receptors in our eyes or phonological processing when the sound of words stimulates receptors in our ears. However, these two processing systems, the orthographic and the phonological, frequently interact when readers read.

> **DIAGNOSTIC PEEPHOLE**
> Is the student's vision sufficiently acute for reading without any eyestrain? If vision is questionable, arrange for the student to have an eye examination.

## Cognitive Processes

Our cognitive processes include ***orthographic*** and ***phonological processing, working and long-term memory, word recognition,*** construction of ***phrase and sentence sense, text building,*** and an ***internal text representation.***

Orthographic processing.     You read in tiny moments of eye fixations on a word or a small group of words. Each fixation usually lasts about a quarter to a half a second. These fixations take up about 90 to 95% of your reading time. After a fixation, your eyes jump to the next fixation. Reading psychologists call the jumps **saccades,** and each saccade takes about 20 milliseconds or 2% of one second (Just & Carpenter, 1987). Bauer (1994) compared reading to a slide show in which our eyes are exposed to about four slides per second. Each slide provides graphic information about the words that we rapidly process into a meaningful mental movie. If we assume that at each fixation skilled readers take in about one word, that means they read at about 240 words per minute (4 × 60). Knowing, as we do, that good readers occasionally take in two words or more at some fixations (and occasionally reread), we could easily justify an average skilled reader's rate of about 300 words per minute.

But do the whole words always translate into meanings or do good readers perceive individual letters and letter patterns before processing the word? Although on the surface good readers appear to grasp words as units, we have evidence that they actually process individual letters of words in the texts they read (Adams, 1990, 1994; McConkie & Zola, 1981). However, good readers link letters into patterns that they have seen over and over again so that they do not always experience the letters as independent units (Ehri, 1991). During a fixation, the visual form of letters combine into groups or units of recognizable letters. The more frequently a reader encounters letters and letter units of two or three letters the more quickly these letters and letter units will activate the meaning for the word they represent.

Among the operations that occur during orthographic processing are the encoding of letter order and the division of long words into parts or syllables. Inspire, conspire, perspire, suspire, transpire. For a struggling reader, grasping the letter order for these words would itself be daunting, but then each word needs to be divided into its meaning-revealing syllables, its prefix and root. While poor readers have trouble reporting letter order in the words they read, good readers rarely make errors of that kind. Good readers have gained sufficient knowledge of letter patterns and their more common associations. That letter pattern knowledge helps to reinforce their perception of printed words. However, weak readers, who lack sufficient knowledge of letter associations, are less able to use their memory of letter patterns to help with word recognition and the reporting of letter order. While a good eighth-grade reader is unlikely to have trouble identifying the pattern of letters that make up *frequent* in the word *frequently,* a weak eighth-grade reader who infrequently reads the word would. Frequent errors in letter order reporting have been interpreted as a manifestation of dyslexia in the form of a perceptual deficit. However, researchers have shown that the root cause of frequent errors in letter order probably arises from poor orthographic training and insufficient opportunities to develop knowledge of letter patterns (Stanovich, 2000).

The other function of the orthographic process is its capacity to break down polysyllabic words, such as *antidisestablishmentarianism.* As you read such words, you may notice that you attack the word by breaking it into syllables (12 in this case) rather than seeing it letter by letter. Good readers are skillful at breaking longer words down into their syllables while weaker readers struggle with such words. Researchers (Adams, 1990; Wilkinson & Silliman, 2000) have shown that good readers use their knowledge of letter strings and associations to break longer words into parts or syllables. Because they have over-learned word patterns and common associations, good readers segment longer words at such a rapid pace that it appears automatic. Less skilled readers, however, may take an uncomfortably long time to pronounce a word like *reverence* yet not identify its meaning. This may be one of several reasons for caution when asking a class of students to engage in round robin reading.

Cat. As a knowledgeable reader, you knew the word at a glance. The reader sees *c* in the word, but, because the whole word lies in our visual span at one fixation, we can also see *a* and *t*. Each letter contributes to heightening excitation for the associated network of the word *cat*. If you were just beginning to read, your recognition of the word *cat* would not have been as automatic. However, because you have read, heard, spoken, and written the word hundreds of times, its pattern recognition is instantaneous. Adams (1990) has pointed out that if beginning readers cannot recognize individual letters and letter patterns automatically and transform those letters into words that have meaning for them, then their frustration will probably keep them from reading at all.

Catalogue. There's that "cat" again. But this is no word-at-a-glance for early or weak readers. For this word, the reader has to have a pretty good knowledge of its spelling pattern and be able to break it down into its parts (Just & Carpenter, 1987). A good reader, skilled in parcing words and nearly automatic when faced with finding information from a catalogue of words, will have little trouble with the associated letter patterns and meaning stored in long-term memory.

A basic question about the processing of letters and words is this: Do readers sound them out? To answer this question, we must look at the role of phonological processing in reading.

Phonological processing.   Phonological processing occurs as letters, associated patterns of letters, or words activate (usually automatically in good readers) their corresponding sounds. But must these sounds always become activated for a reader to become aware of a word's meaning? Or is there a more direct route to meaning? Earlier in the history of reading research, educators widely accepted a "dual-route" model (Stanovich, 1991). According to that model, two pathways following visual stimulation could be taken. One path by-passed phonological mediation and led directly to the lexicon. A second route, more indirect, went through phonological processing, wherein stored spelling-to-sound correspondences were activated. After much investigation, Seidenberg (1985) established that phonological coding was usually involved in accessing a word's meaning, especially in the case of infrequently used words.

However, research (McClelland & Rumelhart, 1986) revealed that several related reading processes, such as orthographic and phonological, could occur at the same time and side-by-side. With "parallel activation models" like those proposed by Perfetti (1985) and Seidenberg and McClelland (1989), phonological activation is a clear result of orthographic activation. If the parallel processing view holds up and becomes standard (Stanovich, 1991), the issue of dual-routes and the question of whether lexical access occurs before or after phonological processing will be a non-issue.

Many other researchers (Adams, 1990, 1994) have confirmed that good readers automatically produce letter-to-sound translations. Rather than being an obstacle to readers, the phonological loop that echoes in sound can support reading in a couple of ways. First, it can function as a back-up system to orthographic processing. Second, it enlarges readers' working memory and thereby enhances comprehension, especially for more challenging texts.

As letters are processed orthographically, their impression activates corresponding sounds that enable us to phonologically process texts. The "feedback" sound of the word may help us process the printed letters more carefully, especially if we are having trouble recognizing an unfamiliar word. We are more likely to pay more attention to letters that could be skipped and to see how letters, when sounded, form recognizable strings. Furthermore, pronouncing a word like *salivate* can activate its potential meanings. And, if both visual and auditory cues are familiar and similar, both orthographic and phonological processing will activate appropriate word meanings.

Because many of the words we read are often repeated and over-learned, we do not have to translate letters and words into sounds to grasp their meaning. Words orthographically processed can be directly recognized with little, if any, recourse to phonological processing. But these over-learned words, such as *dog,* constitute only a small portion of the words we read. Most words, such as *canine,* are encountered infrequently. These infrequently used words often carry much of a text's meaning. And readers processing content area texts, such as those in math or science, frequently encounter large numbers of unfamiliar or new words.

Good eleventh-grade readers can use their phonological backup system to help them understand less familiar words, such as *tangential,* and attack those that are entirely new, such as *inculcate.* Less visually familiar words may, when sounded, trigger stronger associations with word meanings held in long-term memory, as might occur when "tangential" triggers "tangent." And longer words, like "tangential," may have syllables that, when sounded, can help readers dissect and combine word elements to discover meaning. Orthographic knowledge, of course, also helps in these attacks on unknown words, as readers visually associate strings of letters and recall common syllable break-points.

Readers may also pronounce words because they look like others they know. Knowledge of letter–phoneme correspondence isn't the sole mechanism readers use to phonological recode. Researchers (Goswami, 2000; Moustafa, 1997) have found that children use analogies in reading and that their use increases as vocabularies enlarge. If a reader knows how to say the word *light* and comes across the word *fight,* she may be able to analogize from the known pronunciation of -*ight* to the unknown word. Of course, pronouncing a word doesn't magically release its meaning.

> **DIAGNOSTIC PEEPHOLE**
> You can evaluate students' letter–sound or decoding skills and levels of phonemic awareness through an Individual Reading Inventory, Curriculum Based Measurement, or Running Record, each of which will be described in the next chapter.

Without a memory system, stimuli to the sensory system would be senseless data. So before we proceed to word recognition, we will first have to discover what we know about the role of memory in reading.

Working memory.    Without memory you simply could not read this. The letters and words would go through your sensory system and brain as though it were a sieve with no meaningful residue whatsoever. There are brain-damaged individuals who can't remember any new experiences, including what they read. Fortunately, most of us have several forms of memory that, when explained, will help you understand how they help—and limit—reading. What have psychologists learned about memory that would help us understand how it works when we read?

Let's begin with working memory, one of two major memory components depicted in Figure 2.4. Working memory is where we represent the immediate world, actively compute solutions, such as making sense out of this text, and remember the results for rather short periods of time. (Do you remember the first word of the last sentence you read?) Working memory also creates mental and learning bottlenecks. That's because its capacity to hold information is very limited and the limited amount of information it can hold deteriorates rather fast. So what we have is a limited memory bank or cognitive resource to proceed with reading and to keep short-term track of our progress through symbolic representations. Fortunately, mental functions, such as recognizing the meaning of a word, can become automatic and reduce the demands on working memory so that it can work harder on tougher tasks like comprehending more complex passages.

While reading, working memory keeps essential meaning construction data and skills active, including letters and words from the text on the page and knowledge from long-term memory that transfers into working memory. From the text being read, working memory holds orthographic information in the form of letters and phonological responses or analogues in the form of sounds that correspond to the images observed. Dog, as a pattern of letters and /dŏg/ as corresponding sounds, interact to reinforce and maintain meaning in memory. Knowledge and skills transferred into working memory from long-term memory include knowledge networks of many kinds, such as word meanings and text structure knowledge. All of these forms of knowledge and skills enable us to make sense of texts. Working memory also maintains the result of our text building efforts: an active mental text representation that is continually updated as we read. All of these features of working memory are shown in Figure 2.4 where the features of long-term memory are also summarized.

Long-term memory.   What comes into working memory from past learning and experience arrives there only because of its access to long-term memory. *Long-term memory* (LTM) is like the hard disk on a computer that stores large amounts of information until we erase it—or until our hard disk crashes and we lose it. We draw on information stored in LTM to help us deal with issues or problems that are currently alive in working memory. Of course, we have much more storage space for memory in our brains than any mega-gigabyte hard disk. We never seem to run out of room to learn something new—including vocabulary.

How does long-term memory serve readers? Readers hold many forms of information in LTM that have a number of different functions. Forms of LTM that are critically important to reading include declarative, procedural, and conditional knowledge, knowledge of language (orthographic, phonological, lexical, and syntactical knowledge), word analysis skills (encoding productions resulting in word recognition), text-structure knowledge, comprehension strategies, and metacognitive knowledge and strategies. The activation and application of nearly all these forms of knowledge held in LTM is best understood through schema theory (Ruddell & Unrau, 1994).

*Schema theory.*   A **schema** is a knowledge network, an organized cognitive pattern, or a script that guides our behavior, including what we do with information gathered from reading. We can compare it to files of knowledge with associated "slots" that a reader fills with related information gained from a text (Rumelhart, 1980). If readers have activated a schema for knowledge about which they are reading, the schema can provide slots for incoming data, making the reading process relatively effortless. According to schema theory, what we know about grocery stores, restaurants, football, animals, WWII, ecology, and even reading is organized into associated networks or schemata (the plural form of schema).

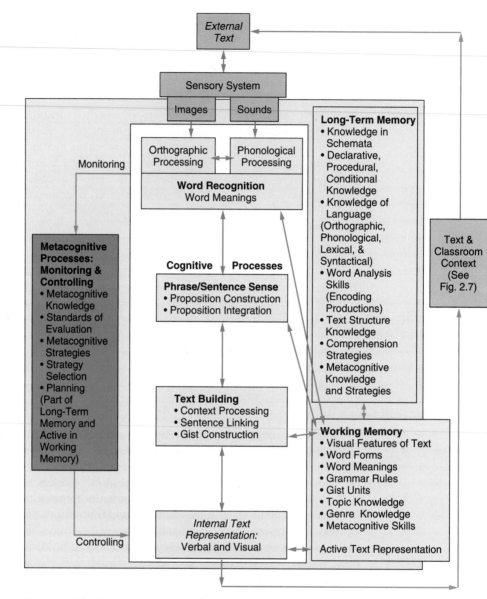

**FIGURE 2.4**  Socio-Cognitive Reading Model Components.

A schema can represent a network of events that commonly occurs when a specific situation arises, like going to a restaurant. As researchers on scripts in memory have observed (Bower, Black, & Turner, 1994; Schank & Abelson, 1977), going to a restaurant triggers a series of events: entering, ordering, eating, and exiting. A series of events occurs within each of these "scenes." When entering a restaurant, the customer looks for a table, decides where to sit, goes to the table, and sits down. When reading a narrative text, readers presented with characters entering a restaurant are likely to activate the "slots" that compose the restaurant script and arouse expectations that may be met by the text or that may distort events that actually are described

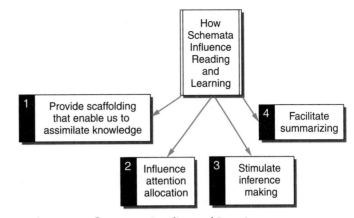

**FIGURE 2.5**   Schemata's Influence on Reading and Learning.

in the text. In short, activated schemata raise readers' expectations that content already known may arise in the text.

However, schemata also serve as knowledge resources that enable us to build new knowledge structures (Spiro, 1988). Accordingly, readers do not always mechanistically fill slots but take chunks of knowledge from many different yet related knowledge structures and assemble new knowledge structures, new meanings. Newly constructed schema allows for more organic, interdependent links than any linear, rigidly conceived schema.

With respect to how schemata affect learning and remembering from text, Anderson (1994) identified several of their functions that are summarized in Figure 2.5:

1. *Schemata provide scaffolding that enable us to create meanings out of new information we read and organize that new knowledge in relation to prior knowledge.* When reading about strategies to motivate your students to learn, your schemata related to motivation and motivational strategies would become activated and guide your comprehension of the text you're reading. How you have organized information about motivation and motivational strategies would then influence how you process, use, or transform new information you acquire from the text. We might add that existing schemata may be modified if new learning compels readers to alter their internalized schemata in the direction of new information. If newly read information does not fit into the slots of readers' existing schemata, that is, if readers cannot connect new material with their existing schemata, readers will often extend more effort attempting to comprehend the text.

2. *Schemata influence attention allocation.* If readers have schemata for a topic, say Dublin, Ireland, those knowledge structures will influence the amount of attention that readers would give to aspects of the text being read, like James Joyce's *The Dubliners.* Knowing something about the topic, readers will focus on those features of the text they deem most important.

3. *Schemata stimulate readers to go beyond the literal to draw less obvious implications and conclusions from text content.* If readers have no pre-existing knowledge about a topic being read, they cannot activate a schema that will help them comprehend either the explicit text or its implications. I encounter this problem when I try to read articles in the journal *Science* about research on genetics or neurotransmitters. However, if readers have a schema for the text, they can use it to make inferences that

enable readers to go beyond what is stated in the text itself. They can also use the schema to fill in knowledge gaps when information may be left out or forgotten. That inferential elaboration and reconstruction can strengthen readers' overall text comprehension.

4. *Schemata facilitate summarizing.* As we discovered earlier, summarizing is an important activity in which good readers engage. If readers have a schema for a topic being read, say motivation, that old network of knowledge about motivation can make summarizing newly acquired knowledge about motivational strategies much less effortful and more comprehensive.

Schemata hold the key to understanding the bottom-up and top-down interactive nature of the reading process. While readers process individual letters and words bottom-up, activated schemata interact with that data and influence the construction of meaning top-down. This construction-integration process occurs after each reading cycle (Just & Carpenter, 1987; Kintsch, 1994). As we will see at a later point in the model's description, readers can activate and apply schemata to build web-like representations of the text rather than rigid, slot-filled representations.

**Declarative, Procedural, and Conditional Knowledge.**    Background knowledge stored as schemata in LTM has been divided into information about what's in the world, how it works, and when to use it. Cognitive psychologists refer to these as declarative, procedural, and conditional knowledge, respectively (Paris, Lipson, & Wixson, 1983). Declarative knowledge is knowledge of facts, objects, events, language, concepts, and theories that contributes to our personal construction and understanding of "reality." Procedural knowledge consists of strategies and skills for using and applying knowledge, from knowing how to replace an electrical wall outlet to starting a barbecue. We may not even be able to describe some of this procedural knowledge, like riding a bicycle or reading the last sentence you read. Finally, conditional knowledge refers to the "when and why" of using information, such as when and why to apply a known classroom management procedure like assertive discipline. When we read, we usually use all three of these forms of knowledge because we must access our memory of facts and words, engage our reading skills, and decide when and why to use our knowledge to facilitate comprehension.

**Language Knowledge.**    To construct meaning, readers must engage various forms of knowledge about language. Readers' language knowledge includes schemata that represent orthographic, phonological, lexical, and syntactical knowledge. Although most of these knowledge forms are well developed before a child even enters school (Heath, 1983), lexical and syntactic knowledge continues to grow throughout the school years.

*Phonological knowledge* is well established in the memories of most children by the time they are 4 years of age (Gibson & Levin, 1985). They can identify words that conform to English phonology in contrast to sound clusters that make no sense, such as *click* versus *dlek* (Morehead, 1971). Some children, however, enter school with English as a second language or with phonological problems that emerge as they learn to read (Stanovich, 2000).

*Orthographic knowledge* accumulates over time as readers phonologically recode words that have similar patterns and as they store similarly spelled sight words in LTM (Ehri, 1994). Readers may also acquire orthographic knowledge as they learn to spell words with similar patterns that are stored in their lexicon. Many spelling patterns, including word roots (in*tend*ed, ex*tend*ing, *tend*ency) and word endings (-ed, -ing, -ency) may be observed by readers and remembered.

*Lexical knowledge* refers to knowledge of words and their meanings. Knowledge of words is closely connected with a reader's background knowledge in the forms of declarative, procedural, and conditional knowledge as well as knowledge of the world in general because it is through words that these forms of knowledge find expression. Furthermore, some researchers (Johnson, Toms-Bronowski, & Pittelman, 1981) have found that words representing concepts are clustered into categories that are arranged in hierachically structured schemata. In turn, these categories are connected with other conceptual structures.

Extensive research on vocabulary (Beck & McKeown, 1991) also indicates that lexical knowledge is directly related to comprehension and meaning construction. Efficient meaning construction demands that readers have a knowledge of concepts, and readers must depend upon their internal lexicon of remembered words as their route to these concepts. How would I ever explain the process of reading to you without having the vocabulary to do so? How would you ever understand it without having the vocabulary I use? The larger a reader's lexicon, the larger is the reader's capacity to understand texts.

While the size of a reader's lexicon is important, so is speed of access to it. Research on lexical access reveals that the meaning of more frequently used words, such as *when*, are more rapidly activated than less frequently used ones (Just & Carpenter, 1987). Fluent readers usually have faster lexical access speeds than poor readers who may have to activate phonological information about a word before gaining lexical access (Stanovich, 2000). Because of the importance of vocabulary to concept development, Chapter 4 focuses on techniques for building word knowledge in content areas.

*Syntactical knowledge,* like phonological knowledge, is well developed before children begin reading. The basic ability to understand and generate language is inborn (Chomsky, 1959, 1965). According to Bruner (1986), we are born with a Language Acquisition Device (LAD) that requires a Language Acquisition Support System (LASS). The Language Acquisition Support System is embedded in our culture, as we saw in the previous chapter, and emerges in various social settings (Vygotsky, 1986). A child's innate capacity to understand and generate syntactical structures will not develop normally if it is not sufficiently stimulated and supported through social interaction.

*Word analysis skills.*   Word analysis enables readers to recognize words, to transform visual symbols in print to mental representations for meaning construction. Word analyzing skills are grounded in each reader's early experiences with print and invented spellings and grow through the school years into the automatic processing of known words (Samuels, 1994) and the conscious analysis of new words (Ehri, 1994).

*Encoding productions.*   Numerous encoding productions are also stored in LTM. Encoding refers to the change or transformation of symbols, whether visual or auditory, into memory patterns. You encoded these words in order to understand them. For encoding to occur, we have to learn many productions. A production is similar to a computer's program because, just like a production, a program states an action that is to be carried out and the conditions that need to be met for that action to take place.

We have in LTM many production rules or statements consisting of IF-THEN connections that are activated under the right conditions, like when we're multiplying numbers or reading. For example, IF 7 × 7, THEN 49. Together, these production rules make up a production system that is just like the computer program I'm using to type this sentence on my monitor. This program has a rule like this: IF I spell *their* "thier", THEN it will underline *thier* in red. Encoding productions and word analysis skills contribute to readers' recognition of words, a process we will examine more closely after we have completed this explanation of the role of LTM in reading.

***Text structure knowledge.***　As readers respond to texts and construct meanings for them, they often try to figure out if the text is narrative or expository. These text structures and strategies for figuring out what form a text is likely to fit are stored as schemata in LTM. These schemata, if appropriately activated, can help readers discover how a writer organized a text and how to organize a mental representation of that text. Narrative text structures follow a "story grammar" that includes setting, initiating event, characters' responses to that event, characters' behaviors, consequences of the behaviors, and a resolution. Although often mixed, expository texts typically take one of six forms: description, sequence, causation, problem-solution, comparison, and persuasion. These text structures are more fully described with examples in Chapter 5.

***Comprehension strategies.***　To the list of resources held in LTM, I would add comprehension strategies. Readers apply these strategies to promote meaning construction and learning from texts under certain conditions, for example, when faced with an unfamiliar text structure, when comprehension breaks down, or when engaged in critical reading. I would also add word identification strategies that may be triggered when less familiar words, like *approbation*, appear in texts and readers may need to analyze the word or use context cues in order to increase the likelihood of its being recognized.

As we saw from our review of characteristics of good readers, they usually have many comprehension strategies stored in LTM that they can activate when they get into trouble reading a challenging text. However, less skilled and struggling readers have far fewer strategies to activate and apply. That is why a major portion of this text presents strategies that you can teach growing readers so that they have more resources to attack challenging texts in the content areas.

Although you will notice in Figure 2.4 that metacognitive knowledge and skills are also housed in LTM, I will discuss them after explaining all other cognitive processes.

Word recognition.　When readers fixate on the word *cat*, orthographic and phonological processing fire up. All of the letters in the word *cat* should be strongly associated because of the word's frequency—even for early readers. We could expect that the reader will see and, most likely, hear *cat* and its letter units as an associated pattern of letters. If the pattern of letters had been C-Y-T instead of C-A-T, some readers' orthographic processors might attempt to process the stimulus pattern in the same way. However, most readers would eventually perceive the set of letters as C-Y-T, the visual stimulus on the page. The automatic response to certain words, such as *cat*, is a result of our learning patterns of associated but individual letters.

The whole word is easier to read than its individual parts because of their being strongly associated.

As beginning readers become more fluent readers, they learn more and more "sight words" or words that readers recognize at a glance and without much in the way of extensive orthographic and phonological processing. These words include *the, and, that,* and (with more practice) words such as *bat, dog, fish,* and *tree.* Some teachers encourage emergent readers to learn sight words and keep word banks displayed on classroom walls. While short function words, frequently repeated words, and easily predictable words may occasionally be skipped, most content words in a text receive direct visual fixation to facilitate word recognition.

Ehri (1994) identified several ways in which a reader can read words:

◆ *Sight.* As we have seen, only familiar words are read by sight. When reading words by sight, readers access their mental dictionary and identify the word's meaning, spelling, pronunciation, and even grammatical roles in sentences. These words are read rapidly as units with no analysis of or breaks between phonemes (or letter sounds). What's an example of a word you read by sight?

◆ *Decoding (or phonological recoding).* This is slower than reading sight words because readers transform the sight of a word into its component sounds by applying their knowledge of the relationship between letters and their sounds (grapheme-phoneme correspondences). Then they search their mental dictionaries for meanings that are associated with that pronunciation. Although you can hear beginning readers decode, more experienced readers do it mentally although you may detect some subvocalizing as they experiment with possible sounds for a word.

◆ *Analogizing.* When analogizing, readers search their memory for known words that have the same parts or spellings as an unfamiliar word. When reading the word *Armorica* as a geographical location mentioned in James Joyce's *Finnegans Wake,* a reader could figure out the meanings of that word by analogizing to America, armor, and amor (love)—all of which lend meaning to Joyce's neologism (or new word making) as he begins his neverending story. Beginning readers use analogies with far less esoteric reading tasks than deciphering Joyce.

◆ *Spelling patterns (or orthographic patterns).* For readers to use spelling patterns to figure out a word's meaning, they need to have the spellings of many words stored in memory to take advantage of pattern recognition. When letter clusters are identified, orthographically associated words are activated. That leads to the word's pronunciation and on to the discovery of its meaning.

◆ *Context.* As readers read, they set up expectations about what's coming next, just as we do when listening to a friend's conversation and anticipating what will next be said. The text that readers have comprehended creates a context in which they can guess the meaning of unfamiliar words. Unfortunately, unfamiliar content words in an informational text often carry an abundance of meaning, and guessing from context may not provide accurate information for understanding of the unfamiliar word.

Word recognition is the foundation of the reading process, and weak word recognition is a strong predictor of problems in reading comprehension (Stanovich, 1991). Without sufficient practice in reading, less efficient readers are unlikely to develop automaticity and speed in word recognition. Slow processing draws on memory capacity that higher level comprehension and text integration require. With

reading for meaning hampered by word recognition problems, struggling readers rarely enjoy reading, become engaged in it, or build knowledge and skills from it.

**Phrase/sentence sense.**   As readers recognize individual word meanings, these individual meanings cohere into longer units of meaning. Effective readers quickly construct phrases and sentences that make sense. To make phrase and sentence sense, readers engage in proposition construction and meaning integration.

***Proposition construction.***   Proposition construction occurs when readers combine individually recognized words and their grammatical forms, inflections, or cues into basic meaning structures. A proposition is the smallest unit of knowledge that can stand as a separate assertion subject to a test of being true or false (Bauer, 1994). Propositions commonly reveal an agent's or an object's condition or action (Just & Carpenter, 1987). For example, the sentence "Sam took the right fork" contains several propositions or meaning structures, some contributing to ambiguity.

1. Sam exists. (Noun function/Subject)
2. A fork exists. (Noun function/Object)
   2.1. Fork may mean eating utensil.
   2.2. Fork may mean farm tool.
   2.3. Fork may mean branch in road.
3. Sam "take" fork. (Past/Verb function)
   3.1. Take may mean grasp with the hand(s).
   3.2. Take may mean to go in a specific direction.

4. Forks can be right or wrong, in terms of correctness.
5. Forks can be right or left, in terms of direction.

To disambiguate this statement and to construct an appropriate clause based on these propositions, readers refer to the context in which the original language occurred.

Part of constructing phrases, clauses, and sentences that make sense depends upon readers' grammatical or syntactical knowledge. That knowledge enables readers to construct a sensible grammatical structure, such as a sentence, from individual words, their endings or inflections, and often their placement in a sentence pattern, such as Subject + Verb + Object. If readers have trouble recognizing how words fit together, including inflected words, into a clause or sentence pattern, then reading slows until readers recognize patterns that make sense (Kintsch, 1994; van Dijk & Kintsch, 1983). The first quatrain from Shakespeare's Sonnet 65 suggests just this problem:

Since brass, nor stone, nor earth, nor boundless sea,
But sad mortality o'ersways their power,
How with this rage shall beauty hold a plea,
Whose action is no stronger than a flower?

More than one reader has slowed down to find the pattern in these words and so to make sense of Shakespeare's question.

Phonological processing promotes meaning construction as well (Adams, 1990, 1994). Although readers process words more or less one at a time, those words must be put into phrases or clauses or sentences to be understood. When we reproduce an utterance based on a text, we usually shape its delivery with intonation that reinforces its sense. Pitches drop. Pauses occur, usually at important junctures in sentences or at their ends. These inner-speech patterns produced through phonological processing help readers construct meaning and reflect on it. Researchers (Waters, Caplan, & Hildebrandt, 1987) have found that if good readers are not allowed to vocalize beneath the surface (subvocalize or use internal and silent speech), their capacity to understand longer and more complex sentences is disrupted. However, if young readers take too long to process individual, unfamiliar words in a sentence, they are likely to have trouble making sense of the sentence because early parts of its meaning will have decayed before sense can be made of the whole. Furthermore, if struggling readers must focus attention on individual letters and syllables, then they have trouble constructing meaningfully worded clauses because capacity for phonological processing is unavailable. Shakespeare's Sonnet reminds us that many struggling readers find frustration aplenty when they encounter unfamiliar words in unfamiliar patterns in his plays.

We must also recognize that as phrases, clauses, and sentences are constructed in what dual coding theorists call the "verbal system," these structures may also interact with corresponding visual imagery developing in the nonverbal system (Sadoski & Paivio, 2001). We can conceive of a reader imagining a fork, either in a road or on a table. This sympathetic nonverbal activity would be especially true of narrative texts eliciting imagery, but, as we will see, imagery may be encouraged to foster comprehension and recall of expository content area texts that are unlikely to promote much imagery naturally. These dual modes of text processing (verbal and visual) will appear again when we arrive at a later section on internal text representation.

***Proposition integration.***    Proposition integration occurs when readers combine simple propositions into more complex units of meaning: grammatical sentences that make sense (Kintsch, 1994). Returning to "Sam took the right fork," we can see that once readers are able to connect which meaning of fork goes with which meaning of "right," they are able to integrate the propositions embedded in the words and construct an unambiguous, meaningful sentence.

As readers integrated propositions into sense-making sentences, schema related to the topic becomes activated (Kintsch, 1994). If the meaning for *fork* is that of eating utensil, then, according to schema theory, we would expect knowledge about eating utensils and perhaps dining to become activated and moved from long-term memory to working memory to influence text comprehension. If the meaning for fork is that of a split in a road, then we would expect a very different kind of schema to be reconstructed from memory and to influence comprehension.

Text building.    Text building takes place as we link and integrate sentences, engage schemata, and form gists or general meanings. Text building results in the construction of an *internal text representation.*

During the building of an internal text representation, readers link sentences containing simpler units of meaning into a more complex, integrated network. That active mental representation of the text is held in working memory and is subject to extension and revision. Some researchers believe that readers infer little beyond what is needed to construct a coherent representation of the text on the page. According to that view, a reader first constructs a text-on-the-page representation from processes such as decoding, word recognition, and proposition formation and then, as a secondary process, interprets that representation (McKoon & Ratcliff, 1992). Research (Long, Seely, Oppy, & Golding, 1996) suggests that weaker readers appear to make fewer inferences and do not expand beyond the text-on-the-page representation, while stronger readers make more inferences and construct richer interpretations of the text.

***Key propositions.***    The development of a text representation is often controlled by key propositions that we construct as we make our way through a text. In expository prose, key propositions may be contained in a paragraph's topic sentence or develop as a reader makes inferences about a text's content. These "macro-propositions," as van Dijk and Kintsch (1983) call them, become organizing principles that influence subsequent text interpretation. What is the following paragraph about?

Tony slowly got up from the mat, planning his escape. He hesitated a moment and thought. Things were not going well. What bothered him most was being held, especially since the charge against him had been weak. He considered his present situation. The lock that held him was strong, but he thought he could break it. He knew, however, that his timing would have to be perfect. Tony was aware that it was because of his early roughness that he had been penalized so severely—much too severely from his point of view. The situation was becoming frustrating; the pressure had been grinding on him for too long. He was being ridden unmercifully. Tony was getting angry now. He felt he was ready to make his move. He knew that his success or failure would depend on what he did in the next few seconds.

When researchers (Anderson, Reynolds, Schallert, & Goetz, 1977) gave this paragraph to a group of men involved with wrestling, they thought the passage was about a wrestler caught in his opponent's "lock." Physical education students also thought it was about a wrestling match. However, most readers take the passage to be about a convict planning a prison escape. Readers' background schema influenced the propositions they constructed as well as their text building and representation processes.

If a reader's adherence to a key proposition is too great, it may distort comprehension of a text, as can activated schema held in LTM. This could happen when a reader ignores text content, such as qualifications of a proposition or information that contradicts it, in order to preserve the reader's beliefs.

Schema activation, which we saw influencing phrase and sentence sense, also continues to play an important role in text elaboration. As schemata are activated, instantiated, or retired, we expand our understanding of a text, in part, because of a schema's important meaning-construction functions. While schemata benefit text building, they may also distort the comprehension of texts, as can macro-propositions. These distortions in comprehension can occur if contradictions arise between a reader's schema and the literal content and intended meaning of a text being read. For example, when a reader's background knowledge of natural phenomena varies from scientific knowledge, their misconceptions may hinder their acquisition of new information that is not consistent with their old misunderstandings (Otero, 1998). Thus, activating prior knowledge does not always facilitate learning if the new information is incompatible with old information.

*Intertextuality.*   As Hartman (1994) has pointed out, however, "reading is more than finding appropriate schema, activating it, and filling in the slots." Intertextuality also shapes text building (Hartman, 1991, 1994). Intertextuality is the process of connecting developing texts with past texts to construct meanings. Those past texts can include not only printed texts but also the texts of movies, television, and other forms of art or cultural communication (Bloome & Bailey, 1992). You can think of intertexuality as the interaction between the text being read and the many "texts" internalized from our cultural experiences. If, for example, your "muggle" (non-magic) students have read the earlier books in J. K. Rowling's *Harry Potter* series, their reading of the later books in the series will be affected by intertextuality, providing a richer, fuller understanding of Harry's growth and development as a wizard. And if you read the Potter books along with the books of the psychologist Carl Jung, you'll discover troves of intertextuality.

Furthermore, as elements of a text begin to form a recognizable text pattern, such as that of an adventure story, a satire, an autobiography, or an argument, the schema for that particular genre may be activated. If so, readers' expectations for the upcoming structure and content of the text may be aroused and affect the text's interpretation (Anderson, 1994; Ruddell & Unrau, 1994). Let's take for our example the reading of Mark Twain's *The Adventures of Huckleberry Finn*. If, upon beginning to read the novel, readers activate an adventure story schema, they may expect to fill the "slots" of that genre with a series of Huck's adventures. With those expectations activated, readers may find it difficult, if not impossible, to experience the novel as a satire about parenthood, religion, education, morality, and human gullibility. However, readers anticipating a satirical novel or attuned to the potential for ironic "slots" are more likely to discover and enjoy Twain's humor.

DIAGNOSTIC PEEPHOLE
You can evaluate students' ability to construct a summary of a text, to make connections between different parts of the text, to generate questions to assess comprehension of text, to detect irrelevant content, and to recognize genres.

Internal text representation (Verbal and nonverbal).  Although the internal text representation appears as a separate entity in the model, it is stored in both long-term memory and working memory. The internal text representation is the text as we currently understand it. We can also activate text we have processed earlier and stored in long-term memory. That text representation may often be brought into working memory when readers are looking back to summarize a text or to interpret newly processed text.

Furthermore, the internal text representation may be both verbal and nonverbal. As a complement to verbal comprehension, imagery's role in reading comprehension is evident from research and from its intuitive appeal. Often, when we read fiction, our minds are vibrant with the images conveyed through a riveting text. However, the storage of imagery occurs in response to reading expository as well as narrative texts.

According to the Dual Coding Theory (Sadoski & Paivio, 2001), our minds operate with two different but connected mental systems that derive from our verbal and nonverbal experiences. While one of these systems is specialized for processing verbal information, the other processes nonverbal information, such as imagery. These two systems can function independently or in parallel through a network of interconnections. The Dual Coding Theory complements the schema theory because it accounts for both the verbal dimensions of comprehension that schema theory does explain and the mental imagery that schema theory does not adequately explain.

Nonverbal imagery.  Mental imagery makes several contributions to reading (Sadoski & Paivio, 2001). First, mental imagery helps readers comprehend texts, both narrative and expository, without any special instruction or training. It appears as a natural and spontaneous process, one that we might extend or expand to facilitate comprehension of all kinds of texts. Second, imagery enhances long-term recall for texts. Concrete sentences and paragraphs, those laden with imagery, are much more likely to be recalled than abstract texts. Imagery, perhaps as mental "pegs" on which to hang related information, appears to facilitate both storage and recall of printed information. Third, while verbal cognition plays a significant part in readers' aesthetic response or emotional reaction to texts, imagery is essential for a "lived" experience of literature. Imagery also contributes to the "lived" experience of other kinds of texts, such as those based on science and history. Some secondary school texts, such as *Biology: Visualizing Life* (Johnson, 1998), have been designed to make use of students' nonverbal systems to increase understanding, comprehension, and recall.

> **DIAGNOSTIC PEEPHOLE**
> In addition to asking readers for a retelling or written rendering of text read to document an internal text representation, you could ask them to draw a picture that represents their understanding of the text and explain verbally the picture's meaning. This visualization technique provides an image revealing elements of each reader's internal text.

## Metacognitive Processes

Following years of research and investigation, educators (Hacker, 1998a) widely agree that the concept of metacognition includes (a) knowledge of one's own knowledge and cognitive processes and (b) the ability to monitor and regulate one's knowledge and cognitive processes.

Metacognitive knowledge usually accumulates over years of experience with learning and problem solving. We learn how we think about ourselves as thinkers, about tasks, and about strategies that help us accomplish tasks (Garner, 1992). Metacognitive self-knowledge is exemplified by a student's knowing that she's better at solving word problems in math than in reading Shakespeare. As a teacher, we would see metacognitive knowledge about tasks in a student who recognizes that he remembers reading about Colonial American history more than the New Deal era in our history because he knows more about early America and is more interested in it. Metacognitive knowledge about strategies appears when a student decides to make a knowledge map to represent information she has just learned about different types of cell division.

Monitoring and control.    Metacognitive monitoring and control includes various kinds of self-assessment and self-management, both of which are of keen interest to educators seeking methods to develop self-regulating learners. When you get bogged down in reading something you're having trouble understanding, like a Shakespearean sonnet or a description of DNA replication, what do you usually do to help yourself understand? The answer you give to this question about how you would cope with a reading bog-down exemplifies metacognitive processes in the form of self-assessment. Acts of reflection on your thinking include discovering knowledge not only about what you know and how you think but also about when and how you use your knowledge and strategies. Do you have a purpose in mind whenever you read? Do you make mental summaries? Do you go back and forth in a text to make connections between ideas? Do you make guesses about a passage's meaning and then check to see if your guess was right?

As the diagram of the model shows (Figure 2.4), ***metacognitive processes*** include not only metacognitive knowledge but also both the monitoring and controlling of cognition while reading. To control the development of texts, we might engage several different metacognitive processes: standards of evaluation, metacognitive strategies, and planning. In some ways, these metacognitive processes function like an executive observing, evaluating, and improving the quality of our reading. Together our metacognitive capacity to monitor and control text building enables us to engage in what Hacker (1998b) calls self-regulated comprehension.

During cognitive processing of text, we generate mental representations of the external text in the form of propositions that are integrated and stored in memory as chunks or networks of information that form or modify schemata held in long-term memory. Perhaps this is happening to you as you read about this model of reading and compare it to your own mental model of what you think happens when a reader reads. As reading progresses, readers construct gists and build an internal text representation, just as you are constructing an internal representation of this reading model. Skilled readers monitor the representational products of the reading process to watch for various kinds of miscues, word recognition problems, incongruities within an evolving text, and incongruities between an evolving text and existing world knowledge or current schemata. Perhaps as you have been reading about this model, parts of it support your existing knowledge of reading while other parts don't fit so well and require your further examination to see if you can accept them.

Among the strategies that good readers may use to enhance their comprehension of a text is the application of ***standards of evaluation.*** Baker (1985) identified a number of comprehension-monitoring standards that influence the quality of the internal text representation. These standards are presented in Figure 2.6 as questions you might ask

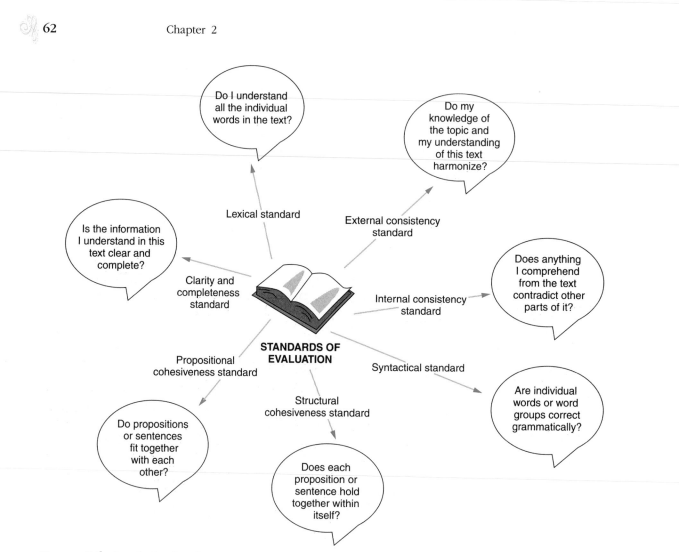

**FIGURE 2.6** Standards of Evaluation.

*Source:* Figure from Baker, Linda. (1985, Spring). Differences in the standards used by college students to evaluate their comprehension of expository prose. *Reading Reserch Quarterly,* 20(3), 297–313. Copyright by the International Reading Association. All rights reserved.

yourself, consciously or unconsciously, about your evolving internal text representation. If you ask yourself these kinds of questions, then you are systematically reviewing your internal text representation. We do know that good readers, those with high verbal ability, use these standards more frequently than readers with less ability (Baker, 1985).

Metacognitive strategies.    Strategic readers also have an assortment of **metacognitive strategies** that they can activate and apply if and when they find that something has gone amiss during the construction of a text representation. Metacognitive strategies are routines or procedures designed to help readers promote the meaning construction process. Garner (1992) defines strategies as "sequences of activities undertaken to reach goals efficiently" (p. 245). Brown, Palincsar, and Armbruster (1984) developed an inter-related set of metacognitive routines they called reciprocal teaching as a procedure to foster comprehension in struggling readers. We will look more closely at the elements of reciprocal teaching (summarizing, questioning, predicting, and clarifying) in Chapter 6.

Strategy selection.   Strategy selection, another critical metacognitive process, includes a broad overview of the entire comprehension problem, resistance to quick-fix solutions, choice of procedures that most closely fit the problems as represented, and a readiness to monitor and modify the strategy selected if it fails to solve the perceived problem. For example, if you were having trouble keeping track of new terms and concepts while reading this chapter, what strategy would you use to address the problem you noticed? If you decided to use a marker to underline new terms and concepts but found that strategy wasn't really working, would you change strategies, perhaps begin to take notes, to rectify your recognition of strategy breakdown?

> **DIAGNOSTIC PEEPHOLE**
> You can discover to what degree your students engage in metacognitive activities through an Informal Reading Inventory, a Metacognition Interview (see Unrau, 1997), or by using the Metacognitive Awareness of Reading Strategies Inventory (MARSI) (see Mokhtari & Reichard, 2002). After you discover how aware they are of their metacognitive processes, you may want to teach them reading strategies they could use to improve their monitoring and control of comprehension.

Metacognitive planning.   When skilled readers encounter comprehension problems while forming a text representation, *metacognitive planning* can enable them to decide on an appropriate course of action to solve the problems. Readers may develop plans, review them, and select the plan that appears to have the most problem solving promise (Davidson & Sternberg, 1998). For example, when readers face a challenging reading task, they may design a plan with subgoals and multifaceted, but related, activities, including using different reading rates, graphic organizers, and textual, technological, and human resources.

If teachers and students learn more about metacognition in reading and learning, will they read and learn more effectively? Much research on developing metacognitive knowledge and applying metacognitive strategies indicates that it does help (Hacker, 1998a). Many of the strategies you will find later in this textbook can be classified as metacognitive, and they have been shown to improve reading and to help students become more self-regulating.

## Text and Classroom Context

Up to now, we have been looking into the "meaning construction zone" within a reader's mind. Sometimes comparing the mind to a computer, I have tried to break apart an organic, instantaneous process that occurs on many levels, frequently at the same time, into its many components. The hypothesized reader constructed all of the knowledge alone, only from interactions with a text. That reader built a unique internal text representation or understanding of a text. But in classrooms, internal text representations rarely stay forever hidden inside students' minds. In class, interpretations of texts get talked through as students and teachers share and reflect upon the meanings they have constructed.

As a classroom teacher, I have often been surprised by what students tell me they think a passage they have read is about. While this happens more frequently when I teach Shakespeare or Emerson than when I teach with standard expository texts far less laced with ambiguity, I am always interested in the roots of diverse interpretations. When teaching poetry, I find the variety of interpretations intriguing, even exhilarating. But I hadn't always found the tensions between interpretations so valuable as opportunities to teach for understanding and for thinking.

During my college training, a form of literary criticism that was having its hayday was "New Criticism." Readers learned to look for meaning in the text itself. We traced imagery, interpreted symbols, examined metaphors, and hunted for mythic allusions that would allow us to open the text to richer readings. Knowledgeable critics with impressive influence held no small power over authors included in the canon as well as meanings that certain texts contained. Because certain critics brought vast amounts of experience, knowledge, authority, and prestige with them to their readings, college sophomores could be intimidated into believing that these "expert" interpretations must be the ones not only respected but acknowledged as supreme. Deferring to expert authority was made easy for most of my classmates. We were told the critics knew what they were talking about.

However, ideals change. And so do the ways educators evaluate the merit of interpreters and their interpretations. With the waxing of reader response theory came the waning of "expert" readings. Much of the support for this shift came from the growing influence of reader response theorists, like Louise Rosenblatt (1978, 1985) and Richard Beach (1993).

According to Rosenblatt's (1978) transactional theory of reading, every act of reading is a transaction between a particular reader and a particular text at a particular time in a particular context. The reader and the text compose a transactional moment. The meaning doesn't pre-exist in the text or in the reader but results from the transaction between reader and text.

In addition, Rosenblatt (1978) believes that readers adopt stances toward texts that guide their processing. Reader's stance refers to the reader's perspective and orientation toward the text. The stance, which directs the reader's focus of motivation and purpose for reading, is to varying degrees under the reader's control. She believes that readers experience texts through two stances on a continuum: efferent to aesthetic. With efferent reading, the reader focuses on information to be taken from the text. With aesthetic reading, the reader becomes absorbed in the imaginative world of character, plot, and setting evoked by the text. Efferent and aesthetic stances may be mixed to different degrees. Or the reader may elect to emphasize one stance over the other. This occurs when a reader adopts the efferent stance when reading Dicken's *Great Expectations* to find out what traits to include in an essay about Pip's growth as a character in the novel. Rosenblatt (1985) has observed a tendency in classrooms to emphasize efferent readings while minimizing aesthetic ones, a tendency that may reduce students' pleasure and enjoyment of transacting with literature.

Some educators and literacy specialists have taken the position that an objective meaning can be found in the text. However, others with a view more similar to Rosenblatt (Bleich, 1980; Culler, 1980; Fish, 1980) have argued that the meaning of a text is a more personal response to be found in the reader's mind, perhaps to be authorized by an interpretive community, but certainly not in an objective text. Meaning may best be understood as a result of the reader's meaning construction that engages readers' unique patterns of background knowledge and cognitive processing. That meaning is not entirely in either the text or the reader but evolves from interactions among reader, text, teacher, classroom community, and context.

With these interacting features in mind, Robert Ruddell and I (Unrau & Ruddell, 1995) designed a model (see Figure 2.7) that represents text interpretation in classroom contexts. The model was induced from numerous studies, both theoretical and empirical (Ruddell & Unrau, 1994), as well as my own classroom teaching experience. The model was designed with a social constructivist perspective of learning in mind. Accordingly, we as teachers create a learning environment that engages students in a meaning negotiation process over texts. During that process, we and our

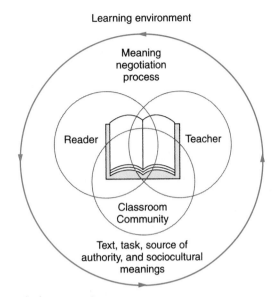

**FIGURE 2.7**  Text and Classroom Context.

students construct and negotiate meanings not only for the text itself but also for tasks, sources of authority, and features of the sociocultural setting.

The text and classroom context includes the text, task, sources of authority, and sociocultural meanings. The design and features of that environment have a strong influence not only on a student's decision to read but also on the ways in which the reading progresses. Our students are more likely to engage in reading if they are motivated, if their prior knowledge is activated, if they feel a personal connection with the tasks they undertake, and if they play a central role in constructing knowledge. In school environments with these features, our students are more likely to read and learn productively (see Chapter 10, "Focusing on Motivation to Read in Content Area Classes"). In a constructivist environment, students will be confronted and will have to solve problems, such as working together with classmates to master solutions to acceleration problems, to negotiate the meaning of poems, or to figure out the basic mechanisms and principles that drive the stock market. Such environments encourage meaningful dialogue, conceptual growth, and flexible understandings.

The meaning negotiation process.    You and your students will negotiate meanings in your classroom. But much more than just the printed text will be read and meanings negotiated. Your students also need to read and construct meanings for the tasks, the authority structure of the classroom, your intentions and expectations, and the sociocultural setting of your classroom.

However, whose meaning will be viewed as valid or correct in a classroom of 25 to 30 students and you? Put in another way, whose standards will endorse the validity of a particular interpretation? Will your interpretation alone dominate discourse? Will your students have a say in what texts mean? Will you suppress your personal beliefs about the meaning of texts while enabling your students to express theirs?

While many interpretations by different readers and us should be brought into the learning environment, I believe that the work of both students and ourselves is to confirm that interpretations are well grounded in both the actual text and in our students' unique responses to the text. Interpretations should be reasonably supported with reference to events, statements, or claims made in the text. As Rosenblatt has written, "Fundamentally, the process of understanding a work implies a recreation of it, an attempt to grasp completely the structured sensations and concepts through which the author seeks to convey the quality of his sense of life. Each must make a new synthesis of these elements with his own nature, but it is essential that he evoke those components of experience to which the text actually refers" (1938, p. 113).

Although classroom negotiation over the meanings of a text may not be its final authority, negotiation distributes many benefits. You and your students share meanings in the classroom community so that, through dialogue, a community of readers comes to hold a range of possible meanings. In Figure 2.7, the three overlapping circles represent the interactive nature of meaning negotiation. Notice, however, that the interactive process, diagrammatically shown, overlaps a real text upon which the dialogue is founded. The diagram demonstrates symbolically that the text itself is not the sole object carrying meaning but that meanings arise from transactions between individuals and the text. During negotiation, your students bring meanings to the interaction, you bring your understandings, and all members of the class interact with the text and each other to clarify meaning.

The Hermeneutic circle.    Texts and their interpretations exist in what is called a ***hermeneutic circle*** (Dilthey, 1976). In that circle, meanings we evoke as readers can perpetually re-emerge in modified or new forms. As you and your students voice your views about a text's meaning, a cycle of hypothesis and confirmation or disconfirmation spins. Furthermore, while the meanings we construct for an entire text influence interpretations of its parts, our understanding of the parts shapes our interpretation of the entire text. Why the ghost of Hamlet's father haunts Hamlet becomes increasingly clear as scene after scene exposes treachery in Elsinore Castle. But will we ever know if Hamlet was truly mad? The cycle of interpretation is represented in Figure 2.7 by the circle with arrowheads surrounding the meaning negotiation process. While reading and forming meanings, you and your students should keep in mind that interpretations are forever reinvented as dialogue, disagreement, and debate deem.

The notion of meanings subject to constant reinvention may be unsettling for some domains of knowledge, such as the physical sciences. In fact, fresh meanings are more likely to spring from literature, poetry, or history than from scientific texts. When reading biology or math texts, the emergence of multiple meanings is likely to be more restricted than it would be when reading history or literature. In part, that condition arises from scientific or mathematical texts having a foundation in meanings that are widely agreed upon within the respective community. In addition, science and math texts are less likely to contain ambiguities that contribute to alternative interpretations. Nevertheless, the history of science tells us that even those meanings that are widely adopted and agreed upon in a scientific community, like Newtonian physics, can be put under such pressure from new research and theory that scientists must renegotiate the old meaning of texts (Kuhn, 1962).

Readers read different kinds of "texts."    We should keep in mind that all learners negotiate several different kinds of meaning: text, task, sources of authority, and aspects of the sociocultural setting. These we will examine separately to understand them more deeply.

*Text meanings.* We know from our understanding of the reading process that different readers construct different meanings for texts because of variables like their knowledge base, processing skills, and emotional states. Different readings may be more likely in some subjects, like English, than similar ones. However, all teachers in all content areas should understand that legitimate divergent meanings may arise in any subject. And, more importantly, we should have some clear ideas about how to cope with multiple interpretations of the same text. Our classrooms can, for example, become forums for the articulation and negotiation of multiple meanings in the hermeneutic circle. While shared meanings become part of the classroom's understanding of a text, those meanings are never fixed forever. They may be reinterpreted as the classroom's conversation continues.

*Task meanings.* Tasks are structured activities that are related to the text and that are designed or selected by either us or our students. Students who are capable and effective may interpret these tasks in different ways. As teachers, we may think we have clearly described an activity or exercise we expect students to complete in a particular way. But we are sometimes surprised, as I have often been, to discover that students have constructed divergent interpretations for the task that, upon inspection, I often see are quite feasible.

Linda Flower (1987) found that students interpreted assignments differently from each other and from the teachers she observed. A teacher may clearly see in her own mind what she wants her student to do when she asks them to analyze their response to a problem they had to solve, like figuring out the causes of the American Revolution. She wants them to step back a little from their problem-solving processes and to reflect on them. However, some students may not have been asked to engage in that form of self-reflection in the past and so find the assignment perplexing, even if fully explained and modeled. Because they lack a clear schema for engaging in self-reflection on their problem-solving processes, students may come up with answers that reveal their representation of the assignment is different from others.

Of some help in these teaching situations are opportunities for discussion about multiple interpretations our students may have in response to an assignment. Such discussions may help our students to see how others in the class have understood the task and to hear us explain our expectations. In any event, we and our students both need to monitor and assess our decisions about the meanings that have been assigned to tasks.

*Source of authority meanings.* In classrooms, we and our students inevitably arrive at an understanding of who is the authority. That authority could reside in the text, our student readers, ourselves, or the classroom community. It could also arise from the interactions among these potential sources of authority as we negotiate meanings.

In "traditional" classrooms, students commonly identify the teacher as the source for authority. When questions about the meaning or interpretation of a text arise during students' learning or classroom discussions, the teacher's understanding of the text is the meaning students usually accept, perhaps as truth. In these classrooms, students have interpreted the learning environment in such a way that the teacher is the source of authority. Some students may question the "truths" that teachers transmit in those classrooms, but most students continue to perceive the teacher as the final arbiter of accuracy. After all, who gives and grades the tests?

In some classrooms, the text may appear to have the ultimate position as authority. When texts have such power, they are frequently consulted to determine their author's possible intentions. If the text holds the position as ultimate source for authority in the classroom, a reader's interpretation could easily be invalidated because it fails to correspond with the teacher's interpretation in the author's meaning. These invalidations of meaning may occur even though we know that readers construct unique meanings because of their personal background knowledge.

At the opposite extreme are those rather rare classrooms in which the only recognized source for the authority of meaning is the reader's mind. In these classes, rare though they are, only the reader's personal interpretations of a text count.

Each of us in our classrooms decide how much time and thought we want to give to negotiation over the source of authority for text meanings. To a significant degree, the content area in which we teach will influence our decisions about appropriate sources of authority. Some of us may find that the text speaks loudest; some may decide our understandings should have most significant authority; some will encourage their students to exercise textual authority; and some will continually negotiate the proper source of authority on different occasions. Just as the meanings of a printed text need not be fixed forever in a specific meaning, the source of authority for a text's meaning is always negotiable.

***Sociocultural meanings.*** Sociocultural meanings are shaped by values and attitudes held in our classrooms, schools, and the larger community within which we and our students live and learn. While we and our students bring our own sociocultural values into the classroom, we also interpret the social life and culture we discover there. In addition, we are likely to interpret aspects of the sociocultural life of the classroom in different ways. For example, in the same classroom, some of our students may believe that their school is a rich ground of resources for learning at the same moment that other students perceive the school as a blackboard jungle of obstruction and frustration. We also construct very different interpretations of our school's sociocultural life. Meanwhile, many of us and our students are likely to share sociocultural interpretations.

To sum up, you and your students read many "texts" in classrooms. The interpretations we construct of these texts often go unexamined. However, if you are aware of the multiple interpretations that your students create, you have distinct advantages during meaning negotiation. You can help your students discover each other's meanings and explore the evidence that contributes to those meanings. In so doing, you can help your students think through their interpretations and modify them in the light of reasoned discussion. Engaging in the process of reflecting rationally on the meanings they have constructed for texts provides you with opportunities to exercise and develop their tools of critical thinking.

Negotiating meanings in a classroom context: An example.　Now that I've explained the model of meaning negotiation in classrooms, I'd like to tell you a story about a story about a story—but you'll see what that's all about before we're done. The story I want to tell is about a series of instructional episodes that took place in my eleventh-grade classroom.

My class of 27 eleventh graders had read Salinger's *Catcher in the Rye* and was about to begin reading his short story entitled "The Laughing Man" (Salinger, 1981). We were late in the second month of the fall semester, so my students were still acclimating to the reader-based environment that I was encouraging with response logs, sharing of responses in small teams, and ample, whole-class discussions about meanings. As an initial task to activate background knowledge and heighten motivation, I asked my students to predict the story's content based on its title. "Knowing what you know about Salinger's writing," I asked them, "What do you think a story entitled 'The Laughing Man' is going to be about?" Several students responded.

*Eric:*       I think it'll be about a crazy person in a mental hospital. He thinks everything's hysterical.

*Sally:*      Maybe it's about the death of a comedian or a clown.

*Margaret:*   I'd expect it to be ironic. Maybe about someone who's depressed and unhappy with their life but puts on a facade by laughing all the time to make people think he is happy.

The predictions often seemed to reflect what students had learned about Salinger's characters and to show that my students' prior knowledge shaped their thinking. Actually, Margaret was not too far off.

***Synopsis of "The Laughing Man."*** A brief summary of "The Laughing Man" is essential for your understanding of the meaning-negotiation that occurred in our classroom:

> John Gedsudski, the story's almost hero, is a shy, rather short law student who goes to New York University and who chaperones and coaches the Comanches, a group of young, energetic boys—mostly about nine or ten years old. One of the Comanches, who is now about thirty-five, tells the story as he remembers John, whom the boys considered just short of heroic. It's baseball season, and the Chief (that's what the boys called John) takes them in his bus to parks where they can play ball. As they traveled to and from parks in the bus, the boys were frequently entranced by the Chief's exciting stories about a mysterious character called the Laughing Man.
>
> The Laughing Man was disfigured as a boy when Chinese bandits put his head in a vice because his missionary parents wouldn't pay a ransom. He grew up among the bandits but was so ugly he would only be tolerated if he wore a mask over his face. Though shunned by people, he befriended animals in the forest. He imitated the bandits' style, soon surpassed them in crime, and aroused their jealousy to such an extent that they longed to kill him. In a short time, the Laughing Man accumulated a fortune, gave most of it to a monastery, but was pursued by an internationally famous detective, Dufarge. He evaded Dufarge with his four friends: a wolf, a dwarf, a Mongolian giant, and a beautiful Eurasian girl. He was never seen without his mask.
>
> Each time the Chief drove the boys to their baseball game, he told them another installment of the story. One unusual day, the Chief stopped his bus on the way to a game to pick up a girl, Mary Hudson. She was, in the boys' eyes, a beauty, but, when she asked to play baseball with them, she got a big "this-isn't-a-girl's-thing" response. She insisted and eventually took center field. Her fielding of the ball was terrible, but she got a hit every time at bat. The team forgave her fielding, and, for over a month, she would join the team a couple of days each week.

One day on the bus while the Comanches waited for Mary Hudson to arrive, John told another episode about the Laughing Man. Through detective Dufarge's cheap trickery, the Laughing Man was captured. He removed his mask, stunning his captors. But Dufarge, who had a coughing fit at the moment of the unveiling, didn't look at the horrid face. Covering his eyes, he emptied his gun at the sound of the Laughing Man's heavy breathing. There the episode ended, even though Mary Hudson hadn't arrived.

Without Mary, the Chief drove the bus to the park where the boys were to play baseball. During the middle of the game, she arrived but refused to play ball. The narrator of the story, who was nine at the time, explains that he couldn't figure out what was going on between the Chief and Mary but that he knew she wouldn't play again. She was crying on a distant bench. When the game was called because of darkness, the Chief went over and held the sleeve of Mary's coat. She broke from him and began running away. He didn't follow.

Back on the bus, the Comanches learned that four of detective Dufarge's bullets hit the Laughing Man. As Dufarge approached, however, the Laughing Man spit out the bullets, a feat that burst Dufarge's heart. But the Laughing Man continued to bleed day after day. The animals in the forest soon summoned the Laughing Man's friend, the dwarf, who came with a fresh supply of eagle's blood, a vital food for the Laughing Man. But when the Laughing Man heard that Dufarge had killed the wolf, Black Wing, he crushed the vial of eagle's blood in his hand. As he died, Laughing Man removed his mask.

At the end of the story, one of the Comanches was crying and the narrator's knees were shaking with emotion.

*Conventional interpretation.*  A conventional interpretation of "The Laughing Man" posits a parallel between events in the Chief's relationship with Mary Hudson and episodes in the story the Chief tells to his Comanches. Often, the Chief is viewed as a mask for the Laughing Man. As the Chief's relationship with Mary dies, so does the famous and beloved masked bandit. The end of the Chief's affair with Mary is transformed through a creative process into the Laughing Man's demise. Although no one in the class predicted that "The Laughing Man" would be a love story or a story about the creative process, in several ways—under its mask—it is both. However, I was careful not to impose or even to reveal this conventional reading to my students. Instead, I tried to remain open to their discoveries.

*Students' initial interpretations.*   When my students finished reading the story, I asked them to write in their learning logs about the story's meaning—or, if they were totally "clueless," as some students said, then to write a summary of it.

Mira and Emily were two students in my class that read "The Laughing Man." Their responses to the story and the classroom context in which we discussed the story exemplify what happens in many classrooms as meanings are negotiated.

Mira, a student who said she "didn't really have an understanding when I first read the story," wrote the following summary of it in her log:

> The story is about a young boy who is reflecting back on his childhood when he was in a boys' group called the Comanches. He is telling us how their "Chief" was adored and loved by all. Even though he wasn't very handsome, the boys still thought of him as gorgeous, and he was their hero. He would take them

to the park on weekends to play ball. Then, after the game on the way home, he would tell them an installment of the Laughing Man. The Laughing Man was a disfigured man who stole and murdered, but he did it for good. The boys all looked up to him. Once the Chief had a girlfriend whom the boys adored, but she left suddenly one day. That day the boys saw the fall of two of their favorite heroes, for that was the day the Chief also killed the Laughing Man.

The summaries that students like Mira wrote represented their understanding of "The Laughing Man" prior to interacting with other readers.

However, even before small group discussion began, other students wrote their initial interpretations of the story instead of summaries. Emily was one of those students. In her log, she wrote:

> Don't judge a book by its cover. The Laughing Man is a made up creative character. He is hideously ugly so he keeps his face hidden. However, the Laughing Man has a beautiful inside. He means well and has a loving soul. . . . When humans saw Laughing Man's face, they were frightened. However, the animals didn't know Laughing Man was ugly. They didn't know the difference between it, so the animals loved Laughing Man. They reached further down than just skin to realize how wonderful Laughing Man was. J. D. Salinger I believe wants us to be mature enough not to judge people by their outside appearance.

Emily's interpretation is one of many different meanings that students initially attributed to the story.

After reading the story and writing summaries or interpretations of it in their logs, students met in small groups to share their journal entries. I introduced this chapter with a description of my students' working in small groups. Their discussions led to significant changes or shifts in meanings not only for smaller parts of the story but also for the story as a whole.

During whole-class discussions, I urged my students to explore these alternative meanings and asked them to explain how they arrived at them. The process contributed to our creating a classroom community meaning for both the story and its parts.

***Interpretations negotiated and reformed.*** A few days after the small group and class discussions, I asked my students to write their current understanding of the story and to describe how and why their interpretation changed—if it had. Most students reported that they had formed or reformed the meanings they had given to the story during or after the small group and class discussions. Mira, whose initial summary was presented earlier, arrived at a meaning that went significantly beyond that initial response. She wrote:

> I think that the story of the Laughing Man that the chief would tell the Comanches was in a sense the way he saw himself. The Laughing Man was an alter ego of John Gedsudski, the Chief. Both were not handsome and shunned by their society and peers. Both had a band of loyal followers who looked up to them. For the Chief, it was the kids; for the Laughing Man, it was a dwarf, a Mongolian, and a beautiful Eurasian girl. At around the time that the Laughing Man is held captive by Dufarge, the Chief is having problems with Mary Hudson. When the Laughing Man gets shot, it is at the same time the Chief and Mary break up. This just enforces my theory that the Chief and the Laughing

Man are one in the same. The Chief takes the installments from his own day to
day life, but he enhances them and makes them more exciting.

Many students like Mira contributed to what became a classroom community meaning for the relationship between the Chief and Laughing Man, that is, that the two
paralleled each other in many ways. As for the vial of eagle's blood that could have
saved the Laughing Man, Mira wrote that it "represents the Chief's love for Mary."

Emily, whose initial, rather stock response to the story was "You can't judge a
book by its cover," later wrote that the story was "tragic." She thought that the Chief
was so hurt and depressed by the break-up of his relationship with Mary that he
"took it out on the players."

That night, driving home on the bus, John began telling the story of the Laughing Man once again. In this final story, John killed the Laughing Man because
Mary left him, and because his love was taken away from him, he did the same
to the Comanches. They loved the Laughing Man so John took him away from
them.

Although Emily interprets the meaning of the Laughing Man's death quite differently
from Mira, Emily wrote that the vial of eagle's blood that might have saved Laughing Man represented John's love for Mary which was crushed.

***Summary of student interpretations.***   In summary, many readers—the initially
"clueless" as well as those who offered early interpretations—began to share a
community interpretation of the story or at least important parts of it. Almost everyone agreed that a close correspondence existed between the Chief's life and that
of Laughing Man. Many came to think that the trouble the Chief was having in his
relationship with Mary translated into the death of Laughing Man. Nevertheless,
many readers still held divergent meanings about several aspects of the story.

Responding to texts in an environment that encouraged the formation and expression of individual interpretations and their negotiation in a classroom community appeared to benefit many of my students. One of them, Sarah, wrote the
following:

Too many teachers think that their understanding is the only correct one. Now
I understand that a story can mean so many things, and as long as you can back
it with at least some good thought, it's right—for yourself. Now I feel I can just
put more of my thoughts out there even if other people don't agree. I basically
think that's why my interpretation of "The Laughing Man" has changed. I think
I have a little more freedom to say what I think.

What is important about "The Laughing Man" example for our discussion is not only
the divergent interpretations of the story by different students but also the dialogue,
the meaning negotiation process, that occurred among students and between students and teacher.

The more you know about meaning construction and negotiation in your classrooms, the more reflective you and your students may become. Teachers who encourage their students' active engagement in meaning negotiation directly contribute
to their students' capacity to think more critically about what to believe about texts
and what actions to take based upon those beliefs. In short, with greater understanding of classroom discourse over texts, you can help students become more critical readers.

# IMPLICATIONS OF THE MODEL FOR TEACHING

Before launching upon this journey into a model of reading, I stated that one of the benefits of having a model could be the hints and clues it gives about intervention strategies that may help struggling readers improve at different points in the reading process. What are these hints and clues to make us better teachers of literacy and content knowledge?

- Background knowledge stored in memory serves as an essential and valuable resource for all readers (see Figure 2.8). We can assess that background knowledge discover methods to activate it, work with students to extend or expand it, and apply procedures to assess its growth.
- Without solid and automatic decoding skills, such as rapid processing of letter–sound correspondences and the application of effective word attack skills, readers will not have enough working memory to construct meaning for texts they struggle to read. We should assess our students' decoding skills to know if assigned texts are manageable.
- Knowledge of word meanings, including immediate access to the meanings of high-frequency words, is critical to the reader's meaning construction process. Building vocabulary knowledge removes obstacles to comprehension.
- Ready knowledge of sentence patterns and structures contributes to more automatic processing when reading. With speedy construction of propositions in the form of phrases and sentences, less working memory must be devoted to basic elements in the meaning making process, and more memory can be allocated to questioning, analyzing, comparing interpretations, and evaluating.
- Readers should be trained and encouraged to monitor continuously the meaning construction process. Readers can be taught to watch for breakdowns in comprehension and for inconsistencies in their internal text representation.
- Comprehension fostering strategies serve readers well. The more effective strategies readers learn and use, the better the chances of high-quality comprehension. Strategies to encourage monitoring and detection of confusion can be taught to students at all reading levels.
- Readers build mental text representation in both verbal and visual forms. Readers can be encouraged to attend to both coding modes to enhance comprehension.
- An examination of the meaning negotiation process in classroom contexts yields several practical suggestions for growing interpretive, thoughtful classroom communities:

  a. Encourage readers in their construction and exploration of meanings.
  b. Use teams to share and shape reader responses to texts.
  c. Encourage and orchestrate more student-to-student interaction patterns rather than student-to-teacher patterns.
  d. Design team activities so that stores of knowledge and interpretations shared will be brought to the whole class for discussion.
  e. Engage in whole-class conversations that build upon reader's individual responses, explanations of their derivation, and comparisons between them.
  f. Discuss standards for the validity of interpretations to enable the interpretive community to acknowledge and understand its assumptions.
  g. Cultivate in readers an evolutionary perspective of texts (a hermeneutic perspective) rather than seeking final, absolute interpretations of texts.
  h. Prompt readers to explain or support their interpretations with reference to reasons, such as evidence from the text interpreted.
  i. Encourage students through instruction and climate control to request from each other explanations for the grounds of text interpretations.
  j. Through classroom activities and interactions, show the importance of dialogue in shaping meanings not only for the printed texts read in class, but also for tasks that are assigned, for sources of classroom authority, and for sociocultural features, such as students' perceptions of their own role and function in classrooms.
  k. Encourage a welcoming, open, inquisitive, questioning, and skeptical spirit with respect to the meaning formation process and the meanings formed.

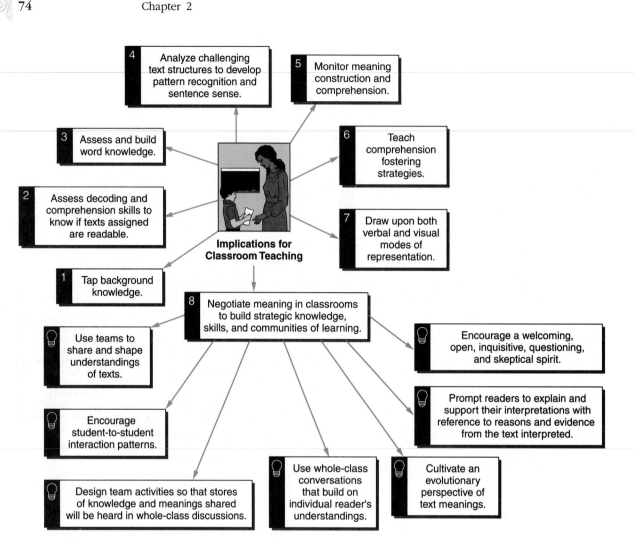

FIGURE 2.8   Implications of Reading Model for Classroom Teaching.

Go to the Double-Entry Journal for Chapter 2 on our Companion Website at www.prenhall.com/unrau to complete your journal entry.

♦ With this reading model as a foundation and reference point, we can identify a range of reading abilities and define several categories of readers that are likely to appear in our classrooms. We can also see what problems plague struggling readers and what skills enhance the performance of highly proficient ones.

DOUBLE-ENTRY JOURNAL: After Reading

Review the description of the reading process you created before reading this chapter. What features, if any, would you add to capture what researchers have found goes on when a reader reads? How could your understanding of reading influence the way you could help students master content knowledge/skills and develop literacy?

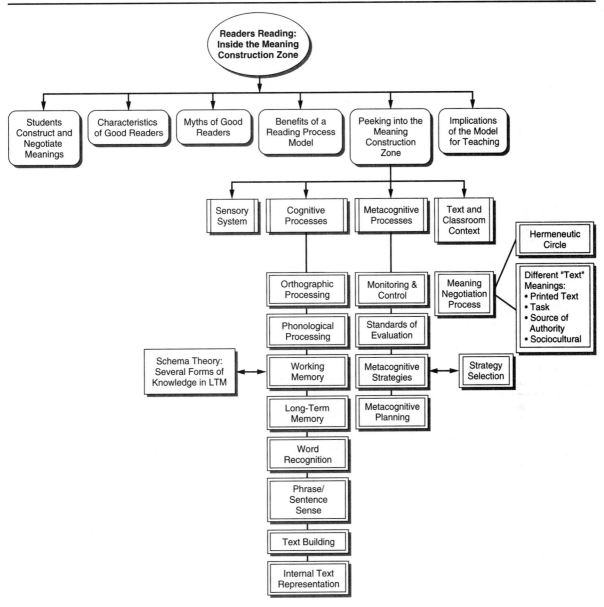

For exercises to clarify your understanding of chapter content, visit the self-assessments for Chapter 2 on our Companion Website at
www.prenhall.com/unrau

# References

Adams, M. (1990). *Beginning to read: Thinking and learning about print.* Cambridge, MA: Bradford Books/MIT Press.

Adams, M. (1994). Modeling the connections between word recognition and reading. In R. B. Ruddell, M. R. Ruddell, & H. Singer (Eds.), *Theoretical models and processes of reading* (4th ed., pp. 838–863). Newark, DE: International Reading Association.

Anderson, R. C. (1975). The notion of schemata and the educational enterprise: General discussion of the conference. In R. C. Anderson, J. Osborn, & R. J. Tierney (Eds.), *Schooling and the acquisition of knowledge* (pp. 415–431). Hillsdale, NJ: Erlbaum.

Anderson, R. C. (1994). Role of the reader's schema in comprehension, learning, and memory. In R. B. Ruddell, M. R. Ruddell, & H. Singer (Eds.), *Theoretical models and processes of reading* (4th ed., pp. 469–482). Newark, DE: International Reading Association.

Anderson, R. C., Reynolds, R. E., Schallert, D. L., & Goetz, E. T. (1977). Frameworks for comprehending discourse. *American Educational Research Journal, 14,* 367–382.

Baker, L. (1985). Differences in the standards used by college students to evaluate their comprehension of expository prose. *Reading Research Quarterly, 20* (3), 297–313.

Bauer, J. (1994). *Schools for thought.* Cambridge, MA: MIT Press.

Beach, R. (1993). *A teacher's introduction to reader-response theories.* Urbana, IL: National Council of Teachers of English.

Beck, I. L. (1989). Improving practice through understanding reading. In L. B. Resnick & L. E. Klopfer (Eds.), *Toward the thinking curriculum: Current cognitive research. Yearbook of the Association for Supervision and Curriculum Development* (pp. 40–58). Alexandria, VA/Hillsdale, NJ: ASCD/Erlbaum.

Beck, I., & McKeown, M. (1991). Conditions of vocabulary acquisition. In R. Barr, M. L. Kamil, P. B. Mosenthal, & P. D. Pearson (Eds.), *Handbook of reading research* (Vol. II, pp. 789–814). Mahwah, NJ: Erlbaum.

Bleich, D. (1980). Epistemological assumptions in the study of response. In J. P. Tompkins (Ed.), *Reader-response criticism: From formalism to post-structuralism* (pp. 134–163). Baltimore, MD: Johns Hopkins University Press.

Bloome, D., & Bailey, F. (1992). Studying language and literacy through events, particularities, and intertextuality. In R. Beach, J. Green, M. Kamil, & T. Shanahan (Eds.), *Multidisciplinary perspectives on literacy research* (pp. 181–210). Urbana, IL: National Council of Teachers of English.

Bower, G., Black, J., & Turner, T. (1994). Scripts in memory for text. In R. B. Ruddell, M. R. Ruddell, & H. Singer (Eds.), *Theoretical models and processes of reading* (4th ed., pp. 538–581). Newark, DE: International Reading Association.

Brown, A. L., Palincsar, A. S., & Armbruster, B. B. (1984). Instructing comprehension-fostering activities in interactive learning situations. In H. Mandl, N. Stein, & T. Trabasso (Eds.), *Learning and comprehension of text* (pp. 255–285). Hillsdale, NJ: Erlbaum.

Bruner, J. (1986). *Actual minds, possible worlds.* Cambridge, MA: Harvard University Press.

Chomsky, N. (1959). A review of B. F. Skinner's Verbal Behavior. *Language, 35*(1), 26–58.

Chomsky, N. (1965). *Aspects of the theory of syntax.* Cambridge, MA: MIT Press.

Culler, J. (1980). Literary competence. In J. P. Tompkins (Ed.), *Reader-response criticism: From formalism to post-structuralism* (pp. 101–117). Baltimore, MD: Johns Hopkins University Press.

Davidson, J. E., & Sternberg, R. J. (1998). Smart problem solving: How metacognition helps. In D. J. Hacker, J. Dunlosky, & A. C. Graesser (Eds.), *Metacognition in educational theory and practice* (pp. 47–68). Mahwah, NJ: Erlbaum.

Dilthey, W. (1976). The development of hermeneutics. In H. Rickman (Ed. & Trans.), *Selected writings.* Cambridge: Cambridge University Press. (Original work published in 1900).

Duke, N., & Pearson, P. D. (2002). Effective practices for developing reading comprehension. In S. J. Samuels & A. E. Farstrup (Eds.), *What research says about reading instruction* (3rd ed., pp. 205–242). Newark, DE: International Reading Association.

Ehri, L. C. (1991). Development of the ability to read words. In R. Barr, M. L. Kamil, P. Mosenthal, & P. D. Pearson (Eds.), *Handbook of reading research* (Vol. 2, pp. 383–417). White Plains, NY: Longman.

Ehri, L. C. (1994). Development of the ability to read words: Update. In R. B. Ruddell, M. R. Ruddell, & H. Singer (Eds.), *Theoretical models and processes of reading* (4th ed., pp. 323–358). Newark, DE: International Reading Association.

Fish, S. (1980). *Is there a text in this class? The authority of interpretive communities.* Cambridge, MA: Harvard University Press.

Flower, L. (1987). *The role of task representation in reading to write* (Technique Rep. No. 6). Berkeley, CA: Center for the Study of Writing.

Garner, R. (1992). Metacognition and self-monitoring strategies. In S. J. Samuels & A. E. Farstrup (Eds.), *What research has to say about reading instruction* (2nd ed., pp. 236–252). Newark, DE: International Reading Association.

Gibson, E. J., & Levin, H. (1985). *The psychology of reading.* Cambridge, MA: MIT Press.

Goodman, K. (1965). A linguistic study of cues and miscues in reading. *Elementary English, 42,* 639–643.

Goswami, U. (2000). Phonological and lexical processes. In M. Kamil, P. Mosenthal, P. D. Pearson, & R. Barr (Eds.), *Handbook of reading research* (Vol. 3, pp. 251–267). Mahwah, NJ: Erlbaum.

Hacker, D. J. (1998a). Definitions and empirical foundations. In D. J. Hacker, J. Dunlosky, & A. C. Graesser (Eds.), *Metacognition in educational theory and practice* (pp. 1–24). Mahwah, NJ: Erlbaum.

Hacker, D. J. (1998b). Self-regulated comprehension during normal reading. In D. J. Hacker, J. Dunlosky, & A. C. Graesser (Eds.), *Metacognition in educational theory and practice* (pp. 165–191). Mahwah, NJ: Erlbaum.

Hartman, D. K. (1991). *8 readers reading: The intertextual links of able readers using multiple passages.* Unpublished doctoral dissertation, University of Illinois, Urbana, IL.

Hartman, D. K. (1994). The intertextual links of readers using multiple passages: A postmodern/semiotic/cognitive view of meaning making. In R. B. Ruddell, M. R. Ruddell, & H. Singer (Eds.), *Theoretical models and processes of reading* (4th ed., pp. 616–636). Newark, DE: International Reading Association.

Heath, S. B. (1983). *Ways with words.* Cambridge, UK: Cambridge University Press.

Jastak, S., & Wilkinson, G. S. (1984). *Wide Range Achievement Test—Revised (WRAT-R) for word recognition.* Wilmington, DE: Jastak Associates.

Johnson, D. D., Toms-Bronowski, S., & Pittelman, S. D. (1981). *A review of trends in vocabulary research and the effects of prior knowledge on instructional strategies for vocabulary acquisition.* Madison, WI: Wisconsin Center for Educational Research.

Johnson, G. (1998). *Biology: Visualizing life.* Austin, TX: Holt, Rinehart and Winston.

Just, A. J., & Carpenter, P. A. (1987). *The psychology of reading and language comprehension.* Boston, MA: Allyn & Bacon.

Kintsch, W. (1994). The role of knowledge in discourse comprehension: A construction-integration model. In R. B. Ruddell, M. R. Ruddell, & H. Singer (Eds.), *Theoretical models and processes of reading* (4th ed., pp. 951–995). Newark, DE: International Reading Association.

Kuhn, T. S. (1962). *The structure of scientific revolutions.* Chicago, IL: University of Chicago Press.

Long, D. L., Seely, M. R., Oppy, B. J., & Golding, J. M. (1996). The role of inferential processing in reading ability. In B. K. Britton & A. C. Graesser (Eds.), *Models of understanding text* (pp. 189–214). Mahwah, NJ: Erlbaum.

McClelland, J. L., & Rumelhart, D. E. (1986). *Parallel distributed processing: Explorations in the micro-structure of cognition* (Vol. 2). Cambridge, MA: MIT Press.

McConkie, G. W., & Zola, D. (1981). Language constraints and the functional stimulus in reading. In A. M. Lesgold & C. A. Perfetti (Eds.), *Interactive processes in reading* (pp. 155–175). Hillsdale, NJ: Erlbaum.

McKoon, G., & Ratcliff, R. (1992). Inference during reading. *Psychological Review, 99,* 440–466.

Mokhtari, K., & Reichard, C. (2002). Assessing students' metacognitive awareness of reading strategies. *Journal of Educational Psychology, 94* (2), 249–250.

Morehead, D. M. (1971). Processing of phonological sequences by young children and adults. *Child Development, 42,* 279–289.

Moustafa, M. (1997). *Beyond traditional phonics: Research discoveries and reading instruction.* Portsmouth, NH: Heinemann.

Otero, J. (1998). Influence of knowledge activation and context on comprehension monitoring of science texts. In D. J. Hacker, J. Dunlosky, & A. C. Graesser (Eds.), *Metacognition in educational theory and practice* (pp. 145–164). Mahwah, NJ: Erlbaum.

Paris, S., Lipson, M., & Wixson, K. (1983). Becoming a strategic reader. *Contemporary Educational Psychology, 8,* 293–316.

Pearson, P. D., Roehler, L. R., Dole, J. A., & Duffy, G. G. (1992). Developing expertise in reading comprehension. In S. J. Samuels & A. E. Farstrup (Eds.), *What research has to say about reading instruction* (2nd ed.). Newark, DE: International Reading Association.

Perfetti, C. A. (1985). *Reading ability.* New York: Oxford University Press.

Pressley, M., El-Kinary, P. B., & Brown, R. (1992). Skilled and not-so-skilled reading: Good information processing and not-so-good information processing. In M. Pressley, K. R. Harris, & J. T. Guthrie (Eds.), *Promoting academic competence and literacy in school* (pp. 91–127). San Diego: Academic.

Rosenblatt, L. M. (1938). *Literature as exploration.* New York: Appleton–Century. (Reprinted 1968, 1976, 1983, 1995.)

Rosenblatt, L. M. (1978). *The reader, the text, the poem: The transactional theory of the literary work.* Carbondale, IL: Southern Illinois University Press.

Rosenblatt, L. M. (1985). The transactional theory of the literary work: Implications for research. In C. R. Cooper (ed.), *Researching response to literature and the teaching of literature* (pp. 33–53). Norwood, NJ: Ablex.

Ruddell, R. B., & Unrau, N. J. (1994). Reading as a meaning-construction process: The reader, the text, and the teacher. In R. B. Ruddell, M. R. Ruddell, & H. Singer (Eds.), *Theoretical models and processes of reading* (4th ed., pp. 996–1056). Newark, DE: International Reading Association.

Rumelhart, D. E. (1980). *An introduction to human information processing.* New York: Wiley.

Sadoski, M., & Paivio, A. (2001). *Imagery and text: A dual coding theory of reading and writing.* Mahwah, NJ: Erlbaum.

Salinger, J. D. (1981). The laughing man. In J. D. Salinger (Ed.), *Nine stories* (pp. 56–73). Boston, MA: Little, Brown and Company.

Samuels, S. J. (1994). Toward a theory of automatic information processing in reading revisited. In R. B. Ruddell, M. R. Ruddell, & H. Singer (Eds.), *Theoretical models and processes of reading* (4th ed., pp. 816–837). Newark, DE: International Reading Association.

Schank, R. C., & Abelson, R. P. (1977). *Scripts, plans, goals, and understanding.* Hillsdale, NJ: Erlbaum.

Seidenberg, M. S. (1985). Constraining models of word recognition. *Cognition, 20,* 169–190.

Seidenberg, M. S., & McClelland, J. L. (1989). A distributed, developmental model of word recognition and naming. *Psychological Review, 96,* 523–568.

Spiro, R. J. (1988). *Cognitive flexibility theory: Advanced knowledge acquisition in ill-structured domains* (Tech. Rep. No. 441). Champaign, IL: University of Illinois, Center for the Study of Reading.

Stanovich, K. E. (1991). Word recognition: Changing perspectives. In R. Barr, M. Kamil, P. Rosenthal, & P. D. Pearson (Eds.), *Handbook of reading research* (Vol. 2, pp. 418–452). New York: Longman.

Stanovich, K. E. (2000). *Progress in understanding reading: Scientific foundations and new frontiers*. New York: Guilford.

Tierney, R. J. (1994). Dissension, tensions, and the models of literacy. In R. B. Ruddell, M. R. Ruddell, & H. Singer (Eds.), *Theoretical models and processes of reading* (4th ed., pp. 1162–1182). Newark, DE: International Reading Association.

Unrau, N. (1997). *Thoughtful teachers, thoughtful learners: A guide to helping adolescents think critically*. Scarborough, Ontario: Pippin Press.

Unrau, N., & Ruddel, R. (1995). Interpreting texts in classroom contexts. *Journal of Adolescent and Adult Literacy, 39*(1), 16–27.

van Dijk, T. A., & Kintsch, W. (1983). *Strategies of discourse comprehension*. New York: Academic.

Volk, P. (1999, September 2). Can you spare 7 minutes of life to read this? *New York Times,* p. B7.

Vygotsky, L. S. (1986). *Thought and language*. Cambridge, MA: MIT Press.

Waters, G., Caplan, D., & Hildebrandt, N. (1987). Working memory and written sentence comprehension. In M. Coltheart (Ed.), *Attention and performance XII: The psychology of reading,* 531–555. Hillsdale, NJ: Erlbaum.

Whimbey, A., & Lochhead, J. (1999). *Problem solving and comprehension* (6th ed.). Mahwah, NJ: Erlbaum.

Wilkinson, L. C., & Silliman, E. R. (2000). Classroom language and literacy learning. In M. L. Kamil, P. B. Mosenthal, P. D. Pearson, & R. Barr (Eds.), *Handbook of reading research* (Vol. III, pp. 337–360). Mahwah, NJ: Erlbaum.

# 3

# ASSESSING READERS AND THEIR TEXTS

After reading Chapter 3, you should be able to answer the following questions:

1. What is diagnostic teaching?
2. What steps are involved in diagnostic decision making about reading?
3. How will diagnostic decision making help me set sound learning goals and develop appropriate instruction for my students?
4. What are major differences between formal and informal assessment and what are some examples of each related to reading?
5. What are portfolios and how will they contribute to assessing student work and to student-led conferences?
6. How can I discover what comprehension strategies my students use and how much metacognitive awareness they have?
7. What categories of adolescent readers am I likely to find in my classroom?
8. How can I determine the readability and accessibility of texts for my students?

DOUBLE-ENTRY
JOURNAL: Before
Reading

If, at the beginning of a class, you wanted to evaluate your students to discover how well they read and what problems they had with reading, what steps would you take?

Now go to the
Double-Entry
Journal for
Chapter 3 on
our Companion Website at
www.prenhall.com/unrau
to fill out your journal
entry.

## DIAGNOSTIC TEACHING

History is littered with examples of solutions that failed because the problems they were to solve were inaccurately described and explained. An eighteenth-century Scottish physician, John Brown, treated diseases by administering large doses of either stimulants or sedatives to his patients. Based on his observations, he concluded that diseases were caused by too much or too little stimulation. As you might guess, his solution caused considerable harm to many people because the basis of the treatment method was wrong.

Describing and explaining how a process works when it works correctly enables us to understand what changes need to be made when a procedure is flawed and does not work. All of us have witnessed successful problem solving moments when we have discovered the right fit between a problem's description and the solution we have selected for it.

Some of these solutions are quite simple. After flipping a light switch in the hallway, a light bulb fails to come on. We examine the bulb, discover the filament is broken, replace the bulb, flip the switch, and illuminate the hallway.

Some problems are far more difficult to solve. We may not be able to describe the problem space so easily as we can describe the problem space of a hallway with a burned-out light bulb. To our misfortune, we may remain in the dark for days or forever.

Without clear descriptions and explanations of learning processes, we are going to have trouble bringing light to the problems our students encounter when trying to learn. Why struggling students cannot create meanings from a text they are trying to read is many a teacher's dark puzzle. Gaining clearer descriptions and explanations of how our students read and why their lights too often fail to go on is the purpose of this chapter.

Teachers, like physicians, can view themselves as diagnosticians. But the illnesses teachers treat are those caused by improper conceptualization, lack of appropriate skills, misconceived strategies, and ineffective thinking. They engage in what Solomon and Morocco (1999) describe as "critical scrutiny" of student output to discover ways to improve performance. While diagnostic teachers carefully examine student work for signs of healthy, productive thinking that leads to correct understanding and good solutions, they also look for signs of conceptualizations and problem solving procedures that are unproductive and ineffective. And, like physicians, diagnostic teachers find ways they can carefully administer new conceptions to students, new procedures, and new strategies that lead to productive thinking and learning.

Throughout our professional careers, we should continue to look upon our work with students as endless opportunities to observe how their minds are working to solve the problems in learning that we and the world present to them. The more we learn over years of careful observation and the more strategies we can bring to bear in helping students solve the problems they face, the better we can be at diagnosing and ameliorating the disorders in learning our students acquire.

Although we will be reviewing standardized, norm-referenced tests as well as other assessment tools, our goal should not be simply the ranking of our students by level of skill or knowledge. The diagnostic teacher's focus should rather be on understanding the features, gross and subtle, of each student's thinking, of each student's mental operations when reading and learning. That knowledge gained from critical scrutiny should then inform teaching practice. The diagnostic teacher emphasizes building the capacity to learn in students over that of depositing information.

When diagnostic teachers view reading (as well as writing) as meaning-making processes, as we've seen they are in the previous chapter, these teachers are far more likely to make efforts to understand how their students make meaning from texts. They look for each student's particular way of comprehending texts, and they try to discover how to improve the quality of that comprehension rather than delivering generic, one-size-fits-all solutions.

## CONTENT TEACHER'S DIAGNOSTIC DECISION MAKING ABOUT READING

I encourage teachers using texts of any kind to use a diagnostic decision-making approach to instruction. It calls for a thoughtful diagnostic assessment of students before, during, and after instruction. The purpose for engaging in that assessment is to develop diagnostic teaching sessions and appropriate reading instruction. Although time away from content coverage is the bane of many a teacher, assessing students and their texts will help you design instruction that accounts for your student's reading level and its further development. That diagnostic approach should be applied to instructional programs that use literacy skills and strategies, like reading, to master knowledge in content courses.

A diagnostic approach to reading assessment for content area teachers answers several questions, some of which Kibby (1995) posits:

1. What is the student's current level of reading ability, and is it satisfactory for the reading expected in the course?
2. Which reading strategies and skills strengthen or limit the student's reading?
3. What factors are associated with the student's reading ability?
4. What instructional conditions most favor the student's learning?
5. What recommendations or referrals will further the student's reading development?

Going through the steps of the diagnostic decision-making process with students enables you to answer each of these questions and provide optimum reading instruction and growth for students in your classes.

In adapting Kibby's (1995) diagnostic decision-making process to middle and high school teaching, I identified seven steps to guide the assessment of students in content classrooms:

Step 1. Begin learning about each student's identity, history, goals, values, and interests.

Step 2. Determine the expected level of reading at which students will need to perform satisfactorily in the course.

Step 3. Assess each student's reading capacity using a standardized reading test, Group Reading Inventory, or Curriculum-Based Measurement. For students reading below grade level or observed to have significant problems comprehending course texts, administer an Individual Reading Inventory (IRI) to clarify instructional needs.

Step 4. Develop an overall literacy profile for the whole class of students, including strengths and weaknesses of the entire group.

Step 5. Inventory and review available teaching strategies and resources.

Step 6. Engage in diagnostic teaching to maximize compatibility between content texts and readers' capacity.

Step 7. Continue instructional monitoring, modifications, and recommendations, including referrals for remedial reading instruction.

In the following discussion, I'll describe each step in more detail, explaining procedures to apply in your classrooms. Figure 3.1, the Content Teachers Diagnostic Decision-Making Model, provides a graphic summary of the process.

## Step 1. Student's Identity, History, Goals, Values, and Interests

Recall that much heard educator's quip, "I teach students—not (fill in the subject)"? Of course, there's much to commend the view that what comes first is the student's mind and not the content knowledge teachers may want to deposit there. There's plenty of evidence on influential teachers (Ruddell, 1995; Ruddell, Draheim, & Barnes, 1990) to assert that students favor and respond favorably to some teachers more than others. Students tend to prefer teachers who take a personal interest in their learning, who ask questions about how they are responding to instruction, who want to engage their students by discovering what interests them and how they can become more interested in a course's content.

None of this is meant to demean the importance of a teacher's knowledge of their subject. As one of the core propositions articulated by the National Board for Professional Teaching Standards puts it: "Teachers know the subjects they teach and how to teach those subjects to students." Both knowledge of your subject *and* of his or her procedures to teach it must enlighten your classrooms.

But for diagnostic teaching, the student must come first. Diagnostic teachers want and need to discover as much as they can learn about their students' identities, their educational histories, their aspirations, their values, and their interests. Although we will investigate these antecedents of instructional engagement much more carefully in Chapter 10 on motivation, diagnostic teachers should be committed to discovering what they can about their students in order to put each student's reading into a living perspective.

Early in the school year, you can discover a lot about your students' reading and attitudes toward reading through surveys and questionnaires. Nancy Atwell (1998), the author of *In the Middle,* has designed a reading survey she gives to her middle school students so she can learn about each student's reading experiences and attitudes at the beginning of the school year. She asks about how they learned to read, why they read, what they think it takes to be a good reader, what kinds of books they like to read, how often they read at home on their own, and how they feel about reading in general. During the first week of school, students complete her surveys,

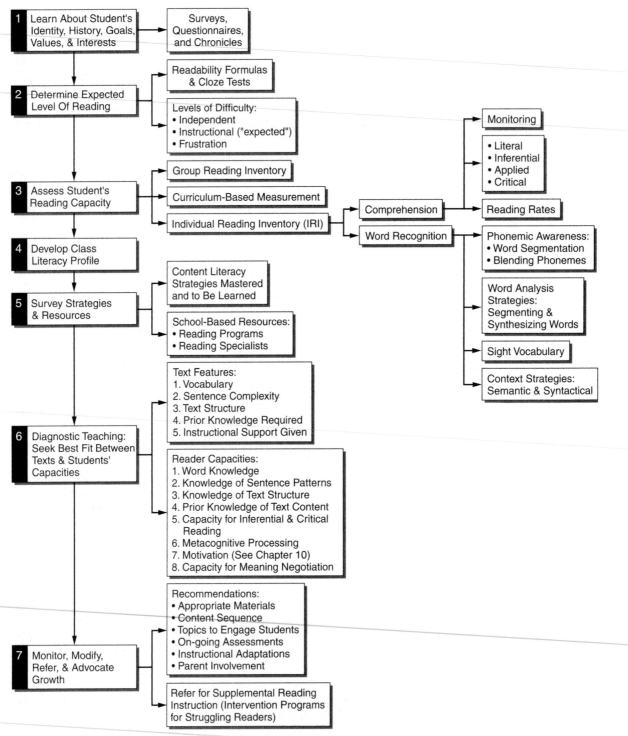

**FIGURE 3.1** Content Teacher's Diagnostic Decision-Making Model.

she reads them over, makes notes about who her students are, and puts the surveys into individual folders for each student.

Jeff Waid, a teacher at Los Angeles High School, keeps a "student chronicle," a continuous and evolving record of each of his students throughout the school year. He starts the chronicle with a Student Information Sheet that provides him with background data about each student's home language, after-school jobs, responsibility for siblings, and personal information about favorite movies and music. (See Figure 3.2.) Early in the school year, Jeff asks students to write an autobiography that includes information gathered through interviews of family members, information about each student's language history, learning goals, and home life. Jeff believes that, by maintaining chronicles for his students, they recognize that their history and home life are valued and "feel confident in bringing their entire experience to bear as readers and writers" in his classroom (Waid, 2002). The evolving chronicles deepen the ways he interacts with them and they interact with him.

## Step 2. Expected Level of Reading

Expected Level of Reading is the level of difficulty that a text presents to a reader. It's the level of reading at which a reader is expected to perform. But at what level *is* the student expected to perform? Levels of reading vary depending on the degree of challenge a text presents to a reader. Usually, the readability of a text is measured with a readability formula or a cloze test. Readability formulas yield a grade level, so a readability level of 9 means that, to successfully construct meaning for that text, a student should be able to read at the ninth-grade level or better. Cloze tests yield categories of text difficulty. These categories span the independent, instructional, or frustration levels. More details about measures of readability will come later in this chapter.

The expected level for satisfactory reading performance in a class is usually the "instructional" which means the reader is reading at grade level. Unlike the independent level, the instructional level assumes that you will provide support for reading texts. However, while some of your students will find the text to be at their frustration level, other students may need more challenging texts in order to grow.

## Step 3. Assess Student's Reading Capacity

The next step entails your assessing each student's current reading capacity to decide if that capacity will enable the student to satisfactorily engage and learn from your content area texts. Your student's silent reading comprehension may be measured with any of several reading comprehension tests, such as the Gates-MacGinitie Reading Comprehension Test. The results of a standardized reading comprehension test may be a percentile rank, a stanine score, a normal curve equivalent (NCE), or a grade equivalent score from a standardized test. I'll explain these scores when we discuss test interpretation later in this chapter. Often scores from standardized reading tests are available in a student's cumulative file. However, if scores are more than a year old, I recommend testing to obtain a more current score.

You can also give your students a Group Reading Inventory (GRI) and/or a Curriculum-Based Measurement (CBM) to assess their capacity to read texts normally given in your content area. The procedures for constructing and giving GRIs and CBMs will also be provided later in this chapter.

# STUDENT INFORMATION SHEET

Please take your time and fill out this sheet as completely and honestly as possible. And hey, please write neatly.

Name _____
               First                     Middle                   Last

The name you go by _____ Birthday _____ Grade _____

Parent(s)/Guardian _____ Relationship _____
                              First        Last

Parent(s)/Guardian _____ Relationship _____
                              First        Last

Address _____ City _____ Zip _____

**TELEPHONE NUMBER** _____

                                Not at all ⟵⟶ Very Well
I speak and understand English (circle one):   1   2   3   4   5
My parents speak and understand English:   1   2   3   4   5

If you speak another language besides English, please answer the following questions:

What other languages do you speak? _____

                 Not Fluently ⟵⟶Very Fluently
How fluently?         1      2      3      4      5

In what other countries have you lived? _____

How long have you lived in the United States? _____

Please describe any special limitations about you that I should be aware of so I can best help you in this class (For instance, do you need to sit close to the front to see?)

_____

Is there anything that prevents you from studying or doing your homework? Please explain (e.g., "I have to share a bedroom with my sister who talks too much and bugs me every time I try to do my work.") _____

_____

_____

If you have a job, where is it? _____

How many hours a week do you work? _____

What are your responsibilities around the house (e.g., chores, caring for brothers and sisters)? _____

_____

_____

FIGURE 3.2 Student Information Sheet.

*Source:* Originally designed by Nick M. Deligencia and modified by Jeff Waid.

**Please do your best to answer the following:**

*What is your favorite:*

**Television Show?** _____

        Why? _____

**Radio Station?** _____

        Why? _____

**Music Group?** _____

        Why? _____

**Individual Singer?** _____

        Why? _____

**Song?** _____

        Why? _____

**Latest Movie?** _____

        Why? _____

**All-time Movie?** _____

        Why? _____

**Actor/Actress?** _____

        Why? _____

What hobbies, clubs, sports, or outside activities have you enjoyed? _____

_____

_____

What are your plans for the future? _____

_____

What are your plans for now? _____

_____

What college would you like to attend? _____

**Please complete the following sentences:**

*The greatest things about me are:* _____

_____

_____

*The greatest problems confronting me now are:*

_____

_____

**In the space below, write down three questions that you would like to ask me.**

FIGURE 3.2    *Continued.*

87

If a student is more than a year below grade level or is manifesting significant frustration in comprehending course reading material, I recommend administration of an Individual Reading Inventory.

An Individual Reading Inventory or IRI generates more detailed information about a student's reading process than standardized reading tests, GRIs, or CBMs. An IRI yields estimates for a student's independent, instructional, and frustration levels and information about performance on different kinds of comprehension and aspects of word recognition. You may not have the time to administer IRIs to all your students because they take between 30 and 45 minutes. However, other specialists in your school could give the inventory and provide you with information about the results.

## Step 4. Class Literacy Profile

After your students have been given tests to measure their reading capacities, you can create a profile for the entire class. That profile should reveal the reading levels for each student as indicated by standardized reading tests, GRIs, and CBMs. Students identified as likely to be struggling readers in your course should be given further diagnostic testing, such as the IRI recommended in Step 3. Their strengths and weaknesses should be taken into account as you design lessons that entail reading. Some of these struggling readers may need additional reading instruction beyond what you could possibly offer. We will discuss the importance of appropriate referral of students like these in Step 7.

Information about all students need not be gathered before instruction begins. As we've seen, diagnostic teaching entails on-going observation and collection of information about students' performance. Group surveys, questionnaires, and standardized group tests can be administered at the beginning of the course or school year. In the case of standardized reading tests, recent information about students' reading performance may be available in their cumulative records. However, we need to be wary of data more than a year old when looking at reading performance.

## Step 5. Teaching Strategies and Resources

At this stage, diagnostic teachers survey the strategies and resources available for their use in helping students read and learn from reading. Resources may include reading specialists in your school or district and reading intervention programs, such as those to be described in Chapter 9. Later in this book I will describe how you can use several strategies to enhance students' reading comprehension. Chapter 4 focuses on vocabulary development. In Chapter 5, I'll explain how to use the Directed Reading–Thinking Activity, Directed Inquiry Activity, graphic knowledge organizers, and other comprehension fostering strategies. In Chapter 6, you'll learn about group methods to promote literacy and learning, including cooperative learning and reciprocal teaching techniques. In Chapter 7, I'll present several strategies to enhance critical responses to texts, such as Inquiry Questions (or IQs), ReQuest, Questioning the Author, the Thesis Analysis and Synthesis Key (TASK), and principles for conducting class discussions to develop critical literacy. And, in Chapter 8, you'll learn about the uses of writing to assess, promote, and observe learning. So even if you are a beginning teacher feeling limited by the number of instructional strategies you currently know, in a few days or weeks you'll be introduced to many more. All can be tried in the diagnostic teacher's classroom to discover how they enable your students to read and learn more effectively.

# Step 6. Diagnostic Teaching

Diagnostic teachers strive for compatibility between their students' reading capacities and course texts. When selecting content textbooks and supplementary reading materials, you should weigh and balance readers' capacities with features of the texts. At the diagnostic teaching stage in the decision-making process, you should have gathered enough information to discover the kinds of instructional conditions generally favorable to your students.

If text comprehension requirements are too great, even readers with good monitoring and control skills, high motivation, and considerable capacity for meaning negotiation over texts in the classroom will need lots of teacher support—or they will be overwhelmed.

Text features.    When evaluating texts that your students will encounter in their reading for your courses, several text features that determine a text's accessibility are taken into account. These features include the text's vocabulary, sentence complexity, structure, prior knowledge expectations, and instructional support provided to facilitate accessibility. The text's vocabulary should be surveyed to discover what types of problems with word recognition and word meanings your students are likely to encounter. Sentence length and complexity, including number of embedded phrases and clauses, should also be examined and evaluated. Fry's Readability Formula, described later in this chapter, will help you evaluate both the challenge of vocabulary and sentences because those features are built into that formula. The kinds of text structures that the author used to convey content are important to assess, as are the forms and depth of prior knowledge expected of readers and the kinds of instructional support, such as graphic organizers, definitions of terms, summaries, and questions, provided in the text.

Reader capacities.    To estimate a text's accessibility to your students, you will need to evaluate several of their capacities as readers. These include their knowledge of words, sentence patterns, and text structure; their prior knowledge related to a text; their ability for inferential and critical thinking; their metacognitive skill; their motivation; and their capacity for meaning negotiation. An assortment of instruments, formal and informal, are described in this chapter and other chapters to help you determine your students' compatibility with the texts they will read.

Finding, adapting, and supporting texts for instruction.    Finding reading materials that fit a specific profile of needs for just ONE struggling reader is challenging. Finding the best fit between available content texts and the composite literacy profile for an entire class is a greater one. However, I have come to believe that good diagnostic teaching requires us to make serious and genuine efforts to attain that best fit. Too often the mismatch between students' reading capacities and course text reading requirements results in massive frustration for both students and teacher.

We should remember, however, that texts that are at students' instructional levels could be made accessible with teacher support. Even texts that are at your students' frustration levels can often be adapted or presented so those students can gain

access to the information in them. Many reading comprehension strategies described in the next chapter help readers construct meaning through directed or guided interaction with challenging texts. At the other end of the spectrum from readers who find content texts frustrating are those who find the texts to be at an easy independent reading level. You'll need to take into account more knowledgeable and skilled readers who may not be sufficiently challenged by the course reading materials to enable them to grow as readers.

Through diagnostic discovery and teaching, you can formulate your lessons to provide greater opportunity for your students to achieve mastery of the material you present to your classes. While teaching, you can observe and collect information that will further inform your instructional decision making. With that knowledge, you can bring to bear your growing arsenal of teaching strategies and resources to provide additional opportunities for your students to learn strategies and skills that will help them grow as readers and learners.

## Step 7. Instructional Monitoring, Modification, and Recommendations

Diagnostic teachers who follow Solomon and Morocco's (1999) suggestions monitor and observe their students' reading and learning in detail and continue to make judgments about (a) students' strategies and comprehension, (b) their acquisition of subject-matter knowledge, and (c) the effectiveness of teaching strategies and practices used in the classroom. You can observe a wide range of factors affecting learning from texts:

- ◆ Your students' levels of interest and motivation,
- ◆ Their responses to success as well as failure,
- ◆ Their attention span,
- ◆ The effects of pace on their learning, and
- ◆ The amount of additional support and review of content required for their success.

Using these observations, you can modify your teaching, note the impact of those modifications, and make recommendations. Those recommendations include the assignment of appropriate materials, the selection of topics to engage students, instructional adaptation, and on-going assessment.

While parental involvement in children's literacy development tends to taper off as children progress through the middle and high school years, I believe parents' continued engagement has many benefits. Keeping parents informed of students' progress in reading development, while sometimes overlooked, is especially important for struggling readers. Parents can offer at-home support for literacy growth as well as encouragement for school-related literacy tasks. In some families, middle and high school students discuss school and independent reading with parents. These discussions can provide students with opportunities to explore aspects of their reading they may otherwise miss. Some teachers promote communication with parents by developing and sending home newsletters that give parents information about the curriculum, including books, their children are covering in school.

Recommendations for individual reading remediation.   Serious reading problems that diagnostic teachers find with individual students are too often ignored or denied because no program has been established to address the literacy needs of struggling readers. As Kibby points out, individual reading remediation should be recommended "even if there are no individual instructional facilities available or funds for such facilities" (1995, p. 53). His rationale for these recommendations make complete sense because parents may not seek alternative reading remediation resources if they are not informed of their children's reading difficulties. Urging students and their families to seek help may prompt school personnel and other educational agencies to provide essential programs for struggling readers who may be at risk of failing and of eventually dropping out of school.

## ASSESSMENT INSTRUMENTS FOR DIAGNOSTIC TEACHING

You are the best assessment instrument your students have. Your observational and interpretive powers compose the most powerful set of reading and learning assessment tools that your students could ever face. What you observe, how deeply you observe, and how you interpret those observations inform critical dimensions of teaching, like your understanding of your students' comprehension levels, skills, and needs. Your observations of your students' behavior in classrooms, how they interact with texts and how they participate in text-based discussions, often yield information and insights far more useful than data from a standardized test. However, both formal and informal reading assessment tools can focus and magnify your observational powers to help you discern what's going on in the minds of your students as they read and learn.

The effective implementation of a diagnostic decision-making process relies upon your understanding of what instruments can facilitate diagnostic work and how to use them. Some of these instruments are formal tests and others are informal assessment instruments. I'll begin by describing formal tests and then turn to informal assessment instruments. We'll approach formal tests by starting with the most widely used international testing programs and then explore national, state, district, school, and classroom testing. We'll also look at differences between norm-referenced and criterion-referenced formal tests. Finally, we'll look at several examples of formal testing instruments that are used to assess groups of students and individual, struggling readers during the diagnostic decision-making process. In short, we'll progress from global to local.

## FORMAL ASSESSMENT

Several features define the difference between formal and informal assessment. (See Table 3.1, Two Methods of Assessment Compared, for a summary.) Formal tests are standardized by having all subjects complete similar tasks and follow similar procedures that enable comparisons between individuals or groups taking the test. Given directions must be followed, and time limits, if provided, must be observed. Formal testing includes international-, national-, state-, and district-level assessment. The instruments used for these large-scale evaluations are usually designed by testing experts. Some formal tests, like the National Assessment of Educational Progress (NAEP) or the Scholastic Achievement Test (SAT), include test items that are usually used once and retired to be replaced by similar but unique items. Other formal tests, like the Gates-MacGinitie Reading Test or the Stanford Achievement Test, include passages and items that are used repeatedly. Reading comprehension tests often have two or more different forms at the same grade levels to measure growth over time.

Formal testing in middle and high schools is extensive. Middle school testing programs often include assessments, such as the Stanford Achievement Tests, the Iowa Test of Basic Skills, or the Texas Assessment of Academic Skills. Teachers may also administer some form of reading test, such as the Nelson-Denny or the Gates-MacGinitie. While all these tests may also appear in high school testing programs, other kinds of "high-stakes" formal testing for college admission, such as the Scholastic Achievement Tests (SAT) or the American College Test (ACT), absorb the attention of thousands of students. Many other state-, district-, or school-sponsored testing programs have flourished in recent years, adding to a test-heavy schedule.

Your role in these testing programs will usually be that of monitor. However, because some of these tests may be aligned to teaching standards and reflect in-

**TABLE 3.1**  Two Methods of Assessment Compared

| | Formal Assessment (aka: "High-Stakes") | Informal Assessment (aka: "Authentic" or "Naturalistic") |
|---|---|---|
| **Purposes, Uses for Data** | • Measurement of student performance, usually in groups, to compare reading levels or determine growth following intervention.<br>• Measure change for state accountability and reward programs.<br>• Determine reading levels to select texts.<br>• Measure reading ranges in a class.<br>• Categorize students, e.g., to identify struggling or delayed readers for further diagnosis or placement. | • Identify qualities of students' reading performance, such as fluency and miscues.<br>• Discover strategy use while reading.<br>• Monitor and detect problems in comprehension.<br>• Resources for teacher team meetings.<br>• Data for benchmarks to monitor development (e.g., CBMs).<br>• Feedback to evaluate effectiveness of teaching. |
| **Designers** | Testing companies and committees of experts. | Teachers, reading experts. |
| **Student Interaction with Tasks** | All subjects complete similar tasks, follow similar procedures, observe same time limits. Students usually complete test in groups according to schedule. | May complete similar or different tasks; procedures usually similar but may vary; time limits less likely. Usually given in small groups or one-on-one. May be repeatedly given to measure progress or monitor development. |
| **Teacher's Role** | Administer test, monitor, interpret results. May do some test preparation. | Observe reading behavior, interact with students, record reading behavior, analyze data. |
| **Method of Measurement** | Multiple choice, other forms of closed-ended questions, quantitative. | Observations, more open-ended questions, qualitative. |
| **Examples** | IEA, NAEP, State Testing Programs (STAR in California, TAAS in Texas), test batteries (Stanford Achievement Test, Iowa Test of Basic Skills), Gates-MacGinitie, Scholastic Aptitude Test (SAT). | Informal Reading Inventory (IRI), Curriculum-Based Measures, Running Record, Cloze, portfolios, teacher-made tests, classroom observations, student self-reports. |

struction, you and your school's administrators may have some significant stake in their outcome. However, the extent of that stake varies from state to state, district to district, and school to school. While some school cultures are test performance sensitive, others are far less so.

## Norm-Referenced Tests

A norm-referenced test is a standardized test that can be used to compare one student's reading performance with that of a reference group. The reference groups are often composed of thousands of students who are drawn from a wide sampling of schools in different communities. Norms are ranges of scores representing an average in a distribution.

Norm-referenced survey reading tests yield several different kinds of scores: raw score, percentile rank, stanine, normal curve equivalent, and grade equivalent score.

The ***raw score*** is nothing other than the total number of items a student got correct on the test or its subparts. The subparts of a norm-referenced reading test usually consist of separate comprehension and vocabulary tests. You can refer to appropriate tables and transform raw scores into more meaningful scores, such as those next described.

The ***percentile rank*** reveals where, in percentage categories from 0% to 99%, a student's raw score lies within a range of scores. It tells the percentage of students in the same grade with lower raw scores. If a student's percentile score is 37, she has done better than 37% of the students in the norm-referenced group who took the test. A percentile score of 50 shows that the test-taker has done better than half the students in the norm-referenced group.

Similar to percentile ranks, ***normal curve equivalents*** (NCEs) present a student's reading level relative to other students at the same grade level. NCEs are based on percentile ranks, but those percentiles have been changed into a scale of equal reading achievement units. Because each NCE unit is equal throughout the scale, they can be used for computing averages and making comparisons between scores.

***Stanines*** divide the spectrum of reading achievement into nine score bands or categories. Because each stanine measures reading in a relatively broad band of achievement, stanines do not encourage focusing on what may be meaningless small score differences.

***Grade equivalent scores*** (GEs) rank students' reading performance within groups that include students from all grades. They characterize performance in terms equal to that of other readers in a particular grade. A grade equivalent of 8.5 indicates that the reader performed as well as the average eighth grader in the sixth month (February) of the eighth grade because the first month (September) would be scored as 8.0. GEs are not standards or criteria to be reached. They are simply measures of performance.

## Criterion-Referenced Tests

While a norm-referenced test yields results that enable comparisons between test takers—and, thereby, may foster competition, criterion-referenced tests are designed to measure a student's performance against a set standard or criterion. Teachers in some states must score at or above a set standard on tests of basic skills, like reading comprehension, essay writing, and mathematics, in order to be eligible to receive a credential.

As a teacher, you may also establish standards of performance on skills or mastery of content material that your students must attain before they can progress to the next unit. Some districts establish literacy criteria, such as a certain level of performance on reading and writing tasks that must be reached before a student can progress to the third grade or from middle to high school. Several states, including New York and California, have high school exit exams that are based on standards that students must meet in order to graduate.

Benchmarks, indicators of performance used to measure students' progress toward skill or content standards, are finding their way into more schools and classrooms. You can set up an assessment system of benchmarks in your own classroom to record and monitor your students' progress in reading, writing, and learning in a content area. Some middle schools use a reading fluency measurement to monitor students' progress in reading at intervals of two or three months throughout the school year. Students use the data to monitor their progress; teachers use it to chart students' growth and identify special needs; and schools use it to quickly spot struggling readers and the impact of intervention programs.

Currently, many states use norm-referenced testing programs that may not be closely tied to a school's, district's, or even state's curriculum. Because criterion-referenced tests provide information about students' mastery of specific, explicit curriculum content, many educators (Calkins, Montgomery, & Santman,1998) are urging their use rather than norm-referenced testing. With criterion-referenced tests, teachers, students, and their parents can know what kind and degree of mastery in reading or any other subject has been established by assessment policy. Furthermore, standards, frameworks, teacher-preparation programs, and mission statements of discipline-based professional organization can be aligned with content criteria. Knowing those expectations, you and your students could work together toward their attainment.

## Assessing the Assessment Instruments

Validity.    To evaluate the quality of assessment instruments, we need to take into account a test's validity and its reliability. For a test to be valid, it must measure what its designers claim it will measure. If test designers say that a test is made to measure reading comprehension but provide no evidence that it actually does measure reading comprehension, we cannot view the test as a valid instrument.

Several concepts of validity are commonly applied: construct, content, predictive, and concurrent (or statistical). ***Construct validity*** refers to the degree to which some theory (or construct) is reflected in a test. Thus, if your students were able to rapidly identify the meaning of words on a test of vocabulary, they would, in theory, have enough automaticity and semantic knowledge to read well. So a test measuring a student's memory for the meaning of a list of vocabulary words would have construct validity as a test of reading. ***Content validity*** refers to the match between the content of a test and the reading or tasks that are taught in the curriculum. A valid test of reading strategy instruction would need to reflect the strategies taught as part of the curriculum. If you taught your students how to activate background knowledge related to a topic about which they were to read and you gave them a test to see if they used that approach when reading, your test would have content validity. ***Concurrent (or statistical) validity*** occurs when performance on a new test is compared to performance on an established test through calculating a correlation between them. If you were to design a new test of reading comprehension and attempt to reveal its concurrent validity, you would compare the results of readers' performance on your test with their performance on an existing test of reading comprehension to reveal the magnitude of the correlation between the two tests.

Lastly, ***predictive validity*** refers to the extent to which a test predicts some specified performance. For example, scores on a standardized reading test are likely to predict students' grades in an English class and have relatively strong correlations.

*Reliability.* A test may measure what it purports to measure at one time. But does it do so consistently? A reliable test is one that consistently measures what it is designed to measure. So, if one of your students retakes a reliable test, you would expect that student to receive approximately the same result.

*Standard error of measurement.* A single resulting score on a test should be viewed as a more or less narrow range or spectrum of scores rather than an absolute point on a scale. That's because no test is perfect, and scores are likely to have errors built into them. Statisticians refer to these errors as the *standard error of measurement* or SEM. An SEM is an estimate of the variance between the score actually received and the score that would result from a "perfect test."

## What Reading Processes Can't Be Adequately Assessed

We can learn quite a lot about our students' reading processes through formal procedures that now exist. With commercial reading comprehension tests, we can measure vocabulary and comprehension of several kinds, such as literal, inferential, applied, and critical comprehension. However, several aspects of the reading process are difficult, if not impossible, for us to adequately quantify or measure with formal, norm-referenced tests. Among those are our students':

- Background knowledge relevant to specific texts encoded in long-term memory (LTM);
- Range of genre knowledge, including poetic language and argumentation, held in LTM;
- Depth of engagement experienced with texts;
- Range of reading strategies (stored in LTM) activated when reading, especially when the going gets tough;
- Capacity to summarize, ask questions, and make predictions while reading (Metacognitive strategies);
- Degree of automaticity in word identification, and
- Application of learning to near and far transfer tasks.

Some of these features can be measured or examined more closely with informal assessment instruments.

## INFORMAL ASSESSMENT

While informal tests may be made to measure any population of students on just about any skill and provide more flexibility in administration, they lack a standard scale (norms) for categorizing or ranking student performance. However, with informal instruments, you can often discover more about students' background knowledge, range of genre knowledge, depth of engagement, strategy use, metacognitive skills, word recognition processes, as well as comprehension. Often informal assessments, like miscue analysis or individual reading inventories, provide detailed information that helps with decision making. Without detailed information about how your students respond to texts often used in your classroom instruction, you will have less information to make informed decisions about what kinds of texts are best used for content instruction. Furthermore, informal assessments can provide insights about how your students think and construct meaning while they read.

Informal assessments of reading are often called "authentic" reading assessments. Usually, "authentic" assessments engage students in the reading of actual texts used in classroom instruction or in tasks undertaken in a natural environment, like a classroom, rather than tasks completed in a clinical or test-structured environment. Often, "authentic" assessments are based on reading materials and tasks normally constituting daily classroom teaching.

Informal or "authentic" reading assessment will also allow you to see more clearly your students' thinking and meaning construction processes. By looking closely at those thinking processes, you can better understand what is working and what is breaking down as your students construct meaning through interaction with content area texts.

Among the informal reading assessments we will review are the Group Reading Inventory (GRI), miscue analysis, running records, Curriculum-Based Measurement (CBM), retellings, comprehension think-alouds, and interviews.

## Group Reading Inventory (GRI)

To discover how your students are likely to comprehend texts used in your class, you can administer a Group Reading Inventory (GRI). Its purpose is to discover which students will probably find a particular textbook frustrating to read and will, therefore, need additional support and guidance to comprehend it. For normal teaching purposes, students should be reading texts at an instructional level, if teachers are to work with the text in class, or at an independent level, if the texts are to be read on their own. With a GRI, you can time students to get a reading rate and test comprehension with a set of questions assessing vocabulary and various forms of comprehension. Because of wide differences in interests and background knowledge, students should be given GRIs for each content area text they are expected to read.

## STEP-BY-STEP: *Group Reading Inventory*

**STEP 1.** From the textbook or other material that students will be reading, select a passage of about 500 words that students have not yet read.

**STEP 2.** Prepare 10 or 20 questions to assess vocabulary, literal comprehension, such as main ideas, details, sequence, and inferential comprehension. The questions may be either multiple choice or open-ended. A sample GRI reading with questions (Rakes & Smith, 1992) appears in Table 3.2.

**STEP 3.** Develop an answer key with original questions and appropriate answers. Identify the type of skill each question requires to answer correctly, such as identifying main ideas or comprehending details. A sample GRI answer key (Rakes & Smith, 1992) appears in Table 3.3.

**STEP 4.** Distribute the passage to students or tell them which pages from their text they are to read and explain that you will be asking them to time themselves. To help in this regard,

**TABLE 3.2**   Sample GRI Reading with Questions

**Directions:** Read the selection beginning on page _____ through page _____ to find out how the early novel developed and the various forms it took. When you have finished reading the selection, raise your hand and you will be given a short questionnaire over the material.

**The Novel**

One of the nicest pleasures in life for many people is to curl up in a comfortable place and read a good novel. Novels have been in existence for a relatively short time, compared to other forms of literature. For example, the drama has existed for centuries, whereas the novel came into being only about three hundred years ago. Basically, a novel can be defined as a long story, written in prose, and having many characters and more than one plot.

Prior to the development of the novel in its present form, stories were often written in verse. These verse stories were known as "romances" during the Middle Ages. Usually the stories revolved around characters, such as kings, queens, knights-in-armor, and other heroes. Rarely were ordinary people and their problems ever subjects for romances—they were considered unfit subject matter for literature.

During the Renaissance, dating between the fourteenth and sixteenth centuries, people began to see that ordinary people and their lives could be interesting and meaningful subjects for stories, often changing their point of view about life and literature.

Among these important changes were the geographical expansions of many countries (etc.)

**Comprehension Questions**

1. What is a novel?
2. What was the "picaresque" novel?
3. Approximately when did the novel come into being?
4. What is a "plot" novel?
5. How did the invention of the printing press affect literature?
6. What are "romances"?
7. How does the "plot" novel differ from the "adventure" novel?
8. If our society were only composed of the very rich and the very poor, with no middle class, what type(s) of novel(s) might we have today?
9. How did exploration affect the merchants?
10. What type of modern literature do you think may have been an outgrowth of space exploration?
11. What are two examples of "adventure" or "journey" novels in English or American literature?
12. How might the mass media (television, newspapers, etc.) negatively affect the novel today?
13. Why did the novel develop the way it did?
14. What social topics might be found in modern novels today?

secure a timing clock that all students can see. Otherwise, write down the time on the board in 10 second intervals. (Later, students will compute a words-per-minute score by dividing the total number of words in the passages they read by the time taken to read them.)

**STEP 5.** When finished reading the passage, students should either close their books or flip their papers over and answer questions you've provided.

**STEP 6.** Review results of the GRI to determine how many students scored at an independent (90% or higher), instructional (70 to 90%), or frustration level (50% or less). Students who comprehend 70 to 75% of well-designed questions based on the passage should be able to understand the text with some instructional support in class. That support should include key vocabulary, study methods, and strategy instruction to promote comprehension.

TABLE 3.3   GRI Answer Key Sample

| Skill | Question and Possible Answer |
|---|---|
| Main Idea | 1. What is a novel? (long, prose story with many characters and more than one plot; Paragraph 1) |
| Context | 2. What was the "picaresque" novel? (stories of adventures of rogues or rascals who traveled about the country; from the Spanish word *picaro* meaning rascal; Paragraph 5) |
| Detail | 3. Approximately when did the novel come into being? (during the Renaissance; between fourteenth and sixteenth centuries; Paragraph 3) |
| Context | 4. What is a "plot" novel? (stories of love between people, set in only one place and having few characters) |
| Detail | 5. How did the invention of the printing press affect literature? (large quantities of books available at reasonable cost) |
| Context | 6. What are "romances"? (stories written in verse usually about kings, queens, knights, or other heroes; Paragraph 2) |
| Detail | 7. How does the "plot" novel differ from the "adventure" novel? ("plot" novels are usually set in one place and have fewer characters) |
| Inference | 8. If our society were only composed of the very rich and the very poor, with no middle class, what types(s) of novel(s) might we have today? (answers will vary) |
| Detail | 9. How did exploration affect the merchants? (gave them more markets in which to sell products) |
| Inference | 10. What type of modern literature do you think may have been an outgrowth of space exploration? (science fiction) |
| Detail | 11. What are two examples of "adventure" or "journey" novels in English or American literature? (*David Copperfield, Oliver Twist, Huckleberry Finn, Robinson Crusoe*, or *Joseph Andrews*) |
| Inference | 12. How might the mass media (television, newspapers, etc.) negatively affect the novel today? (answers will vary) |
| Main Idea | 13. Why did the novel develop the way it did? (people were becoming more practical and realistic; discovered that the "ordinary" could make good stories; other varied answers) |
| Inference | 14. What social topics might be found in modern novels today? (answers will vary) |

**Performance Levels**

| | |
|---|---|
| Independent: | 0–2 questions missed |
| Instructional: | 3–6 questions missed |
| Frustration: | 7 or more questions missed |

**Reading Rate**

Words-per-minute rate = Total number of words read/Time = _____.

## Miscue Analysis

Miscues are oral reading responses that vary from those expected. Kenneth Goodman (1969, 1994) has observed that mistakes in oral reading should be viewed as miscues in a "psycholinguistic guessing game" rather than errors because these mistakes are actually attempts to construct meaning. Examining miscues can help you understand how a reader decodes texts and tries to make sense of them.

Miscue analysis is often done as part of a larger informal reading inventory (IRI), but a miscue analysis can be done independently. Certain kinds of miscues that are judged "mistakes" but should be scored as word recognition miscues are described

**TABLE 3.4**    Word Recognition Miscues That Are Scored

| Miscue | Example | Comments |
|---|---|---|
| Use of nonsense word or mispronunciation | (regmint)<br>The ~~regiment~~ went on to defeat the enemy. | Reader attempts pronunciation but produces a nonsense word. |
| Substitution | when<br>~~want~~ | An incorrect real word gets spoken in place of one on the page. |
| Omission | For the first time, Fanny ran behind the tall ~~Blue~~ Spruce. (Reader leaves out Blue.) | Reader does not appear to notice that any word was skipped. |
| Reversal | He stood on the ~~pad~~. (The word *pad* is pronounced "dap.") | Reader reverses words or letters. |
| Insertion | The (puffy) blue cloud floated all the way to Toledo. ("Puffy" inserted.) | Word or series of words that are not in the text are inserted. |
| No attempt to pronounce a word | Jamie looked into the ~~sarcophagus~~ and fainted. (Reader does not say word.) | Reader refuses to say a word that the teacher says so assessment can go on. |

**TABLE 3.5**    Word Recognition Miscues That Are NOT Scored

| Miscue | Example | Comments |
|---|---|---|
| Self-corrections | Jaime went to the store (door). (Reader says "door" first, then corrects without prompting.) | After making an error, reader recognizes the mistake and corrects it. |
| Repetition | Alex listened to the ("the" repeated) hit album six times. | Reader repeats word or phrase at least once. |
| Pause | (…)<br>Take my (purse) and throw it into the lake. | Reader makes long pause before pronouncing a word correctly. |
| Missing the Point | Two independent sentences separated by a period are read as if they were one sentence. No stopping point intoned. | Reader pays no attention to periods, commas, or other points of punctuation. |

in Table 3.4. Other miscues not scored as mistakes are listed and explained in Table 3.5. Although procedures for scoring miscues during an oral reading analysis or an IRI vary among authors, the rationale for including items to be scored or not scored on a miscue analysis are based on recommended procedures in Burns and Roe (1999), McCormick (1999), and Wilde (2000).

## Running Records

A running record is an informal oral reading assessment that you can use to discover if material you present to your students is at a manageable reading level and what strategies your students use to decode difficult words. It's relatively quick and easy. As your student reads, you record his performance using predetermined miscue guidelines. For miscues, you can use a system like that provided in Table 3.4.

TABLE 3.6   Running Record Guidelines

| Degree of Difficulty | Percentage of Correct Responses |
|---|---|
| Easy | 95–100% |
| Instructional | 90–94% |
| Hard | 80–89% |

*Source:* From Thomas G. Gunning. *Assessing and Correcting Reading and Writing Difficulties,* 2e. Published by Allyn & Bacon, Boston, MA. Copyright © 2002 by Pearson Education. Reprinted by permission of the publisher.

Running records can be used with any text your student reads. Mark miscues in a copy of the text your student is reading. When a miscue occurs, circle the word or mark the text and note the kind of error the student made.

To calculate the percentage of correct responses, you can simply divide the number of words correctly read by the total number of words in the reading. Although running record standards for determining degree of text difficulty vary somewhat, Gunning (2002) offers guidelines in Table 3.6 that you could apply.

If one of your students has less than a 90% correct response rate and manifests other behaviors that indicate problems in comprehension, such as the inability to answer basic comprehension-check questions, the text you are asking him to read may simply be too difficult.

While similarities between running records and both IRIs and miscue analysis are apparent, the merit of the running record is that it can be done on the spur of the moment with little advanced preparation. However, planned running records with pre-selected texts of 200 words or so can also be used with each of your students to obtain benchmarks of individual student and even whole-class progress.

## Curriculum-Based Measurement (CBM)

The oral reading fluency of students and their improvement can be quickly and efficiently assessed with Curriculum-Based Measurement (CBM). Fluency can be measured by counting the number of words a student reads correctly in one minute. Researchers (Fuchs, Fuchs, & Hosp, 2001) have gathered evidence to demonstrate that oral reading fluency serves as an indicator of reading competence.

CBMs provide useful information to both teachers and students. Measuring and monitoring changes in a student's fluency while reading curriculum-based texts provides indications of a student's reading development in your content area classroom. Data from CBMs can help you decide what kinds of texts your students can read at an instructional level, their responsiveness to content area instruction, and their need for reading intervention programs. Meanwhile, CBM data can help students monitor their own growth in reading and serve as the basis for graphs of reading progress in a student's portfolio.

An initial CBM provides a baseline for students' reading fluency, an opportunity to observe miscues, and a method of determining the degree of difficulty that a particular text is likely to present to individuals and, collectively, to a class. The miscues will provide you with data to use as the basis for developing helpful instructional programs tailored to individual students or small groups of students sharing similar reading problems.

Although you can conduct CBM data for oral reading fluency by determining the number of words a student reads correctly in one minute (Fuchs, Fuchs, & Hosp, 2001), I suggest using a two-minute reading to increase the accuracy of the measurement. During a one-minute reading, a student may encounter unfamiliar words that significantly reduce their fluency rate. More time reading improves the chances that you will get a more accurate picture of your students' general fluency. It takes a little more time and a little more math, but it yields a more reliable measurement.

## STEP-BY-STEP: *Curriculum-Based Measurement (CBM)*

**STEP 1.** Select a passage of about 600 words from a language arts, history, or science text designed for the grade level the students are currently in or are about to enter. Make sure the passage has a reasonable starting point with respect to content and does not include a large number of specialized words infrequently encountered in students' reading at their grade level.

**STEP 2.** For the student copy, type the text in approximately the same font and size as the original.

**STEP 3.** For the teacher's copy, produce the same text as you did for the student copy; however, on the right hand side of the page, make a column for line-by-line cumulative word counts. At the top of the page, create space for the Student's Name, Grade, Date, and Assessing Teacher. On the bottom of the page, create a rate box with space for the following information: Words Read in Two Minutes, Total Number of Scored Miscues, Total Number of Words Correctly Read in Two Minutes, and Average Number of Words Correctly Read in One Minute (or Correctly Read Words ÷ 2).

**STEP 4.** Using the student copy of the text, the student reads aloud for two minutes. When exactly two minutes are up, put a slash mark after the last word read.

**STEP 5.** As the student reads, the assessing teacher marks miscues on the teacher's copy by putting a line through miscued words or writing in an inserted word. Miscues are responses to texts that differ from expected responses. They occur when the reader reads words that are different from those on the assessor's copy. Miscues include use of nonsense words, substitutions (e.g., ran for rain), omissions, reversals (words not read in the correct order are miscues), inserted words, and no attempt to say a word. However, self-corrected words, repeated words, hesitations, words read with an accent or dialect, and improper intonation resulting from ignored punctuation marks are all scored as correct. (See Tables 3.4, 3.5, and earlier section on Miscue Analysis for further explanation and examples.)

**STEP 6.** Observing a reader's problem-solving strategies while reading a text is quite instructive. Teachers should observe carefully what readers do when they encounter a difficult word. Do they try to sound it out, use context cues, ask for help, give up? Do some of the mistakes make sense? For example, Gunning (2002) emphasizes the importance of observing semantic (was for were) or graphic (letter for leather) similarities between miscues and the actual text. How well does the reader monitor the reading process? How are errors corrected? Answers to questions like these provide insights into students' reading strengths and clues about ways struggling readers can be helped. In the Observations Box, write answers to any of these questions or other observations made during the assessment.

**STEP 7.** After a student reads the text for two minutes, the assessing teacher calculates the student's oral fluency rate or number of words correctly read in one minute. This is done by dividing the total number of words read correctly in two minutes by 2. For example, in the first minute of reading a selection from her world history textbook, Maria read 73 words and in the second minute she read 66 for a total of 139. However, she made 5 miscues which reduced the total number of correctly read words to 134. After dividing by 2, Maria's average number of words read correctly was 67. (See Figure 3.3.)

**STEP 8.** Oral fluency rates should be kept for each struggling reader and, if possible, for each student. The same text can be used at three points over the traditional academic year to measure oral fluency development: September, January, and May. Minor variations in this schedule should not affect results. However, frequent use of the same text is likely to result in learning that could influence the CBM's validity. CBM data for an entire class or grade level can also be calculated and graphically displayed to show development over time.

**STEP 9.** Teachers can also calculate CBM rates for any other text they wish by following the guidelines provided above. Such information will help teachers decide on the appropriateness of a text for a given student or even for a whole class and the amount of instructional scaffolding that students may need to read the text successfully.

## Informal Assessments for a Closer Look at Comprehension Processes

Neither a standardized reading test nor a miscue analysis provides detailed information about a reader's comprehension process. While an oral reading and miscue analysis provide valuable information about a reader's decoding skills and processes, they do not tell the whole story about what meanings that reader constructed. Nor do standardized reading tests, such as the Gates-MacGinitie, which often depend upon a student's recognition rather than recall to answer multiple-choice items. Other procedures, including retellings, think-alouds, and interviews, magnify a student's thinking while reading and furnish more detailed information about comprehension. That information can help you understand how thoroughly your students comprehend narrative or expository texts, how they organize knowledge, and what they do when meaning-making breaks down.

### Retellings

A retelling is just what its label indicates. After a student reads a narrative or expository text, she tells you what meanings she constructed. Rather than mere recognition, retellings require recalling knowledge from a reading selection.

## STEP-BY-STEP: *Retelling*

**STEP 1.** Select a text, narrative or expository, that is difficult enough to engage a student in using strategies to make sense out of challenging reading materials. If possible, choose a text that is not at the reader's frustration level.

Student's Name  Maria Russell                Grade: 6        Date: 9/15/2002

Teacher's Name  Joseph Knell

| Text: *Ancient World: Adventures in Time and Place* | Word Count |
|---|---|
| *omitted* -ed *omitted* -d (Banks, et al., 2000) Pericles became Athens' leader in 462 B.C. He quickly acted to boost the role of poor or working citizens in government. Pericles said that citizens *help* should be paid when they held a government job or *as* served on a jury. A jury is a group of citizens chosen to hear evidence and make decisions in a court of law. This money would allow farmers and other working citizens to take time off / from work so they could serve in government. Democracy Grows | 73 wpm |
| Pericles won enough votes in the citizen assembly for his bill to become law. As a result, many citizens were able to become involved in government during Athens' Golden Age. Even the poor citizens could *would* accept important jobs in government. Look at the diagram on page 356. What kinds of jobs did citizens do / to keep Athens running smoothly? | 66 wpm |
| All citizens were now able to take part in votes that affected their own lives. When they voted for Athens to go to war, for example, it meant that they themselves would fight. Unlike many other city-states, citizens made up the bulk of the Athenian army and navy, not a group of hired soldiers. | |

**RATE CALCULATION**

Total Number of Words Read in Two Minutes: _139_

Total Number of Scored Miscues: _5_

Total Number of Words Correctly Read: _134_

Average Number of Words Correctly Read in One Minute
  (Words Correctly Read in Two Minutes ÷ 2) _67_

**Observation Box**

Maria read haltingly but at a consistent pace. At a couple of points, she did not read as though she knew a sentence came to an ending. That suggests that she may not be paying attention to units of meaning while she reads. Her comprehension of informational text should be monitored. Her average number of words read correctly per minute (67) also suggests that she is having trouble with decoding and recognizing words. She clearly did not automatically recognize several words in the passage, such as *held, served,* and *allow.* The passage, according to a readability formula, is written at a 5.8 grade level. However, she clearly has difficulty with the passage and will need significant scaffolding to help her comprehend this text.

FIGURE 3.3    CBM Data Sheet (SAMPLE FORMAT).

**STEP 2.** Create an outline of the selected text that includes the main points and supporting details. The outline will serve as your guide and as a source for generating probing questions to prompt the recall of information the student omitted from the retelling.

**STEP 3.** Explain to your student that you will request a retelling after reading and then have him read the text silently. Observe your student's behavior while reading the selection to identify any strategies used to aid comprehension, such as previewing the selection, rereading sections, and so forth.

**STEP 4.** Ask students to retell everything that they can remember about the passage they read without referring to the text. It's important to ask for all the reader can recall. Otherwise, a superficial summary may be recited.

**STEP 5.** You can use the outline you created in step 2 to get an estimate of the percentage of the text that your student recalls.

**STEP 6.** If a reader missed important elements in the text that are noted in the outline, you should ask follow-up questions, or probes (McCormick, 1999). These probes can also elicit levels of comprehension beyond the literal level, such as understandings about a story's themes or generalizations that might be drawn from an expository text.

Some teachers prefer to tape record retelling sessions so that they can compare the retelling with the text's outline. You, too, may find this an efficient method. McCormick (1999) points out that some students may provide a disorganized retelling that suggests poor comprehension. However, that may not be an accurate impression. The student may comprehend successfully but structure the retelling poorly. Practice in retelling usually remedies disorganized responses.

If time for retellings is limited or you are working with large groups, students could write out summaries of the texts they read. While some things may be lost using this method, such as opportunites to probe for details, other things are gained, such as time and a written record that can be scored and kept on file.

## Comprehension Think-Alouds

An effective way to discover how your students think when they read is to do a Comprehension Think-Aloud with them. During think-alouds, readers describe their thoughts as they form meanings through interaction with the text. The think-aloud provides a view of cognitive processes that readers use to make sense of what they are reading. Struggling readers often have trouble carrying out processes that good readers engage in automatically, processes we saw when we reviewed their qualities in Chapter 2. You'll recall that, among other things, good readers activate background knowledge, make predictions, form mental images as they read, monitor their comprehension progress, and fix up problems as they go along. While doing think-alouds with your students, you can watch for examples of these processes.

To show students how to do a think-aloud, you should demonstrate the process first. You may activate background knowledge and associate a story's or article's title to concepts held in long-term memory. You may admit moments of confusion, use fix-up strategies, and discuss multiple meanings as you work through ambiguities. However, you should try to keep your associations close to the text and limited in length. Your demonstration then serves as a model that your students can use to understand what they will do when engaged in a think-aloud.

**TABLE 3.7**    Think-Aloud of "Sea Fever"

| "Sea Fever" by John Masefield | R. Silva's "Thinking Aloud" |
|---|---|
| I must go down to the sea again,<br>    to the lonely sea and the sky,<br>And all I ask is a tall ship<br>    and a star to steer her by,<br>And the wheel's kick and the wind's song<br>    and the white sail's shaking<br>And a gray mist on the sea's face<br>    and a gray dawn breaking. (pause) | After reading the first section of the poem aloud, Mrs. Silva said, "First of all, I would go back and reread it silently." After doing so, she said, "I think it's a sailor or somebody who's working on a ship who needs to be back on the ocean again, to feel what it's like to be out there again. He needs a tall ship to guide him through the seas and a star to let him know where he's going. He hears wind and sees gray mist, and that's how he sees the sea, feels it." |
| I must go down to the seas again,<br>    for the call of the running tide<br>Is a wild call and a clear call<br>    that may not be denied; (pause) | "Something is calling him (or her) there. He (or she) has a need to be there. The running tide and the wild call are things asking him to come." |
| And all I ask is a windy day<br>    with the white clouds flying,<br>And the flung spray and the blown spume,<br>    and the sea-gulls crying. (pause) | "To make this day complete, it would be a nice windy day with the white clouds flying above spraying ocean water, and sea gulls crying above." |
| I must go down to the seas again<br>    to the vagrant gypsy life,<br>To the gull's way and the whale's way<br>    where the wind's like a whetted knife;<br>(pause) | "This and the previous passage actually remind me of *Charlotte Doyle* by Avi and the men who were on that ship…. They just loved the sea. It was their way of life. At the end (of the novel), she feels called back to the boat." |
| And all I ask is a merry yarn<br>    from a laughing fellow rover, | "She missed the camaraderie she had there. That's what he misses besides the sea. Having peace within himself." |
| And a quiet sleep and a sweet dream<br>    when the long trick's over. | I next asked Mrs. Silva if she had any other comments about what the author was conveying to the reader or how she would express the poem's main idea. She said, "Everyone has a place where they want to be, and his place is on the sea." |

To investigate how different readers in a Los Angeles middle school culture construct meaning for John Masefield's "Sea Fever," I videotaped think-alouds by a teacher and sixth-grade students. The videos were intended not only to demonstrate the think-aloud technique but also to observe meaning construction in process and to study differences between expert and novice readers. To help you "hear" what the middle school teacher, Remi Silva, said in response to the poem, I present the poem on the left and her comments on the right in Table 3.7. We began the think-aloud session with my asking Mrs. Silva to read the poem aloud, pause at points indicated, and tell us what was going on in her mind to make sense of the poem.

This think-aloud shows students how a teacher constructs meaning for a complex reading task. Unlike the other students videotaped, for example, Mrs. Silva pauses to say she wants to reread the poem to get into it before explaining what she's gotten out of it. As she explains her understanding of the poem's meaning, she makes an important intertextual connection with *The True Confessions of Charlotte Doyle* by Avi. That "young adult" novel is about a 13-year-old girl who makes a life-changing voyage to America from England in 1832. She's the only passenger on a ship with a tyrannical, cruel captain and a mutinous crew with whom she eventually unites but not before winning their trust. After Charlotte arrives safely in America and rejoins her family, she decides to abandon the comforts of home for the adventures of the sea. This intertextual link helps Mrs. Silva put "Sea Fever" in context, make sense of its language, and compare the sea-enchanted Charlotte to the poem's sailor who also becomes feverish for the sea.

One of the sixth graders, Liliana, who also completed a think-aloud for "Sea Fever," had a remarkably different intertextual link. The connection she made reveals both her struggle to make sense of the poem and her use of background knowledge to do so. She made an intertextual connection between "Sea Fever" and a movie entitled *Free Willy*. In that film, a young boy and his family conspire to free a whale from captivity. To this young reader, the poem was not about a man yearning for the sea and the sailor's life but about people and animals interacting, about people wanting to protect and help animals so they won't lose their friendships or families. The sea gulls were crying because they wanted men to stop trying to get the whales, and the wind wanted a knife to free the whales. Comparing the two think-alouds reveals how differently two readers can interpret the same text and activate background knowledge that sustains or elaborates upon the meanings they construct. Comparing the think-alouds also reveals the potential power they hold in helping teachers see and understand their students' meaning construction processes.

## STEP-BY-STEP: *Doing a Comprehension Think-Aloud*

**STEP 1.** Select a passage of about 200 words that is new to the reader and at the instructional level. It should challenge but not overwhelm the reader. You should pre-read the passage and identify one or more sentence chunks of text with stop-points.

**STEP 2.** Explain to the reader that the passage will be read in segments marked with stop-points and that at those points he will explain what meaning has been gained from the text. Forewarn the reader that you may ask a few questions, such as "What do you think this is about?" to encourage the development of text-based hypotheses.

**STEP 3.** Prepare to record the session so that you can make a transcription of it along with your observations of the student's meaning construction processes.

**STEP 4.** After the think-aloud is complete, talk with the student about what he observed and learned from doing a think-aloud.

**STEP 5.** Analyze the results to determine if the reader:
- Formulates hypotheses.
- Provides information to support the hypotheses generated.
- Draws upon background knowledge and makes intertextual connections, such as those Mrs. Silva and Liliana made.
- Uses strategies, such as rereading, to cope with breakdowns in comprehension.
- Uses strategies to figure out the meaning of unfamiliar words.
- Notices inconsistencies between interpretations and the textbase.
- Understands the gist of the passage.

## Interviews and Interactions

You can learn much about your students' reading habits, preferences, and processes simply by talking with them, asking questions, and being observant during instructional interactions.

Discovering how your students decode texts provides diagnostic information that can influence your decisions about promising interventions to improve struggling readers' word identification abilities. Interviews, careful observation, and questions all can help. Gunning (2002) suggests a "word identification interview" based on questions that, when answered, lead to insights about how a student thinks and creates meaning while reading. He suggests word identification questions such as these:

- How do you feel about reading?
- What is the hardest thing for you to do when you read?
- Why do you think it's hard for you to recognize words when reading?
- Why do you think it's hard to learn words?
- What would make it easier?
- What makes it hard to figure out some words?
- What kinds of words are hardest to learn?

Answers to questions like these may amplify and clarify clues and hints about reading problems that trouble struggling readers in your classes. You may have made some diagnostic discoveries through standardized tests or informal assessments, but talking with your students about how they read can release information that sharpens your diagnosis and points to sensible intervention instruction.

Comprehension processes can also be made clearer through several informal assessment procedures. You can include questions like these during interviews with students about comprehension:

- How do you know you understand something you are reading?
- Do you ever notice when you're reading that you can't make any sense out of it? What do you do when that happens?
- When, if ever, do you ask yourself questions about what you're reading?
- Do you ever ask yourself questions about the book you're reading and then try to answer them as you read along?
- Do you ever find yourself guessing what's going to happen next in a story?
- When you're having trouble understanding a book, do you let your teacher know?
- What are some things you do to help yourself when you're having trouble understanding what you're expected to read?
- What are some things teachers do that help you understand your reading assignments?

Obtaining answers to these questions and others like them will help you see what strategies students use to construct meanings for text and to discover what kinds of strategic instruction would benefit your struggling readers.

Reading workshops.  In her work with middle school students, Nancie Atwell (1998) has discovered that as a teacher she is "always beginning," an approach to teaching that indicates her readiness to look at her students and their work through fresh eyes. But she has a clear and structured curriculum to build her students' strengths as readers. She has developed an organized and effective system to get to know her students, how they read, and how they feel about reading. In many ways, she exemplifies a diagnostic approach to teaching reading.

By looking carefully at what Atwell believes students often learn about reading from the lessons we teach in classrooms, she has made some memorable discoveries. Among the lessons that students have sometimes unintentionally learned are these:

- ◆ "Errors" in comprehension or interpretation will not be tolerated.
- ◆ There is one interpretation of a text: the teacher's (or the teacher's manual).
- ◆ Reading requires memorization and mastery of information, terms, definitions, and theories.
- ◆ Reading is a waste of class time.
- ◆ There's another kind of reading, an enjoyable, secret, satisfying kind you can do on your free time or outside of school.

As a teacher of English, Atwell had the opportunity to design instruction to radically change the way reading is taught and the way her students approach it. The radical vehicle she designed for that change is the reading workshop.

To prepare for these workshops, she asks herself a number of questions most content teachers and all diagnostically oriented teachers might benefit from asking themselves at the beginning of a school year:

- ◆ How do I talk with kids about their reading in ways that move them forward?
- ◆ How do I organize myself? How do I arrange to keep track of each reader's activity, accomplishments, problems, pace, and growth?
- ◆ How do I provide models of the kinds of reading I want kids to engage in?
- ◆ How do I assess students' reading so it reflects what I ask of them as readers, doesn't put them in competition with each other, and makes sense to them and to their parents?
- ◆ How can I use mini-lessons to advance students' learning?
- ◆ What behaviors do I want to see in the reading workshops? How do I encourage them? Which should I mandate?
- ◆ How and when do I demonstrate my experiences as a reader? To what ends?

Even before she begins teaching through the workshop approach, Atwell (1998) surveys her students to discover what she can about their experiences and attitudes as readers. She asks them how they learned to read, why they think people read at all, what it takes to be a good reader, what kinds of books they like, how they decide which books they will read, how often they read at home, and how they feel about reading. After giving these surveys during the first week of school, she reads them over, highlights features important to reading, and begins to get to know her kids.

## Portfolio Assessment in Content Area Classrooms

**What are portfolios?**   For diagnostic teaching, portfolios provide an extraordinary means of discovering how each of your students reads, writes, thinks, and grows. Furthermore, portfolio assessment encourages your students to look more carefully at their own work and reflect upon it. Basically, a portfolio is a collection of work. But that collection of work can be selected, organized, analyzed, and reviewed so that it provides a kaleidoscopic as well as microscopic view of each student's engagement in content area learning. The portfolio can reveal how much work your

students are doing, how well they are doing it, what kinds of help they need to progress, and how they conceptualize their own progress. Moreover, thoughtful observation of students' portfolios can guide productive classroom instruction because, as you perceive your students' learning needs, you can formulate plans to address them. Those diagnostically responsive plans could include individual instruction, cooperative learning teams, mini-lessons, or whole-class teaching.

Benefits and limitations of portfolios.    In comparison with standardized, formal testing, portfolios have several distinctive advantages. While standardized tests are one-shot, often high stakes performances, portfolios allow on-going assessment. Standardized tests often communicate a formal judgment about one-time outcomes rather than a developmental perspective over time. With standardized tests, goals for improving performance are more removed from immediate classroom achievement. With portfolios, your goals for improvement are formed on the basis of immediate prior classroom accomplishments. While standardized test results rarely provide direct information to you or your students about what could be done to improve performance, portfolios provide avenues for clear and direct intervention. After taking a standardized test, students are given a score, perhaps one that is machine generated and printed out. With portfolios, your students can assess their own achievement and progress. They must be accountable to their own sources of evidence. When formal, standardized tests are used to assess students' learning and achievements, the tests may not be directly aligned with your classroom teaching. However, the content of your students' portfolios reflects directly your standards and your classroom teaching practices.

However, portfolios have their drawbacks in comparison with formal testing. To gain validity and increase reliability, portfolio scoring requires the development of rubrics or scoring guides. Reading the content of the portfolio and scoring that content, usually with rubrics, takes patience and time. Even by using rubrics and exercising patience, standardized tests usually have greater statistical validity and reliability. Furthermore, standardized tests are often easier to administer and definitely easier to score.

Using portfolios in the content area to examine student work.    What goes into a student's portfolio? Although portfolios can function as showcases for your students' best works, their value as an assessment tool resides in their allowing both you and your students to examine individual student work emerging from classroom assignments. To fulfill their function as mirrors of students' reading, writing, and thinking in a content area, you must decide what materials will reflect your students' learning achievements, progress, and problems. The choices are many: homework assignments, quizzes, tests, a graph of grades received, reading logs, learning logs, responses to readings, lab reports, questionnaires, notes on lectures, responses to discussions, drafts of papers from first to last revision showing progression of thought and organization, letters to you from your students and from you to your students.

You and your students can examine individual items, such as an essay, to identify strengths, areas of growth, and specific needs for further development. When you have a writing conference with a student, both of you can look over the student's work to identify those specific aspects of writing that need to be addressed for the student writer to progress. If a problem in writing, such as pronoun-antecedent agreement, troubles only one of your students, you can reach out to that particular student and help her address it in her writing. If the problem troubles many of your students, you can design a mini-lesson for the whole class that addresses that weakness. (See Chapter 6 on mini-lessons.) What I've described is how I've used portfolios when teaching eleventh graders in English. However, portfolios can be used in similar ways to diagnosis and design instruction for students in math, science, social studies, or other content area classes.

Linnea Dahl, an English teacher in an arts "magnet" high school (Los Angeles County High School for the Arts), asked her seniors near the end of their high school careers to reflect on portfolios of work that they kept all year. She designed a series of three lessons that included a reflective essay on their portfolios and their evaluation.

For the first assignment, Linnea asked her students to complete a planning sheet that included several tasks. She asked students to select the best six assignments in their portfolios and rank them. Any written assignments they turned in during the year that had more than five mistakes had to be revised. She also asked them to reflect on any other written work they had done throughout high school, including any pieces they had published. She then asked them to "Look at what you have to work with. What is your initial reaction?" Students were to compose a "freewrite" focused on what their portfolio said to them about who they were as seen through their written work in high school.

For the second assignment, Linnea's seniors had to examine and write about all the writing in their class portfolio. They could also include material from other sources. To help them plan a reflective essay on their history as a writer, she composed another planning sheet. In it she explained that the portfolio essay should "delve into the person that the writing has come from" and be a comparison between early and more recent efforts. Explicit prompts called out for students to

- Describe how they saw themselves as writers earlier in high school and "what kind of writer you are now."
- Target areas of specific improvement and areas where they still lacked confidence.
- Examine ways their personalities influenced their writing.
- Define future writing challenges and how they will be met.

- ◆ Identify what they would like someone to "really see or understand" about their writing.

She gave them two weeks to complete the essay and asked them to express how they honestly felt about writing.

The third assignment was an independent evaluation of their essays. Earlier Linnea and her students developed a criteria chart that she used to prepare a rubric or scoring guide. Using that rubric, students had to assess their work, give themselves a grade, and (with reference to the rubric) explain how they arrived at that grade. Linnea, using the same rubric, also evaluated their portfolios and met with them when differences in ratings arose. She added her perceptions of their writing and its development that they may have overlooked. Linnea decided to use this portfolio evaluation process in lieu of a final examination grade.

In response to this assignment, one of her seniors wrote the following:

Throughout most of high school I wrote papers in the standard, simple format for the sole purpose of getting a grade. There was no personal flair to them and they did not reflect my personality, but I found this acceptable since I had little attachment to the assignment. I told myself that if the paper was only for class and therefore was of no particular significance to me, then it was alright (sic) for me to do a mediocre job. I never felt satisfied with these papers. I was timid and embarrassed to turn them in because I knew that, despite there (sic) adequate outward appearance, they were not work I could honestly be proud of.

My analytical/academic writing is the most obvious example of how my uncommitted feelings influence my work. I have always wanted to write well, but I was not willing to put my heart into the writing. The essay I wrote on *Slaughterhouse Five* is a good example of my writing, not at its worst, but far from its most stimulating. It is not always clear what I am talking about and although there are sections of inspired thought when it seems that there is a real connection or realization taking place, such as in the last paragraph, those tidbits are few and far between. Writing analysis of books is not difficult for me since I am generally perceptive to themes and subtleties in writing, but I am still searching for a way to make the process of writing, and the subsequent paper, more interesting and alive.

My more inspired writing comes when I am involved in a more creative pursuit, such as playwriting. The new morning elective playwriting class has been such an inspirational experience for me and has allowed me to discover a wonderful new way with which to express myself. . . .

The writer goes on to describe a couple of his plays that show how he is moving toward a "more defined personal style." This activity not only allowed Linnea's students to explore the development of their writing, it also gave them an opportunity to explore aspects of their identities, who they are, and who they are becoming in terms of evolving literacies.

Portfolios and the student-led conference.   Portfolios can also be the engines that power student-led conferences. A student-led conference is a meeting at school between a student and parent or other adult over course work kept in a portfolio (Austin, 1994). Student-led conferences have many benefits:

- Students must be responsible and accountable to themselves, their teachers, and their parents,
- Students communicate course curriculum and expectations to their parents,
- Students must keep track of their work and its progress,
- Students have to organize and maintain a portfolio of their work,
- Students review the portfolio's documents and write periodic self-evaluations,
- Students conduct conversations with their parents about their school work,
- Students must be ready to refer to evidence in their portfolio that supports claims they make about their academic progress as well as problems in learning, and
- Students construct learning goals that are based on their portfolio and conference and that are shared with the student's parent(s) and the teacher.

In summary, these benefits contribute to your students' becoming more self-regulated and motivated learners in all content area classrooms. Although student-led conferences have been more widely used in middle schools, their value in high school instruction has, I believe, often been overlooked. They can vitalize and deepen students' engagement.

But how can you build student-led conferences into your instructional plans? At the beginning of the school year, you should notify parents that their student will be maintaining a portfolio of work in your course and that parents will be invited to school so that their child can discuss the portfolio. You can notify parents at an open house or have each student write a letter home describing student-led conferences and explaining what their parents' role in them will be. In one way or another, parents learn that they will be meeting with their children at least twice during the school year to talk about the portfolio, its contents, and their child's progress.

What goes into portfolios for student-led conferences? One answer is *everything*. Another is to let the student decide. Yet another is what makes the student's work in the course look good. Still another is to include documents that show learning. None of these answers is ideal. Some teachers believe it is best to analyze their state or local standards, curriculum goals, instructional strategies, and assignments to determine which documents and data are to be included and the rationale for their inclusion. I believe that last solution, though requiring some decision making on your part, holds considerable promise for the success of student-led conference portfolios.

At the beginning of the course, you should let your students—as well as their parents—know what will be kept in the portfolio and how to maintain it. Knowing that the contents of the portfolio will be presented to parents often serves as a significant motivator for students—and as a focus of interest to parents. A list of standards and portfolio items that demonstrate their realization can be affixed to the file's inside front cover. Graphs of grades to track test and quiz performance could also be displayed. If desired, the portfolio could also include learning logs, letters (to teachers or other students about course material), attendance records, lecture notes, and more.

In preparation for a student-led conference, each of your students should

1. Review the work in the portfolio,
2. Write a report that covers the period under review, and
3. State a learning goal that will be evaluated as part of the next student-led conference and reasons for choosing it.

You can give your students specific questions to answer as part of their covering report. These questions can focus on specific kinds of work, like essays, logs, lab reports, chapter tests, projects, cooperative team presentations, and the like. Documents in the portfolio then serve as evidence for claims about learning and performance that your students make in their reflections. The review and report then serve as a context for each student stating a learning goal and reasons for working toward its achievement.

Teachers using student-led conferences usually write letters to parents letting them know when the conference will be held and what aspirations the teacher and student have for the meeting. You can explain that you'll be available in the "conference room" for consultation should the need arise. In the letter, you can also provide some guidelines to parents that will help them understand how their responses to their student's work can have a positive, motivating effect. In addition, you may wish to have your students write a welcoming invitation to their parents to attend the student-led conference. And it's not a bad idea to include an RSVP with the student's invitation that will enable you to plan for refreshments or surrogate parents if required.

As orchestrators of student-led conferences, you will have to schedule times for parents to come to school. Most teachers schedule no more than 10 student-led conferences to be held in the same room simultaneously. The length of the conference depends on the amount of material to be reviewed. However, conferences usually run about 45 minutes or so. During the conference, you'll roam, troubleshoot, but (most importantly) shadow presentations to get a sense of how they are progressing.

Part of preparation for student-led conference day is practice. Students, even those having done conferences in the past, may need rehearsal time. Some teachers recommend using education students from a nearby college as rehearsal parents (Austin, 1994). In some classes where cooperative learning groups have been established and the climate is supportive, students could practice presenting their portfolio to another member of their co-op team. For the rehearsal, a list of procedures will help your students know and remember what steps they should take—from introducing parents to the teacher at the beginning to thanking parents for attending at the end. These directions can even be tailored to the specific content of key documents in the portfolio to make sure they are covered during the student-led conferences.

You are likely to have some students whose parent cannot attend the conference, and, of course, you'll wonder to whom the student can present their portfolio. Usually, teachers find other teachers or administrators to serve as parent surrogates during the student-led conferences. Ideally, teachers serving as parent surrogates have the student who will present the student-led conference as a student in their own classes. That way your colleague will learn much about how a student they are teaching is performing in other classrooms with other teachers. Such interactions can be quite enlightening for teachers.

After the student-led conference, you should plan to give your students an opportunity to debrief and discuss the event. Following the discussion, students benefit from writing a report that they give to you to read. The discussion and report can include the following:

◆ What went well,
◆ What needs some improvement,
◆ What the student got from the experience, and
◆ What the student thought the parents got from it.

The report can help you make decisions about modifications to the student-led conference process and lead students to consider how they might improve their next conference presentation. Of course, this concluding report gets filed in their portfolios.

Stephanie Pearson, a middle school teacher in Los Angeles, engages her students in after-conference reflections. One of her students, Grace, had a range of comments about how things went during the conference, what could have gone better, what she gained from the experience, and what she thought her dad gained. Grace felt the conference went well "because I felt that I was speaking a littler clearer to my father. Also, I explained about what I was doing in class. I felt I did an okay job explaining what it was we do in class." She felt things might have gone better "if maybe he wasn't in a rush to go home and work. Then I probably could of talked a little more." She wrote that she would have told him more about the process her class went through when writing essays. As for what she gained, Grace wrote that she thought she could have spoken "a little louder and clearer to my dad 'cause I don't talk a lot. Also it showed how much I knew about the class and what the goals and points of it were." She felt that the conference helped her dad get a "better understanding of what I'm doing in class and if I was doing good."

## Reading Strategies Inventories

Two informal instruments to be reviewed in this section include a diagnostic reading series to gauge a student's comprehension skills and an inventory to measure metacognitive awareness of a student's reading strategies. The "Comprehensive Assessment of Reading Strategies" (Curriculum Associates, 1998) gives students opportunities to assess and practice their own comprehension skills. The "Metacognitive Awareness of Reading Strategies Inventory" or MARSI (Mokhtari & Reichard, 2002) is designed to evaluate students' awareness and use of reading strategies while reading content area texts.

Comprehensive assessment of reading strategies.  The "Comprehensive Assessment of Reading Strategies" (Curriculum Associates, 1998) provides feedback and practice for students, especially those in grades 6 through 8, on reading skills or objectives and feedback to teachers about student skill levels, information that can inform further instruction in reading. Although originally designed for use with students up to and through middle school, the series can be used to assess high school students' mastery of comprehension objectives, especially students who are delayed or struggling readers. Reading comprehension skills or objectives, as they are called in some standardized test programs, include summarizing, finding a word's meaning from its context, making inferences, recalling facts and details, understanding sequence, making predictions, comparing and contrasting, recognizing cause and effect, identifying an author's purpose, finding the main idea, and distinguishing between fact and opinion. Some of these objectives, such as finding the main idea, entail basic understanding of a text while others, such as comparing and contrasting, require analysis and evaluation that are forms of critical reading. The assessment consists of 10 reading selections accompanied by 12 questions, one for each comprehension skill. This diagnostic series can also help you design instruction to improve student performance by identifying strengths and weaknesses in student skills usually assessed on standardized reading tests.

Metacognitive awareness of reading strategies inventory.  The MARSI assesses reading metacognition of students in grades 6 through 12. While making students more aware of what they do when coping with content-area reading, MARSI helps teachers understand the instructional needs of their students. Mokhtari and Reichard identified three categories (or factors) into which their inventory items fell: Global

## TABLE 3.8    Metacognitive Awareness of Reading Strategies Inventory (Version 1.0)

*Directions*: Listed below are statements about what people do when they read *academic* or *school-related materials* such as textbooks or library books. Five numbers follow each statement (1, 2, 3, 4, 5), and each number means the following:

- **1** means "I **never or almost never** do this."
- **2** means "I do this **only occasionally.**"
- **3** means "I sometimes do this" (about **50%** of the time).
- **4** means "I **usually** do this."
- **5** means "I **always or almost always** do this."

After reading each statement, **circle the number** (1, 2, 3, 4, or 5) that applies to you using the scale provided. Please note that there are **no right or wrong answers** to the statements in this inventory.

| Type | Strategy | Scale |
|------|----------|-------|
| GLOB | 1. I have a purpose in mind when I read. | 1  2  3  4  5 |
| SUP | 2. I take notes while reading to help me understand what I read. | 1  2  3  4  5 |
| GLOB | 3. I think about what I know to help me understand what I read. | 1  2  3  4  5 |
| GLOB | 4. I preview the text to see what it's about before reading it. | 1  2  3  4  5 |
| SUP | 5. When text becomes difficult, I read aloud to help me understand what I read. | 1  2  3  4  5 |
| SUP | 6. I summarize what I read to reflect on important information in the text. | 1  2  3  4  5 |
| GLOB | 7. I think about whether the content of the text fits my reading purpose. | 1  2  3  4  5 |
| PROB | 8. I read slowly but carefully to be sure I understand what I'm reading. | 1  2  3  4  5 |
| SUP | 9. I discuss what I read with others to check my understanding. | 1  2  3  4  5 |
| GLOB | 10. I skim the text first by noting characteristics like length and organization. | 1  2  3  4  5 |
| PROB | 11. I try to get back on track when I lose concentration. | 1  2  3  4  5 |
| SUP | 12. I underline or circle information in the text to help me remember it. | 1  2  3  4  5 |
| PROB | 13. I adjust my reading speed according to what I'm reading. | 1  2  3  4  5 |
| GLOB | 14. I decide what to read closely and what to ignore. | 1  2  3  4  5 |
| SUP | 15. I use reference materials such as dictionaries to help me understand what I read. | 1  2  3  4  5 |
| PROB | 16. When text becomes difficult, I pay closer attention to what I'm reading. | 1  2  3  4  5 |
| GLOB | 17. I use tables, figures, and pictures in text to increase my understanding. | 1  2  3  4  5 |
| PROB | 18. I stop from time to time and think about what I'm reading. | 1  2  3  4  5 |
| GLOB | 19. I use context clues to help me better understand what I'm reading. | 1  2  3  4  5 |
| SUP | 20. I paraphrase (restate ideas in my own words) to better understand what I read. | 1  2  3  4  5 |
| PROB | 21. I try to picture or visualize information to help remember what I read. | 1  2  3  4  5 |
| GLOB | 22. I use typographical aids like boldface and italics to identify key information. | 1  2  3  4  5 |
| GLOB | 23. I critically analyze and evaluate the information presented in the text. | 1  2  3  4  5 |
| SUP | 24. I go back and forth in the text to find relationships among ideas in it. | 1  2  3  4  5 |
| GLOB | 25. I check my understanding when I come across conflicting information. | 1  2  3  4  5 |
| GLOB | 26. I try to guess what the material is about when I read. | 1  2  3  4  5 |
| PROB | 27. When text becomes difficult, I reread to increase my understanding. | 1  2  3  4  5 |
| SUP | 28. I ask myself questions I like to have answered in the text. | 1  2  3  4  5 |
| GLOB | 29. I check to see if my guesses about the text are right or wrong. | 1  2  3  4  5 |
| PROB | 30. I try to guess the meaning of unknown words or phrases. | 1  2  3  4  5 |

## Scoring Rubric

Student name: _____ Age: _____ Date: _____

Grade in school: ❑ 6th  ❑ 7th  ❑ 8th  ❑ 9th  ❑ 10th  ❑ 11th  ❑ 12th  ❑ College  ❑ Other

1. Write your response to each statement (i.e., 1, 2, 3, 4, or 5) in each of the blanks.
2. Add up the scores under each column. Place the result on the line under each column.
3. Divide the subscale score by the number of statements in each column to get the average for each subscale.
4. Calculate the average for the whole inventory by adding up the subscale scores and dividing by 30.
5. Compare your results to those shown below.
6. Discuss your results with your teacher or tutor.

| Global Reading Strategies (GLOB subscale) | Problem-Solving Strategies (PROB subscale) | Support Reading Strategies (SUP subscale) | Overall Reading Strategies |
|---|---|---|---|
| 1. _____ | 8. _____ | 2. _____ | GLOB |
| 3. _____ | 11. _____ | 5. _____ | PROB |
| 4. _____ | 13. _____ | 6. _____ | SUP |
| 7. _____ | 16. _____ | 9. _____ | |
| 10. _____ | 18. _____ | 12. _____ | |
| 14. _____ | 21. _____ | 15. _____ | |
| 17. _____ | 27. _____ | 20. _____ | |
| 19. _____ | 30. _____ | 24. _____ | |
| 22. _____ | | 28. _____ | |
| 23. _____ | | | |
| 25. _____ | | | |
| 26. _____ | | | |
| 29. _____ | | | |
| ____ GLOB score | ____ PROB score | ____ SUP score | ____ Overall score |
| ____ GLOB mean | ____ PROB mean | ____ SUP mean | ____ Overall mean |

*Key to averages:* 3.5 or higher = high    2.5–3.4 = medium    2.4 or lower = low

*Interpreting your scores:* The overall average indicates how often you use reading strategies when reading academic materials. The average for each subscale of the inventory shows which group of strategies (i.e., global, problem solving, and support strategies) you use most when reading. With this information, you can tell if you score very high or very low in any of these strategy groups. Note, however, that the best possible use of these strategies depends on your reading ability in English, the type of material read, and your purpose for reading it. A low score on any of the subscales or parts of the inventory indicates that there may be some strategies in these parts that you might want to learn about and consider using when reading.

*Source:* Metacognitive Awareness of Reading Strategies Inventory (Version 1.0) by Mokhtari and Reichard, from "Assessing students metacognitive awareness of reading strategies" in *Journal of Educational Psychology, 94* (2), 249–259. Copyright © 2002 by the American Psychological Association. Reprinted with permission.

Reading Strategies, Problem-Solving Strategies, and Support Reading Strategies. Global Reading Strategies include setting a purpose for reading, activating prior knowledge, and skimming to note text structure. Problem-Solving Strategies include adjusting reading rates, rereading, and visualizing information presented. Support Reading Strategies include taking notes while reading, underlining, and asking self questions. The inventory itself, including information about the category to which each strategy belongs and a scoring rubric, is in Table 3.8.

## CATEGORIES OF ADOLESCENT READERS

With our cognitive model, a battery of reading assessment tools, and ample research on struggling as well as skilled readers (Beers, 1998; Hacker, 1998; Spear-Swerling & Sternberg, 1996), we can now identify several categories of readers you are likely to find in many of your classrooms. (See Table 3.9.) These categories range from non-decoders who have little, if any, alphabetic knowledge and little, if any, knowledge of letter–sound correspondences to highly proficient readers who can integrate ideas and information from many genres, make meaning from texts with challenging syntax and rhetorical devices, and comprehend specialized content.

I did not design this system of categories to serve as a classification system that identifies the underlying cause of a student's reading problem. We often can't diagnose specifically what has caused the condition we encounter in struggling readers. Causal factors are frequently so complex and interactive that attribution to a specific cause or even a constellation of causes is an impossible dream. So these categories are based on symptoms that struggling readers present. However, discovering your struggling readers' symptoms is likely to give you some hints about possible causes that we can visualize and understand with reference to our cognitive model of reading. Having some idea of the possible causes provides us with the potential to apply sensible interventions that stand a reasonable chance for improving reading.

## Who Can Be Helped and How?

Most struggling readers who fit in the categories described in Table 3.9 can be helped with appropriate interventions, such as programs that build phonological processing, word recognition, and strategic knowledge and skills. Slow comprehenders may benefit from activities that increase automaticity, such as learning sight-words, and abundant practice in reading. Students lacking topic knowledge can be provided with information that facilitates comprehension. However, some struggling readers who also fit these categories are less likely to respond to appropriate instruction because of underlying limits, such as deficits in working memory and phonological processing problems that may be biologically based (Stanovich, 1990; Stanovich & Siegel, 1994).

Students with monitoring and control problems can be helped with activities that build metacognitive skills and strategies. Lacking the ability to detect comprehension problems, struggling under an illusion of knowing, or failing to activate strategies to repair reading problems can sometimes be improved through strategies like reciprocal teaching or collaborative reading.

Students in the "Disengaged" category who are unmotivated or uncommitted to reading, who do not see themselves as readers, and who even have negative attitudes toward those who do read may have disconnected because they had few enjoyable experiences with reading as young children. Beers (1998) found that children with negative attitudes toward reading had parents who read to them infrequently and for short periods of time. They remembered few, if any, enjoyable reading experiences. None the less, students with positive attitudes toward reading could remember many enjoyable and worthwhile reading episodes with their parents. Beers also found that even reluctant readers with quite negative attitudes can become more engaged in reading if they can:

**TABLE 3.9**   Categories of Adolescent Readers

1. *Non-Decoders or Weak Decoders:* Non-alphabetic readers who have not grasped the alphabetic principle that each speech sound has a graphic representation; very impaired reading comprehension and word recognition; little letter–sound or phonological knowledge; profound spelling difficulty.

2. *Compensatory Readers:* Grasp alphabetic principle; impaired word recognition and reading comprehension; limited orthographic and phonological knowledge; use sight-words and sentence context to compensate for lack of phonological knowledge; significant spelling difficulty.

3. *Slow Comprehenders or Non-Automatic Readers:* Accurate but non-automatic, effortful word recognition; naming-speed correlated with slowness in word recognition; lack of practice reading also contributes; use sentence context to help with word recognition; impaired reading comprehension; significant spelling difficulty.

4. *Delayed Readers:* Slow acquisition of automatic word recognition skills; few comprehension strategies, lack awareness of text organization; impaired reading comprehension; lag behind others of similar age; some difficulty with spelling; attribute problems with reading to ability ("stupid") rather than to lack of effort; thus, use fewer strategies; questions arise about cause of strategy deficits.

5. *Readers with Monitoring Difficulties:* Fail to monitor comprehension; experience "illusions of knowing"; root of monitoring difficulty may lie in one or more of the following areas (Hacker, 1998):
   ● Lack linguistic or topic knowledge to detect dissonance,
   ● Have linguistic and topic knowledge but lack monitoring strategies,
   ● Have knowledge and strategies but lack conditional knowledge about when and where to apply them,
   ● Comprehension and/or monitoring demand too much of readers' memory and other resources, and
   ● Lack motivation to engage in monitoring.

6. *Readers with Control Difficulties:* Fail to execute control over perceived breakdowns in reading process; root of control difficulty may lie in one or more of the following areas (Hacker, 1998):
   ● Lack knowledge needed to control problems monitored,
   ● Have knowledge needed to control problems but lack strategies to apply their knowledge,
   ● Have strategies for application but lack conditional knowledge about when and where to apply them,
   ● Comprehension and/or control demand too much of readers' memory and other resources, and
   ● Lack motivation to engage control resources.

7. *Readers Lacking Specific Topic Knowledge:* Decode but trouble making meaning because of weak topic knowledge in particular domain, including vocabulary, specifically in relation to subject of current reading; these readers may attain proficiency in some topic domains.

8. *Sub-Optimal Readers:* No problems with word recognition; limited repertoire of basic comprehension strategies; few higher-level language skills/strategies, such as knowledge of different genre, syntax sophistication, grammar mastery; adequate spelling skills.

9. *Disengaged or Inactive Readers:* Have adequate to advanced knowledge base, skills, and strategies but lack motivation or sufficient degree of connection with schooling to read; don't make time in their schedules for reading; may also be seen as disaffiliated or disidentified readers.

10. *English Learners:* Includes students in "immersion" programs, English as a Second Language programs; Bilingual programs; programs using specially designed academic instruction in English techniques.

11. *Advanced, Highly Proficient Readers:* See qualities of good readers that begins Chapter 2.

◆ Choose their own books,
◆ Select books with lots of illustrations,
◆ See a movie based on the book and then read it,
◆ Have books read aloud to them, and
◆ Respond to reading books by creating art works.

Additional strategies to engage struggling readers may be found in Chapter 10, which focuses on motivation to read in content area classes.

In any case, we need to carefully evaluate our students to determine the full range of their reading strengths and problems. In some instances, you will be able to evaluate your students with activities and instruments described and explained in this chapter. Other students with profound reading problems may require a thorough evaluation by trained reading specialists, special education teachers, or school psychologists to discover the strengths, weaknesses, and appropriate educational programs for those students.

# ASSESSING TEXTS: READABILITY AND ACCESSIBILITY

No matter how much you learn about your students' reading skills and attitudes, you'll still need to evaluate the books you are going to ask your students to read. If you don't evaluate the books you expect them to read, you may be presenting your students with reading that is far too difficult, too easy, too "inconsiderate," too inaccessible, or simply too unfriendly. Our purpose is to work toward a good fit between students and the texts to be read. Instruments available to help us engage in that evaluation include readability formulas, cloze tests, and text evaluation scales.

## Readability Formulas

What features would help us to determine a text's level of reading difficulty? Should we depend on the text's engagingness, its predictability, its decodability, its text structure, the number of unfamiliar words in it, its content or ideas or themes, or perhaps its literary elements? The determination of text difficulty presents teachers, text makers, standards writers, and curriculum developers with significant challenges.

Readability formulas, which were used throughout most of the twentieth century to determine grade-level difficulty, usually depend upon two primary variables to determine a grade-level score: sentence length and word difficulty. The grade-level score tells us what level of reading achievement a student should have to successfully comprehend the text. If the calculation for a specified text yields a score of 10, students should supposedly be able to read at the tenth-grade level in order to understand the text. However, several important variables that predict reading difficulty or ease are not included in readability formulas.

Readability formulas spit out narrow, specific numbers. However, you'll be wise to think of those grade-level numbers as elastic measures, loosely calibrated. You should not assume that a student reading at the tenth-grade level on a standardized reading test could easily comprehend a content area text written at the tenth-grade level according to a readability formula. Too many critical variables are either questionably represented in the formulas or entirely left out of them. That is why educators have tried to find other methods of establishing text difficulty (Hiebert, 2002).

Among the variables questionably represented in readability formulas are sentence length and word difficulty, their two main components. The reason that sentence length is not always a good predictor of grade-level complexity is that short sentences may be difficult to understand if their structure and content is complex: "To be or not to be, that is the question." However, long sentences could be quite easy to follow if their structure and meaning is quite simple. Furthermore, word length does not always correspond to level of difficulty. Take the short words *epic, protist,* or *value.* Each is two syllables, but each is quite complex in meaning. Longer words, however, might not be so challenging, even to younger readers: *Disneyland, gymnasium, Mississippi, auditorium, portfolio.*

Among the variables not represented at all are background knowledge, paragraph structure, level of abstraction, and reader interest in a topic. Whether or not a reader has background knowledge to activate in response to a text can strongly influence level of comprehension. For example, readers having lots of background knowledge about biology may have no problem whatsoever with the word *protist,* while a student with little biology background would be left guessing.

Paragraphs that have clear topic sentences and that are clearly developed are usually far easier to comprehend than paragraphs with implied topic sentences and ambiguous development. E. M. Forster, the English author of *Aspects of the Novel* and *A Passage to India,* struggled to make his sentences and paragraphs models of clarity. Other authors, like the English romantic poet Coleridge, believed that readers should have to be willing to work to get an author's meaning. Of course, a reader's work might pay off in the quality of understanding gained.

Highly abstract texts with few, if any, vivid examples or illustrations that evoke visual imagery are often far more difficult to comprehend than texts with examples that excite visual imagery. Some philosophical texts, for example, are quite difficult to read because they treat abstract metaphysical problems and may have few examples that make their import graphically clear.

Lastly, reader motivation can significantly affect comprehension. At risk of gender stereotyping, I would suggest that an adolescent girl faced with a text in which she may have little or no interest, such as *Car and Driver* magazine or *A Military History of the Napoleonic Wars,* could find reading the text to be an uphill march, whereas *Seventeen* or Alcott's *Little Women* may be more engrossing.

**The Fry Readability formula.**   Keeping these limitations in mind, let's take a look at one of the most popular readability formulas, namely the Fry Readability Graph (Fry, 1977). Designed to measure the grade level of a text from grade 1 through college, the Fry depends upon only sentence length and word length in 100-word passages. Instead of using only one passage of 100 words to determine grade level, Fry suggests using three and calculating an average. Fry claims that his readability graph predicts text difficulty within one grade level.

## STEP-BY-STEP: *Calculating Readability with Fry's Formula*

Fry (Fry, Kress, & Fountoukidis, 2000) provides the following directions for calculating the difficulty level of a text:

**STEP 1.** Randomly select three sample passages and count out exactly 100 words beginning with the beginning of a sentence. Count proper nouns, initializations, and numerals.

**STEP 2.** Count the number of sentences in the hundred words estimating length of the fraction of the last sentence to the nearest one-tenth.

**STEP 3.** Count the total number of syllables in the 100-word passage. If you don't have a hand counter available, an easy way is to put a mark above every syllable over one in each

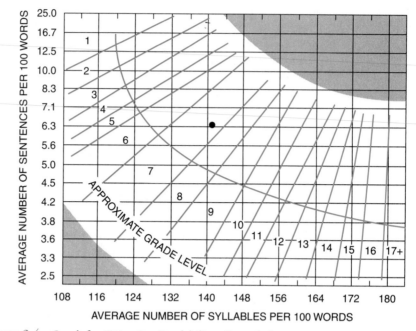

**FIGURE 3.4**    Graph for Estimating Readability—Extended.

*Source:* "Fry's Readability Graph: Clarifications, validity, and extension to Level 17," *Journal of Reading, December 1977, 21* (3), p. 249.

word, and then when you get to the end of the passage, count the number of marks and add 100. Small calculators also can be used as counters by pushing numeral "1," then push the "+" sign for each word or syllable when counting.

**STEP 4.** Enter on a graph the *average* sentence length and *average* number of syllables; plot a dot where the two lines intersect. The areas where a dot is plotted will give you the approximate grade level. (See Figure 3.4.)

**STEP 5.** If a great deal of variability is found in syllable count or sentence count, putting more samples into the average is desirable.

**STEP 6.** A word is defined as a group of symbols with a space on either side; thus, "Joe," "IRA," "1945," and "&" are each one word.

**STEP 7.** A *syllable* is defined as a phonetic syllable. Generally, there are as many syllables as vowel sounds. For example, *stopped* is one syllable and *wanted* is two syllables. When counting syllables for numerals and initializations, count one syllable for each symbol. For example, "1945" is four syllables, "IRA" is three syllables, and "&" is one syllable.

The worksheet in Table 3.10 outlines the procedure for calculating the score based on the number of sentences and the number of syllables in each of three 100-word passages.

*Cloze tests.*    Cloze procedures have several uses: (a) to determine the readability of a passage, (b) to test a student's reading ability for placement, and (c) to teach comprehension strategies or review content knowledge. Our primary purpose here is to understand how the cloze test can be used to determine the readability of a text or an estimate of how competently a student can read a given text.

Cloze tests, originally conceived by Taylor (1953), work because of our mind's tendency to create closure. This propensity to create visual as well as verbal closure ap-

TABLE 3.10    Fry Readability Graph Worksheet

| | Number of Syllables | Number of Sentences |
|---|---|---|
| **Passage 1**　(page:　) | _____ | _____ |
| **Passage 2**　(page:　) | _____ | _____ |
| **Passage 3**　(page:　) | _____ | _____ |
| **Totals** | _____ | _____ |
| **(Divide totals by 3.)** | | |
| **Average** _____<br>(Enter averages on graph to plot intersection.)<br>**Grade Level**  (+ or − 1) | | _____ |

pears to be founded in what German psychologists referred to as gestalts or forms that we perceive in our environment. In verbal contexts, we want to close in blank gaps with meaningful words. How well we close in those gaps depends on our background knowledge and facility with language. As readers interact with a text that has words missing, those readers often think of words that fit the author's meaning exactly. In fact, authors who fill in blanks systematically in their own writing do so at a statistically higher rate than competent readers, a discovery that has been used to detect plagiarism.

## STEP-BY-STEP: *How to Administer a Cloze Readability Test*

When using the cloze procedure to determine text readability, you can take the following steps to prepare, administer, score, and interpret it.

**STEP 1.** Preparation

1.1. Select two passages of about 300 words from a text that your students have not yet read but will be assigned. Two passages are chosen to increase the accuracy of the procedure.

1.2.  For each passage, leave the first sentence as written. However, starting with the second sentence, you should delete each fifth word and put in a blank space about 10 to 15 spaces in length. Delete exactly 50 words but retain the last sentence as written. A sample cloze passage appears in Figure 3.5.

**STEP 2.** Administration

2.1. Begin by asking students to read over the entire passage first.

2.2. Then, ask them to go back and fill in each blank with the word they believe was deleted.

2.3. If students have problems filling in a word, tell them to skip it, complete the rest of the passage, and return to the blank for another try.

2.4. The test is not timed.

2.5. A short practice test helps to prepare students for the actual testing.

2.6. While some students experience cloze testing as an entertaining and challenging puzzle, others may find it quite frustrating and require some encouragement.

**STEP 3.** Scoring

    3.1. When scoring the cloze test, only exact words replaced are correct.

    3.2. Correct spelling of replaced words is not required.

    3.3. To calculate percent of correct words, divide 50 into the total number of correctly replaced words. If Cynthia replaced 30 words correctly, her score would be 60%.

    3.4. When using two passages to increase accuracy, the percentages of correctly replaced words for each passage are averaged. If Cynthia got 60% on the first passage and 68% on the second, her average would be 64%.

**STEP 4.** Interpretation

    4.1. Criteria for determining reading levels were developed by Bormuth (1968):

| PERCENTAGE CORRECT | READING LEVEL |
|---|---|
| 57% or more | Independent level |
| 44–57% | Instructional level |
| Below 44% | Frustration level |

    4.2. Students scoring over 57% can probably read and understand most of the tested text on their own.

    4.3. Students scoring between 44 and 57% can probably read the material tested with supportive teaching of vocabulary, comprehension strategies, and study guidelines.

    4.4. Students scoring below 44% will probably have so much difficulty with the tested text that you will have to find alternative texts or methods of teaching the content knowledge you want those students to learn.

*Benefits and limitations of cloze testing.*    On the benefits' side, cloze tests are relatively easy to prepare, administer, and score. They can help you get a rather quick fix on how each of your students is likely to engage and comprehend specific content texts. That's more than you'll get after calculating a readability formula for a textbook. Although the cloze procedure remains controversial, researchers (Shanahan & Kamil, 1984) have found fairly high correlations (.6 to .8) between cloze tests and standardized reading comprehension tests using multiple-choice items. For determining students' reading levels, Cziko (1983) demonstrated that these tests are valid and reliable measures.

However, cloze tests tell us very little, if anything, about our students' capacity for higher-order thinking in the form of interpretive or inferential comprehension. Many standardized reading tests assess that form of comprehension, as do most IRIs.

In addition, many students get quite frustrated when taking a cloze test. I've even heard many teachers in credential programs complain of their frustration when I've asked them to complete a cloze test on a text that's being used in a teacher preparation program. Middle and high school students may need substantial encouragement and a clear message that their performance on the "test" will not be averaged into their course grade!

## Friendly Text Evaluation Scale

There are dimensions of texts that none of the more traditional instruments we've covered manage to measure. For example, how accessible is the text to its readers? Henry Singer (1992) developed a scale to help educators determine the "friendliness"

Your dermis also has tiny muscles that are attached to the hairs in your skin. When you are cold __1__ afraid, the muscles contract, __2__ the hairs upright. This __3__ process happens in the __4__ of other mammals. The __5__ of a cat, for __6__ , will stand up when __7__ cat is threatened by __8__ dog, making the cat __9__ larger and more dangerous. __10__ the cat is cold, __11__ fur fluffs up and __12__ more air near its __13__ . Because trapped air is __14__ good insulator, this __15__ the cat stay warm. __16__ . muscles in your skin __17__ just like those of __18__ cat. However, because you __19__ have fur, you just __20__ goose bumps—a leftover __21__ our evolutionary past.

__22__ skin, like all other __23__ parts of your body, __24__ nourishment to live. This __25__ is supplied by blood __26__ courses through tiny blood __27__ in the dermis. In __28__ to carrying nutrients, the __29__ in these vessels carries __30__ waste products and helps __31__ body temperature. Blood radiates __32__ into the air as __33__ passes near the surface __34__ the skin. If your __35__ becomes too hot, the __36__ blood vessels enlarge, allowing __37__ blood to flow through __38__ dermis near the body __39__ . This increased flow of __40__ is easy to see __41__ light-skinned people as their __42__ becomes reddish during strenuous __43__ .

Sweat is another way __44__ your body removes excess __45__ . Your skin contains __46__ 100 sweat glands per __47__ centimeter. The evaporation of __48__ from the surface of __49__ skin removes heat much __50__ efficiently than simply radiating heat from the blood into the air. Without sweat, you would have great difficulty cooling your body on a hot day or after exercising.

FIGURE 3.5    Sample Cloze Passage.

*Source:* Excerpt from *Holt Biology: Visualizing Life,* by G. B. Johnson. Copyright © 1994 by Holt, Rinehart and Winston. Reprinted by permission of the publisher.

of a text. His Friendly Text Evaluation Scale can help you focus on a text's organization, consistency, and cohesiveness as well as on its capacity to explain concepts clearly. This Friendly Scale also includes several items focusing on a text's instructional devices, their variety, and their effectiveness. Information of this kind provides a different view of texts from those generated by readability formulas and cloze tests. The entire Friendly Text Evaluation Scale is present in Table 3.11.

After reading this text book, I invite you to apply the "Friendly Text Evaluation Scale" to these pages. And I hope you and your instructor will let me know what needs to be done to improve the book's accessibility.

DOUBLE-ENTRY JOURNAL: After Reading

Go to the Double-Entry Journal for Chapter 3 on our Companion Website at www.prenhall.com/unrau to complete your journal entry.

Having read this chapter, how would you modify (if at all) your plan to evaluate the reading performance of students at the beginning of a new class? Besides evaluating your students' reading levels, how would you approach teaching "diagnostically" in your content area? What benefits would you expect to gain from that approach?

**TABLE 3.11**   Friendly Text Evaluation Scale

*Directions:* Read each criterion and judge the degree of agreement or disagreement between it and the text. Then circle the number to the right of the criterion that indicates your judgment.
1.  SA = Strongly Agree
2.   A = Agree
3.   U = Uncertain
4.   D = Disagree
5.  SD = Strongly Disagree

| I. Organization | SA | A | U | D | SD |
|---|---|---|---|---|---|
| 1. The introductions to the book and each chapter explain their purposes. | 1 | 2 | 3 | 4 | 5 |
| 2. The introduction provides information on the sequence of the text's contents. | 1 | 2 | 3 | 4 | 5 |
| 3. The introduction communicates how the reader should learn from the text. | 1 | 2 | 3 | 4 | 5 |
| 4. The ideas presented in the text follow a unidirectional sequence. One idea leads to the next. | 1 | 2 | 3 | 4 | 5 |
| 5. The type of paragraph structure organizes information to facilitate memory. For example, objects and their properties are grouped together so as to emphasize relationships. | 1 | 2 | 3 | 4 | 5 |
| 6. Ideas are hierarchically structured either verbally or graphically. | 1 | 2 | 3 | 4 | 5 |
| 7. The author provides cues to the way information will be presented. For example, the author states: "There are five points to consider." | 1 | 2 | 3 | 4 | 5 |
| 8. Signal words (conjunctions, adverbs) and rhetorical devices (problem–solution, question–answer, cause–effect, comparison and contrast, argument–proof) interrelate sentences, paragraphs, and larger units of discourse. | 1 | 2 | 3 | 4 | 5 |
| Discourse consistency | | | | | |
| 9. The style of writing is consistent and coherent. For example, paragraphs, sections, and chapters build to a conclusion. Or they begin with a general statement and then present supporting ideas. Or the text has a combination of these patterns. Any one of these patterns would fit this consistency criterion. | 1 | 2 | 3 | 4 | 5 |
| Cohesiveness | | | | | |
| 10. The text is cohesive. That is, the author ties ideas together from sentence to sentence, paragraph to paragraph, chapter to chapter. | 1 | 2 | 3 | 4 | 5 |

| II. Explication | SA | A | U | D | SD |
|---|---|---|---|---|---|
| 11. Some texts may be read at more than one level, (e.g., descriptive vs. theoretical). The text orients students to a level that is appropriate for the students. | 1 | 2 | 3 | 4 | 5 |
| 12. The text provides reasons for functions or events. For example, the text, if it is a biology text, not only lists the differences between arteries and veins but also explains why they are different. | 1 | 2 | 3 | 4 | 5 |
| 13. The text highlights or italicizes and defines new terms as they are introduced at a level that is familiar to the student. | 1 | 2 | 3 | 4 | 5 |
| 14. The text provides necessary background knowledge. For example, the text introduces new ideas by reviewing or reminding readers of previously acquired knowledge or concepts. | 1 | 2 | 3 | 4 | 5 |
| 15. The author uses examples, analogies, metaphors, similes, personifications, or allusions that clarify new ideas and make them vivid. | 1 | 2 | 3 | 4 | 5 |

| | | SA | A | U | D | SD |
|---|---|---|---|---|---|---|
| 16. | The author explains ideas in relatively short active sentences. | 1 | 2 | 3 | 4 | 5 |
| 17. | The explanations or theories that underlie the text are made explicit (e.g., Keynesian theory in Samuelson's economic text, Skinner's theory in Bijou and Baer's *Child Development*, behavioristic or gestalt theories in psychology texts). | 1 | 2 | 3 | 4 | 5 |

| III. Conceptual Density | SA | A | U | D | SD |
|---|---|---|---|---|---|
| 18. Ideas are introduced, defined, or clarified, and integrated with semantically related ideas previously presented in the text and examples given before additional ideas are presented. | 1 | 2 | 3 | 4 | 5 |
| 19. The vocabulary load is appropriate. For example, usually only one new vocabulary item per paragraph occurs throughout the text. | 1 | 2 | 3 | 4 | 5 |
| 20. Content is accurate, up-to-date, and not biased. | 1 | 2 | 3 | 4 | 5 |

| IV. Metadiscourse | SA | A | U | D | SD |
|---|---|---|---|---|---|
| 21. The author talks directly to the reader to explain how to learn from the text. For example, the author states that some information in the text is more important than other information. | 1 | 2 | 3 | 4 | 5 |
| 22. The author establishes a purpose or goal for the text. | 1 | 2 | 3 | 4 | 5 |
| 23. The text supplies collateral information for putting events into context. | 1 | 2 | 3 | 4 | 5 |
| 24. The text points out relationships to ideas previously presented in the text or to the reader's prior knowledge. | 1 | 2 | 3 | 4 | 5 |

| V. Instructional Devices | SA | A | U | D | SD |
|---|---|---|---|---|---|
| 25. The text contains a logically organized table of contents. | 1 | 2 | 3 | 4 | 5 |
| 26. The text has a glossary that defines technical terms in understandable language. | 1 | 2 | 3 | 4 | 5 |
| 27. The index integrates concepts dispersed throughout the text. | 1 | 2 | 3 | 4 | 5 |
| 28. There are overviews, proposed questions, or graphic devices such as diagrams, tables, and graphs throughout the text that emphasize what is to be learned in the chapters or sections. | 1 | 2 | 3 | 4 | 5 |
| 29. The text includes marginal annotations or footnotes that instruct the reader. | 1 | 2 | 3 | 4 | 5 |
| 30. The text contains chapter summaries that reflect its main points. | 1 | 2 | 3 | 4 | 5 |
| 31. The text has problems or questions at the literal, interpretive, applied, and evaluative levels at the end of each chapter that help the reader understand knowledge presented in the text. | 1 | 2 | 3 | 4 | 5 |
| 32. The text contains headings and subheadings that divide the text into categories that enable readers to perceive the major ideas. | 1 | 2 | 3 | 4 | 5 |
| 33. The author provides information in the text or at the end of the chapters or the text that enables the reader to apply the knowledge in the text to new situations. | 1 | 2 | 3 | 4 | 5 |
| 34. The author uses personal pronouns that makes the text more interesting to the reader. | 1 | 2 | 3 | 4 | 5 |

SCORE          TOTALS _____

Add the numbers circled.

Score range: 34 to 170.

INTERPRETATION OF SCORES

A score closer to 34 implies the text is friendly; scores closer to 170 suggest the text is unfriendly.

*Source:* Singer, H. (1992). Friendly texts: Description and criteria. In E. K. Dishner, T. W. Bean, J. E. Readence, & D. W. Moore (Eds.), *Reading in the content areas* (3rd ed., pp. 155–168). Dubuque, IA: Kendall/Hunt.

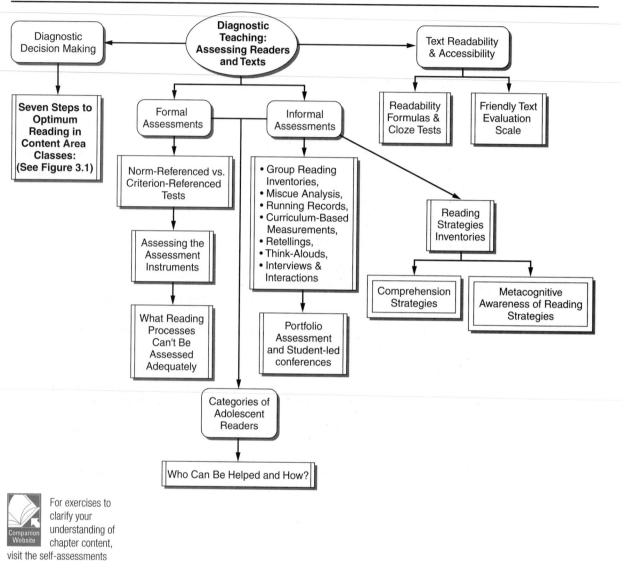

For exercises to clarify your understanding of chapter content, visit the self-assessments for Chapter 3 on our Companion Website at www.prenhall.com/unrau

# References

Atwell, N. (1998). *In the middle: New understandings about writing, reading, and learning.* Portsmouth, NH: Heinemann.

Austin, T. (1994). *Changing the view: Student-led parent conferences.* Portsmouth, NH: Heinemann.

Banks, J. A. (2000). *Ancient world: Adventures in time and place.* New York: McGraw-Hill/National Geographic.

Beers, K. (1998). Choosing not to read: Understanding why some middle schoolers just say no. In K. Beers & B. G. Samuels (Eds.), *Into focus: Understanding and creating middle school readers* (pp. 37–63). Norwood, MA: Christopher-Gordon Publishers.

Bormuth, J. R. (1968). The cloze readability procedure. In J. R. Bormuth (Ed.), *Readability in 1968.* Champaign, IL: National Council of Teachers of English.

Burns, P. C., & Roe, B. D. (1999). *Informal reading inventory: Preprimer to twelfth grade.* Boston, MA: Houghton Mifflin.

Calkins, L., Montgomery, K., & Santman, D. (1998). *A teacher's guide to standardized reading tests.* Portsmouth, NH: Heinemann.

Curriculum Associates. (1998). *Comprehensive assessment of reading strategies: Books 2–8.* North Billerica, MA: Curriculum Associates, Inc.

Cziko, G. A. (1983). Another response to Shanahan, Kamil, and Tobin: Further reasons to keep the cloze case open. *Reading Research Quarterly, 18,* 361–365.

Davey, B. (1983). Think-aloud—modeling the cognitive processes of reading comprehension. *Journal of Reading, 27,* 44–47.

Fry, E. (1977). Fry's readability graph: Clarifications, validity, and extension to level 17. *Journal of Reading, 21,* 242–252.

Fry, E., Kress, J., & Fountoukidis, D. (2000). *The reading teacher's book of lists* (4th ed.). Paramus, NJ: Prentice Hall.

Fuchs, L., Fuchs, D., & Hosp, M. K. (2001). Oral reading fluency as an indicator of reading competence: A theoretical, empirical, and historical analysis. *Scientific Studies of Reading, 5* (3), 239–256.

Goodman, K. (1969). Analysis of reading miscues: Applied psycholinguistics. *Reading Research Quarterly, 5* (1), 9–13.

Goodman, K. (1994). Reading, writing, and written texts: A transactional sociopsycholinguistic view. In R. B. Ruddell, M. R. Ruddell, & H. Singer (Eds.), *Theoretical models and processes of reading* (4th ed., pp. 1093–1130). Newark, DE: International Reading Association.

Gunning, T. G. (2002). *Assessing and correcting reading and writing difficulties* (2nd ed.). Boston: Allyn & Bacon.

Hacker, D. J. (1998). Self-regulated comprehension during normal reading. In D. J. Hacker, J. Dunlosky, & A. C. Graesser (Eds.), *Metacognition in educational theory and practice* (pp. 165–191). Mahwah, NJ: Erlbaum.

Hiebert, E. H. (2002). Standards, assessments, and text difficulty. In A. Farstrup & S. J. Samuels (Eds.), *What research has to say about reading instruction* (3rd ed., pp. 337–369). Newark, DE: International Reading Association.

Johnson. G. B. (1998). *Biology: Visualizing life.* Austin, TX: Holt, Rinehart and Winston.

Kibby, M. W. (1995). *Practical steps for informing literacy instruction: A diagnostic decision-making model.* Newark, DE: International Reading Association.

McCormick, S. (1999). *Instructing students who have literacy problems* (3rd ed.). Columbus, OH: Merrill.

Mokhtari, K., & Reichard, C. A. (2002). Assessing students' metacognitive awareness of reading strategies. *Journal of Educational Psychology, 94* (2), 249–259.

Rakes, T. A., & Smith, T. L. (1992). Assessing reading skills in the content areas. In E. K. Dishner, T. W. Bean, J. E. Readence, & D. W. Moore (Eds.), *Reading in the content areas: Improving classroom instruction* (3rd ed., pp. 399–426). Dubuque, IA: Kendall/Hunt.

Ruddell, R. B. (1995). Those influential literacy teachers: Meaning negotiators and motivation builders. *The Reading Teacher, 48,* 454–463.

Ruddell, R. B., Draheim, M., & Barnes, J. (1990). A comparative study of the teaching effectiveness of influential and non-influential teachers and reading comprehension development. In J. Zutell & S. McCormick (Eds.), *Literacy theory and research: Analyses from multiple paradigms* (pp. 153–162). Chicago, IL: National Reading Conference.

Shanahan, T., & Kamil, M. L. (1984). The relationship of three concurrent and construct validities of cloze. In J. A. Niles & L. A. Harris (Eds.), *Changing perspectives on research in reading/language processing and instruction* (pp. 334–338). Rochester: National Reading Conference.

Singer, H. (1992). Friendly texts: Description and criteria. In E. K. Dishner, T. W. Bean, J. E. Readence, & D. W. Moore (Eds.), *Reading in the content areas* (3rd ed., pp. 155–168). Dubuque, IA: Kendall/Hunt.

Solomon, M. Z., & Morocco, C. C. (1999). The diagnostic teacher. In M.Z. Solomon (Ed.), *The diagnostic teacher: Constructing new approaches to professional development* (pp. 231–246). New York: Teachers College Press.

Spear-Swerling, L., & Sternberg, R. J. (1996). *Off track: When poor readers become "learning disabled."* Boulder, CO: Westview Press.

Stanovich, K. E. (1990). Explaining the differences between the dyslexic and the garden-variety poor reader: The phonological-core variable-difference model. In J. K. Torgesen (Ed.), *Cognitive and behavioral characteristics of children with learning disabilities* (pp. 7–40). Austin, TX: Pro-Ed.

Stanovich, K. E., & Siegel, L. S. (1994). Phenotypic performance profile of children with reading disabilities: A regression-based test of the phonological-core variable-difference model. *Journal of Educational Psychology, 86,* 24–53.

Taylor, W. (1953). Cloze procedure: A new tool for measuring readability. *Journalism Quarterly, 30,* 415–433.

Waid, J. (2002). Through the looking glass and back: The pursuit of National Board for Professional Teaching Standards certification. Unpublished master's thesis, California State University, Los Angeles.

Wilde, S. (2000). *Miscue analysis made easy: Building on student strengths.* Portsmouth, NH: Heinemann.

# 4 VOCABULARY AND CONCEPT DEVELOPMENT IN THE CONTENT AREAS

After reading Chapter 4, you should be able to answer the following questions:

1. What is the relationship between decoding and word recognition?
2. Why is knowing a word so complicated?
3. What have researchers learned about teaching vocabulary?
4. How could you help students learn and use strategies to discover the meanings of unknown words?
5. How would you approach the design of vocabulary instruction as part of a unit in your discipline?
6. How can you help students learn new words through "just reading"?

DOUBLE-ENTRY
JOURNAL: Before
Reading

How do you feel about encountering and learning new words? What methods have you used to learn them? How could you heighten your students' awareness and appreciation of words?

 Now go to the
Double-Entry
Journal for
Chapter 4 on
our Companion Website at
www.prenhall.com/unrau
to fill out your journal
entry.

Words are small wonders. When spoken, they're puffs of air. When written, they're jiggles on paper. These puffs and jiggles enable us to communicate, to convey our love, to pursue justice, to contain our histories, and to carry on our culture. As a teacher, your words serve as a bridge for your students to enter new worlds of knowledge, new fields of understanding. As your students acquire subject matter vocabulary, they acquire the tools to work and to communicate in that field. Vocabulary, the repertoire of words people use to understand their world and to express their perceptions of it, is the best single indicator we have of intelligence (Sternberg, 1988). The purpose of this chapter is to provide you with the knowledge and strategies to help your students gain the vocabulary they need to grow and to succeed.

## WORDS IN A MODEL CONTEXT

If you focus on the role of words in the model of reading presented in Chapter 2, you will soon see that neither word knowledge nor its acquisition is simple. Being able to read a word, either a basic word such as *cat* or a complex one such as *catalogue*, requires considerable background knowledge and skill—not to mention intricate cognitive processes we are still discovering. If you consider how much word knowledge students need to approach proficient comprehension in a content area such as history, math, biology, or physics, you can begin to appreciate the complexity of vocabulary development.

I want to connect this chapter's discussion of word learning to reading processes in the sociocognitive model of reading that I presented earlier. Making that connection is more likely to convince you that word learning, word recognition, and comprehension are integrated. To recognize a word when reading, a reader must have command of knowledge and skills that take years to develop. Without the ability to decode a word or recognize it, a reader is lost.

### Decoding

If you envision the reading process as presented in Chapter 2 and read about the importance of reading readers, you already know that, without adequate decoding ability, your students will struggle when trying to read. If the texts you give them contain many unfamiliar words, they will experience varying degrees of frustration. One way or the other, you will have to find some way to cope with their weaknesses and their strengths.

Many educators believe that word-level decoding is a bottleneck in readers' meaning construction efforts. If readers can't decode a word, they simply can't understand it. And, if large portions of working memory are tied up in decoding, comprehension is likely to falter (Samuels, 1994). For better understanding and fluency, readers need to acquire greater automaticity when decoding. Efficiency in reading depends upon rapid word recognition that can't occur without fluid decoding.

While meaning cues in the context of a word make important contributions to word recognition (Goodman, 1996), the scientific evidence we have favors letter-sound cues as most important in skilled decoding (Nicholson, 1991; Pressley, 2000). Inferences about word meanings from contexts have proven to be problematic because readers can infer incorrectly (Miller & Gildea, 1987). After first seeing a less familiar word, sounding it out to trigger recognition is a next step but hardly the last, for readers must attend to that word's meaning within its larger context.

## The Lexicon in Long-Term Memory

As depicted in the model, readers' knowledge of words and their meanings is stored in long-term memory. As readers recognize words and activate their meanings, they construct a mental representation for the text. With a lexicon of recallable words, readers access their knowledge of concepts, just as these words are helping you access your understanding of the reading process. The more words that a reader has stored for activation, the greater the reader's chances of understanding content area texts. As we learned, speed of access to word meanings also contributes to fluent reading. Every reader's working memory functions better if not taxed by having to struggle with either decoding a word or accessing its meaning.

Although some earlier research showed that word training did not result in better comprehension, Tan and Nicholson (1997) found that weak readers who practiced recognizing "target words" visually until they could do so automatically benefited significantly from the training in comparison to a control group. In the control condition, subjects engaged in discussion about the meaning of "target words" but never saw them. Visual word recognition appeared to be a key to better comprehension. Other research (Breznitz, 1997) also confirmed that comprehension improved when subjects could decode words rapidly. As we have seen, this probably results from struggling readers gaining more working memory capacity to construct extended meaning.

## THE COMPLEXITIES OF SIMPLY KNOWING A WORD

Knowing a word appears to be a fairly simple form of knowledge; however, beneath that appearance of simplicity, we quickly discover how complicated knowing a word really is. Nagy and Scott (2000) identified five aspects of word knowledge complexity:

1. Knowing a word is not a yes–no dichotomy but a matter of degrees. Students know words on a continuum from complete ignorance of a word to proficiency in crafting sentences with that word.

2. Knowing a word entails many dimensions of knowledge. These dimensions include knowledge of a word's spoken form, written form, grammatical form, conceptual meaning, synonyms, antonyms, frequency of use, and responsiveness to contexts.

3. Words frequently have many meanings. To know a word well implies knowing much more than a single memorized definition. Many words, such as *rose* or *fork,* have multiple meanings and nuances within individual meanings.

4. Knowledge of a single word isolated from all others is impossible. Words live and acquire meanings in interconnected networks. That is especially true of words germane to academic disciplines, such as words used by geologists or physicists.

5. What it means to know a word is dependent upon the kind of word you are talking about knowing. For example, knowledge of an article, such as *the,* or of a conjunction, like *and,* is quite different from knowledge of nouns such as *conjugation, polynomial,* or *catalyst.*

Although most researchers and teachers have recognized the complexity of word knowledge for many years, traditional vocabulary instruction, such as memorizing definitions for a weekly quiz, often fails to take that complexity into account. One implication arising from a recognition of word knowledge complexity is that explicit instruction in word definitions must be supplemented with multiple and varied exposure to target words. Knowing a word well entails knowledge of how that word works in our language system, how it is used in multiple contexts, and what you can do with it, not simply what it means in isolation. As Nagy and Scott (2000) insightfully observe, "In most cases, knowing a word is more like knowing how to use a tool than it is like being able to state a fact" (p. 273).

## Word Counts

How many words do students know? How many do they usually learn each year? Answers to these questions depend upon several prior questions: What counts as a word? What does it mean to know a word? What dictionary or list of words will be used to measure totals and rates of growth? How will that body of words be sampled? What populations will be sampled to determine size and growth rates? Because different researchers (Beck & McKeown, 1991) have answered these questions differently, the answers to our questions about total words known and rates of growth vary.

As for vocabulary size, estimates for college students vary from 19,000 to 200,000. For first graders, estimates range from 2,500 to 25,000. As part of an extensive study of vocabulary development, Biemiller and Slonim (2001) estimated the number of words at each **Living Word Vocabulary (LWV)** grade level and the proportion of those that were root words. The LWV is a comprehensive assessment of 44,000 word meanings known by children through high school and into adulthood (Dale & O'Rourke, 1981). Root words were defined as **morphemes,** having only one meaning and distinct from derived, inflected, or compound words based on that root. If a reader understands *plan* as a root word, she would also understand *planned, planning,* and *unplanned.* Biemiller and Slonim estimated that 67 to 80% of eighth graders knew about 22,000 LWV meanings and about 11,000 root words while 67 to 80% of twelfth graders knew about 30,500 LWV meanings and about

15,000 root words. After their review of relevant research, Beck and McKeown concluded that "absolute statements about vocabulary size of various populations cannot be made" (1991 p. 794). However, we know that huge individual differences in word knowledge among students exist. For example, in Smith's (1941) study, high-performing seniors in high school knew about four times the words that low-performing seniors knew. Furthermore, high-performing third graders knew as many words as low-performing seniors in high school.

As for rates of growth, they extend from 1,000 per year to 3,500 per year for children in first through fifth grades. Nagy (1988a) has argued that 1,000 words per year is "unrealistically low." More realistically, research evidence would support the claim that at least some children learn 2,000 or more words each year (Nagy & Scott, 2000). While some children from grades 1 through 5 learn at these higher rates per year, students whose background has not provided a substantial language base need to gain knowledge of words at twice the pace or more of their more fortunate peers. Although Biemiller and Slonim (2001) present evidence that schooling does help to close the gap in the early grades, Stanovich (1986) has demonstrated that students with a shallow literacy base because of limited language development slip further and further behind as time goes by. This tendency of achieving students to enrich their vocabularies while underachieving students become further impoverished is one that most teachers meet and make efforts to mitigate.

## High- and Low-Frequency Words

Readers are exposed to words at different rates or frequencies. Although exposure to words varies along a continuum, reading specialists tend to think of words as belonging in two extreme categories: high- and low-frequency words. ***High-frequency words*** are the shortest, most frequently occurring ones and, oddly enough, are a source of difficulty for many struggling readers. Quite a few of these high-frequency words, such as *the, of,* or *would,* don't carry a heavy load of meaning. They are usually abstract function words. Even though students may process and reprocess some of these high-frequency words hundreds of times, words such as *where* or *were,* some students still have trouble with them. For fluent readers, however, most of these high-frequency words are "sight words," words that are instantly recognized and processed orthographically without analysis.

Educators (Fry, Kress, & Fountoukidis, 2000; Zeno, Ivens, Millard, & Duvvuri, 1995) have compiled lists of the words that appear most often in textual materials that school children read. Fry, Kress, and Fountoukidis observed that the first 25 words on their "instant word" list make up about one-third of everything in print, while the whole list of 100 words makes up about half of all written material (see Table 4.1). Kucera and Francis (1967) discovered that, in a sample of 1,000,000 words of adult text, 50% was composed of only 133 words.

Most students learn these high-frequency, or "instant" words, early in their reading career, many by about the third or fourth grade, or earlier. However, some students continue to struggle with them, in part because of limited practice or weak orthographic processing (Gunning, 2002). Some of these students can gain greater automaticity through reading a wide range of "easy" books, through reading more frequently, or through "repeated reading" (Samuels, 1994). When doing repeated readings, a student

**TABLE 4.1**   Instant Words or High-Frequency Words

| First Hundred | | | |
| --- | --- | --- | --- |
| **Words 1–25** | **Words 26–50** | **Words 51–75** | **Words 75–100** |
| the | or | will | number |
| of | one | up | no |
| and | had | other | way |
| a | by | about | could |
| to | word | out | people |
| in | but | many | my |
| is | not | then | than |
| you | what | them | first |
| it | were | so | been |
| he | we | some | call |
| was | when | her | who |
| for | your | would | oil |
| on | can | make | its |
| are | said | like | now |
| as | there | him | find |
| with | use | into | long |
| his | an | time | down |
| they | each | has | day |
| I | which | look | did |
| at | she | two | get |
| be | do | more | come |
| this | how | write | made |
| have | their | go | may |
| from | if | see | part |

*Source:* From *The Reading Teacher's Book of Lists* (p. 47), by E. B. Fry, J. E. Kress, and D. L. Fountoukidis, 2000. Copyright © 2000 by John Wiley & Sons, Inc. This material is used by permission of John Wiley & Sons, Inc.

chooses a passage that presents a challenge to fluent reading and makes a record of word-recognition errors and speed for the passage. The student, like a pianist learning to play a score, then practices rereading the passage independently, working as needed with particularly challenging words, until ready for another testing for time and errors. When the student reads the passage with fluency, it's time to move on to a new selection. If you have students who have problems with high-frequency words, their difficulty may signal a need for attention to delayed reading development. Chapter 9 will present information to help you and your colleagues address these problems.

For our students, ***low-frequency words*** usually carry more content area knowledge. Unfortunately, readers encounter these low-frequency words far less often. Carroll, Davies, and Richman (1971) discovered that 90% of texts they analyzed were constructed of 5,000 common words. But many less common words also appear in those texts. The remaining 10% of the words (about 80,000) accounted for 94% of all the other words readers had to understand. These are words of good coinage (e.g., *metaphor, surgeon, pepper, magic, algorithm, spruce, assembly, concerto, syntax, verdict*) that can be exchanged for meaning if that meaning can be activated in long-term memory following orthographic and phonological processing (see

Chapter 2). Of course, context can contribute to correct interpretations of low-frequency words as well.

Furthermore, a low-frequency word for one reader may not be for another. Because one of your students may spend a lot of time reading about car engines and tinkering with his own car's engine, the word *torque* may be a relatively high-frequency word for him although that same word could easily fall within another student's low-frequency list. Determining a word's degree of frequency depends on the reading experience of the reader. Consequently, the speed with which weaker readers recognize low-frequency words is likely to be slower, especially for words with an irregular letter–sound pattern.

Greater knowledge of lower frequency words contributes directly to higher scores on tests of word knowledge. And, it follows that bigger banks of lower frequency words will translate into better reading comprehension for a wide variety of texts. Most standardized reading tests are composed of a vocabulary section and a reading comprehension section that are highly correlated and combined to yield a total reading score. The more word knowledge a reader has, the higher the score on the reading test.

Knowing what we do of high- and low-frequency words, we can see what our word knowledge instructional challenge will be: Discover ways to enable our students to acquire low-frequency words that permeate our content area teaching.

## Flashbacks: The Return of the Vocabulary Card

Among the purposes for encouraging a lot of reading are that it can build fluency through practice and provide opportunities for incidental learning of vocabulary. But there are other ways to build speed in struggling readers. Although most of your students will have gained automatic recognition of sight words, some may not. While you probably will not have to take your entire class through sight-word training, some students may require that kind of instruction. If so, you may have a specialist or assistant who could help these delayed readers increase word recognition speed through drilling students on those "instant" words. (See Table 4.1.) Practice should continue until targeted high-frequency words are recognized immediately. Some computer-based reading programs can also help struggling readers gain automaticity with high-frequency words.

How many millions of students have used flashcards to learn words? Long ago, even before television, maybe before radio, students helped themselves learn vo-

*Source:* CALVIN AND HOBBES © Watterson. Reprinted with permission of UNIVERSAL PRESS SYNDICATE. All rights reserved.

cabulary by putting unknown words on one side of a card and, on the opposite side, the meaning, part of speech, and a sentence using the word correctly. Recent research (Tan & Nicholson, 1997) suggests that this ancient technique could be effective in helping readers recognize words more quickly so that text in which the words were embedded could be understood better.

## What Do We Know about Teaching Vocabulary?

Many teachers have not found effective techniques for teaching word knowledge to their students, and researchers in the profession have not shown much commitment to investigating how teaching vocabulary could improve. Teachers have long believed that teaching vocabulary is essential to their students' reading comprehension (Anderson & Freebody, 1981). Although teachers say they believe vocabulary learning should reflect in-depth knowledge of words learned, their instructional actions, as some researchers (Konopak & Williams, 1994) have observed, don't reflect that belief because their teaching about words tends to lack integration and depth. Often, instruction consists of paraphrasing sentences that contain unfamiliar words or demonstrating how a new word might be used in context (Scott & Butler, 1994). Furthermore, a survey of leading reading professionals indicates that interest in vocabulary has been rated in the lowest category of interest, "cold," for several years (Cassidy & Cassidy, 1999–2000, 2000–2001, 2001–2002; Cassidy & Wenrich, 1997, 1998). While interest in vocabulary may have been cold over the past few years, 75% of the reading specialists surveyed believed it should be "hot" because of its great importance.

As long ago as the mid-1970s, researchers (Becker, 1977) claimed that one of the major contributing factors to the failure of disadvantaged children in our schools was inadequate vocabulary knowledge. One transparent implication was that students received inadequate vocabulary instruction.

When I began to teach English in the 1960s, I taught my students vocabulary from lists of words students were expected to know. Usually, I took words from novels or essays we were reading as a class. In one school where I taught, lists were compiled by the English department for specific grade levels and English teachers were expected to cover all the vocabulary for the grade level they taught. When my students and I disagreed over a word's meaning or when a word had multiple meanings, such as "fray," we'd agree on a specific dictionary definition that students would have to know for their Friday vocabulary quiz. It seemed like a sensible approach. It had its merits. Parents approved. It worked like a current SAT word list. All of us, to the best of my knowledge, used an approach that emphasized students' looking up the word's definition and composing a sentence using it "appropriately." At the time I had some misgivings about the process, but I hung with it. Years later, research began to emerge that confirmed my misgivings about the definitional approach we used.

## Traditional Methods

Why has some "traditional" vocabulary instruction failed to increase comprehension? Nagy (1988a) believes that most vocabulary instruction simply does not provide students with the in-depth knowledge of words needed for comprehension. Memorizing definitions, which Nagy described as one form of "traditional" vocabulary instruction, isn't enough to produce in-depth knowledge of words needed to augment comprehension. Just giving students the definition of words or asking them to look up the definitions of words, writing them down, and memorizing those definitions usually does not result in sufficient information to enable a student to understand the word's meaning in context or to use it correctly. According to Nagy, only a superficial knowledge of words occurs through that definitional approach to vocabulary instruction.

However, a review of several definitional word-learning studies (Blachowicz & Fisher, 2000) indicates that teaching definitions does result in learning and, when combined with other related activities, such as writing, produces even better results. Other researchers (Nist & Olejnik, 1995) have confirmed that having access to adequate dictionary definitions improves independent word learning. The quality of the definitions influenced the degree to which students were able to learn new words independently. Better definitions led to better word learning. The researchers suggested that looking up words in a dictionary might not always be the worst way to learn words.

A second "traditional" approach to vocabulary instruction that Nagy (1988a) identified was using context to infer the meaning of words. While this is an important means of vocabulary growth, he does not believe it is effective for teaching new meanings, especially when compared to other, more direct instructional methods. Most contexts are "relatively uninformative" because a single context rarely provides sufficient information for productive inference about unfamiliar word meanings.

What constitutes inadequate vocabulary instruction? Like many answers related to word knowledge and word learning: That depends. However, some researchers (Nagy, 1988a) have identified features of "traditional" vocabulary instruction that studies have revealed to be ineffective. One of these features is simply teaching definitions of vocabulary words.

Nagy (1988b) argues that a combination of a definitional and a context approach is more effective than either in isolation. Providing students with the meaning of a word or the resources for looking it up together with natural contexts in which the word is used makes the word's meaning more concrete. Vocabulary instruction needs to offer students both adequate definitions and examples of the word's use in real-world contexts.

## Principles to Guide Vocabulary Learning

Although research on vocabulary instruction had been sparse up to the mid-1970s, several hundreds of studies and summaries of studies focused on vocabulary instruction have since been published (Blachowicz & Fisher, 2000).

Educators (Baumann & Kaméenui, 1991; Irvin, 1990; Ruddell, 1994) have distilled much of what has been learned from 25 years or so of research into a set of insights that teachers could apply to their classroom instruction. After reviewing the research, Blachowicz and Fisher (2000) identified four main principles to guide vocabulary instruction:

1. Students should be active learners as they acquire specific vocabulary and strategies to enlarge their vocabulary base.
2. Students benefit from personalizing the learning of words.

3. Students gain from immersion in words.
4. Students augment their vocabulary through repeated exposure to words.

These principles for learning words can be applied in many different contexts, including struggling readers and English language learners. From these principles, we can conclude that to teach new words, we need to immerse our students in active and repeated opportunities to integrate word instruction with knowledge students have already acquired in our discipline.

## Creating Word-Rich Environments for Harvesting Word Knowledge

Students, especially those who have had fewer opportunities for language development and may be losing ground, need an environment of exposure to print that fosters word knowledge. According to the environmental opportunity hypothesis (Stanovich, Cunningham, & West, 1998), vocabulary differences that we see in our students result from varying opportunities that they have had to learn words. In accord with this theory, some students with opulent vocabularies have thrived in language-rich environments while others with impoverished vocabularies eked out their word knowledge from desert-like conditions. Countering this hypothesis is the belief that experiential factors make little if any difference in vocabulary development because differences in word knowledge among individuals result from variations in cognitive mechanisms and their efficiency in extracting meaning from contexts.

Without engaging in extended debate over the nurture vs. nature issue, perhaps we could cut to what should be done to promote word learning in our classrooms if we accept both the environmental opportunity and the cognitive efficiency hypotheses with a little modification. If we accepted both hypotheses, we'd want to provide our students with every opportunity for word growth in a word-rich environment while giving them strategies to harvest that environments' word crop. We could develop an ecology for vocabulary growth in our students and give them tools to prosper in it. If we knew what nurtured word-knowledge proliferation for our students, we could manipulate the environment to provide that nurturing or to create niches for word knowledge to thrive.

As noted, exposure to a word-enriched environment alone may not lead to its efficient uptake and use. Internalized strategies can have a strong facilitating effect on word learning and knowledge acquisition (Sternberg, 1987, 1988). Researchers (Pressley, 2000) have shown that strategic instruction can improve student reading and learning from texts.

We know that learning individual target words does improve comprehension when those words are related to the material that students are reading (Beck, McKeown, & Omanson, 1987). Pressley (2000) believes that more evidence favors vocabulary instruction than mitigates against it.

## Fostering Word Consciousness

While immersing students in word-rich environments, making students active learners of words, personalizing their word learning, and repeatedly exposing students to new words all contribute to vocabulary instruction, we can also foster "word consciousness" in other ways. To Anderson and Nagy (1992), consciousness of words includes both awareness of them and interest in learning them. Word consciousness motivates word learning. To foster word consciousness Graves and Watts-Taffe (2002) make several specific recommendations that can be integrated into daily instruction:

♦ *Model, recognize, and encourage attention to word usage.*   You are a model of the importance of words and how they are used whenever you communicate with your students. You can acknowledge the challenge of new words in reading assignments and in students' use of words in their speaking and writing. You can also encourage your students to become more aware of how they use words to convey their perceptions and understanding of concepts in your content area. Implementing "The Daily Word" demonstrates your attention to the importance of words and their proficient use. Words speak volumes.

♦ *Promote word play.*   Your enjoyment of words, their sounds, and their use contribute to a word-aware environment in your classroom. No matter what discipline you teach, words are actors. They strut and struggle across the stage of every classroom. Awareness of the verbal tricks those actors play in puns, cliches, metaphors, and inappropriate applications add significant dimensions of understanding and humor to teaching. Encouraging your students to play with words provides opportunities for them to discover the character of words and the myriad of roles they play.

♦ *Involve students in investigations.*   When students embark on an original investigation or research an aspect of the discipline you teach, they can be encouraged to pay special attention to vocabulary. Students can watch for ways different authors writing about the same topic use words differently to convey meaning. For example, students could attend to less familiar words encountered during their discovery. If investigating a current event, students can discover how writers published in two or three different newspapers or magazines use different words to describe and to analyze it. A student might tally the number of unfamiliar words in each article and reflect on the significance of those differences. *The American Heritage Word Frequency Book* (Carroll, Davies, & Richman, 1971) would facilitate their tallying of less frequently used words.

## GAINING WORD KNOWLEDGE THROUGH STRATEGY INSTRUCTION: PLANNING FOR SECONDARY SCHOOL WORD LEARNING

Knowing, as we do, the importance of vocabulary growth and instruction to the development of students' knowledge base and content area, what can we do to enhance their opportunities to gain word knowledge both in school and out of school?

To introduce word-learning strategies that can be used in either middle or high school classrooms, I will describe instructional decisions I would make if I were teaching a ninth-grade world history class. I'm assuming that students in my class of 30 range in reading ability from fourth to eleventh grade; that they come from many cultural backgrounds, including African-American, Hispanic, and Asian; and that their motivation is, so to speak, all over the map. A few of these students are academic achievers, several are pleasant but quietly passive, and some are completely disidentified with school.

The text we use for world history is chronologically organized. The social studies department selected it three years ago. It is written at about the ninth-grade level (which is beyond the reach of some struggling readers in the class) and has been well designed by a staff of specialists and teachers providing clearly written prose accompanied by colorful supporting pictures, end of chapter questions, and a glossary. From past years of teaching, I know that if I just assign a section of the text to read, very few students will come to class having read the assignment. Many students find the text inaccessible, "boring," or both in spite of its lively writing style. I have learned that one of the major problems many students have with the text is their limited vocabularies. The text, though written at about a ninth-grade level, is at a frustration level for more than a third of my students, some of whom are English language learners. Many others need instructional support to comprehend it. Very few can read it independently with reasonable comprehension.

Some of my teaching colleagues have more or less given up on using the text. Instead, they lecture. They require students to take notes. Some have students read out loud to each other and paraphrase the text. Others use videos that parallel the text's content and discuss the videos with students. But these approaches do little to build weaker students' reading capacity or vocabulary.

In my first year, I was stunned to discover that most of my ninth graders were reading on the fifth-grade level, some on the third- or fourth-grade levels. Reading the social studies text was frustrating for them because they simply didn't have the reading tools to understand what they read. But I learned that I could help many of them if I gave them lots of support, "scaffolding," and some pre-reading vocabulary instruction.

To make the text more accessible, I'd begin by working out a vocabulary instruction program for the first two or three months of the school year. I'd review my teaching goals and standards and the material students would be reading. Based on a review of that material, I'd make decisions about which vocabulary I thought my ninth graders would find unfamiliar. Then I'd create two categories of words: Those I thought would be essential to the students' understanding of the texts to be assigned and those I considered less essential. I'd also provide student with the opportunity to let me know which words they know and want to know by using a Word-Knowledge Check and a Vocabulary Self-Collection Strategy (VSS). These strategies are described later in this chapter.

## Addressing Vocabulary

To demonstrate how I would address vocabulary instruction, I will assume that I'm to teach a part of the chapter in the text covering ancient Greece. That chapter includes not only sections on the rise of Athens, Greek government, and war and conflict between Greece and her neighbors, it also includes a section on Greek art, culture, and philosophy. I'm going to focus on the art, culture, and philosophy section to illustrate vocabulary instruction.

To help make these vocabulary instruction choices, I would keep in mind Allen's (1999) 10 decision-making questions:

1. Which words are most important to understanding the text?
2. How much prior knowledge will students have about this word or related concept?
3. Is the word encountered frequently?

4. Does the word have multiple meanings?
5. Is the concept significant and does it therefore require pre-teaching?
6. Which words can students figure out from context?
7. Can some words be grouped together to enhance understanding of a concept?
8. What strategies could I use to help students integrate the concept (and related words) into their lives?
9. How can I make repeated exposures to the word/concept possible, productive, and even pleasant?
10. How can I help students use the word/concept in meaningful ways in multiple contexts?

Keeping these guidelines in mind, I went through the section they were to read on arts and philosophy to identify essential and less essential words. Essential words I defined as those required to grasp the central ideas and concepts presented in the reading. So I got my essential list together:

> *Acropolis, polis, politics, culture, philosophy, systems of thought, adhere, tragedy,* and *comedy.*

Under less essential words I grouped those that I thought most students would recognize or that were not necessary for them to comprehend the basic information given. My less essential list of words (and concepts) that I could teach while we discussed the reading or afterward included:

> *Architecture, Parthenon, Athena, cutting-edge, philosopher, Socrates, Pericles, government, prefer, mask,* and *scholar.*

After a first reading of the text, students could add unfamiliar words to the list through the Vocabulary Self-Collection Strategy or VSS (Haggard, 1982, 1986). I'd suspect that some words I selected for the less essential list would appear on students' VSS lists.

After deciding on the vocabulary I thought was essential for my students to understand an upcoming reading on Greek culture, I had a reservoir of strategies to draw upon: a Word-Knowledge Check, the keyword method, word maps, word parts, interconnected concepts, and crossword puzzles.

## Word-Knowledge Check

A **_Word-Knowledge Check_** is a technique to let you know how well your students know certain words. Researchers (Dale, 1965; Paribakht & Wesche, 1997) have hypothesized several stages of word knowledge that are reflected in a Word-Knowledge Check's five levels of word awareness. (See Table 4.2.) Because I selected words and concepts that I suspected my students would not know, using a Word-Knowledge Check will confirm or correct my hunches. I would ask students to look over the words and tell me their level of familiarity with each word.

## Keyword Method

Pressley and his associates (Pressley, Levin, & Delaney, 1983; Pressley, Levin, & McDaniel, 1987) have developed and empirically verified the effectiveness of the

TABLE 4.2   A Word-Knowledge Check

|  | I never saw it before. | I heard it but don't know what it means. | I recognize it in context as related to something I know. | I know it well. | I can use it in a sentence. |
|---|---|---|---|---|---|
| polis |  |  |  |  |  |
| politics |  |  |  |  |  |
| culture |  |  |  |  |  |
| philosophy |  |  |  |  |  |
| systems of thought |  |  |  |  |  |
| adhere |  |  |  |  |  |
| tragedy |  |  |  |  |  |
| comedy |  |  |  |  |  |

mnemonic keyword method. ***Mnemonic*** means a systematic procedure designed to improve memory use. Although the method was first designed to help second-language learners acquire vocabulary (Atkinson, 1975), the ***keyword method*** works well in helping native speakers learn new words in their mother tongue.

The process can be broken down into three steps: recoding, relating, and retrieving.

1. When *recoding,* you select part of the unknown word that looks or sounds like a word you know. For example, I would like to learn the vocabulary word *adhere* and notice that the word sounds like "add here."
2. When *relating,* you relate the recoded word to the unknown word's definition using some image. I imagine adding Post-its that say "here" on them to an ad for glue.
3. When *retrieving,* you need to think of the keyword for the newly learned word. When I see the word *adhere,* I would picture the image of those Post-its being added to the glob, reminding me that adhere means to stick to something or to obey.

## Word Maps

I would use three kinds of word maps with these ninth-grade students, and I'd use them with younger and older students as well: Question Map, Structured Overview, and Concept Mastery Map.

A ***Question Map*** allows students, perhaps working in small groups, to generate questions about important words and concepts. Students can list any and all questions they have about an unknown or unfamiliar word or concept and have no concern about being wrong. As an example, I elected to work with the word *philosophy,* a word so full of juice for me that I had to pick it. So my Question Map

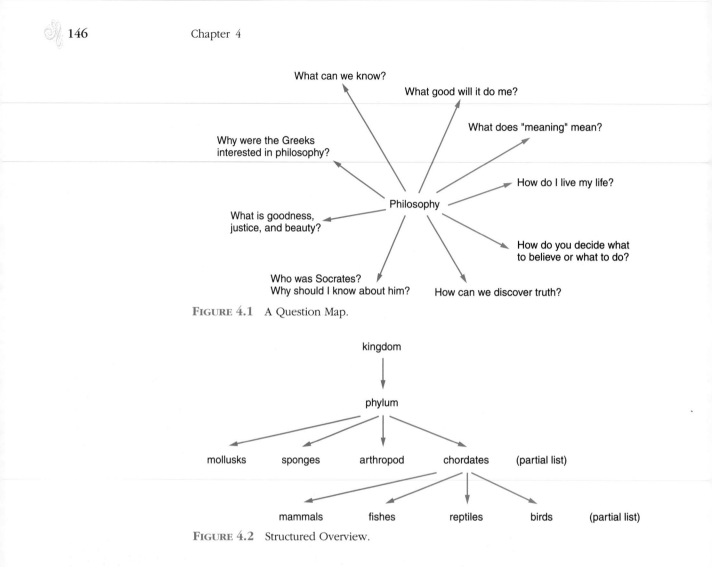

**FIGURE 4.1**    A Question Map.

**FIGURE 4.2**    Structured Overview.

(Figure 4.1) presents the kinds of questions I suspect students would generate, along with several that I would add.

A **_Structured Overview_** is for concepts that have subordinate and superordinate relationships, like the concept _phylum_ used to exemplify this kind of map in Figure 4.2. To practice this method of organizing the relationships between concepts, you could create a structured overview for this chapter. It would show how concepts are organized and presented. Some writers and readers find that graphically organizing material in this way after reading about it or before writing about it serves them well.

A **_Concept Mastery Map_** graphically presents information about a word or concept, how it interrelates with other knowledge, and how you might integrate it with memory enhancing features. Its oval or circular format suggests how concept mastery is interrelated with many forms of knowledge. The rectangles to be filled in around the oval or circle going clock wise from high noon include:

- Concept (or word) and its dictionary definition,
- Example from reading or real life,
- Original sentence using word,

- ◆ Antonym,
- ◆ Word origin,
- ◆ Synonym,
- ◆ A situation in which you'd use the concept or word, and
- ◆ Something you'd like to know about the concept or word.

The format and an example using the concept of *comedy* are in Figure 4.3.

## Word Parts

Knowing roots, prefixes, and suffixes helps readers learn unfamiliar words (Baumann et al., 2002; Nagy & Anderson, 1984). Researchers (Nagy & Scott, 2000) have also found that it contributes to reading ability through the high school level. To help students understand how words are created, you can focus on word parts (prefixes, suffixes, and roots) when studying new words and show them how parts of one word may appear in many other words.

While the effects of teaching word parts appears to degrade over time (Baumann et al., 2002), we know that knowledge of morphemes is important to vocabulary growth. I took Latin in high school, and, while I was far from a fluid translator of Caesar's *Gallic Wars*, I did learn enough Latin vocabulary to help me understand several English word roots and prefixes. Thompson (1958) combined 14 roots and 20 prefixes into 14 "master words" that, if mastered, provide readers with a useful set of roots and prefixes that apply to over 14,000 words in *Webster's Collegiate Dictionary*. (See Table 4.3.)

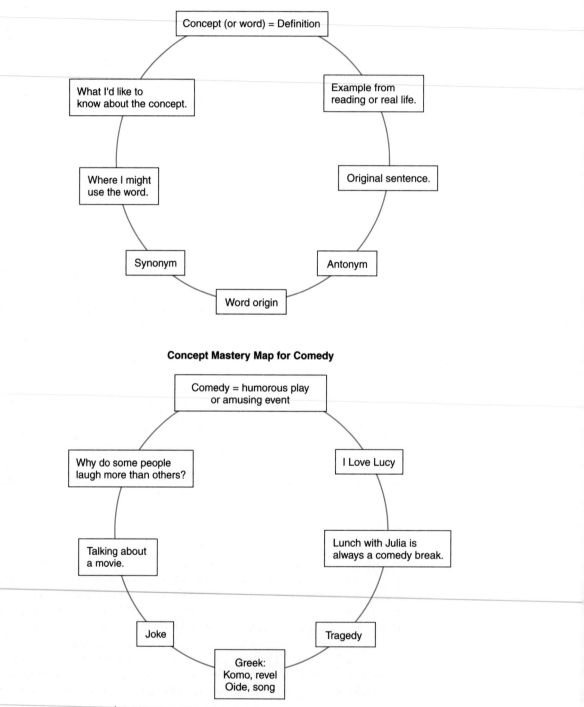

**Concept Mastery Map**

Concept (or word) = Definition

What I'd like to know about the concept.

Example from reading or real life.

Where I might use the word.

Original sentence.

Synonym

Antonym

Word origin

**Concept Mastery Map for Comedy**

Comedy = humorous play or amusing event

Why do some people laugh more than others?

I Love Lucy

Talking about a movie.

Lunch with Julia is always a comedy break.

Joke

Tragedy

Greek: Komo, revel Oide, song

FIGURE 4.3   Concept Mastery Map.

TABLE 4.3   Fourteen Words: Keys to the Meaning of 14,000 Words

| Word | Prefix | Common Meaning | Root | Common Meaning |
|------|--------|----------------|------|----------------|
| 1. aspect | Ad-/As- | (to, toward) | Specere | (see) |
| 2. detain | De- | (away, down) | Tenere | (hold, have) |
| 3. epilogue | Epi- | (upon) | Legein | (say, study of) |
| 4. indisposed | In- Dis- | (into) (apart, not) | Ponere (pos) | (put, place) |
| 5. insist | In- | (into) | Stare | (stand) |
| 6. intermittent | Inter- | (between, among) | Mittere | (sent) |
| 7. mistranscribe | Mis- Trans- | (wrong) (across, beyond) | Scribere | (write) |
| 8. monograph | Mono- | (alone, one) | Graphein | (write) |
| 9. nonextended | Non- Ex- | (not) (out, beyond) | Tendere | (stretch) |
| 10. offer | Ob- | (against) | Ferre | (bear, carry) |
| 11. oversufficient | Over- Sub- | (above) (under) | Facere | (make, do) |
| 12. precept | Pre | (before) | Capere | (take, seize) |
| 13. reproduction | Re- Pro- | (back, again) (forward, for) | Ducere | (lead) |
| 14. uncomplicated | Un- Com- | (not) (with) | Plicare | (fold) |

*Source:* Adapted from Thompson, E. (1958). News, Letters, and Notes: The Master Word Approach to Vocabulary Training. *Journal of Developmental Reading, 2,* 62–66.

You can also teach word parts on an ad hoc basis in your content area. If you have texts with words that are unknown to your students and that have Latin or Greek roots or word parts, that could be the time for you to teach those word parts to your students. For example, in the text on Greek history that I've imagined teaching to ninth graders, I would teach students about the roots of several important words: *philosophy, polis, politics, acropolis, comedy,* and *tragedy.*

In this lesson with so many of the words having their origin in Greek, going to the roots seems a natural instructional step. Philosophy comes directly from the Greek words *philos,* meaning friendly, dear, or loving, and *sophia,* meaning wisdom, which together mean a lover of wisdom. Polis means a Greek city-state, and politics (the art of government) has its root in polis. Acropolis also has its root in polis with *acr-,* meaning topmost or beginning, in front of it, just like *acr*ophobia, or fear of heights. Comedy finds its root in the Greek words for revel, *komo,* and song, *oide.* Tragedy comes from two Greek words: *tragos,* meaning goat, and *oide,* which you now know means song, or put together mean "goat song." Some scholars believe that tragedy had its roots in Dionysian rituals that involved the hero's becoming a "scapegoat," a sacrifice to cleanse or purify the community of evil.

I happen to like words a lot (Would you have guessed?) and believe that teaching word parts can help students improve their reading and ability to learn more effectively. So teaching the origins of words and how they work in our language is a pleasure for me. However, I've noticed that all my students have not always resonated with that pleasure even though I have tried to ignite a similar pleasure in them. You'll have to discover how word-part instruction in your content area teaching can best contribute to your students' knowledge and their word consciousness.

## Vocabulary Self-Collection Strategy (VSS)

The main purpose of VSS is to enable students to integrate new content words into their vocabularies (Haggard, 1982). Students identify and select words they want to know because those words are important for understanding a passage or because of their curiosity.

## STEP-BY-STEP: *Vocabulary Self-Collection Strategy (VSS)*

**STEP 1.** You can begin VSS instruction after any learning event, especially after your students have read a text for the first time. When using VSS, I ask my students to note the words they want to learn as they read. I also explain that they or a team with which they work will nominate a certain number of those words and that many of them will appear on the vocabulary list related to their reading. In this way, students feel they have some control over what they will learn. I also explain that I can nominate a certain number of words. The number of words I ask students to nominate depends upon the density of unfamiliar words in the text being read. However, as a rule of thumb, I ask individuals or groups to select about five words.

**STEP 2.** Whether I have individuals or groups submitting VSS words, I ask students to answer several questions (Ruddell, 2001):

2.1. Where did you find the word? (Please provide page number and sentence.)

2.2. What do you think the word means in the context?

2.3. Why do you think the class should learn this word? (or) What is the importance of this word to the topic we are reading about?

**STEP 3.** If working in teams, students can answer the above three questions for words the team selects and report to the whole class about those words.

**STEP 4.** After I review all the submissions, I select a reasonable and representative number of words for our class list. Alternatively, you can set up a system whereby each team has control over the number of words that will join the list, such as two, and you can also contribute two. If you have about five teams, you will wind up with 12 vocabulary words.

## Activities to Master VSS and Other Important Words

You can use some of the activities I have already described, such as the keyword method, word maps, and word parts, to help students learn more about the vocabulary words obtained from the VSS exercise. Knowing that a variety of techniques and repeated exposures in learning new words show benefits (Beck & McKeown, 1991), you can incorporate other activities into your lessons that have research support. Researchers (Blachowicz & Fisher, 2000) have confirmed the benefits of semantic relatedness techniques, including semantic maps, synonym webs, and semantic feature analysis.

Semantic maps.    Although the term ***semantic map*** often refers to any graphic organizer showing a relationship between words, I am using the term for a specific format that includes a theme or concept at the map's heart, important ideas or terms highlighted with boxes or circles, and lines connecting related ideas or concepts that are not hierarchically organized. When using semantic maps for vocabulary instruction, you control the terms and concepts for which your students will contribute related concepts and specific examples.

## STEP-BY-STEP: *Semantic Maps*

**STEP 1.** Before or after a first reading of a text, you write the word you want your students to explore in the center of a blackboard. If you want your students to integrate related words, write them on an adjacent board.

**STEP 2.** Talk with your students about the target word, its meanings, and its use in the text from which it came. Ask students what they know about the concept or word.

**STEP 3.** As your students generate related words, concepts, ideas, and examples, jot these down on the board. Add your own related ideas as your discussion with the class proceeds.

**STEP 4.** Ask your students to copy the semantic map into their notebooks or journals so they can add to it as their knowledge of the target word expands.

Once you have modeled semantic maps with your class, such as the example using the vocabulary word *architecture* (see Figure 4.4), you can ask students to try completing them on their own. You can start them on their way with a partially completed map they will use as a base for elaboration, and you can provide related words you would like them to integrate. As they become more adept at completing semantic maps, you can give them a target word and ask them to complete the map on their own.

Synonym webs.    While a semantic map includes all types of concepts related to the target word, a ***synonym web*** limits the exploration of semantic relationships only to words similar in meaning. When students are trying to learn words with multiple

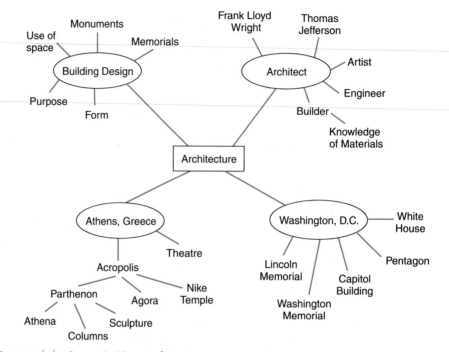

**FIGURE 4.4**    Semantic Map: Architecture.

meanings, words on our list such as ***adhere*** or ***systems,*** synonym webs are particularly helpful.

## STEP-BY-STEP: *Synonym Webs*

To have small groups construct synonym webs, I have adapted Blachowicz and Fisher's (1996) suggestions into the following steps:

**STEP 1.** Ask students working in teams of 3 or 4 to generate all the synonyms they can for the target word. Then have each team use a thesaurus to add to their team's list of synonyms.

**STEP 2.** Ask the team to categorize the words they listed. Each team should discover which words seem to cluster or cohere in some way. You can work with teams needing help with building categories. Students should be ready to explain how the meanings connect.

**STEP 3.** Each team makes a web to demonstrate patterns of relationship.

**STEP 4.** The teams present their web to the class.

**STEP 5.** Students, using their team's web as a base, extend that web with ideas presented by other teams. They copy their web and its extensions into their journals.

Figure 4.5 shows a possible synonym web for the word *system.*

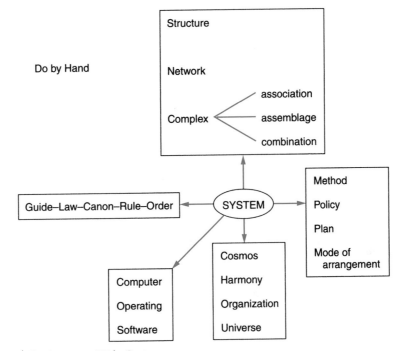

**FIGURE 4.5**   Synonym Web: System.

Semantic feature analysis.   As we saw in Chapter 2, readers use knowledge networks and structures (schemata) to help them make sense of their reading. These networks, if externalized, can show us how students organize knowledge about their world into categories. If we can get our students to activate and compare some of their existing categories with new or unfamiliar words and concepts they encounter, their learning of new words can be facilitated. However, there are many instructional variations of ***semantic feature analysis.*** What they all have in common is a grid with shared semantic features plotted against a list of related words. For example, features attributable to Greek gods are listed down the left-hand column and the names of several gods across the top. Notations in the columns indicate students' awareness of connections between features listed and Greek gods.

## STEP-BY-STEP: *Semantic Feature Analysis*

**STEP 1.** Select a category. A likely candidate for a unit on ancient Greek civilization is a category like mythology.

**STEP 2.** You then generate names of concepts or objects related to the category. Eventually, students should help in this step. In the case of mythology, I might suggest words like *Aphrodite*, *Athena*, *Eros*, *Hades*, *Hermes*, *Poseidon*, *Prometheus*, and *Zeus*. These names are placed at the top of each column.

**TABLE 4.4** Semantic Feature Analysis: Identity of the Gods

| | Names of Greek Gods | | | | | | | |
|---|---|---|---|---|---|---|---|---|
| **Features** | **Aphrodite** | **Athena** | **Eros** | **Hades** | **Hermes** | **Poseidon** | **Prometheus** | **Zeus** |
| **Titan (Elder gods)** | — | — | — | — | — | — | ✔ | — |
| **One of the 12 Olympians** | ✔ | ✔ | — | ✔ | — | ✔ | — | ✔ |
| **One of the "lesser" Olympian gods** | — | — | ✔ | — | — | — | — | — |
| **Supreme ruler** | — | — | — | — | — | — | — | ✔ |
| **Of no mother born** | — | ✔ | — | — | — | — | — | — |
| **Immortal** | ✔ | ✔ | ✔ | ✔ | ✔ | ✔ | ✔ | ✔ |
| **Brought fire to earth** | — | — | — | — | — | — | ✔ | — |
| **Married** | — | — | — | ✔ | ? | ? | ? | ✔ |
| **Messenger of the gods** | — | — | — | — | ✔ | — | — | — |
| **Ruler of the Underworld** | — | — | — | ✔ | — | — | — | — |
| **Guide of the dead to the Underworld** | — | — | — | — | ✔ | — | — | — |

**STEP 3.** You next list in lines to the left of the columns features attributable to the concepts or objects identified in the previous step. For our example, one or more of the gods are: immortal, married, one of the 12 Olympians, of no mother born, and so on.

**STEP 4.** Students put "+" signs where connections occur, "–" signs where they don't, and "?" where students are uncertain.

Table 4.4 shows an example of a semantic feature analysis on the identity of Greek gods.

## GROWING WORD KNOWLEDGE: JUST READING

"What is needed to produce vocabulary growth is not more vocabulary instruction but more reading," wrote Nagy (1988b). That need for more reading is pursued here; however, I'll encourage some further vocabulary instruction to increase the likelihood that more words will be learned.

I'd like to begin this discussion about promoting vocabulary growth by focusing on general word knowledge development through just reading and the impediments of struggling readers. From the fifth grade on, avid readers process millions of words each year. The California Department of Education's *English-Language Arts Content Standards* (1998) call for students in the eighth grade to read one million words on their own in addition to books read for their English class. By the twelfth grade, the Standards call for students to read two million words on their own besides class assignments. According to Stanovich (1993), reading volume is an "explanatory variable" that predicts cognitive outcomes and trends.

Why does reading build vocabulary knowledge? More exposure to moderate- and low-frequency words occurs in reading material more often than in speech, including TV and radio talk (Hayes, 1988). And that reading is a source for lower frequency words that contribute to better performance on vocabulary tests. For many researchers, reading is a more potent source for vocabulary growth than oral language exposure (TV, radio, etc.). Most of one's vocabulary appears to be learned outside of school. In school or out, talking is "no substitute for reading" (Stanovich, 1993).

To appreciate the potential value of reading to develop vocabulary over watching a film adaptation of the same novel, let's look at what Baines (1996) discovered when he compared the language of three novels with their film versions. The novels he selected have been required reading over the past 35 years in the secondary English curriculum, and the film versions of those novels have been widely acclaimed. Baines found that what gets reduced when a novel moves from page to screen is the number of polysyllabic words, the complexity of sentence structure, the amount of lexical diversity, and the complexity of dialogue, plot, character, and theme.

While all of these reductions should be of concern, we are especially interested in lost vocabulary. To illustrate the kinds of loss in lexical diversity and polysyllabic words, we're going to focus on *To Kill a Mockingbird* by Harper Lee. The information in Table 4.5 provides a measure of the total number of different words found in a 2,500 word sample from the novel and from the film script and the number of one-, two-, and three-or-more-syllable words from novel and script. A similar pattern appeared for samples of both *Wuthering Heights* and *Of Mice and Men*.

Another indicator of lexical diversity can be found in the number of different words beginning with different letters. Table 4.6 shows the number of words beginning with the letter U in the samples of 2,500 words from the script and from the novel.

With film's reliance on visual image and condensed dialogue to convey information, the language of novels gets condensed, simplified, or eliminated. With reduced lexical diversity and more familiar monosyllabic words, viewers of the film who eschewed the book would have had few, if any, chances to gain word knowledge.

Print exposure is associated with vocabulary knowledge and the growth of general knowledge (Stanovich, 1993). Reading appears to be an "uniquely efficacious way of acquiring vocabulary" and serves as an "unparalled" tool for building content

TABLE 4.5   Lexical Diversity and Polysyllabic Words in *To Kill a Mockingbird*

| Title | Lexical Diversity* | One-syllable | Two-syllable | Three-or-more Syllable |
|---|---|---|---|---|
| *To Kill a Mockingbird* (novel) | 870 | 148 | 568 | 154 |
| *To Kill a Mockingbird* (film script) | 642 | 259 | 316 | 67 |

*Number of different words in a 2,500 word sample.

**TABLE 4.6**   The Letter U Beginning Words in *To Kill a Mockingbird*

| Script | | Novel | | |
|---|---|---|---|---|
| ugly | upstairs | unceiled | unique | upon |
| under | us | uncontrollable | unless | upstairs |
| until | used | uncrossed | unlighted | us |
| up | | under | unpainted | use |
| | | undress | until | used |
| | | unhitched | up | |

knowledge structures. As readers acquire content area knowledge, that knowledge contributes to their efficiency when processing information. Electronic sources (TV, radio) commonly lack both depth and conceptual richness provided by print. "Only print provides opportunities for acquiring broad and deep knowledge of the world," writes Stanovich (1993).

According to Stanovich (1993), most of the enormous differences in vocabulary knowledge between high- and low-performing students can be attributed to what students do outside of school—not in it. Non-school reading can account for most of the differences between successful and struggling readers, including differences in word knowledge. Summer break reading has accounted for more of the gap between high- and low-achieving students than in-school reading (Hayes & Grether, 1983).

"For unto every one that hath shall be given, and he shall have abundance; but from him that hath not shall be taken away even that which he hath." That line from the Gospel, according to Matthew, provides the allusion for what Stanovich (1986) has called the "Matthew effects." Students who have already acquired reading skills and extensive word knowledge have a strong base on which to build. Students with few skills and less word knowledge must try to learn with what they have in spite of their overall tendency to fall farther behind. It's a "rich-get-richer, poor-get-poorer" scenario, and Stanovich provides ample evidence to support the Matthew effects allegation.

As teachers, we have the challenge of reversing the downward spiral of struggling readers who frequently find themselves enmeshed in reading materials that are too difficult for them to use as a source for learning in our classes. Much of that difficulty arises from low-frequency, content area vocabulary that impedes their efforts to comprehend.

However, immersion in literature and reading may not be the best pathway to gaining extensive word knowledge. Some students can read avidly but make only minor gains in vocabulary if they have little inclination to understand words they don't know. Many bright and avid readers with good comprehension show only mild interest in independently pursuing the meanings of unfamiliar words in novels they read, including those required for their honors and Advanced Placement English courses. Context doesn't seem to provide sufficient cueing for these students to discover a word's meaning. They may also lack strategies to take words apart or resources to discover their meanings. So, given that immersion itself doesn't lead directly to word-knowledge growth, we'd best look for ways to help students acquire strategies that could make their vocabulary acquisition while roaming in the orchards of independent reading more fruitful.

Fortunately, strategies for the acquisition of vocabulary through independent reading have been developed. Some are rather basic, others quite complex. We'll review both. You can decide which approaches you can offer for your students' use.

## Word Play: Language Games in Contexts

More than half a century ago, Gray (1946) had a superb moment of synthesis. He pulled together several strategies that he believed could help a reader figure out the meaning of a word when encountered in a text. Gray labeled the four-step method simply *CSSD: Context, Structure, Sound, and Dictionary.* What Gray encouraged was an early form of metalinguistic awareness or word consciousness, including the ability to reflect on and manipulate language structures (Nagy & Scott, 2000). To figure out the meaning of an unknown word, Gray recommended that readers first look for cues in the context of the text that would contribute to figuring out the word's meaning. Second, readers should attend to the word's structure, looking for roots, prefixes, or suffixes that could provide clues to meaning. Third, readers should sound out the word in hopes of triggering like-sounding known words. And lastly, readers can use a dictionary to discover meaning. But do good readers use a system like this to detect the meanings of unknown words when reading?

## Looking Closely at Students Constructing Word Meanings

When Harmon (2000) listened carefully to think-alouds that revealed how avid middle school readers figured out the meaning of unfamiliar words encountered in independent novel reading, she discovered they did not use the same problem-solving pattern each time they encountered an unknown word. Each approach was unique and engaged various strategies in non-linear order. First, she found that students she listened to drew more upon a text's immediate context and events (bottom-up) rather than upon more global (top-down) background knowledge to figure out words. Second, when they used content connections, which they did in nearly every unknown word instance to discover word meanings, they focused on immediate events and on language structures much more often than they applied ideas beyond the text. Third, they used word-level analysis, that is, looking at word parts, while attending to context determiners of meaning. Fourth, syntax proved to be an essential cueing element to help these students discover unknown word meanings. Fifth, they frequently used synonyms as substitutions for unknown words and often found that strategy enhanced their incidental word learning. And as a last resort, these young readers used a dictionary when they were baffled or, in a couple of instances, to confirm their guess. Most importantly for Harmon was her observation that these readers did not follow a sequential use of strategies, as Gray's CSSD sequence seemed to urge.

Harmon (2000) found that these students used a variety of strategies on a highly personal or idiosyncratic basis. They did not use the same approach to unknown words repeatedly but approached each unknown uniquely. While one of these students did use orthographic clues to help her figure out by analogy what a word might mean, the sound of unknown words seemed to be of little importance to them. The implication for instruction we could derive from Harmon's work is that students need not or should not be expected to apply unknown word discovery strategies in any rigid or sequential order. We would be wiser to help them build a repertoire of strategies that they can evoke on a case-by-case basis.

## Using Context Efficiently

To move in the direction of helping students learn an assortment of strategies to discover word meanings, I'm going to focus on context for two reasons: First, students apparently learn more words from context than we could ever teach them explicitly and, second, we have learned more about how readers' minds work when extracting meaning from context. If we can teach our students how to improve their use of context to gain word knowledge, they can become more effective independent word learners for life.

Much of what I have to explain to you about context comes from the work that Robert Sternberg has done on verbal intelligence. He has constructed a componential theory of verbal intelligence that includes three parts: information-processing components, context cues, and moderating variables. Sternberg's (1985; Sternberg & Powell, 1983) research has both confirmed this theory and found that it serves as a foundation for training students in using context to learn words. However, other researchers (Beck & McKeown, 1991) have reported that studies of instruction in using context to derive word meanings have revealed that those skills are not easily influenced but that the procedures deserve further study because of their importance.

*Information-processing components.* I've written the following paragraph to present an unfamiliar word (for some) in a context that could contribute to discovery of the word's meaning.

> *As night settled over the dark mansion on the hill, the necromancer gathered all the deceased mother's relatives in the library. He lit the candles and pulled the thick curtains shut. If only he could contact her and bring her into the room, he told them, they might convince her to release her son from the madness into which he had descended.*

In accord with Sternberg's theory, when you encounter unfamiliar or new words like *necromancer*, three different knowledge acquisition processes apply.

First, you separate irrelevant from relevant information in pursuit of a meaningful definition of a new word. This process is called ***selective encoding.*** Although the meaning of *necromancer* isn't directly related to lighting candles or shutting curtains or night falling, you would be on target in giving relevance to summoning the spirits of the dead and trying to release a young man from the grip of madness.

Second, you combine as many of the relevant cues as you can into a working definition. That's called ***selective combination.*** The business of summoning a spirit of the dead and asking it (her?) to influence the state of mind of her son are relevant elements that need to be combined to figure out the meaning of *necromancer.*

Third, you connect new word knowledge with old knowledge in a process called ***selective comparison.*** You may have stored away in memory some remembrance of eerie things past, like the summoning of the dead to communicate with them in the hope of discovering something about the future or of influencing its outcome. Several novels and movies use such devices to forward their narratives.

That activated memory would help you conclude or confirm what a necromancer does—or, better yet, is supposed to do.

Context cues.    In the minds of good readers, there are eight cues that operate on the three information-processing components just discussed (Sternberg, 1987). When I first read about them, I realized that many of my students and I use these cues without thinking about them or without having a name for them. I'll present them here and talk about how you could help your students learn about them and their use after:

1. *Temporal cues* relating to the duration or frequency of the unknown word or the time at which the word can occur (Our necromancer worked at dusk but isn't restricted to dusk-only spirit summoning);
2. *Spatial cues* indicating where the word could exist or occur (Our necromancer works in a mansion but, if he were really good at his work, he could probably work in an outhouse);
3. *Value cues* suggesting the worth or attitudes related to the word (This necromancer could help a troubled person and his family);
4. *Descriptive cues* that convey the word's physical properties (size, weight, smell, color, etc.) (Necromancers are usually in human form, but with improved robotics, who knows?);
5. *Function cues* providing information about the unknown word's purposes or what it can do (Our necromancer apparently rouses spirits of the dead and asks them to do things);
6. *Causal/Enabling cues* that relate what could cause the word to occur or enable it to exist (Our necromancer apparently has gone to work because of a young man's madness and a family's concern about it);
7. *Class membership cues* give information about the categories to which an unknown word might belong (This necromancer clearly isn't a fish or a quarterback as much as he's a conjuror); and
8. *Equivalence cues* that tell us what the word is similar to (synonyms) or different from (antonyms).

To help students learn about these cues, you can play "Twenty Questions" with unknown vocabulary words in context. You're familiar with the usual first "Twenty Questions" question: Is it animal, vegetable, or mineral? To apply "Twenty Questions" to the discovery of word meanings, players can ask the following questions based on the eight context cues:

1. When does Y (unknown word) happen? or How long does Y go on when it happens?
2. Where does Y exist or occur?
3. What value does Y have?
4. If it has them, what are Y's physical properties?
5. What does Y do, if anything?
6. What causes or enables Y to occur?
7. Into what categories does Y fall or fit?
8. To what words is Y similar or different?

The possibility of answering questions like these depends on several moderating variables, such as the number of cues arising from the context that contribute to making a good guess about an unknown word's meaning.

**Moderating variables.**    Sternberg (1987) also found several ***moderating variables*** that can make it easier or harder to apply encoding, combining, and comparing information about words in context to the eight context cues.

1. If the unknown word occurs more than once, the number and usefulness of context cues increases. (Necromancer occurred only once in the passage.)
2. If the unknown word appears in multiple contexts (in different subject matter, for example), more context cues are likely to occur and contribute to word meaning discoveries. (Necromancer occurred in only one context.)
3. If an unknown word is critical to comprehending a passage, a reader's motivation to understand the word is heightened. (Knowing the meaning of necromancer wasn't critical to comprehending the passage, but that knowledge might have helped a reader understand the passage more fully.)
4. If cues in context are distant from the unknown word, they are less likely to be seen as relevant and therefore less likely to be selected for encoding. (Cues in the necromancer passage are quite close to the "unknown" word.)
5. If a text contains many unknown words, the reader may not be able to discern which cues are relevant to which unknown words. (You probably had no problem understanding any of the other words in the necromancer passage and may not even had a problem with the "unknown" word.)
6. If the reader has background knowledge related to a context cue, that knowledge could enable the reader to use the cue more productively in figuring out the word's meaning. (If a reader had read books or seen movies that contained necromancy, then figuring out the meaning of necromancer from the context would be facilitated.)

## Applying Theory to Practice to Teach Learning from Context

Sternberg (1987) doubts that any effort to teach the learning of words from contexts will have any significant effect unless we apply two principles:

1. *Students must learn how to learn from context so they can teach themselves.* They need to understand how information processes, context cues, and moderating variables influence word learning from contexts before they can do it on their own. And they must learn to do it on their own because you and I cannot possibly teach them every word they need to know. We know from research that students learn between 2,000 and 3,000 words and more each year. That's a long vocabulary list to test every Friday of every school year.

2. *Students must be convinced that learning how to use context to figure out the meaning of words is worthwhile to them.* You might explain to them that every moment of their lives is lived in contexts, and they might want to figure out what's going on in those contexts because, if they do, they may perform a lot better. One way to figure out what's going on in the context of reading is to learn how to discover the unknowns, the black holes, when in that context. As Sternberg (1987) put it when asked why context was so effective for learning from everyday life, "Because context, whether verbal or otherwise, forms the milieu in which we live. We need to learn from it to survive, or to survive well."

To these two principles a third principle based on Harmon's (2000) work on detecting unknown word meanings should be added:

3. *Use strategies flexibly rather than in a linear sequence.* Harmon's research revealed that, for students in her study, each unknown word presents a fresh learning challenge that calls for unique strategy applications. No two unknown word puzzles are alike, nor are two discovery solutions the same.

## Handing Context Tools to Students

Sternberg (1985) designed a six-lesson training intervention to help high school students use context to decipher the meanings of unfamiliar words. The intervention focused on the following seven topics:

1. Students learned about context and how to use it to discover the meaning of unfamiliar words.
2. Students learned from examples how context could be used in a variety of ways to gain word knowledge.
3. Using the game "Twenty Questions," students learned informally about context cues and how to spot them. With sentences containing unknown words, students tried to figure out a word's meaning by generating and answering questions.
4. After becoming aware of context cueing through "Twenty Questions," students learned about four specific cues: temporal, spatial, descriptive, and equivalence. Then, practicing what they learned, they tried to figure out the meaning of unknown words that were embedded in example sentences.
5. Students next learned how to paraphrase sentences that contained unknown words. By reprocessing such sentences, students had to grapple with likely unknown word meaning.
6. Students learned about two more cues, function and causal/enabling, and practiced figuring out unknown words using those kinds of cues.
7. Students applied all they had learned to discovering the meaning of mystery words, neologism, embedded in sentences and paragraphs.

Sternberg and his colleagues then compared the performance of the trained students with a control group and found that the trained students did significantly better in pre- to post-testing.

This six-lesson training program for teaching students to use context effectively could serve as a model. It could be adapted to literacy programs in middle or high school and reinforced throughout the curriculum so that students would be reminded of its usefulness in all content area reading.

In the next section on the use of cloze passages, I will introduce to you a method to help students learn more about figuring out the meaning of unfamiliar words. The various cloze techniques provide opportunities for you to engage your students in discussions about strategy use in unknown word detection.

## Practicing Cloze Passages from Content Area Texts

Removing words from a passage and asking readers to "fill in the blank" is usually called a *cloze* procedure. Teachers use cloze passages with every fifth word removed to determine the difficulty of a text, a procedure described in Chapter 3.

When reading a cloze passage, readers use their knowledge of context, concepts, and strategies to create a meaningful passage. Students who successfully fill in more of the blanks are more likely to comprehend the larger text from which the passage came. However, you can use the cloze procedure to train students in the use of context to figure out unfamiliar words and improve comprehension. By so doing, students become empowered to build their own vocabularies and become better independent readers.

The three forms of cloze presented, regular cloze, zip cloze, and maze close, will provide you with an array of options to use with your students. Each cloze format can help your students become more aware of cues they could use to decipher a passage. These gains in awareness are more likely to accrue to your students if you can discuss their meaning-discovery process in class, identifying strategies applied as you proceed. You can make these strategies visible simply by asking your students to explain why they made the word choices they did for the blank spaces in the passages.

To facilitate classroom discussion of strategies used to discover possible meanings for omitted words in a cloze passage, I would suggest distributing copies of the passage to students AND making an overhead of the passage that you can project on a screen for all to see. First, let each student work independently on filling in the blank spaces. Then project the passage on the screen and ask for solutions. That's your chance to probe strategy use so that students can see what strategies worked and why they worked.

Regular cloze.    In a ***regular cloze*** passage, you can select significant content words for deletion, not every fifth word, from any book. It's important to choose interesting passages that have some degree of predictability so that your students will not be frustrated to distraction. Some students find cloze passages an interesting puzzle, but others find them very frustrating. How you present these cloze passages to your students will influence how they respond. Making it into a game-like discovery process works to their advantage.

Although I'm going to use a selection from a chemistry text to show you how cloze procedures can be used in all content classes, you have to keep in mind your students' reading capacities—as well as their word problem solving skills. You may want to begin with more high-interest, easy-reading texts from a magazine or newspaper related to your content field before diving into the text itself. That's going to be your judgment call.

The passage I've selected from a popular high school chemistry text (Wilbraham, Staley, Matta, & Waterman, 2000), ironically enough, happens to be headed "Word Equations." I've deleted content words, the discovery of which will require students to apply their knowledge of science.

> *Every minute of the day chemical _____ take place _____ both inside you and around you. After a meal, a series of complex chemical _____ take place as your body digests food. Likewise, plants use sunlight to drive the _____ processes needed to produce plant growth. Although the chemical _____ involved in _____ and digestion are quite different, both of these chemical _____ are necessary to sustain life. What are some other _____ necessary for life?*

Or for something a little more challenging for students who have gained more background knowledge:

*In water or aqueous solutions, hydrogen ions ($H^+$) are always joined to water molecules as _____ ions ($H_3O^+$). The _____ ions are themselves solvated to form species such as $H_9O_4^+$. Hydrogen ions in aqueous solutions have several names. Some chemists call them protons. Others prefer to call them hydrogen ions, _____ ions, or _____ protons. In this textbook, either $H^+$ or $H_3O^+$ is used to represent _____ ions in _____ solution.*

Zip cloze.    Readers, especially those struggling with challenging texts, sometimes become totally lost in a cloze passage. Their internal text representation simply doesn't consolidate. Under these frustrating conditions, readers may be unable to persevere. To help them, Blachowicz and Fisher (1996) suggest using ***zip cloze,*** a procedure named by second graders. Zip cloze is best used with an overhead of the passage that you plan to use. However, instead of leaving a blank space for a deleted word, you put a piece of masking tape over it. As the students discuss and discover which word works for a deleted word, you zip off the tape and reveal the correct word when they have guessed it. Students get immediate feedback and can use that information to help them guess other deleted words in the passage. Keep in mind, however, that discussing the strategies that students use to detect deleted words is central to this instruction. By the way, teams of students could prepare zip cloze overheads for use in class.

Maze cloze.    Students needing more structure and practice in discovering deleted words may benefit from maze cloze. With the ***maze cloze*** procedure, you provide students with several choices of possible words to make sensible meaning out of sentences in a passage. You can begin with highly predictable text passages and progress to more challenging ones from content area texts, like the first year algebra book on graphing systems of equations that I've used to develop this example:

If a system of two linear equations has no solution, then the graphs of the two equations must be (perpendicular, intersecting, parallel) lines.
If a system of two linear equations has exactly one solution, then the graphs of the two equations must be (perpendicular, intersecting, parallel) lines.
If a system of two equations has an infinite number of solutions, then the lines have the same (formula, slope, length) and x- and y-intercepts.

As with other cloze formats, discussing reasons for selecting specific words over others lies at the heart of the exercise. In the example of maze cloze with math, students can see how important background knowledge is to understanding the meaning of words, for without knowing the mathematics relevant to these statements, students could only guess which word works.

## A SUMMARY OF RESEARCH INFORMING INSTRUCTION IN VOCABULARY DEVELOPMENT

In condensing what we know about word learning so that knowledge could inform classroom instruction, I would have to include the following:

1. Word recognition and word knowledge are essential for a reader to construct meaning from texts.

2. Students acquire between 2,000 and 4,000 words per year during middle and high school.

3. Research has shown that several instructional techniques, such as keyword and semantic relatedness strategies, have significant effects on vocabulary learning.

4. Teachers cannot possibly teach as many words as students learn during their secondary school years.

5. Students learn many words incidentally by inferring meaning from context. To learn more than 3,000 words per year, students need to read between 500,000 and one million words.

6. Some research has shown that instruction in using context to improve word learning has significant effects.

7. Motivation, as well as cognition, is important to learning words. Word consciousness promotes motivation.

8. Educators are not sure about best practices for teaching word knowledge in middle and high school classrooms. Tension exists between those advocating just more reading and those advocating instructional intervention to build vocabulary directly.

From this digest of research information, what's a teacher in the content areas to do? Three general, overlapping teaching purposes emerge: (a) Foster word consciousness among your students. (b) Find and apply vocabulary building techniques that help students comprehend content area texts. (c) Encourage more independent reading while providing strategy instruction in gaining vocabulary.

## DOUBLE-ENTRY JOURNAL: After Reading

What are three concrete steps you could take to increase your students' awareness of words, especially in your content area? What strategies for heightening word awareness and word learning would you build into your instructional program? Explain why you think these strategies would work with your students in your subject.

Go to the Double-Entry Journal for Chapter 4 on our Companion Website at www.prenhall.com/unrau to complete your journal entry.

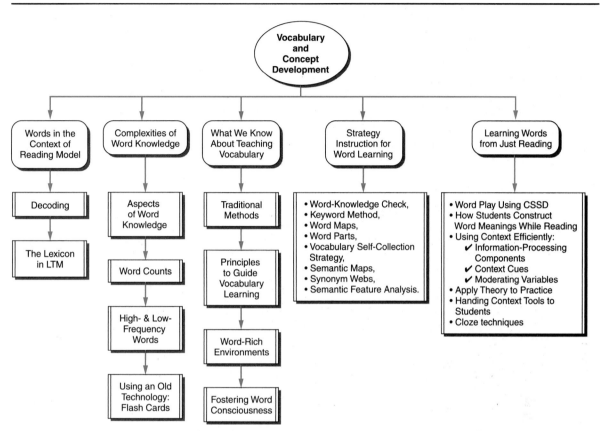

For exercises to clarify your understanding of the chapter content, visit the self-assessments for Chapter 4 on our Companion Website at www.prenhall.com/unrau

# References

Allen, J. (1999). *Words, words, words: Teaching vocabulary in grades 4–12*. York, ME: Stenhouse Publishers.

Anderson, R. C., & Freebody, P. (1981). Vocabulary knowledge. In J. T. Guthrie (Ed.), *Comprehension and teaching: Research reviews* (pp. 77–117). Newark, DE: International Reading Association.

Anderson, R. C., & Nagy, W. E. (1992, Winter). The vocabulary conundrum. *American Educator, 15,* 14–18, 44–47.

Atkinson, R. C. (1975). Mnemotechnics in second-language learning. *American Psychologist, 30,* 821–828.

Baines, L. (1996). From page to screen: When a novel is interpreted for film, what gets lost in translation? *Journal of Adolescent and Adult Literacy, 39,* 612–622.

Baumann, J., Edwards, E. C., Font, G., Tereshinski, C., Kame'enui, E. J., & Olejnik, S. (2002). Teaching morphemic and contextual analysis to fifth-grade students. *Reading Research Quarterly, 37*(2), 150–173.

Baumann, J. F., & Kaméenui, E. J. (1991). Research on vocabulary instruction: Ode to Voltaire. In J. Flood, J. M. Jensen, D. Lapp, & J. R. Squire (Eds.), *Handbook of research on teaching the English language arts* (pp. 604–632). New York: Macmillan.

Beck, I., & McKeown, M. (1991). Conditions of vocabulary acquisition. In R. Barr, M. L. Kamil, Mosenthal, P. B., & Pearson, P. D. (Eds.), *Handbook of reading research* (Vol. II, pp. 789–814). Mahwah, NJ: Erlbaum.

Beck, I. L., McKeown, M. G., & Omanson, R. C. (1987). The effects and uses of diverse vocabulary instructional techniques. In M. G. McKeown & M. E. Curtis (Eds.), *The nature of vocabulary acquisition* (pp. 147–163). Hillsdale, NJ: Erlbaum.

Becker, W. C. (1977). Teaching reading and the language arts to the disadvantaged—What we have learned from field research. *Harvard Educational Review, 47,* 518–543.

Biemiller, A., & Slonim, N. (2001). Estimating root word vocabulary growth in normative and advantaged populations: Evidence for a common sequence of vocabulary acquisition. *Journal of Educational Psychology, 93*(3), 498–530.

Blachowicz, C., & Fisher, P. (1996). *Teaching vocabulary in all classrooms*. Columbus, OH: Merrill.

Blachowicz, C., & Fisher, P. (2000). Vocabulary instruction. In M. L. Kamil, P. B. Mosenthal, P. D. Pearson, & R. Barr (Eds.), *Handbook of reading research* (Vol. III, pp. 503–523). Mahwah, NJ; Erlbaum.

Breznitz, Z. (1997). Effects of accelerated reading rate on memory for text among dyslexic readers. *Journal of Educational Psychology, 89,* 289–297.

California Department of Education. (1998). *English-Language Arts content standards for California public schools, kindergarten through grade twelve*. Sacramento: California Department of Education.

Carroll, J. B., Davies, P., & Richman, B. (1971). *The American Heritage word frequency book*. Boston: Houghton Mifflin.

Cassidy, J., & Cassidy, D. (1999–2000). What's hot, what's not for 2000. *Reading Today, 17*(3), 1, 28.

Cassidy, J., & Cassidy, D. (2000–2001). What's hot, what's not for 2001. *Reading Today, 18*(3), 1, 23.

Cassidy, J., & Cassidy, D. (2001–2002). What's hot, what's not for 2002. *Reading Today, 19*(3), 1, 18.

Cassidy, J., & Wenrich, J. (1997). What's hot, what's not for 1997. *Reading Today, 14*(4), 1, 28.

Cassidy, J., & Wenrich, J. (1998). What's hot, what's not for 1998. *Reading Today, 15*(4), 34.

Chall, J. S. (1987). Two vocabularies for reading: Recognition and meaning. In M. G. McKeown & M. E. Curtis (Eds.), *The nature of vocabulary acquisition* (pp. 7–17). Hillsdale, NJ: Erlbaum.

Curtis, M. E. (1987). Vocabulary testing and vocabulary instruction. In M. G. McKeown & M. E. Curtis (Eds.), *The nature of vocabulary acquisition* (pp. 37–51). Hillsdale, NJ: Erlbaum.

Dale, E. (1965). Vocabulary measurement: Techniques and major findings. *Elementary English, 42,* 82–88.

Dale, E., & O'Rourke, J. (1981). *The living word vocabulary: The words we know.* Boston: Houghton Mifflin.

Dixon, R. C., & Jenkins, J. R. (1984). *An outcome analysis of receptive vocabulary knowledge.* Unpublished manuscript, University of Illinois, Champaign-Urbana.

Fry, E. B., Kress, J. E., & Fountoukidis, D. L. (2000). *The reading teacher's book of lists* (4th ed.). Paramus, NJ: Prentice Hall.

Goodman, K. S. (1996). *On reading.* Portsmouth, NH: Heinemann.

Graves, M. F. (1987). The roles of instruction in fostering vocabulary deveopment. In M. G. McKeown & M. E. Curtis (Eds.), *The nature of vocabulary acquisition* (pp. 165–184). Hillsdale, NJ: Erlbaum.

Graves, M. F., & Watts-Taffe, S. M. (2002). The place of word consciousness in a research-based vocabulary program. In A. Farstrup & S. J. Samuels (Eds.), *What research has to say about reading instruction* (3rd ed., pp. 140–165). Newark, DE: International Reading Association.

Gray, W. S. (1946). *On their own in reading.* Chicago: Scott-Foresman.

Gunning, T. G. (2002). *Assessing and correcting reading and writing difficulties* (2nd ed.). Boston: Allyn & Bacon.

Haggard, M. R. (1982). The Vocabulary Self-Collection Strategy: An active approach to word learning. *Journal of Reading, 27,* 203–207.

Haggard, M. R. (1986). The Vocabulary Self-Collection Strategy: Using student interest and world knowledge to enhance vocabulary growth. *Journal of Reading, 29,* 634–642.

Harmon, J. M. (2000). Assessing and supporting independent word learning strategies of middle school students. *Journal of Adolescent & Adult Literacy, 43*(6), 18–27.

Hayes, D. P. (1988). Speaking and writing: Distinct patterns of word choice. *Journal of Memory and Language, 27,* 572–585.

Hayes, D. P., & Grether, J. (1983). The school year and vacations: When do students learn? *Cornell Journal of Social Relations, 17*(1), 56–71.

Irvin, J. L. (1990). *Vocabulary knowledge: Guidelines for instruction.* Washington, DC: National Education Association.

Kameenui, E. J., Dixon, R. C., & Carnine, D. W. (1987). Issues in the design of vocabulary instruction. In M. G. McKeown & M. E. Curtis (Eds.), *The nature of vocabulary acquisition* (pp. 129–145). Hillsdale, NJ: Erlbaum.

Konopak, B. C., & Williams, N. L. (1994). Elementary teachers' beliefs and decisions about vocabulary learning and instruction. In C. K. Kinzer & D. J. Leu (Eds.). *Multidimensional aspects of literacy research, theory and practice: Forty-third yearbook of the National Research Conference* (pp. 485–495). Chicago, IL: National Reading Conference.

Kucera, H., & Francis, W. N. (1967). *Computational analysis of present-day American English.* Providence, RI: Brown University Press.

Miller, G. A., & Gildea, P. M. (1987). How children learn words. *Scientific American, 257*(3), 94–99.

Nagy, W. E. (1988a). *Vocabulary instruction and reading comprehension.* Tech. Rep. No. 431. Center for the Study of Reading.

Nagy, W. E. (1988b). *Teaching vocabulary to improve reading comprehension.* Newark, DE: International Reading Association.

Nagy, W. E., & Anderson, R. C. (1984). How many words are there in printed school English? *Reading Research Quarterly, 19,* 304–330.

Nagy, W. E., & Herman, P. A. (1987). Breadth and depth of vocabulary knowledge: Implications for acquisition and instruction. In M. G. McKeown & M. E. Curtis (Eds.), *The nature of vocabulary acquisition* (pp. 19–35). Hillsdale, NJ: Erlbaum.

Nagy, W. E., & Scott, J. A. (2000). Vocabulary processes. In M. L. Kamil, P. B. Mosenthal, P. D. Pearson, & R. Barr (Eds.), *Handbook of reading research* (Vol. III, pp. 269–284). Mahwah, NJ: Erlbaum.

Nation, I. S. P. (1990). *Teaching and learning vocabulary.* Boston, MA: Heinle & Heinle Publishers.

Nicholson, T. (1991). Do children read words better in context or in lists? A classic study revisited. *Journal of Educational Psychology, 83,* 444–450.

Nist, S. L., & Olejnik, S. (1995). The role of context and dictionary definitions on varying levels of word knowledge. *Reading Research Quarterly, 30,* 172–193.

Paribakht, T. S., & Wesche, M. B., (1997). Vocabulary enhancement activities and reading for meaning in second language vocabulary instruction. In J. Coady & T. Huckins (Eds.), *Second language vocabulary acquisition* (pp. 174–200). Cambridge: Cambridge University Press.

Pressley, M. (2000). What should comprehension instruction be the instruction of? In M. L. Kamil, P. B. Mosenthal, P. D. Pearson, & R. Barr (Eds.), *Handbook of reading research* (Vol. III, pp. 545–561). Mahwah, NJ: Erlbaum.

Pressley, M., Levin, J. R., & Delaney, H. D., (1983). The mnemonic keyword method. *Review of Educational Research, 2,* 6–91.

Pressley, M., Levin, J. R., & McDaniel, M. A. (1987). Remembering versus inferring what a word means: Mnemonic and contextual approaches. In M. G. McKeown & M. E. Curtis (Eds.), *The nature of vocabulary acquisition* (pp. 107–127). Hillsdale, NJ: Erlbaum.

Ruddell, M. R. (1994). Vocabulary knowledge and comprehension: A comprehension-process view of complex literacy relationships. In R. Ruddell, M. Ruddell, & H. Singer (Eds.), *Theoretical models and processes of reading* (4th ed., pp. 414–447). Newark, DE: International Reading Association.

Ruddell, M. R. (2001). *Teaching content reading and writing* (3rd ed.). New York: John Wiley & Sons.

Samuels, S. J. (1994). Toward a theory of automatic information processing in reading revisited. In R. B. Ruddell, M. R. Ruddell, & H. Singer (Eds.), *Theoretical models and processes of reading* (4th ed., pp. 816–837). Newark, DE: International Reading Association.

Scott, J. A., & Butler, C. E. (1994). *Language arts in the 1990s: A survey of general practices with an emphasis on the teaching of vocabulary in literature-based classrooms.* Paper presented at the annual meeting of the American Educational Research Association. New Orleans, LA.

Smith, M. K. (1941). Measurement of the size of general English vocabulary through the elementary grades and high school. *Genetic Psychological Monographs, 24,* 311–345.

Stanovich, K. E. (1986). Matthew effects in reading: Some consequences of individual differences in the acquisition of literacy. *Reading Research Quarterly, 21*(4), 360–406.

Stanovich, K. E. (1993). Does reading make you smarter?: Literacy and the development of verbal intelligence. In H. Reese (Ed.), *Advances in Child Development and Behavior* (Vol. 24, pp. 133–180). San Diego, CA: Academic Press.

Stanovich, K. E., Cunningham, A. E., & West, R. F. (1998). Literacy experiences and the shaping of cognition. In S. Paris & H. Wellman (Eds.), *Global prospects for education: Development, culture, and schooling* (pp. 253–288). Washington, DC: American Psychological Association.

Sternberg, R. J. (1985). *Beyond I. Q.: A triarchic theory of human intelligence.* Cambridge, UK: Cambridge University Press.

Sternberg, R. J. (1987). Most vocabulary is learned from context. In M. G. McKeown & M. E. Curtis (Eds.), *The nature of vocabulary acquisition* (pp. 89–105). Hillsdale, NJ: Erlbaum.

Sternberg, R. J. (1988). *The triarchic mind: A new theory of human intelligence.* New York: Viking.

Sternberg, R. J., & Powell, J. S. (1983). Comprehending verbal comprehension. *American Psychologist, 38*(8), 878–893.

Tan, A., & Nicholson, T. (1997). Flashcards revisited: Training poor readers to read words faster improves their comprehension of text. *Journal of Educational Psychology, 89,* 276–288.

Thompson, E. (1958). The "master word" approach to vocabulary training. *Journal of Developmental Reading, 2,* 62–66.

Wilbraham, A., Staley, D., Matta, M., & Waterman, E. (2000). *Chemistry* (5th ed.). Menlo Park, CA: Prentice Hall.

Zeno, S. M., Ivens, S. H., Millard, R. T., & Duvvuri, R. (1995). *The educator's word frequency guide.* Brewster, NY: Touchstone Applied Science Associates.

# 5 STRATEGIES TO ENHANCE COMPREHENSION

After reading Chapter 5, you should be able to answer the following questions:

1. How do comprehension enhancing strategies help students activate background knowledge, set purposes, and promote deeper engagement while reading?
2. Which comprehension strategies help students activate and integrate knowledge?
3. How do reading strategies, like SQ3R and PLAN, facilitate independent student study?
4. Why does knowledge of text structures enhance comprehension?
5. How would you use outlines, graphic organizers, and concept maps to help your students organize information acquired through reading?

DOUBLE-ENTRY
JOURNAL: Before
Reading

Now go to the
Double-Entry
Journal for
Chapter 5 on
our Companion Website at
www.prenhall.com/unrau
to fill out your journal
entry.

Have you ever thought about the strategies you use to comprehend what you read? What strategies were you taught in school to improve your reading comprehension? Have you discovered any on your own? Which of these strategies do you use when you read? Why are they useful to you? What strategies would you teach to your students and how would you convince them that these strategies help comprehension?

In this chapter, I'll present numerous strategies to improve comprehension and learning in content areas. We know that good readers are strategic and that struggling readers can become better if they learn to use strategies appropriately (Gersten, Fuchs, Williams, & Baker, 2001). Looking back at the model of reading presented previously (Chapter 2) should clarify why strategies enable readers to comprehend better. When readers build a text representation, they draw upon their long-term memory for background knowledge. Without strategies that enable readers to make connections between their own background knowledge and a new text, readers are less likely to activate information that will help them organize and comprehend new knowledge. As readers link sentences into more complex networks, they can apply graphic organizers to help them represent ideas expressed in a passage. During text building, readers with summarizing strategies construct gists for passages. With knowledge of text structures, readers can see how an author has organized information into a plan to convey the passage's main ideas. Without knowledge of text structures, readers may simply accumulate random pieces of information rather than build a coherent pattern to represent a text's meanings. But these strategies to connect with background knowledge, summarize, and construct internal text structures must be stored in a reader's long-term memory and accessible for application at appropriate times.

Readers who lack reading strategies, such as those that will be presented in this chapter, can acquire and apply them in their content area courses. We know from extensive research (Hattie, Biggs, & Purdie, 1996) that strategies to improve learning are best taught in specific contexts and through tasks that are in the same subject as the target content. So, if you wanted to teach your biology students to use a reading strategy to improve their comprehension of the biology text, you would increase your likelihood of success if you taught students the strategy using biology readings. Embedding teaching strategies in our course content is the underlying reason for teachers in all content areas to learn and apply literacy enhancing strategies such as the ones we are about to discover in this chapter.

## COMPREHENSION-ENHANCING STRATEGIES TO ACTIVATE AND INTEGRATE KNOWLEDGE

Researchers have conducted many studies to discover the effects of activating background knowledge before learning new information related to that knowledge. In general, these studies confirm that activating relevant background knowledge heightens both understanding and retention of new knowledge (Corkill, 1992; Mayer, 1984; Pressley et al., 1990; Pressley et al., 1992). However, if prior knowledge is lacking or weak, strategies to activate background knowledge before acquiring new, related knowledge may be counterproductive (Alvermann et al., 1985). On balance, engaging students in activities that heighten their awareness of prior knowledge is a sensible and productive instructional approach. We'll explore several of these knowledge activation strategies that students not only can use to increase their understanding and recall of texts but also to motivate them to engage in reading.

## Double-Entry Journal (DEJ)

For this and every other chapter, you are asked to create a journal entry. This activity was designed to activate your own prior knowledge. You can also ask your students to participate in the ***Double-Entry Journal (DEJ).*** Readers should be encouraged to write responses using 150 to 250 words to answer the questions before the reading and approximately the same number of words to answer questions that follow the chapter. As you might have guessed, this particular form of DEJ is so called because the reader writes before reading and after reading the text (Vaughan, 1990).

The before reading questions are intended to get readers thinking about the topics to be explained and explored in the text as well as to have readers activate relevant background knowledge. The post-reading questions are designed to help readers integrate new knowledge into existing knowledge networks or modify them to accommodate the new information.

Although some teachers like to have students use a notebook dedicated to DEJs, I have found it more effective to have students write and label the entries as "Pre-Reading" and "Post-Reading." In part, I've adopted that format because increasing numbers of students e-mail assignments to me rather than turning in notebooks for evaluation. Which method you elect will depend upon your own preferences and the benefits you think will come to your students from a particular format.

When I assign DEJs, I ask students to be sure they have completed them before class because I use the DEJs to begin a class discussion. For example, I would use students' DEJ responses for this chapter by asking students at the start of class to get together in teams of three or four to share their pre- and post-reading entries.

The classroom scenario might work like this: I would ask the teams to discuss among themselves the reading comprehension strategies each of them had used or been taught and to compile a list of them. Then I would have one team member report to the class on strategies his or her team members mentioned. These I would list on the board so that I would know which strategies were already familiar to some class members and which were unfamiliar. I would then know which teams or students I might call upon to talk about their experiences with a particular comprehension fostering strategy. I would also know which strategies, if new to all, might require more time to explain and practice.

## STEP-BY-STEP: *How to Design and Implement DEJs*

**STEP 1.** Before designing DEJs, read carefully the targeted text.

**STEP 2.** Identify some of the key topics or concepts from the reading selection that readers are likely to have encountered in the past.

**STEP 3.** Formulate questions or request responses that will activate information about those topics or concepts. Keep in mind that you want to activate relevant knowledge during this pre-reading activity.

**STEP 4.** Formulate post-reading questions or response prompts that will require readers to review the reading selection in order to reflect productively. Identify aspects of the reading that are likely to lead either to growth in knowledge or understanding, or to applications of knowledge for problem solving. Using those, I generate post-reading prompts.

**STEP 5.** Ask students to write about 150 to 250 words in response to both pre- and post-reading prompts. The appropriate length of written response will vary from class to class and from text to text.

**STEP 6.** Provide opportunities for students to meet in pairs or small groups to read and share their DEJs during class time, perhaps in preparation for a class discussion.

**STEP 7.** After students read their partner's DEJ, I usually ask students to comment on them by initially asking them to simply find a sentence they like, underline it, and writing a brief marginal statement explaining why it was selected. As weeks go by, I ask partners to write more extensive commentary in response to a DEJ. For example, in response to a partner reading the DEJ for this chapter, I would ask that he identify a strategy or an idea in the DEJ and write about how that strategy or idea could be adapted to his own content area instruction.

For the DEJ I developed for this chapter (that I hope you responded to before you began reading the chapter), I wanted my readers to focus on comprehension strategies and activate knowledge about those they use when reading. I also wanted readers to think about how those strategies worked for them, which strategies they would consider teaching to their own students, and how they would get their students engaged in learning them. But that's not the end of the DEJ story. You will come upon another DEJ at the end of this chapter. At that point you'll be asked to write more about strategies I've covered. I don't want to give away the surprise ending, but I'm likely to ask you once again to reflect on strategies presented here, ask you to tie them to what you knew about strategies before, and maybe ask you to reconsider how and why these strategies are likely to help your students.

## Anticipation Guide

An **Anticipation Guide** is a list of statements you generate about a subject that your students react to before they read about it. After your students complete the Anticipation Guide, you conduct a conversation with them to identify their preconceived ideas and attitudes about the topic. As you talk about their knowledge and beliefs, you can encourage your students to connect what they will learn with

**TABLE 5.1**   Anticipation Guide Example

If I were to have designed an Anticipation Guide for Chapter 2, "Readers Reading: Inside the Meaning Construction Zone," I could have done so as follows:

*Directions:* Below you see several statements about reading. If you agree with the statement, put a check next to the sentence under YOU. If you disagree, leave the space blank. After you have read the related selection, put a check in the AUTHOR column if the statement is consistent with the author's beliefs. You may also indicate in your column any change in beliefs you had as a result of your reading the selection.

| YOU | AUTHOR | Statement about Reading |
|---|---|---|
|  |  | 1. Good readers can read at 1,000 words a minute and more while maintaining good comprehension. |
|  |  | 2. Good readers both make inferences and test them while reading. |
|  |  | 3. Good readers don't subvocalize. |
|  |  | 4. Good readers clarify for themselves why they are reading. |
|  |  | 5. Good readers read only the key words. |
|  |  | 6. Good readers always recognize words as wholes. |
|  |  | 7. Good readers never look back. |
|  |  | 8. Good readers make sure the meanings they are constructing while reading are internally consistent and compatible with what they know and what makes sense. |

what they already claim to know. By getting them to connect what they know with what they may learn, you can deepen their engagement and purpose for reading.

STEP-BY-STEP: *How to Prepare and Present Anticipation Guides*

**STEP 1.** Read the text you are going to assign and identify key concepts you would like your students to understand, challenge, or both.

**STEP 2.** Compose six to eight statements that are likely to challenge your students' beliefs about the topic or express an opinion about it.

**STEP 3.** Arrange the statements in a True–False or You–Author format (see Table 5.1).

**STEP 4.** Ask students to complete the Anticipation Guide individually before reading the text to which it relates.

**STEP 5.** Discuss their responses, making efforts to highlight possible conflicts between their beliefs and the content of the text they are to read.

**STEP 6.** After the discussion, ask students to read the material.

**STEP 7.** Ask students to review their responses to the Anticipation Guide when they complete their reading of the text material. Students should put a check in the AUTHOR column if the statement is consistent with the author's belief. Students should also identify any changes in their own beliefs about the topic.

## Directed Reading-Thinking Activity (DR-TA)

Before you read further, what do you think a Directed Reading-Thinking Activity is? What do you think a teacher would do to conduct one? What would a student do who was engaged in one? Remember to pause for a moment to tell yourself what you think.

Designed by Russell Stauffer (1969), the ***Directed Reading-Thinking Activity (DR-TA)*** engages students in making predictions about a text, reading the text, and discovering the accuracy of those predictions. Although developed in the 1960s, the DR-TA is still recognized as an effective tactic to advance comprehension and develop metacognitive skills. When making a prediction about a text, students activate background knowledge. After prereading the text and making stop points, I begin by explaining that there really are no right or wrong responses because all will be guessing. Some may guess more luckily than others, but I encourage all responses—warm or cold. I urge students to remember their predictions because they will get a chance to test, verify, or modify them. When reading the text, students find out if the text confirms their hypotheses or if they need to change them.

For example, I asked you to make a prediction about what a DR-TA was before you read the description. You activated knowledge about these associated words to see if you could predict what the essence of the activity was. Now that you've gotten a brief description of the activity, you should be able to confirm your prediction or modify it to conform to what you have learned.

## STEP-BY-STEP: *How to Do a DR-TA*

**STEP 1.** Decide what text you are going to use to conduct the DR-TA. The text could be part of a chapter in a content textbook, the first section of a novel or story, a poem, or an article.

**STEP 2.** Read the text and mark promising stop points where you will ask students to make predictions about what will happen next or what will be examined next. Start by asking something like, "Looking at the title, what do you think this story (or chapter or article) is going to be about?" After the title, break the text at sensible points, such as at headings or after a couple of meaty paragraphs if the text is extensive and complex.

**STEP 3.** To reduce students' temptation to read ahead, provide them with a sheet of paper to cover the text and ask them to slip it down the text only as far as your next stop point. (You can also later use the same sheet of paper to have students make a graphic organizer or map of the information given in what they've read.)

**STEP 4.** Get your questions ready so that at stop points you will be prepared to guide student responses. As students respond, you might ask some students to explain why they thought what they did. Ask questions like "Given what the author has already written, what do you think will happen next?" "Why do you think so?" or "What topic do you think the writer will explain next?" "Why?"

There are a few points to keep in mind when doing DR-TAs. First, I explain to teachers that they have to keep flexible about the choice of text when doing a DR-TA. Some texts are much more amenable to DR-TAs than others. I had excellent experience with texts that are more figurative or narrative. Highly literal texts may work less well; however, you should experiment with your students to see what works with them.

Second, teachers need to be patient when first trying DR-TAs. Students may not respond enthusiastically the first time teachers try it. Students may need to warm up to the technique and to build some trust in teachers' accepting their guesses. Some students hate making any kind of mistake in class because they don't want to look foolish. So it may take a few times before the DR-TA begins to look like a vehicle students will want to ride. I often tell my students about a class I observed over several days while a new teacher I was supervising tried to get his sometimes disengaged, sometimes sleepy students to respond to a DR-TA. The first day only three or four students got engaged while a couple of students had their heads on desks. The second day I observed the teacher using a DR-TA no heads were down, and there was a sense of modest excitement in the air. After he had tried the activity three or four more times, most students had gained enough interest and trust in the process that they were contributing to a lively discussion about their reading. It became safe to be wrong and fun to discover whether or not guesses were on target.

Third, as students warm-up to DR-TAs, their motivation to read a text rises. That's actually one reason I usually ask students to cover the text we're reading with a sheet of blank paper. Covering the texts reduces the temptation to read ahead, a temptation that seems to grow on some students as their motivation to read heightens.

Lastly, DR-TAs should not be used too frequently. Although they are relatively easy to prepare compared to other reading activities, their interest to students can be kept alive if their welcome isn't worn out by too much use.

As an example of a DR-TA in action, I'm going to walk you through how I've used it to teach poetry to high school students, some of whom are less than ecstatic when I present them with a poem to discuss. Often, I find that the roots of their distaste are grounded in their feelings of inadequacy and confusion as they face lines of words lying like mysteries they must solve and do so without looking too stupid. However, DR-TA spreads poetic kindness. Why? Because students don't have to have the right answers to the meaning of each mysterious line. DR-TA promotes speculation, or guessing about interpretations, which is just what students need to do when faced with new, unfamiliar language.

Figure 5.1 shows you where I'd put stop points for a DR-TA using Robert Browning's "My Last Duchess." When I presented this poem, I put it on a transparency, covered all the text before projecting it, and then revealed only those lines before my next "stop point" question. In this figure, I've signaled stop points (SP) I think work well with the poem and questions I'd ask students to speculate upon. Remember, I'm trying to encourage them to speculate, to make guesses, to hypothesize about the meaning of words as I guide them through the poem.

## Know-Want to Know-Learned (K-W-L) Strategy

Before setting out to teach about a topic, teachers frequently want to discover what their students already know about it and what more they would like to learn. To gather that information and more, Ogle (1986) developed the **K-W-L strategy** by which teachers can find out what their students already know (K), what they would like to learn (W), and (following reading and instruction) what they learned (L). As

| My Last Duchess **(SP1)** | **(SP1)** Given this title, what do you think this poem will be about? |
|---|---|

That's my last duchess painted on the wall,
Looking as if she were alive. I call
That piece a wonder, now; Fra Pandolf's hands
Worked busily a day, and there she stands.
Will 't please you sit and look at her? **(SP2)** I said

**(SP2)** What do you think is happening in the poem? Why? Who is present? Where are they?

"Fra Pandolf" by design, for never read
Strangers like you that pictured countenance,
The depth and passion of its earnest glance,
But to myself they turned (since none puts by
The curtain I have drawn for you, but I)
And seemed as they would ask me, if they durst,
How such a glance came there; so, not the first
Are you to turn and ask thus. **(SP3)** Sir, 'twas not

**(SP3)** What do you think now about who's talking to whom and where? What do you predict will happen?

Her husband's presence only, called that spot
Of joy into the Duchess' cheek; perhaps
Fra' Pandolf chanced to say, "Her mantle laps
Over my lady's wrist too much," or, "Paint
Must never hope to reproduce the faint
Half-flush that dies along her throat." Such stuff
Was courtesy, she thought, and cause enough
For calling up that spot of joy. She had
A heart—how shall I say?—too soon made glad,
Too easily impressed; she liked whate'er
She looked on, and her looks went everywhere. **(SP4)**

**(SP4)** What has happened? Which of our hunches about what is going on are being confirmed in the poem? What do you think of the duke? Why do you think that? What impression of the duchess do you have?

Sir, 'twas all one! My favor at her breast,
The dropping of the daylight in the west,
The bough of cherries some officious fool
Broke in the orchard for her, the white mule
She rode with round the terrace—all and each
Would draw from her alike the approving speech,
Or blush, at lest. She thanked men—good! but thanked
Somehow—I know not how—as if she ranked
My gift of a nine-hundred-years-old name
With anybody's gift. **(SP5)** Who'd stoop to blame

**(SP5)** Which of our impressions of the duke are being confirmed? Do you have more thoughts about his character? What do you predict he'll do about the duchess?

This sort of trifling? Even had you skill
In speech—(which I have not)—to make your will
Quite clear to such a one, and say, "Just this
Or that in you disgusts me; here you miss,
Or there exceed the mark"—and if she let
Herself be lessoned so, nor plainly set
Her wits to yours, forsooth, and made excuse,
—E'en then would be some stooping; and I choose
Never to stoop. **(SP6)** Oh, sir, she smiled, no doubt,

**(SP6)** What other qualities of the duke emerge?

Whene'er I passed her; but who passed without
Much the same smile? This grew; I gave commands;
Then all smiles stopped together. **(SP7)** There she stands

**(SP7)** What do you think he has done?

As if alive. Will 't please you rise? We'll meet
The company below, then. I repeat,
The Count your master's know munificence

*Continued*

**FIGURE 5.1** DR-TA for "My Last Duchess," by Robert Browning.

| | |
|---|---|
| Is ample warrant that no just pretense<br>Of mine for dowry will be disallowed;<br>Though his fair daughter's self, as I avowed<br>At starting, is my object. **(SP8)** Nay, we'll go<br>Together down, sir. Notice Neptune, though,<br>Taming a sea horse, thought a rarity,<br>Which Claus of Innsbruck cast in bronze for me! **(SP9)**<br><br><br><br>*Note:* Fra Pandolf and Claus of Innsbruck are imaginary artists<br>from the Renaissance. | **(SP8)** What are the duke's<br>plans? How do you think they<br>fit with our impression of his<br>character?<br>**(SP9)** Do these last lines<br>confirm anything we said<br>about the duke earlier or add<br>anything new? |

**FIGURE 5.1**    *Continued.*

I'll expalin after giving you step-by-step procedures for doing a K-W-L. I use K-W-Ls in teaching my own university classes when I want to know what students already know about something like cooperative learning or qualitative research and what they would like to learn.

## STEP-BY-STEP: *How to Do a K-W-L*

**STEP 1.** Ask students to fold a sheet of paper into three columns and to label the first column with a K, the second with a W, and the third with an L.

**STEP 2.** Explain to students that the first column (K) is for them to write all they know about the topic for the activity. This part of the exercise activates students' background knowledge. Before filling in the column, students could get together in small groups of three or four to talk about what they know.

**STEP 3.** Working alone or in their small groups, students generate questions that they place in the "Want to know" (W) column.

**STEP 4.** The teacher helps students organize the information on their K-W-L sheets. This can be done by asking students to report what they know and want to know while someone writes the information on the board. As an alternative, one student in each group can be responsible for writing up the information.

**STEP 5.** The students read the text that the teacher divides into reasonable sections. After students read a portion of the text, they should refer to their questions to see if they have been answered or if they have additional questions to write on their lists.

**STEP 6.** After completing their reading, students write down what they have learned in the "L" column. Students can then share that information with others in their group and class.

**STEP 7.** Students acknowledge not only what they have learned, but they also take note of what questions remain unanswered.

As a follow-up, many educators combine K-W-Ls with maps so that the knowledge they gain can be consolidated. We will be covering graphic organizers in the next section of this chapter.

I often use K-W-Ls in my own teaching. In one case, I was preparing to teach credential candidates about cooperative learning, a topic we'll take up in the next chapter, and I wanted to know what my students knew and what they wanted to learn about it. After we studied cooperative learning, I returned the K-W-L charts to my students for them to complete and enable me to discover what they had learned—or wanted to learn more about. One of my students, a musician I'll refer to as Nadia who was preparing to teach music in secondary schools, completed her K-W-L chart as shown in Table 5.2.

While I addressed most of the "Want to know" items on Nadia's list, I didn't fully address her question about the use of cooperative learning strategies in the creative arts. We discussed in class how "naturally" cooperative learning practices meshed with teaching music (five musicians were in my class), how an ensemble of band or choir members could constitute a team, and how they could be assigned roles to complete their musical tasks successfully. While I adapted curriculum to the musicians' questions, I focused more on integrating literacy into cooperative learning activities.

## The Prereading Plan (PreP)

Judith Langer (1981, 1982) developed a strategy to encourage students to think about ideas associated with topics or concepts about to be encountered in a reading assignment. Through the ***Prereading Plan (PreP),*** you can prepare your students to read by having them recollect prior knowledge and reflect on the sources of that knowledge. After class discussion, but before jumping into the actual reading, you should prompt your students to think about the effects the discussion had on their thinking about the topic and to articulate any changes in their knowledge and understanding.

**TABLE 5.2**   K-W-L Chart on Cooperative Learning

| Know | Want to Know | Learned |
|---|---|---|
| 1. Works in groups<br>2. Groups are often made up of different levels of students<br>3. Some believe it enables students to build social & learning skills necessary to integrate with colleagues in the "real" world<br>4. Can be problematic if some students do all the work and others "freeload"<br>5. Some believe it helps all students to function at a higher level<br>6. Can support a classroom goal/ atmosphere of creativity & encouragement | 1. What *really* are the benefits of co-op learning?<br>2. What are the best ways to engage students through cooperation?<br>3. Are some methods of engaging students better than others?<br>4. Does co-op learning benefit all students?<br>5. How do I assess students who have worked cooperatively?<br>6. How would co-op learning work in a creative arts setting? | 1. More specific ways to implement co-op learning<br>2. The parameters including delegating authority, roles, individual accountability, shared responsibility, mixing of levels, complex tasks<br>3. More about how to arrange groups in a sensitive manner to ensure the success of the group<br>4. Some examples of what *not* to do (e.g., limiting the student by *always* working in groups or placing them in difficult situations)<br>5. Assessment can take various forms based on assignment |

## STEP-BY-STEP: *How to Do a PreP*

Langer (1981) described the three phases of the process in the following words:

**STEP 1.** *Initial associations with the concept.* In this first phase you can say, "Tell anything that comes to mind when (for example) you hear the word Congress." As your students tell what ideas initially came to their minds, you should jot each response on the board. During this phase, your students have their first opportunity to find associations between the key concept and their prior knowledge. When this activity was carried out in a middle school class one student, Bill, said, "important people." Another student, Danette, said, "Washington, D.C."

**STEP 2.** *Reflections on initial associations.* During the second phase of PreP, you should ask, "What made you think of . . . (the response given by a student)?" This phase helps your students develop awareness of their network of associations. They also have an opportunity to listen to each other's explanations, to interact, and to become aware of their changing ideas. Through this procedure, they may weigh, reject, accept, revise, and integrate some of the ideas that came to mind. When Bill was asked what made him think of important people, he said, "I saw them in the newspaper." When Danette was asked what made her think of Washington, D.C., she said, "Congress takes place there."

**STEP 3.** *Reformulation of knowledge.* In this phase, you ask your students the following: "Based on our discussion and before we read the text, have you any new ideas about (for example) Congress?" This phase allows students to verbalize associations that have been elaborated or changed through the discussion. Because they have had a chance to probe their memories to elaborate on their prior knowledge, the responses elicited during the third phase are often more refined than those from the first. This time, Bill said, "Lawmakers of America." And Danette said, "U.S. government part that makes the laws."

Once your class has been PrePed for a reading, you will have a clearer idea of the knowledge base that students will bring to it. Students whose network of associated ideas may not be as rich as others are likely to need additional support and guidance when trying to comprehend the reading. If only a few students have much knowledge to share, that may indicate that some further preliminary teaching, mid-way discussion, or post-reading comprehension activities are warranted for the entire class.

## Directed Inquiry Activity (DIA)

A strategy that activates students' topic knowledge while providing both purposes for reading and some degree of teacher control over concepts students must master is the ***Directed Inquiry Activity (DIA).*** Keith Thomas (1986) developed DIAs to enable teachers to guide their students' inquiry and discovery.

Teachers frame inquiry questions based upon the texts their students will be reading. These questions answer any or all of the questions about who, what, when, where, why, and how. After students are given the questions, they survey and skim their text for information. This overview is intended to give students information to predict answers to the teachers' inquiry questions. As students make predictions, the teacher puts them on the board or records them for later use.

### STEP-BY-STEP: *How to Do a DIA*

**STEP 1.** Review or write the content mastery goals for the body of material about to be taught.

**STEP 2.** Compose several inquiry questions based on the goals and the text to be read (See Figure 5.2).

**STEP 3.** Distribute questions to students.

**STEP 4.** Have students skim the text to discover what information will help them answer the questions. Discuss with students how they think the questions will be answered.

**STEP 5.** As students make their predicted answers, ask students to explain why they think the answers they predict will be accurate. How does their prereading guess connect to their background knowledge and their brief review of the text?

**STEP 6.** Have students read the text carefully.

**STEP 7.** After students have read the text, return to a discussion about the correct answers to your inquiry questions. This discussion, together with their reading of the text, should provide students with knowledge to clarify, modify, or extend their predicted answers.

These DIA Questions are based on a chapter entitled "The Heritage of Ancient Greece" from a secondary level textbook, *World History: Patterns of Civilization,* by B. F. Beers (1993).

1. Looking at a map of ancient Greece, how do you think geography influenced its economy and society?
2. What historical events laid the groundwork for the rise of the Greek City-States?
3. What form of government guided the city-state and society of Athens?
4. How did society in the city-state of Sparta differ from that in Athens?
5. How did the Persian and Peloponnesian Wars shape Athens' history and government?
6. What contributions did the Greeks make to drama, philosophy, and the arts?
7. What were Alexander the Great's ambitions and achievements?

**FIGURE 5.2**   DIA Sample Questions.

## SQ3R

Like the Directed Inquiry Activity, **SQ3R** (Robinson, 1946) is designed to help students set purposes for reading and engage them in reading for answers to significant questions. Furthermore, the method urges readers to survey what is to be read, generate self-posed questions, and review what has been covered in the text. SQ3R stands for Survey, Question, Read, Recite, and Review.

When I use SQ3R, I begin by looking over the reading material to get an impression of its scope and depth (Survey). Then, I use headings in the text to pose questions to myself (Question). These questions then contribute to my purpose for reading (Read). While reading, I watch for textual information that will contribute to my answering the questions I've posed for myself (Recite). And, after reading the passage and answering my questions, I go back over the material I've covered (Review).

If I were to use SQ3R on this description of SQ3R, I'd begin by (a) surveying or skimming the section, noting introductory sentences and getting a sense of the text's length. Then I'd (b) ask myself a question: What is SQ3R? How is it going to help me enhance my reading comprehension since that's what this whole chapter is about? Should I teach it to my students? Now for the 3Rs: I'd (c) read the section with the purpose of answering my question(s), (d) recite to myself the answer(s) I'd constructed from reading the text, and (e) review the entire section after completely reading it.

While more than half a century old and the most often taught independent reading strategy, SQ3R as a system appears to improve comprehension about as well as just rereading (Caverly, Orlando, & Mullen, 2000). When texts are more challenging, however, SQ3R is effective with weaker readers. To gain that effectiveness, students must learn each step in the strategy and how to apply it. Even more important, students must believe in the procedure to make the effort needed to complete its steps. While effective with some students, SQ3R is not useful with low-ability readers who struggle with word recognition and comprehension problems.

## PLAN

David Caverly and his associates (1995) developed a variant of SQ3R that was found to have significant effects on the reading performance of secondary students. The strategy is called **PLAN,** an acronym for four separate tactics: Predict, Locate, Add, and Note. The separate tactics are integrated to facilitate comprehension before, during, and after independent reading.

When *Predicting* a text's content before a careful reading, students draw a likely representation of a text after previewing it. A student's map or diagram represents the author's key ideas taken from the title, headings and sub-headings, and graphs or charts. The map or diagram reveals the student's predictions about the text's meaning and its importance to the reader. A sample of the Predicting phase of PLAN appears in Figure 5.3. After previewing a chapter on natural resources in their social studies textbook, *The United States Yesterday and Today* (Helmus, Toppin, Pounds, & Arnsdorf, 1988), middle school students collaborated on creating the map with teacher guidance.

When *Locating,* students indicate with a check mark (✓) on the map those concepts they find familiar and with a question mark (?) those that are unfamiliar to them. In doing this before reading, students are assessing their schemata (or lack thereof) related to the text's content. Knowing what is known and unknown helps students assess depth of prereading concept mastery, focus attention, and select appropriate reading rates.

During reading, students engage in *Adding* words and phrases to capture the meaning of unfamiliar concepts labeled with question marks while elaborating on familiar ones that they checked. When a student reads a text and finds no content

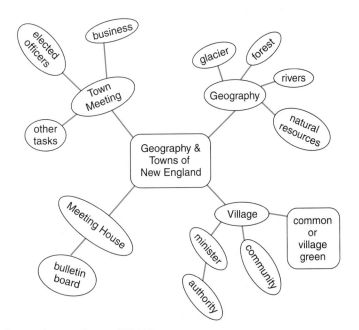

**FIGURE 5.3**   Predicting Phase of PLAN.

addressing concepts affixed with question marks, that may mean that the student overlooked important text content. Selective rereading may be the next tactic to engage.

After reading, students *Note* new understandings of concepts on their maps or reconstruct a new map integrating the newly learned with the formerly known. Predictions made early may need to be modified in the light on a closer reading of the text. Follow-up *Noting* may also include writing a summary of the text, a log entry, or notes and questions for a discussion.

## Making Reading Meaningful

A few years after Ellen Langer, a professor of psychology at Harvard University, wrote *Mindfulness* (1989), she turned her attention to writing *The Power of Mindful Learning* (1997). In the earlier book, Langer shows what she means by mindfulness and how we can become more mindful in many dimensions of our daily lives. She explains that a mindful person demonstrates several key characteristics when approaching an activity: (a) the creation of new categories, (b) openness to new information, and (c) an implicit awareness of multiple perspectives. She contrasts this mindful state with mindlessness (which I've enumerated with negative numbers to emphasize how they subtract from learning): ($-1$) entrapment in old categories, ($-2$) automatic behavior that blocks attention to new signals, and ($-3$) vision limited to a single perspective.

In *The Power of Mindful Learning,* Langer presents a creative alternative to two prevalent methods of teaching. The first of these two methods, exemplified by lecturing, is top-down. We listen and learn. The second, exemplified by direct experience, structured practice, and memorization, is bottom-up. We repeat and learn. The third alternative she suggests is "sideways" learning, the goal of which is to maintain a mindful state. When engaged in sideways learning we manifest these characteristics:

- ◆ openness to novelty,
- ◆ alertness to distinction,
- ◆ sensitivity to different contexts,
- ◆ implicit, if not explicit, awareness of multiple perspectives, and
- ◆ orientation in the present.

From her research with Matt Lieberman (1995) on mindful learning, we can discover approaches that hold out the promise of improved reading comprehension. She asked two groups of ninth graders to read two different essays from their literature anthology. One group was instructed to simply learn the material. The second group was told, as described below, *to make the material meaningful to themselves:*

> This may entail thinking about how certain parts of the information remind you of past, present, or future experiences, how the information could be important to yourself or someone else, or simply finding some significance of the story in relation to anyone and/or anything. Remember, what is meaningful to one person is not necessarily meaningful to another.

After a twenty-minute reading period, all students were tested. Students in the second group, the make-it-meaningful-to-yourself group, who did not resort to memorization in order to perform well on the test outperformed all others by recalling more information from the reading. They also wrote essays judged better by a group of evaluators; however, we are looking most closely at reading comprehension and performance.

In a related experiment, Lieberman and Langer (1995) investigated the effects of mindful reading with tenth graders. To make an episode about the enactment of the Kansas–Nebraska Act from a high school history text meaningful, students were asked to read it from the perspective of the United States Senator who presented the legislation. Students were to think about how they would feel and what they would think if they were in the Senator's situation or how they would see things from the perspective of the Senator's grandchild. The control group was only asked to learn the passage.

Students in both the experimental and control groups were tested on the chapter at the end of the class period and one week later. As in the earlier experiment, students reading mindfully scored better on recall of information on both tests. Essays they wrote were also judged to be more creative and insightful.

In sum, these investigations reveal that, if students can make material more meaningful by adopting different perspectives and discovering that information is context-dependent, they can improve the quality of their comprehension and understanding of texts. The studies also validate an alternative to the technique of finding ways to make the content of reading selections "relevant" to students' interests and values. In Langer's experiments, the attitudes of students in relationship to the reading material were changed. The researchers guided students into discovering approaches to texts that made them more personally meaningful. Teachers can replicate these mindful, "sideways" learning practices by encouraging students to read from multiple perspectives, become more sensitive to different contexts, be alert to drawing distinctions, and create new categories.

## STEP-BY-STEP: *How to Help Students Make Reading Meaningful*

**STEP 1.** Explain to your students what a mindful learning orientation is and that you want to encourage them to approach all their reading more mindfully.

**STEP 2.** One way to approach reading more mindfully is to entertain and adopt multiple perspectives. Rather than simply reading text from the perspective of a student who just wants to get through the reading and, hopefully, to learn it, ask students to create a perspective that would make the text especially important to them or to someone they know. For example, if they were to read a chapter about the history of World War I, how would the content of that chapter be perceived by a cadet at West Point, who was in training to be a military leader? As an alternative, students could try to discover how information they are to read reminds them of past, present, or future experiences or events. Explain to students that what is meaningful to one reader will not necessarily be meaningful to another reader.

**STEP 3.** Ask students to write down what they found as a way to make the reading meaningful to them and take a few minutes to share those perspectives in class.

## TEXT STRUCTURE

What do the "Three Little Pigs," "Cinderella," and the Biblical story of Job have in common? All share a pattern of narrative development called story grammar (Stein & Glenn, 1979; Trabasso & Stein, 1997). A narrative's structure, or its story grammar, typically consists of (a) a setting, (b) an initiating event signaling change, (c) characters' goal-defining responses to the initiating event, (d) characters' goal-directed behaviors, (e) the consequences of those behaviors, and (f) a resolution. Teachers of young readers in the elementary grades have recognized that children who have a sense of story structure seem to ask good questions about stories and to comprehend them better. Furthermore, many studies show the effectiveness of using story-grammar elements to help students, including struggling readers, comprehend narrative texts (Gersten, Fuchs, Williams, & Baker, 2001). While knowledge of story structure clearly helps readers understand narratives, does knowledge of expository text structure help readers comprehend expository passages, such as those found in history, science, or math textbooks?

To answer this question, we can draw two conclusions from research connecting knowledge of expository text structure to its comprehension: (a) The ability to identify and use expository text structure contributes to comprehension, and (b) readers comprehend some expository text structures more easily than others (Gersten, Fuchs, Williams, & Baker, 2001). One of the factors complicating comprehension of expository passages is that they may contain not one text structure but several mixed together. Beside that, a reading of today's front page newspaper stories will quickly convince you that expository texts frequently include story-grammar elements, like settings and characters who get themselves into trouble even worse than the Three Little Pigs.

Nevertheless, with knowledge of text structures, readers can approach texts with expectations and a plan of attack (Englert, 1990). If readers recognize that a text has a particular structure, they can expect elements of the text to contribute to that known structure. With knowledge of text structures, readers can organize the text mentally as they read it. Without that knowledge, readers cannot approach texts with such expectations or plans. Instead, these readers pick and choose information more randomly (Meyer, Brandt, & Bluth, 1980).

## Types of Text Structures

In work spanning over twenty-five years, Bonnie Meyer and her colleagues (Meyer, Brandt, & Bluth, 1980; Meyer & Freedle, 1984; Meyer & Poon, 2001) have focused on the impact that text structure has on the amount and kind of information readers remember. Text structures arise from the way their authors organize information. Meyer and her colleagues identified five ways to organize discourse: Description, sequence (including ordering by time or events), causation, problem-solution (including effect or evaluation of the solution), and comparison. A sixth text structure, persuasion or argument, will be presented in Chapter 7.

## Effects of Text Structure Knowledge

From studies of text structure knowledge effects that Meyer and her associates (Bartlett, 1978 ; Meyer, Brandt, & Bluth, 1980; Meyer & Freedle, 1984) conducted with high school and college students, she distilled several major findings:

◆ Ideas at the top of a text's structure are remembered better than those lower in a text's hierarchy. For example, in a magazine article about supertankers, readers are far more likely to remember the top-level of the problem presented (oil spills) and its solution (training, ground control stations, improved tanker design) than they are lower-level descriptions of specific tanker accidents and the number of birds destroyed.

◆ A text's overall plan and major relationships between its paragraphs have a more powerful effect on its recall than the organization of details. For example, if readers see that a text's overall structure is problem-solution, as was the case in the oil spill article, they will remember it better.

◆ Some top-level text structures, such as causation and comparison, facilitate readers' recall of a text's content more than others. For example, descriptions of a specific tanker accident in England's North Sea is less likely to be remembered than a cause-effect relationship (oil spills causing thousands of birds to die).

◆ Strategic instruction in the recognition and use of top-level structures improves students' capacities to remember the content of texts. For example, after students were given direct instruction in text structures over five 1-hour sessions during their English classes, they demonstrated statistically superior recall of texts in comparison to their pretraining scores and in comparison to a control group. Students who received the training also demonstrated performance advantages across the curriculum (Bartlett, 1978).

## Five Basic Text Structures

The five discourse patterns Meyers identified (description, sequence, causation, problem-solution, and comparison) appear in newspapers, scientific writing, political speeches, and (of course) school texts. To help your students know when an author is organizing information into one of these five text structures, they will benefit from definitions, identifying cues, likely contexts, and examples of each type.

Description.   Descriptive texts provide information about the specific attributes of a topic and, perhaps, its setting.

*Cues:* The organization of text structure is based on a listing of attributes or features. This text structure may include explicit language to draw a reader's attention to several attributes of a topic and enumerate them as "first," "second," "third," and so forth. Signaling words or phrases include the following: for instance, for example, such as, includes, consists of.

*Contexts:* Description of a painting, a living room, a person's face, a garden, an event reported in a newspaper or magazine, a battle scene, a product for sale, or the features that make up story grammar.

*Example:*

New, spacious, detached Mediterranean townhouse for sale. The unit consists of 3 bedrooms, 2.5 bathrooms, an office upstairs, and approximately 2,431 square feet with a huge deck off the living room that overlooks a grove of lemon trees. The gourmet kitchen has a slab granite counter top, GE appliances, oak cabinetry, tile floors, and a convection oven. The master suite has a walk-in closet, marble fireplace, and a spa tub with shower. This townhouse has a convenient location on a tree-lined street just a few steps from shopping and award-winning schools.

**Sequence.** Texts using sequence as their organizing principle group ideas on the basis of time or order.

*Cues:* Texts using sequence present items serially and progress orderly or chronologically. Signaling words or phrases include the following: at the beginning, next, then, later, over time, and at last.

*Contexts:* Directions for assembling a bookcase from packed parts, oatmeal cookie recipe, history of battles in World War I, stages of cognitive development from infancy to adulthood, procedures for a chemistry experiment.

*Example: To Die For Chocolate Chip Oatmeal Cookies:*

1. Heat oven to 350 degrees.
2. Beat 1/2 cup butter and 1 cup of brown sugar until creamy.
3. Add 1 teaspoonful of vanilla and 1 egg. Beat well.
4. Sift together 1/2 cup flour, 1/2 teaspoon baking soda, 1/2 teaspoon cinnamon, and 1/4 teaspoon salt. Add to bowl of ingredients and mix well.
5. Stir in 1 1/2 cups of uncooked old-fashioned oatmeal.
6. Stir in 7-ounce package of chocolate chips and 1 teaspoon of grated orange rind.
7. Drop rounded tablespoonfuls of dough onto an ungreased cookie sheet.
8. Bake 'til golden brown, about 10 to 12 minutes.
9. Cool on a well-greased cookie sheet for about 5 minutes.
10. Remove to wire rack and hide from sight immediately to reduce risk of immediate consumption.

**Causation.** Using causation text structure, writers present cause-and-effect relationships between ideas or concepts. Usually, effects come before their causes. To enhance comprehension, readers should look for causes when effects begin to appear in texts.

*Cues:* Texts organized with a cause-effect structure include phrases or words that signal causal analysis, including the following: reasons for this, because, was caused by, so.

*Contexts:* A medical manual explaining causes of illnesses, historical factors contributing to outbreak of war, reasons why animal species are becoming extinct, compilation of computer glitches and their possible causes, why a president's administration flourished, or features leading to a nation's economic expansion.

*Example:*

Many reasons lie behind a good reader's performance. First, good readers activate and connect with the knowledge base related to the subject of the reading. Second, good readers monitor their comprehension process while reading and recognize those moments of mental blackout and misunderstandings that lead us into confusion. Third, good readers pay attention to the spectrum of information they are reading and categorize it from important to unimportant, giving priority to major content and secondary attention to trivia. Fourth, good readers both make inferences and test them while reading. Fifth, good readers periodically review what they have read and ask themselves questions about the reading. Sixth, good readers do not ignore comprehension breakdowns or lapses. They take steps to correct comprehension once problems are recognized. Seventh, good readers also clarify for themselves why they are reading and try to understand what is expected of them as readers and learners. Eighth, good readers make sure the meanings they are constructing while reading are internally consistent and compatible with what they know and what makes sense. This constitutes part of their internalized standards of text evaluation. And ninth, good readers have knowledge of text structures that they can use to organize and remember information as they read.

Problem-solution.   In problem-solution text structures, ideas are presented in two sections: a problem section and a solution section. Sometimes this text plan appears in a question-answer form. The question presents a problem while the answer provides its solution. Some problem-solution plans also include an evaluation or consequences of solutions provided.

*Cues:* Problem, solution, question, answer, reasons are many.

*Contexts:* Papers published in scientific journals, newspaper editorials, history texts, political and policy documents, advertisements.

*Example: Rat Allergy*

Psychologists who work with rats and mice in experiments often become allergic to these creatures. This is a real hazard for investigators who spend hours a week running rats in experiments. These allergies are a reaction to the protein in urine excreted by rats when they get upset.

At a meeting sponsored by the National Institutes of Health, Dr. Andrew Slovak, a British physician, recommended that experimenters be kind to rats and mice. Psychologists who pet and talk softly to their rats are less often splattered with urine and the protein that causes the allergic reaction. (Adapted from Meyer, Young, & Bartlett, 1989, p. 137.)

Comparison.   Texts organized under this principle relate ideas in terms of their differences and similarities. Different points of view may be expressed about the same issue, as occurs in political debates or pro and con statements in newspapers and magazines.

*Cues:* On the other hand, in contrast, from another perspective, however.

*Contexts:* Debate-like material or political speeches comparing the value of different solutions, perspectives, purposes, or policies.

*Example:*

Both the North and South sides had certain advantages at the beginning of the Civil War. The North possessed approximately three-fourths of the nation's wealth and had more than twice the manpower of the South. In addition to its vast farmlands, the North also operated almost all the factories in the country.

The Navy, which was solely in the hands of the North, assured control of the entire coastline of the Confederacy. The South, on the other hand, was fighting a defensive war and did not have to carry the fighting to Northern soil. It was blessed with splendid officers and a fighting breed of men accustomed to riding and the use of firearms. Moreover, its cause was popular with many of the European powers.

## Levels of Text Structure

Texts in the content areas include multiple text structures. Main ideas expressed in text structures at the top of the hierarchy will be fleshed out with details expressed in other text structures at lower levels. For example, the top-level structure for an article on oil tankers could be problem-solution: We can prevent oil spills from supertankers by training personnel who operate the ships, designing better tankers, and installing control stations. Meanwhile, lower level text structures, including causation, description, and sequence, provide information to support and explain in detail the text's main problem-solution plan of organization (Meyer, Young, & Bartlett, 1989).

We know from research that a good predictor of readers' recall of passages is whether or not they recognize and use a passage's top-level structure to organize their recall of the passage (Meyer, Brandt, & Bluth, 1980). When information high in the hierarchical structure of a passage is remembered better than lower level information, that phenomenon is called levels effect. If readers attend to and recall higher level text structure and the information expressed in it, that reveals the readers' responsiveness to the relative significance of ideas represented in a passage. The reason for the levels effect may be attributed to more attention being given to high-level content or to the repeated processing of the main idea while reading a lower level text (Meyer, 1984).

## What's the Structure?

Recognizing that students who are unaware of text patterns have trouble both comprehending and writing content materials, Janet Richards and Joan Gipe (1995) created a game to help students recognize common text structures. Before introducing the game, Richards and Gipe teach their students major content writing patterns using passages from the students' textbooks covering various subject areas. With text passages on a transparency, they show the text structure to students and point out the kinds of connective words and phrases typically used with a particular text pattern.

## STEP-BY-STEP: *What's the Structure?*

**STEP 1.** To conduct "What's the Structure?" with the text structures we have included here, you should put your students into groups of six or eight.

| 1. | 2. | 3. |
|---|---|---|
| What are the connective words and phrases in the passage? How is information in the passage organized? | How do the connective words and phrases provide clues to the writing pattern or combination of patterns in the passage? What is the top-level text structure? | Why do you think the author of this passage used this particular text structure? |

| 8. | | 4. |
|---|---|---|
| Write a short summary of the information in the passage and share it with others in your group. | **What's the Structure?** | What other text structures at lower levels, if any, does the author use in this passage? |

| 7. | 6. | 5. |
|---|---|---|
| What are the most important ideas in the passage? | Create a map showing how the facts and concepts in the passage are connected to each other. Share your map with other group members. | Share some connections between the facts and concepts in the passage and your own experiences and background knowledge. |

**FIGURE 5.4**    Game Board for What's the Structure?

*Source:* Richards, Janet Clarke, & Gipe, Joan P. (1995, May). Open to Suggestion: What's the Structure? A game to help middle school students recognize common writing patterns. *Journal of Reading*, 38 (8), 667-669. Copyright by the International Reading Association. All rights reserved.

**STEP 2.** Give each group a game board modified from one that Richards and Gipe designed (see Figure 5.4) and five packets of color-coded cards that contain text from content area books. Packets of red cards will contain identical copies of a description passage; green cards will contain copies of a sequence passage; blue will contain causation; yellow will have problem-solution; and orange will have a comparison passage.

**STEP 3.** A student in each group begins the game by selecting a packet of cards and giving one card in the packet to each group member. After players read the passage on the card, you circulate among the groups giving suggestions and encouragement while students respond to the numbered activities (1 through 8) on the game board (Figure 5.4) and collaborate toward solutions.

**STEP 4.** The game goes on until cards with passages illustrating all five writing patterns have been distributed and discussed, using the game board to guide discussion.

To continue practice with text structure passages of different kinds, students can bring passages they find to class for inclusion in future episodes of "What's the Structure?" Students can also be encouraged to use these text plans to help them organize and write their own content passages that can also be included among the passages when the game is played.

## STRATEGIES TO ORGANIZE KNOWLEDGE (KNOWLEDGE ORGANIZERS)

After reading, students frequently benefit from constructing a representation of what they discovered and learned. These representations help students remember information needed to study for examinations or to use in research projects. Four general methods or categories of knowledge representation from which students benefit are outlines, Cornell notes, graphic organizers, and concept maps.

### Outlines

For many years, teachers have encouraged students to write a formal outline after they have read a selection in order to see the structure and sequence of information presented in the reading. That more traditional, linear approach to organizing knowledge sequentially works well for many students. Main points and supporting details can be built into an outline that reflects the author's knowledge structure as depicted in the reading. Of course, readers who are expected to create outlines should have the reading skills necessary for identifying main ideas and supporting evidence or detail. Many comprehension fostering strategies already presented, or to come, will contribute to students identifying key ideas and their supporting claims.

There are two kinds of outlines in general use: topic outlines and sentence outlines. ***Topic outlines,*** as their name implies, are outlines that organize information by key concepts or key words. They demand of readers the capacity to capture the gist or essence of passages and paragraphs as well as subordinate ideas and the ability to state those gists and subordinate ideas in the readers' own concise words. Readers compose ***sentence outlines*** by stating key and subordinate concepts in complete sentence form.

There are several formats currently in use to identify levels of subordination in an outline. The more traditional pattern begins with Roman numerals identifying superordinate or main ideas. The next level of importance is represented with capital letters. Below that come Arabic numerals followed by lower-case letters. Traditionally and logically, outlines are balanced in that at least two numbers or letters make up each lesser section of an outline. An outline sequence and its balanced structure are shown in Figure 5.5.

To guide students' development of formal outlines, you can point out that numbers and letters used in the overall structure signal the importance of terms and concepts in an outline. Similar numbers and letters mark points of more or less equal importance in the outline. Information of relatively little importance to the knowledge contained in the reading is excluded from the outline. When reading a text, students can use its headings to help them identify main points, subordinate points, and the text's overall organization. The topic sentences of paragraphs also signal information of significant importance in the text.

### Note Taking (From Lectures and Readings)

The ***Cornell Note Taking System*** was developed at Cornell University's Reading Research Center over many years (Pauk, 1989). Although useful for taking lecture notes, the Cornell method adapts readily to taking notes while reading to gather

I. The Greek City-States
  A. Early City-States
    1. Greek Colonies
       a. Colonies put Greeks in touch with other Mediterranean societies.
       b. Contact with others led to sharing of ideas.
    2. Rise of tyranny
       a. Military service was every citizen's duty.
       b. Citizen-soldiers demanded greater voice in government.
       c. Discontent led to rise of tyrannies.
       d. In some city-states, democracy replaced tyranny as a form of
          government.
  B. Foundation of Democracy in Athens
    1. Beginnings of reform
       a. Solon and his reforms in Athens.
       b. Unrest persisted.
       c. Tyrannical government of Pisistratus emerged.
    2. Cleisthenes and movement toward democratic government
       a. Made the Athenian Assembly into a lawmaking body.
       b. Granted citizenship to some immigrants and slaves.
       c. Extended power of citizens through use of ostracism or temporary exile
          of citizen from city-state.

**FIGURE 5.5**  Outline Structure.

*Source:* Adapted from "The Heritage of Ancient Greece," a chapter in *World History: Patterns of Civilization,* by B.F. Beers, 1993.

main and supporting concepts for study. When using the Cornell system for taking lecture notes, students using ordinary ruled paper draw a two inch wide left margin and take notes only to the right of that margin. After class, students reorganize and rephrase their notes for clarity and accuracy. In the left margin, they insert questions, headings, and cues to facilitate learning and mastery of content. When review time arrives, students cover notes in the right column and use cues in the left margins to trigger content recall. Not surprisingly, the quality and quantity of a student's notes correlates highly with their achievement (Armbruster, 2000).

Adapting and extending the Cornell method to reading is quite simple. I've added a bell or whistle from research on note taking from textbooks (Caverly, Orlando, & Mullen, 2000), such as the importance of recognizing text structure to find "big ideas" and the need to explicitly teach note-taking strategies.

The format for taking notes from texts that I've adapted from the Cornell method is illustrated in Figure 5.6. It includes the following:

1. Reference to the assignment read at the top of the note page,
2. Right-column space for notes from the reading (especially key or "big" ideas and supporting concepts), types of text structure recognized or imposed when the text structure is not clear to a reader, and key terms, and
3. Left-column space for questions generated during or after reading that relate directly to notes in the right-column and unanswered questions generated from the reading. The questions in the left-column should be crafted to guide review of the reading material for class discussion and tests.

| Reading Assignment<br>Text: *Call to Freedom*          Chapter: 5<br>          (Stuckey & Salvucci, 2000) | Date: 10/11/xx<br>Pages: 136–138 |
|---|---|
| **Questions<br>(after reading)** | **Key and Supporting Concepts<br>(while reading)** |
| What are revivals? | Revivals: public church meeting where large groups of people gathered to hear sermons given by preachers. People sometimes renewed their religious commitment during an emotional ceremony. |
| What was the Great Awakening? | Great Awakening: unorganized, widespread movement of evangelical Christian church meetings where emotional sermons were delivered.<br>Important leaders:<br>Jonathan Edwards. Gave dramatic sermons like "Sinners in the Hands of an Angry God."<br>George Whitefield: Began giving revivals in the south and later in New England that drew thousands. |
| Effects of G.A. on Churches? | Divided some churches into traditionalists and members following evangelical preachers.<br>Old Lights = traditionalists<br>New Lights = followers of G.A.<br>Some Old Light ministers opposed G.A. because they doubted that it could actually awaken one's inner spiritual life (Charles Chauncy, minister of Boston's First Church). |
| **Unanswered Questions** | **Types of Text Structure Recognized** |
| Why was the Great Awakening so appealing to some colonists? | Description (Revival, Great Awakening)<br>Comparison (Old & New Lights) |

**FIGURE 5.6**   The NoteTaker.

# Graphic Organizers

***Graphic organizers*** help students organize knowledge and see more clearly how elements in a text are related to each other. In addition to an all-purpose cluster organizer, the graphic organizers presented here will enable students to represent visually the variety of text structures we just explored. These organizers graphically capture description, sequence, causation, problem-solution, and comparison.

Clusters.   Clusters are visual arrangements of terms, events, people, or ideas. They have a couple of purposes, including an alternate form of outlining, a strategy for studying, and a method of brainstorming. They help us see how things relate or connect, and they may confirm the adage that a picture is worth a thousand words.

As an alternative to a linear outline designed to represent information presented in a lecture or a reading, clusters enable listeners to more freely and visually arrange ideas, events, dates, and people. As students read, they can draw clusters of ideas

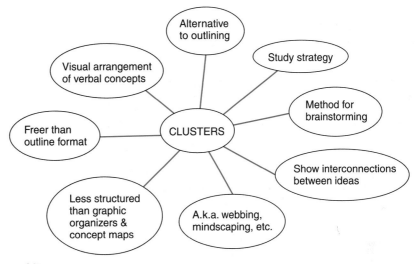

**FIGURE 5.7**   Clustering.

that may in turn be connected to other concept networks to produce a mental map of inter-related ideas.

Clustering is also known as mind-mapping, semantic mapping, mindscaping, and webbing. Hyerle (1996) refers to clusters as brainstorming webs. They are a little like sand-play or sketching because the process is loose—certainly less structured than graphic organizers to come later.

To make a cluster, students write a key word in the center of a page, circle the word, and place associated words or ideas around the key word and connect them with a line. The example in Figure 5.7 began with the key word: clusters.

Students can effectively use clusters for taking notes from lectures or from reading content textbooks, developing presentations, and initially organizing ideas for essays or research reports. While clusters are helpful visual representations of ideas, they are rudimentary forms of visual thinking. Organizers and content maps are more structured ways to represent knowledge and its branches.

Graphic organizers to represent text structures.   Organizers are useful ways for readers to present their understanding of what they have read in visual terms. Once learned, these organizers can be used across the disciplines as need arises. For example, the process organizer could be used to show how to run an experiment, take a photograph, or write a research paper in English.

*Characteristics organizer.*   Textbooks in all content areas, including math, history, and science, describe the characteristics of many concepts they present. Readers can better comprehend, understand, and perhaps remember these characteristics when using a ***characteristic organizer.*** To create this form of organizer, your students should first draw a circle or ellipse and put the target term in it. They then encircle the target term with characteristics and draw lines or arrows between the term and each characteristic.

If you return to the "house for sale" example of descriptive text structure (p. 188), you can see that townhouse would be the target term and characteristics

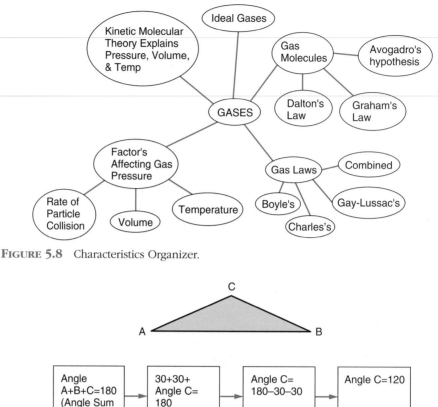

**FIGURE 5.8**   Characteristics Organizer.

**FIGURE 5.9**   Process Organizer.

of the townhouse would be placed in bubbles around the target and connected to it. Characteristics organizers also display much larger bodies of text. A whole chapter entitled "The Behavior of Gases" from a high school chemistry text (Wilbraham, Staley, Matta, & Waterman, 2000) could be visually summarized in a characteristics organizer as shown in Figure 5.8.

*Process organizer (flow chart).*   A ***process organizer*** does what it says it does: organizes a process. If students read about a process, such as making a cake, a federal law, or a Frankenstein monster, they can use the process organizer to visualize and describe the steps in the process. Process organizers display sequence text structures that present ideas in terms of time or order. You could use one to display the recipe for chocolate chip oatmeal cookies given earlier as an example of sequence text structure. Revealing its applicability to other sequences, the process organizer in Figure 5.9 depicts the steps needed to solve the following geometry problem: Two angles of an equilateral triangle (A and B) each have a measure of 30 degrees. Find the measure of the third angle (C).

*Cause-effect organizer.*   ***Cause-effect organizers*** are designed to graphically represent an array of causes that contributed to some specific event. They depict causation text structures, such as the passage explaining the causes behind a good reader's performance. In Figure 5.10, the information constituting the cause-effect organizer

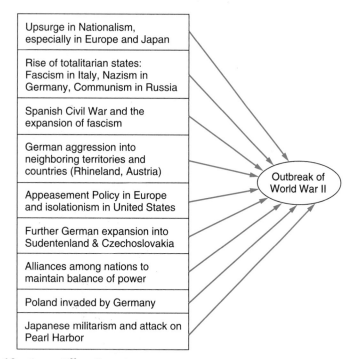

FIGURE 5.10   Cause-Effect Organizer.

for World War II's outbreak came from two chapters, "The Rise of Totalitarian States" and "The World at War," in a high school level world history text (Beers, 1993).

*Problem-solution-evaluation organizer.*   Organizers can provide a visual method to represent texts that are problem-oriented, as is the case with problem-solution text structures. The passage on teenage pregnancy that illustrated problem-solution text structures could easily be depicted in a ***problem-solution-evaluation organizer.*** In Figure 5.11, I've diagrammed an article from the *New York Times* presenting the problem of water flow in the Florida Everglades and the threat of reduced water to animal and plant habitats (Stevens, 1999). I've also presented the proposed solution and an evaluation of its results.

*Compare/contrast organizer.*   ***Compare/contrast organizers*** can take many graphic forms, including the one shown in Figure 5.12. In this case, the theatrical concepts of comedy and tragedy are compared and contrasted. With an organizer of this kind, readers can summarize similar features of two concepts and their unique characteristics. The example used to illustrate a comparison text structure (p. 189) focused on the advantages that the North and the South had at the beginning of the American Civil War. Because that text did not include characteristics common to both sides, the midsection of shared features in a compare and contrast organizer would not be needed.

    Methods of representing texts come in an infinite variety. With the graphic organizers shown in this chapter as a base, you can encourage your students to explore new approaches to depicting graphically the texts they read. In Chapter 7 on critical reading, we will explore a method to take apart written arguments, organize them in a chart, and discover how their elements work together.

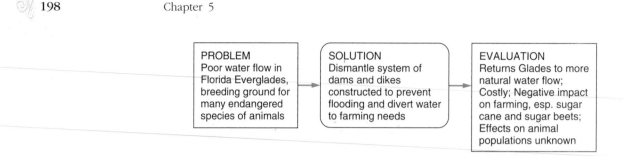

FIGURE 5.11    Problem-Solution-Evaluation Organizer.

FIGURE 5.12    A Compare and Contrast Organizer.

# Concept Mapping

Concept Mapping pushes graphic organizing into even more meaningful realms of student learning. Although they may demand more time, analysis, and creativity than the organizers I have already presented, Concept Maps are much more likely to show how concepts are linked to each other and to a learner's prior knowledge.

While looking for a sound method of capturing what students know about a topic before and after instruction, Novak and his colleagues (1991, 1998) came upon Concept Maps as a means of representing students' knowledge structures. A *concept map* is a method of showing key concepts and their relationships in graphic form. Novak examined students' reports of learning concept words and propositions. These indicators of a student's understanding could be configured into a constellation of concepts and propositions to represent the knowledge that the student constructed. Given a set of concepts, students can arrange them to show how they relate to the students' current knowledge structure and how connections between the concepts can be described. In Figure 5.13, you can examine an example of a Concept Map showing key ideas and principles of good concept maps that Novak himself created.

Novak attributes the inspiration for his Concept Maps to Ausubel's (1968) theory of meaningful learning. In contrast to rote learning, meaningful learning relates to relevant aspects of a learner's existing knowledge structure. For example, if you simply ask students to memorize by rote the definition of a Concept Map, that is less meaningful than asking your students to construct a Concept Map showing how it is related

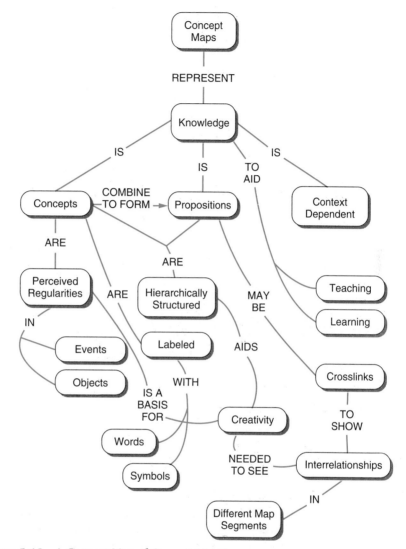

FIGURE 5.13   A Concept Map of Concept Mapping.

*Source:* From *Learning, Creating, and Using Knowledge: Concept Maps as Facilitative Tools in Schools and Corporations,* by J. D. Novak, 1998, Mahwah, NJ: Lawrence Erlbaum Associates. © 1998 by Lawrence Erlbaum Associates. Reprinted with permission.

to their prior knowledge about ways to organize information. One of Ausubel's contingent principles is that learners must be free to choose meaningful learning as a means of constructing new knowledge representations in long-term memory.

Simply teaching students to do Concept Maps and providing them with opportunities to practice mapping skills may enhance their recall of texts they read but do not explicitly map. Researchers (Chmielewski & Dansereau, 1998) have conducted studies using a Concept Mapping strategy. In comparison to a control group, students who were taught how to construct Concept Maps demonstrated better recall of both macro- and micro-level concepts in articles they read but never mapped. It is quite possible that training and practice in mapping texts enable readers to attend to the structure of passages and to watch for key concepts along with their relationships to other concepts and subconcepts.

## STEP-BY-STEP: *How to Design a Concept Map*

**STEP 1.** Formulate a question that relates to the knowledge domain or problem to be mapped. Identify 10 to 20 concepts pertaining to that question and list them separately on Post-its or 3 × 5 cards, limiting each concept to one or two words. Maps may also be constructed electronically using an appropriate computer program to make, move, and connect labeled concepts.

**STEP 2.** Place the most inclusive or most general concept(s) at the top of the map.

**STEP 3.** Choose 2 to 4 subconcepts to put under each of the most general concepts. If more than 4 subconcepts cluster around a single superordinate concept, try to find a concept of intermediate inclusivity to build into your hierarchy.

**STEP 4.** Define the relationships between concepts, draw a line between them, and use a few linking words to clarify the relationship. The hierarchical relationships constructed allow a structure of meaning for the knowledge domain to emerge.

**STEP 5.** Revise the map's structure. Add, remove, rearrange concepts and their relationship. This process of revision may occur several times.

**STEP 6.** Try to identify cross-links between concepts located in different regions of the map and connect these with descriptive linking words.

## Tech Tip:

You can download Concept Map software developed at the Institute for Human and Machine Cognition at the University of West Florida. This software can be used to create simple and highly complex multimedia concept maps. Several samples of Concept Maps and a tutorial accompany the IHMC Web site whose address is: *http://cmap.cognist.uwf.edu/download/files/cmapForm.html*.

You can also use Inspiration, a software program from Inspiration Software (*www.inspiration.com*) that enables users to electronically design knowledge organizers, including webs, idea maps, and Concept Maps. This software transforms hierarchical outlines into graphic forms and diagrams into outlines. By inserting a web address into either a diagram or outline, Inspiration automatically creates a hyperlink.

Go to the Double-Entry Journal for Chapter 5 on our Companion Website at www.prenhall.com/unrau to complete your journal entry.

DOUBLE-ENTRY JOURNAL: After Reading

What new comprehension fostering strategies did you discover and which of the strategies in this chapter would you teach to your students? Why do you think these strategies would help your students? More specifically, how does knowledge of text structure make sense as a comprehension fostering strategy in the context of the model of reading presented in the early part of this text?

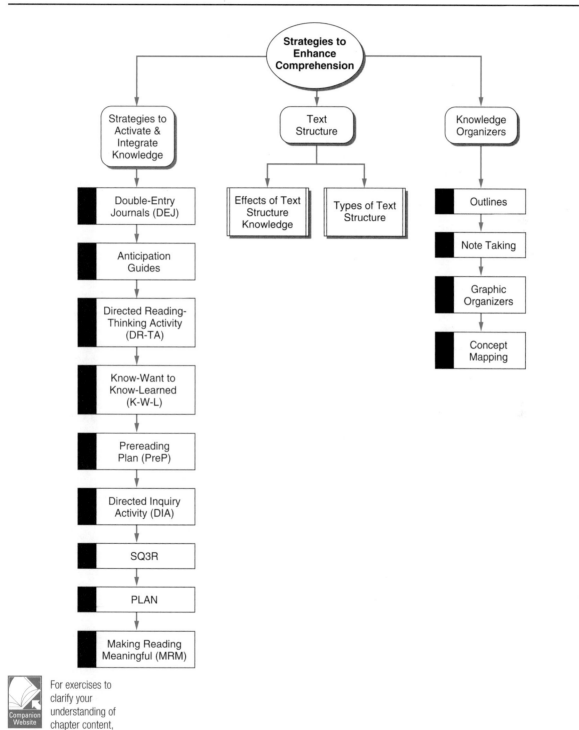

For exercises to clarify your understanding of chapter content, visit the self-assessments for Chapter 5 on our Companion Website at www.prenhall.com/unrau

# References

Alvermann, D. E., et al. (1985). Prior knowledge activation and the comprehension of compatible and incompatible text. *Reading Research Quarterly, 20,* 420–436.

Armbruster, B. (2000). Taking notes from lectures. In R. Flippo, & D. Caverly (Eds.), *Handbook of college reading and study strategy research* (pp. 175–199). Mahwah, NJ: Erlbaum.

Ausubel, D. P. (1968). *Educational psychology: A cognitive view.* New York: Holt, Rinehart & Winston.

Bartlett, B. (1978). *Top-level structure as an organizational strategy for recall of classroom text.* Unpublished doctoral dissertation, Arizona State University.

Beers, B. F. (1993). *World History: Pattern of Civilization.* Englewood Cliffs, NJ: Prentice Hall.

Caverly, D., Mandeville, T., & Nicholson, S. A. (1995). PLAN: A study-reading strategy for informational text. *Journal of Adolescent & Adult Literacy, 39*(3), 190–199.

Caverly, D., Orlando, V., & Mullen, J. (2000). Textbook study reading. From R. Flippo & D. Caverly (Eds.), *Handbook of college reading and study strategy research* (pp. 105–147). Mahwah, NJ: Erlbaum.

Chmielewski, T. L., & Dansereau, D. F. (1998). Enhancing the recall of text: Knowledge mapping training promotes implicit transfer. *Journal of Educational Psychology, 90*(3), 407–413.

Corkill, A. J. (1992). Advance organizers: Facilitators of recall. *Educational Psychology Review, 4,* 33–67.

Englert, C. (1990). Unraveling the mysteries of writing through strategy instruction. In T. Sruggs & B. Y. L. Wong (Eds.), *Intervention research in learning disabilities* (pp. 186–223). New York: Springer-Verlag.

Gersten, R., Fuchs, L., Williams, J., & Baker, S. (2001). Teaching reading comprehension strategies to students with learning disabilities: A review of research. *Review of Educational Research, 71*(2), 279–320.

Hattie, J., Biggs, J., & Purdie, N. (1996). Effects of learning skills interventions on student learning: A meta-analysis. *Review of Educational Research, 66* (2), 99–136.

Helmus, T. M., Toppin, E. A., Pounds, N., & Arnsdorf, V. (1988). *The United States yesterday and today.* Lexington, MA: Silver Burdett & Ginn.

Hyerle, D. (1996). *Visual tools for constructing knowledge.* Alexandria, VA: Association for Supervision and Development.

Langer, E. (1989). *Mindfulness.* Reading, MA: Perseus Books.

Langer, E. (1997). *The power of mindful learning.* Reading, MA: Addison-Wesley.

Langer, J. A. (1981). From theory to practice: A prereading plan. *Journal of Reading, 25,* 152–156.

Langer, J. A. (1982). Facilitating text processing: The elaboration of prior knowledge. In J. A. Langer & M. T. Smith-Burke (Eds.), *Reader meets author/bridging the gap* (pp. 149–162). Newark, DE: International Reading Association.

Lieberman, M., & Langer, E. (1995). Mindfulness and the process of learning. In P. Antonacci (Ed.), *Learning and context.* Cresskill, NJ: Hampton Press.

Mayer, R. E. (1984). Twenty-five years of research on advance organizers. *Instructional Science, 8,* 133–169.

Meyer, B. J. F. (1984). Text dimensions and cognitive processing. In H. Mandl, N. Stein, & T. Trabasso (Eds.), *Learning from texts* (pp. 3–52). Hillsdale, NJ: Erlbaum.

Meyer, B. J. F., Brandt, D., & Bluth, G. (1980). Use of the top-level structure in text: Key for reading comprehension of ninth-grade students. *Reading Research Quarterly, 16,* 72–103.

Meyer, B. J. F., & Freedle, R. (1984). The effects of different discourse types on recall. *American Educational Research Journal, 21,* 121–143.

Meyer, B. J. F., & Poon, L. (2001). Effects of the structure strategy and signaling on recall of text. *Journal of Educational Psychology, 93,* 141–159.

Meyer, B. J. F., Young, C. J., & Bartlett, B. J. (1989). *Memory improved: Reading and memory enhancement across the life span through strategic text structures.* Hillsdale, N.J.: Erlbaum.

Moore, M. (1975). *Paragraph development.* Boston, MA: Houghton Mifflin Company.

Novak, J. D. (1991). Clarify with concept maps. *The Science Teacher, 58*(7), 45–49.

Novak, J. D. (1998). *Learning, creating, and using knowledge: Concept maps as facilitative tools in schools and corporations.* Mahwah, NJ: Erlbaum.

Ogle, D. (1986). K-W-L: A teaching model that develops active reading of expository text. *The Reading Teacher, 39,* 564–570.

Pauk, W. (1989). *How to study in college* (4th ed.). Boston: Houghton Mifflin.

Pressley, M., Woloshyn, V., Lysynchuk, L. M., Martin, V., Wood, E., & Willoughby, T. (1990). A primer of research on cognitive strategy instruction: The important issues and how to address them. *Educational Psychology Review, 2,* 1–58.

Pressley, M., Wood, E., Woloshyn, V. E., Martin, V., King, A., & Menke, D. (1992). Encouraging mindful use of prior knowledge: Attempting to construct explanatory answers facilitates learning. *Educational Psychologist, 27,* 91–110.

Richards, J., & Gipe, J. (1995). What's the structure? A game to help middle school students recognize common writing patterns. *Journal of Reading, 38*(8), 667–669.

Robinson, F. P. (1946). *Effective study* (2nd ed.). New York: Harper & Row.

Stauffer, R. (1969). *Teaching reading as a thinking process.* New York: Harper & Row.

Stein, N. L., & Glenn, C. (1979). An analysis of story comprehension in elementary school children. In R. O. Freedle (Ed.), *New directions in discourse processing* (pp. 53–120). Norwood, NJ: Ablex.

Stevens, W. (1999, February 22). Everglades restoration plan does too little, experts say. *New York Times,* p. A1.

Stuckey, S., & Salvucci, L. K. (2000). *Call to freedom: Beginnings to 1914.* Austin, TX: Holt, Rinehart and Winston.

Thomas, K. J. (1986). The Directed Inquiry Activity: An instructional procedure for content reading. In E. K. Dishner, T. W. Bean, J. E. Readence, & D. W. Moore (Eds.), *Reading in the content areas* (2nd ed., pp. 278–281). Dubuque, IA: Kendall/Hunt.

Trabasso, T., & Stein, N. L. (1997). Narrating, representing, and remembering event sequences. In P. W. vanden Broek, P. J. Bauer, & T. Bourg (Eds.), *Developmental spans in even comprehension and representation* (pp. 237–270). Hillsdale, NJ: Erlbaum.

Vaughan, C. L. (1990). Knitting writing: The double-entry journal. In N. Atwell (Ed.), *Coming to know: Writing to learn in the intermediate grades* (pp. 69–75). Portsmouth, NH: Heinemann.

Wilbraham, A., Staley, D., Matta, M., & Waterman, E. (2000). *Chemistry.* Menlo Park, CA: Prentice Hall.

# 6

# Collaborating for Literacy and Learning: Group Strategies

After reading Chapter 6, you should be able to answer the following questions:

1. How would you apply whole-class methods, such as oral reading and discussion techniques, to integrate literacy development with growth in content knowledge?

2. What small-group methods, including cooperative learning activities, could you apply to integrate literacy development with growth in content knowledge?

3. What principles guide acknowledged forms of cooperative learning and what activities demonstrate these principles?

4. What is reciprocal teaching? How does it help readers improve comprehension? How would you use it in your classroom?

5. How would you integrate tutoring, including peer, cross-aged, and professional variations, into your content area instructional program?

DOUBLE-ENTRY JOURNAL: BEFORE READING

Now go to the Double-Entry Journal for Chapter 6 on our Companion Website at www.prenhall.com/unrau to fill out your journal entry.

What are your memories of group work in your middle and high school classes? How were they organized? How did they contribute to your learning? What kinds of whole-class, small-group, and paired activities do you plan to use in your teaching?

## Building Muscle Power Cooperatively (by Cindy Thai)

I held this cooperative learning activity in the weight room so students in my health education class, where I was teaching a unit on muscular strength and endurance, would be able to explore the possibilities of different exercises. I used a Jigsaw activity while teaching the unit. Students would have to read and understand their health textbooks and supplementary reading materials I handed out. I wanted my students to identify and demonstrate several exercises for each muscle group. I divided the class into five cross-ability, cross-status teams (Home Team A to Home Team E) and asked them to come up with a team name as their first Home Team task. I explained to them that at least one member of their Home Team would become a member of an "Expert Team" and that each "expert" would return to the Home Team to teach all the team members what the expert had learned. Then I put a chart up on the wall like this one:

| EXPERT TEAM NUMBER | MUSCLE GROUP EXERCISED |
|---|---|
| Expert Team One | Biceps and triceps |
| Expert Team Two | Deltoid and pectoralis major/minor |
| Expert Team Three | Trapezius and latissimus dorsi |
| Expert Team Four | Quadriceps and hamstrings |
| Expert Team Five | Gastrocnemius, soleus, & abdominals |

Next, I explained to my students that each Expert Team would have to identify the muscle groups they were assigned, create at least two exercises for each muscle group, and teach the exercises to their Home Team. While the Expert Teams were working on their tasks, I walked around the room monitoring and coaching the teams. After all the Expert Teams completed their task and returned to their Home Teams to teach the exercises, we had a full-class discussion to clarify any possible confusion. After completing the activity, I was convinced again that Jigsaw is an excellent way to encourage students to participate in group settings of different ethnic, cultural, and racial backgrounds.

In the cooperative learning episode that opens this chapter, Cindy Thai controlled the selection of text materials, the tasks that students were to undertake, the structure of the activities, and the means of its evaluation. Her teaching demonstrates how teachers' decisions about texts, tasks, and tactics shape classroom environments and learning. As we saw in the model of reading presented in Chapter 2, our classrooms play a pivotal role in students' comprehension of texts. Meanings for what they read get negotiated every day as our students interact with texts and with each other. But other elements of meaning beyond printed texts, elements that shape learning in classrooms, also get negotiated. These other classroom elements include the assignments we give, sources of classroom authority over text interpretation, and aspects of the social and cultural setting.

Into learning environments like those Cindy created, we and our students bring many meanings even before we begin to discuss our understandings of a specific text. Participants in the classroom bring their cultural heritage, their literacies, and their interpretations of the text to be discussed. As the discussion and dialogue proceed, students and teacher negotiate meanings informed by their individual backgrounds and perspectives.

During the dialogue among participants in the class, meanings are forged that the classroom community shares. These widely held interpretations form a set of expectations or assumptions on which subsequent meanings are likely to be based. All class members participate in this culture-creating endeavor. However, the teacher's role is of central importance because the teacher usually brings extensive knowledge of the subject and pedagogical tools to build classroom cultures.

When organizing for instruction, some teachers begin with whole-group instruction and progress to individual applications of concepts first presented to the whole group. The gradual release model of instruction (Pearson, 1985; Wood, 2001) demonstrates this progression (see Figure 6.1). According to the model, instruction begins with teachers explaining and demonstrating what students are to learn in whole-class settings. At the next level of small groups, students begin to take responsibility that the teacher releases to them when he believes they sufficiently understand concepts or skills they will eventually master. These groups may be pre-structured cooperative learning groups that enable students to share responsibility for each other's mastery of the material. At the next level, teachers ask students to work in pairs to practice and to reinforce what they've learned. Ultimately, what students have learned can be independently applied to other subject areas or problem spaces.

A gradual release model may not always be the best instructional model to follow. For some instructional situations, moving from individual input to small groups and then to whole-class discussion works better, especially if you want to get shy students to talk about their personal meanings or opinions first. That's the pattern I frequently followed when I wanted to encourage students to interpret texts in my classroom, share their interpretations in small groups, and then discuss interpretations in a whole-class

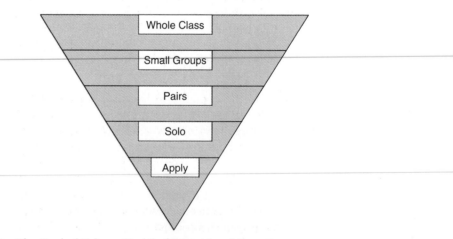

**FIGURE 6.1**    The Gradual Release Model of Instructional Grouping.

setting to discover what class-wide meanings we could negotiate. Although the underlying structure of this chapter moves from whole-group to individual applications, I definitely want you to remain free and ready to use instructional patterns that are completely opposite. You, of course, will have to decide which models (and which variations of those models) in which situations will work best for your content area classes.

## Whole Groups

Whole-class settings provide rich opportunities for teacher-student interaction of many kinds. Most typically, however, a teacher stands in front of a classroom of students, delivers information to them, instructs them to take notes, and expects them to demonstrate an understanding of what was delivered. When lecturing to students during my first months of teaching, I soon discovered that 80% of what I said went directly through them and out the window. Okay, so maybe 90%. I had few techniques to engage students even though I believed what I had to say was of at least some significant value. I'd gone to college and listened to professors deliver lots of information that I thought was both informative and interesting. Why not do the same for my students? While lecturing works well for the delivery of some information, as it does when teachers of history weave students into an engaging narrative of events with heavy consequence, I'm going to focus primarily on whole-class reading strategies, like oral and guided reading, and on class discussion methods. I'm adopting this focus primarily because this chapter is intended to present group strategies to acquire not only content knowledge but also literacy skills—not lecture techniques, although some of the strategies presented in this chapter, if integrated with lectures, should more deeply engage students in learning from lectures.

### Whole-Class Reading Methods

Many teachers ask their students to read aloud in class. While a student reads, others follow along in their own books. One student after another reads row by row as the teacher says, "Next." It's a popular strategy to cover both narrative and expository texts. Sometimes it's called Round Robin reading and, though widely tried, it doesn't always fly.

Why is this traditional classroom practice so popular? Opitz and Rasinski (1998) observed that teachers often use Round Robin reading to address classroom control and management issues, not to develop reading skills or improve comprehension. Ruddell (1997) notes that teachers sometimes use it when they are so frustrated by students' not doing their reading assignments that the only way they have left to make sure everyone at least hears the text content is to read it out loud in the classroom. However, researchers have found that Round Robin reading may actually get in the way of your developing more skilled readers. Among the undesirable effects of the practice are the following:

♦ *Its tendency to arouse undue anxiety in readers who may then come to loath reading rather than pursue it.* Some students, waiting for their turn to read, spend their anticipation time trying to deal with trembling hands and upset stomachs.

♦ *It diminishes readers' self-monitoring and self-regulation of reading.* During round robin reading other students often correct miscues and errors before the reader has a chance to self-correct. The practice may lead away from the ideal of developing self-regulating readers.

♦ *It may stimulate excessive sub-vocalization.* We know that sub-vocalization can help readers comprehend texts and that skilled readers rarely sub-vocalize every word in a text. However, if students slow down their reading rates to repeat each word to themselves as a student reads aloud in class, that practice could transfer to silent reading tasks, stimulate excessive sub-vocalization, and slow readers' rates through habituation.

♦ *It may reduce attention to meaning construction.* In anticipation of reading aloud to the class, students look ahead to see what they are expected to read and to rehearse their lines. However, that means they pay less attention to comprehending the whole text. Furthermore, those who've read ahead are likely to get in trouble when called upon to read but don't know the place to start.

♦ *It uses time that could be better spent on more meaningful and engaging activities.* Students could be developing other reading skills or building and extending their knowledge base rather than consuming time with an activity that has less educational value.

All in all, teachers should evaluate the usefulness of Round Robin reading. Although it may have a constructive place in some classrooms, more productive oral reading practices are available as strategies from which teachers can choose.

## Alternatives to Round Robin Reading

Reading aloud to students.    Students of all ages often find pleasure in having teachers read to them. Even middle and high school students are frequently delighted when their teachers read aloud. A poem, a humorous story, a passage from a book you're reading, or a newspaper editorial all provide a means to begin a class and open communication. Also, when reading aloud, you model proficient reading. The implication for students is that you would like them to read with similar fluidity and expression. For that reason, practicing the selection before reading it aloud is beneficial.

Following your reading, you should allow some time to talk with students about what you've read. You may just ask for general responses or form specific questions about the reading for students to answer. Either way, engaging students in some conversation after the reading has multiple benefits, including your discovering of the quality of their listening comprehension for different kinds of texts at different levels of difficulty.

Shared reading.    While reading aloud to students brings enjoyment to many, shared reading brings important added benefits. **Shared reading** combines your reading aloud plus your students following your reading in their own texts. Janet Allen (2000), in identifying its purposes, wrote that shared reading:

- Demonstrates fluid reading to students so they can experience the flow and charm of good writing;
- Builds bridges between texts and students' lives;

◆ Provides practice in strategies that make a text comprehensible;
◆ Models fluent reading that students can imitate in their independent reading; and
◆ Helps students build knowledge of texts and their world.

Even students who have trouble decoding can focus on comprehension rather than worrying about pronunciation. They can visualize the story, ask themselves questions about it, make predictions, analyze its components, and connect it with their own experience. With practice, readers can transfer these strategies to their own independently read texts.

Think-alouds.    When discussing reading assessment in Chapter 3, I explained how you can use comprehension think-alouds to discover how your students make meaning from texts, including those in the content areas. You can also use think-alouds as alternatives to Round Robin reading by asking students to share their associations to passages from a text with others in the class. You can watch for and emphasize processes that good readers engage in when they read, such as

◆ activating background knowledge,
◆ making predictions,
◆ forming mental images as they read,
◆ monitoring their comprehension progress, and
◆ fixing up comprehension problems as they arise.

Before students practice doing think-alouds on their own, you'll need to demonstrate the procedure for them. For guidelines to the procedure, see Chapter 3, Table 3.8 (A Think-Aloud of "Sea Fever"), and the following description of how to do think-alouds in class.

## STEP-BY-STEP: *Think-Alouds in Class*

**STEP 1.** When you demonstrate think-alouds, select passages that are likely to reveal the cognitive processes of engaged reading. Choose passages that are likely to challenge some of your students, passages that include comprehension problems, such as unfamiliar vocabulary or concepts and complex sentence structure.

**STEP 2.** Read the passage you intend to use for demonstration before sharing it with your class and identify several think-aloud pause points for yourself. At those points you will share with your class the associations stimulated by the content of the passage. You might want to make a few notes to focus and limit your associations.

**STEP 3.** You should begin by reading the passage aloud to your students. At points you've identified, pause and talk out your associated thoughts, as Mrs. Silva did with "Sea Fever," so that students can hear what you do to construct meaning.

**STEP 4.** After your demonstration, ask students to share their "think-aloud" thoughts and associations to parts of the same passage you used.

**STEP 5.** After demonstrating think-alouds yourself, ask for a volunteer to do a think-aloud with a text appropriate for the class, perhaps a text that the class is currently reading. Before giving it to the volunteer, prepare the passage by identifying several think-aloud pause points. Remind the student that at those points she should share the associations stimulated by the content of the passage. As appropriate and needed, you can ask questions, such as these recommended by Gunning (2002), to get more information about the student's construction of meaning:

- ◆ What was the selection mainly about?
- ◆ How did you get the main idea of the selection?
- ◆ What were you thinking about as you read the selection?
- ◆ What do you think will happen next in the selection? Why do you think so?

**STEP 6.** After you and the volunteer have demonstrated the technique, ask for and answer any questions about doing a think-aloud.

**STEP 7.** Next, identify and prepare with stop points an appropriate passage for your students to practice think-alouds in pairs. After pairing students, ask them to practice thinking aloud together.

**STEP 8.** After all dyads have had an opportunity to practice, pause and talk with students about what they observed and what they learned from doing think-alouds themselves.

Encouraging imagery to enhance comprehension.  You'll remember our learning about the Dual Coding Theory (DCT) in connection with our model of reading (Sadoski & Paivio, 2001). Briefly, DCT presents us with the notion that we have two processing systems, one verbal and one non-verbal. The non-verbal system includes imagery that helps us comprehend and remember texts, especially those stimulating the mental production of images, like narratives. However, you can also encourage students to develop imagery with expository texts.

## STEP-BY-STEP: *How to Induce Imagery*

**STEP 1.** To introduce this strategy to students, you should select a descriptive passage of about 200 words from a story. (I've included a sample from the fairy tale "The Frog Prince" to serve as a promising passage for this exercise.) Such a passage is likely to demonstrate how readers form mental images when reading. Put the passage on a transparency.

**STEP 2.** Make sure each student has a sheet of blank paper and a pencil, pen, or crayon with which to draw.

**STEP 3.** Read the passage aloud to your students while they follow.

**STEP 4.** Cover or remove the text and ask students to draw the image they formed in response to the descriptive text.

**STEP 5.** Ask students to form groups of two or three, share their drawings, and explain their meaning to others in the group. Ask students to explore similarities and differences between the images they created and the text from which they created the images.

**STEP 6.** Talk with students about how imagery can enhance comprehension and recall of texts they read in the content areas.

An example of image-rich descriptive writing comes from Grimms' "The Frog-Prince."

One fine evening, a young princess went into a wood and sat down by the side of a cool spring of water. In her hand, she had a golden ball, which was her favorite plaything, and she amused herself with tossing it into the air and catching it again as it fell. After a time, she threw it up so high that when she stretched out her hand to catch it, the ball bounded away and rolled along upon the ground, till at last it fell into the spring. The princess looked into the spring after her ball, but the spring was very deep, so deep that she could not see the bottom of it. Then she began to lament her loss, and said, "Alas! If I could only get my ball again, I would give all my fine clothes and jewels, and every thing that I have in the world." Whilst she was speaking, a frog put its head out of the water, and said, "Princess, why do you weep so bitterly?" (The rest, of course, is magic.) (Grimm, J., & Grimm, W., 1823/1971)

After demonstrating this imaging strategy with descriptive narratives, you can show students how it can be applied to informative or expository texts. Passages from many content area texts could serve as vehicles for demonstration; however, history and science texts often work especially well.

Read to discover.    To encourage reading for a purpose, you can have your students silently read a text that will be used as a resource for subsequent activities (Opitz & Rasinski, 1998). Following their silent reading, students can read aloud in class sections of the text they found particularly meaningful, exciting, or informative and explain why they found them so. They can also use what they read silently as a source of information to answer questions that you'll ask. Students also discover that reading for a purpose enhances attention and aids comprehension.

## STEP-BY-STEP: *How to Conduct a "Read to Discover" Session*

**STEP 1.** All students read silently (perhaps as their homework assignment) a particular text.

**STEP 2.** On 3 × 5 cards, write questions of various kinds about the text. These questions may vary from asking students to select and read a passage that they enjoyed, liked best, or found meaningful to reading a section that addresses more specific cognitive questions. For example, students might be asked to read a passage that explains the causes for an event, such as the American Revolution in a U.S. history class, or the physiological effects of a particular drug, such as caffeine, in a health education class (see Figure 6.2). You can also ask your students to read the topic sentence in an important paragraph and two or three sentences that support it.

**STEP 3.** Distribute the question cards to students. This could be done by having students pull questions from a "Read Aloud Bag" or by deciding which students could be optimally challenged with specific questions you write and giving those directly to specific students you think would benefit from finding and reading the answers aloud. Or you can pull cards from the question bag yourself, read the question to the whole class, give time for students to find the answer in their texts, call upon students who raise their hands when they find the answer, and request that the student read the appropriate text aloud.

1. What is ecology?
2. What is an ecosystem?
3. How do the organisms in an ecosystem get their energy?
4. What is an ecological pyramid?
5. What is a trophic level?
6. Which organisms are in the first trophic level?
7. Why do ecologists assign organisms in an ecosystem to a trophic level?
8. About what percentage of the total energy at trophic level 3 can be found in organisms at trophic level 4?

**FIGURE 6.2**   Sample Questions for a 10th Grade Biology Class "Read Aloud Bag" from a Chapter Entitled "What Is an Ecosystem?" in *Biology: Visualizing Life*.

*Source:* From *Holt Biology: Visualizing Life* (pp. 253–258), by G. B. Johnson. Copyright © 1994 by Holt, Rinehart and Winston. Reprinted with permission of the publisher.

## Whole-Class Discussions

Jennifer walks into one of her classes, sits down, takes out her notebook, copies the outline from the board, and then spends the better part of 40 minutes listening to her teacher, Mr. Delbanco, talk while she takes notes. The delivery is one way. Students ask few, if any, questions. In fact, when students ask questions, the teacher says he has a lot to cover and little time to cover it. He's caught in the crossfire between coverage and understanding with little time for the latter. He believes he's doing the best instructional thing he can to "prepare these kids for college." Jennifer keeps reading sections of her textbook as assigned and taking her lecture notes, but she knows she isn't learning much that she'll retain. What she's expected to know is delivered to her, deposited for a later withdrawal. She rarely participates in thinking much about course content, and she can't recall talking with any of her classmates about it—other than confirming the time for the next multiple-choice test.

In another of her classes, Jennifer is often asked, as part of her homework assignment, to bring three questions to class that she has about the previous day's lecture-discussion, about her reading, or about her project. Her teacher, Ms. Travaille, often begins the economics class by posing one of Jennifer's questions, one of her classmate's, or one of her own to the whole class. Sometimes they have to write for a few minutes about the question while things get settled down. When Ms. Travaille is ready, she asks students to share their answers, usually with a classmate first, and then moves into a whole-class discussion about their answers.

Through negotiated construction of meanings similar to the process described in Chapter 2, Ms. Travaille's students build deeper understandings of economic principles and practices. Into her economics classroom, students bring different meanings for the texts they read, the lectures they hear, and the discussion they engage in. From their discussions, common understandings of economic concepts and issues emerge. Students also construct and negotiate meanings for tasks, sources of authority, and other features of the classroom.

To guide her lecture-discussion session, Ms. Travaille often puts a set of questions on the board so students know what territory they will explore that day. Jennifer knows that the questions are a kind of map telling her where they'll go and what they're expected to know. But she usually has to actively take the journey with her teacher and classmates in order to discover or construct her answers. Her teacher works as a kind of guide suggesting they look this way or that, sometimes giving hints but rarely giving outright answers without students getting into the venture. Earlier in the year, Ms. Travaille taught her students about the Cornell Note Taking System and reminds them about its value as a study strategy. Jennifer often thinks her way to understandings in this class by applying the Cornell method—unless she's having an "off day." Usually, she senses that she'll remember the terrain she's covered, perhaps not every square inch but certainly the landmarks, the major sites, and the important vistas.

Ms. Travaille puts into practice important principles that enable her to cover her economics course content and address the state's standards while providing ample time for her students to interact, to discover, and to build understandings. What principles does she apply? She has put into practice several of them, some of which James Barton (1995) identified as those contributing to effective classroom discussions:

◆ Conducting a whole-class discussion is an art form, not unlike conducting an orchestra or playing in a jazz ensemble. But like conductors or musicians, teachers have to prepare and practice for class discussions. They need to know the material, discover main themes, prepare questions, and listen very carefully to the substance, texture, and tone of students' contributions.

◆ Talking enables students to construct new meanings, extend old ones, and make fresh connections between branches of knowledge and personal understandings. Teachers can encourage or guide students to make connections between branches of knowledge that may have been neglected or ignored and the current focus of discussion.

◆ Students can develop listening and speaking skills while interacting over and learning the course content. Teachers who listen effectively serve as models to their students. When needed, teachers can ask students to practice explicitly specific listening skills, such as rephrasing or summarizing what another student has said before extending the conversation.

◆ Students can acquire and practice thinking strategies during conversations about concepts and ideas in the course curriculum. During discussions, teachers can guide students so that they learn to differentiate opinion from supporting evidence or provide explanatory bridges between opinions and reasons supporting an opinion.

◆ All students should become part of the conversation. To work toward that goal, teachers need to monitor patterns of participation among students and to diagnose possible causes for non-participation. Some students may feel that they have little or nothing to contribute, that they can't put their thoughts into words, that they are confused, that they have been excluded from the dialogue, or that they don't want to say something dumb in front of everyone. Once a teacher has figured out what's at the root of the passivity, measures can be taken to draw in reluctant students.

Like Ms. Travaille, Barton (1995) believes that well orchestrated discussions depend upon the teacher having a clear instructional focus. Ms. Travaille thinks through the material she needs to convey to students until she has a clear grasp of what she wants her students to understand, why she wants them to understand it, and how she is going to guide them toward that understanding. The questions she puts on the board act as landmarks or beacons that signal to students where they need to direct their attention and what they need to understand.

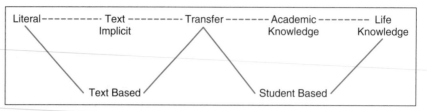

**FIGURE 6.3**   Continuum of Discussion Questions.

*Source:* Adapted from a figure from Barton, James. (Febuary 1995). Conducting effective classroom discussions. *Journal of Reading,* 38 (5), 346-350. Copyright by the International Reading Association. All rights reserved.

How to make good discussion questions.    Barton (1995) presented a system of five categories for organizing discussion questions that covers a spectrum from text-based questions to experience-based questions (see Figure 6.3). Effective discussions include questions covering the entire spectrum. However, students are likely to be most comfortable with literal questions although they require that students have done their reading and know how to search it, if needed, for correct answers.

The other four categories of questions take students beyond the literal and into what may be less familiar territory. This is the terrain that Ms. Travaille likes to roam with her students as she explores for deeper understanding and connections. She poses *text implicit questions* when she asks her students to make inferences based upon the text they are reading. For example, she asked Jennifer's class to explain why the author of an article on obesity among teenagers mentioned that schools often encourage consumption of rich junk foods by selling them on campus but didn't say anything about why schools sold them or why they simply didn't stop providing them. When Ms. Travaille asked Jennifer's class to think of ways to apply the idea of supply and demand to our global water access, she was asking a *transfer question* that required her students to think about how the idea of supply and demand for cars could apply to a natural resource. Ms. Travaille posed an *academic question* to connect her students' understanding of information in economics to other subject domains when she asked them to look for connections between their understanding of a stock's price-earnings ratio and an athlete's workout program. And, when Ms. Travaille asked Jennifer and her classmates to discuss the connections between a company merger plan and starting a new friendship, she was asking them a *life knowledge question* in which they had to relate their academic learning about mergers to their personal life experience. Ms. Travaille explained to her students that every answer they gave didn't have to be "right on the money." She wanted them to approach these questions creatively, sort of like writing a draft of a paper that would undoubtedly have to be rewritten. That way she was providing a safe space for exploration and affirming that searching for answers was a creative process that promoted learning.

The purpose of whole-class discussion is to engage students in content- or issue-focused interactions. Through these interactions between teacher and students or among students themselves, students can build understandings of key ideas and make links between what they already know and what they are learning. Although some educators believe that a teacher's role is to do as little as possible during discussions (O'Flahavan, Stein, Wiencek, & Marks, 1992), I believe that a teacher's active engagement in the design, development, and review of classroom conversations is optimum in the content areas. You are, in a sense, the lead instrumentalist in a jazz band who wants to develop a musical theme, encourage its exploration, and engage your musicians creatively. But you want your players to listen attentively to each other so they can each contribute to the performance. Accordingly, the teacher's multifaceted role is

◆ to decide on a discussion's purposes, including the concepts, processes, or skills students are to gain, and how those purposes tie to long-range learning goals,
◆ to set the stage and initiate conversation,
◆ to guide its development by clarifying concepts or making connections between them that will deepen understanding,
◆ to monitor the discussion's content and the degree to which students understand it,
◆ to facilitate interaction that will deepen engagement among participants,
◆ to help students internalize skills or rigorously examine concepts,
◆ to offer opportunities to students for summaries, reviews, and moments of reflection, and
◆ to analyze and reflect upon the lesson in order to learn what worked, which students need further instructional support, and what next instructional steps to take.

Without your active participation, discussions become vulnerable in too many classrooms to off-target drift. This is not to say that you should dominate dialogue important to students although not on your agenda. That would be both educationally inappropriate and psychologically oppressive. However, you will need to make judgments about the direction and value of the conversation as it evolves and, if too far off course, ask students to reflect on how the line of discussion contributes to learning goals or deepens understandings of the content or issues upon which the discussion is focused. Perhaps most important of all, you can use each of your whole-class discussion episodes as chapters upon which to reflect for the purpose of making future decisions about how best to conduct future discussions.

# Mini-lessons

A central feature of Nancy Atwell's (1998) teaching is the *mini-lesson,* a forum for sharing the teacher's knowledge and strategic skill with students. The mini-lesson sharing goes both ways, however, because students also share their knowledge, contributing to the growth of a classroom community. Although Atwell's mini-lessons used to be five to ten minutes long, she extended them to twenty minutes to allow for more interaction. Topics for the mini-lessons arise from her analysis of students' reading, their reading logs, their letters to her about their books, and their participation in classroom conversations. Through close observation and analysis, she decides what students must learn to gain greater competence as readers and learners. The decisions she makes about what should come next form the foundation for the mini-lessons.

To get students to think about and internalize reading strategies that good readers use, Atwell presents mini-lessons about a variety of reading-related topics:

◆ short- and long-term memory,
◆ schema theory,
◆ reading paces,
◆ considerate and inconsiderate texts,

- comprehension strategies,
- various methods of monitoring comprehension while reading,
- how readers respond to unfamiliar words, and
- how to cope with standardized reading tests.

However, concentrated interaction with readers over the texts they read is at the core of Atwell's approach to teaching reading. Although she prepares her students for these interactions at the beginning of the year by explaining schema theory and other reading processes, she demonstrates how students can put that theory into daily practice while reading throughout the school year. During the yearlong reading workshops interspersed with mini-lessons, she learns much from students' responses and class discussions. During these discussions, she carefully notes her students' comments about their reading processes and their responses to books and texts. It's this information that, when analyzed, helps her make subsequent decisions about the content of future mini-lessons.

You can also grind the grains of information you gather from your students over their reading into mini-lessons. If you're a math teacher and discover that your students have trouble translating problems written in English into algebraic terms, you can design mini-lessons to address the specific kinds of problems your students encounter during translations. If you're a history teacher and notice that few of your students are questioning their text's assumptions or making connections between parallel ideas or events, you can offer mini-lessons that focus on "questioning the author" to improve your students' critical thinking. To read the cues that students present in their written work and during class discussion is the key to opening students' minds to improved reading through mini-lessons and content learning workshops.

Jeff Waid, whose "student chronicles" I introduced in Chapter 3, discovered early in the school year that several students in his honors ninth-grade English class needed help with subject-verb agreement. Three-fourths of the students in that class were or had been ESL students with first languages other than English contributing to their English agreement problems. To address these difficulties, Jeff designed a mini-lesson on subject-verb agreement that helped students understand the roots of their grammar problem and methods to reduce its prevalence in their written work.

## COOPERATIVE LEARNING

So what exercises best flatten tummies? This chapter began with a description of Cindy Thai, a health education teacher, using Jigsaw to help her students understand muscle groups and how to strengthen them. She got her students into home and expert teams, gave them access to their health textbooks and supplementary reading materials, assigned muscle groups to each team, and asked each team to develop a presentation, including a couple of exercises for their muscle group. While Cindy's teams successfully presented exercises that would guide her students toward flatter tummies, what principles are likely to guide you toward more successfully using cooperative learning strategies?

# Principles of Cooperative Learning

Several principles of cooperative learning formulated by its inventors and innovators (Johnson & Johnson, 1999; Kagan, 1992: Slavin, 1995) typically guide its classroom applications. These principles, which are based on their creators' research and practical experience, have helped me make decisions about the design and use of cooperative learning activities in classrooms.

1. *Heterogeneous groups.* Researchers (Lou,1996) have found that although, medium-preformance students learn best in homogeneous groups and high-performance students do well in either homogeneous or heterogeneous groups, low achieving students perform best in heterogeneous groups. Furthermore, mixing students by both performance and status traits (like ethnicity, group affiliation, or gender) is likely to yield other benefits, such as improved interethnic and interpersonal understanding. Because of these reasons, many educators prefer to create heterogeneous teams when using cooperative learning strategies.

2. *Group accountability.* Students in teams should know that their team has a specific goal or goals that each member is working to achieve. Without a clearly expected outcome in the form of a product or performance, teams drift.

3. *Positive interdependence.* Group goals, usually in the form of a group reward, and accountability are connected with team interdependence. Activities are designed so that team members must swim together or sink together as they work toward a common objective. If one person can float on the work of others, something is amiss with the activity's design.

4. *Individual accountability.* Each team member must be held accountable for his or her participation in the team's work. Individual accountability arises from specifically tailored jobs (individual task specialization) for each team member or from holding each member accountable for performance on a test of knowledge or skills learned in the team but tested independently.

These principles serve as foundational concepts to design and implement cooperative learning activities of many kinds. However, you are likely to encounter other principles that some practitioners advocate. For example, Slavin (1995) endorses activities that can be adapted to students' individual needs and provide for equal opportunities of success for all team members. In the case of adaptation for individual needs of struggling readers, for example, cooperative learning activities that involve reading would take into account those readers performance levels and provide them with skill-appropriate reading tasks and strategies. In the case of equal opportunities for all to succeed, team members would be awarded improvement points to reward the effort and growth of lower performing students.

Cooperative learning practitioners have different attitudes toward competition between teams in classrooms. Some (Slavin, 1995) advocate team competition to heighten team cohesion and suggest the use of games or tournaments that engage teams in competition for rewards. Others (Johnson & Johnson, 1999) advocate cooperatively designed activities both within and between teams and see little advantage in competition between individuals or teams.

Researchers (Antil, Jenkins, Wayne, & Vadasy, 1998) who have examined conceptions of cooperative learning and its prevalence in classrooms found that few teachers used acknowledged forms of cooperative learning. When these researchers boiled cooperative learning down to two fundamental principles—positive interdependence and individual accountability—only about 25% of teachers who said they used "cooperative learning" and who were interviewed actually applied the two fundamental principles. Only 5% of teachers met a more restrictive five principle standard that included reflection on group process and its evaluation (Johnson & Johnson, 1999). Most teachers used their personally constructed version of cooperative learning, usually a less formal approach than that advocated by either Johnson and Johnson (1999) or Slavin (1995).

From my perspective, positive interdependence and individual accountability are essential to any small group activity that flies the banner of cooperative learning. As Slavin (1995) reported, cooperative learning activities that include individual accountability produced significantly more gains than those group endeavors without individual accountability. Including additional principles, such as heterogeneous groups, opportunities to reflect on group process, and equal opportunities for success, into the design of cooperative learning activities may simply enhance their impact.

## Informal Group Methods to Support Learning and Literacy

Before we get to more formal cooperative learning activities that may take more than a day to complete, I want to alert you to a couple of informal cooperative activities that facilitate learning and discussion. These activities can complement and enliven a more traditional lesson through guided interaction.

Numbered Heads Together.   When teaching or reviewing material that has more or less objective answers, like parts of speech in a grammar exercise, answers to math problems worked out individually, or the meaning of terms in a science class, **Numbered Heads Together** can help students learn or prepare for a quiz (Slavin, 1995). It's basically a game played between teams of four or five members, each of which is given a number and each of which provides individual accountability for learning. Once teams are formed, you present problems or questions to the whole class and give time for teams to figure out solutions or share answers so that any team member could respond successfully. Then you call out a number, say "3," and the 3s in each group who believe they can answer the question or explain the problem's solution raise their hands. You then call on one of the number 3s whose hand went in the air. If the student responds correctly, her team gets a point. Tallies can be kept on the board as the game progresses.

Think-Pair-Share.   When I'm presenting ideas to a class, seeking some interpretation of a text, or discussing various opinions about a topic, I sometimes use **Think-Pair-Share** to enrich the conversation and keep students engaged. Although Lyman (1981), who developed this activity, suggested having students sit in designated pairs, I usually ask my students to find informally a partner in the classroom. During my lesson, I may stop and ask students to take a minute to explore in a brief writing or journal entry an idea I've presented. Then I ask each student to find a partner, share written work, and discuss related ideas. These Think-Pair-Share activities may last only a few minutes, and I may do more than one during a class period. If so, I usually ask students to find a new partner to share and discuss what they've written during the individual thinking phase of the activity.

After students have completed a round of Think-Pair-Share, I try to bring out what they have written and discussed by asking students to share with the whole class. That sharing gives me a pretty good idea of what's on my students' minds, what needs clarifying, and how to extend conversations begun in pairs. As I continue with my presentation of ideas, I can incorporate aspects of students' sharing of ideas. After I asked students in a teaching for thinking course to jot down the names of three individuals who have shaped our current culture of ideas, I asked them to find a partner and share who got on their lists and why. After pairing and sharing, we had an animated whole-class discussion about who was on students' lists, how they got there, and what influence they had on today's thought.

## Cooperative Learning Activities with Integrated Literacy Goals

Group Investigation.    The roots of **Group Investigation** stretch back to John Dewey (1970) and his belief that cooperation and discovery in the classroom teach students how to live in a democratic society. As in democratic communities, the growth of group investigation requires interpersonal dialogue and collaborative inquiry. Through small group peer interaction, students pursue challenging, perhaps interdisciplinary learning goals.

*Learning goals for Group Investigation.*    A major learning goal commonly sought through Group Investigation is good solutions to complex problems in a specific discipline or across disciplines. Students working in small groups can use their analytical intelligence (Sternberg & Spear-Swerling, 1996) to recognize and define a problem; formulate strategies to solve it; gather, analyze, and synthesize information relevant to the problem; allocate their time and resources to address the problem; and evaluate the success of their proposed solutions. Examples of problems across disciplines that teachers may have students address include global warming or endangered species; the investigation of trigonometry functions, their discovery, structural variety, and applications; life in France during the French revolution; the legacy of nineteenth-century Romantic poets in Britain; and obesity in American culture. You can present to your students a broad problem or issue and students can then break the larger problem into smaller segments that will be the focus of each team's investigation.

Although the outcome of a Group Investigation can include a PowerPoint presentation that will engage your students' literacy skills, I would encourage you to integrate reading texts, printed and/or electronic, to gather information and writing text to demonstrate understanding of ideas or concepts contributing to each team's "product." When including reading and writing skills, you can build in opportunities to develop your students' reading and writing proficiencies, including presentation of reading or writing strategies. Using writing in the form of journal entries, essays, reports, and reflections gives you multiple opportunities to monitor and evaluate not only group progress but also individual contributions.

*Cooperative planning in teams.*    Engaging student teams in cooperative planning to address a problem lies at the heart of Group Investigation. While you coordinate, they decide which aspect of the problem to investigate, strategies to apply, information to gather, time and personal resources to dedicate, and methods for evaluating their solutions. Positive interdependence arises from the equitable division of labor among group members.

Because interactive planning does not come built in to every student who walks into your classroom, you will have to test your students' group-planning skills. They will undoubtedly need some guidance and structure that you can provide to augment the likelihood of each team's success. Whole-class discussions about the assignment help, as do structured reports from each team and continuous monitoring of progress toward learning goals. Start small and grow. Single day projects might best come before extended investigations.

*Coordinating Group Investigations: The hats teachers wear.* When doing Group Investigations, you will play several roles. First, you'll need to make choices about broad topics for investigation related to your long-term or standards-based instructional goals. You may also want to break the broad category down into several lesser topics. Teams may then choose from those subtopics or, if instructionally advantageous, you can assign subtopics to teams. Second, you will need to serve as a monitor and facilitator of team planning. Students will have questions about what to do, who's to do it, and when it's to be done. Your guidance will provide solutions during their organizing episodes, and your knowledge of resources will help them realize those solutions. Schedules for work completion might also be needed for longer projects. Before teams begin to carry out their plans, I would recommend that you review their subtopic proposals so that your learning goals are aligned with their task proposals. Third, you should consider using a rubric to evaluate team products and individual contributions. (See Chapter 8 on rubrics to assess writing.) A rubric will also alert teams and individual team members to the criteria that will be applied when their projects are completed. Those criteria will also enable students to see outcome expectations clearly. Fourth, when subtopic projects are completed, you will need to facilitate their presentation to the class and, perhaps, whole-class evaluation of each team's project. Lastly, all aspects of the curriculum related to the broad topic you select may not be covered through subtopic projects and presentations. In that event, you can fill in or elaborate through whole-class instructional methods and individual assignments.

## STEP-BY-STEP: *How to Do a Group Investigation*

When implementing Group Investigation, you and your students will go through several stages (Sharan & Sharan, 1992; Slavin, 1995).

**STEP 1.** *Getting Students Into Teams.* After you have selected the broad topic, students can review resources related to that topic and make subtopic proposals. You can present the broad topic or problem to the class, ask them what they would like to know about it, and record their interests and questions. You might then add subtopics that students did not identify and that supplement your instructional goals. When all potential subtopics have been described, students select their subtopics and teams depending on their interests. I suggest developing a procedure for team membership, such as giving students a list of all possible subtopics and asking them to rank the top 3 or 4 they would like to in-

Team name: _____

Team members: _____

Team subtopic: _____

What questions we plan to answer or problems we'll investigate and solve: _____

_____

_____

A list of our resources to accomplish the above: _____

_____

Who will do what: _____

_____

When we'll get things done: _____

_____

What we think we'll do for a presentation (not required info at this time): _____

_____

_____

FIGURE 6.4    Team Planning Worksheet.

vestigate. Then you would work on putting teams together, with student interests and the principle of heterogeneity guiding their team building. Before students actually meet in their teams, you may need to survey materials students can access to accomplish their teams' purposes. Students in higher grades may be given more responsibility for finding resources and bringing them to class for team use.

STEP 2. *Planning for Learning about the Subtopic.* Students need to meet in their teams to decide what they will study or what problem they will solve, how they will go about their work, who will do what and when, and what kinds of products or outcomes they will create. Each team could submit a worksheet (see Figure 6.4) describing their program and schedule so you can see what each team member will be individually accountable for with respect to the group outcome.

A team's subtopic can be further segmented into mini-topics. After discussion and identification of mini-topics whose investigation can contribute to the team's subtopic presentation, each team member selects a mini-topic. Team members can share resources they uncover while pursuing their mini-topics.

STEP 3. *Engaging in the Investigation.* With the information they gather, students analyze their data, propose solutions, organize information, and reach conclusion. The team's work should be designed so that each member contributes and so that you can monitor each student's contribution. Usually, students interact over their resources, decide how resources will be applied to their problem, discuss their understandings of texts, clarify meanings, and pursue conclusions for their products and presentations.

If teams divide their subtopic into mini-topics, each team member works independently and interacts with the team to report on problems and progress. Each team member also prepares a mini-topic presentation to give to his or her own team. These individual mini-topic presentations will contribute to the team's presentation to the whole class later in the process. Using mini-topics for which each team member is responsible makes each member's contributions more transparent and ensures individual accountability. These mini-topic presentations can be in the form of written reports that could, like the team's presentation, be evaluated.

**STEP 4.** *Designing the Final Report or Presentation.* After stating and sharing their team's central findings and their rationale, groups decide what they'll present and how they'll present it. Because the integration of literacy growth into content learning is a primary instructional aim, I recommend that reports or presentations be written. Other forms of presentation can accompany the written products, such as debates, quiz shows, simulations, art or theatrical work, and PowerPoints or multimedia shows that draw upon the multiple intelligences of group members. You or a student committee can coordinate team presentations.

**STEP 5.** *Presentations.* Group presentations should be made to the whole class and can actively involve all students in the class. For example, if a team is presenting what they learned about a trigonometric function, like tangent or cosine, students in the whole class could engage in solving or creating problems that entail the application of those functions and meet at learning stations to share their solutions. Students should also be involved in assessing the quality of a team's presentation. If you design with your class or present a rubric to guide the evaluation of presentation, students can apply that rubric to team presentations.

**STEP 6.** *Assessment.* Teams should engage in self-evaluation and receive assessment feedback from other students and from you. An important aspect of cooperative learning is learning about group processes and how members contribute to team effectiveness. Students can discuss how they completed their work, how they felt about the process, and how they solved problems as a team to complete work on their subtopics. After students evaluate a team's presentation to the whole class, these evaluations can be given to each team.

In alignment with research and my own observations, I also hold students individually accountable for learning about concepts, ideas, or solutions that each team presented, including those presented by their own team. The form of that accountability is usually a test of the material covered. I have made lists of study questions to guide students' individual learning based not only upon what teams presented but also on material related to the broad topic that I presented to the whole class. With information about how teams performed and about how individuals performed on tests covering the material presented, I can get a pretty clear picture of how well each student in the class engaged in learning and mastering key concepts and knowledge.

If teams break their subtopic into mini-topics, products can be generated that enable assessment at four points: When the whole class assesses the team's subtopic presentation, when other team members assess individual mini-topic contributions to the team's effort, when team members evaluate their own team's whole-class presentation, and when the teacher evaluates both individual and team learning and performance.

**Group Reading Activity (GRA).** Like Group Investigation, a ***Group Reading Activity*** (Manzo & Manzo, 1997) divides a complex learning task into smaller segments that each team addresses cooperatively. If you were asking a class to undertake a GRA focused on the American Civil War, you would divide the history text into roughly equal segments, as I've done in Table 6.1.

TABLE 6.1   Group Reading Activity Team Assignment Example

| Section | Pages | Assigned Group |
|---------|-------|----------------|
| The Roots of Civil War | pp. 225–231 | |
| The Alignment of the States | pp. 232–238 | |
| The Battles Begin | pp. 238–243 | |
| Life Back Home | pp. 244–260 | |
| Final Fighting | pp. 260–266 | |
| The War's Consequences | pp. 266–273 | |
| Beginning Reconstruction | pp. 274–280 | |

Assign students to teams of 4, determine the total number of teams composed, and then divide the text into roughly equal segments, one for each team. The Civil War reading assignment (Table 6.1) for each team arose from their being 28 students in the history class. With 4 students in each team, 7 assignments were needed.

When students meet in their teams, they have several tasks to complete that lead to a class presentation. After all presentations are completed and before assessing students individually for their understanding of the text, the teacher and students decide what still needs to be covered to ensure that learning goals or standards have been met for topics included in the GRA.

## STEP-BY-STEP: *How to Do a Group Reading Activity (GRA)*

**STEP 1.** Select text material that aligns with your lesson's learning goals and pertinent standards.

**STEP 2.** After creating 4-person teams, decide how many teams you'll have in a particular class. Divide the section of text material in the GRA into appropriate sub-sections for each team to read, as exemplified in Table 6.1.

**STEP 3.** All students should read all team assignments, perhaps for homework the evening before beginning the GRA.

**STEP 4.** You should assign one section to each team. For each team's reading assignment, explain to teams that they will need to identify the most important concepts or ideas in the material they will read, to decide what additional material they may need to cover relevant text topics, and to decide how to present the text's content to the rest of the class. Presentations may take a multitude of forms, including written reports, debates, simulations, round-table discussions, and audiovisuals.

**STEP 5.** After appointing a friendly critic from each team, you should explain to the whole class that the critic is to visit another team to hear its presentation and to offer constructive suggestions for improvement.

**STEP 6.** Let critics hear other team presentations and provide recommendations that presenting teams can use to improve their work. The visiting critic's constructive suggestions guide a team's revision before whole-class presentations begin.

**STEP 7.** Review each team's presentation yourself, provide your own suggestions, and give teams time to digest all recommendations for improvement.

**STEP 8.** Schedule and hear team presentations.

**STEP 9.** Engage in a whole-class discussion to make sure key concepts are covered, misunderstandings clarified, and questions answered.

Jigsaw II.    When concept acquisition rather than skill acquisition is your learning goal, *Jigsaw II* (Slavin, 1995) may be your instructional vehicle. Originated by Elliott Aronson and his colleagues (1978), Jigsaw works like interlocking parts forming a whole picture. In Slavin's Jigsaw II, texts provide the raw material that all "home team" members read and use to teach each other. You assign students in a home team chapters to read and give them expert sheets that identify topics to master or questions to answer while reading. Students with the same topic, but from different home teams, meet together in "expert teams" when they finish reading. They discuss the topics, answer their questions, and become "experts." They then return to their home team and take turns teaching other cooperative team members the material they have mastered. Students next take a test to evaluate their command of the material, and those test scores become team scores. Slavin used an individual improvement score system to provide for individual differences and success for all. Team success motivates all members to engage in learning. Positive interdependence with every student contributing to his or her team's success lies at the heart of this activity. Although some teachers initially balk at complications connected with planning and organizing a Jigsaw II event in class, I have often used the activity and found it effective.

## STEP-BY-STEP: *How to Do a Jigsaw II Activity*

**STEP 1.** Decide on what students are to read and study to address your learning goals and standards. On the day before you plan to begin the Jigsaw II activity, assign the reading material to be covered so that all students will have read it.

**STEP 2.** Compose several questions for the expert sheet. Slavin advises teachers to formulate questions that are relevant to topics that appear throughout a chapter or unit. If we were to use Jigsaw II to cover the Civil War rather than a group reading activity, we would have to write expert sheets for each section that team members were to master. For example, if an expert Civil War team were to focus on "The Battles Begin" text, I would provide each student with a set of topics or questions to guide and focus their reading in preparation for expert team discussion. Those questions might look something like this:

1. What brought about the fall of Fort Sumter?
2. What general strategies for war did the Union and the Confederacy adopt?
3. What was the significance to the Confederacy of the outcome of the First Battle of Bull Run?

4. What was the outcome of the Battle of Antietam and why was it significant to the Union forces?

5. What is an ironclad and why did it change naval warfare?

**STEP 3.** Create heterogeneous home teams so that the number of team members corresponds to the number of topic questions on the expert sheet. If you have five students in the home team, you'll need five topic questions and five expert teams. You'll also need at least 25 students in your class to have five expert teams. If you have more than 25, you can have more than one member of a team become an expert on the same topic or question.

**STEP 4.** One question on the expert sheet should be assigned to at least one member of the home team.

**STEP 5.** Ask all students with the same question to meet in an expert team to address that question and be ready to explain the answer to their home team. You should monitor discussion and preparation for teaching the home teams as expert teams interact.

**STEP 6.** When ready, expert team members should return to their home teams to explain answers and concepts to their home teammates. Further discussion may arise in the home team as teaching progresses.

**STEP 7.** After home teams have heard from all "experts," you can convene a whole-class discussion to cover any loose ends, confusion, or further questions.

# RECIPROCAL TEACHING

Although ***reciprocal teaching*** depends upon small-group interaction for its effectiveness, it was not originally designed as a cooperative learning activity. In its original, experimental form, reciprocal teaching engaged only a struggling reader and a researcher in a series of prescribed interactions to enhance comprehension. However, the reciprocal teaching method worked for certain students, and its original form morphed into a variety of applications, one of which engaged four students working collaboratively—if not in an acknowledged cooperative learning format. While earlier comprehension strategies in this and the previous chapter were designed to help readers' cognitive processing before, during, and after reading, reciprocal teaching was intended to foster *meta*cognitive processing. More specifically, reciprocal teaching helps readers monitor and control comprehension, important functions of metacognition that we explored in Chapter 2. Following years of research and investigation, educators widely agree that metacognition while reading consists of two fundamental dimensions: monitoring and controlling comprehension.

## A Brief History of Reciprocal Teaching

Charles has an IQ of about 70 and reads on a third-grade level, four years behind his peers in reading comprehension. In spite of his being enrolled as a special education student and receiving several forms of remedial reading instruction, he's made little progress. He can read aloud seventh-grade texts at about 90 words per minute with few errors, but he can't tell you much about what he's read. He has great difficulty answering the most basic questions you ask him about passages he reads.

When you ask him to ask you a question based on his reading of a passage, he can't do it. He makes only statements about the passages. You often require students to read their textbooks as part of their homework assignments, and you have learned that Charles cannot do homework assignments that require him to read the text and respond to it. He simply doesn't understand what he's reading well enough.

After reviewing the behaviors of good readers, Annemarie Palincsar (Brown, Palincsar, & Armbruster, 1984; Palincsar, 1982) created reciprocal teaching to address the needs of inadequately mediated learners who, like Charles, had trouble with reading comprehension. These struggling readers may have lacked parental modeling, such as question-answer sessions over a book read together. Disadvantaged students who can decode but not comprehend quickly may have missed important nurturing in literacy. Once at school, teachers take over the parenting role to model and promote effective reading and learning strategies. This they do by showing their curiosity about what is read, generating questions, making predictions, and searching for evidence to validate their conclusions and inferences. Good teachers become models of comprehension fostering strategies that children internalize thorough social interaction in the classroom.

## Original Reciprocal Teaching Model

If students lack reading strategies because they have not had enough interactive experience with more able readers to develop good reading tactics, couldn't these struggling readers learn strategies by interacting with teachers who modeled strategic reading? Couldn't these struggling readers, like Charles, imitate and internalize those strategies? These are the questions Palincsar, Brown, and their colleagues (Brown, Palincsar, & Armbruster, 1984; Palincsar, 1982) asked. They identified activities underlying traditional reading education practices and theoretical treatments before selecting four particular skills for strategy instruction. These four were (a) summarizing, (b) questioning, (c) clarifying, and (d) predicting. Researchers had explored the effectiveness of these skills in isolation but had not combined them to confront the problems of readers with poor comprehension. As a package of activities, they were embedded in a training procedure called reciprocal teaching that mimicked parent-child interaction over books. In its earliest experimental forms, Palincsar and Brown used reciprocal teaching as a training strategy with seventh- and eighth-grade students who had adequate decoding skills, but whose comprehension scores were, on average, three years below grade level. "Adequate decoding skills" meant that students could read grade-appropriate texts at rates of 80 words per minute with no more than two errors. In this early model of reciprocal teaching, each student worked with one of the researchers. Together both would silently read a passage, usually about one paragraph long, in an appropriately challenging book. Whoever was in the role of "teacher" first, perhaps the researcher, summarized the passage, clarified complex or misleading parts of the text, asked the student a teacher-like question based on the main idea, and made a prediction about where the text was going. While providing suggestions and encouragement, the experimenter tried to keep the dialogue informal. Then, they reversed roles, and the "student" became the "teacher" for the next passage, sometimes delighting in asking the adult a question about the text. At first, students would sometimes have difficulties putting the gist of a passage into their own words and would need some coaching from the adult who would provide prompts, nudges, and hints along with praise for progress. After several sessions, perhaps six to ten, students became more adept at capturing the essence of a passage, asking a question, and making a prediction. All in all, students had about 20 reciprocal teaching sessions.

Eventually, with sufficient modeling, students were able to perform these reading strategies on their own. They had internalized the reading comprehension strategies through social interaction during several one-on-one sessions with a trained "teacher." Students' performance on experimenter-designed quizzes to determine their comprehension improved from an average of about 15% to rates of 80 to 90% after instruction in reciprocal teaching. Although performance fell off somewhat after half a year, students' performance again improved after one day of training "booster" sessions.

Through training in reciprocal teaching, Charles, who was actually a student in one of Palincsar and Brown's studies, made impressive progress in overcoming his frustrations with reading comprehension. He learned to give concise summaries, answer 80 to 90% of the comprehension questions, and formulate appropriate questions after reading passages. In addition, his comprehension score on the Gates-MacGinitie, a standardized reading test, improved 20 months.

 STEP-BY-STEP: *How to Do Basic One-On-One Reciprocal Teaching*

**STEP 1.** Determine your student's capacity to decode text by having him or her read from a text appropriate to his or her grade level. As a general guideline, if students are unable to read grade-appropriate texts at rates of 80 words per minute with no more than two errors, they would most likely benefit from instruction in decoding skills prior to or along with comprehension fostering activities. (See Chapter 9, "Struggling Readers and English Learners," for appropriate intervention programs.)

**STEP 2.** Create and administer a 10- or 20-item comprehension quiz based on the text you have selected. If students who appear to be able to "read" the text do not perform satisfactorily on the quiz, that is, they answer less than half the questions correctly, they are likely to be candidates for reciprocal teaching.

**STEP 3.** Arrange for a series of 20 training sessions about ½-hour to 45-minutes in length.

**STEP 4.** Identify appropriately challenging "instructional" level texts for the student. Books should be neither at the frustration level nor at the independent reading level for the student. Be ready to change texts if the ones selected are either too difficult or too easy.

**STEP 5.** Prepare in advance the length of passages you and your student will read. However, maintain flexibility. You may have to change the size of passages you have planned to use as you see how your student responds to the text.

**STEP 6.** Begin by reading the first passage silently together. (If decoding itself is a challenge, the text can be read aloud and followed.)

**STEP 7.** Do not start by having the student summarize, question, clarify, and predict. But do begin with you as the teacher demonstrating these skills for the student. Initially, you may need to look at the text as you summarize, ask questions, and make predictions. However, try to work toward doing so without looking at the text. Your student may also begin by needing to consult the text, but the point is to construct a gist that can be put into the reader's own words without consulting the text frequently.

**STEP 8.** After completing the first passage, change roles. Now the student will adopt the role of the teacher. Read the next passage silently (or aloud if decoding presents a problem) and have the student summarize, clarify, ask a question of you, and make a prediction about where the text is going. You may have to do some guiding during the first few rounds, but provide help, support, and especially praise following moments of success. Try to keep the atmosphere informal while still being structured.

**STEP 9.** Continue this process until you have completed the session.

**STEP 10.** Following each session, I'd recommend writing a log describing your student's response to reciprocal teaching. Note the appropriateness of the text you selected. Note your student's progress in response to your modeling. Watch for skills that may need more deliberate demonstration at the next session. And indicate your student's general response to this reading game.

## Variations of Reciprocal Teaching

**Early modifications.**   Teachers and researchers have been prolific in creating variations on the theme of reciprocal teaching. However, Brown and her colleagues (Brown, Palincsar, & Armbruster, 1984) were themselves innovative. After the success of their initial studies, they replicated reciprocal teaching's key steps with classroom teachers in school settings rather than with researchers. This time they selected for their sample seventh- and eighth-grade students from the poorest reading groups in classrooms and students in reading groups that met in a resource room. While these students were about 2½ years behind in reading comprehension, they had to meet the decoding requirement for inclusion in the training. Teachers received three training sessions in reciprocal reading, including a video of the researchers using the strategy. The researchers showed teachers how to help students who became overly detailed in summarizing and who were unable to generate appropriate teacher-like questions. Teachers also had opportunities to practice the procedure with students not taking part in the innovation. The results of this second study of reciprocal teaching in the natural setting of school classrooms was quite similar to the one-on-one study previously described. Students improved in the ability to summarize, ask questions, participate in dialogue about passages read, and answer comprehension questions. Students also transferred their newly acquired skills to other reading and learning tasks.

**Later applications.**   Although numerous teachers and researchers have applied reciprocal teaching in their classrooms, we are going to examine more closely its implementation in a couple of schools, one a middle school, the other a high school.

Faced with hundreds of underprepared readers, Cindy Lenners and Kelly Smith (1999), who were teaching at Harden Middle School in Salinas, California, modified the original model of reciprocal teaching so that they and other teachers in their school could help their students become more skilled readers. In their approach to reciprocal teaching, Lenners and Smith focused on question asking early and extensively. They begin by distinguish between "on-the-surface" and "under-the-surface" reading. **_On-the-surface reading_** reveals an understanding of what was said in the text or what happened and can be demonstrated through literal retelling, simplistic paraphrasing, and summarizing. **_Under-the-surface reading_** gets at what the text means and includes connecting the text to the reader's life, to other texts, and to background knowledge, filling in knowledge gaps, clarifying, making predictions, questioning, evaluating, challenging, and reflecting. These differences in levels of reading are important because training in reciprocal teaching entails learning how to ask more and better questions. To teach students their variation of reciprocal teaching, Lenners and Smith encourage teachers to model all aspects of the dialogue, including reading aloud, generating both on- and under-the-surface questions, clarifying, summarizing, and predicting. They also encourage teachers to help students understand the function of different question-word categories. If the student is trying to generate on-the-surface questions, they will want to use question words such as Who? Where? When? What? and sometimes How? If under-the-surface questions are being generated, students should think of using question words such as these: Why? How? Would? Should? Could?

Question generation appears to be a critical factor in reading comprehension improvement. Several researchers (Rosenshine, Meister, & Chapman, 1996) reviewed 26 intervention studies that taught students to generate questions as a way to improve comprehension and found that some procedural prompts were more successful than others in improving students' comprehension performance. The most successful prompts were the following:

1. Signal words, such as those included in Lenners and Smith's (1999) intervention (e.g., who, where, how),
2. Generic question stems (e.g., "What are the strengths and weakness of . . . ?"), and
3. Story-grammar categories that helped students generate questions about a story's setting, main character, main character's purposes, and obstacles the main character confronted.

The form of question generation emphasized in training provided for teachers and students through Lenners and Smith's model is primarily that of signal words, such as who, where, and why, with some question stems, especially for under-the-surface questions, such as hypotheticals in the form of "If . . . , then would . . . ?"

In their adaptation of reciprocal teaching, Lenners and Smith (1999) have students work in pairs or groups of four who proceed in a cycle that I called a "Metacognitive Merry-Go-Round" to improve reading through self-regulation (Unrau, 1995). Let's say the group consists of Alice, Brenda, Carlos, and David (A, B, C, & D, for short). The process begins with A reading a passage silently or out loud and asking an on-the-surface question and an under-the-surface question. Then B, C, and D attempt to answer the questions. A proceeds to ask for or to give a clarification, perhaps by saying, "Do you need anything clarified?" A next summarizes the text she read and B, C, and D add to that summary. To complete the first cycle, A makes a prediction and gives some evidence for making it. Finally, B, C, and D agree or disagree with the prediction and provide their evidence. The next cycle begins with Brenda (B) playing the reader role. If working in pairs rather than a team of four, students modify the procedures described above by having only B do all tasks that B, C, and D are expected to do.

Although the original experimental model for reciprocal teaching engaged struggling readers in only a 20-day intervention program, Lenners and Smith (1999) encourage middle and secondary teachers to implement and practice reciprocal teaching activities for many months or years in their classrooms. They also believe in the importance of teachers knowing how to train extensively their own students in reciprocal teaching practices, such as question asking of many kinds. Allowing teachers to experiment with transplanting the strategy into their own classrooms is another important principle these teachers advocate. These practices appear to be paying off in improved student reading and learning performance.

In a test of reciprocal teaching's impact on high school students in remedial reading classes, Alfassi (1998) investigated the method's impact compared with a control group that was given a traditional method of remedial reading based on skill acquisition. The study would be a test and a stretch for reciprocal teaching because, in past studies, it was applied primarily to elementary and middle school students, often in more experimenter-controlled or lab settings which were quite different from remedial reading classrooms. Students in the study received training in reciprocal teaching for 20 days, the usual training time, and then five days of introduction to the four primary processes followed by three weeks of activities using the method.

Reciprocal teaching met the challenges of its being taught to high school students, whose reading struggles have persisted over many years, and of its being taught in remedial reading classes that created a more authentic or natural setting for the method's implementation. The researcher found that the study supported the implementation of the method in large, intact, remedial reading high school classes. In addition, it lent credence to strategy instruction with long-struggling, high school-aged readers who needed to internalize metacognitive strategies, such as self-assessment and self-regulation, while reading.

## Features Contributing to Reciprocal Teaching's Success

Several studies (Carter, 1997; Marks, 1993; Rosenshine & Meister, 1994) have concluded that reciprocal teaching in various forms improves the comprehension of struggling readers. However, its success may depend on its including specific elements. A review of reciprocal teaching's implementation in classrooms indicates that its success may be attributable to several factors:

1. Students should be carefully evaluated to make sure that they can decode an appropriate grade-level text at a reading rate of at least 80 words per minute with no more that two errors. If students are unable to decode at that standard, they probably need other kinds of reading interventions, such as some form of corrective reading program that emphasizes the growth of decoding skills. (To accomodate weak decoders, texts could be read aloud.)

2. During training, teachers should thoughtfully regulate the level of text difficulty. If needed, students can begin with single sentences for summarizing, asking questions, clarifying, and predicting. They can then progress to single paragraphs, two or more paragraphs, and on to longer selections of 800 or more words. Later, students could select or be given appropriately challenging grade-level texts with which to learn and practice reciprocal teaching strategies.

3. Teachers (tutors, peers, etc.) of reciprocal teaching should be thoroughly trained in its basic activities: summarizing, questioning, clarifying, and predicting. That training should include an understanding of direct instruction, provision for ample practice, an understanding of monitoring and control over reading comprehension, and the evaluation of teachers who will be trained and who will serve as models.

   3.1. Teachers should learn to give students direct instruction in learning to summarize a passage. With the goal of enabling students to clearly explain to students the steps essential to quality summarizing, I have used a procedure called single-sentence summaries. To create the strategy, I reviewed work on summarization (Day, 1980, 1986; Kintsch & van Dijk, 1978) and orchestrated

1. Reader reads section aloud to partner. *Using own words, reader summarizes the section in one sentence.* Partner assists and records the summary.
2. Partner reads the *next* section aloud. *Using own words, partner summarizes the section in one sentence.* Reader assists and records the summary.
3. Continue to switch roles following the pattern established above.

*Summarizing Hints:*
1. Drop out information that is not of central importance. (Avoid trivialities.)
2. Don't repeat any information. (Avoid repetition.)
3. In place of a list of examples, use a general term that includes all the items on the list.
4. Look for the topic sentence in the paragraph. It can help you identify and state the main idea.
5. If you can't find a topic sentence in the paragraph, make one up that you think expresses the paragraph's core meaning. Try to define the paragraph's controlling idea.

*Summaries*
¶ 1.


¶ 2.


¶ 3.

**FIGURE 6.5**   Single-Sentence Summaries.

summarizing procedures so that students work as collaborating partners (see Figure 6.5). A single-sentence summary sheet can be designed to fit the number of paragraphs or sections students are to summarize with a number identifying each paragraph or section.

3.2. Teachers should be trained to understand the range of questions that students can ask and the most effective means by which to teach question generating methods to students. Studies (Rosenshine, Meister, & Chapman, 1996) suggest that best practices include initially using single-word and stem prompts to help students generate questions on the surface level and beneath the surface. As students internalize question-asking procedures, these structured prompts should be gradually withdrawn. Lenners and Smith (1999) developed a procedure to help students learn how to ask on-the-surface and under-the-surface questions. I have modified their procedure somewhat and include it as Figure 6.6. As was done with a single-sentence summary sheet, a question log can be designed to reflect the number of paragraphs or sections students are to base their question generation on.

3.3. Teachers need to understand the role of clarifying in the reciprocal teaching process and the different kinds of clarifying that might be done during the activity.

---

1. Reader reads section aloud to partner. Reader asks an on-the-surface question. Partner repeats the question and then answers. Partner records question on log.

2. Partner asks an under-the-surface question. Reader repeats the question and answers. Reader records question on log. Switch roles and go on.

| On-the-Surface Questions (When, Where, What, Who) | Under-the-Surface Questions (Why, How, Would, Should, Could) |
|---|---|
| ¶ 1. | |
| ¶ 2. | |
| ¶ 3. | |

---

FIGURE 6.6   On-the-Surface and Under-the-Surface Question Log.

   3.4. Teachers should be able to explain, demonstrate, and teach predicting in reciprocal reading.

   4. Sensitive interaction and modeling of strategies are essential. Teachers need to develop scaffolding for each student's response, regression, or progression. Through reciprocal teaching, teachers provide students with a progressively challenging scaffold that they use to gain comprehension strategies. As readers become more competent, teachers ask the readers to become increasingly responsible for more comprehension tasks while increasing the challenge in progressive, manageable degrees.

   5. Teachers should evaluate students' progress toward mastery of summarizing, questioning, clarifying, and predicting. Mastery-level criteria can be established, and students can be continuously evaluated to determine whether or not they have met the criteria. Students not meeting the criteria may need further instruction.

   6. Essential, too, is the frequent assessment of target students' progress with comprehension quizzes and checks on development of dialogue. Both the degree and quality of students' internalization of strategies need to be assessed.

   7. The training should provide bridges and maps to show teachers and students how the strategy applies across the curriculum.

   8. Teachers should be organized to coach each other, perhaps with some form of a Critical Friends Group program (see Chapter 12).

   9. Teachers and administrators ought to be committed to infusing reciprocal teaching over the long haul, including the provisions of training to new teachers and students as they enter the school or district.

Many of these principles have contributed to the success of earlier reciprocal teaching efforts in several different educational settings, from elementary school to the university. Certainly, teachers need to discover how reciprocal reading may best be adapted for their students in their classrooms. However, these guidelines, if applied, will increase the likelihood that reciprocal reading interventions that you plan in your classroom or school will help struggling readers improve their comprehension and enjoyment when reading.

## TUTORING: WORKING IN PAIRS

To promote collaborative learning and literacy in a variety of graduated forms, this chapter began with whole-group instruction techniques, moved on to small-group formats, including cooperative learning and reciprocal teaching, and will now focus on pairs, specifically tutoring pairs. Tutoring can take a variety of forms, including peer tutoring, cross-age tutoring, and adult-literacy tutoring in which a trained college student, adult volunteer, or teacher works one-on-one with a tutee. Although teachers can gain much diagnostic knowledge from one-on-one tutoring and give strategic instruction to students in need of special scaffolding, time limits teacher-student tutoring opportunities. So we'll start our discussion of tutoring with student-to-student interaction and progress to adult-student models.

### Peer Tutoring

Peer tutoring engages students of similar age and grade in helping each other master a domain of knowledge or skill. The practice has both advantages and some drawbacks. The advantages include cognitive growth through peer empathy with a learner's frustration and more supportive classroom climates arising from pro-social cooperation.

On occasion, peer tutors echo the adage "Been there; done that." Having had problems in learning they have overcome and sharing a "cognitive framework," peer tutors can help their classmates understand topics that teachers may struggle to convey (Cohen, 1986). Most teachers have had moments in class when calling on a student to explain a concept or process was just the magic needed to move beyond a

sticking point. On more than one occasion while teaching an English class, I've answered a student's question about the motives behind a character's behavior with reasonable clarity, but some students found my explanation difficult to grasp. I could see perplexity written on their faces. So I'd call on a savvy student to explain in his own words the point I was making. And "Presto!" like pulling a rabbit from an empty black hat, confused students grasped the point. That magic can also occur in peer tutorials.

Competitive, tense, "Wha'd'ja get?" classrooms can become more conducive to learning with a dash of cooperation. Peer tutoring puts students in pro-social cooperative roles helping classmates learn. Building those supportive relationships can significantly change a classroom climate. We know that school climates improve when cooperative learning programs are effectively developed (Slavin, 1995). The same cooperative dynamics that contribute to those changes work in peer tutoring relationships within classrooms.

While peer tutoring enables students to help each other learn, every peer tutoring relationship a teacher engineers does not always result in a well-built bridge for learning. Personalities clash sometimes when the chemistry of one learner collides with that of another. Or a tutee's self-worth may suffer from feeling stigmatized as less capable than a tutor from the same class, and so a tutee may resist help or advice. However, the likelihood of problems arising from putting peers together for tutoring drops with appropriate training, placement, assignment, and assessment. Even those few resisters may discover the benefits of tutoring and seek it rather than resist it.

**Guidelines for tutoring from research.**    Because I've focused this discussion of group methods on the development of reading, I want to provide you with research-based guidelines for developing and implementing reading tutorials. Martha Rekrut (1994) compiled a set of useful guidelines that her investigation of relevant research generated. These guidelines answer many questions that teachers interested in using reading tutorials ask.

1. *What elements of reading are amenable to tutorial work?* While many elements make a friendly fit, a tutor might focus on word recognition to build fluency, vocabulary development in content areas, comprehension strategies like SQ3R and PLAN, text structure, and graphic organizers. When pairing a tutor with an English learner, a focus on oral reading, rereading, and vocabulary development would be productive.

2. *Should tutors be high-achieving students?* That's not essential. Research indicates that any level achiever may become a commendable tutor. What tutors of any achievement level avoid, however, is making and announcing value judgments to the tutee.

3. *What about training?* Training in interpersonal, management, and content skills are essential. Tutors should have both initial training and ongoing coaching. Debriefing of tutorial sessions helps tutors reflect on their practice and work out problems that arise during tutoring sessions.

4. *Are same-sex or opposite-sex pairs better for tutoring?* Rekrut (1994) recommends same-sex partnering because she has found that cross-gender pairing "sabotages both content and skill acquisition." She indicates from her review of research that pairing older girls with younger boys usually works well, however.

**Paired reading.**    Paired reading is an effective method of helping struggling and reluctant readers. Topping (1987) found that routine dyadic reading helped struggling readers improve both their word recognition and their comprehension. It's a form of one-to-one tutoring in which a proficient reader, who models and supports good reading, is paired with a struggling reader. The "proficient" reader may be a more able student reader, a teaching assistant, or a parent. While Figure 6.7 provides a flow chart of the Paired Reading procedure (Scoble, Topping, & Wigglesworth, 1994), steps in the strategy are given here:

## STEP-BY-STEP: *How to Do Paired Reading*

**STEP 1.** Identify a struggling reader, henceforth, the tutee, and a tutor who will work constructively with the tutee.

**STEP 2.** Provide the tutor with an orientation toward dyadic reading that includes some basic, common sense rules about working one-on-one with a student having a history of reading frustrations. Explain that the tutee needing support with reading selects books or magazines and can change texts when desired. The tutor explains the procedure outlined below to the tutee before they begin their work.

**STEP 3.** Tutee and tutor start by reading the same text aloud together, a kind of reading duet.

**STEP 4.** When the tutee wants to read aloud alone, she should signal the tutor to stop vocalizing. The tutor encourages the tutee while reading progresses.

**STEP 5.** At appropriate points, tutee and tutor should pause to talk about the text and make sure that the meaning-making process is sensibly progressing. The tutor can simply ask, "What's going on here?" or "What do you think is happening up to now?"

**STEP 6.** If the tutee makes a mistake or miscue, the tutor should wait to see if it is corrected. If the miscue is not corrected and it could affect the meaning of the passage, the tutor can ask the tutee what the miscued word is and how it contributes to the meaning of the passage. If the tutee does not know the word, then the tutor can explain it as needed. Then the two read together again until the student gives the signal for reading aloud independently.

Guided reading. Although often used in the elementary classroom (Fountas & Pinnell, 1996), guided reading works well with struggling readers in the middle and high school (Allen, 2000). While it can be used in small groups and even whole classes, guided reading is a highly effective tutoring tool if properly used. Its purpose is to develop independent, proficient readers who can summarize and question the meanings they construct, who can form opinions based on the reading of a text and support those opinions with reference to the text.

Teachers and tutors use guided reading to help struggling readers learn and apply comprehension strategies so that they can move toward independent, silent reading. To use guided reading, tutors need to carefully read texts they will use with tutees and make plans to engage them in a challenging dialogue. During the guided reading process, tutors model ways to make personal and critical connections with texts on multiple levels. As Allen (2000) points out in *Yellow Brick Roads,* tutors using guided readings focus on process rather than outcomes with their tutees by asking questions like these: How do we know that? What other choices did the character have? Why do you think that? What is likely to happen next? What words in the text helped us make

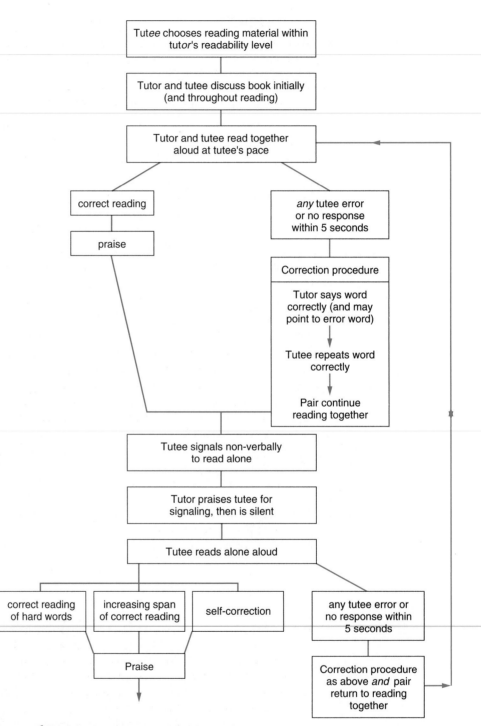

**FIGURE 6.7**  Paired Reading Procedure.

*Source:* Figure from Scoble, John, Topping, Keith, & Wigglesworth, Colin. (1988, Febuary). Training family and friends as adult literacy tutors. *Journal of Reading*, 31(5), 410-419. Reprinted with permission of the International Reading Association.

**TABLE 6.2** Question Categories for Guided Readings

| | |
|---|---|
| **Personal Response Questions** | How would you feel under those circumstances?<br>How would you respond to a comment like that? |
| **Metacognitive Response Questions** | Does this passage make sense to you?<br>When did you notice you were confused with what was going on? |
| **Connection Response Questions** | How would your best friend react to a situation like that?<br>What was the author trying to do for you as a reader when she set up that comparison? |
| **Critical Response Questions** | How does this boyfriend compare to her other boyfriend in the story?<br>How would you change this explanation to make it clearer to you? |
| **Surface-Features-of-Text Questions** | How does the title connect with the story?<br>How do the chapter headings help you understand this chapter? |

that discovery? Furthermore, tutors make every attempt to generate questions rooted in their tutee's responses while they are making meaning rather than depending on predetermined questions, such as those at the end of a story in a school anthology.

Allen (2000) recommends the exploration of five different question categories that tutors can use during guided reading. These categories are described in Table 6.2. Tutors can also use the categories to explore think-alouds that will give their tutee ideas about how to respond to a text and construct meaning from it.

A key to success with guided readings is the choice of texts, if tutors have a choice. Allen (2000) suggests that the texts be "interesting, informative, short." However, guided readings can also be based upon the content area text tutees are expected to read. A tutor may have to do quite a bit of scaffolding to help a tutee understand the text, but the experience will help a tutor or teacher become more deeply aware of the kinds of challenges students face when trying to read materials for a class.

## Cross-Age Tutoring

Alexandra, a high school junior, got credits for enrolling in a tutoring program at her school in which she would help first and second graders learn to read. Alexandra was herself a struggling reader. But what made the group of tutors Alexandra joined special was that all of the tutors-in-training were expecting to give birth to their own children in a matter of months. This cross-age tutoring program would help her prepare to teach her own child how to read.

Customarily, cross-age tutoring pairs an older student with a younger one. The more proficient reading tutor serves as a model to a less proficient tutee seeking to develop reading skills. The tutor scaffolds reading instruction while taking into account the tutee's background knowledge, reading skills, and pace. In some cross-age tutoring models, tutors make significant gains in their own reading proficiency (Jacobson et al., 2001).

In a tutoring program studied by Douglas Fisher (2001), middle school tutors benefited because they engaged in authentic literacy events with first and second graders, got to emulate effective instructional models, received feedback from their tutoring efforts, and integrated writing with their tutoring assignment. In the program Fisher (2001) investigated, the middle school tutors were students significantly below average in reading competency and were enrolled in a reading class. The tutees they tutored attended a nearby elementary "feeder" school for the middle school. The reading class teacher developed reading lessons for the tutors. On the day before the tutors went to the elementary school to tutor, the teacher modeled the lesson in the reading class and gave tutors time to practice with each other. The next day they went to the elementary school to tutor. After tutoring with their first- and second-grade tutees, the tutors spent the following day back at their middle school debriefing, writing about their tutoring experiences, and preparing for the next day's tutoring episodes.

The typical lesson plan included five phases. First, tutors introduced the literature they would teach to their tutees, showed the book's pictures to the tutees, and asked them to predict from those pictures what the story would be about. Second, tutors focused on the story's challenging vocabulary by reading each unfamiliar word to the tutee who then read the word back to the tutor. Third, tutees wrote the words down, wrote a definition, drew a picture revealing each word's meaning, and wrote a sentence using each word. Fourth, the tutors read the book to their tutee. Finally, the tutees wrote in their journals describing their feelings about the book.

Variations on the model of cross-age tutoring I've just described are plentiful. Some pair struggling or outstanding high school students with delayed readers in middle or elementary schools. For example, Connie Juel (1991) paired student athletes with at-risk children, gave the athletes authentic reasons to practice reading, and improved reading performance. Some programs train high school seniors for tutoring incoming freshmen known to be struggling readers. Programs, such as the one Alexandra entered at the beginning of this section, train pregnant adolescent girls for tutoring first graders so that, as new mothers, these one-time tutors can transfer their tutoring skills to reading time with their own children. These cross-aged tutoring programs often reveal not only improved reading performance for both tutor and tutee but also improved attitudes toward reading (Haluska & Gillen, 1995; Potter, 1997).

## Adult-Student Tutoring

Components of effective literacy tutorials.    Reviewers (Juel, 1993; Wasik, 1998) of formal literacy tutoring programs for younger struggling readers have identified several practices contributing to their success. Lessons should have a balanced instructional design that includes reading of familiar texts to gain fluency, work on word and letter-sound correspondences, writing, and inclusion of a variety of texts to incorporate various reading strategies. Furthermore, Wasik (1998) has identified eight features contributing to tutorial success:

1. Supervision by a reading specialist,
2. Continuous coaching for tutors,
3. Structured sessions with a balanced design, such as that described earlier,
4. Consistent and intensive sessions,
5. High-quality materials,

6. Periodic assessment of progress, including that of high-frequency word recognition,
7. Consistent attendance,
8. Coordination between tutorial content and classroom teaching.

These features have been incorporated into many tutoring programs, including those in the federally funded America Reads program that prepares volunteers and work-study students in colleges and universities to tutor children in kindergarten through third grade (Morrow & Woo, 2001).

Features similar to those that contribute to tutorial success with younger readers work well with adolescent readers (Brown, 1996), including:

1. Reading familiar material to build confidence and fluency,
2. Reading aloud to the student to promote the enjoyment of reading,
3. Maintaining a running record of the texts that tutees read,
4. Work on words and letters, including "basic" or frequently used words,
5. Writing down dictated stories for readers to read and edit, and
6. Reading of new materials, including read-alouds of which the tutor makes a running record during the session following the introduction of a new text.

Brown also includes methods not only to develop comprehension but also to develop vocabulary and competence in writing.

**Teachers tutoring struggling readers.** To help beginning teachers learn to assess struggling readers, apply reading strategies, and foster literacy in the content areas, I ask credential candidates in my classes to engage in a literacy tutorial focused on reading development. The tutorial serves as an important fieldwork episode in which emerging teachers create and sustain a one-on-one relationship with a student who may be "at-risk" and who is not "at home" with reading.

I explain to my students that the individual tutorial and the subsequent case study that they will write based on it should include at least six components:

1. *Assessment of the tutee's reading and writing abilities and attitudes.* Information about a student's reading and writing performance can be gathered from that student's current and former teachers, from formal assessment that includes standardized testing information usually available in a student's cumulative file, and from informal assessment sources like a Curriculum-Based Measurement (CBM), Group Reading Inventory (GRI), running records, cloze tests, and interviews (see Chapter 3).

2. *Instruction designed to foster fluency and reading comprehension.* Based on the results of the assessment information, teachers design and implement a series of lessons that focus on the development of fluency, reading comprehension, and the use of writing to learn strategies. I ask teachers to convene no less than 10 separate sessions of about 45 minutes, gear instruction to the needs of the student, and engage in instruction within a specific content area. (The tutorial may cover more than one subject area, but it should focus on one, such as science or history).

3. *A field journal for observational and/or field notes that traces the tutorial's progress.* Tutors use a field journal to keep track of tutoring events and to record observations and impressions as the tutorial develops. I ask tutors to include their field notes as an appendix to their written case study.

4. *A 10-minute uninterrupted video of their interaction with the tutee during a tutoring session.* Tutors describe in writing their learning goal and instructional challenges during the video-taped episode, why they pursued the learning goal they pursued, how effective they believe the instructional episode was, what they would change if they could do an "instant replay," and where they will next take their tutee based on what transpired during the video-taped session.

5. *Evaluation of progress made during the tutorial.* In order to gauge the impact of the tutorial, tutors use their on-going, benchmark, or formative evaluations as evidence upon which to measure progress. Tutors sometimes collect additional assessment information that might include (but is not restricted to):

- Readministration of a CBM, GRI, or cloze test using texts similar to the first round of testing. If the tutorial has a short run (less than 12 to 15 sessions), indications of progress on these instruments is, in my experience with them, rather unlikely. But breakthroughs happen.
- A portfolio of the student's work (completed in the tutorial and/or in the tutee's other classes).
- Talks with a tutee's teacher about in-class and homework performance.
- Written measures, such as summaries or recall protocols.

6. A reflection on their tutoring experience. What did tutors discover about their tutees or themselves during the tutorial? After reflection on the tutorial, what would tutors have changed, done more of, or done less of? What did tutors learn that could be transferred to small-group or whole-class instruction?

Guidelines for the reading tutorial.   When students in my credential classes asked me to help them get started on their reading tutorials, I drew up the following practical guidelines:

1. Know your tutee's background, resources, interests, motivation, and obstacles to learning. Form a positive relationship.
2. Assess the tutee's ability to read. For a quick assessment, use an oral reading test.
   2.1. To evaluate reading fluency, you can give your tutee a CBM using passages from one of your tutee's content area textbooks. (See Chapter 3 for procedures.)
   2.2. To determine the challenges presented to your tutee by a content area textbook, you can develop and administer a GRI based on the same textbook you used for the CBM above. (See Chapter 3 for procedures.)
   2.3. *REMEMBER:* Some students can decode but struggle with comprehension. So ask your tutee some questions about the reading he is doing. A good way to find out if tutees get the main idea is to ask for a summary in their own words of a specified section of text. Then ask a few questions that require the tutee to clarify meanings or make predictions about what's to come. Your judgment on this will be critical. Do tutees really get the meaning of what they're reading or are they just reading words?
3. Set some goals. Design a program that's responsive to your tutee's reading level, school learning situation, and interests.
4. Check to see if your tutee has a grasp of letter-sound relationships for a vocabulary of 100 basic words. (See Chapter 4 on vocabulary.)
5. Include basic vocabulary (as needed) in the tutorial and build your tutee's word knowledge. (See Chapter 4 on vocabulary.)

6. Help your tutee to read strategically, purposefully. Teach your tutees strategies that will help them become more independent, self-regulated readers but provide scaffolding so your tutee can grow with your cognitive support. Use strategies like the following:
   Paired and guided reading
   VSS, Key Word Method, and Word Maps (Chapter 4)
   Anticipation Guides, DR-TA, DIA (Chapter 5)
   SQ3R and PLAN (Chapter 5)
   Text structure instruction (Chapter 5)
   Graphic organizers, Concept Maps (Chapter 5)
   Reciprocal teaching
   However, a few strategies well-mastered will serve your tutee better than a glut of tactics barely understood. Select wisely.
7. Have your tutee write before, during, and after reading. Use strategies like the DEJ, freewrites, question papers, and RAFT. Have tutees keep a log (see Chapter 8).
8. Some tutees need help getting organized to learn and managing their time. As you work with your tutees, continue to evaluate their work habits and time allocation to see how effectively and efficiently they learn. Suggest changes to improve effectiveness.
9. Keep in mind that you are the tutor. Develop an understanding, but a professional relationship. Your approach and expectations can influence your tutee's productivity and learning.

**Impact of reading tutorials on credential candidates.** While evidence of benefits to those tutored are prevalent (Wasik, 1998), I investigated the tutor side of the "tutor + tutee = learning" equation (Unrau, 1996). I wanted to know what teachers-in-training would gain from the experience of tutoring a struggling reader with strategies like those described in this book. Research and my teaching experience indicated that some credential candidates resisted the infusion of literacy strategies into their content areas and the transfer of techniques into their future classrooms (Hollingsworth & Teel, 1991; O'Brien & Stewart, 1992; Stewart & O'Brien, 1989). The reasons for this resistance to acquisition and transfer could lie in many quarters, including feelings of inadequacy, lack of training or confidence, lack of instructional time in the schools to integrate literacy strategies, and belief that such instruction should be the province of the English teacher.

My purpose for the investigation of the tutorial was simple: I wanted to know how credential candidates were affected by tutoring a struggling reader. I also wanted to know if tutorials helped these new teachers gain strategic knowledge about reading and apply that knowledge in their content area classrooms.

I had a hunch that tutorials could help satisfy new teachers' needs for independent practice and internalization of reading strategies. If tutorials were utilized as opportunities to practice and internalize knowledge, then the possibility for transfer of strategic knowledge from the university to the schools might improve. However, the usefulness of these tutorials needed to be assessed to find out which strategies got transferred to the tutorial and to discover the extent to which students found the tutorial valuable and why.

To gather information to answer my questions, I read the case studies of 178 student teachers who completed a content area literacy course, took notes from those sections of each case study that addressed relevant questions, and had all 178 student teachers complete a questionnaire.

After reviewing the information I collected from reading case studies and from the questionnaires, I was able to draw a few tentative conclusions:

1. After taking a course in content literacy, beginning teachers rarely reported no inclination to develop the reading and/or writing ability of their students. About 4% of the sample indicated that they did not think they should be expected to include the teaching of reading and/or writing in their content area. Keep in mind that the sample included teachers from all content areas normally taught in the middle and high school curriculum, including music, art, and physical education.

2. Among the most frequently used strategies in the tutorials were DR-TA, reciprocal teaching, Vocabulary Self-Collection Strategy, K-W-L, and quickwrites. Among those strategies least used were DEJs, DIAs, and PreP, and other strategies that require substantial teacher preparation time because texts being taught must be read and materials prepared in advance.

3. Well over 60% of all candidates in the sample indicated that they gained confidence by applying strategies in their tutorials. Sixty-six percent agreed that the tutorial helped them to diagnose student learning problems more confidently, and 64% agreed that they felt their confidence increased as the tutorial progressed. Even a larger percentage felt a sense of satisfaction in their role as tutors.

4. About 80% of the candidates said that the tutorial gave them an understanding of how they could use reading and/or writing strategies in their classes. That would suggest that, having gained an understanding of their application, they would actually use them.

5. A large percentage of the sample (85%) agreed that the tutorial gave them a chance to learn something important about themselves as teachers. About the same percentage agreed that the tutorial helped them to find out the problems students have in reading.

6. Although the tutorial took a significant amount of time, only about one of four candidates agreed that the tutorial took too much of their time and should be eliminated as part of the course because it contributed little or nothing to their understanding of students as learners. More than half of all candidates agreed that they wished the tutorial could continue.

Many comments that candidates made on their questionnaires and in their case studies provided further indicators that beginning teachers valued the tutorials and learned from them. New teachers discovered that tutees with limited English proficiency, with learning disabilities, with low self-esteem, and with little or no parental support often had complex literacy and learning problems to overcome. One student teacher whose tutee was a 13-year-old "hard-headed, antagonistic young lady" with *cholo* (gang) affiliations in South Central Los Angeles wrote the following: "Angie was not the only one who learned how to summarize a passage and develop questions effectively. During our first sessions, I felt quite uncomfortable doing our reciprocal teaching exercises. As we went along, however, I felt much more comfortable. The same holds true for other strategies I employed. Because I actually used DR-TA, DIA, and mapping activities with Angie, I would be much more comfortable in adopting and adapting them in my curriculum." Experience with Angie strengthened this student's "resolve to incorporate reading and writing activities in my curriculum."

In summary, the vast majority of new teachers in the research I conducted said they were motivated to integrate literacy strategies into their content areas. Through the tutorial they got an opportunity to try numerous techniques to improve reading; many learned much about the literacy difficulties their tutees and future students face; and most new teachers concluded that the tutorial had considerable merit and value for them.

But what do these teacher candidates, such as yourself, really do about integrating literacy to promote learning in their content area classrooms in the years after they have received their teaching credentials and settled into their classrooms?

DOUBLE-ENTRY
JOURNAL: After
Reading

Go to the Double-Entry Journal for Chapter 6 on our Companion Website at www.prenhall.com/unrau to complete your journal entry.

Having read this chapter on group strategies, how would you modify your list of whole-class, small-group, and paired activities you would use in your instructional program to enhance literacy and learning? With reference to the model of reading in Chapter 2, how do you think the collaborative methods you have included on your list promote both learning and literacy?

# CHAPTER 6 GRAPHIC SUMMARY

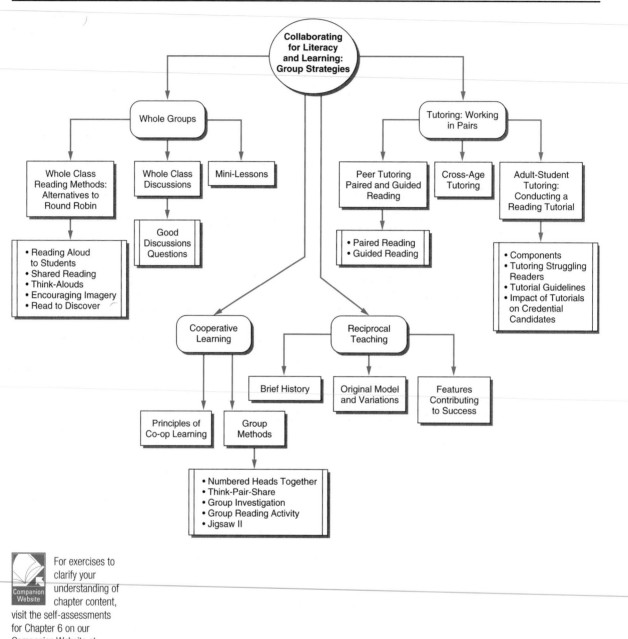

For exercises to clarify your understanding of chapter content, visit the self-assessments for Chapter 6 on our Companion Website at www.prenhall.com/unrau

# References

Alfassi, M. (1998). Reading for meaning: The efficacy of reciprocal teaching in fostering reading comprehension in high school students in remedial reading classes. *American Educational Research Journal, 35*(2), 309–332.

Allen, J. (2000). *Yellow brick roads: Shared and guided paths to independent reading 4–12.* Portland, ME: Stenhouse Publishers.

Antil, L., Jenkins, J., Wayne, S., & Vadasy, P. F. (1998). Cooperative learning: Prevalence, conceptualizations, and the relation between research and practice. *American Educational Research Journal, 35*(3), 419–454.

Aronson, E., Blaney, N., Stephan, C., Sikes, J., & Snapp, M. (1978). *The Jigsaw classroom.* Beverly Hills, CA: Sage Publications, Inc.

Atwell, N. (1998). *In the middle: New understandings about writing, reading, and learning* (2nd ed.). Portsmouth, NH: Heinemann.

Barton, J. (1995). Conducting effective classroom conversations. *Journal of Reading, 38*(5), 346–350.

Brown, A. L., Palincsar, A. S., & Armbruster, B. B. (1984). Instructing comprehension-fostering activities in interactive learning situations. In H. Mandl, N. Stein, & T. Trabasso (Eds.), *Learning and comprehension of text* (pp. 255–285). Hillsdale, NJ: Erlbaum.

Brown, O. M. (1996). *Tips at your fingertips: Teaching strategies for adult literacy tutors.* Newark, DE: International Reading Association.

Carter, C. J. (1997, March). Why reciprocal teaching? *Educational Leadership, 54*(6), 64–68.

Cohen, J. (1986). Theoretical considerations of peer tutoring. *Psychology in the Schools, 23*(2), 175–186.

Day, J. (1980). *Training summarization skills: A comparison of teaching methods.* Unpublished doctoral dissertation, University of Illinois, Champaign-Urbana.

Day, J. (1986). Teaching summarization skills: Influences of student ability level and strategy difficulty. *Cognition and Instruction, 3*(3), 193–210.

Dewey, J. (1970). *Experience and education.* New York: Collier.

Fisher, D. (2001). Cross age tutoring: Alternatives to the reading resource room for struggling adolescent readers. *Journal of Instructional Psychology, 28*(4), 234–241.

Fountas, I., & Pinnell, G. S. (1996). *Guided reading: Good first teaching for all children.* Portsmouth, NH: Heinemann.

Grimm, J., & Grimm, W. (1823/1971). *Grimms' Fairy Tales.* Middlesex, England: Penguin Books.

Gunning, T. G. (2002). *Assessing and correcting reading and writing difficulties* (2nd ed.). Boston, MA: Allyn & Bacon.

Haluska, R., & Gillen, D. (1995). Kids teaching kids: Pairing up with cross-grades pals. *Learning, 24*(3), 54–56.

Hollingsworth, S., & Teel, K. (1991). Learning to teach reading in secondary math and science. *Journal of Reading, 35,* 190–194.

Jacobson, J., Thrope, L., Fisher, D., Lapp, D., Frey, N., & Flood, J. (2001). Cross-age tutoring: A literacy improvement approach for struggling adolescent readers. *Journal of Adolescent and Adult Literacy, 44*(6), 528–536.

Johnson, D. W., & Johnson, R. T. (1999). *Learning together and alone: Cooperative, competitive, and individualistic learning.* Boston, MA: Allyn & Bacon.

Johnson, G. B. (1998). *Biology: Visualizing life.* Austin, TX: Holt, Rinehart and Winston.

Juel, C. (1991). Cross-age tutoring between student athletes and at-risk children. *The Reading Teacher, 45,* 178–186.

Juel, C. (1993). What makes literacy tutoring effective? *Reading Research Quarterly, 31,* 268–289.

Kagan, S. (1992). *Cooperative learning resources for teachers*. San Juan, CA: Kagan Cooperative Learning.

Kintsch, W., & van Dijk, T. (1978). Toward a model of text comprehension and production. *Psychological Review, 85*(5), 363–394.

Lenners, C., & Smith, K. (1999, September). *Explicit Instruction of Comprehension Skills.* Workshop presented at Burbank Middle School, Burbank, CA.

Lou, Y. (1996). Within-class grouping: A meta-analysis. *Review of Educational Research, 66*(4), 423–458.

Lyman, F. (1981). The responsive classroom discussion. In A. S. Anderson (ed.), *Mainstreaming Digest.* College Park: University of Maryland, College of Education.

Manzo, A., & Manzo, U. (1997). *Content area literacy: Interactive teaching for active learning* (2nd ed.). Upper Saddle River, NJ: Merrill.

Marks, M. (1993). Three teachers' adaptations of reciprocal teaching in comparison to traditional reciprocal teaching. *Elementary School Journal, 94*(2), 267–283.

Morrow, L. M., & Woo, D. G. (2001). *Tutoring programs for struggling readers: The America Reads challenge.* New York: Guilford Press.

O'Brien, D., & Stewart, R. (1992). Resistance to content area reading: Dimensions and solutions. In E. D. Dishner, T. W. Bean, J. E. Readence, & D. W. Moore (Eds.), *Reading in the content areas: Improving classroom instruction* (3rd ed.). Dubuque, IA: Kendall/Hunt.

O'Flahavan, J. F., Stein, C., Wiencek, J., & Marks, T. (1992). *Interpretive development in peer discussion about literature: An exploration of the teacher's role.* Paper presented at the 42nd annual meeting of the National Reading Conference, San Antonio, TX.

Opitz, M. F., & Rasinski, T. V. (1998). *Good-bye Round Robin: 25 effective oral reading strategies.* Portsmouth, NH: Heinemann.

Palincsar, A. (1982). *Improving the reading comprehension of junior high students through reciprocal teaching of comprehension-monitoring strategies.* Unpublished doctoral dissertation, University of Illinois at Urbana-Champaign.

Pearson, P. D. (1985). Changing the face of reading comprehension instruction. *The Reading Teacher, 38,* 724–738.

Potter, J. (1997). New directions in student tutoring. *Education + Training, 39*(1), 24–29.

Rekrut, M. D. (1994). Peer and cross-age tutoring: The lessons of research. *Journal of Reading, 37*(5), 356–362.

Rosenshine, B., & Meister, C. (1994). Reciprocal teaching: A review of the research. *Review of Educational Research, 64* (4), 479–530.

Rosenshine, B., Meister, C., & Chapman, S. (1996). Teaching students to generate questions: A review of the intervention studies. *Review of Educational Research, 66* (2), 181–221.

Ruddell, M. R. (1997). *Teaching content reading and writing* (2nd ed.). Boston, MA: Allyn & Bacon.

Sadoski, M., & Paivio, A. (2001). *Imagery and text: A dual coding theory of reading and writing.* Mahwah, NJ: Erlbaum.

Scoble, J., Topping, K., & Wigglesworth, C. (1994). Training family and friends as literacy tutors. In M. C. Radencich (Ed.), *Adult literacy: A compendium of articles from the Journal of Reading* (pp. 219–226). Newark, DE: International Reading Association.

Sharan, Y., & Sharan, S. (1992). *Group investigation: A strategy for expanding cooperative learning.* New York: Teacher's College Press.

Slavin, R. (1995). *Cooperative learning* (2nd ed.). Needham Heights, MA: Allyn & Bacon.

Sternberg, J. R., & Spear-Swerling, L. (1996). *Teaching for thinking.* Washington, DC: American Psychological Association.

Stewart, R., & O'Brien, D. (1989). Resistance to content area reading: A focus on preservice teachers. *Journal of Reading, 33,* 395–401.

Topping, K. (1987). Paired reading: A powerful technique for parent use. *The Reading Teacher, 40,* 608–614.

Unrau, N. (1996, April). *Using tutorials to teach literacy strategies across the content areas: Do they work for pre-service teachers?* Paper presented at the annual meeting of the American Educational Research Association in New York City.

Unrau, N. (1995, May). *Tactics to engage readers in reflection and self-regulation: Paths to critical literacy across the curriculum.* Paper presented at the Annual Convention of the International Reading Association, Anaheim, California.

Wasik, B. A. (1998). Volunteer tutoring programs in reading: A review. *Reading Research Quarterly, 33,* 266–292.

Wood, K. (2001). *Literacy strategies across the subject areas.* Boston: Allyn & Bacon.

# 7 CRITICAL READING

After reading Chapter 7, you should be able to answer the following questions:

1. Why do students need to read more critically?
2. What conceptions of critical thinking apply productively to improve critical reading?
3. What activities foster critical reading?
4. What is critical literacy, how is it different from critical thinking, and how can it heighten students' "critical consciousness"?

**DOUBLE-ENTRY JOURNAL: Before Reading**

Now go to the Double-Entry Journal for Chapter 7 on our Companion Website at www.prenhall.com/unrau to fill out your journal entry.

If you "shift gears" into reading texts more critically, under what circumstances does that shift occur? What do you do differently when you read "critically"? How would you teach your students critical reading of texts in your content area?

## THE NEED FOR MORE CRITICAL READING

Even though about three out of four students in eighth grade and twelfth grade develop basic reading skills appropriate to their grade level (Mullis, Campbell, & Farstrup, 1993), only about three in one hundred perform at advanced levels. At these advanced levels, readers analyze meanings and explicitly support their analysis with examples. In addition, they make connections between the texts they read and their understanding of the world. They can "synthesize and critically examine information" in texts as well as demonstrate strength in dealing "objectively and critically" with the text (p. 85).

Throughout middle and high school, students are expected to read hundreds of pages of informative texts that provide them with knowledge about history, geography, government, mathematics, biology, chemistry, health, and other fields. The majority of students reading informative texts at the basic level can identify the central purpose of straightforward texts. They can understand explicitly stated information and can connect information given at different points in a text's development. However, very few of these students can compare and contrast information within a text, draw upon knowledge from other areas, or form opinions about what they've read and use evidence from it to support their opinions. For example, only a very small percentage of students can read different accounts of a similar event, such as the battle of Lexington, decide which passage they would select as most reliable, and provide reasons for their choice based on information in the passage.

With regard to arguments, such as those formulated for newspaper and magazine editorials, many students have difficulty detecting patterns in argument development and identifying claims made in those arguments. Like many of her classmates, Allison, the pseudonym for an eleventh grader I taught, had trouble analyzing arguments. She often struggled to identify the thesis in an argument. She also had problems sorting through, classifying, and evaluating the quality of evidence used to support a thesis after we had identified it. Like many of her classmates, she rarely paused to reflect upon and examine the assumptions or values that were beneath the claims or the selection of evidence to support those claims. She also avoided a careful consideration of counterclaims and counterevidence. More importantly, she had rarely been encouraged to read so that she could construct different perspectives of a written argument to compare their relative merits.

With an explosion of information available over the Internet and on thousands of Web sites comes a myriad of opportunities for students like Allison to be misinformed and manipulated. Exercising common sense when it comes to cyberspace messages intended to dupe readers may be the best way to exorcise electronic hoaxes and tomfoolery. But the mindful reading of more extended informative and argumentative texts requires something more: The development of skills and application of strategies for more critical responses to texts.

Although many of us would like to promote the capacity of our students to read more mindfully at advanced levels, we have known for decades that they engage in thoughtful, critical reading infrequently (*A Nation at Risk,* 1983; Applebee, Langer, & Mullis, 1985, 1988; Boyer, 1983). In a "report card" compiled for the NAEP and entitled *Who Reads Best?,* Applebee, Langer, & Mullis (1988) note that, while proficient readers have a variety of "meaning-making strategies," efforts to improve students' ability "to reason more effectively about what they read" ought to be one of the schools' central goals. Students, they write, "must develop the ability to synthesize, analyze, and extend their ideas and their knowledge" (p. 11).

Research shows that students, such as those with basic reading strengths, could benefit from programs and strategies that empower them to read informative and argumentative texts more adequately, more thoroughly, more planfully, and more constructively. In this chapter, I plan to review with you a number of strategies intended to help students become more proficient readers of expository texts and arguments. I will focus on approaches and activities designed to help students respond more thoughtfully to texts, to ask more questions about texts and their authors, to analyze arguments, and to improve the quality of their work when evaluating texts. You will also learn how to facilitate the examination of texts in classroom contexts and how to engage students in critical literacy to develop their "critical consciousness."

## What Is Critical Reading?

When considering what helps students read more critically, I inevitably plunge into a closely related field: critical thinking. Critical thinking has been around for a very long time. Some teachers model their critical thinking program on Socrates' methods of questioning, methods he used to pursue "truth" about 2,500 years ago. Since the 1930s, the tide of enthusiasm for critical thinking in our nation and in individual states has risen and fallen. However, its level of importance in any classroom depends of one central factor: how the classroom teacher's mind works. If you are disposed to thinking critically, if you pursue reasons, look at things from multiple perspectives, seek, apply, and monitor strategies, evaluate the consequences of your beliefs and decisions, and reflect on your thinking and that of others, then critical thinking will be at high water marks and your students will flourish in thoughtful teaching.

But what is critical thinking and how does it help us develop a clearer idea of critical reading? Critical thinking has been defined in several different ways, most of which share common concepts such as analysis, reasoning, and the weighing of evidence. In *Thoughtful Teachers, Thoughtful Learners* (Unrau, 1997), I drew upon the work of Robert Ennis (1996) and defined **critical thinking** as "reasoned reflection on the meaning of claims about what to believe and what to do." So, for example, when a writer asserts that a school voucher program will remedy educational ills, a critical reader begins to comb through the argument to clarify and examine the meanings of this claim and the evidence that supports it. Voters in many states, including California, have engaged in just such tasks. Usually, voucher initiatives include state payments per pupil for attendance at public or private schools and leave the choice to students and their families. However, critical readers and thoughtful voters who evaluate a voucher program proposal should engage in its close examination to weigh its costs and benefits: What kind of voucher program is the writer proposing? Who will be eligible for it? How much money will the voucher provide? What ills will be remedied? How does a reader know that they will be remedied? What "price" will schools that students leave have to pay? What will the program cost the state and how certain are we of those cost estimates? (In the case of California's voucher Proposition 38, the *Official Voter Information Guide* (2000) indicated that fiscal impact to the state could range from a cost of $2 billion to a savings of $3.4 billion.) How will federal funds to the state be affected? What schools will benefit from the program? Does the writer address counterarguments to the proposal? Is the writer biased, and do biases affect the writer's assessment of the program's value and effectiveness? As these questions indicate, when engaged in critical thinking, readers use strategies to analyze and to evaluate at deeper levels the claims made in texts.

Like many other educators promoting teaching for thinking, I never believed that simply teaching skills and strategies to enable critical thinking would ever be sufficient for the development of thoughtful, reflective students or critical readers. The development of students' motivation and dispositions to engage in productive thinking and critical reading are essential. Students must develop a desire to think and read critically, and I do not believe there is any quick-fix strategy that will spark that desire. If you can start or detect in your students a small flame burning, that flame must be fed. Initiating that flame can be viewed as a teaching triumph and fanning it, a victory.

No device for igniting a skeptical spirit of critical reflection when reading books, watching evening news, or facing any of life's choices is foolproof. However, you can serve as a model of thoughtful learning, as a provider of effective thinking and reading strategies, and as an encourager for engagement in critical responses to texts. When responding to texts, you can reveal your thinking about that text's contents and context, show students what claims should be thoughtfully examined, and demonstrate your search for valid evidence to support those claims. Besides providing models of thinking for students to emulate, you can also directly teach strategies to take arguments apart, lay out their pieces, and make judgments about each part's value to the whole. Furthermore, you can encourage signs of thoughtful response that students manifest to all kinds of texts. You can create and nourish classroom climates for questioning, analysis, and reflection that help each of your students become a more self-regulated thinker and learner.

Jason Agliolo, one of my former students, teaches Trigonometry at Bell Gardens High School. I watched a video of Mr. Agliolo trying to teach his students, many of whom are English learners, how to use trig functions (sine, cosine, tangent ratios) to solve "real world problems." As he put it, most of his students "decode quite rapidly and actually string sentences together quite cohesively, but their understanding of meaning is often lacking." That presents Mr. Agliolo with one of his instructional challenges. How can students read a math problem to detect essential information, transform that information into visual images to represent the problem, and then proceed to solve it?

To help his students transform text into drawings, Mr. Agliolo first models how he constructs meaning from the word problem, depicts the problem pictorially, and solves it. When constructing meaning, he reads and rereads the problem aloud, asks himself questions about it, and draws a representation that reflects the language of the word problem. As he does so, he demonstrates critical reading by reasoning about the meaning of claims made in the problem, making connections between its parts, and, after creating a picture on the board, checking for evidence in the language of the word problem to confirm the accuracy of his picture.

Then he asks several students to read another similar problem aloud and peppers them with questions. By doing so, he said that his students "develop a sense of ownership in the process and begin to take some stock in the meaning negotiation process." After several readings of the problem and a battery of questions about it, one of Mr. Agliolo's students goes to the board, follows his demonstration of pictorially representing the problem, checks its accuracy, and solves it.

As teachers, we are challenged every day during every class to observe the quality and effectiveness of our students' approaches to problems and decision making. This detective work will enable us to see what works well for our students and where improvements need to be made. In a graduate course I've taught to promote teaching for thinking, I ask teachers of math, science, foreign languages, and just about every other subject to watch and record their students' thought processes and reasoning—especially when patterns of ineffective problem solving and thinking begin to appear. By reflecting on students' thinking, you can discern problems in cognition that you could then address. One math teacher, for example, saw that students in his eighth-grade honors class were so eager to get to the right answer that they usually did not show their work. Without seeing the steps they took to solve problems, he could not detect errors in their thinking. With a few adjustments, like only giving credit for homework assignments that showed all the steps students used in their problem solving, checking homework regularly, and returning it promptly, he detected several errors in students' problem-solving performance and guided his students toward visible improvements. Later in this chapter, you will read about another teacher who wanted to see how her students constructed meanings when reading their math text. With a colleague, she developed Socratic Seminars to facilitate and witness reasoning about math concepts and their application.

## ACTIVITIES TO FOSTER CRITICAL READING

### Inquiry Questions (IQs)

"The important thing," said Albert Einstein, "is not to stop questioning." We can help students avoid this dark risk by using Inquiry Questions. **Inquiry Questions (IQs)** are intended to encourage readers to ask themselves questions as they read and learn. IQs are based on Bloom's (1956) *Taxonomy of Educational Objectives,* in particular those in the cognitive domain. Bloom hypothesized the existence of six cognitive domains that have gone on to influence both the development of curriculum and its assessment. Those domains include the following: knowledge, comprehension, application, analysis, synthesis, and evaluation. Frequently, thinking in the last three of these domains is referred to as "higher order" thinking. However, we can help develop more mindful readers through the asking of questions in all domains.

7-16 ©1997 Wiley Miller DIST. BY UNIVERSAL PRESS SYNDICATE

*Source:* NON SEQUITOR © Wiley Miller. Dist. by UNIVERSAL PRESS SYNDICATE. Reprinted with permission. All rights reserved.

Educators who have written objectives for units or lessons have usually become familiar with Bloom's taxonomy of cognitive objectives. For nearly 50 years, the taxonomy has helped teachers clarify their purposes for teaching. The cognitive domains are reviewed in Table 7.1, and associated stem words that you can use to develop IQs are given. You can use these stem words to explore and deepen your students' reading assignments and to demonstrate to students how they can continually question whatever they read.

## STEP-BY-STEP: *Inquiry Questions (IQs)*

**STEP 1.** Identify the passage(s) that students are to read and study.

**STEP 2.** Based on the six cognitive objects, decide what topics and concepts you want your students to be able to recall, understand, apply, take apart, put together in novel ways, and evaluate.

**STEP 3.** Formulate questions based on different cognitive objectives that will facilitate inquiry into topics and concepts you deem essential. As you form these questions, keep in mind that you can use the stem words in Table 7.1 to prompt your question generation for the various objectives.

**STEP 4.** Use your IQs to guide and strengthen your inquiry with your students.

**TABLE 7.1**   Inquiry Questions

| Cognitive Domain | Stem Words for Questions | Examples of Inquiry Questions (IQs) |
|---|---|---|
| *Knowledge:* The recall or remembering of information learned previously. Includes facts as well as generalizations. | who, what, when, where, retell, list, define, name, state, etc. | Who was the first president of the United States? How would you define "hero"? |
| *Comprehension:* The understanding or grasping of facts and ideas without connecting them to other concepts or seeing their implications. | explain, which, predict, illustrate, summarize, what, conclude, rephrase. | What would you include in a summary of the Declaration of Independence? What do you predict will happen next? How would you illustrate the order of operations? |
| *Application:* Use of knowledge, including ideas or procedures, in new contexts. | apply, solve, test, how, demonstrate. | How would you use the FOIL method to multiply polynomials? |
| *Analysis:* Taking apart or breaking down knowledge to reveal its hidden structure, as in reading between the lines. | analyze, classify, categorize, how, explain, what, discriminate. | What are the differences between comedy and tragedy? What are the facts and opinions expressed in this argument about global warming? |
| *Synthesis:* Putting together or combining old knowledge into new forms. | create, formulate, make up, suggest. | How would you formulate an argument supporting the view that all students should become critical readers? |
| *Evaluation:* Judging the value or worth of material used for specific purposes. | judge, assess, defend, evaluate. | How would you evaluate Marx's *Communist Manifesto?* How would you defend standards-based instruction? |

**STEP 5.** As a follow-up of students' learning, develop activities, projects, text prompts, and problems that will enable you to assess the degree to which your students have mastered the topics and concepts explored through your IQ-guided discussion.

Paul Perez, a music teacher whose high school memoirs began this book, developed the following set of IQs to use with students who had read about jazz trumpeter Louis Armstrong and listened to several of his recordings, including those with Ella Fitzgerald and Bing Crosby:

1. What experience did Armstrong gain while playing second trumpet in Joe "King" Oliver's band? (Knowledge)
2. Why is the role of the second trumpet important in a song's harmonic structure? (Comprehension)
3. How would you demonstrate that Armstrong's use of harmony in the King Oliver band is similar to his harmonic singing with Ella Fitzgerald or Bing Crosby? (Application)
4. How would you explain the differences between a melodic line and a harmonic line? (Analysis)

5. How did Armstrong's experience as a second trumpet player in his early career benefit him in his later sessions with Bing Crosby and Ella Fitzgerald? (Synthesis)
6. How effective was Armstrong's use of harmony as a second trumpeter and singer in terms of form and aesthetics? (Evaluation)

Mr. Perez gave his last IQ to his students as a prompt for an essay in which they were to present their opinions and support them with reference to readings and recordings.

## Questioning the Author (QtA)

***Questioning the Author (QtA),*** a teaching strategy developed by Beck and her associates (1997), is intended to help students engage in the thoughtful construction of texts. Researchers found that using QtA brought about several changes in classroom interaction, including students talking twice as much as they had in traditional classrooms while initiating more questions, comments, and student-to-student interactions. Although the strategy can be used with both expository and narrative texts, we are going to explore QtA's use in helping students to comprehend and question more challenging expository texts.

The primary purpose for QtA is to shift your work from checking for comprehension by asking comprehension-type questions ("What . . . ?") to helping your students construct and explore meanings. Rather than encouraging a view of text as given authority in black and white, you can use QtA to present texts as some person's ideas in writing that may not always be clear and comprehensible. Authors (except this one, of course) are fallible.

I'll present the procedure for QtA in the following four sections: queries, planning, discussion, and implementation. Figure 7.1 summarizes the QtA procedure.

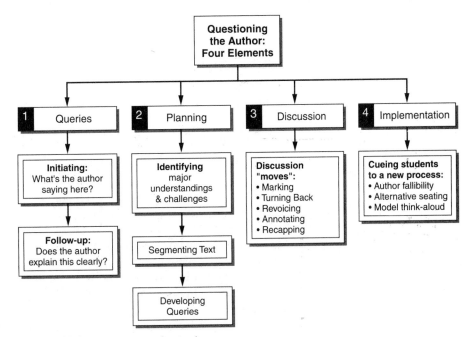

**FIGURE 7.1** Questioning the Author.

**Queries.**    Queries, unlike many teacher-made questions, are not intended to evaluate readers' understanding of a text. Rather they are intended to help students grasp ideas presented in a text, be used while students read the text, facilitate discussion about the author's ideas, and support student-to-student dialogue. Analysis and engagement are the desired effects of Queries that are designed to make students do more work on meaning construction.

For our focus on expository texts, Queries are of two major kinds: Initiating and Follow-up. *Initiating Queries* are intended to open the text to class-wide construction of meaning, understanding, and discussion by focusing on central text ideas. Their purpose is to provide guidance for inquiry and exploration. To initiate meaning construction work on the part of students, Beck and her associates (1997) recommend three types of Initiating Queries:

1. What is the author trying to say here?
2. What is the author's message?
3. What is the author talking about?

*Follow-up Queries* are intended to provide focus and guide the discussion while helping students to integrate meanings and make connections with other ideas. The questions that you ask are intended to urge readers to look more deeply into an author's language and network of ideas. Follow-up Queries, such as the following two suggested by Beck and her associates (1997), urge students to look beneath the surface of the author's words:

1. What does the author mean here?
2. Does the author explain this clearly?

Follow-up Queries can also prompt students to make connections with stored knowledge or with information read earlier in the text:

1. Does this make sense when related to what you know about this topic?
2. How does this connect to what the author told us before?

Furthermore, Follow-up Queries, such as these, can help readers speculate on an author's purpose in providing certain information in a text:

1. Why do you think the author tells us this now?
2. Does the author tell us why this information is given?

Lastly, you can go beyond Beck and her associates' Query types by guiding students toward the critical examination of positions an author takes, directly or indirectly, about a topic. These suggested *Critical Thinking Queries* can probe an author's reasoning and marshalling of evidence:

1. If the author is trying to persuade us of something, what do you think that is?
2. Why has the author organized his ideas as they are presented in the text?
3. Does the author give us enough evidence to support his conclusions?

**Planning.**    Beck and her associates (1997) suggest that we compare preparing to use QtA with rehearsing a play for production. When producing a play, director and actors carefully take apart the script, make decisions about actors' movements on stage, and practice responding to cues. Directors have much to anticipate in terms of audience reaction and potential problems. How a director and actors prepare radically affects what audiences experience and understand.

You will act as both director and performer when engaged in preparing and presenting a QtA lesson. As director, you "block" (or decide) what will be discussed and anticipate how a lesson will play on the classroom stage. Because teachers, like actors, cannot know in advance what will develop during the performance, you must be ready to improvise.

Planning entails three distinct phases: (a) identifying major understandings and potential problems, (b) segmenting text, and (c) developing queries.

1. *Identifying major understandings and potential problems.* Like a director and an actor, you begin working with a text by giving it a close reading. One of the purposes for the close reading is to identify the major understandings that students should gain from reading the text. The second purpose is to anticipate and solve potential problems that may arise in teaching the text, including difficult concepts or dense passages. Accomplishing these dual purposes clears the way for the author's entry into the classroom and sets the stage for a conversation that engages readers with the author. The core of that conversation is Questioning the Author.

2. *Segmenting text.* Following a close reading of the text, identifying major understandings, and anticipating problems with the text's comprehension, you next segment the text. By segmenting a text, Beck and her associates (1997) mean the identification of stop points at which you'll initiate questioning and discussion. Major understandings you want your students to gain drive decisions about where to segment. At times, a single sentence that has a bearing on a major understanding may signal a stop point. Much longer passages and sets of paragraphs may be summarily dealt with. Asterisks in the text can be used to identify segments.

3. *Developing queries.* Queries, as we have already learned, are of several kinds. Initiating Queries launch discussions. Follow-up Queries help students look beneath the text's surface, make intertextual connections, speculate on an author's purposes, and, in general, deepen discussion and the exploration of the text. Critical Thinking Queries guide students into an examination of an author's reasoning, organization of evidence, and conclusions based on that reasoning and evidence.

Discussion.   Beck and her associates (1997) draw an analogy between solving a maze and comprehending a text. However, you won't lead your students through the maze. Rather you will support your students in their own maze journey, their own meaning construction, as they work toward the goal of understanding. Discussions are where students do much of the work of making sense of the text.

During QtA discussions, students work together with each other and you to build ideas that are discovered in the text. Discussions are composed of two components: your role and your students' contributions. Students are active participants who develop and connect ideas encountered in the text. They share in the investigation and construction of meaning.

You will use your planning to motivate and guide students' contributions rather than to dominate the classroom discussion. You guide students in the exploration of ideas, think ideas through in relation to the text, and extend them where possible. As you differentiate among all the students' contributions, you shepherd those contributions toward the goal of meaning construction.

Beck and her associates (1997) describe six kinds of discussion moves that you can apply to orchestrate and promote your students' comprehension and questioning of the text: marking, turning back, revoicing, modeling, annotating, and recapping.

1. *Marking*. You use marking to draw attention to particular ideas that are critical to major understandings. You may mark a student's contribution by echoing the observation or by explicitly acknowledging that someone is on to something significant, as in stating that a student is making a "very important point." Through marking you send a signal to readers that an idea is of special value.

2. *Turning back*. Turning back has a couple of meanings. On the one hand, it refers to turning responsibility back to readers for digging more deeply into ideas and clarifying their meaning. Teachers using this form of turning back often guide students toward idea elaboration and interconnection with other students' meanings. When used another way, turning back refers to turning students' attention back to the text in order to clarify their thinking. This could occur when students make statements about the meaning of a text that the text itself contradicts. In either meaning of turning back, you should avoid jumping in to explain the text's meaning. You should, however, transfer responsibility for understanding to students.

3. *Revoicing*. When you "revoice," you interpret what students are saying about a text and echo the ideas you hear, as you do when you "listen actively." This helps students express their ideas so that they become part of the discussion.

While marking, turning back, and revoicing are discussion interventions that nudge your students toward meaning construction, the next three moves engage you more directly in the meaning construction process.

4. *Modeling*. Through modeling, you attempt to make visible to students reading processes that are usually invisible. By revealing these reading processes, you provide opportunities for students to imitate questioning, intertextual links, and expert problem solving while grappling with text construction. When doing a comprehension think-aloud, Mrs. Silva explained her understanding of "Sea Fever" through an intertextual connection with a young adult novel about a girl who makes a life-changing voyage to America (see Chapter 3). Without making her thinking visible, we could never see how her mind made meaning, and students might not realize how their intertextual links contribute to comprehension.

5. *Annotating*. When annotating, you offer information to students that an author may have left out of the text. Without that information, students would encounter grave difficulties in constructing appropriate meanings for the text. The information could include not only fleshing out assumptions but also making tricky connections in reasoning.

6. *Recapping*. When students are ready to consolidate their understanding of a text and move on to the next passages, you can use this discussion move. By summarizing major understandings and concepts, you signal students that they have grasped the essentials and are ready to progress further. You can also call on your students to recap, a move that extends responsibility to the class members for constructing and organizing text meanings.

**Implementation.**   Because QtA varies from traditional text-oriented questioning for comprehension, you can provide cues to students that they are about to engage in a more active classroom reading process. One way to send that message is to begin by presenting to students the idea of "author fallibility" and the notion that texts are merely an author's ideas in print. Authors may not always present knowledge in language that is easily accessible to students, so students will sometimes have to work very hard to construct appropriate meanings when texts seem confusing and hard to understand.

Another way to cue students is to put them in a new configuration in the classroom. Beck and her associates (1997) suggest using a U-shape seating arrangement that helps students watch and interact with each other while providing easier teacher movement among students during discussion.

A third cue to prepare students for QtA is to present a model think-aloud with a text that you think will be challenging for your students. After selecting, reading for major understandings, and segmenting the text, you can show the students how to proceed to construct meaning together through discussion. The purpose of the modeling here is to show students the kinds of thinking that an expert goes through to construct a text's meaning and to give students a clear idea of the work they will be expected to do to make sense of and to question challenging texts.

## STEP-BY-STEP: *Questioning the Author (QtA)*.

**STEP 1.** Read the text you plan to help students construct and examine.

**STEP 2.** Identify the major understandings you want your students to gain and the potential problems you anticipate students may have in grasping the text's meaning.

**STEP 3.** Segment the text by identifying stop points where you want to begin questioning and discussion. Place asterisks in the text to identify stop points.

**STEP 4.** Develop queries for the stop points you have selected. Formulate Initiating Queries to start discussion, Follow-up Queries to probe beneath the surface and discover connections within the text as well as between students' knowledge and that the author presents , and (where appropriate) Critical Thinking Queries to examine an author's argument, evidence, and reasoning.

**STEP 5.** Provide cues to your students that they are about to engage in something different from traditional comprehension questioning. Arrange the desks in a U-shape. Establish the notion of "author fallibility."

**STEP 6.** When engaged in discussion, use the following discussion "moves" to help students construct the text and question the author's ideas: marking, turning back, revoicing, modeling, annotating, and recapping.

## Editor Interviews

As we have seen, Questioning the Author (QtA) makes the writer of a text more accessible to students. Editorials in newspapers and magazines provide opportunities to meet the editor. **Editor Interviews** permit students to assume the persona of a newspaper or magazine editor and make an appearance in the classroom so that students can talk their way into and through arguments.

Having a conversation with the writer of an argument provides students with an opportunity to raise questions in a social setting, to construct an understanding of a text, and to explore the strengths and weaknesses of an author's reasoning. Because bringing writers of arguments, like newspaper or magazine editors, to class is not usually feasible, we can ask students to immerse themselves in a writer's reasoning and then to role-play that writer. Students who role-play the writer benefit from a thorough study of a writer's argument while students who talk with the student-as-author get a chance to examine many facets of an argument in dialogue. Students can discover more about a writer's purposes, methods, likely beliefs, and thoroughness. They may also find alternative ways to view important or controversial issues.

A student asked to role-play the writer of an argument, such as a newspaper editorial, should be given time to carefully read and analyze the argument. Additional time to gather information related to the argument presented always contributes to a student's readiness. When the student-as-writer is prepared, other students can initiate the conversation in the classroom.

Before proceeding with the interview, however, students should formulate specific questions they could ask the interviewee. You can encourage question-generation for the interview by placing students in small teams to review the argument and design questions to ask the "editor." A set of basic questions is provided here as a springboard:

- What was your purpose in writing this piece?
- Why is this argument important to you?
- Would you please summarize your argument for us?
- How did you organize the presentation of your ideas?
- How much research did you do before you finished?
- Do you make any assumptions about the ideas you present?
- What is the best counter-argument that you can think of?
- Why should I agree with your argument?
- What do you consider your most persuasive premise or rationale for supporting your thesis? Why?
- How does your opinion about this topic bias your writing about it?
- What, if anything, could or would change your mind about the position you took?
- If you were to rewrite the argument today, what would you change, why would you change it, and how would you change it?

For students to see what they need to do to prepare and to perform in an Editor Interview, teacher modeling is helpful. For this, you should familiarize yourself not only with the editorial you select to demonstrate an Editor Interview but also with sufficient background knowledge germane to the argument. Ask yourself the "springboard" questions above, and, if you can answer them, you should be ready to dive in.

## STEP-BY-STEP: *Editor Interviews*

**STEP 1.** Select an editorial from a newspaper or magazine that fits with your curriculum purposes and/or will engage the interest of your students.

**STEP 2.** Ask all students to read and study the editorial, its position, and the argument it presents.

**STEP 3.** Ask a student to prepare to "visit" the class as the editorial's writer. Provide time for the student to prepare by gathering background information about the editorial and its bearing on current events. (Prior to having a student role-play the editor, I encourage you to initially show how to prepare and engage in an Editor Interview with the class.)

**STEP 4.** Ask students to formulate questions about the editorial to which the "editor" can respond. (This could be done in cooperative teams.) Students begin the question-generation process with a set of "springboard" questions such as the ones provided in this chapter. However, editorial-specific questions should also be formulated to address the specific content of the editor's argument.

**STEP 5.** The student role-playing the editor should make a brief, general introduction to the class (perhaps putting the editorial in current context) and then request questions from the audience.

**STEP 6.** The rest is largely dependent on the preparation and improvisational skills of both the student-as-editor and the students-as-interviewers.

## ReQuest

Much like reciprocal teaching, **ReQuest** is a strategy to get students to think while they read. Originally developed by Manzo (1969) for one-on-one interaction, ReQuest can be used with a whole class. The strategy encourages student questioning while you serve as a model questioner.

In Manzo's original one-on-one guidelines for ReQuest, the teacher and a student read the text silently, one sentence at a time. They then took turns asking each other questions about what they had read. The student asked a question, and then the teacher asked a question. Like reciprocal teaching, the student was told to ask questions like those generated and delivered by the teacher. In short, the teacher severed as a model for the questioning process. Both teacher and student closed their text while being asked questions. "I don't know" answers were deemed unacceptable because, Manzo believed, the student could at least try to explain why he could not answer. If questions or answers were unclear, requests for clarification were encouraged. Participants prepared to support answers with references to the text. If uncertain about an answer, the text would be consulted.

My experience with the whole-class version of ReQuest has been stimulating, but students and even teachers I have trained to use ReQuest tend to ask "on the surface" or literal questions. That certainly has put me on the spot from time to time because I don't always remember all the details in a passage, especially longer sections of text. But I believe there are benefits from students observing that teachers don't absorb every detail when reading and can't answer every question students ask. Among the benefits are their seeing we are not total sponges and that it's okay for them to have limited memory as well.

However, getting an avalanche of literal questions may signal that students are having trouble generating more "under the surface," inferential, or applied questions. And that signal means we need to design instruction so that students have more opportunities to learn how to generate questions of different kinds. Here our modeling of questions during ReQuest may help, especially if we point out what kinds of questions we are asking and why we are asking that type. You could also do some "under the surface" question training as described in the explanation of reciprocal teaching (see Chapter 6). Also you could review the Inquiry Question (IQ) chart with your students to show them the range of questions they can create. You should observe the kinds of questions your students ask during ReQuest and note the evolution in the kind and quality asked.

## STEP-BY-STEP: *ReQuest*

**STEP 1.** You and your whole class of students silently read the same passages that you previously segmented. One-by-one sentence speed would be appropriate for a whole class of struggling readers. Longer passages, perhaps a paragraph or more in length, will be appropriate for some classrooms.

**STEP 2.** After closing the book, you should respond to student questions. (You have a choice at this step either to take all the questions from students or to take fewer questions, even just one, before asking students a question. I prefer the latter method.)

**STEP 3.** Now you ask the students questions. (Again, you have a choice: to ask a bunch of questions at one time after receiving all the students' questions or to ask one question and then turn it over to the class for their next question in ping-pong fashion. I prefer the ping-pong method.)

**STEP 4.** The next passage (or sentence) is silently read, and steps 2 and 3 are repeated.

**STEP 5.** When you sense that most of your class could make good predictions about where the text is going next, ask students to formulate a purpose-setting question for the remainder of the reading. For example, a student might ask a question that she believes the remaining text will answer.

## Socratic Seminars

Math textbooks have traditionally been the source of assigned problems after a teacher introduces a new concept and demonstrates its mathematical applications. Few teachers engage students with the text as a source of useful strategies or to promote reasoned mathematical discourse. When conversations occur in math, they are about answers and errors—not about the textbook.

Michael Tanner and Leah Casados (1998) explored an alternative to using math texts, an alternative that could be used with any content area text: the Socratic Seminar. **The Socratic Seminar** envisioned and implemented was to help students discover ideas through a teacher's skilled questioning and guided dialogue, as did Socrates himself. After reading a text, students participating in the Seminar would construct understandings of that text through discussion and reason about those understandings. To a significant degree, this process parallels the meaning negotiation process described in the model of reading when teacher and students negotiate interpretations they bring into the classroom context (see Chapter 2).

To prepare for a Socratic Seminar, you need to become familiar with the text students read, whether it be about math or any other subject. Familiarity entails knowing what concepts the author presents and how they are presented, including author's use of headings, vocabulary, organization, and examples. To implement a Socratic Seminar, take the following steps:

## STEP-BY-STEP: *Socratic Seminars*

**STEP 1.** Select and prepare the text by focusing on key concepts and strategies presented, essential related background knowledge, and vocabulary to be taught.

**STEP 2.** Write out questions that will facilitate students' analysis, application, and synthesis of the information presented, such as "What applications can you see for the law of sines and cosines? Are there any new ideas in this section? What steps does the author recommend?" Also develop metacognitive questions that will help students focus on thinking about strategies acquired and applied, such as "How is this strategy useful? When would you use it? What was confusing in this reading? How did we resolve the confusion?"

**STEP 3.** Prior to the Seminar, assign the reading and arrange one circle of desks inside another to create a circle of observers around a "fishbowl" of discussants.

**STEP 4.** Give students a set of guidelines. The following are adapted from Tanner and Casados (1998):

- Focus on selected content.
- Listen to each other.
- Talk only if you are in the "hot seat."
- Inner circle students talk to each other.
- Outer circle students take notes on content and interaction.
- Time limited to 20 minutes plus 5 to 10 minutes for debriefing.
- Inner circle students get two tokens (worth 5 points each) that must be used during the Seminar discussion.
- Each time an inner circle student speaks, she places a token in a box at the center.
- Students may speak more than twice, but twice is the minimum.

**STEP 5.** The teacher begins the discussion with a question, guides students in reconstructing the author's meanings, and helps students to construct their own meanings that are useful (in the case of math) for doing math.

**STEP 6.** As a student goes to the hot seat to speak, he puts a token into the box, sits down, speaks, and leaves the seat. (When students become comfortable participating in the Socratic Seminar, you may want to phase out the hot seat.)

**STEP 7.** When the discussion is completed, the teacher gives or requests a summary statement.

**STEP 8.** The teacher then conducts a debriefing of the Seminar in which both inner and outer circle students participate. Sample questions about interaction include: "Did all inner circle students participate? Was the discussion clear? How did the discussion contribute to your understanding?" Here the metacognitive questions formed in Step 2 can also be asked to help students look at what process or strategy was useful, why it was useful, and when to apply it.

Tanner and Casados (1998) assure us that, while the first Seminar in math was "only satisfactory," discussion about what worked and what could be done so that the Seminars worked better led to significant improvements. Initially, students were quiet and a little uncomfortable, but with some teacher encouragement and question rephrasing they soon warmed to the process. Eventually, students articulated math strategies in their own words and made metacognitive observations about how

| Student's Name _____ Author/Title _____ |

1. What topic is being judged?

2. What basic claim (B) is made about that topic?

3. Antithesis (A): What would a reader most likely be for or against if he were opposed to the writer's claim about the topic?

4. What supports the basic claim and the antithetical claim?

| Basic Thesis Supports | Antithesis Supports |
| --- | --- |
| C. | A. |
| C. | A. |
| C. | A. |
| C. | A. |

5. Are any unclear, complex, or "loaded" words in the piece? (If so, identify and clarify them.) [Use other side of TASK, if needed, for phases 5, 6, and 7.]

6. Evaluate supports for both thesis and antithesis. Identify any questionable inferences, irrelevant supports, fallacies, or other weaknesses in arguments.

7. If you recognize any assumptions, values, or ideological influences in the basic thesis or its supports, what are they? Do any of them shake the validity of the claim?

8. State the full thesis in the following form: "Although A (the antithesis or one of its strongest supports), B (the basic claim) because C (a major cause for belief in the basic claim)."

9. Is the full thesis debatable yet supportable beyond a reasonable doubt, unsupportable, or too complex to support?

10. If needed, revise original claim and repeat TASK.

FIGURE 7.2   Thesis Analysis and Synthesis Key (TASK).

they learned. They made connections between the text and background knowledge to construct meanings and engage in mathematical dialogue.

## TASKing in Pairs

From research I had done on writing (Unrau, 1992), I discovered that students often improve the quality of their thinking if explicitly guided through a procedure. To help students analyze arguments, I developed a procedure called *TASK,* which stands for *Thesis Analysis and Synthesis Key* (see Figure 7.2). TASK guides readers through several stages as they take apart an argument. Readers first identify the topic of the argument they are reading and then state in their own words the central claim or thesis the writer has made about that topic. Once the thesis has been stated, the readers identify the argument's antithesis (or create one if the writer made no mention of any counterargument). Having articulated both the thesis and antithesis, readers next list the supports given for the thesis and the antithesis (if given). If no antithesis was provided, readers then generate evidence and reasons they believe would support the student-created antithesis and list those.

Following the analysis of the argument to identify and list supports for both the thesis and the antithesis, readers identify any unclear terms, perplexing concepts, or emotionally weighted language that appears in either the thesis or antithesis. After that, readers evaluate the soundness of the supports for the thesis and antithesis. That includes noting any fallacies discovered. Then, the readers identify any assumptions, values, or influences of ideology on the antithesis or its supports because these may strongly bias an argument. Acknowledging their presence can help readers understand the underlying principles that may be driving an argument even though those under-the-surface principles are not explicitly stated.

Readers next put together several elements of the analysis into a sentence. That sentence takes the following form: Although A, B because C. Here A stands for some antithesis or support for the antithesis. B stands for the basic claim made in the argument, and C is one of the primary supporting reasons for believing in B. Having created this sentence, readers have the gist of the argument in a nutshell.

## STEP-BY-STEP: *TASKing in Pairs*

**STEP 1.** Pair two students who are to read an argument on a controversial issue.

**STEP 2.** Decide which student will become an expert for the argument's thesis and which will become an expert on the argument's antithesis.

**STEP 3.** Pro and con students receive and complete a separate thesis analysis and synthesis key (TASK) while discussing the argument.

**STEP 4.** Students discuss what topic is being judged (less any judgment the text may make about the topic).

**STEP 5.** Pro-person states the thesis while con-person states the antithesis or a strong counterclaim opposing the thesis. If no antithesis or counterclaim is stated, con-person creates an appropriate counterclaim to the thesis.

**STEP 6.** Pro-person identifies supports for the thesis and lists them.

**STEP 7.** Con-person identifies all the supports for the antithesis or counterclaim and lists them. If no supports for the antithesis or counterclaim are presented in the argument, the con-person generates them.

**STEP 8.** Pro-person identifies any unclear, perplexing, or emotionally charged language used in the antithesis or counterargument. Con-person explains, expands, and tries to cleanse the argument of emotionally charged language.

**STEP 9.** Con-person identifies any unclear, perplexing, or emotionally charged language used in the thesis. Pro-person explains, expands, and tries to cleanse the argument of emotionally charged language.

**STEP 10.** Pro-person inspects and evaluates the supports for the antithesis or counterclaim by identifying questionable logic, irrelevant supports, fallacies, and other points of weakness in the counterclaim.

**STEP 11.** Con-person inspects and evaluates the supports for the thesis or major claim by identifying questionable logic, irrelevant supports, fallacies, and other points of weakness in the thesis.

**STEP 12.** Pro-person tries to identify any assumptions, values, or influences of ideology on the antithesis or its supports.

**STEP 13.** Con-person tries to identify any assumptions, values, or influences of ideology on the thesis or its supports.

**STEP 14.** Together, the Pro and Con-persons synthesize the argument into one sentence in the following format: Although A (where A is the counterclaim or one of its strongest supports), B (where B is the thesis or basic claim) because C (where C is a major reason for belief in the basic claim).

**STEP 15.** Pro and Con experts prepare to present their side of the argument to the class for further discussion.

## Understanding Critical Literacy

While strategies like TASK contribute to readers' development of critical thinking, making more critical readers can also be achieved through the practice of critical literacy. However, "critical" takes on a somewhat different meaning in the term critical literacy from the meaning it has in the term critical thinking. In addition, the practices and outcomes of this form of critical reading are also different.

From the teachings of Paulo Freire (1993/1970), a Brazilian educator who worked extensively with the impoverished, arose the practice of critical literacy. Differing from critical thinking, as we shall see, ***critical literacy*** focuses on ways in which reading and writing help students to understand daily political processes for the purpose of living more freely in a democratic society. Engaging in critical literacy practices enables readers to see their world more clearly, to understand how it works, to "rewrite" that world with their interests written in, and to take more liberating action within it. Critical literacy's intent is to emancipate, to empower those subordinated and marginalized.

In his widely read *Pedagogy of the Oppressed,* Freire (1993/1970) presents his method for developing "critical consciousness," the capacity to perceive social, political, and economic contradictions and to act against oppressive forces. He focuses on the roots of oppression and methods of unearthing them for close examination. Through reflection on the forces of oppression, the oppressed will be liberated. Liberation will come through critical dialogue with the oppressed that aims at reflection on an individual's specific situation.

Freire encourages educators to eschew the "banking" model of education in which knowledge is deposited and withdrawn. To be avoided is teacher-talk like this: "Listen to my lecture and regurgitate my words on the exam." The new capital must be language that liberates and transforms individuals through reflection on their immediate life and dialogue about it. Critical dialogue leads to humanization rather than dehumanization.

To engage the oppressed in critical dialogue for the purpose of developing a critical consciousness, you pose problems revealing dilemmas in the historical and lived reality of your students' world, for example, cliques in school cultures. Critical analysis of each individual's situation leads to the discovery of reality and its presentation as a problem to students. How do cliques form and function in the school culture? Dialogue and critical analysis are intended to reveal contradictions embedded in that reality, such as the tension between inclusion and exclusion from a clique, and to discover each inhabitant's degree of awareness of those contradictions. The function of dialogue and action is to resolve the contradictions in favor of transcending their limitations, or of gaining liberation from the contradictions.

According to Freire (1993/1970), there can be no true dialogue without critical thinking. Problem posing and dialogue about those problems turns students into critical thinkers.

However, Freire's (1993/1970) conception of critical thinking is different from the one introduced earlier in this chapter. For him, critical thinking "discerns an indivisible solidarity between the world and the people and admits of no dichotomy between them." It is thinking that "perceives reality as process, as transformation, rather than as a static entity." Critical thinking for him never disengages from action. He contrasts his conception of critical thinking with naïve thinking, the intent of which is to accommodate to things as they are. For the student engaged in Freire's form of critical thinking, the aim is the continuous transformation of reality for the purpose of its humanization.

You and your students, as coinvestigators, together investigate what he calls the "thematic universe." That thematic universe is composed of many interacting themes, including ideas, values, concepts, and aspirations, that reflect a given epoch. The "fundamental theme of our epoch," as Freire sees it, is domination. You can help individuals externalize their thematics by making explicit their consciousness of the real world.

## STEP-BY-STEP: *Critical Literacy in the Classroom*

**STEP 1.** Adopt an historical and theoretical perspective of critical literacy. Allan Luke (2000) described what he did to engage students in "redefined" critical literacy when he taught in Australia. But first, a little history. Australian educators in the 1980s faced criticism of a curriculum based on whole language, process writing, and personal growth models that dominated instruction. That criticism led to a new focus on how texts worked. To get at how they work, educators borrowed strongly from the field of critical discourse analysis. From different theoreticians and practitioners of critical discourse analysis came the views that:

- Texts are an interplay of conflicting voices,
- Students need tools to gain access to historical and cultural positions,
- Students need to discover whose purposes and ends are fulfilled in texts,
- Discourse constructs identities for readers, defines who they are, and positions them,
- Readers construct multiple meanings for texts,
- Words are cultural coins with exchange value in communities, and
- The development of a "critical consciousness" could liberate oppressed peoples by making them aware of dominant social, political, and economic forces and leading them to action.

**STEP 2.** Applying these principles in classrooms, you could stimulate debate over what a text is trying to do, what ideologies are driving it, and how students can apply those ideologies in various domains of interest. As Luke (2000) puts it, the purpose of critical literacy is to create classroom climates in which both you and your students collaborate to discover how texts construct your students' worlds, cultures, and identities "in powerful, often overtly ideological ways" and use the texts to reconstruct those worlds. "The *redefinition of critical literacy* (my emphasis) focuses on teaching and learning how texts work, understanding and re-mediating what texts attempt to do in the world and to people, and moving students toward active position-taking with texts to critique and reconstruct the social fields in which they live and work" (p. 453).

**STEP 3.** The kinds of questions you could pose in relation to a text may be categorized into four sets of practices necessary for critical literacy. These categories and questions include the following:

- *Coding Practices.* How does the text work? How is it designed? What are its features?
- *Text-Meaning Practices.* How are ideas related to each other within the text? What cultural resources would help us make sense of this text? What cultural readings and interpretations can we construct from the text?
- *Pragmatic Practices.* What do we do, as readers, with the text? How does its function shape its form?
- *Critical Practices.* What is the text attempting to do to us, individually? Whose interests are served through the agency of this text? Whose voices and interests are expressed? What positions are conveyed? Who is being left out?

**STEP 4.** Ask your students to apply questions from the four categories above and write responses in their journals to a particular text you want to examine.

**STEP 5.** Create teams of three to five students, ask students to share answers to their questions in their teams, and arrange for one member of each team to report to the whole class.

**STEP 6.** Guide a whole-class discussion using team reports and individual student's journal entries as springboards. Rather than asking students questions about the text that have already-known answers, keep in mind that teachers practicing critical literacy ask themselves questions such as these:

- How can we approach this text so that we can use it as a tool to raise critical consciousness?
- What will the text tell us about how society works and how we arrived at our current social status?
- How can we approach this work so we can understand social forces that oppress and exploit people, that lead to alienation?

Drawing upon a "social issues" curriculum used in an Australian secondary school, Luke (1995) provides an example of text analysis. For him, models of critical reading foreground political power and knowledge relations expressed in texts. One of the questions students should ask about the following passage is "What is this text trying to do to me?"

> Think of your own family. You are probably aware that you belong to a separate group in society. You feel that you are in some ways "different" from the Browns or the Smiths across the road. Each member of your family plays a number of roles. You may look up to your father or mother as the "head of the family" or the "family breadwinner." Your mum or dad, for their part, will expect you to behave in certain ways—to help out with the dishes or in the garage, for example. (p. 107)

According to Luke (1995), a critical reading of this text should highlight its "monocultural social order" based on a "version of the ideal, Anglo-nuclear family" with the Browns and Smiths living across the road and expecting their children to do dishes and clean garages. Luke also sees the text as telling readers what to do when they begin reading: "Think of your own family." The author(s) constructed a role the reader is to assume when engaging with the text. For practitioners of critical literacy (Luke, 1995), critical discussion of texts laden with values and ideologies but presented as "nonfiction" begins with questions that reveal how authors "construct and position human subjects and social reality": How does this text work? What cultural interpretations can we construct from the text? What do we do with the text? What does the text do to us?

## Ophelia Re-Visioned through Critical Literacy

Looking at the classroom instruction of two Australian teachers, Bronwyn Mellor and Annette Patterson (2000), we can discover how they taught classical Shakespeare from a critical literacy perspective. One of their guiding principles was that students should reflect critically not only on what they are reading but also on how they are reading it. Mellor and Patterson planned to help students see how readers construct divergent meanings for the same character by looking at interpretations of Hamlet's sometime sweetheart, Ophelia, at two ends of a continuum. At one end of the continuum was Ophelia, the virginal innocent, and at the other end was Ophelia, the sexually wise wanton.

Mellor and Patterson (2000) asked students to decide how they would describe Ophelia's character and qualities by responding to the following scenes:

*Scenes with her father and brother:*

a. Ophelia is totally subservient.
b. Ophelia is obedient but not without spirit.
c. Ophelia's obedience is a pretense.

*Scenes with Hamlet:*

a. Ophelia is shocked and upset by Hamlet's ungentlemanly behavior.
b. Ophelia answers Hamlet's innuendo and abuse as best she can.
c. Ophelia flirts knowledgeably with Hamlet.

*The mad scenes:*

a. Ophelia's madness is the tragic breakdown of a total innocent.
b. Ophelia's madness is the result of the repression of her identity and her sexuality.
c. In Ophelia's madness is proof of her sexual knowledge and lack of innocence.

After students decided on their readings of Ophelia's behavior, Mellor and Patterson discussed the possible sources for their interpretations. After presenting students with these influences, students explored how they could have constructed their readings.

What makes this approach different? The assumptions underlying it. Now we can work under the assumptions that a text will yield multiple readings, that you can help students see what has contributed to these different readings, and that contradictions in readings can be examined through discussion and dialogue. Working under these assumptions, students are no longer expected to find the meaning the author intended to inscribe. Rather, readers are constructed by their interpretations of a text that delivers various visions of reality. Critical literacy is tied to Freire's belief that in reading we engage in an interpretation of reality, of the world in which we live. Reading texts in school creates capital that students use in economies of symbols to express and exchange value and power, such as during a classroom discussion or when writing an essay.

In Australia, Luke (2000) writes, literacy is about social power. An education through critical literacy goes beyond skill acquisition. It engages students in the analysis and reconstruction of their worlds.

In this chapter, we have examined why students in a democratic society need to expand their basic reading abilities so they can analyze texts, identify claims, search for evidence, question perspectives, and evaluate conclusions. I've provided several strategies, including Inquiry Questions, Questioning the Author, Re-Quest, Socratic Seminars, and TASK, that promote the development of students' critical reading. I've also introduced critical literacy as a method to increase students' awareness of how texts define and shape their readers and how marginalized readers can be empowered through textual analysis. However, presenting strategies and methods to students does not ensure their use. Dispositions to read critically require nurturing, and as teachers, we nurture those dispositions every time we ourselves model the critical reading of texts of all kinds. Keep in mind: Questions open minds.

---

**DOUBLE-ENTRY JOURNAL: After Reading**

Go to the Double-Entry Journal for Chapter 7 on our Companion Website at **www.prenhall.com/unrau** to complete your journal entry.

How have you modified, if at all, your conception of critical reading now that you have read this chapter? What strategies or approaches to critical reading development in your content area could you add to those you described in your prereading DEJ? How could you integrate critical literacy into your content area instruction?

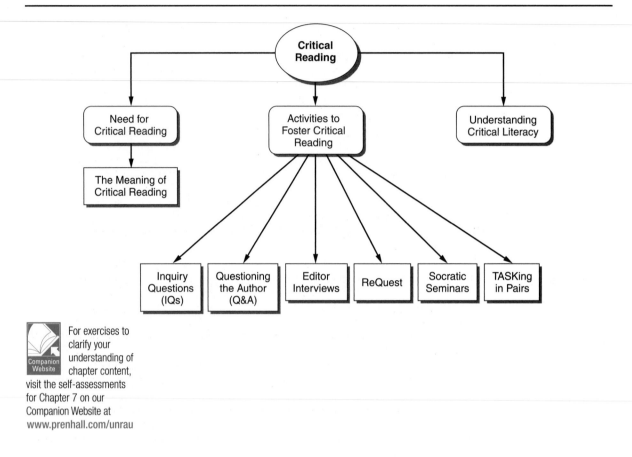

For exercises to clarify your understanding of chapter content, visit the self-assessments for Chapter 7 on our Companion Website at www.prenhall.com/unrau

# References

*A nation at risk: The imperative for educational reform* (1983). Washington, DC: Government Printing Office.

Applebee, A. N., Langer, J. A., & Mullis, I. V. S. (1985). *The reading report card, progress toward excellence in our schools: Trends in reading over four national assessments, 1971–1984.* Princeton, NJ: Educational Testing Service.

Applebee, A. N., Langer, J. A., & Mullis, I. V. S. (1988). *Who reads best?* Princeton, NJ: Educational Testing Service.

Atwell, N. (1998). *In the middle: New understandings about writing, reading, and learning.* Portsmouth, NH: Heinemann.

Beck, I., McKeown, M. G., Hamilton, R. L., & Kucan, L. (1997). *Questioning the author: An approach for enhancing student engagement with text.* Newark, DE: International Reading Association.

Bloom, B. S. (Ed.). (1956). *Taxonomy of educational objectives: Handbook I: Cognitive domain.* New York: David McKay.

Boyer, E. (1983). *High school: A report on secondary education in America.* New York: Harper and Row.

Ennis, R. H. (1996). *Critical thinking.* Upper Saddle River, NJ: Prentice Hall.

Freire, P. (1993/1970). *Pedagogy of the oppressed* (M. B. Ramos, Trans.). New York: Continuum.

Luke, A. (1995). When basic skills and information processing just aren't enough: Rethinking reading in New Times. *Teachers College Record, 97*(1), 95–116.

Luke, A. (2000). Critical literacy in Australia: A matter of context and standpoint. *Journal of Adolescent and Adult Literacy, 43*(5), 448–461.

Manzo, A. V. (1969). The ReQuest procedure. *Journal of Reading, 13,* 123–126.

Mellor, B., & Patterson, A. (2000). Critical practice: Teaching "Shakespeare." *Journal of Adolescent and Adult Literacy, 43*(6), 508–517.

Mullis, I. V. S., Campbell, J. R., & Farstrup, A. E. (1993). *NAEP 1992 reading report card for the nation and the states.* Princeton, NJ: Educational Testing Service.

Official voter information guide. (2000). < *http://Vote2000.ss.ca.gov/VoterGuide/home.htm*> Accessed 2002 July 10.

Tanner, M. L., & Casados, L. (1998). Promoting and studying discussions in math classes. *Journal of Adolescent and Adult Literacy, 41*(5), 342–350.

Unrau, N. (1992). The TASK of reading (and writing) arguments: A guide to building critical literacy. *Journal of Reading, 35* (6), 436–442.

Unrau, N. (1997). *Thoughtful teachers, thoughtful learners: A guide to helping adolescents think critically.* Scarborough, Ontario: Pippin Press.

# 8 WRITING TO ASSESS, PROMOTE, AND OBSERVE LEARNING

After reading Chapter 8, you should be able to answer the following questions:

1. What developments have taken place over the past 25 to 30 years to support the uses of writing in classrooms across the curriculum?

2. What is the "process approach" to writing and how do teachers engage students in it?

3. What do we know about the effects of writing on learning?

4. How can writing serve as a tool to construct knowledge in classrooms across the disciplines?

5. How can you use writing to assess, promote, and observe learning?

6. What factors should you consider in deciding what kind of writing assignments to give to your students and how to respond to the writing they submit?

| DOUBLE-ENTRY JOURNAL: Before Reading | Recall three or four specific examples of how your high school or college instructors used writing to promote your learning. What were you learning and how did writing help you learn? How would you use writing to help your students learn? |

Now go to the Double-Entry Journal for Chapter 8 on our Companion Website at www.prenhall.com/unrau to fill out your journal entry.

## WRITING IN THE CONTENT AREAS

Do students write better or more in school today than they did 30 years ago? Although the *Writing Report Card for the Nation and the States* (Greenwald, Persky, Campbell, & Mazzeo, 1998) reveals that only one out of four students can write at a "proficient" level, showing "solid academic performance and competency over challenging subject matter," we have no compelling evidence that writing skills of today's middle and high school students have changed much since the 1970s. And, even though computers would seem to encourage more writing in the school, whether or not students in today's secondary schools write more or less than they did in 1970 is a tough question to answer because data is difficult to obtain.

Although we don't know for sure if the quality or amount of writing students do in school has changed over the past 25 or 30 years, we do know that four major educational developments during that time should support and encourage the use of writing in content area courses. First, researchers and teachers have learned more about the writing process, how to engage students in it, and how to adapt it to the needs of urban classrooms. Second, researchers and teachers have been drawn to the promise of writing to learn. Third, many teachers across the curriculum have become intent upon engaging their students in the construction of knowledge through exploration and discovery rather than through memorization. And fourth, the National Writing Project was born and expanded to serve teachers across the disciplines. These four broad developments have contributed to major changes in teaching and learning in many classrooms.

### How Process Upstaged Product

Prior to the 1970s, writing in classrooms was product-centered. Teachers and researchers focused on instructional strategies that got students to write and on evaluating their written products. Since the 1970s, writing as a process in a context has struggled to upstage and replace the formerly dominant product perspective. However, product-oriented writing has not been pushed into the wings. As our national educational drama plays year after year, writing-as-product strolls or struts back to center stage and delivers its hegemonic oratory—and its pleas for grades.

Decades of research on writing have led to several significant generalizations about what happens when writers write. To define what was known about writing and what needs to be learned, several researchers at the Center for the Study of Writing (Freedman, Dyson, Flower, & Chafe, 1987) pulled together a set of generalizations about the nature of the writing process:

♦ Writing consists of several main processes—planning, transcribing text, and reviewing—which do not occur in any fixed order; rather, thought in writing is not linear but jumps from process to process in an organized way which is largely determined by the individual writer's goals (Emig, 1971; Flower et al., 1989; Flower & Hayes, 1981).
♦ The writing process is a hierarchically organized, goal-directed, problem-solving process (Bereiter & Scardamalia, 1980; Flower & Hayes, 1981).
♦ Experts and novices solve the problems posed by the task of writing differently (Flower, 1979; Flower & Hayes, 1977; Perl, 1979).
♦ The nature of the writing task changes the writer's strategies (Applebee, 1984; Carey et al., 1989; Emig, 1971).

If you reflect on your own writing experiences, you are likely to find personal evidence for these observations and insights.

Some of these discoveries about the nature of writing contributed to what was and is widely called the "process approach" to teaching writing. Usually, "writing as a process" gets broken down into several steps or stages: prewriting, drafting, revising, proofreading, and publishing (Michigan State Board of Education, 1994). In each stage, the writer engages in different activities, such as those described in Table 8.1.

However, these stages are not linear. Researchers have repeatedly confirmed that the writing process is recursive in nature and encourage teachers to create environments where students can rethink ideas and ways to express them at all stages of composition.

Classroom instruction across America now reflects the process approach to writing. In the *Writing Report Card for the Nation and the States* (Greenwald, Persky, Campbell, & Mazzeo, 1998), about 9 out of 10 students in grades 8 and 12 report that their teachers always or sometimes ask them to write more than one draft of a paper. Furthermore, students in the eighth and twelfth grades who were always asked in their classes to write more than one draft performed better on measures of writing achievement than their peers who were only sometimes or never asked to write

**TABLE 8.1**    The Process of Writing

| Prewriting | Drafting | Revising | Proofreading | Publishing |
|---|---|---|---|---|
| Planning by: | Constructing a preliminary form | by: Reviewing or reflecting on | one's work by: Preparing for publication by: | Sharing with a target audience by: |
| • Clustering, • Listing, • Brainstorming, • Researching, • Note taking | • Writing drafts, • Selecting a format, • Deciding on an audience | • Rethinking, • Adding, • Dropping, • Rearranging, • Rewriting | • Polishing, • Correcting spelling, punctuation, and grammatical problems | • Reading, • Displaying, • Anthologizing, • Submitting for publication |

multiple drafts. As for prewriting activities, the majority of students at both grades 8 and 12 report that their English teachers asked them to plan their writing at least once a week. Students who planned their writing also demonstrated higher levels of writing achievement.

Many of the generalizations about writing that researchers and educators induced, such as the "process approach," had been derived from laboratory-like conditions rather than the natural context of classrooms. Freedman and her colleagues (1987) foresaw a need for educators to become more aware of other dimensions that influence writing, including the effects of social contexts on the writing process. Out of these purposes grew studies that investigated many aspects of writing, including "situated learning" (Freedman, Flower, Hull, & Hayes, 1995). Their purpose was to discover what goes on when students learn in specific situations, like multicultural urban classrooms.

In one such study, Sarah Freedman and her collaborators (1999) investigated literacy processes in urban classrooms. She engaged 24 Boston, Chicago, New Orleans, and San Francisco area teachers of English and social studies in university-supported teacher-research projects. The teachers in the network she established examined their classroom literacy and learning practices and described what they did and saw in order to serve as models for other teachers facing multicultural classrooms across America. Teachers formulated their own research questions, and their search for answers guided their investigation of the perplexing teaching situations in which they worked. They met in groups from time to time to share their findings and to find encouragement and direction from collaborating teachers.

Writing played an important role in many of these teachers' classrooms (Freedman et al., 1999). With teacher guidance, students used writing for a multitude of purposes: to record connections between personal experiences and reading experience, to promote learning in geography, to shape the stories of their lives, to confront racism, to expand their ethnic identity, and to understand their feelings of marginality.

These teachers did not universally embrace a process approach to teaching writing. Some, agreeing with Delpit's (1986, 1988) critique of process writing and advocacy of explicit instruction in literacy skills, believed that their students needed a much more structured approach than the process pedagogy provided. One of these network teachers argued that the process approach held students responsible for what they haven't been taught and haven't learned. Their non-standard English, while expressive of their own lives, would not empower them in the wider world. Her teacher-research question was "How can I help students internalize correctness so it becomes a part of their repertoire?" Although she used a red pen to mark errors, gave grammar mini-lessons daily, and varied in other ways from a process-writing pedagogy, she had very mixed feelings about doing so. However, her teacher-research confirmed for her that she was on the right track with her multicultural students (Freedman et al., 1999).

As for writing instruction in multicultural urban classrooms, these teacher-researchers learned some important lessons about how their work could benefit the educational community with which they shared it. One of the general findings that emerged from these inquiries was that, if teachers wanted to achieve high standards for writing while empowering their students, they would need to teach explicitly the conventions of standard edited English. That guideline applied to both non-native speakers of English and those speaking a nonstandard dialect. Teachers should also provide explicit instruction in other writing skills and knowledge, including composition structures and writing styles. The script for the process approach to teaching writing, as some teachers saw it, got modified in urban classrooms to meet the specific learning needs of diverse students.

These new discoveries about the writing process and its use in the social context of school were not the only elements drawing teachers' attention to writing. Teachers were also lured by the value of writing to learn.

## The Promise of Writing to Learn

Writing can work as a cultural tool to build and examine knowledge (Vygotsky, 1978). But before a writer externalizes knowledge as written text, she engages in what Vygotsky called "inner speech," a form of self-talk in which the talker (and writer) tries to make sense of her thoughts. Unfortunately, inner speech does not always enter consciousness in standard English. Especially for struggling writers, it emerges in fragments with words and details left out. Coherence and structure may also be left out (Everson, 1991). Nevertheless, if we can provide an instructional environment in which students can externalize their inner speech, writing can serve as a medium for learning.

And plenty of research supports the claim that writing promotes learning (Durst, 1987; Langer & Applebee, 1987; Newell, 1998). Newell & Winograd (1995) found that, in comparison to studying without writing, studying with writing yields a considerable advantage. Writing then presents itself to teachers as a tool with considerable promise. In fact, Newell (1998) believes writing offers at least three promises:

- ◆ Writing provides a means to explore and make sense of ideas and experiences.
- ◆ Writing can alter both the role of teachers (by transforming them from evaluators to collaborators) and students (by transforming them from memorizers to meaning-makers) while changing the value of knowledge in the content areas (by transforming it from facts to ways of understanding one's culture, one's traditions, and one's self).
- ◆ Writing across the disciplines can help students learn about the wide range of genres and formats used in various content areas.

These are functions of critical importance for writing to perform in our classrooms. It's a tool for discovery, for changing the way students learn, and for bridging students into the forms of writing that are common in each content area.

Types of writing.    But not all kinds of writing produce the same results. Different types of writing foster different kinds of learning and reasoning (Newell, 1998):

- ◆ *Restricted writing.*    This form of writing, exemplified by answering study questions focused on comprehension of a text, usually engages students' minds in a basic search and transcription process. For example, after reading passages about Andrew Jackson's presidency, students are asked to explain in writing the doctrine of nullification and Jackson's response to it. Little or no composing or transformation of knowledge occurs when students engage in this form of writing. Teachers can use it for a couple of instructional purposes: (a) to review content of a text before a test or class discussion and (b) to prepare students for a more complex instructional task, such as comparing alternative theories or explanations once individual explanations have been comprehended (Newell & Winograd, 1995).

◆ *Summary writing.* This form of writing focuses on ideas at a deeper level than a mental review but at a more superficial level than analytic writing. Summaries do require students to compress and integrate information to capture the gist of a text while representing the original text's structure. So knowledge does get transformed to some degree. But students emerge with a distillation of the original text rather than an analysis or evaluation of it. Like restricted writing, summary writing can prepare students for more complex tasks.

◆ *Analytical writing.* This form of writing engages students in reformulating and extending the text. In science, a student could analyze and compare two different explanations of a laboratory event. In history, students could analyze multiple text sources to answer complex inquiry questions, such as those about the origins of WWI, its consequences, and how the war might have been avoided. In English, a student could analyze a character, such as Hester Prynn or Willy Loman; state a theme and justify it; or inspect the effects of setting in a novel. These manipulations of ideas to organize an argument or to persuade a reader of a student's position are likely to create a more enduring representation of content through reformulation and integration (Langer & Applebee, 1987; Newell, 1998; Newell & Winograd, 1995).

**Effects of writing on learning.** So certain forms of writing support certain kinds of learning. This looks like important pedagogical knowledge for us to have. If we want students to learn a lot of general information about a chapter in a history text, we'd better think through what kind of writing (if any) we think they should do. Would asking students to "write a report" on the chapter lead to the kind of knowledge we'd like our students to gain for an examination testing their comprehension of the whole chapter? Probably not.

Studies have clearly shown that different kinds of writing (analytical or summary) activate quite different kinds of cognitive processes that result in students' learning different things, perhaps even important things. However, they may not be things we're planning to include on an exam.

Penrose (1989) found that whether or not writing promotes learning depends on what kind of writing and learning we're talking about. In her study, students read two academic articles during two different sessions. During one session, students were assigned a written "report" on the text. During the second session, students were instructed to "study for a test" using whatever strategies they thought would work. After completing the assigned tasks, students took a test that included four different types of comprehension questions: simple recall of facts, complex recall of two or more related facts, main idea, and application.

The results overall showed that, when students studied rather than wrote, they scored higher on the comprehension test. Writing failed to result in higher scores on any comprehension measure. Furthermore, students spent about 35% more time on the writing task. This finding does not mean that students weren't learning when they were writing their report. For those reports, some students organized or transformed information in the text as they reflected on its significance to them as learners. Unfortunately, they were constructing or manipulating knowledge that didn't contribute enough to their overall understanding of the article to show that they had comprehended it at levels that students who simply studied the article did.

Now comes an important variable that Penrose might have used to discover the effects of specific kinds of writing on learning. What would have happened to students' comprehension scores if she had asked them to write a *summary* rather than a report and included specific expectations with respect to the summary's content and structure? As we saw earlier, summary writing has some rather specific effects on knowledge construction. Students writing summaries are more likely to condense the original text rather than reflect upon or evaluate some aspect of it. That condensation in memory might prove to be helpful in answering comprehension questions of various kinds.

In a follow-up analysis of her study, Penrose (1992) looked more carefully at task representation, noting that other studies (Flower et al., 1990) have confirmed that students often interpret writing assignments in ways that differ from their teacher's and from other students' interpretations. How a writer interprets an assignment influences what kind of learning will occur. Penrose (1992) observed that students, while focusing on the analysis of a single aspect of the text they read, may not have taken in the broader picture. In so doing, students may not have attended to individual facts, knowledge of which was tested through comprehension questions. She concluded that what students learned was more dependent on their interpretation of the writing tasks than on the tasks as she intended them.

Other researchers besides Penrose have questioned claims that writing is a unique tool to promote learning. Ackerman (1993) finds that many writing-to-learn accounts "overstate" the power of writing as a medium for learning and ignore other study tools that could be equally facilitative. As we've seen so far, writing does not inevitably lead to learning of any specific kind.

What is to be learned from this discussion focused on the promise of writing to learn? One implication is that you will need to let your students know more clearly what kind of writing you want them to do and what you want them to learn from the writing. Rubrics for an assignment, delivered to students when the assignment is given, can make more explicit both what you want students to do and to learn. We will further examine rubrics later when we discuss responding to students' writing. A second implication is that individual differences play a central role in connecting writing to learning. What students bring to a writing assignment shapes what they will learn from it. But part of what they learn may well be how experts in a discipline, like history or biology, reason, construct knowledge, and write about their fields. In summary, writing holds a lot of promise for us as a tool for learning; however, you will need to put significant thought into the selection and presentation of writing assignments for that promise to be realized in learning.

## Writing Furthers Constructivism

We've seen that reading is a meaning construction process, and I've given you a model of reading that shows how readers construct meaning. Researchers (Emig, 1971; Flower & Hayes, 1977) have also provided ample evidence to show us that writing is also a meaning construction process that activates knowledge held in memory, including world knowledge, text structure knowledge, metacognitive knowledge, and knowledge of the mechanics of writing. While writing itself is constructivist, writing can also be used to promote constructivism in the form of knowledge-building classrooms in which students use writing to learn through inquiry.

When I, as an English teacher, first engaged my high school juniors in inquiry projects that required extensive research, I don't think I knew how important writing would be to help me and my students achieve our goals. I used writing to discover what they wanted to do and to monitor where students were going, how they were getting there, and how well the journey was going for each of them. Writing helped them ride out the bumps and find productive roadways. Without constantly writing back and forth, in logs and letters, I would have been lost in the dust.

I enjoyed designing units that opened opportunities for students to explore topics, usually of their own choice, and to build on their knowledge base. Using inquiry or discovery methods, I engaged students in projects and problem solving. I used writing to facilitate their growth of understanding rather than depositing what I knew in their minds in order to withdraw those deposits on the next examination for an accounting. Students, meanwhile, constructed knowledge as they made connections between what they knew and new information they discovered. I had them writing lots of summaries although I did so, not because of what I knew about research at the time, but because it felt like the right thing to do. Sometimes, although not always, my classroom became a community of learners using writing to become both more knowledgeable and more thoughtful.

Similarly, in history classes using a constructivist perspective, students are not simply told about the events of World War I through lectures even though teachers may use lectures at some times. Instead, students read and discuss textbook chapters about World War I along with original documents describing historical events leading up to America's engagement in the war, the war's battles, and its aftermath. They might be presented with topics for inquiry:

- What economic and political relationships prevailed among European countries in 1914 before the outbreak of war?
- At what points and in what ways could the series of events that led to the outbreak of war in Europe have been broken?
- Which battles best typified battlefield tactics and the kind of suffering soldiers endured during the war?
- Looking back, was America's decision to enter the war a good decision? Should America have entered the war or should it have maintained an isolationist policy?
- Looking forward, what can we learn from the events of World War I that could inform our foreign policy and decision making in the twenty-first century?

Students, perhaps working in cooperative learning teams, engage in gathering and interpreting information that help them to answer these questions. They prepare documents for the teacher and the class that reveal their discoveries and their answers to these questions. But how could a teacher move these students forward, observe their work, and offer productive suggestions? What better tool than writing?

Through writing, students record their discoveries in the form of notes and summaries, guided by the teacher's questions and recommendations. After discussing their discoveries in their teams, they write about their discussions in journals. As they move toward answering their team's major questions, they draft and share their analyses and arguments. Finally, they compile a final copy of their documents for the teacher and use their writing as a basis for their presentation to their classmates who engaged in similar inquiries and writing in their own teams. In this way, class-rooms become communities to promote learning and scholarship through inquiry and the construction of knowledge.

Teachers across the land and across the disciplines realized the potential of writing to learn and to construct knowledge. The use of writing in content area courses gathered so much attention that it became a movement called Writing Across the Curriculum (or WAC). At first, colleges tended to lead the WAC movement. But secondary school teachers, like myself and thousands of others, quickly followed. Teachers reading professional educational journals published by national organizations of social studies, science, and math teachers or teachers attending professional conferences soon learned about WAC. They discovered how they could use writing in their specific disciplines to support learning.

## The National Writing Project (NWP)

In the early 1970s, several teachers, teacher educators, and professors in the San Francisco Bay Area became interested in finding a format in which teachers using writing in the schools could meet with other teachers to improve student writing. In 1974, James Gray (2000) and his colleagues at the University of California, Berkeley, broke new educational ground with the first Summer Institute of the Bay Area Writing Project (BAWP). About 25 teachers from high schools in the Bay Area and institute organizers, including some of BAWP's later leaders, such as Mary Ann Smith, Mary Kay Healy, and Miles Myers, listened to and gave presentations about writing, the writing process, and the use of writing to promote learning. They also wrote a lot because advocates believed that the process of writing could be best understood by writing. Although the BAWP model of teachers teaching each other worked, Gray (2000) believes it took a few more summers for fine-tuning, like interviewing Institute applicants before inviting them and extending invitations to elementary as well as high school teachers.

During the school year, BAWP ran workshops for schools and districts. After some misfires, Gray discovered a few guidelines that worked. Workshops would consist of several sessions, usually about 10, focused on one Writing Project teacher's 2- to 3-hour presentation. Teachers in the workshops wrote and shared their writing in response to the presenter's demonstration of a teaching method. Having seen what can happen when teachers were required to attend in-service programs, Gray insisted that teacher attendance be voluntary. Elements like these combined to produce workshops much in demand by schools and districts within driving range of BAWP Fellows.

BAWP also held monthly meetings during the school year to which teachers from the Bay Area came to give and get ideas about writing in their classrooms. Many of those attending taught English, but all teachers of all grades and of all content areas were encouraged to attend. I had the pleasure of sharing ideas about writing with many enthused, inspiring teachers and discovered a multitude of approaches and strategies that I used in teaching social studies and English.

BAWP caught on. Soon teachers and teacher educators representing campuses in California and other states heard about BAWP's successes and wanted to model a teacher development program along similar lines. By the late 1970s, the stage was set for the emergence of the National Writing Project (NWP). During the 1980s and 1990s, NWP sites sprang up at about 150 universities. These sites housed writing project centers to which teachers of all disciplines were invited to do essentially what was done at the first BAWP meetings: share ideas with other teachers to improve student writing. NWP sites have trained and served well over a million teachers.

Among the basic assumptions that continue to guide the NWP work are the following:

- Teachers learn well from other teachers because of their credibility.
- Writing is a tool that facilitates learning in science, math, history, and other disciplines as well as in English.
- Teachers who teach writing write.
- To be effective, professional development programs must be on-going so that teachers come together throughout their careers to exchange ideas about writing.
- Teachers must be free to participate voluntarily in NWP programs.
- Knowledge about teaching writing comes from both research and classroom practice.
- The NWP encourages the critical examination of a variety of approaches to the teaching of writing and promotes no single writing pedagogy.
- Working together, teachers and universities can guide and support school reform (National Writing Project, 2001).

In general, the National Writing Project has a progressive and constructivist theory informing its practices. Students learned to write by writing, as did teachers, and learning wasn't something teachers deposited in their students' minds. Students used writing to explore ideas and construct knowledge. Meanwhile, teachers reflected on their practice, shared ideas with other teachers, and built communities of learners.

Across the country, teachers at all grade levels attend NWP Summer Institutes, participate in NWP-supported in-service workshops, and share in monthly meetings where teacher-to-teacher contacts foster effective writing practices in the schools. In these various settings, teachers present the problems and successes they have in teaching their students to learn and to write.

In summary, these four developments in education had significant effects on the uses of writing in content area classrooms. First, new discoveries about the writing process provided reasons to displace earlier product-centered views of writing and to engage students in the development of more process-oriented writing skills, such as planning and editing. Second, writing held out an appealing promise to teachers: students could learn through using the tool of writing. Third, constructivism encouraged teachers to focus more intently on helping their students to build knowledge, and writing served as a flexible but durable tool to do that building. And, fourth, with the development of the National Writing Project, teachers could find universities and sites where their efforts to infuse and to improve writing across the disciplines would find strong support and guidance.

## CATEGORIES OF WRITING

Animals often slip neatly into a biological category like a bear into its cave or a hermit crab into its shell. But, when it comes to writing, different types of writing don't always fit easily into a category. Some types of writing creep around looking for the appropriate category to slip into. Of course, categories of discourse go all the way back to Aristotle's *Rhetoric,* and some teachers still use his system of classification. Educators have created several other category systems (or typologies) to describe the uses for writing in school (Applebee, 1981; Britton, 1970; Moffett, 1989). Currently, the National Assessment of Education Progress (Greenwald, Persky, Campbell, & Mazzeo, 1998) evaluates three categories of writing in the schools: narrative, informational, and persuasive writing.

I wanted a set of categories that reflect the ways teachers use writing to engage students in knowledge construction and learning across the curriculum. Keeping that goal in mind, I decided on three learning related categories to capture the purposes for teachers assigning writing: to assess learning, to promote learning, and to observe learning. Of course, a teacher can combine these purposes so that two or even three purposes could be combined and pursued in one assignment.

I pondered over the title of this chapter because I was concerned about putting writing to assess learning before writing to promote or observe it. However, research indicates and everyday observations in schools confirm that writing to assess learning dominates the reasons for its use (Applebee, 1984; Britton et al., 1975). Perhaps I can persuade you to expand its uses so that the value of the tool of writing can further enrich your students' learning and development.

## Writing to Assess Learning

Many teachers like to give multiple choice tests because they believe such tests are more objective. Some teachers feel obligated to give multiple choice tests because they believe the practice will help prepare students for high-stakes standardized testing. In spite of these considerations, teachers still argue that writing is the most efficient way to assess what students have learned. Teachers have good reasons for their argument about writing to assess learning. When composing, students can't guess what answer is correct. They have to construct and organize knowledge from what they have learned and stored away.

Writing can have multiple purposes, but teachers tend to use it primarily to evaluate previous learning. According to Applebee's (1981) study of writing in the secondary school, teachers most frequently ask students to write for the purpose of discovering what they have learned. Using that information, teachers can assign a grade to the degree of content mastery students demonstrate. However, always putting yourself in the role of examiner and grader of your students' writing limits the instructional purposes and potential of writing. Applebee (1984) found that giving students opportunities to use writing to explore ideas, to promote understanding of concepts, to have a dialogue with the teacher, or to address readers other than the teacher-as-grader were limited. These alternative purposes for asking students to write enrich instruction, as we'll discover.

Applebee (1984) also found that of the four uses of school writing he identified (mechanical, informational, personal, and imaginative), informational writing was the most frequently required. Furthermore, across all content areas analytical writing was the category of informational writing that teachers asked students to engage in more than half of the time. When doing analytical writing, students draw generalizations or make classifications based on the examination of information or data. For example, in a chemistry lab report, students would be expected to analyze the results of an experiment in order to draw conclusions about it. However, Applebee (1984) found that, as students moved from observation and summary to analysis and argument, they tended to apply rigid, formulaic approaches. With these approaches, students would simply fill in slots of information. While these formulaic approaches to writing, like the five-paragraph essay format, often help students initially to grasp the structure of a report or an essay, these same structures could limit students' analytical thinking and writing.

A couple of developments in the writing field can heighten students' essay-writing expectations and outcomes: Engaging students in the writing process and using rubrics to evaluate performance. When students get opportunities to plan, draft, seek response, revise, edit, and publish, we know they are more likely to produce essays of finer quality. In addition, using a well-designed rubric or scoring guide gives students a clear picture of the criteria you will use to evaluate their work. Knowing, in advance, what standards will be applied to judgments about their writing provides students with clear targets to seek. Many schools and districts now have generic rubrics they encourage their teachers to use. A sample of a six-level rubric for rating eighth graders' persuasive writing from the NAEP's *Writing Report Card* (Greenwald et al., 1998) can be found in Table 8.2. When NAEP readers use these rubrics for scoring, they are trained with "anchor papers" that represent student writing at each of the six levels. Although generic rubrics abound and can be useful in some assessments, I'd encourage you to develop rubrics tailored to the specific writing assignment you give and the expected learning outcomes you have.

## Writing to Promote Learning

Exploratory uses of writing.   Exploratory writing can play a central and catalytic role in all the disciplines. In *Writing to Learn,* Zinsser (1988) posited two categories for writing that augment learning: explanatory ("writing that transmits existing information or ideas") and exploratory ("writing that enables us to discover what we want to say"). Because of the belief and hope that exploratory writing can help us discover what we want to say, I have opted to put our more adventuresome strategies in an exploratory category of their own. These strategies promote both engagement with what is to be learned and learning itself.

***Exploratory writing*** enables students to travel through uncharted knowledge domains and (maybe) discover emerald cities of understanding. All this travel comes quite cheaply, too. But (of course) there is a price to pay: Students are expected to be making sense of ideas, constructing new understandings, making new connections, and generating questions as they go, sort of like Dorothy's journey in the Land of Oz with the Lion, the Tin Man, and the Straw Man. As a teacher, I use exploratory writing to deepen students' engagement with the course content and monitor their understanding. While I'm always hoping to discover their interests in reading assignments, I also use these exploratory writings to discover if students are doing their reading homework. When I use them, I seek these kinds of outcomes:

◆ Connecting students to background knowledge, including other texts,
◆ Constructing and sorting out meanings,
◆ Discovering questions and possible answers, and
◆ Reflecting on one's thinking or problem-solving process (metacognition).

Engaging students in one or more of the exploratory writing strategies that I will present below is quite likely to promote learning. However, many of them still need to be studied empirically to discover how and to what degree they actually do promote learning.

**TABLE 8.2**    Grade 8 Persuasive Scoring Guide

<table>
<tr><td>

**6    Excellent Response**
- Takes a clear position and develops it consistently with well-chosen reasons and/or examples across the response.
- Is well organized with strong transitions.
- Sustains variety in sentence structure and exhibits good word choice.
- Errors in grammar, spelling, and punctuation are few and do not interfere with understanding.

**5    Skillful Response**
- Takes a clear position and develops it with reasons and/or examples in parts of the response.
- Is clearly organized, but may lack some transitions and/or have occasional lapses in continuity.
- Exhibits some variety in sentence structure and some good word choices.
- Errors in grammar, spelling, and punctuation do not interfere with understanding.

**4    Sufficient Response**
- Takes a clear position and supports it with some reasons and/or examples.
- Is organized with ideas that are generally related, but there are few or no transitions.
- Exhibits control over sentence boundaries and sentence structure, but sentences and word choice may be simple and unvaried.
- Errors in grammar, spelling, and punctuation do not interfere with understanding.

**3    Uneven Response** (may be characterized by one or more of the following):
- Takes a position and offers support, but may be unclear, repetitive, list-like, or undeveloped.
- Is unevenly organized; the response may be disjointed.
- Exhibits uneven control over sentence boundaries and sentence structure; may have some inaccurate word choices.
- Errors in grammar, spelling, and punctuation sometimes interfere with understanding.

**2    Insufficient Response** (may be characterized by one or more of the following):
- Takes a position, but response may be very unclear, very undeveloped, or very repetitive.
- Is very disorganized; thoughts are tenuously connected OR the response is too brief to detect organization.
- Minimal control over sentence boundaries and sentence structure, word choice may often be inaccurate.
- Errors in grammar or usage (such as missing words or incorrect word use or word order), spelling, and punctuation interfere with understanding in much of the response.

**1    Unsatisfactory Response** (may be characterized by one or more of the following):
- Attempts to take a position (addresses topic) but response is incoherent OR takes a position but provides no support, may only paraphrase the prompt.
- Has no apparent organization OR consists of a single statement.
- Minimal or no control over sentence boundaries and sentence structure, word choice may be inaccurate in much or all of the response.
- A multiplicity of errors in grammar or usage (such as missing words or incorrect word use or word order), spelling, and punctuation severely impedes understanding across the response.

</td></tr>
</table>

*Source:* From the *NAEP Writing Report Card for the Nation and the States* (p. 144), by E. A. Greenwald, H. R. Persky, J. R. Campbell, and J. Mazzeo, 1998, Washington, DC: U.S. Department of Education. © 1998 by the U.S. Department of Education.

I've already explained a couple of strategies in Chapter 5, "Strategies to Enhance Comprehension": Know-Want to know-Learned strategy (K-W-L) and Double-Entry Journals. Both are used to activate, connect with, and extend background knowledge. However, there are several other writing strategies that engage students in the exploration and formation of knowledge. These include Admit Slips and Exit Passes,

Freewrites, Question Papers, Skeletons, RAFTing, Journals (or Logs), and Quick-writes (such as DEAD, for Drop Everything And Draft).

***Admit Slips and Exit Passes.***   Ever stand in front of a class, ask your students if they have any questions, and meet with a resounding stillness? When you want to get more response from them in the way of questions, try **Admit Slips.** They're none other than 3 × 5 cards you give to students for the purpose of their writing down questions about what you've been studying in your course. At the beginning of class, they might write questions in response to the following circumstances: A reading assignment done for homework, yesterday's lecture or discussion, a review of material to be covered on the next test, or a new topic you're about to study. When class begins, you can flip through the Admit Slips, find a few appropriate questions, and ask your students to try answering them or answer them yourself. One of my students wanted me to follow-up on a concept that arose during our previous class session and asked on her Admit Slip, "What is a miscue? Could you give us more examples?" The question enabled us to review miscue analysis and explore examples.

Ever wonder if your students got anything out of the lecture on Reconstruction that you spent the last 45 minutes giving, or the video on mitosis and meiosis they just watched, or a team's presentation on factoring polynomials? When you want to know, try **Exit Passes.** These are 3 × 5 cards on which you ask your students to write a three or four sentence summary of what went on in class that you want them to tell you about. That summary goes on the front of the card. On the back, have students write a question relevant to the material covered in class that day: Something they want to know more about, some assumption they want to challenge, or some point they would like clarified. These passes are collected as students leave your class. You can review them before the next class meeting. You might even give them a quick grade and then use them to guide instructional decisions about how you'll begin tomorrow's class. One of those questions ("If I give writing assignments to promote learning, how do I deal with the avalanche of papers?") might be just the ticket to an effective warm-up writing exercise to tie tomorrow's instruction to today's.

***Freewrites.***   **Freewrites** go all the way back to the 1960s, to the time of "freeing up" in American culture, the era of America's "greening" and the casting of flowers by San Francisco hippies. During that time, a professor from America's heartland, Ken Macrorie (1968), published the first edition of his *Writing to Be Read*. In that book, he advocated "writing freely" to get closer to a writer's "honest voice" and the "truth" of the writer's world. He began by encouraging teachers to encourage students to write freely without focus for 10 minutes about whatever came to mind. Forget spelling, punctuation, or grammar. Just get all your non-stop thoughts down on paper. This was new, luscious stuff in classrooms where teachers were trying to shake off the restrictions and constrictions of the 1950s and open windows to a whiff of freshness in student writing. Macrorie's (1970) purpose was to release "the natural urges of the writer to discover, to invent, to play with words" (p. viii).

Freewrites (aka "the 5 minute essay") live a somewhat different life in my classrooms because I assign *focused freewrites* that can be used in any content area classroom. This more restricted form of writing, also encouraged by Macrorie (1970), provides students with time before or after a class to clarify their thoughts about a topic. I began using them in my social studies and English classes during the early

1970s and have found them useful throughout my teaching career in secondary schools and college classrooms. While they still have the discovery element of freewrites without a focus, focused freewrites enable students to reflect on specific issues, kinds of learning, or metacognitive aspects of learning. Among their benefits, focused freewrites can:

- promote students' active engagement with course content,
- get students using technical vocabulary of the discipline,
- encourage good listening since students must put knowledge into their own words,
- provide a window on students' thinking,
- set the stage for further inquiry, and
- enhance communication between teacher and student.

Andrews (1997) suggests looping freewrites to explore new concepts or topics. Following a 3- to 5-minute freewrite about a particular idea, Andrews asks her students to summarize what they've written in one sentence. Then she asks them to fold their papers so only the summarizing sentence appears and pass them along to another student who reads that sentence and continues to write about the focus topic with the classmate's sentence as a starting point. She repeats that looping process several times. Throughout the process, students explore their understanding of a topic and respond to their peers' perspectives. At the end of the activity, students get their original paper back, share final sentences, and engage in discussion.

I like to use them after a class discussion to focus attention on what was learned, how it was learned, and what questions remain unanswered. For a focused freewrite, students could be asked to summarize what they learned and to compose questions to be asked at the beginning of the next class. Before the next class, you can review what your students have written to find out if they understood your points of instruction, to identify concepts that bear reteaching, and to select questions to which you will respond. You can also make comments on the papers, reinforce growing understandings, and answer questions that arise.

Or you may elect not to collect the freewrites but to have students use them with each other. For example, after composing the freewrites, students could get together in pairs or teams to read and respond to each other's understandings, misunderstandings, and questions. The freewrites could then be placed in a portfolio for you to review at the end of a week or a unit to make sure students have grasped the meaning and purpose of your instruction. As Young (1997) relays, some teachers allow their students to consult their portfolio of freewrites—but not their books or lecture notes—during an open-portfolio exam. That higher stakes use of freewrites motivates students to make them accurate and lucid.

*Question Papers.*    I learned about **Question Papers** from the Bay Area Writing Project. As mentioned earlier, one element of the BAWP model is teachers teaching other teachers how to use writing in their classrooms, no matter what the subject area. What I learned from one of these teaching-fellows is the usefulness of the Question Paper. When writing a Question Paper, students cannot write anything but questions while reading or after reading an assignment. Students can't write much that's wrong when writing a Question Paper, but they can write much that opens texts and authors to extensive questioning. But don't kid yourself about these question papers not being capable of showing you how well your students understood what they've read. The kinds of questions a student writes reveal much about the level of comprehension that student experienced and the level of doubt and curiosity engendered.

In some ways, the Question Paper is like the focused freewrite. However, rather than writing statements for a pre-determined period of time, say 10 minutes, students write down all the questions they can generate in response to a reading or a lecture. The process can have a rather liberating, spontaneous, and sometimes humorous quality. Usually, the Question Papers get shared in class on a voluntary basis or you could collect them, preview them, determine which papers in particular you would like to have read aloud, and ask their writers to read them in class.

*Skeletons.*   I learned about ***skeletons*** from Bob Pressnall, a middle school teacher who was co-director of BAWP (Bay Area Writing Project) and who used them primarily for helping students revise their writing. However, skeletons (as you'll see) promote exploration, controlled and structured exploration.

Pressnall (1995) originated skeletons in the middle of the night after a challenging day with his students' sketchy or "skeletal" papers. He decided his students needed an exercise to show them how to "hang meat on the bones" of their papers. So the next day he gave them a skeleton:

> I walked into class late. The teacher looked at me. I sat down and opened my book. I heard footsteps approach. The teacher cleared her throat. I looked the teacher in the eye.

He explained to them that each sentence in the skeleton was a bone and that their job was to "bring the skeleton to life with muscle, blood, fur, claws, guts and a beating heart." He asked them to write between one and three sentences or phrases between each of the bones he gave them. The results were astounding. Students who had written little in the past wrote much more with skeletons.

When reviewing a unit on the Civil Rights Movement, he gave them another skeleton to bulk up:

> In the 1960s Dr. King, Rosa Parks, Malcolm X, Thurgood Marshall and others tried to change a few things. They had many goals. They tried many tactics. They met resistance. They met success.

With expository skeletons like these, students could explore what they knew about the Civil Rights Movement, fill out the bones of history, and consolidate their learning for the test to come.

I'm sure you can see how similar skeletons could serve as a structure for your students to explore domains of knowledge in your content area before, during, or after an instructional episode.

*RAFTing.*   Students, like Huck Finn floating down the wide Mississippi, can explore the environment of any content area through RAFTing. ***RAFTing*** (Santa, 1988) consists of four components that guide and stimulate student exploration of content knowledge: Role, Audience, Format, and Topic. When RAFTing, students are their own navigators. They decide who they want to be (Role), to whom they want to address their discourse (Audience), in what form they want to write (Format), and what topic or question they wish to pursue (Topic). RAFTing puts the rudder of choice in your students' hands for a while, giving them time to process more abstract content knowledge in more concrete, even narrative modes. And, as the NWP recommends, you can RAFT along with your students.

Students need some instruction in RAFTing before leaving the shore. You can provide a demonstration, and they can follow your example. It's likely to save some from drowning in freedom. Although T (for Topics) is the last letter of the acronym, choice of topic comes first. You can show students what kinds of questions you would ask about topics your class is currently covering. If, for example, my class were reading Twain's *Huckleberry Finn,* I might become Mark Twain (Role) and write a letter (Format) to Huck (Audience) explaining why I decided to float him down the river (Topic). Or, if I were teaching about the three branches of government, I could become one of the Chief Justices and compose a brochure to new members of Congress explaining to them how I saw my function, especially in relation to Congress and the President. Table 8.3, a matrix of RAFT examples, shows the strategy's versatility.

To help each other generate ideas for RAFTing, students can meet in teams. After collaborating, each student should turn in his choice of Role, Audience, Format, and Topic before beginning the written voyage so that you know where each plans to travel. However, you ought to recognize that currents can carry students to different destinations from an initial pre-departure itinerary.

*Journals and logs.* **Journals** in all content areas provide opportunities for students to heighten "low-stakes" processing and reduce apprehension over "high-stakes" products that teachers grade. Each time teachers ask students to compose in journals, they individualize instruction, forcing passive learners to become actively engaged. Fulwiler (1986) pointed out that he used journals for multiple purposes:

- to stimulate discussion,
- to start small group activities,
- to clarify hazy issues,
- to reinforce learning, and
- to stimulate imagination.

When teaching high school, I had my students bring a notebook to class at the beginning of the school year. I requested a bound notebook of at least 100 pages of 8 1/2 × 11 inch lined paper. They wrote in it three or four times a week as part of their in-class or homework assignment. I've asked students to use the notebook for Double-Entry Journals, Dialogue Journals, Learning Logs, and Reading Response

**TABLE 8.3**   RAFTing Examples

| Role | Audience | Format | Topic |
|------|----------|--------|-------|
| Newspaper reporter | Readers in 1826 | Obituary | Thomas Jefferson |
| Mitochondria | Other cell structures | Operations memo | What functions I have. |
| Holden Caufield | Phoebe | Letter | What happened to me during my college years. |
| Moon | Sun | Instructions | How I move in the solar system. |
| Pythagorian Theorem | Statue of Liberty | Love note | How I can figure out your height from your shadow. |

Logs. I'll give you examples of how I've promoted learning with each of these journal variations.

The journals served as a bridge that kept me informed about what my students were learning—and not learning. They kept us connected. They enabled us to pass information back and forth, to understand each other's understandings. Now that I'm teaching at a university, I still ask students to keep a journal of one kind or another. And they still serve as a bridge between us.

I've already shown you how I would use DEJs. I designed one into the structure of each chapter in this book.

***Learning Logs*** are records of what students have learned or what they are struggling to understand. Frequently, I asked students to use their notebooks as a Learning Log to summarize assigned reading, whether the reading was of narrative or expository texts. I explained to them that I expected the summaries to capture the gist of what they learned from their reading. Initially, some students wrote in too much detail, and some couldn't capture the essence of a reading. But, by providing daily feedback and giving examples of logs that successfully summarized a reading, students gradually improved. Taking a few moments at the beginning of the class and as part of my checking attendance, I could walk through a classroom of 30 students to determine who did the work. If I found students who were not doing well or not doing anything, I checked their work in more detail every day. After a couple of weeks, I'd collect all the notebooks and take a few hours to read some entries more carefully. Some students believed I overworked them with this read-to-write routine, but I believe many students improved their capacity to summarize texts and to comprehend them. Samples of learning logs and reader response logs (presented next) can be found in Chapter 2 where I document students' interpretations of Salinger's "The Laughing Man" and show how those logs became part of our negotiation over the text's meanings.

***Reader Response Logs*** are closely related to Learning Logs. However, the Response Logs focus on interpreting texts, on making inferences from texts rather than on summarizing them. As a teacher committed to encouraging reader response regardless of a text's content, I wanted to make sure my students made meaning when they read and that the meaning making went beyond the literal or surface level. So I frequently encouraged interpretation of text through a variety of strategies and activities. Frequently, I pursued subsurface meanings through probing questions that students would have to answer. These questions required students to go beneath the surface. When reading expository texts, questions required students to examine an author's assumptions, to challenge conclusions, to weigh evidence. When reading narrative texts, questions made students analyze character and setting or to articulate and support a work's themes. Elsewhere, I've gone into more detail about how reader response can be encouraged in all the content areas (Unrau, 1997).

***Dialogue Journals,*** as I've used them, encourage students to construct meanings for specific passages and write about those understandings. When using this variation, I ask students to select a passage from the text assigned and to write about their interpretation of it. This I've usually accomplished by asking students to fold a notebook page in half, transcribe the passage in the left-hand column, and provide in the right-hand column an explanation for why they selected that passage and what its meaning or significance is for them. When I read these journal entries, I get an impression of a student's engagement with a text and how much they care about understanding it.

***Reading Journals,*** as enacted in Nancy Atwell's (1998) reading workshops, consist of letters written between students and between student and teacher. These epistolary reading journals are quite different from Reader Response Logs by being more individually tailored to each student's personal reading. At the beginning of the school year, Atwell writes a letter to her students in which she lets them know the purposes and procedures that will govern the reading journals. The journal will be a place for each student to carry on discussions with the teacher or with friends about the "books, readings, authors, and writings. You'll think about literature in letters to me and friends; we'll write letters back to you. Our letters will become a record of the thinking, learning, and reading we did together" (p. 296).

Atwell then provides some ground rules. Letters are to be no shorter than a page and are to explore aspects of the book read, such as what the reader liked or didn't, how the author wrote, and how the reader read the book. Each student has to write at least a letter a week to Atwell or to a friend in the class. Atwell expects one letter in every 2-week period. The journal gets passed to the person to whom the letter is written. If it's to a friend in class, the writer of the letter should (usually) expect a response in one day. Atwell writes back to her students right after school. From Atwell's examples, a teacher can easily tell that she's having a good time learning about her students, their reading, and how she can help them learn more from what they read.

A variation of Atwell's Reading Journal is the **Two-Way** or **Dialogue Journal.** With this format, student and teacher become engaged in a written conversation over not only material read but also other course content. Like the reading journal, the Two-Way Journal gets passed back and forth between student and teacher so that each gets a better idea of what the other has to say about topics being covered in class. For example, my students were doing research projects related to major issues that our society would have to face in this new century, like pollution and limited energy resources. I had to keep up with what they were discovering, so I asked them to use their journals to write to me weekly. That way I would know what progress they were making and what problems they were having. I, in turn, could write back to them to encourage their successes and give suggestions to help with the problems that cropped up. The entries also served as a window through which I could observe their evolving work, and they could reflect on their project's phases.

For example, as a reader response, I might ask students to summarize and comment on a chapter of a novel or on an essay by Emerson, Carl Sagan, or Joyce Carol Oates. Sometimes I stopped in the middle of a whole class discussion and asked students to describe in their journals what we were discussing, to identify points we were making, to clarify the discussion's relevance to the book we were talking about, or to ask questions elicited by our conversation. I used this approach to get students to negotiate over the meaning of a story we were reading, like those in J. D. Salinger's *Nine Stories*. Because some of those stories had multiple layers of meaning, our use of journals and follow-up discussions helped students understand aspects of the stories they may otherwise have missed (Unrau & Ruddell, 1995).

**DEAD (Drop Everything And Draft) and SNAP (Stop Now And Process).**    I use both of these strategies spontaneously and at ANY time during class. Some teachers may call them quickwrites. If I want to know to what degree students are engaged in what I want them to learn, if I want to get students back on task, if I want to find out what they are struggling to understand, I say, "Let's play DEAD for a few minutes." That's assuming I've already explained what I mean by playing DEAD to the class. **DEAD** stands for "Drop Everything And Draft." It's a kind of "time-out" to reflect on what's been going on; for instance, "Let's play DEAD for

3 minutes." While playing DEAD, students are to explain what they have been learning in class, how it relates to what we have already covered, what they're having trouble understanding, and/or what they'd like to hear more about so they can understand it better. Ironically, playing DEAD can bring students back to life from semi-conscious states. I vary DEAD with **SNAP,** which means "Stop Now And Process," as in "SNAP to it."

These suggested writing strategies to promote learning work best if embedded in the architecture of your classroom structure. Young (1997) makes three recommendations that serve as sensible guidelines:

1. Writing should be integrated into the life of the class because it contributes to creating an interactive climate. If these kinds of writing activities are not discussed with the class, their social and cognitive potential won't be realized. Students will view them as "tacked on."

2. You should explain to your students why you are asking them to do the writing assigned because some students may perceive it as "busywork." You are building a community in which students can explore and construct knowledge central to your discipline. Writing works well as a tool to achieve those community and knowledge-building ends.

3. You should see value in reading what you have assigned your students to write. If it's pure drudgery to you, it's unlikely to contribute to the learning community you want to create. We'll talk about methods of managing paper load in an upcoming section ("Responding to Writing") if you want to assign writing but are concerned about how you'll manage.

Before concluding this section on exploratory writing, I offer a word or two about how to grade them or if they should be graded at all. While some teachers try to set up a system whereby these kinds of writing activities are not graded, I would recommend quite strongly that you devise a grading scheme for them. I used a ✓, ✓+, ✓−, 0 system for daily writing activities and found it amenable to my grading methods. You may want to explore alternative methods of evaluating and grading exploratory writing assignments.

## Writing to Observe Student Work

Few forms of student work reveal thinking and learning as transparently as writing. It makes thinking visible. It confirms progress in learning. It also shows breakdowns in both thinking and learning. But observing those breakdowns can provide teachers with fresh instructional challenges.

As a facilitator in seminars organized to support teachers pursuing National Board of Professional Teaching Standards Certification, I've observed how important the analysis of student work, especially student writing, has been. Seasoned teachers seeking National Board Certification must look closely at their students' writing. Through close examination of students' writing, teachers strive to discover the degree to which learning goals have been achieved, to find evidence of how students are reasoning, and to discover what they could do to move students to a higher level of mastery. Candidates for certification must analyze their students' work to discover weaknesses in conceptual understanding and to decide what next instructional steps they would take to strengthen that understanding.

Several National Board candidates have reported that completing entries for the National Boards has forced them to pay much more attention to collecting, organizing, and analyzing their students' writing. They have grown far more concerned about what to look for in their students' work. In the past, they tended to evaluate their students' work to give it a grade, but they didn't examine the processes through which students went to produce the products graded or ponder the problems their students encountered. Now they approach their students' work differently. They have gained greater sensitivity to their students' thinking, reasoning, and problem solving as they are expressed in students' writing.

The movement from grading to understanding student work has also been pushed by reform groups, such as the Coalition of Essential Schools, the Annenberg Institute for School Reform, and Harvard University's Project Zero. Educators in these organizations have urged teachers to examine student work in collaborative teams and to reflect on perceived patterns and obstacles to learning. Through inquiry and reflection, teachers deepen their understanding of their students and of the impact of their instruction. Especially encouraged is the examination of student work that reveals complex processes and problem solving, such as written documents and, better yet, portfolios of written documents that may show the evolution of a student's writing and thinking. In general, these educators and organizations (Allen, 1998) facilitate an examination of individual pieces of student work, not piles of it, to describe and learn from it with colleagues—not alone. Instead of rushed discussions in hallways or lunchrooms, they encourage organized, purposeful, structured meetings set aside specifically to look at the work of their students and to converse about it.

## STEP-BY-STEP: *A Protocol for Looking at Student Work*

The value to participants of meeting over student work can be heightened by a couple of guidelines and a protocol to direct events (Seidel, 1998). The guidelines or rules of engagement are (a) that participants withhold judgments about the quality of the work examined and (b) that as little information as possible about the writer and the context for the writing be initially revealed. With these guidelines in place, a facilitator takes the presenter and participants through the following phases of the protocol:

**STEP 1.** Silently, everyone reads the written text that a presenting teacher copies and brings to the session.

**STEP 2.** Focusing first on describing the work, all participants discuss its elements.

**STEP 3.** Participants then raise questions about the work, its author, and the context in which it was written.

**STEP 4.** Participants next speculate on what they believe the student was working on or attempting to accomplish when the text was constructed.

**STEP 5.** Throughout the above four phases, the presenter remains quiet. However, at this time, the presenter responds, adding observations of the text and answering as many of the questions raised as he can.

**STEP 6.** As a whole group, presenter and readers weigh alternative teaching moves or instructional directions that the presenting teacher could take to support and challenge the writer of the text.

**STEP 7.** At the end of the discussion over learning challenges to student and instructional challenges for the teacher, the whole group reflects on the process, identifies points of satisfaction or frustration and clarification or confusion for the purpose of enhancing the next session.

Having witnessed and led teacher sessions conducted with the above protocol or ones similar to it, I have learned a few things worth passing along to you.

1. Facilitators are important and require some training. If no one in your region is available to help with training facilitators, resources are available. These include a user friendly but rigorous book, *Looking Together at Student Work* (Blythe, Allen, & Powell, 1999) designed to help teachers and teacher leaders organize student work sessions. A video of the process in action, *Looking at Student Work: A Window into the Classroom,* is also available (Annenberg Institute for School Reform, 1999). Even if seasoned teacher teams, such as those commonly formed in middle schools to serve a group of students, decide to engage in the protocol, a trained facilitator is an asset.

2. Provision of ample time for description of a student's work, discussion of instructional challenges, and review of the protocol process is essential. Too little time constricts, even frustrates participants. I've seen teachers enter into constructive conversations only to be stopped because time ran out or other activities were scheduled.

3. Suitable settings for the discussions contribute to the likelihood of their success. If discussions must take place in crowded, noisy facilities, teachers are less likely to concentrate and engage productively in the close reading of student work and careful analysis required by the protocol process. A relatively quiet, unperturbed room promotes the promise of these discussions over student writing.

These suggestions may help you and your colleagues engage in what I have found to be rich opportunities to gain valued insights into the work of students. Often these student work sessions clarify instructional challenges for teachers that, in turn, heighten the meaningfulness of teaching while supporting students in their growth.

**Individual teachers looking at student work.**   Seeing the immense challenge and value of engaging seasoned teachers in looking closely at their students' writing, I have moved pre-service and freshly credentialed teachers to look more carefully at student work. That includes teachers of math and biology as well as those teaching English and social studies. Some of my students are currently "intern" teachers, which means that they have a bachelor's degree, passed basic competency testing, and are working as teachers full time while pursuing a preliminary or clear credential. However, they do have access to their students' work.

Access to student work empowers teachers. They can look closely at their students' individual performance and begin to make informed judgments about what next steps could be taken to move students closer to mastery. But what should a teacher, new or experienced, look for when looking at student work? Here are several suggested focal points for speculation, observation, and reflection:

◆ How has the student represented the assignment to himself or herself?
◆ What strategies has the student used to solve the problem(s) that the assignment presented?
◆ How well did the problem-solving strategies work?
◆ How close did the student come to meeting your learning goal or performance objective?

- What (other than failed strategies) kept students from gaining a higher level of success?
- After examining the student's work, what are all possible aspects of the work that you could pursue as teaching challenges?
- How would you rank these aspects from least to most challenging?
- Which one or two of these teaching challenges will you pursue? Why have you elected to focus on these?
- How will you pursue the most important one or two of these teaching challenges? What instructional moves will you make?
- How will you assess the degree to which your students met this new learning goal?

**Teachers looking at student work to inform instructional decisions.**   As I saw the potential for improved instructional decisions through closer observations of student work, I began to ask pre-service and in-service teachers in my courses to look more carefully at student writing. Both pre-service and in-service teachers reported that they found these activities "eye-opening." The reason that teachers found these activities enlightening lies in their strong tendency to use writing primarily to grade knowledge acquisition rather than to inform instruction. By shifting their focus from grading to observation of writing for instructional purposes, teachers began to see what next teaching challenges made most sense for their current students. They wrestled with immediate learning problems that impeded students' growth rather than plunging forward with their curricular agenda which tended to ignore the unpleasant realities of students' inability to master significant skills and knowledge.

I assigned "looking at student work" projects in courses where teachers were at different levels of mastery, ranging from pre-service to well-seasoned. In the "Learning from a Student Work Assignment" Step-by-Step box, you will see what I expected new teachers who sought their credential in English to do. If teachers were not currently teaching, I arranged for them to collaborate with a teacher "on track" who would allow pre-service or "off-track" teachers to work with her class in order to complete this "hands-on" assignment. Some of the ideas for the assignment came from work done by the National Board for Professional Teaching Standards and an educational reform group called the ATLAS Communities, a partnership of the Coalition for Essential Schools, Project Zero (Harvard University), and the Yale Child Study Center School Development Program.

 ## STEP-BY-STEP: *Learning from a Student Work Assignment*

A written report emerging from the inspection of student work should take the form indicated in the following step-by-step list:

**STEP 1.** Provide a brief description of the subject, class, kinds of students, classroom climate, and other factors that contribute to the context for the assignment.

**STEP 2.** Describe the assignment, why you gave it, and how it relates to your larger goals. Make a reasonable attempt to select (or design) an assignment that is grounded in your knowledge of your students, that provides them with a reasonable challenge, and that will reveal the range of their knowledge and/or skills in your classroom. Select (or design) an assignment that involves lots of thinking and that gives students some freedom in how they approach the task you give (or gave) them.

**STEP 3.** Using a scoring guide or rubric, separate student work into three sections: high, middle, and low. Provide a brief description of the three categories and what differentiates them. What kinds of thinking differentiate the upper and lower third? What kinds of skills appear in one category that may not appear in the other? What other characteristics make them different?

**STEP 4.** Describe the work of one student in the lower third that you would like to examine in more detail. This should not be a student who is in special education unless you work as a special education teacher. What characteristics emerge from the work? Do you notice any patterns in the student's performance? List your empirical observations of the student's work in a bulleted format. REMEMBER TO INCLUDE A COPY OF THIS STUDENT'S WORK WITH YOUR DESCRIPTION OF IT, PLEASE.

**STEP 5.** Interpret that work. After completing your description, try to make sense out of what the student was doing and why he was doing it that way. Look for patterns in the evidence that provide clues to how and what the student was thinking. Generate as many different interpretations of what the student was trying to do as you can. Link your interpretations to evidence in the student's work. Try to figure out what the student was thinking and why, what the student understood and didn't understand, and how the student interpreted the assignment.

**STEP 6.** Compare work of the student you selected to focus upon with work of others in the class. Explain how the work of the student you selected to examine in detail compares with the work of other students in your class whom you think did a more successful job. How did the other students go about completing the assignment? Did the other students appear to have understandings that the one you selected to examine in detail did not have? To what do you attribute the success of students who did well in the assignment you gave to your class?

**STEP 7.** Describe implications for your practice. Based on your observations and interpretations of the work turned in by the one student you focused upon who performed in the lower third of your class, discuss implications for your teaching and assessment in the class. Pay special attention to the following:

+ What steps could you take next with this student?
+ What teaching strategies would be most effective?
+ What other information about this student's work would help you make instructional decisions? What kinds of assignments or assessments would provide that information?

**STEP 8.** Reflections on the process. What did you learn about your student, your class, and yourself from this investigation? Use the following questions to guide your reflection:

+ Why did you see this student work as you did? What does this tell you about what is important to you?
+ What questions does the inspection of the student's work raise for you?
+ How does what you see and think about the student work compare with what you do in the classroom?
+ What intrigued or surprised you when looking at this student's work?
+ What did you learn about how this student thinks and learns?
+ What about your analysis of the work helped you discover the above?

- ◆ Are there things you would like to try in your classroom as a result of looking at this student's work?
- ◆ What does this investigation of your student's work make you think about in terms of your own practice and about teaching and learning in general?

**Teacher's example of "looking at student work".**    This assignment resulted in many remarkable discoveries, far more than I could ever describe here. However, I can share with you the work of one teacher, Maria Vega, whose findings enabled her to focus on specific teaching challenges in her ninth-grade Humanities class.

Maria teaches her Humanities class at Bell High School in the Los Angeles Unified School District. She described her "sheltered" class as one "designed for a wide spectrum of students." She referred to the class as "sheltered" because many of the 25 boys and 13 girls in it had recently left English Language Development (ELD) classes. Humanities traditionally covers culture, art, and literature from different periods; however, students taking the Humanities course need additional help with reading and writing skills, so Maria has altered the curriculum to accommodate for their literacy needs.

The short-story writing assignment Maria gave to her class for this look at student work was part of a unit on Hispanic culture. Students had read stories from Cisneros' *The House on Mango Street* and *Woman Hollering Creek*. After they had read the latter of these, Maria asked her students to write an original folk tale that included a conflict. Part of her rationale for a series of writing assignments based on conflict came from her knowing that all ninth graders in the LAUSD would be asked to write an essay on conflict for the District-wide Performance Assignment. Maria explained various kinds of internal and external conflicts to her students, divided them into groups to select a conflict, and asked them to write a scenario involving the conflict they selected. Students then read these folk tales to the class, and students tried to figure out what kind of conflict the folk tale contained. This was but the first in a series of conflict exercises that led to her main assignment: a short story that turned on conflict. Students began the short story writing with a "Story Map Worksheet" that helped students to plan their stories before beginning to write them.

When Maria got the stories back, she used a rubric to separate them into three categories. The top third consisted of "interesting, original stories." Students writing these stories recognized the centrality of conflict, had a good understanding of their task, and put in "a lot of effort." Often, writers of these stories were "gifted" or honors students who always tried hard. The lowest third of story writers put "little or no effort into school." While understanding different conflicts, they were not excited by or interested in developing that aspect of their stories.

Maria focused on the work of one student, Hector, in the lowest category. In describing his work, she noted that he did not complete written warm-up exercises to prepare students for writing the short story, but he did participate orally. He tried to incorporate conflict, even mentioned the word as he attempted to describe a run-in between police and a group of criminals, the "Mocha Orejas," who kidnap people. After kidnapping a person, they call his family, request ransom, and, if the ransom doesn't come quickly, they cut off their victim's ear and send it home. If money doesn't come after that, other body parts arrive at the family's front door. Hector then wrote in his story that one day the police captured the leader and his band. As Maria noted, Hector did not develop his story. His writing shows that, while he struggled with sentence structure, punctuation, and spelling, he seemed most eager to be done with it "as quickly as possible." Unlike other students who asked Maria for her help, Hector turned his story in on the last day without having asked her one question.

Looking at her students' work, Maria saw many implications for her classroom practice. With regard to Hector, she would no longer take his work without his showing it to her for review before turning it in. Maria feared his shyness would prevent him from approaching her, so she thought she would pair Hector with another peer who wrote well and could work with him. She saw that in cooperative groups Hector interacted productively and contributed to the writing of the conflict scenario that each co-op team had written as another exercise.

Maria, when reflecting on the entire process of looking at her students' work, also realized that she was going to have to spend more time teaching grammar to her entire class. Because the cooperative learning activities worked well, she thought she would design grammar activities that could be done in small groups followed by quizzes to assess how much students mastered. However, because the class included a wide spectrum of students, she worried that covering basic grammar could bore more advanced students. While Maria flirted with differentiated instruction, she was unsure of just how to make it an integral part of her diverse class. Returning to the effectiveness of small groups, she did reiterate that students may not have understood various kinds of conflict had they not been working collaboratively. Hector, in particular, "works better in groups. He seems to be more motivated." She hypothesized that, because the focus was not on him, he could blend in with the rest of the group members to get work done and ask them to clarify concepts he could not grasp.

In spite of a large, diverse class with many struggling readers and writers, Maria used her observations of student work to inform productive instructional moves that could benefit not only the Hectors in her class but also students functioning at other levels. Rather than assigning a grade and returning the stories the students wrote, she was able to take a few additional minutes, analyze the work she witnessed, and make both short- and long-range decisions that would build essential skills and knowledge that her students will need to survive high school.

## THE TEACHERS' DILEMMA: WHAT KIND OF WRITING SHOULD I ASSIGN?

When I look back on my first experiences as a social studies and English teacher in a high school and think about what place writing had, I cringe. In spite of what I considered high-quality training in college and in my credential program, my grip on the writing component of my program was—well—loose. That was in 1966. That was before process-oriented writing instruction, before writing-to-learn strategies, before constructivist perspectives, and before the National Writing Project would influence almost every American teacher's training and understanding of teaching. As a student teacher in a tenth-grade classroom in a struggling section of Brooklyn, New York, I turned to writing as a way of getting students to express themselves. The school was tracked, and the English department chair assigned me to the lowest track because, as he put it, "You won't do much damage there."

One of my writing assignments was based on having students write a poem that was based on the work of Edgar Lee Masters' *Spoon River Anthology,* a collection of poems about people living in the fictional town of Spoon River. Several of the students wrote exceptional portraits of individuals they had known. Their poems emerged as sketches, miniature pictures much like those Masters had created. I was impressed with their writing and showed some of these poems to the department chair who, after reading them, said, "They plagiarized these." He doubted that the fact of my having watched these students compose the poems in my classroom had any effect whatsoever on their being plagiarized.

In small part, I've written this chapter so that your decisions about the use of writing in whatever courses you teach will be more informed than mine were. Even though, as I look back, I'm astonished that I had as much good luck as I did.

What kinds of writing assignments you give to your students will depend on several related considerations: Your beliefs about what students should know and be able to do in your subject area, your state or local standards, and your commitment to knowing your students and how they learn. Once you have clarified these considerations, then you can think seriously about the role that writing will have in your classroom.

Although I've tried to be fair about providing you with research information about writing and about the kinds of support you can get from colleagues in groups like the National Writing Project, there are other factors you should consider in making your decisions. When deciding whether or not to assign writing and what kind of writing to assign, you'll need to take into consideration these benefits:

- Writing paves a pathway into a new discipline, its writing strategies and techniques, and the ways people think who work in those disciplines.
- Writing, including exploratory writing, should not be overlooked as a window for viewing the minds of your students, how they think, and how they process information as they create and explore new knowledge.

These alone are compelling reasons to use writing in every class.

Because every teacher in every class creates a unique teaching environment and opportunity, few generalizations that I know about writing apply to all classrooms. However, I have some subject-specific suggestions that you may find helpful, especially if you are in your first year or two of teaching.

For English teachers, I can't emphasize enough the importance of one main message: Write, write, write. Almost all the main goals of English instruction throughout middle and high school depend on writing. A recent National Teacher of the Year, Marilyn Whirry, who taught high school English and must have developed the capacity to read in her sleep, assigned 32 essays each academic year. If you don't like to write yourself, work on changing your attitude toward writing. If you don't write well, work on improving your writing. But don't tell your students that you either don't like to write or can't. If you wonder why I'm telling you this, it's because I've heard teachers of English give their students these kinds of messages. As an English teacher, you can frequently use writing to evaluate, promote, and observe learning. And, of course, writing should be an integrated and integrating aspect of your daily instruction.

For social studies teachers, I would say almost the same thing that I've said for teachers of English. However, I know that social studies teachers also worry about covering domains of knowledge they are expected to teach and that lots of writing can impede the amount of territory they can cover in a school year. Knowing that, I still encourage you to find ways to use writing that go beyond evaluating what your students have mastered. You can use writing in the social sciences to construct knowledge, synthesize it, and puzzle over its mysteries. All kinds of exploratory writing, like Admit/Exit Slips or Journals, will enable you to discover what your students know, how deeply they know it, and how they have made connections or seen patterns. And it can help you understand how they think and reason so that you can promote their critical reflection.

For science teachers, the potential for writing is limitless. In a practical vein, students need to learn how to compose lab reports. That is one essential skill to master on their way to understanding the scientific method and entering a scientific field. But writing can serve in several other important ways in the science classroom. Focused freewrites for the first 5 or 8 minutes in biology, for example, can open you and your students to the adventure and excitement of discovery. And they can provide you with opportunities for insights into the lives and minds of your students. That's what John Dorroh's (1993) Expressive Model (EM) notebooks did for him as his students who wrote about viruses or enzymes or scores of other biology topics. As the Writing Project encourages, Dorroh wrote with his students and sometimes read aloud his entries along with theirs. He believes that writing-based instruction enlivened his classroom and enabled him to make bonds with students he never experienced before.

For teachers of math, writing can be a hard sell. In part, that is because new teachers of math may never have had a math teacher who creatively used writing to promote learning mathematics. However, researchers on writing in the math classroom have looked at student-generated questions, journal writing, written explanations, and other forms of expressive writing. They are, as Menon (1998) notes, "unanimous" in their support of writing to learn mathematics. The effects included increased student ownership, improved monitoring and diagnosis of learning difficulties, diminished math anxiety, and heightened motivation. Writing can also promote key ideas contained in the National Council of Teachers of Mathematics *Principles and Standards for School Mathematics* (NCTM, 2000). Among those principles are that students communicate mathematical concepts clearly and coherently, that they organize arguments, and that they understand their own and other's problem-solving processes. Writing serves as a means to those ends. Joseph and Nancy Martinez (2001) suggest several math writing activities for middle and high school math instruction. Students keep logs in which they describe the step-by-step process they use to solve problems along with commentaries, write and solve each other's math word problems, and practice translating math-speak into everyday language. When writing process logs, students use a format the Martinez's (2001) developed that includes several question prompts, such as:

- How many steps are involved in this problem?
- What mathematical operations are involved?
- What will you do first?
- Then what?

By completing these worksheets, students translate math concepts and procedures into ordinary language.

As I've shown how writing can be productively used not only in English classes but also in social studies, science, and math classes, it can also be used in other content areas. I've know many teachers of art, music, health, vocational technology, and physical education who have designed and implemented exciting programs with writing as a tool to achieve their ends. Teachers of art have students keep journals that describe the effects of new drawing, painting, or ceramic techniques they've learned. Music teachers use writing to keep in contact with performance progress and troubles of students in bands, orchestras, and choirs. Students in health classes use writing to explore their understanding of health issues, like diets, sexually transmitted diseases, and anger management. Teachers of woodworking, metal shop, or electronics have students describe in their own words techniques demonstrated in class. And physical education teachers ask athletes to keep records of their workout programs, their performance on teams, and their attitudes toward competition. In all these content areas, writing has served to create bonds between student and teacher while contributing to the development of knowledgeable learning communities.

## RESPONDING TO WRITING

One of the points of resistance among teachers when it comes to making decisions about whether or not to assign writing for any purpose (for evaluation or exploration) is the problem of responding to it. Multiple choice and short answer tests, while providing little information about how your students think or learn, do have an overwhelming strength: They are relatively easy to grade. Asking students to write for any reason activates a network of more complicated questions: What will I ask them to write about? How much will I ask them to write? How will I support or guide their writing? How will I respond to their papers? In effect, this last question is so overwhelming to some teachers that they completely avoid assigning any significant written work of any kind.

Helpfully, Peter Elbow (1997) suggests we look at assigning and responding to writing along a continuum from lowest to highest stakes. Low-stakes assignments are

usually nonevaluative, like freewrites, DEJs, journals, logs, and other forms of exploratory writing. They get students more involved in the content of the course, show us how they approach that content, and tell us about how well they understand it. Furthermore, they encourage students to keep up with their reading for the course because they usually have to read assignments in order to write about them. High-stakes writing assignments, like essays that culminate a unit or that we use on an exam to assess mastery, are more likely to fall in the category of informational writing.

As for responding to writing, Elbow (1997) again envisions a low- to high-stakes continuum which includes the following:

- Zero response (lowest stakes),
- Minimal, nonverbal, noncritical response,
- Supportive response—no criticism,
- Descriptive or observational response,
- Minimal, nonverbal critical response, and
- Critical response with diagnosis and advice for improvement (highest stakes).

As you would suppose, there are links between low-stakes assignments and low-stakes response. For example, low-stakes assignments, like freewrites that provide students with opportunities to create and explore meanings, correspond with low-stakes responses, like simply reading the freewrite or giving it a check mark, a minimal and noncritical response.

Let me make a confession: I rarely sit down in a mood of excited anticipation with piles of student papers before me. In over 25 years of teaching high school English and more than 10 years of teaching undergraduate and graduate students in colleges and universities, I can't recall many times when I relished the event. When I began teaching high school, I sometimes assigned essays that would be due on Friday in all my classes. I looked forward to a weekend with nearly a hundred and fifty papers to read. And, of course, I wanted to correct every grammatical problem, give students helpful commentary for the growth of their writing, and inspire their future development as writers. With stacks of papers on my desk, I felt that I was about to swim the English Channel, cross the Mohave Desert barefoot, and ascend Mt. Everest. I wondered if I had the stamina for the job.

Somehow I got through. As I look back, I realize that I've read and responded to many thousands of student papers in various stages of development from first to "final" drafts. But you need not do what I did in my first years of teaching. My earliest solution to the problem of assigning and responding to my students' writing was not my best solution. I often did not even structure instruction so that I knew students paid attention to the corrections and commentary I gave them. I guess I thought all my students would so value my comments that they would learn directly from what I'd noted on their papers. Of course, I soon learned otherwise.

Fortunately, I discovered more productive solutions to the pile of students' written papers and to my discovery that students could ignore my work. Here are a few suggestions that kept my students writing and helped me maintain a sense that my time was being well used for the purpose of improving my students' writing and thinking.

- Rather than giving extensive commentary on all papers, provide a quick-grade system, such as check, check-plus, or check-minus, for selected assignments.
- If you use peer-editing procedures, provide well-structured feedback sheets so that students can fill them out in detail.

◆ Develop and use rubrics that you give to students before they compose papers you assign. That way they know what criteria you will apply to the evaluation of their papers. You can then assign grades from 1 to 4 or 1 to 6 based on the dimensions of the rubric you develop. Of course, grading with rubrics doesn't give students the detailed commentary they need to make specific kinds of corrections and to improve. However, rubrics work well for many assignments. And you can add commentary and make specific corrections as you see fit.

◆ Develop mini-lessons and mini-assignments to help students with writing problems that appear on many papers. If several students are writing fragments or comma splices, then develop a 10- or 15-minute lesson to address a specific problem. Expect, however, that one mini-lesson may not solve the problem.

◆ If you have a choice, don't assign major writing projects that come due in all classes at the same time. Schedule assignment deadlines so that you can comfortably manage the paper load.

◆ Explain to students that they will be writing more than you can read and grade because you want them to write as much as possible. Explain that you will read and grade only one out of two or even three lengthily written assignments. Explain to them that you may select any of the papers they write for possible grading.

◆ Read selectively. Identify a limited number of elements you will address in responding to a paper. For example, if a student is having problems with topic sentences, then focus on that issue: Point out paragraphs lacking topic sentences, provide sample topic sentences, or ask a student to compose topic sentences for paragraphs needing them and to resubmit the paper before giving it a grade.

◆ Write your comments in pencil. It not only looks less intimidating than a red pen, it also can be erased if you want to change the way you have framed a suggestion after reading it to yourself.

◆ If you provide commentary for corrections and want to make sure students read and learn from your recommendations, ask students to correct their errors or submit revisions (with the previous draft) BEFORE you give out a grade. All too often, teachers will spend hours writing suggestions for improvement, give papers back to students, and discover that students ignore those hours of work. Students are less likely to ignore your work if they don't get a grade until they act on your corrections and commentary by submitting a revision that reflects or incorporates your recommendations. Not all teachers comfortably embrace this practice. However, wanting to see some evidence that students read what I've written, I find it comforting when students turn in their revisions. The revisions serve as signs that my efforts to improve their writing skills have been acknowledged.

In closing, I want to share with you a hope. I customarily ask teachers with whom I work if they use writing in their content area classes. Many say they do. However, many don't. Here are five answers I've heard from teachers when I've asked them about using writing in their classes:

1. "I don't teach writing. English teachers do that."
2. "I don't have time to read piles of students' writing."
3. "Our state testing program is forcing us to teach to the test. It doesn't ask students to write anything about my content area."
4. "If I start having students write in my class, we're going to get too far behind in the curriculum. My colleagues will wind up with students unprepared for next year's content. And you know who'll get blamed?"

5. "Students don't expect to do much—if any—writing in my course. They think it's weird if I assign writing in _____." (Fill in the blank: math, science, history, health, physical education, music, art, etc.)

I hope that, after reading this chapter, these will not be among the answers you would give me if I were to ask you, "Do you use writing in your classes to help students and yourself learn?"

---

**DOUBLE-ENTRY JOURNAL: After Reading**

 Go to the Double-Entry Journal for Chapter 8 on our Companion Website at www.prenhall.com/unrau to complete your journal entry.

After reviewing your before-reading DEJ, what additional activities might you add to your list of strategies to help your students learn? What kinds of writing would you assign in your content area? How would you use writing in your content area to assess learning?

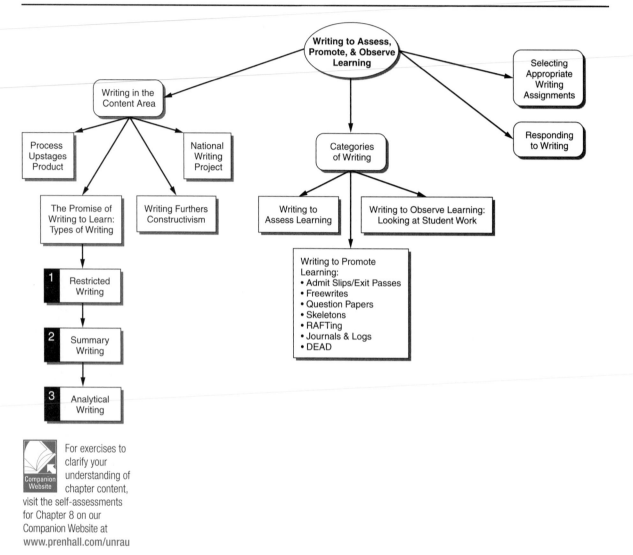

# References

Ackerman, J. M. (1993). The promise of writing to learn. *Written Communication, 10,* 334–370.

Allen, D. (1998). *Assessing student learning: From grading to understanding.* New York: Teachers College Press.

Andrews, S. E. (1997). Writing to learn in content area reading class. *Journal of Adolescent & Adult Literacy, 41*(2), 141.

Annenberg Institute for School Reform. (1999). *Looking at student work: A window into the classroom* [Video]. New York: Teacher College Press.

Applebee, A. N. (1981). *Writing in the secondary school.* Urbana, IL: National Council of Teachers of English.

Applebee, A. N. (1984). *Contexts for learning to write: Studies of secondary school instruction.* Norwood, NJ: Ablex.

Atwell, N. (1998). *In the middle: New understandings about writing, reading, and learning.* Portsmouth, NH: Heinemann.

Bereiter, C., & Scardamalia, M. (1980). From conversation to composition. In R. Glaser (Ed.), *Advances in instructional psychology, Vol. 2.* Hillsdale, NJ: Erlbaum.

Blythe, T., Allen, D., & Powell, B. (1999). *Looking together at student work: A companion guide to assessing student learning.* New York: Teachers College Press.

Britton, J. (1970). *Language and learning.* Middlesex, England: Penguin Books.

Britton, J., Burgess, T., Martin, N., McLeod, A., & Rosen, H. (1975). *The development of writing abilities (11–18).* London: Macmillan.

Carey, L., Flower, L., Hayes, J. R., Schriver, K. A., & Haas, C. (1989). *Differences in writers' initial task representations* (Tech. Rep. No. 35). Berkeley, CA: Center for the Study of Writing at UC, Berkeley and Carnegie Mellon University.

Delpit, L. (1986). Skills and other dilemmas of a progressive black educator. *Harvard Educational Review, 56,* 379–385.

Delpit, L. (1988). The silenced dialogue: Power and pedagogy in educating other people's childen. *Harvard Educational Review, 58,* 280–298.

Dorroh, J. (1993). Reflections on expressive writing in the science class. *Quarterly of the National Writing Project and the Center for the Study of Writing and Literacy, 15*(3), 28–30.

Durst, R. K. (1987). Cognitive and linguistic demands of analytic writing. *Research in the Teaching of English, 21* (347–376).

Elbow, P. (1997). High stakes and low stakes in assigning and responding to writing. In M. Sorcinelli & P. Elbow (Eds.), *Writing to learn: Strategies for assigning and responding to writing across the disciplines* (pp. 5–13). San Francisco: Jossey-Bass Publishers.

Emig, J. (1971). *The composing process of twelfth graders* (Research report no. 13). Urbana, IL: National Council of Teachers of English.

Everson, B. J. (1991). Vygotsky and the teaching of writing. *Quarterly of the National Writing Project and the Center for the Study of Writing and Literacy, 13*(3), 8–11.

Flower, L. (1979). Writer-based prose: A cognitive basis for problems in writing. *College English, 41,* 19–37.

Flower, L., & Hayes, J. R. (1977). Problem-solving strategies and the writing process. *College English, 39,* 449–461.

Flower, L., & Hayes, J. R. (1981). A cognitive process theory of writing. *College Composition and Communication, 32,* 365–387.

Flower, L., Schriver, K. A., Carey, L., Haas, C., & Hayes, J. R. (1989). *Planning in writing: The cognition of a constructive process* (Tech. Rep. No. 34). Berkeley, CA: Center for the Study of Writing at UC, Berkeley and Carnegie Mellon University.

Flower, L., Stein, V., Ackerman, J., Katz, M. J., McCormick, K., & Peck, W. C. (1990). *Reading-to-write: Exploring a cognitive and social process.* New York: Oxford.

Freedman, S. W., Dyson, A. H., Flower, L., & Chafe, W. (1987). *Research in writing: Past, present, and future* (Tech. Rep. No. 1). Berkeley, CA: Center for the Study of Writing at UC, Berkeley and Carnegie Mellon University.

Freedman, S. W., Flower, L., Hull, G., & Hayes, J. R. (1995). *Ten years of research: Achievements of the National Center for the Study of Writing and Literacy* (Tech. Rep. No. 1C). Berkeley, CA: Center for the Study of Writing at UC, Berkeley and Carnegie Mellon University.

Freedman, S. W., Simons, E. R., Kalnin, J. S., Casareno, A., & The M-CLASS teams. (1999). *Inside city schools: Investigating literacy in multicultural classrooms.* New York: Teachers College Press.

Fulwiler, T. (1986). Journals across the disciplines. In T. Newkirk (Ed.), *To compose: Teaching writing in the high school* (pp. 186–197). Portsmouth, NH: Heinemann.

Gray, J. (2000). *Teachers at the center: A memoir of the early years of the National Writing Project.* Berkeley, CA: National Writing Project.

Greenwald, E. A., Persky, H. R., Campbell, J. R., & Mazzeo, J. (1999). *The NAEP 1998 writing report card for the nation and the states,* 144. Washington, DC: U.S. Department of Education.

Langer, J. A., & Applebee, A. N. (1987). *How writing shapes thinking.* Urbana, IL: National Council of Teachers of English.

Macrorie, K. (1968). *Writing to be read.* Rochelle Park, NJ: Hayden Book Co.

Macrorie, K. (1970). *Telling writing.* New York: Hayden Book Co.

Martinez, J. G., & Martinez, N. C. (2001). *Reading and writing to learn mathematics: A guide and a resource book.* Boston: Allyn & Bacon.

Menon, R. (1998). Mathematics and language. In A. McIntosh & N. Ellerton (Eds.), *Research in mathematics education: A contemporary perspective.* Perth, Australia: MASTEC, Edith Cowan University.

Michigan State Board of Education. (1994). *Assessment frameworks for the Michigan high school proficiency test in communication arts, Part I: Writing.* Lansing, MI: Michigan Department of Education.

Moffett, J. (1989). *Bridges: From personal writing to the formal essay* (Occasional Paper No. 9). Berkeley, CA: Center for the Study of Writing.

National Council of Teachers of Mathematics. (2000). *Principles and standards for school mathematics.* Reston, VA: NCTM.

National Writing Project. (2001). NWP assumptions. Retrieved July 20, 2001, from *http://www.writingproject.org/About/assumptions.html.*

Newell, G. E. (1998). "How much are we the wiser?": Continuity and change in writing and learning in the content areas. In N. N. Nelson & R. C. Calfee (Eds.), *The reading-writing connection: The yearbook of the National Society for the Study of Education* (pp.178–202). Chicago, IL: University of Chicago Press.

Newell, G. E., & Winograd, P. (1995). Writing about and learning from history texts: The effects of task and academic ability. *Research in the Teaching of English, 29,* 133–163.

Penrose, A. M. (1989). *Strategic differences in composing: Consequences for learning through writing* (Tech. Rep. No. 31). Berkeley, CA: Center for the Study of Writing at UC, Berkeley and Carnegie Mellon University.

Penrose, A. M. (1992). To write or not to write: Effects of task and task interpretation on learning through writing. *Written Communication, 9*(4), 465–500.

Perl, S. (1979). The composing processes of unskilled college writers. *Research in the Teaching of English, 13,* 317–336.

Pressnall, B. (1995). Skeletons out of the closet: The case of the missing 162%. *Quarterly of the National Writing Project and the Center for the Study of Writing and Literacy, 17*(3), 20–25.

Santa, C. (1988). *Content reading including study systems.* Dubuque, IA: Kendall/Hunt.

Seidel, S. (1998). Wondering to be done: The collaborative assessment conference. In
    D. Allen (Ed.), *Assessing student learning: From grading to understanding* (pp. 21–39).
    New York: Teachers College Press.

Unrau, N. (1997). *Thoughtful teachers, thoughtful learners: A guide to helping adolescents
    think critically*. Scarborough, Ontario: Pippin Press.

Unrau, N., & Ruddell, R. (1995). Interpreting texts in classroom contexts. *Journal of
    Adolescent and Adult Literacy, 39*(1), 16–27.

Vygotsky, L. S. (1978). *Mind in society*. Cambridge, MA: Harvard University Press.

Young, A. (1997). Mentoring, modeling, monitoring, motivating: Response to students'
    ungraded writing as academic conversation. *New Directions for Teaching and Learning,
    69*, 27–39.

Zinsser, W. (1988). *Writing to learn*. NY: Harper & Row.

# 9 STRUGGLING READERS AND ENGLISH LEARNERS: ADDRESSING THEIR COGNITIVE AND CULTURAL NEEDS

After reading Chapter 9, you should be able to answer the following questions:

1. What elements contribute to the struggling readers' comprehension problems?

2. What are the main features of five middle and/or high school level reading intervention programs: Corrective Reading, LANGUAGE!, Reading Apprenticeship, READ 180, and Success for All?

3. What could keep "just read more" solutions to secondary reading problems from working?

4. What five hypotheses contribute to Krashen's theory of second language acquisition?

5. What do we know about how long it takes for an English language learner to become proficient?

6. What practices exemplify Specially Designed Academic Instruction in English (SDAIE)?

7. How can learning strategies be integrated into English language instruction?

DOUBLE-ENTRY
JOURNAL: Before
Reading

Now go to the
Double-Entry
Journal for
Chapter 9 on our
Companion Website at
www.prenhall.com/unrau
to fill out your journal entry.

If many of your English-speaking students were reading two or more grade levels below their assigned grade, what would you do to help them comprehend reading assignments and to catch up? If you have several English learners in your class, what accommodations would you make in your instruction to help them grasp the course content?

## ADDRESSING THE FRUSTRATIONS OF STRUGGLING READERS

### How Serious Are Reading Problems in Our Middle and High Schools?

In spite of reports in the media that there is an adolescent literacy crisis in America, substantial evidence indicates that, for the most part, students on average are reading at least as well now as they did 30 years ago (Klenk & Kibby, 2000). But that's not the end of the story. The magnitude of reading problems that middle and high school students bring with them to their content area classrooms has been established (NAEP, 1998). Some students arrive in middle and high schools unable to read grade-level text fluently or comprehend its meaning. Although most students grasp literal meanings, they have significant difficulties with more complex reading tasks. In hundreds of urban and suburban schools, teachers work in content area classrooms with students who are reading many grade levels below their age-equivalent classmates. Although the incidence of struggling readers varies from school to school and classroom to classroom, they comprise about 25% of all middle and high school students. If you teach in classrooms with significant numbers of struggling readers, you will soon be convinced that you are in the midst of a serious literacy problem. Furthermore, urban centers are not alone in their struggles with literacy. Many students in rural schools throughout the country struggle with similar reading problems (Stephens, 1993). The discrepancy between expected reading ability and real capacity creates instructional havoc for teachers nationwide.

A middle school discovers its struggling readers.   Here is a specific example of the problem content area teachers face every day in their classrooms. This data comes from a Los Angeles middle school that gave about 1,550 of their students the Gates-MacGinitie reading test near the beginning of the school year. It's important to point out that the students taking the reading test included neither 267 students designated for special education classes nor about 150 students who were in English as a Second Language programs. What we found disturbed many teachers while clarifying for them the roots of one of their major instructional frustrations: Students could not read the texts they were asked to read.

We found that among sixth graders 11% were reading at their grade level while nearly 60% were reading below the fourth-grade level. Unfortunately, as these students progressed through their middle school grades, their reading levels may not have improved in accord with their age-mates nationwide. Among seventh graders, we found that 5% read at or above grade level while 55% still read below the fourth-grade level. And among eighth graders, 2% read at their grade level or above while about 45% continued to read below the fourth-grade level. In this school, the teaching problems became abundantly clear to all. Teachers in the content areas attempting to teach from texts written at or near grade level in science, history, mathematics, and English found that large numbers of students faced frustration when attempting to read the texts they were expected to read. As was reported in the *Los Angeles Times* (Sahagun, 2000), one administrator said teachers were "astounded" and "appalled" by the actual results of the reading test.

While struggling readers abounded at this Los Angeles Unified School District (LAUSD)-middle school, the presence of struggling readers—sometimes in fairly large numbers—in nearly all our middle and high schools is pretty much a given. The greater difficulty lies with teachers at the middle and secondary levels not being prepared to address the reading challenges they face.

Certainly teachers can learn strategies to heighten engagement and improve comprehension, strategies such as DR-TA, K-W-L, and reciprocal teaching. But, when faced with struggling readers manifesting reading levels far below their grade levels, teachers face problems of a much different dimension. Few, if any, middle and high school teachers have any training in diagnosing and teaching students with profound reading limitations. Most teachers have spent years gaining mastery over their particular fields, such as math, biology, or history. And often their greatest sense of competence and their deepest interests lie in their subject area. Most of these teachers have little motivation to drop their domain of competency to take up the teaching of reading—even though they recognize that these students will make little or no progress in the classes they are teaching because of profound literacy limitations.

**Finding the roots of reading problems.**   What are the specific problems behind the relatively weak reading performance of these middle school students? For the most part, we excluded students designated as needing special education intervention and many learning English as a second language. Naturally, large numbers of students are still learning academic English. Nevertheless, we suspected that weak decoding skills, few sight-words (such as *and* or *ran*), deficient word attack skills, and general lack of automaticity in processing words, phrases, and clauses contributed to the struggles these students experienced when they tried to read. Extensive fluency research supports the observations made here (Klenk & Kibby, 2000). But that's not the whole of the problem. Listening to these students read, studying their efforts to make meaning, and talking with them about strategy use, we, like Peterson, Caverly, Nicholson, O'Neal, and Cusenbary (2000), found that many students were limited by other important factors. Among them were limited vocabulary, background knowledge, capacity to make inferences, awareness of text structure, reading strategies, and motivation.

## Choices of Strategies and Programs to Help Struggling Readers

As teachers and administrators faced their literacy problem and the implications began to sink in, they discovered a parallel dilemma: What kind of instruction would help all these struggling readers? Few on the staff of nearly 100 teachers had much training in reading and no reading specialist to serve them.

They got some hope from a state project that funded demonstration middle schools. If they could get a grant, they could get money to address their students' literacy needs, including staff development in reading strategies and programs. They formulated and submitted their program focused on help for struggling readers. Fortunately, it was approved.

The committee drafting the grant proposal wrestled with decisions about strategies and programs that would provide the faculty with real hope that struggling readers would benefit. The proposal that emerged addressed two populations of struggling readers: those whose problems with decoding impeded fluency and those whose problems with comprehension kept them from understanding their content area texts.

The committee gathered information about strategies to help students struggling with comprehension in content area courses. Teachers could learn and implement these strategies across the curriculum. They included many of the strategies you have learned about in Chapters 4 through 8, including vocabulary development techniques, anticipation guides, Directed Reading-Thinking Activity, K-W-L, graphic organizers, think-alouds, reciprocal teaching, ReQuest, and writing-to-learn strategies. All of these could support instruction for struggling readers in content classrooms. The problem was limited to which strategies to present to all faculty for implementation. However, the selection of a program that could benefit readers struggling with decoding and fluency presented a greater dilemma.

Although information about some reading intervention programs and their effects are now available (Peterson et al., 2000), the Demonstration Grant committee had limited access to descriptions of these programs and evaluation of their effectiveness based on rigorous research. Because few resources for information about intervention programs exist, some of the programs available are presented here, but first a word about research.

## The Problem of Research Supporting Reading Intervention Programs

While I'd like to refer you to indisputable evidence supporting particular reading intervention programs for struggling readers, I cannot. That is primarily because much of the research that has been conducted to document the efficacy of existing intervention programs does not meet rigorous research standards. As Allington (2001) has pointed out, advocates of a particular program or method tend to generate biased research. Reviews of a particular approach or experiments designed to evaluate programs tend to become contaminated.

Thorough research of intervention programs will require money, time, resources, and skills not yet dedicated to that challenge. Perhaps in years to come with rigorous research supported and guided by legislation like the Reading Excellence Act (REA) passed in 1998, we will be able to rely on credible findings upon which to base decisions about which reading intervention programs work best for whom.

In the meantime, we have to exercise vigilance and scrutinize critically the results of research that has been completed. In many instances where I have described reading intervention programs, I have provided research data indicating the magnitude of the intervention's effect.

## INTERVENTION PROGRAMS FOR STRUGGLING READERS

If students cannot read or write well, they inevitably encounter frustration in most of their content area classes. In this way, literacy problems contribute to students' poor academic achievement. Several theories have been developed to explain and predict early high school dropouts, including deviant behavior, bonding with anti-social peers, growing up in poverty, low school affiliation, and parents' lack of education combined with their low educational expectations. However, the strongest predictor of school dropout before completing the tenth grade is poor academic achievement (Battin-Pearson et al., 2000). To prevent dropout, we should do all we can to support the academic success of students. Catching literacy problems early and providing effective intervention programs can prevent progressive disengagement from school and eventual departure from schooling.

### Features and Functions of Reading Intervention Programs

A multitude of middle and high schools, especially those in urban centers, have elected to confront their students' reading problems head on by implementing reading programs. Knowledge about the design, implementation, coordination, and evaluation of these reading programs is of critical importance to a growing number of teachers.

Teachers and school decision makers must be alert to elect, train for, and implement intervention programs that have a good chance of solving the reading problems that their students manifest. Frequently, attempts to address students' reading problems miss the mark because the severity and depth of the reading problems have not been accurately plumbed and gauged. Because of weak diagnostic efforts, teachers and administrators may elect to implement programs too shallow to remedy their students' reading problems. Weak decoders and weak comprehenders will not make much progress unless the roots of their decoding and comprehending difficulties are directly addressed. That is why there are few benefits for struggling readers from brief in-service workshops for content area teachers on comprehension strategies.

If the struggling readers in their schools stand any chance at all of having their reading needs addressed, teachers must know and understand the reading process as well as the basics of reading programs and their implementation. That knowledge and understanding will be essential if programs are school-wide and require all teachers to serve as teachers of reading for at least part of their day. It is also essential if teachers are involved in decision making about selecting and implementing a reading program that affects a smaller portion of students in the school as a whole. At times, resources and needs dictate partial implementation of a reading program so that it addresses readers in the lowest 10% or 15% of their class or grade.

The programs that we are going to examine in the next section of this chapter have a number of features in common. Most of these reading programs may be implemented school-wide or partially, depending on a school's needs and resources.

Unless otherwise noted, these programs address the needs of struggling readers in grades six through twelve. All have some system for individual student evaluation and grouping. All include comprehension strategies to develop more strategic reading approaches. However, training, implementation, and costs vary.

There are differences between the programs. While some rely on direct instruction, others are more student-centered. Most of them have the capacity to help students who cannot decode text sufficiently to progress in their reading. The creators of programs that don't address decoding problems recognize that some students may need instruction in decoding to benefit from their approach to reading improvement.

As we progress through each program, we will review its history of development, purposes, base in research and theory, implementation (including curricular and instructional approach, materials designed for the program, methods of placement and advancement, and teacher training), and evidence of the program's effectiveness. The five programs reviewed (and presented alphabetically) are Corrective Reading, LANGUAGE!, Reading Apprenticeship, READ 180, and Success for All Middle School.

A caveat.   It's a tad spooky and it may appear somewhat kooky, but the assumptions about reading and what promotes it that underlie some of these approaches have contributed to impressive levels of distrust and contempt among their advocates. Perhaps you've heard of the reading wars. Most of the battles have been waged in the trenches of elementary reading instruction. However, rifle fire and some heavier shells have been exchanged by parties with a stake in the war's expansion into middle and high school reading intervention and instruction. I advocate a "what works" approach. Unfortunately, as of this writing, precise answers to questions about what works dwell in the future.

## Corrective Reading

History of development.   The primary authors of *Corrective Reading (CR)* are Siegfried Engelmann and his associates, including Susan Hanner and Gary Johnson (Engelmann et al., 1998). *CR* was first published in 1978 and has been through various revisions. The reading program, consisting of several levels, relies upon direct instruction to help struggling readers master basic decoding and comprehension skills.

Purpose.   The program is designed to assist middle and high school non-readers or struggling readers who have weak decoding skills, weak comprehension skills, or both. Although the program has been used with students who have English as their second language, the program's designers recommend that students should, as a minimum, speak and understand easy conversational English.

Research and theory.   CR is based on principles of Direct Instruction (Gersten, Woodward, & Darch, 1986; Kaméenui & Carnine, 1998). These principles include teaching for mastery, content presented in skill sequences, explicit and integrated strategy instruction, use of placement tests, close teacher monitoring and coaching, scripted lessons to improve communication, and common lesson formats. In the domain of decoding research, Grossen (n.d.) cites findings supporting phonemic awareness, explicit phonics, letter-sound relationships, blending, the early and consistent use of decodable texts, daily performance measures, and the correction of every oral reading error. In the domain of comprehension research, she cites findings supporting the use of interspersed questions, inclusion of expository text structures, teaching of background knowledge, direct instruction of vocabulary, and the teaching of underlying concepts and strategies.

## Implementation

*Materials' structure and design.*    Materials for the program's implementation include student books, consumable workbooks, and teacher presentation books and guides. The program is packaged at four levels of decoding and comprehension:

- Level A Decoding (65 lessons): Word attack basics, explicit sound-spelling relationships.
- Level B1 & B2 Decoding (65 lessons each): Refining word attack skills, letter-word discrimination, word endings.
- Level C Decoding (125 lessons): Affixes, vocabulary, reading expository texts, sequencing, improving reading rate, etc.
- Level A Comprehension (72 lessons): Vocabulary, basic reasoning, analogies, recitation, etc.
- Level B1 & B2 Comprehension (72 lessons each): More advanced reasoning, analyzing sentences, vocabulary development, sentence writing, etc.
- Level C Comprehension (149 lessons): Absorbing, using, and communicating information.

*Instructional process and lesson time.*    Knowledge of letter-sound correspondence and development of comprehension is transmitted through direct instruction in a scripted presentation. Through exercises and examples, teachers present progressively complex skills and strategies to students. Each lesson takes 35 to 45 minutes of direct instruction and independent student work.

*Placement, assessment, and advancement.*    The program comes with an individually administered decoding placement test that measures each student's accuracy and oral reading rate. While students read from one of the four progressively more challenging parts of the test, the test's administrator records each decoding mistake the student makes and determines the time needed to read the part. Students are placed at an appropriate level in the program depending upon both the number of errors they make and their reading rate.

For comprehension placement, teachers give students an individually administered oral test and a group administered written test. Each level is designed with periodic mastery tests to determine student progress. However, teacher observation is also a critical means of measuring progress.

*Management of students at multiple levels.*    Struggling readers need to be placed in levels (A, B1 or B2, and C) that are compatible with their current reading capability. According to *CR* guidelines, homogeneous grouping of students whose diagnostic test scores indicate placement at the same level will permit optimum growth in reading.

*Training.*    Two forms of training are currently available. One training format, provided by the publisher, requires a full day. A second format developed under the auspices of Dr. Grossen requires three days plus periodic in-class follow-ups from a trainer.

Evidence of effectiveness.    Generally, advocates cite the effectiveness of direct instruction through reference to "Follow Through," an extensive, government sponsored research program comparing 13 instructional models and finding direct instruction to be the most effective (Adams & Engelmann, 1996). More specifically, Grossen (n.d.) cites studies showing that students in CR programs accelerated their reading growth significantly beyond that of control groups. Findings of faster than normal rates of improvement in learning are said to be consistent across most studies reported. Grossen, a professor of special education at the University of Oregon, has helped several middle schools in California, especially Goethe Middle School in Sacramento, use CR with struggling readers (Grossen, 1998, 2000). Results in several California middle schools reveal reading growth rates significantly above state averages on standardized tests.

Commentary.    Trainers emphasize the importance of adherence to the scripted design of CR. Wavering from the program's script can affect results significantly. Supportive coaching by specialists in direct instruction often improves teacher and student performance in CR classrooms. Some teachers, upon hearing that the program is structured, sequenced, and scripted, back away—especially initially. Advocates of CR explain that teachers need to understand reality-distorting myths about direct instruction (Kozloff, LaNunziata, Cowardin, & Bessellieu, 2000). CR has had extensive use in special education settings where teachers working with learning disabled students have found the program useful and effective.

# LANGUAGE!

History of development.    LANGUAGE! was developed by Jane Greene (1998), former teacher of English and reading specialist, in the early 1990s. Her goal was the development of a comprehensive literacy curriculum for delayed readers that included literature, language, and composition.

Purpose.    The program can assist middle and high school non-readers or struggling readers who have poor decoding skills, weak comprehension skills, or both. Students should, as a minimum, speak and understand easy conversational English. LANGUAGE! serves basically the same population as that served by Corrective Reading.

Research and theory.    Greene cites evidence from research proving the central relevance of learning to decode single words rapidly, of phoneme awareness to acquire reading skills, and of abundant practice in reading decodable text at an independent reading level. She also cites research documenting the effectiveness of direct teaching of structured language (Greene, 1998).

Implementation
***Materials' structure and design.***    The curriculum has three levels and a total of 54 units (see Table 9.1):

- ◆ Level One (Books A, B, & C with six units each): phonemic awareness, sound-letter correspondence, decoding, fluency in passage reading, vocabulary development, comprehension, introduction to grammar, writing, and supplementary reading.

**TABLE 9.1** Curriculum Content and Materials

| Curriculum Level | Content Covered | Materials Required | Support Materials |
|---|---|---|---|
| **Level 1**<br><br>**Readability:**<br>Primer–2.5<br><br><br><br><br>**Units 1–18** | Phoneme awareness<br><br>Phoneme-grapheme correspondence<br><br>Decoding, encoding, accuracy, and fluency in reading<br><br>Vocabulary, comprehension, and supplementary reading<br><br>Figurative language and idioms<br><br>Writing and editing practice | Instructor's Manual<br><br>Sounds & Letters (book & cards)<br><br>*Student Mastery Books A, B, & C*<br><br>*J&J Language Readers* (Level 1) | *J&J Vocabulary Cards* (Level 1)<br><br>Practice Instructor's Manual<br><br>*Practice Workbooks A, B, & C*<br><br>LANGUAGE! Categories<br><br>Degrees of Reading Power (DRP) BookLink |
| **Level 2**<br><br>**Readability:**<br>2.5–6.0<br><br><br><br>**Units 19–36** | Syllabication<br><br>Morphology<br><br>Syntax mastery for comprehension, reading, and listening<br><br>Expanding grammar and composition through narrative and expository writing | Instructor's Manual<br><br>*Student Mastery Books D, E, & F*<br><br>*J&J Language Readers* (Level 2) | Same as above plus:<br><br>*LANGUAGE! Roots*<br><br>*Morphemes for Meaning* |
| **Level 3**<br><br>**Readability:**<br>6.0–9.0<br><br>**Units 37–54** | Greek morphology<br><br>Literacy concepts<br><br>Achieving mastery of vocabulary, English grammar, and usage | Instructor's Manual<br><br>*Student Mastery Books G, H, I*<br><br>*J&J Language Readers* (Level 3) | Same as above. |

*Source:* Reprinted with permission of Sopris West Educational Services, 800-547-6747, LANGUAGE! by Jane Greene, copyright 2000.

- ◆ Level Two (Books D, E, & F with six units each): Three new strands include syllabication, morphology (Latin roots, prefixes, and suffixes), and sentence structure or syntax. Composition and grammar development continue.
- ◆ Level Three (Books G, H, & I with six units each): Two new strands include Greek morphology and literary concepts (theme, plot, character development, point of view, etc.). Although literature was read in earlier levels, it was not directly studied as it is at this level. Grammar and writing development continue.

All levels include supplementary reading integrated into the curriculum to provide practice in reading decodable, connected texts at students' independent reading levels. A student's test score on Degrees of Reading Power, a criterion-referenced reading comprehension test, can be linked with books at that student's reading level. During training, teachers implementing the program also learn to use sounds, letter cards, and a drill book.

*Instructional process and lesson time.*   Teachers teach each unit's content directly, sequentially, and cumulatively. Each level of 18 units takes about one year of study to complete.

*Placement, assessment, and advancement.*   Group administered, code-based test combined with standardized test scores, writing samples, and teacher observation determine placement. Students must demonstrate 80% mastery of a unit's tasks before progressing to the next unit. After showing mastery, teacher initials the record of student progress and that student advances to the next unit.

*Management of students at multiple levels.*   Although the program is designed for individual instruction in heterogeneous classes, teachers can better serve groups of students placing at the same level.

*Training.*   Training by a certified trainer takes about five full days using the authorized manual during which components of the program are explained. A professional development course syllabus is required for participation in the training program and provides teachers with groundwork for the program's implementation. Follow-up classroom coaching is a key component to training.

Evidence of effectiveness.   Greene (1996, 1998) cites a study showing that on average students trained in LANGUAGE! gained more than three grades over a 6-month instructional period in word identification, spelling, comprehension, and composition. As with CR, results in several California middle schools reveal reading growth rates significantly above state averages on tests used state-wide (Moats, 2001).

Commentary.   LANGUAGE! may require more training time than CR because the LANGUAGE! curriculum contains more components and is somewhat more complex in design. Originally, it was less structured and scripted than CR and so took more time to prepare. However, Greene has designed a sequence of lessons compiled from the program's resources to facilitate implementation.

LANGUAGE! includes supporting materials that teachers may opt to use with the core curriculum. These supporting materials include the following:

- *LANGUAGE! Roots:* provides practice in roots, prefixes, and suffixes from Latin and Greek.
- *Sounds of Our Language* audiotape: provides teacher practice with all phonemes learned in the professional development course for teaching LANGUAGE!
- *LANGUAGE! Categories:* presents groups of words that students put into categories.
- *Morphemes for Meaning:* cards containing suffixes, roots, and prefixes to directly teach methods of combining morphemes for vocabulary development.

# READ 180

History of Development.   Ted Hasselbring (1991) and his associates at Peabody College of Vanderbilt University developed READ 180 in the late 1980s and 1990s. In the Peabody Learning Lab, developers designed READ 180 with interactive computer technology to engage and accelerate reluctant or struggling readers. In literacy class-rooms, the multimedia lab is combined with literacy workshops (Allen, 1995). Developers implemented, refined, and tested READ 180 as part of the Orange County (Florida) Literacy Project from 1994 through 1999.

**Purpose.**    READ 180 is tailored to address characteristics of middle and high school struggling readers that have been found through numerous studies. These characteristics include

1. an inability to form mental models of texts because of weak vocabulary and background knowledge,
2. lack of phonemic awareness and decoding skills,
3. low levels of engagement with reading,
4. inability to relate to and process content area texts, and
5. lack of success in traditional classrooms.

To address these traits of struggling readers, READ 180 includes

1. vocabulary on topic CDs and content-related videos to build mental models for content-related reading;
2. software that models fluent reading, offers practice in rapid word identification to build automaticity, and requires demonstration of skill mastery before progressing;
3. skill-appropriate, age-appropriate, and motivating content to build vocabulary, fluency, and comprehension;
4. age-appropriate literature and interface to support and motivate reluctant readers with CD-ROMs linking curriculum content in math, science, social studies, and art with program passages; and
5. CD-ROMs that deliver and manage individualized reading and vocabulary adjusted to each student's skill level within a 90-minute instructional model.

**Research and theory.**    Research enabled designers of READ 180 to identify characteristics of struggling readers and discover appropriate methods and technologies to address weaknesses while building on strengths. Developers of READ 180 repeatedly refer to work conducted by Samuels (1994a, 1994b) who has done extensive research on word recognition and developed a theory of automatic information processing in reading that informs repeated reading practices. Developers also cite research on vocabulary instruction (Beck, Perfetti, & McKeown, 1982), the use of technology to drive literacy growth in at-risk students (Hasselbring, 1991), and the Matthew effect, which hypothesizes that those with reading skills prosper while those without fall farther and farther behind (Stanovich, 1986).

## Implementation
*Materials' structure and design.*    Curriculum is organized into two stages:

♦ Stage A for grades 4 through 6 and Stage B for grades 6 and above. Materials for each stage are provided to support the program's three basic components.
  1. *Instructional Reading* is supported by five CD-ROMs covering nine topics. Each topic includes videos and activities in four zones: reading (decoding, flu-

ency, vocabulary, comprehension instruction), word study (decoding and word recognition), spelling, and "success" (application and practice in comprehension skills). [Requires student workstations, teacher workstation, and a network server to install centralized database.]

2. *Modeled Reading* is supported by 12 cassette audiobooks presenting a model reader and a coach for reading strategy development.
3. *Independent Reading* is supported with 30 leveled paperbacks for Stage A and 40 for Stage B. These provide independent reading practice at students' current levels.

♦ To encourage and foster daily student-teacher interaction, the program comes with additional teacher support materials:
1. Teacher's guide with lesson plans to support every topic, audiobook, and paperback.
2. Teacher's resource book including graphic organizers, writing assignments, and class management materials.
3. Reading strategies book for teacher-directed instruction in word study, vocabulary, and comprehension.

*Instructional process and lesson time.*   Class sessions are designed to take 90 minutes each day. Each session includes five parts:

1. Whole-class instruction (20 minutes);
2. Instructional reading with READ 180 software (20 minutes);
3. Modeled or independent reading with READ 180 audiobooks or paperbacks (20 minutes);
4. Small-group teaching that includes guided reading, instruction in comprehension skills, and fluency practice (20 minutes); and
5. Whole-class wrap-up including journal writing, self-assessment, or discussion (10 minutes).

*Placement, assessment, and advancement.*   Individual, computer-driven tests are used to measure each student's decoding and comprehension skills for appropriate placement. The management program has a self-contained system to record students' progress, including length of time on computer, number of sessions, and percent of fluent words practiced in each lab. Records can be printed out for consulting. READ 180 can assess the following skills with built-in tools: reading fluency, comprehension, vocabulary, and spelling. Individual reports can be generated for each of four "Learning Zones": Reading, Word, Spelling, and Success. The "Reading Counts! Report" also monitors student progress in book completion, primarily for independent reading.

*Management of students at multiple levels.*   The program is designed for groups of 20 students who are near the same reading level. However, instruction provided through software is individualized. One stage serves 60 students. Reading materials are provided at students' reading level measured in **lexiles,** a popular readability formula that permits construction of a common scale for texts and their readers. The lexile scale ranges from First Grade (200 to 370) through to 1,600. As a touchstone, Rowling's *Harry Potter and the Goblet of Fire* has a lexile of 880, and the lexile range for eighth graders is 805 to 1,100 (MetaMetrics, 2000).

***Training.***   Initial introduction and on-going support for the program are essential. Building a classroom environment and familiarity with materials, including computer programs, may take several days of training. Teachers need time to develop strategies for literacy workshops. Maintenance and periodic evaluation of system function are important.

**Evidence of effectiveness.**   The program was implemented and evaluated in numerous middle and high schools in Florida's Orange County as part of the county's literacy initiative. As measured by the Stanford Achievement Test, reading comprehension grade equivalency of students in the Middle School Literacy Program increased from a mean of 2.6 to 3.6 (Blasewitz & Taylor, 1999). Over one year, gains of students in grades 6, 7, 8, and 9 who were participating in the program were significantly larger than control groups. In one study, ninth graders gained three years in reading level (Taylor & Sulzer, 1997). In their assessment, Peterson and her associates (2000) rated the program as "promising."

## Reading Apprenticeship (RA)

**History of development.**   The Reading Apprenticeship (RA) program grew out of the work of two classroom teachers and two researchers at WestEd, a non-profit center for research and development of educational programs (Schoenbach, Greenleaf, Cziko, & Hurwitz, 1999). The researchers served on a project called the Strategic Literacy Initiative (SLI) whose purpose was to design and implement a model of professional development that could be used in secondary schools to improve student literacy. Their collaboration with classroom teachers resulted in a site-based literacy intervention model that engaged cross-disciplined teams of teachers in discussions and writing about literacy practices. Reflection and professional exchange beat at the heart of the model, similar to the National Writing Project model of teacher-to-teacher interchange. Although the RA model could augment the reading development of all readers, I've included it here because of its applicability to struggling readers.

**Purpose.**   The developers of RA recognized that most American students fall short when trying to reach higher levels of literacy competencies and that most teachers find it nearly impossible to integrate constructivist strategies into their instructional programs. Thus, these educators designed a case inquiry–based approach to improve secondary teachers' competency in literacy instruction and content area reading. Teachers become "masters" in their craft and work with their student "apprentices" whom they guide toward higher levels of expertise. The expertise of teachers as readers in their content areas forms the foundation of this approach to improving adolescent reading (Jordan, Jensen, & Greenleaf, 2001).

**Research and theory.**   The designers of this model embrace Vygotsky's beliefs that social contexts and language-based communication promote cognitive development. During "metacognitive conversations," four dimensions of classroom life overlap and support RA: the social, personal, cognitive, and knowledge-building dimensions (Schoenbach, Greenleaf, Cziko, & Hurwitz, 1999).

Case methods and teacher inquiry or action research influenced the development of RA. Believing that teachers will become more engaged and committed to teaching reading when they understand it and their students' struggles with it, developers focused on using cases to promote inquiry-based teacher development. Teachers become seriously engaged as learners about their students and their practice rather than brushing on acquired strategies that may not fit students' literacy needs. Through the study of multimedia and print-based cases, including student work, interview excerpts, and classroom observations, teachers look deeper into the problematic literacy performance of students struggling to learn.

## Implementation

***On-site reading intervention course development.*** Teachers and WestEd's SLI staff created a yearlong, "mandatory elective" called Academic Literacy that was required of all freshman (Schoenbach, Greenleaf, Cziko, & Hurwitz, 1999). Its goal was to prepare all students to read challenging texts in various content areas with success throughout high school. The course was designed to examine reading with students as apprentices to their teachers as master readers. The learning goals reflected the four dimensions of classroom life constituting RA's theoretical foundation. The curriculum consisted of four units: Reading Self and Society, Reading Media, Reading History, and Reading Science and Technology. A Sustained Silent Reading (SSR) program with required amounts of reading and responsive writing began with the beginning of the course. All four of the units included SSR and other key instructional strategies, such as reciprocal teaching and its four components (see Chapter 6).

***Engaging students.*** Teachers worked to engage students in social and personal dimensions by forming communities of readers dedicated to investigating and improving reading. Teachers gave students a vocabulary to talk about reading, encouraged think-alouds while reading difficult texts, permitted confusion about reading challenging texts, built student confidence, and helped students develop an identity as readers. Meanwhile, teachers strongly supported SSR by using logs and book sharing techniques.

***Teaching students reading strategies for all content area reading.*** Teachers engage students in acquiring cognitive tools for solving the problems that reading comprehension presents. Strategies, such as reciprocal teaching, are taught in context. Teachers model reading through think-alouds (see Chapters 3 and 6). Students learn that technique and then use it in pairs. As students move through the curriculum's units, they acquire more discipline-specific knowledge and strategies for reading in subject areas, such as history or science. Apprenticeship strategies, including reciprocal teaching and recognizing text structures, are integrated into the subject areas to build ways of reading into the disciplines.

***Training.*** Teachers attend Institutes for Reading Apprenticeship where SLI staff members work with instructional leaders in an extended inquiry-based development experience designed to build capacity for site-based implementation and literacy improvement. Participants, preferably in site-based teams, return to their schools and districts to implement the RA framework and procedures. Participants become more aware of their invisible reading processes in order to make them visible to their student apprentices in various content areas. Participants also learn comprehension strategies, such as reciprocal teaching, that become part of an RA classroom. They also learn to engage students in "metacognitive conversations" about reading processes.

RA has no pre-packaged program, software, or workbooks. The investment lies with teacher training and development. A specific tool likely to help, at least initially, is a guidebook entitled *Reading for Understanding* (Schoenbach, Greenleaf, Cziko, & Hurwitz, 1999).

**Evidence of effectiveness.**   To measure growth, the designers of Academic Literacy used the Degrees of Reading Power (DRP) test, which is based on a modified *cloze* procedure (see Chapter 3). On average, the ninth graders gained 4 DRP units, a gain corresponding to an increase in independent reading from the ability to read *Charlotte's Web* (50 DPR) to the ability to read *To Kill a Mockingbird* (54 DPR). That is substantially more, the authors claim, than one year of expected growth in reading at the ninth-grade level, which is about 2 DPRs (Schoenbach, Greenleaf, Cziko, & Hurwitz, 1999).

**Commentary.**   RA programs can be designed to focus on struggling readers or extend to an entire school's population. Building a community of committed teachers ready to reform a school's reading program is key to successful RA implementation. Elements built into RA programs increase the likelihood that teachers would learn and be moved to integrate strategic instruction in reading into their content area classes.

## Success for All (SFA)

**History of development.**   Success for All (SFA) (Slavin, Madden, Dolan, & Wasik, 1996a) was initially designed to address lagging literacy among disadvantaged children in urban elementary schools. SFA focused primarily on first graders because one main principle of the program was to help readers get reading right the first time without requiring remedial programs. Expanding the program to address students in pre-kindergarten through grades 5 or 6, Robert Slavin, the program's chief architect, built in several key features: systematic phonics to develop decoding, one-on-one tutoring, explicit strategy instruction to assist comprehension, family support programs, and professional development. Begun in the 1980s, SFA has grown and produced significant results (Hurley, Chamberlain, Slavin, & Madden, 2001).

A middle school model of SFA has been piloted extensively. Many features from SFA's elementary model were transferred to its middle school program, including (a) a school-wide curriculum, (b) periodic reassessment, (c) family support, (d) tutoring, and (e) a program facilitator.

**Purpose.**   The main purposes of the Success for All Middle School program include:

- ◆ Assessment of students' strengths and weaknesses,
- ◆ Instruction to fill in their gaps,
- ◆ Building bridges to more challenging content, and
- ◆ Practical applications for knowledge gains.

As a school-wide program, SFA targets reading in all classes. SFA's stated reading goal is to increase the number of students reading at or above grade level by 20% each year. Non-readers are grounded in the basics of reading; advanced readers are given challenging literacy activities to help them grow. Other purposes for the program include improvement of school climate and implementation of an academically rigorous curriculum in math, science, and social studies.

Research and theory.   SFA Middle School program is based on the extensively researched SFA elementary school model (Slavin, Madden, Dolan, & Wasik, 1996a). Both SFA programs draw upon research and theory related to cooperative learning, one-on-one tutoring for delayed or struggling readers, and school-home connections. Adhering to the "small is better" theory, students are placed in "houses" with four teachers, a key concept of the middle school *Turning Points* reform program to foster the creation of learning communities (Carnegie Council on Adolescent Development, 1989; Jackson & Davis, 2000). Schools adopting SFA are encouraged to provide teachers in the same house with a common planning time to organize and coordinate instruction, another *Turning Points* recommendation.

Implementation.   Because SFA is a school-wide program, all aspects of the school's curriculum, organization, and management are affected. At least 80% of the administrative staff and faculty must indicate by secret ballot their desire to become a SFA Middle School site.

***Required and recommended elements.***   SFA Middle School programs have several required and some strongly recommended elements. The required elements include:

- A 2-hour Core Humanities Class integrating social studies and language arts. Students learn and apply reading and writing strategies while investigating real-world problems in cooperative groups.
- Forty to sixty minutes dedicated to reading instruction. Reading is not only integrated into all classes, but children are assessed and grouped to facilitate growth in literacy skills and strategies appropriate to their levels of achievement. Children are assessed and regrouped at 8-week intervals. Those reading below grade level participate in a reading intervention program, "Reading Roots for Older Readers," especially designed for struggling readers. Students at or above grade level in reading focus on developing research and study skills and other activities.
- Heterogeneous groups except for homogeneous reading (and some math) groups.
- "Houses" composed of four classes of students with four teachers, usually two covering the humanities, one for science, and one for math.
- Professional or paraprofessional reading tutors for at least 20% of all sixth-grade struggling readers.
- Use of the SFA Middle School curriculum for the humanities and reading.
- Use of SFA Middle School classroom management and teaching strategies.
- Incorporation of SFA Middle School Family Support Program.
- At least one full-time, in-school facilitator to support program implementation.

The recommended elements include:

- Common meeting and planning time for four teachers in each house.
- Commitment of all team teachers to teach a reading section.

***Support programs and personnel.*** Schools adopting SFA should consider site-based management orchestrated by a school improvement team. The principal's primary purpose is to assist in the implementation of elements that make SFA work, including curriculum, staff development, planning, and participation on key committees. Together with the principal's support, a school facilitator who is highly qualified should have the sole obligation of making certain that all the gears of SFA are well-oiled and running smoothly. Teachers require training for SFA, particularly in cooperative learning strategies that are central to SFA's realization, classroom management strategies, and aspects of the SFA curriculum. Because family support and community involvement are integral components of SFA, teams that include parents and community members from each school develop services that extend regular instruction to address students' needs.

Evidence of effectiveness. SFA Middle School has been piloted in well over 30 school sites. Anecdotal information about its effects on reading are positive; however, research-based findings for reading improvements compared to control groups, although being conducted, have yet to be reported. SFA's elementary school model has a broad research base developed over 15 years. Findings on multiple measures of reading development in grades 1 through 5 confirm that SFA's effects are significantly better than control cohorts (Slavin et al., 1996b) and carry over into grades 6 and 7. Growth in reading among students in the lowest 25% of their grades was especially positive. Researchers (Madden, Slavin, Karweit, Dolan, & Wasik, 1993) found that SFA students not only read better than those in a control school but were also much less likely to be designated as special education students or to fail a grade. The outlook for the SFA Middle School program with respect to its effects on reading is promising.

## The "Just Read More" Program

In his review of research on reading and intervention programs for struggling readers, Allington (2001) identified an elegantly simple solution: Just read more. National Assessment of Educational Progress data in the *Reading Report Card for the Nation and the States* (1999) tell this story of correlations: the more minutes per day that students read, the higher they score on tests of reading achievement. No extensive teacher training. No one-on-one tutoring. No fancy computer programs. No cooperative learning enterprises in literacy. Just more reading. A middle school student who reads 40 minutes a day will read about 2,400,000 words a year and is likely to score in the 90th percentile.

To increase their students' volume of reading, schools could simply set aside a minimum of 90 minutes per day for *actual* in-school reading. Allington (2001) writes that schools should look closely at their daily schedules to discover how they can reduce wasted time that can be allocated to reading. Many schools, he believes, could find 30 to 50 more minutes for reading and still have plenty of time for all the other subjects.

In grades 6 through 12, teachers could select texts that increase reading opportunities. Too often an anthology in an English class and one history book suffice as reading material for an entire year of English and social studies. If teachers provided more novels, plays, and collections of stories or essays along with several books to accompany the study of history, students could expand their volume of reading many fold.

Some states have established volume of reading standards. In New York State, the English Language Arts Core Curriculum calls for students in all grades to read 25 books or their equivalent across all content areas per year (New York State Education Department, 1997). In California, eighth graders are expected to read 1,000,000 words while eleventh and twelfth graders should reach 2,000,000 (California Department of Education, 1998).

But to expand the volume of reading, teachers and schools need to enhance access to books. That means more books in every backpack, classroom, bookroom, home, and library. McQuillan (1998) pointed out a very high correlation (.85) between library adequacy and NAEP reading achievement scores. However, the existence of a relationship between books on hand and the presence of better readers does not mean that books alone caused reading improvement. Other factors that contribute to good reading, like abundant family support for reading and learning, are likely to occur in communities where books are plentiful.

## ENGLISH LEARNERS

Struggling readers, most of whom speak English with at least conversational proficiency, constitute a large portion of students with exceptional language and cognitive needs. However, another large and growing number of students present classroom teachers with even more profound language, cognitive, and cultural challenges because these students have not acquired conversational or academic proficiency in English.

The number of students in classrooms who are English learners varies dramatically across America. About 15% of all public school teachers have one English learner in their classroom (August & Hakuta, 1997). In some regions, very few classrooms have any English learners at all. In other regions, classrooms with over 80% of students identified as English learners are not unusual. In many districts, English learners are grouped together in English as a second language (or ESL) classes. In classes with even a few students who are struggling with English as their second (or

third?) language, teachers must be ready to adopt strategies that will address these special language, cognitive, and cultural needs.

Looking more closely at the numbers of English learners across America, we discover estimates of about three and a half to four million. About 40% of that total number of students attend schools in California where one out of four students is an English learner. That comes to about one and a half million students in California who are trying to learn English while keeping up in their content area classrooms.

Recently, the level of foreign born living in New York City has increased to 40% of the city's population, a level not reached since 1910. Always a melting pot, New York now has more rapidly growing populations of people from the former Soviet Union, Mexico, the Dominican Republic, and South Asia ("40 Percent in NY," 2000).

Experts in demographics predict that more and more states and cities will have to address the needs of English learners in the years to come as increasing numbers of immigrants, especially from Central America, South America, and Asia, arrive in the United States seeking access to education. While California, Texas, and New York now have the largest numbers of English learners, many other states, like Georgia, North Carolina, Oregon, and Kentucky, have had large percentage increases over the past 10 years (Zhao, 2002). Programs and strategies to respond to the needs of English learners are now and will become of critical importance.

## Federal Law and English Learners

In accord with the Civil Rights Act and its interpretation by the U.S. Supreme Court (*Lau v. Nichols,* 1974), states and school districts are obligated to provide educational services to limited-English-proficient (LEP) students. The law requires that each educational system "take appropriate action to overcome language barriers that impede equal participation by its students in its instructional programs." "Appropriate action" does not mean that schools must provide instruction in a student's primary language nor does the law specify any other specific methods. For the most part, "appropriate action" has been guided by three principles arising from another federal law decision (*Casteneda v. Pickard,* 5th cir. 1981):

1. *Use sound theory.* Some experts must view the educational theory forming the base for instruction as sound.
2. *Provide adequate support.* The school system is obligated to provide resources, procedures, and personnel to implement effectively the theory's practice in classrooms.
3. *Achieve results.* The program's implementation must result in students actually overcoming English language barriers to equal participation in a school's instructional programs. The program should not result in students revealing academic deficits.

## A Glossary of Acronyms and Abbreviations

So many acronyms and abbreviations arise in discussions and descriptions of English learner services that a glossary is essential. The glossary will also serve as an introduction to a number of concepts and programs helpful to teachers who work with English learners.

- EL stands for English Learner(s). The term has been widely used in discussions about students acquiring English as their second language.
- L1 stands for an English Learner's first language.
- L2 stands for the target language that a student is acquiring. In most cases in our classrooms and schools, L2 would be English.
- ESL stands for English as a Second Language and usually refers to classes in which students learn English as a second (or perhaps third, even fourth) language. Although teachers may be fluent in their students' native language, teachers in these classes usually communicate only in English. However, students may communicate (on the side) in their L1.
- ELD stands for English Language Development.
- ELL stands for English Language Learner. At times in writing about these students, writers refer to them as ELLs.
- LEP stands for Limited-English-Proficient students. They have acquired some degree of oral fluency in English. However, they are not yet able to communicate comfortably in academic English or in many interpersonal situations requiring English.
- FEP stands for Fluent-English-Proficient students who have acquired and use English in both academic and social situations with a significant degree of ease.
- CLAD, in California, stands for Cross-cultural, Language, and Academic Development. From approved teacher credential programs in the state, teachers receive a CLAD Credential after completing programs that include emphasis and curriculum on students' diverse cultures and languages. The credential authorizes them to provide instruction to limited-English-proficient students.
- BCLAD stands for Bilingual, Cross-cultural, Language, and Academic Development. Students completing a bilingual program that also includes an approved program in the study of culture, language, and diversity of the classroom receive a BCLAD credential.
- SDAIE stands for Specially Designed Academic Instruction In English. When using SDAIE methods, teachers modify their teaching of the curriculum to make it more accessible to students. These methods will be described in a later section of this chapter.
- SAE stands for Students Acquiring English and is used by some educators to emphasize the positive development in knowledge that English learners undergo rather than the implicit deficits of designations like LEP.

## Toward a Theory of How a Second Language Is Learned

Stephen Krashen (1981, 1995) has put forward five hypotheses that, when conjoined, build a valid theory for second language acquisition. We'll review each of these five hypotheses to see how they contribute to an overall explanation of how students learn English—or how any person learns a second language.

Acquisition-learning hypothesis.   How do we gain language facility? Do we mainly absorb language through interaction with others using it to communicate or through intentional study of grammar, syntax, and vocabulary? According to Krashen, language acquisition is mainly an unconscious process that results from using a new symbol system to communicate with others. However, we clearly do learn language from its conscious, systematic study.

**Natural order hypothesis.**    In what order are the elements of a second language learned? The natural order hypothesis asserts that some general order of acquisition exists; however, the particulars of that order are not clearly known for every language.

**Monitor hypothesis.**    Krashen hypothesizes that second-language learners must have some kind of monitoring system that will enable the new language speaker to recognize when some language form or construction is simply not right. When that recognition occurs, the L2 speaker self-corrects if the correct language forms can be adequately remembered. This process is much like metacognition, our capacity to observe mental operations, to think about mental processes, and to make appropriate adjustments in our thinking so that we can be more successful in communicating or problem solving. For this system to work, a speaker of a new language needs to know L2's linguistic rules, to focus on L2's correct expressive forms, and to have time to reflect on L2's proper use. Unfortunately, reflective conditions are often lacking in the midst of communicating in a new tongue.

**Input hypothesis.**    As I read the Spanish newspaper in Los Angeles, *La Opinion,* listen to the radio news in Spanish, or watch a movie in Spanish, I frequently find myself striving to master a syntactic structure that is just a little beyond my current capacity to comprehend. Sometimes it's an inflected verb form used in a new sentence pattern. Sometimes it's a string of unfamiliar *palabras* that leave me searching for context cues to figure out their meaning—like you may be trying to do with the word *palabras* if you don't happen to be familiar with the word in Spanish.

This mental phenomenon of my grasping what's a little beyond me is a concrete example of Krashen's input hypothesis. It states that we acquire a new language by learning language that contains linguistic structures (or meanings) just a tad beyond what we know. We may comprehend well at stages 3, 4, 5, or the $i$ stage, but then we stretch for the next stage of mastery, $i + 1$, where $i$ represents our current level of competence and 1 stands for the stage we're about to acquire. In Krashen's (1995) words, "We acquire (not learn) language by understanding input that contains structures that are just beyond our current level of competence" (p. 100). By understanding the meaning of what we read or hear, we acquire language—not by explicit study of the isolated structures we are learning.

The input hypothesis helps to explain what is called the *silent period* in language acquisition. That's the period of time that the learner of a new language says nothing. Usually, lots of language is getting in. So much may be getting in that it creates a kind of mental din of words and sounds out of which little meaning can be constructed. That is what I experience now when I hear a broadcast or conversation in Russian. Although I studied the language many years ago, I used it so infrequently over the years that almost all my knowledge of it has deteriorated. All I hear is a din of sounds, few of which I can recognize. I would surely be silent at a Russian dinner party where guests spoke only in Russian. However, that silent period is of great importance for learners of new languages. We're getting lots of incomprehensible information that will take time to sort out, digest, and understand before we're ready to produce comprehensible information ourselves in that new language.

**Affective filter hypothesis.**    When attempting to speak Spanish, I frequently become anxious about making mistakes because I haven't become sufficiently fluent and confident in the language to always enjoy its social use. I tend to become hypercritical when I need to loosen up and let language (even with its mistakes) just flow.

Krashen identified three affective filters that may cause us to inhibit second language acquisition and use. These three include anxiety, motivation, and self-confidence. With high anxiety accompanied by low motivation and low self-confidence, language acquisition may become stymied. But, when we feel more relaxed, more motivated, and more confident, our affective filters are less active, a condition that makes acquiring and conversing in L2 much easier and more effective.

Consolidating Krashen's theory.    Krashen (1995) may have summarized his theory best when he wrote, "People acquire second languages when they obtain comprehensible input and when their affective filters are low enough to allow the input in" (p. 101). As teachers of students who are learning English as well as content knowledge, we need to keep in mind the importance of keeping anxiety low while keeping motivation and self-confidence high so that students receive "comprehensible input."

Having presented a theory of second language acquisition, let's turn to an important and related pedagogical question: How long does it take English learners to become proficient?

# How Long Does It Take for an English Learner to Become Proficient?

There are legal requirements for schools to provide appropriate programs for English learners, and a multitude of programs have been implemented. However, the length of time such services should be provided has been much debated and remains controversial.

Several researchers (Collier, 1987; Cummins, 1981; Hakuta, Butler, & Witt, 2000; Mitchell, Destino, & Karam, 1997) have tried to determine approximately how long it takes to learn English. Some estimated that it takes up to 10 years for a student to become fully proficient in English, that is proficient enough to be competitive with native speakers of the same age in an academic setting.

Part of professing "proficiency" entails proclaiming some level of accomplishment. But what level of achievement or mastery of English signals "proficiency"? The ability to use English in academic settings would seem to signal academic English proficiency. And that level is clearly essential for success in school. Nevertheless, different standards define proficiency.

In his discussion of students learning English as a second language, James Cummins (1984) identified two levels of proficiency. He used the terms *basic interpersonal communication skills* (BICS) to describe proficiency in social settings and *cognitive academic language proficiency* (CALP) to identify proficiency in classroom settings. In a sense, Cummins is referring to distinct discourse communities in which students communicate. One is highly conversational and personal while the other is more formal and abstract. In his research, Cummins found that ELLs took about 2 years to acquire age-appropriate conversational proficiency, what he called (BICS) and about 5 to 7 years to acquire academic proficiency (CALP). We must be careful not to assume that a student who has attained basic interpersonal communication skills (BICS) is just as proficient in cognitive academic language proficiency (CALP). Knowing how to get along on the playing field in English doesn't indicate that a student knows how to use English successfully in a math, science, or history class.

In an attempt to determine reasonable time expectations for achieving proficiency in English, Hakuta, Butler, and Witt (2000) examined four sets of data. The four studies included two school districts in the San Francisco Bay Area and two in Canada. The researchers came to a "clear conclusion" that oral proficiency took from 3 to 5 years to develop while academic English proficiency took 5 to 7 years. The findings of the two school districts in Canada strengthened these findings. Furthermore, the findings of Hakuta and his associates more or less confirm Cummins' estimates of time to proficiency.

What factors could affect length of time needed to gain proficiency? Some educators favor bilingual education programs because of the benefits to students such programs are said to yield. However, Hakuta and his colleagues (2000) point out that the presence or absence of bilingual education programs had no effect on the time taken to achieve oral and academic proficiency. Only 1 of the 4 districts, one located in the San Francisco Bay Area, offered a bilingual education program. However, Hakuta and his colleagues analyzed the data from that district's students and found no significant differences in language proficiency between students who were in its bilingual program and those in its English-only program.

One factor the Hakuta team (2000) did identify that had a significant effect on learning rate was socioeconomic status. Students attending schools with lower rates of poverty learned to become proficient more quickly than those students from schools with higher rates of poverty. Furthermore, students who had parents with higher levels of education reached English proficiency earlier than students from families where parents had less education.

## Programs for English Language Learners

Several programs used extensively to help English learners acquire proficiency can be identified and described. Even though we can label and describe these programs, we must keep in mind that wide variations exist within each of the specific program categories. Often the discrepancies arise from differences between espoused pedagogy and actual classroom practice.

Here we will define and briefly review seven different instructional approaches to address the needs of English learners: English as a second language (ESL), content-based ESL, sheltered English, structured English immersion (SEI), transitional bilingual education, maintenance bilingual education, and two-way bilingual programs (see Figure 9.1).

◆ *English as a second language (ESL-only):*   Using an ESL approach, teachers aim instruction at students to develop English language skills, such as grammar, vocabulary, and oral competency. Academic content areas are de-emphasized.

◆ *Content-based ESL:*   Using this approach, teachers structure ESL instruction around academic content. Generic English language skill development is not emphasized. The next two programs, Sheltered English instruction and structured English immersion, are often categorized as forms of content-based ESL.

◆ *Sheltered English instruction:*   Teachers provide EL students with subject matter instruction in English. Teachers modify instruction so that content will be

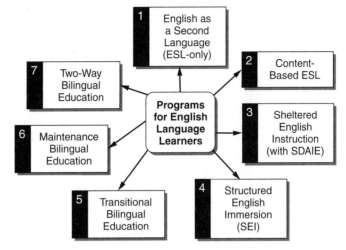

**FIGURE 9.1**  Programs for English Learners.

accessible to students at their level of English proficiency. In these classrooms, teachers commonly apply Specially Designed Academic Instruction in English (SDAIE), the principles and practices of which we will review later in this chapter. Sheltered English instruction and structured English immersion (the next program category) are so similar that the program labels are sometimes interchanged.

♦ *Structured English immersion (SEI):*   All students learning English, regardless of their first language, are grouped together. Instruction is given only in English with little or no L1 support. However, teachers adapt instruction to fit the level of their students' English competency so that content is comprehensible. Lessons in mathematics, for example, are carried on in English but at a level appropriate for English learners in the class. In some states, the passage of state laws mandating SEI programs (unless parents explicitly request alternatives) has caused their rapid expansion while bilingual programs have contracted.

♦ *Transitional bilingual education:*   Although teachers provide some instruction in students' native language, the aim of transitional bilingual programs is to transition to English as soon as possible. Bilingual teachers of these classes shift to English as rapidly as they can. Students are tested periodically for replacement. During the 1990s, 50% of English learners were in transitional bilingual programs (August & Hakuta, 1997).

♦ *Maintenance bilingual education:*   Teachers provide large amounts of instruction to students grouped according to their native language. Maintenance programs differ from transitional programs in that teachers who run maintenance bilingual programs aim to develop English fluency while developing academic proficiency in L1.

♦ *Two-way bilingual programs:*   Teachers using two-way programs serve in classrooms that are split roughly in half between native English speakers and English learners who share the same native language. Teachers have as their objective the development of proficiency in both languages for both groups of students they teach. Maintenance and two-way bilingual programs are relatively rare (August & Hakuta, 1997).

## California's English Learners' Programs: An Example of the Teacher's Challenge

California's educators faced a challenging task in 1998 after citizens passed Proposition 227, an initiative directly addressing the education of English learners in the state. The proposition specified the kinds of instruction to be provided to English learners and the expected time frame for that instruction. "Children who are English learners shall be educated through sheltered English immersion during a temporary transition period not normally intended to exceed one year." The statute uses the terms "sheltered English immersion" and "structured English immersion" interchangeably.

Furthermore, the statute permits parents to request a waiver from the structured English immersion program so that their children could be taught English and the content curriculum through bilingual education or other recognized methods. Prior to the passage of the proposition, many administrators in California schools with English learners automatically placed most students in bilingual education classes, most of which were Spanish bilingual.

In order for students to receive structured immersion rather than submersion and possible drowning in English, the Department of Education clarified that the structured immersion program must have the following components:

- a curriculum specifically designed for English learners,
- teachers who have received training in second-language acquisition methods, and
- instructional strategies designed for language learning.

Although not an English-only program, structured English immersion makes far less use of non-English languages for instruction than bilingual methods.

## Principles Guiding English Learners' Instruction

To help educators address the challenges of Proposition 227, the California Department of Education also convened a 35-member task force charged with developing recommendations that would give school systems guidance in designing programs for English learners. The task force identified several central questions that California educators would need to answer in order to serve English learners in accord with the new statute. Among those questions were the following:

- What is the responsibility of the school to English learners?
- What does it mean to know a language?
- How will English acquisition and academic progress be assessed?

These were and continue to be tough questions to answer.

However, in their report *Educating English Learners for the Twenty-First Century* (1999), the task force formulated a number of principles to guide educators in answering these questions and implementing programs for English learners. Several of these principles may help teachers address the problems of English learners not only in California but also in states across the country.

- *All teachers will be professionally prepared, qualified, and authorized to teach English learners.* To accomplish this, the task force recommended extensive staff development to include training in accelerated English-language acquisition, training that would go beyond the foundation that CLAD certificated teachers would already have. Also recommended was greater emphasis in administrator and teacher credentialing programs on literacy development, language-acquisition strategies, assessment, and content instruction. (Some states, such as Maryland, require twice as much course work on reading instruction as other states to obtain teaching credentials and to prepare teachers to address instructional challenges English learners present in content courses.)

◆ *Educators of English learners will systematically assess student performance by using valid measures and will review performance results to ensure that instruction is aligned with English-language development standards and each student's needs.* To reach this goal, the task force recommended the development of state-wide performance standards for each designated level of English-language proficiency. These standards should be clustered by grade spans so that teachers will have a meaningful context for levels of proficiency and will be able to focus instruction and assessment on the standards. Teachers should also have access to diagnostic assessment instruments and training in their use so they can focus on language learning. The state should also develop a statewide instrument appropriate for the assessment of English learners language acquisition.

◆ *Instruction, evaluation, and accountability of English learners will be most effective when instructional decisions are based on meaningful data related to student performance.* The task force, as should be clear from these last two principles, was intent on effective diagnostic and standards-based evaluation of English learners. Part of this continuing assessment program included the creation of criteria for the redesignation of English learners as fluent speakers of English only when they had reached grade-level standards in both English-language proficiency and core academic subjects. Should English learners fail to achieve grade-level standards in a reasonable amount of time, additional services should be provided. These could include extended-day instruction, summer school, and Saturday classes.

◆ *All schools will provide effective, up-to-date materials, technology, and equipment for English learners.* The task force recommended that the state budget have funds specifically for instructional materials and software designed to teach English learners. The state's department of education should publish information to help practitioners select teaching materials for English learners. More specifically, these materials should directly help teachers develop students' interpersonal communication skills, comprehension of oral and written language, and academic English. Classes in the content area should include Specially Designed Academic Instruction in English (SDAIE) and English as a Second Language (ESL) techniques.

◆ *All English learners will have access to the same challenging core curriculum and receive the necessary support to achieve the high standards expected of all students.* The task force emphasizes the importance of English learners progressing in their development of content knowledge as well as English-language proficiency. With state funding, instruction outside the regular school day is recommended for English learners.

◆ *Rapid and effective acquisition of academic English in the structured English immersion process will be a focus and priority for all students who have less-than-reasonable proficiency in English.* The task force recommends that teachers use strategies that help English learners in three communication modes they identified: interpersonal, interpretive, and presentational. Also recommended are teacher guidelines for the implementation of the structured English immersion process. SDAIE is considered "an acceptable approach" in content areas for English learners who have progressed beyond beginning levels.

◆ *Instructional programs for English learners with reasonable fluency in English in mainstream classrooms or alternative courses of study will use the learner's language, literacy skills, and sociocultural experiences so that students acquire advanced reading and writing skills in English as well as content knowledge.* The task force recommends that teachers learn to use "sheltered instruction" as a method to help students master content area curriculum. Schools should also provide English learners with access to resources in their primary language to facilitate learning content in English-language mainstream classrooms.

## Sheltered English Instruction and Structured English Immersion

By design, English as a Second Language (ESL) programs help English learners gain proficiency in English as quickly as possible. Two content-based ESL programs that share many features merit our special attention because of their wide use. Sheltered English instruction and structured English immersion, as we have seen, are labels for content ESL programs that are often used interchangeably, as they are in the case of California's Proposition 227.

When teaching English learners through sheltered English instruction, teachers modify the content curriculum and its delivery to make it more accessible to students. One of the most prevalent modes of modification for English learners is Specially Designed Academic Instruction in English (SDAIE). Among the practices recommended (Chamot & O'Malley, 1994; Schifini, 1994) for SDAIE are the following:

- ◆ The level of students' English language fluency determines language objectives;
- ◆ Instruction provides access to grade-appropriate core curriculum in content areas;
- ◆ Instruction is organized around content that is appropriate for a specific grade;
- ◆ Language and content are integrated;
- ◆ Students' interests and background knowledge, including that of their culture, form the base upon which teachers build;
- ◆ Students are explicitly taught learning strategies to build content knowledge, English proficiency, and problem solving;
- ◆ Instruction allows English learners to process content in multiple forms: reading, discussing, drawing, questioning, dramatizing, writing;
- ◆ Content becomes organized into meaningful learning sequences;
- ◆ Levels of language use are modified during classroom instruction;
- ◆ Speech rates may become slower;
- ◆ Content may be repeated;
- ◆ New words are defined in context;
- ◆ Idiomatic speech, jargon, and slang are limited;
- ◆ Complex or sophisticated language expressions are paraphrased for understanding;
- ◆ Meaning is dramatized with actions, gestures, and facial expressions;
- ◆ Visual aids, including graphs, maps, and pictures, make content more concrete;
- ◆ Verbal expression is supported with films, videotapes, and bulletin board displays;
- ◆ All students, with appropriate sensitivity to levels of English proficiency, are drawn into participation;

- ◆ To facilitate interpersonal and academic language development, students work and learn in many grouping formats, including pairs, small groups focused on cooperative learning, and skill-building teams; and
- ◆ Multiple assessment methods (performance-based, standardized, diagnostic, portfolio, self) enable students to demonstrate language and content knowledge growth and discover avenues for further development.

## Cognitive Academic Language Learning Approach (CALLA)

CALLA is a content-based ESL approach for English learners (Chamot & O'Malley, 1994). However, it is quite different from sheltered instruction because it arises from a cognitive model of learning and its strategy-based instruction is integrated into both content and language learning. CALLA, its creators explain, has three components:

1. It uses content drawn from grade-level curriculum that content area teachers identify.
2. Language activities are added to the content to build vocabulary, oral skills, and reading and writing abilities designed to help students think through the concepts being learned.
3. Explicit instruction in learning strategies are seen as essential to both content and language comprehension, storage, and recall of information.

Learning strategies, as mentioned in the last of these three components, vitalize much of Anna Chamot's work on second language acquisition (Chamot, 1995; Chamot, Barnhardt, El-Dinary, & Robbins, 1999; Chamot, Keatley, & Mazur, 1999). She believes that strategies for learning or activities that enhance learning should play a pivotal role in teaching second language learners for several reasons. First, learning strategies are dynamic processes that underlie productive learning. Second, active learners learn better. Third, students can learn strategies and transfer them to new tasks. Fourth, research shows that school-related language learning is more effective when students learn and use strategies.

Drawing on research in strategy instruction, Chamot identifies three types of learning strategies: metacognitive, cognitive, and social/affective (Brown & Palincsar, 1982). Metacognitive strategies include planning, monitoring, and evaluating. When planning, for example, students can use advanced organization to preview a text in social studies to identify its organizing principle and skim it to grasp the gist of its content. That strategy will enable learners to plan what steps they will take to accomplish the learning tasks they face. ("Since this section on the French Revolution is entitled 'The Reign of Terror,' what does that tell me about its content? What's my purpose for reading this section?"). Cognitive strategies include elaboration of prior knowledge, note taking, grouping to enhance recall, and linguistic transfer. For example, a reader approaching a social studies text in L2 could make personal connections with the text's content ("What do I already know about France, especially during the period of the Revolution? What experience have I had connected to revolutions?"), jot down key words and concepts in abbreviated form ("How can I best organize this information about the French Revolution? Outline? Concept map? Graphic organizer?"), and make connections with the native language ("What terms or historical names can I recognize because of similarities to my first language?"). Social/affective strategies include cooperation and self-talk. An example of this form of strategic learning lies in working cooperatively with others to solve problems in L2 ("Who should I ask in class to help me understand Robespierre's role in the Revolution?"). We know that such collaboration is one of the most productive paths to language learning.

CALLA includes several reading strategies that are explicitly taught and that expand students' array of strategic approaches to learning. Among these are the following:

◆ *English learners activate and elaborate prior knowledge.* Students work alone or in cooperative groups to jot down or illustrate what they already know about a topic about which they are going to read. (Students gather in teams to list what they know as a group about the French Revolution.)

◆ *English learners set a purpose and plan for reading.* After students decide why they are reading a text, they create a plan to help them see how they will approach a text to learn from it. (After reviewing what needs to be read about the French Revolution, a student sets a purpose for reading, decides what to focus upon, and selects a means for organizing knowledge gained.)

◆ *English learners monitor their comprehension through self-questioning.* Students ask themselves questions about texts, such as "Does this make sense to me?" As students become aware that their comprehension is breaking down, they can activate fix-up strategies. (A student reading about Robespierre's role in the French Revolution asks himself if he understands what he's read, discovers he's not sure, and decides to reread the text.)

◆ *English learners self-evaluate and assess their progress toward the purpose they set for reading a text.* These self-assessments can take the form of conferences with the teacher, discussions in small groups, written summaries, retellings, and journals. (After writing summaries, students reconvene in their team to discuss questions based on their reading about the French Revolution.)

None of these strategies should be taught in isolation, according to Chamot and O'Malley (1994). The strategies should be integrated and practiced with content reading. Furthermore, English learners should "experience" an entire text before trying to comprehend each individual word. To do this, Chamot and O'Malley suggest listening to the text, reading familiar words for the gist, or engaging in a form of reciprocal teaching in which students can help each other comprehend the text.

Through CALLA, English learners read "authentic" texts from different content areas, such as literature, science, history, and math. In literature, they could read stories and poems, in math, word problems. While learning to read in the content areas, students learn academic language skills through listening, talking, reading, and writing. The variety of strategies and activities included in CALLA (which, ironically, means "keep quiet" in Spanish) promotes development of both basic interpersonal communication skills and cognitive academic language proficiency.

Researchers (Chamot, Dale, O'Malley, & Spanos, 1992) compared ESL math students who received extensive instruction through CALLA with a control group. They found that students in high implementation classrooms performed better on measures of problem solving and mentioned the use of metacognitive strategies more frequently.

## How Can We Know Which Programs Serve English Learners Best?

Claiming that any one program for English learners has research-based merits that far exceed any other program would, at this point, be far from prudent. In their review of research on English-language learning reported in a National Research Council study, August and Hakuta (1997) argue that policy decisions with regard to educating English-language learners have been based on a "paucity of research and a predominance of politics" (p. 23). Several issues have often inflamed the debate over English-language instruction: the pursuit of "affirmative ethnicity" through bilingual education, the establishment of English as the official language of the United States, and national immigration policies. "When ably used by politicians who wish to define themselves to voters or by the media when they wish to create controversy," write August and Hakuta (1997), "the educational debate over how best to teach language-minority students is over-whelmed by these controversies" (p. 14).

A review of more than 30 empirical studies (August & Hakuta, 1997) whose purpose had been to verify school and classroom practices promoting effective English-language learning from elementary through high school gave little firm evidence in the form of student outcomes supporting any single instructional feature or practice. The review did suggest the importance of key attributes contributing to classrooms and schools whose English-language learning instruction worked. Evidence supported a spectrum of effective school attributes, among which were the following:

- a supportive school-wide climate;
- solid leadership in planning, coordinating, and administering programs;
- customized learning environments to reflect classroom contexts;
- use of native language and culture (but no clear answer to questions about the role that native language and culture should have in English-language learning);
- a balance of both basic and higher order skill instruction;
- direct instruction in skills;
- student-directed activities;
- strategies that enhance understanding;
- opportunities for practice, discussion, and review;
- organized, purposeful, and frequent student assessment;
- staff development for all teachers; and
- parent-school involvement.

Over the past decades, increasing numbers of schools and districts have looked to research on effective schools to guide their reform efforts. About 15% of the nation's school districts use attributes of effective schools, like those described above, to design their programs, including English-language learner instruction.

Extensive research is needed on a wide range of critical questions and programs to help us make more informed decisions about the best practices for English learners. Fortunately, August and Hakuta (1997) compiled a comprehensive summary of work completed by a National Research Council committee charged with the development of a research agenda to improve schooling for limited-English-proficient and bilingual students. The committee identified the following research priorities of particular importance to classroom teachers:

- What programs work and under what conditions?
- What are the characteristics of effective practice with English learners?
- What role does level of proficiency in English play in content area learning?
- What, if any, modifications in language use could teachers make that would make complex subject matter more accessible to English learners?
- What practices are most effective for students who have had limited prior formal schooling before entering middle or secondary school?

- What factors contribute to students' continued classification as English learners even after numerous years in U.S. schools? How can we better meet their English-language development needs?
- How do English-language learners affect content area teachers and their classrooms?
- What English literacy instructional program or approach is best for children of different ages, for those with different native languages, for those whose native language is not written, or for those whose parents are not literate in English?
- How do teachers' attribution of status to a language affect their instructional work?

Beyond these important research questions, Hakuta and his associates (Hakuta, Butler, & Witt, 2000) recognize that we need to know more about how long it takes English learners to learn basic oral English skills and how long it takes them to learn sufficient academic English to no longer be handicapped in classrooms without specially designed instruction for their language needs.

The National Clearinghouse for Bilingual Education (NCBE) maintains an online resource (*www.ncbe.gwu.edu/index.htm*) for research and classroom strategies related to teaching English language learners. NCBE is funded by the U.S. Department of Education's Office of Bilingual Education and Minority Languages Affairs whose purpose is to collect, analyze, and disseminate information about effective education for linguistically and culturally diverse learners.

Although the problems that teachers face in classrooms with increasing numbers of English learners are often complex, we have many promising strategies to make English-language learning more efficient and effective. With insistence from educators that practices be based on careful research, we can over time increase the number of strategies available to teachers, our understanding of how those strategies work, and our skills in using them with English learners at different stages of proficiency. There are no easy answers to educating English learners, but we must continue to ask provocative questions that promote further inquiry and discovery.

## DOUBLE-ENTRY JOURNAL: After Reading

Revisit your DEJ written before reading this chapter. How would you revise your approach to those English-speaking students who were at least a couple of grades behind in their reading? In what ways would you modify or amplify your approach to English learners in your content area class?

 Now go to the Double-Entry Journal for Chapter 9 on our Companion Website at www.prenhall.com/unrau to fill out your journal entry.

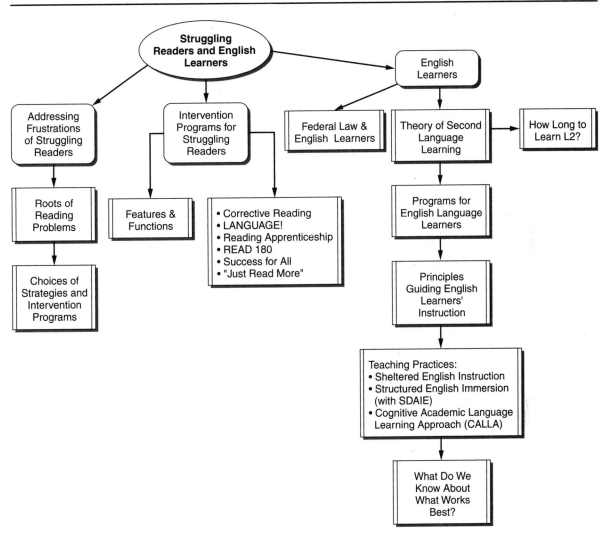

```
                    ┌─────────────────┐
                    │   Struggling    │
                    │ Readers and English │────────────────┐
                    │    Learners     │                    │
                    └─────────────────┘                    ▼
                      │         │                    ┌──────────┐
                      │         │                    │ English  │
                      ▼         ▼                    │ Learners │
```

Struggling Readers and English Learners

- English Learners

Addressing Frustrations of Struggling Readers

Intervention Programs for Struggling Readers

Federal Law & English Learners

Theory of Second Language Learning

How Long to Learn L2?

Roots of Reading Problems

Features & Functions

- Corrective Reading
- LANGUAGE!
- Reading Apprenticeship
- READ 180
- Success for All
- "Just Read More"

Programs for English Language Learners

Choices of Strategies and Intervention Programs

Principles Guiding English Learners' Instruction

Teaching Practices:
- Sheltered English Instruction
- Structured English Immersion (with SDAIE)
- Cognitive Academic Language Learning Approach (CALLA)

What Do We Know About What Works Best?

For exercises to clarify your understanding of chapter content, visit the self-assessments for Chapter 9 on our Companion Website at www.prenhall.com/unrau

# References

Adams, G. L., & Engelmann, S. (1996). *Research on Direct Instruction: 25 years beyond DISTAR*. Seattle, WA: Educational Achievement Systems.

Allen, J. (1995). *It's never too late: Leading adolescents to lifelong literacy*. Portsmouth, NH: Heinemann.

Allington, R. L. (2001). *What really matters for struggling readers: Designing research-based programs*. New York: Longman.

August, D., & Hakuta, K. (1997). *Improving schooling for language-minority children: A research agenda*. Washington, DC: National Academy Press.

Battin-Pearson, S., Newcomb, M. D., Abbott, R., Hill, K., Catalano, R. F., & Hawkins, J. D. (2000). Predictors of early high school dropout: A test of five theories. *Journal of Educational Psychology, 92*(3), 568–582.

Beck, I., Perfetti, C. A., & McKeown, M. G. (1982). Effects of long-term vocabulary instruction on lexical access and reading comprehension. *Journal of Educational Psychology, 74*, 506–521.

Blasewitz, R. B., & Taylor, R. (1999). Attacking literacy with technology in an urban setting. *Middle School Journal, 31*(3), 33–39.

Brown, A. L., & Palincsar, A. S. (1982). Inducing strategic learning from texts by means of informed, self-control training. *Topics in Learning and Learning Disabilities, 2* (1), 1–17.

California Department of Education. (1998). *English-Language Arts content standards for California public schools, K–12*. Sacramento, CA: CDE Press.

Carnegie Council on Adolescent Development. (1989). *Turning points: Preparing American youth for the 21st century*. New York: Carnegie Corporation of New York.

Casteneda v. Pickard, 648 F .2D 989 (5th cir., 1981).

Chamot, A. U. (1995). Learning strategies in listening comprehension: Theory and research. In D. Mendelsohn & J. Rubin (Eds.), *The theory and practice of listening comprehension for the second language learner* (pp. 13–26). San Diego, CA: Dominie Press.

Chamot, A. U., Barnhardt, S., El-Dinary, P. B., & Robbins, J. (1999). *The learning strategies handbook*. White Plains, NY: Addison Wesley Longman.

Chamot, A. U., Dale, M., O'Malley, J. M., & Spanos, G. (1992). Learning and problem solving strategies of ESL students. *Bilingual Research Journal, 16* (3–4): 1–33.

Chamot, A. U., Keatley, C., & Mazur, A. (1999). Literacy development in adolescent English language learners: Project Accelerated Literacy (PAL). Paper presented at the 1999 Annual Meeting of the American Educational Research Association, Montreal, Canada.

Chamot, A. U., & O'Malley, J. M. (1994). Instructional approaches and teaching procedures. In K. Spangenberg-Urbschat & R. Pritchard (Eds.), *Kids come in all languages: Reading instruction for ESL students* (pp. 82–107). Newark, DE: International Reading Association.

Collier, V. (1987). Age and rate of acquisition of second language for academic purposes. *TESOL Quarterly, 21*, 617–641.

Cummins, J. (1981). Immigrant second language learning. *Applied Linguistics, 11*, 132–149.

Cummins, J. (1984). *Bilingualism and special education: Issues in assessment and pedagogy*. Clevedon, UK: Multilingual Matters.

*Educating English learners for the twenty-first century* (1999). Sacramento,CA: California Department of Education.

Englemann, S., Carnine, L., Johnson, G., Hanner, S., Osborn, S., & Haddox, P. (1998). *Corrective reading: Decoding and corrective reading: Comprehension*. Columbus, OH: SRA/McGraw.

40 Percent in NY are foreign-born, study finds. (2000, July 24). *New York Times,* p. A18.

Gersten, R., Woodward, J., & Darch, C. (1986). Direct instruction: A research-based approach to curriculum design and teaching. *Exceptional Children, 53*, 17–31.

Greene, J. F. (1996). Middle and high school students: Effects of an individualized structured language curriculum. *Annals of Dyslexia, 46*, 97–121.

Greene, J. F. (1998, Spring/Summer). Another chance: Help for older students with limited literacy. *American Educator, 22,* 74–79.

Grossen, B. (n.d.). *The research base for Corrective Reading, SRA.* Columbus, OH: SRA/McGraw-Hill.

Grossen, B. (1998). C. M. Goethe Middle School: An evidence-based middle school model. Retrieved July 6, 2001 from World Wide Web: *http://www.higherscores.org.*

Grossen, B. (2000). BIG gets largest test gains in state for low performing school. *Higher Performing Schools.* Retrieved July 6, 2001, from *http://www.higherscores.org.*

Hakuta, K. Butler, Y. G., & Witt, D. (2000). *How long does it take English learners to attain proficiency?* University of California Linguistic Minority Research Institute Policy Report 2000–1. Santa Barbara, CA: UC Linguistic Minority Research Institute.

Hasselbring, T. (1991). Improving education through technology: Barriers and recommendations. *Preventing School Failure, 35,* 33–37.

Hurley, E., Chamberlain, A., Slavin, R., & Madden, N. (2001). Effects of Success for All on TAAS reading scores: A Texas statewide evaluation. *Phi Delta Kappa, 82*(10), 750–756.

Jackson, A., & Davis, G. (2000). *Turning points 2000: Educating adolescents in the 21$^{st}$ century.* New York: Teachers College Press.

Jordan, M., Jensen, R., & Greenleaf, C. (2001). "Amidst Familial Gatherings": Reading Apprenticeship in the middle school classroom. *Voices from the Middle, 4*(8), 15–24.

Kaméenui, E. J., & Carnine, D. W. (1998). *Effective teaching strategies that accommodate diverse learners.* Upper Saddle River, NJ: Merrill.

Klenk, L., & Kibby, M. W. (2000). Re-mediating reading difficulties: Appraising the past, reconciling the present, constructing the future. In M. Kamil, P. Mosenthal, P. D. Pearson, & R. Barr (Eds.), *Handbook of reading research* (Vol. III, pp. 667–690). Mahwah, NJ: Erlbaum.

Kozloff, M., LaNunziata, L., Cowardin, J., & Bessellieu, F. B. (2000). Direct instruction: Its contributions to high school achievement. Retrieved July 14, 2001, from *http://www.uncwil.edu/people/kozloffm/dihighschool.html.*

Krashen, S. (1981). *Second language acquisition and second language learning.* London: Pergamon Press.

Krashen, S. (1995). Bilingual education and second language acquisition theory. In D. B. Durkin (Ed.), *Language issues: Reading for teachers* (pp. 90–115). White Plains, NY: Longman.

Lambert, B. (2000, July 24). 40 Percent in NY are foreign born, study finds. *New York Times,* p. A18.

Lau v. Nichols, 414 US 563 (1974).

Madden, N. A., Slavin, R. E., Karweit, N. L., Dolan, L. J., & Wasik, B. A. (1993). Success for All: Longitudinal effects of a restructuring program for inner-city elementary schools. *American Educational Research Journal, 30,* 123–148.

McQuillan, J. (1998). *The literacy crisis: False claims, real solutions.* Portsmouth, NH: Heinemann.

MetaMetrics (2000). The Lexile framework for reading. Durham, NC: MetaMetrics, Inc. Retrieved July 7, 2002, from *http://lexile.com.*

Mitchell, D., Destino, T., & Karam, R. (1997). *Evaluation of English language development programs in the Santa Ana Unified School District: A report on data system reliability and statistical modeling of program impacts.* University of California, Riverside: California Educational Research Cooperative. Available on *http://cerc.ucr.edu/publications.*

Moats, L. C. (2001). When older students can't read. *Educational Leadership, 58,* 36–40.

National Assessment of Educational Progress. (1999). *Reading report card for the nation and the states.* Washington, DC: U.S. Department of Education.

New York State Education Department (1997). *English Language Arts resource guide.* Retrieved September 1, 2002, from *http://www.nysed.gov.*

Peterson, C., Caverly, D., Nicholson, S., O'Neal, S., & Cusenbary, S. (2000). *Building reading proficiency at the secondary level: A guide to resources.* Austin, TX: Southwest Educational Development Laboratory.

Sahagun, L. (2000, March 27). School strains under effort to end social promotion. *Los Angeles Times*, p. A1.

Samuels, S. J. (1994a). Word recognition. In R. B. Ruddell, M. R. Ruddell, & H. Singer (Eds.), *Theoretical models and processes of reading* (4th ed., pp. 359–380). Newark, DE: International Reading Association.

Samuels, S. J. (1994b). Toward a theory of automatic information processing in reading, revised. In R. B. Ruddell, M. R. Ruddell, & H. Singer (Eds.), *Theoretical models and processes of reading* (4th ed., pp. 816–837). Newark, DE: International Reading Association.

Schifini, A. (1994). Language, literacy, and content instruction: Strategies for teachers. In K. Spangenberg-Urbschat & R. Pritchard (Eds.), *Kids come in all languages: Reading instruction for ESL students* (pp. 158–179). Newark, DE: International Reading Association.

Schoenbach, R., Greenleaf, C., Cziko, C., & Hurwitz, L. (1999). *Reading for understanding: A guide to improving reading in middle and high school classrooms.* San Francisco: Jossey-Bass.

Slavin, R. E., Madden, N. A., Dolan, L. J., & Wasik, B. A. (1996a). *Every child, every school: Success for All.* Newbury Park, CA: Corwin.

Slavin, R. E., Madden, N. A., Dolan, L. J., Wasik, B. A., Ross, S. M., Smith, L. J., & Dianda, M. (1996b). Success for All: A summary of research. *Journal of Education for Students Placed at Risk, 1,* 41–76.

Stanovich, K. E. (1986). Matthew effects in reading: Some consequences of individual differences in the acquisition of literacy. *Reading Research Quarterly, 21,* 360–406.

Stephens, M. A. (1993). *Developing and implementing a curriculum and instructional program to improve reading achievement of middle-grade students with learning disabilities in a rural school district.* Unpublished doctoral dissertation, Nova University, Ft. Lauderdale, Florida.

Taylor, R., & Sulzer, D. (1997). *Literacy program report.* Orange County Public Schools, Orlando, FL.

Zhao, Y. (2002, August 5). Waves of pupils lacking English strain schools. *New York Times,* pp. A1, A11.

# 10 FOCUSING ON MOTIVATION TO READ CONTENT AREA TEXTS*

After reading Chapter 10, you should be able to answer the following questions:

1. How do personal identity, expectations, and self-efficacy contribute to developing an intention to read?

2. What kinds of goal orientations and task values can students adopt and which are more likely to heighten motivation to learn?

3. What can be done to enhance students' connections with the texts available to them?

4. What's the connection between teacher engagement and student engagement?

---

*This chapter took its inspiration from a chapter that Robert Ruddell and I wrote (Ruddell & Unrau, 1997). That chapter was published in *Reading Engagement,* a volume edited by John Guthrie and Allan Wigfield. Ruddell, Guthrie, and Wigfield's ideas contributed to this chapter's structure and content.

5. What elements could you include in an achievement-related instructional program that are likely to affect student motivation to read?

6. How can teachers influence motivation through the classroom community, through an assessment and reward system, and through autonomy support?

---

**DOUBLE-ENTRY JOURNAL: Before Reading**

Before you read beyond this sentence, write down all the goals and reasons you can that could possibly explain why you would read this chapter.

 Now go to the Double-Entry Journal for Chapter 10 on our Companion Website at www.prenhall.com/unrau to fill out your journal entry.

---

## MS. HAWTHORNE'S FRUSTRATION

At one low point during her first year at Jefferson Middle School, Ms. Hawthorne asked her eighth-grade social studies students how many of them completed their homework assignment to read eight pages about the origins of the American Civil War for today's lesson. The day's lesson activity depended upon students' having done their reading. In her class of 29, 13 students raised their hands. Ms. Hawthorne faced a dilemma, perhaps a civil war of her own. How could she go ahead with her lesson activity knowing that more than half the students had not read the section of the book they needed to know to engage productively in the activity?

Thinking she was going to have to delay an investigation of the Civil War's causes to investigate the causes of her own students' lack of responsibility, Ms. Hawthorne asked them why they hadn't done their reading.

"It was soooooo boring," one student groaned.

"I couldn't understand it," said another. "There were too many words I didn't know, so I just stopped."

"I just couldn't get around to it," another coolly dropped.

Clearly, Ms. Hawthorne saw signs of disengagement and frustration.

Ms. Hawthorne's battle is repeated thousands of times every day in classrooms all over America. Some teachers faced with this frustration respond to their students' resistance, malaise, or laziness by trying to find activities that will get them engaged. They try games, which sometimes help. They resort to videos, which can augment instruction. They do a round-robin reading in class that takes the whole period and that few students follow. So they summarize and review the reading's content. Or they lecture. In one way or another, they retreat from requiring that students read the assigned work on their own. But none of these methods directly helps students learn to read texts effectively or learn from them.

When Ms. Hawthorne asked her colleagues what they did, several said the sensible thing to do was just to lecture and have students take notes. Or, they suggested, have students do their reading in class. Other teachers believed that a more sensible approach is to tell students that all texts are not equally exciting. Reading *Seventeen, Road and Track,* an article on Eminem, or Harry Potter's latest adventure is likely to be more immediately interesting than reading the history, science, or English text. However, learning to read important texts directly relates to students' future welfare. So, some argue (Jago, 2000), teachers must insist that students have a responsibility to read about the history of the American Civil War, the functions of DNA, and the adventures of Huckleberry Finn.

Placing these demands on students sounds entirely reasonable. Whether or not students will join our side in the struggle to read and learn more effectively when given these demands is, unfortunately, not always predictable. However, we can go beyond clarifying that students have obligations to learn and demanding that they do so.

As teachers, we all learn quite early on that a substantial canyon too often lies between students' mastering skills and applying them to learn. Inertly sitting on one side of the canyon with disengaged skills and knowledge, students may have little disposition to get to the other side of the canyon to use what they know and can do to discover new territory, new knowledge. Far too often middle and high school teachers tell me that in some of their classes they can't get more than 1 out of 4 students to read assignments they give for homework. These are assignments given to disengaged students who can read but are not motivated to do so.

As teachers, we also learn that not being motivated to read is most often part of a larger motivational quandary. It's not just reading that students are not motivated to do. Often it's learning in general or doing any school work. In fact, we have evidence that levels of motivation decline as students progress from elementary to middle school and on to high school (Sethi, Drake, Dialdin, & Lepper, 1995).

Motivation lies at the heart of classroom instruction (Good & Brophy, 2000). When we look at what's happening in a classroom, motivation is one factor we never want to overlook. Some classrooms buzz with learning. In others, some students are only a heartbeat or two from death. The clock's countdown is their sole life support.

When asking questions about students' motivation, we are asking about what got them fired up in the first place, which direction they are headed, how hard they will work to get there, and how long they are likely to go at it. What moves students, like Ms. Hawthorne's, to read? How might their skills as readers grow? What kinds of activities might be used in her social studies classes to promote literacy engagement?

## FACTORS AFFECTING MOTIVATION TO READ

We are far more likely to understand why our students want to read or decide not to read if we look upon their motivation as a system or network of interacting factors, not any single cause (Alderman, 1999). Many factors contribute to a student's engagement in reading and learning. While some are more directly and more immediately teacher-controlled or teacher-influenced, other factors, mostly under stu-

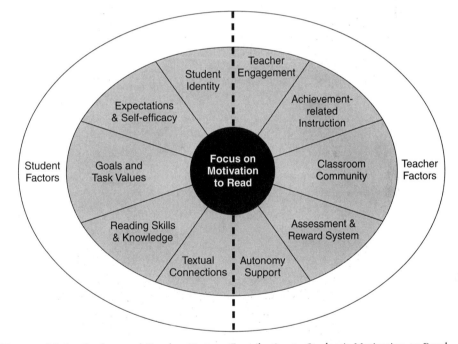

**FIGURE 10.1**   Student and Teacher Factors Contributing to Student's Motivation to Read.

dent control, may be only indirectly affected through our decisions and behavior. And, although we might like the situation to be otherwise, some student factors are probably completely independent of our classroom decisions.

Using an image to help us render, understand, and recollect motivational factors, we can envision the eye as a metaphor for focusing motivation. In Figure 10.1, "Student and Teacher Factors Contributing to Student's Motivation to Read," the inner circle, the focus of motivation, may be seen as the pupil. Factors influencing the focus of motivation radiate out from the pupil and form a larger concentric circle around it, somewhat like the eye's iris. Perhaps this metaphor will help us see more clearly the complex array of features and processes that affect the intention to read.

# The Focus of Motivation

At the center of Figure 10.1 lies the *focus of motivation*. It may be compared to the eye's pupil focusing motivation not in response to light but in response to the confluence of many motivational factors that influence readers. This focus is the center point of the mind's intent, of its direction, purpose, and intensity when interacting with a learning environment. In describing the factors that influence the focus of motivation, we aspire to the ideal of the optimally self-regulated reader.

In the sections below, I'll describe and explain student and teacher motivational factors with the ultimate purpose of discovering what kinds of decisions a teacher could make to optimize motivation for reading. Student factors influencing motivation to read are on the left side of Figure 10.1. These include personal identity, expectations and self-efficacy, goals and task values, reading skills and knowledge, and textual connections. Teacher factors influencing motivation to read are on the right side of Figure 10.1. These include teacher engagement, achievement-related instruction, classroom community, assessment and reward system, and autonomy support. Although I've placed these motivational factors in two categories, they can and do interact with each other. For example, a teacher's assessment and reward system could influence a student's expectations and self-efficacy.

## Student Factors Contributing to Student's Motivation to Read

Student identity.    Adolescence is an extended period of self-exploration and self-discovery. As we know, middle and especially high school provides adolescents with several years to create and to find an identity. Most students spend these years exploring who they are and what they might become in a stage Erik Erikson (1968) labeled identity vs. role confusion. According to Erikson, core identity includes two aspects of self: a sense of self garnered from the integration of many selves or aspects of those selves that have been tried on, played out, rejected, or embraced and a sense of self as an organizing agency that enables self-representation.

*Self-schema.*    The first sense of self in past, present, and future arises from self-schema. Students access past, current, and future self-schemata as facets of their self-system (Markus & Nurius, 1986). Those lived, remembered, and possible selves influence each student's behavior and thus motivation. Images of the self shape the choices made, the actions carried out, and the possibilities pursued or resisted. Garcia and Pintrich (1994) demonstrated that self-schemata contribute to a student's desire to develop literacy skills or to a diligent avoidance of that project. Students can be torn by tension over who they are becoming. One's self-schema can generate an identity perceived by ourselves and others in a range from loathed to loved, failed to fulfilled, incompetent to incomparable.

An example will illustrate the self-schema's motivational strength. Jimmy Santiago Baca is a poet and a teacher who discovered the power of literacy in prison. He went on to win an American Book Award and found Black Mesa Enterprises, an organization that provides young people with alternatives to violence through a language-centered community. However, he struggled with a self-schema that profoundly rejected literacy before becoming a writer. While he was in jail, Jimmy confronted a self-schema that announced:

Sissies read books. You couldn't do *anything* with a book. You couldn't fix a '57 Chevy with a book. You couldn't take money from some hustler with a book. You couldn't convince or persuade anybody with a book. Books were in the way. And not only that, they were the great enemy. Books were where you found the pain. Books were where you found the shame, and books were where you found the lies that my grandparents had been lazy Mexicans and that I was no good, that I couldn't be as good as the next person. *That's* what was in books. So why should I go open a book and give myself all this pain? I didn't *need* that. I would rather go numb with a good bottle of tequila.

However, literacy, the power of words, and another possible self pulled him into what he calls "the fiercest typhoon I have ever been in and from which I have never escaped. I have continually swirled like a leaf" (Moyer, 1995, pp. 35–36).

***Ego-identity.*** The second organizing agency of our identity Erikson (1968) referred to as ego-identity, the "actually attained but forever-to-be-revised sense of reality of the Self within social reality" (p. 211). Erikson's conception of identity is tied to his theory of identity formation through the life cycle. Students' lives can be viewed as psycho-histories that, if examined closely, reveal the outcome of the various crises through which they have passed in home, community, and school on their way to manifesting their current role and identity as a student.

Viewing a student as an individual passing through a "forever-to-be-revised sense of reality of the Self" provides us with a perspective that is both practical and theoretically powerful. The concept of identity organizes selves in a social environment, whether school or home, and establishes a composite of sustainable self-impressions that provides an internal, personal core of self-reference.

The concept of identity also enables us to understand the motivation of students-as-readers at a deeper level. Engaged and responsive teachers are likely to recognize that their students' identities, and thus their students' motives for learning, are shaped by crises of identity before and during schooling as well as by identifications with family, community, and cultural figures.

The sociocultural orientations that students bring to school influence their sense of membership and style of school involvement (Newmann, 1992). Students with little hope that academic success will eventuate in vocational or professional success are unlikely to invest energy in a school's vision of their future. Others, who believe that working hard in school will pay off in the realization of personal and professional dreams, are far more likely to participate in a school's cultural and curricular programs.

Knowing the connection between identity and school performance, teachers understand that many young people, especially those attending inner-city schools, may perceive themselves excluded from the school's culture and seek identity affirmation and affiliation elsewhere, such as in gangs or on the streets (Heath & McLaughlin, 1993). While a sense of school membership is the basis for educational engagement (Wehlage et al., 1989), some students may disidentify with student roles and academic expectations as early as the middle school years. Gang life may be their source of socialization and identity (Vigil, 1993). A "negative" identity, in comparison to community norms, could be more assuring to these adolescents than a sense of having no identity at all. Even a culture of violence and drugs provides meaning to those who have not found it elsewhere. However, some more fortunate at-risk students may discover programs that affirm a positive identity in the schools, such as community service programs, or a teacher who builds bridges to a more promising vision of life.

On occasion, a student alienated from both home and school finds solace in reading. Such was the case for Robin, a high school drop-out who became one of my credential students striving to become a teacher.

By the time that I dropped out of school in the tenth grade, I had attended 6 high schools in 3 states. With the exception of one teacher, who had a profound impact on my life, virtually nothing that occurred within the walls of these schools influenced me in a significant manner. Throughout my formal education, I got to experience several different types of being "the Other." . . . Because we moved around so much, we put little effort into making a connection with our peers after the second or third grade. Then, in a classic case of being in the wrong place at the wrong time, my sibling and I got to enjoy the experience of being bused out of Boston (to school) in the mid-to-late 1970s.

Ironically, I believe that riding buses may have had the most significant impact on the development of my personal literacies and my identity. I didn't realize it at the time, but those hours spent traveling to and from my dysfunctional, overcrowded home and the hostile environment of my school were the only real moments of peace and solitude that I had. How did I ever find peace and solitude on a crowded bus? I read.

Although attracted and attached to being a "nihilistic punk rocker," Robin read her way into "testing out new identities to replace the identity with which I was no longer comfortable." Her discovery of characters struggling with alienation and entrapment in stifling identities helped her find a voice to articulate her own dilemmas. Unfortunately, for many students deeply alienated from home and school, reading is not likely to be the route to self-discovery.

Expectations and self-efficacy.    Perceptions of ability and the expectations they trigger constitute major factors in current views of motivation. Expectations that shape students' behavior come in two main categories: self-expectations and teacher expectations. However, the expectations of teachers may become self-expectations, as Good and Brophy (2000) suggest. We are going to look into both kinds.

*Self-expectation,* what a student expects of his own behavior, is often shaped by the expectations of others, especially teachers. Covington (1992) has explored the relationships between ability attributions and expectations. He has noted that students' personal expectations influence their level of aspiration. That level of aspiration, in turn, may be affected by the expectations of others, especially teachers in school settings.

It is of critical importance that teachers communicate positive beliefs and attributions to young learners. We know that children achieve at a higher level in classrooms where teachers expect all children to learn (Stipek, 1993). From studies of teachers and their students, we know a strong relationship exists between a teacher's beliefs about her own ability to teach students and the students' beliefs about their own abilities and chances for success (Midgley, Feldlaufer, & Eccles, 1989). Students who had high-efficacy teachers, teachers who were task-oriented and believed their efforts would result in incremental student growth, became significantly more positive (or demonstrated less negative change) compared to students who had low-efficacy teachers and who developed more negative beliefs during the school year.

What we believe we are capable of doing or learning constitutes our ***self-efficacy.*** A student's self-efficacy is one predictor of her motivation for engaging in reading (Schunk & Zimmermann, 1997). Accordingly, a student with high self-efficacy will work harder, longer, and more willingly than one with low self-efficacy. Furthermore, Bandura (1986) found that self-efficacy judgments influence not only what activities a student will undertake and what will be avoided but also the amount of effort and time that students will expend in the pursuit of the activity.

Studies of self-efficacy are frequently linked to the attribution theory which had its origins in the study of what people think causes behavior to occur (Schunk, 1994). A teacher like Ms. Hawthorne, who believes that continued effort will lead to student success, is more likely to design lessons that provide her students with knowledge of strategies and opportunities to apply and evaluate their use. Likewise, students who believe that effort applied over time will lead to incremental improvements in such things as reading and writing are likely to persist in mastering challenges.

Alderman (1999) suggests several methods for acknowledging your students' competency and developing self-efficacy.

- ◆ When students do think-alouds, you can direct attention to effective strategies they use to comprehend texts.
- ◆ As a teacher, you can use think-alouds to model how you make sense of difficult passages in your textbook.
- ◆ After identifying peer models who demonstrate effective strategy use and persistence in learning, you can ask these students (without inflaming competition) how they figured out the meaning of a difficult passage so that their problem-solving strategies become visible and, perhaps, capable of being emulated.
- ◆ You could also tell a story about how you solved or overcame a difficult reading and learning problem.

Self-efficacy can also be developed through goal setting and strategy instruction, both of which will be discussed in this chapter.

*Teacher expectations* can become self-fulfilling. If a teacher expects certain behaviors from a student, her behavior is likely to influence how her student behaves. Good and Brophy (2000) created a model to describe the process whereby a teacher's expectation evokes the expected student behavior:

1. At the start of the school year, a teacher develops expectations for each child's behavior and achievement.
2. Based on expectations for each student, the teacher behaves differently with each.
3. The teacher's behavior communicates expectations about how each student is to behave and perform.
4. This treatment is likely to affect students' self-concept, achievement motivation, and goal setting.
5. The teacher's expectations will get reinforced when students begin to conform to the teacher's expectations.
6. Eventually, this process influences student motivation and performance. High expectations for students will motivate them to perform at or near their potential; low expectations for students will result in students not performing as well as they might have if they were expected to do better.

According to Good and Brophy, self-fulfilling prophesies created through a teacher's expectations occur if and only if each aspect of their model is present. If, for example, a student rejects or resists the teacher's expectations, then the model's predictions would fail. When teaching, Ms. Hawthorne tries to monitor the expectations she develops for her students. She notes how those expectations influence her behavior toward them and pays special attention to negative expectations that crop up because they could adversely affect a student's motivation to achieve.

## Goals and task values

***Goals.*** Goals have both direction and intensity. The ***direction of a goal*** refers to its location in an instructional setting and the sequence of actions that need to take place to reach that goal. If Ms. Hawthorne's goal were to have all her students complete a reading assignment for homework, her students could take a number of different actions, like taking the book home for study, that would move them in the direction of reaching the goal. If students balk or resist aligning with Ms. Hawthorne's goal direction because they refuse to adopt the goal or because students have other goals that are more important to them, she is going to have a very long day.

Besides students' accepting the direction of the goal, they also need to be willing to work hard enough to attain the goal. That's the goal intensity variable. A reader's ***goal intensity,*** the energy allocated for specific goal achievement, varies. Many factors affect goal intensity: the value placed on the goal, the difficulty of reaching the goal, the resources that can be activated to achieve the goal, the goal-seeker's level of self-confidence, and quite a few other factors that we'll look at later in this chapter. If students adopt the goal and are willing to make the effort needed to achieve it, Ms. Hawthorne is more likely to find significant satisfaction in her day's work.

If you value reading this text and understanding it, if you perceive the goal as within your reach, if you think you have the resources (such as background knowledge and reading skills) to achieve the goal, if you're feeling confident about your abilities in relation to the goal's attainment, then you're likely to be a motivated reader.

Do different goal orientations make a difference in student achievement? To answer that question, we'll first need to explore achievement goals and the difference between what motivational psychologists call mastery goals and performance goals. If a student asks herself whether or not her reading of a book is leading toward her becoming a more competent student or merely toward the demonstration of her superior skills in comparison to her classmates, she is, according to Nicholls (1984), questioning ***achievement goals.*** Achievement goal theory stresses the engagement of the learner in selecting, structuring, and making sense of achievement experience.

Meece (1994) points out that research has focused on two kinds of achievement goals: ***mastery, learning, or task-oriented goals*** and ***performance or ego-oriented goals.*** Those seeking learning goals are intrinsically motivated to acquire knowledge and skills that lead to their becoming more competent. A student seeking to master an understanding of DNA to satisfy her curiosity exemplifies learning goals. Those pursuing performance goals are eager to seek opportunities to demonstrate their skills or knowledge in a competitive, public arena. A student would be manifesting performance or ego-oriented goals if she were motivated to read her stories to her classmates primarily to show others her skills as a storyteller.

Many researchers (Ames, 1992; Dweck & Leggett, 1988) believed that a learning or mastery goal orientation yields multiple benefits that include higher levels of interest, self-efficacy, persistence, and performance. They also believed that performance goal orientations, in contrast, generated fewer benefits in terms of motivation, strategy use, and outcome. This would especially be the case if a student were only concerned with performing to outdo his classmates and had little concern for mastery.

But couldn't a student avoid performance opportunities as well as seek them? And couldn't that make a difference with regard to the impact of performance goals on behavior and learning? Several researchers (Elliot, 1997; Pintrich, 2000a, 2000b) have found evidence for different directions and intensities of motivation arising from what they call **approach performance goals** and **avoidance performance goals.** If a student were focused on approach performance goals, he would want to perform in class to show others his skills, perhaps to show them off in order to impress his classmates with his accomplishments. If, however, he were focused on avoidance performance goals, he would attempt to avoid appearing incompetent, ignorant, or foolish. That avoidance orientation would most likely result in his avoiding opportunities to read his stories to classmates because he would fear their disapproval or disdain.

If students seek to do well in comparison to others and also embrace mastery goals, argues Pintrich (2000b), they would be adopting an orientation at least as healthy and productive as those students adopting only mastery goals. Researchers (Hidi & Harackiewicz, 2000) have found that students influenced by both performance *and* mastery goals achieved at higher levels than students influenced by only one or the other goal orientation. These findings suggest that students' motivation to read and learn could be heightened through the positive interaction of mastery and performance goals. Learning about something that will help a reader to master a valued task, such as designing an electric car, while demonstrating to friends how well she reads can occur simultaneously among teenagers.

What might move a student toward one or the other orientation? Perceptions of personal ability constitute one critical factor influencing patterns of achievement (Meece, 1994). If students believe they can become better readers by making an effort, they are more likely to embrace a mastery goal orientation. They see themselves as able to improve by degrees over time through making an effort to master challenging tasks. A student who, over time, acquires knowledge and skills that lead to perceptions of incremental growth in competency exemplifies a mastery orientation. Through making that effort to acquire knowledge and skills, the student's feelings of self-worth and competence are likely to increase.

Learners who adopt an ego or performance orientation look upon their abilities as more or less stable or fixed capacities that they judge in comparison to others, such as their colleagues, peers, or classmates. If, for example, a student must make more of an effort, these ego or performance-oriented learners judge that classmate as having less ability when the outcomes are similar. Performance-oriented learners become preoccupied with ability and see it as basic to success in school performance. In an illustrative Calvin and Hobbes cartoon, Calvin, who appears to embrace performance goals, sees that Susie is hitting the books and asks her, "What are you doing? Homework?" To that question, a studious looking Susie, who seeks to master knowledge, replies, "I wasn't sure I understood this chapter, so I reviewed my notes from the last chapter and now I'm rereading this." In response to Susie's mastery oriented explanation, Calvin exclaims, "You do all that **work**?!" He then walks out of the cartoon box saying, "Huh! I used to think you were smart."

Among children, these goal orientations appear to result, at least in part, from their internalizing parental perspectives, especially the mother's view, of effort and ability in learning (Ames & Archer, 1987). But school learning environments have also been found to shape students' goal orientations. Mastery goal states can be induced in students if teachers create environments that accentuate self-improvement, discovery, engagement in meaningful tasks, and practicality while diminishing the importance of competition, demonstration of intellectual skills, outperforming others, and public evaluative comparisons (Ames, 1992; Hagen & Weinstein, 1995). Influential teachers, teachers who embrace a mastery or task orientation toward learning not only build such environments in their classrooms but also serve as models of learning with whom students can identify as they build their identity as students. Like "beating the odds" teachers we met in the first chapter of this book (Langer, 2001), these teachers provide challenging and meaningful learning goals that engage their students until they understand core concepts and are ready to apply them. Once their students master core concepts, these teachers extend understanding by showing students how newly conquered concepts are interconnected with other domains of knowledge, even across disciplines. However, mastery-oriented teachers would also be wise to acknowledge that nurturing student interests as well as providing opportunities and rewards for performance may be critically important for less motivated readers whose mastery orientation needs to be cultivated and developed over time.

Here we return to the influence of the teacher's expectations on students, especially in relation to the teacher's degree of emphasis on task/mastery goals. When looking at the differences in students' strategy-use patterns in high- and low-mastery classes, Meece (1994) found significant differences between teachers' expectations for students. In the high-mastery classes, teachers expected students to understand, apply, and make sense of their learning while in low-mastery classes students spent more time memorizing information and had few opportunities to actively construct meaning or apply their learning in new situations. Such examples illustrate how teachers' expectations can potentially shape students' literacy performance. Teachers can promote literacy engagement by emphasizing a mastery orientation that stresses conceptual understanding, provides for collaborative learning, minimizes social competition, and allows students to participate in curricular decision making.

For example, at Foshay High School in Los Angeles, Myra LeBendig pushed for conceptual understanding through whole-class discussion (Langer, 2001). She taught her students how to work and learn in a community that depended upon discussion to exchange, explore, clarify, and shape ideas. She challenged students to understand works like Ellison's *Invisible Man* from multiple perspectives and to connect those perspectives with their own ethnicity and identity. As she taught for understanding, she urged her students to make sense of literary works they read and apply what they learned to their own lives.

Such examples illustrate how teachers' expectations can potentially shape students' literacy performance. However, as Hidi and Harackiewicz (2000) point out, teachers seeking to motivate the academically unmotivated need to recognize that mastery and performance goals interact and develop hand-in-hand over time. Students who lack mastery goals for academic success may need some forms of external intervention and reward on the road to developing sustained interests and task-directed goals.

*Task values.* Wigfield and his associates (Wigfield, 1994; Wigfield & Eccles, 1992) have identified and investigated a number of interacting components that make up an individual's perception of task values. These components include the following:

- attainment value (or the importance a learner attributes to a task),
- intrinsic interest value (or the task's subjective interest to a learner),
- utility value (or the usefulness of a task in light of a learner's future goals), and
- the cost of success (or the "down side" of accomplishing a task, such as anxiety arousal).

He and his colleagues (Meece, Wigfield, & Eccles, 1990) have investigated the connections between the subjective value adolescents place on various activities and what choices they make with regard to the activities. He has found that students' subject task values predict their actual decisions to take certain courses. This discovery suggests, he believes, that if students claim to value reading, there is a greater likelihood that they would engage in that activity. Most students usually weigh the value of a task, such as a reading assignment, before undertaking it. Their appraisal of its worth helps them answer the question, "What will I get out of doing this specific reading task?" When asked what they valued most in their reading and language arts classes, middle school students preferred free reading time the most (Ivey & Broaddus, 2001).

Reading skills and knowledge. Reading skills and knowledge refers to cognitive processes and resources that enable a reader to undertake a reading task. These resources provide tools to accomplish the tasks for which readers are motivated. However, the equipment a reader brings to bear on a reading task will affect motivation as well. How well the resources and tools work to enable a reader to make sense of the texts she reads influences her motivation to continue reading—and to enjoy it—or to stop.

We have already explored in depth the reader's text-processing resources. Here, we can provide only a reminder of them. The cognitive model of reading that we explored included several key components and processes that enable us to read. To delve into the details of those components and how they work, please review Chapter 2.

The model consists of four major components:

1. A *sensory system* stimulated by external texts;
2. *cognitive processes* that include word recognition, long-term and working memory, construction of phrase and sentence sense, text building, and an internal text representation;
3. *metacognitive processes* that monitoring and control our cognitive processes; and
4. a *classroom context* wherein texts are read, interpreted, comprehended, discussed, analyzed, and evaluated.

When describing the model in Chapter 2, I magnified each component enabling us to look much more closely at how its parts contribute to the reading process as a whole. All the components, including a model of text interpretation in the classroom context, have been magnified to reveal their details and functions in Figures 2.4 and 2.8 in Chapter 2.

Ms. Hawthorne knows that her students' motivation can rise or fall based on her instructional decision making. If she asks students to complete reading assignments that are at the frustration level, their motivation is very likely going to take a serious hit. Even if she asks them to complete reading assignments at the instructional level and provides no support, her students are likely to struggle. Some may come through; many may not. So she has to be knowledgeable about the readability levels of texts she assigns to her students and the capacity of her students to process those texts successfully.

Ms. Hawthorne can enhance her students' motivation by making instructional decisions that take into account their text-processing resources. But to take those resources into account, Ms. Hawthorne needs to know what they are. She can discover a great deal of information about them by taking a diagnostic perspective. With that perspective, she can learn about the strengths and weaknesses of her students' cognitive and metacognitive processes as well as their knowledge of the classroom context and their ability to engage with it when interpreting texts.

Like all responsive, engaged teachers in whatever content area, Ms. Hawthorne plans to discover how well her students read. She has several means of assessing their reading. Many of these methods we already met in Chapter 3, "Assessing Readers and Their Texts." Among the assessment methods she might use are the following:

♦ *Student records.*   Most schools and districts require some battery of tests to monitor student academic development. Teachers may need assistance when interpreting these scores. Counselors, whose professional preparation usually includes training in diagnostic and achievement testing, can usually assist in interpretation of scores as teachers' needs for help arise.

♦ *Diagnostic testing.*   Many teachers administer some type of formal or informal reading test. Several of these are reviewed in Chapter 3. Among the informal measures are Individual Reading Inventories (IRI), Group Reading Inventories (GRI), Curriculum-Based Measurements (CBM), and Metacognitive Awareness of Reading Strategies Inventory (MARSI).

♦ *Student interviews and surveys.*   Helpful information about student's reading processes and strategies can be gained through discussions with students. An exemplar of such thoughtful discovery is Nancie Atwell's *In the Middle* (1998). In that book, she describes several methods for monitoring student reading, conducting reading conferences, developing reading self-evaluations, and running reading surveys. All of these approaches enabled her to learn more about how and why her students read.

◆ *Classroom observation.* Observing students' reading behavior frequently provides a wealth of information about their habits and tactics. That information can arise from many different classroom reading activities: observing students reading aloud or silently, listening to students talk with each other about their reading, noting how they negotiate meanings of texts during classroom discussions, and seeing how they write about what they've read.

## Textual connections

***Interesting texts.*** Guthrie and Wigfield (2000) define interesting texts as "single-authored works in which the text matches the topic interest and cognitive competency of the reader." As bees with flowers, so are students with interesting books: there's more buzz. Students spend more time reading these texts than those they find uninteresting. Furthermore, in a study of high school students, topic interest was positively related to quality of experience during reading and to quality of text learning (Schiefele, 1996). One of the hallmarks of successful Sustained Silent Reading programs is access to an abundance of high-interest books in classrooms (Pilgreen, 2000). By surveying students about their reading interests, more books with appeal can join classroom and school libraries. Matching texts to both students' interests and reading levels, as is done with programs like Reading Counts!, also promotes their motivation to read.

***Intrinsic "flow" state.*** If you have ever been completely absorbed or consumed by a sporting activity, like tennis, or by playing a musical instrument, you have experienced the "flow" of intrinsic motivation. According to Csikszentmihalyi (1990a, 1990b), motivation is closely related to ***autotelic experiences*** that are self-contained and self-rewarding. Autotelic experiences are not pursued for any future purpose or goal but for their intrinsic worth, their enjoyment. While autotelic comes from the Greek words *auto* (for self) and *teles* (for meaning), he has also referred to the autotelic experience as "flow," an optimal psychological experience that puts consciousness on a special level.

When readers experience a sense of "flow" while reading, they are enjoying the reading process as a self-justifying event. To experience this intrinsically rewarding "flow" while reading, readers must attain a balance between reading challenge and reading ability. Many students have experienced frustration when trying to read books that were too difficult for them to enjoy reading on their own. Many have also known profound boredom when trying to read texts that were too simplistic for them or of no interest. If students can discover an optimal balance between challenge and ability, they are likely to enter and enjoy more fully the flow of reading (Csikszentmihalyi, 1990b).

Ms. Hawthorne knows that reading she assigns in her course does not always evoke "flow" experience for her students. However, she mixes into her curriculum opportunities to read engaging historical narratives, biographies, or other informative texts more likely to consume students' attention and heighten their enthusiasm. She watches for moments in the present when she can bring to her students' awareness the intrinsic pleasure of reading and reliving moments in the past.

***Stance.*** In literacy studies, ***stance*** pertains to the perspective and orientation that a reader adopts toward a particular text. By guiding the reader's perspective and purpose, instructional stance influences a reader's motivation to read. Rosenblatt (1978) strongly influenced the field with her identification and elaboration of two stances: efferent and aesthetic. When adopting the ***efferent stance,*** the reader concentrates on ideas and concepts to be taken away from a text. When taking an ***aesthetic stance,*** the reader enters the text world through imagination and feeling so that attention is on what the reader is living through while engaged in the reading episode rather than on gathering information. When reading stories about people in times past, students can adopt an aesthetic stance and enter the "old fashioned" world created in their imaginations. Readers are more likely to experience the intrinsic enjoyment of flow and a deeper engagement with a text during aesthetic readings that draw readers into narrative and imagery.

These are not either-or stances; rather, they are on a continuum along which the degree of emphasis may change. To varying degrees, the reader can control stance. While progressing through a text, the teacher may encourage an instructional stance that guides readers toward an aesthetic or efferent engagement or an integration of both. For example, Ms. Hawthorne could ask her students to read *The Red Badge of Courage,* a novel by Stephen Crane about the American Civil War. When reading about the young soldier's first tastes of war, students could be encouraged to take an aesthetic stance by focusing on the sound and sense of bullets and smoke, the images of wide-eyed soldiers slumbering in death, and the horror aroused against Nature's serene backdrop. Later, when analyzing what the author did to create the panorama of battle, Ms. Hawthorne could focus her students' attention on the writer's techniques, the imagery he painted into the battlefield to convey a vivid sense of war's destruction and devastation. According to Rosenblatt (1985), teachers favor that more efferent, analytic stance at the expense of aesthetic readings. Often preferring an efferent stance, teachers expect students to analyze texts rather than urging students to live through the experiences depicted in the literature they read. That over-emphasis on efferent readings may, in some instances, reduce the value and enjoyment of transactions with literature that students have. However, an emphasis on efferent responses may help students develop analytical skills that build critical thinking.

## Teacher Factors Contributing to Student's Motivation to Read

As we've already seen, you can do several things to influence your students' motivation to read and engage in learning. Perhaps you can't transform all the traits and habits that compose your students' identities so that they identify with school, see value in all its aspects, and align their goals with your daily curriculum. But you can discover what those identities are, what values your students hold, what aspiration they have, and what reading skills they have to pursue their studies. Over time, you can affect their expectations and their self-efficacy. In many instances, you can exercise control over the texts your students read or even choose to read. These are not inconsequential factors that you might influence.

We turn next to motivational factors over which you usually have more control. These factors include teacher engagement, your achievement-related instructional program, the classroom community, your assessment and reward system, and the autonomy support you can provide for your students.

Teacher engagement. Like your students whose identity affects their learning, you have an identity that influences your motivation to teach. You would probably not be reading this if you had not made some important decisions about your occupational

role, decisions that your identity shaped and that will shape your identity. You have made and acted on role decisions that your students, still envisioning their vocational future, will probably be thinking about for a few years. But how you see yourself functioning as a teacher, what commitments you hold, and what beliefs guide your practice will strongly affect the level of your teaching engagement and the kinds of interactions you have with your students. You may not enjoy complete control over all the elements of your identity, but you probably have control over some.

We know that teachers can be influential. How they influence their students depends upon who they are and how they engage in their work as teachers. Because responsive, reflective teaching of literacy does not occur without a responsive, reflective teacher, we'll explore the characteristics that such teachers bring to teaching. From the study of influential teachers, their behavior in the classroom, and their impact on students (Ruddell, 1994, 1995; Ruddell, Draheim, & Barnes, 1990; Ruddell & Haggard, 1982), we can garner insights into responsive teachers as well as ways they promote literacy engagement.

Influential teachers may be defined as teachers who have been identified by a former student as having had a significant impact on the student's academic or personal success in school. From studies of influential teachers, we know that they share characteristics in several areas that include the following:

- They show that they care about their students.
- They manifest excitement and enthusiasm about what they teach.
- They adapt instruction to the individual needs, motives, interests, and aptitudes of their students while having high expectations for them.
- They use motivating and effective strategies when they teach, including clarity in stating problems, use of concrete examples, analysis of abstract concepts, and application of concepts to new contexts.

- They engage students in a process of intellectual discovery.
- They help their students in understanding and solving their personal and academic problems.

High-achieving students, those more motivated for learning, can identify at least twice as many influential teachers as their lower achieving counterparts. When I ask my students who are seeking their teaching credentials to talk about their influential teachers, I frequently discover they have had at least one or more, sometimes within their own families. Whether high or low achieving, students see their influential teachers having clear instructional goals, plans, and strategies that contribute to a classroom learning environment which the teacher closely monitored (Ruddell, 1994, 1995). Furthermore, by emphasizing intrinsic over extrinsic motivation, these influential teachers elicit students' internal motivation by stimulating intellectual curiosity, exploring their students' self-understanding, and focusing on problem solving.

The pattern of engagement demonstrated by the influential teachers that Ruddell studied also appears in a study of secondary science teachers. John Eichinger (1997) found that, as successful college science students looked back on their middle and high school science teachers, those students identified many features in the characteristics and methods of their teachers that reflected the "influential teacher" pattern. Successful science students perceived their influential teachers to be knowledgeable, enthusiastic, and effective communicators who were committed, friendly, competent, and creative. By the way, non-science majors looking back on their secondary school science instruction were especially appreciative of their more patient and caring science teachers.

A study of the effects of teacher engagement on the achievement and motivation of tenth graders generated findings important to our discussion. Knowles's (1999) concept of teacher engagement consisted of a cluster of four positively correlated characteristics:

1. Pedagogical knowledge in the content area,
2. Pedagogical knowledge about student motivation,
3. Teachers' intrinsic motivation toward teaching, and
4. Teachers' self-efficacy toward teaching.

She found that teachers' engagement predicted tenth-grade student achievement and motivation. Her finding suggests that, if we want to positively influence our students' achievement and motivation, we might give serious thought to building our knowledge of student motivation, enhancing our subject domain knowledge, and cultivating our own motivation to teach.

Evidence indicates that problems with student learning are tied to teacher detachment and alienation from their work. These are teachers who "taught their first year for 35 years" and who, at the end of a school year, hardly know their students' names. Most students find learning in these teachers' classrooms an uphill grind, frequented by few vistas of delight. But even communities struggling with lower social and economic status can have schools with involved and caring teachers. When looking into schools with engaged teachers serving disadvantaged students, Louis and Smith (1992) found four types of teacher engagement:

1. Engagement with the whole school as a social unit.
2. Engagement with students as unique individuals.

3. Engagement in the academic achievement of students and colleagues.
4. Engagement with the teacher's own subject.

They focused their inquiry on how these forms of teacher engagement can be reinforced. With respect to teacher culture, they found several elements that positively affected teacher engagement: A strong sense of participating in a school with a common mission, an emphasis on closeness and helping among colleagues, and a demand for active problem solving among fellow teachers. With respect to school leadership, they found a style that promoted engagement: Principals delegated and empowered, spent time on daily routines, buffered teachers to reduce distractions from teaching, and confronted unengaged teachers. Louis and Smith (1992) found that teachers in schools promoting teacher engagement gave freely to realize their instructional goals and student achievement; however, they had access to supportive social structures within their schools to carry them through episodes of frustration and disenchantment. Many of these features also occurred in "beating the odds" classrooms that Langer (2000, 2001) investigated and that I explore in the first and last chapters of this book.

Evidence for the reciprocal effects of teacher behavior and student engagement have also been found (Skinner & Belmont, 1993). Researchers discovered that, while students who showed higher initial engagement got more engaged responses from their teachers, those students who were less engaged or disengaged received fewer such responses, perhaps undermining their motivation further. Perhaps the rich do get richer, at least as far as support for motivation in classrooms gets distributed.

## Achievement-related instruction

***Learning over performance.***   As we saw when looking at the kinds of goals that drive student achievement, a learning or mastery goal orientation has a number of distinct advantages over a performance orientation, including the fostering of long-term achievement through belief in incremental improvement through effort (Ames, 1992; Meece, 1994). So, in designing lessons, a learning goal orientation might guide your curricular and instructional decisions. Even though your students may themselves prefer performance (or ego-oriented) goals and glorify ability, you can set up instruction to emphasize effortful mastery of knowledge and skills rather than their public display for personal status gains. All the instructional elements, including strategy instruction, authentic instruction, and an emphasis on higher order thinking, we're about to review have been shown to augment students' engagement. Furthermore, they can all enhance a learning goal orientation.

***Strategy instruction.***   Integrating strategic instruction with content area reading can positively influence your students' motivation (Guthrie, Wigfield, & VonSecker, 2000; Shuell, 1996). As Guthrie and Wigfield (2000) point out, **strategy instruction** includes a teacher's direct instruction, scaffolding, and guided practice when students are reading to learn. Because success in reading assignments encourages engagement and strategies promote success, strategy instruction is both empowering and motivating. However, because many reading strategies are not easily internalized, they take time and perseverance to acquire. Students must also learn when specific strategies are best applied. Several strategies shown in Figure 10.2 and others described in this text (Chapters 4 through 9) are designed to increase students' self-efficacy.

***Authentic work.***   **Authentic work** has been defined as "tasks that are considered meaningful, valuable, significant, and worthy of one's effort" (Newmann, Wehlage,

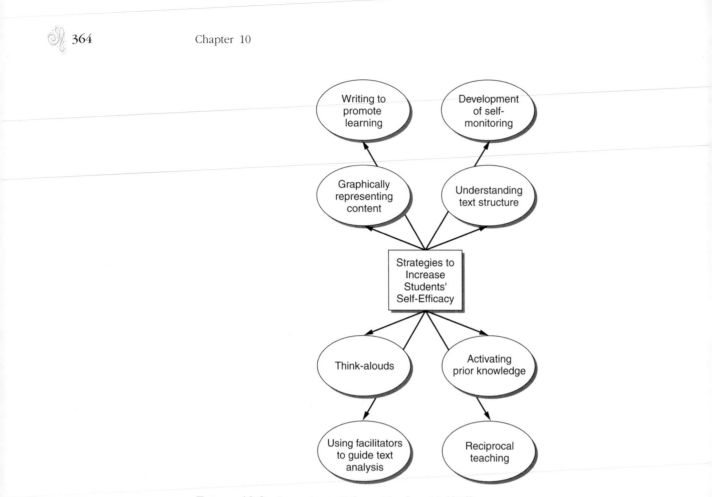

**FIGURE 10.2**    Strategies to Enhance Students' Self-Efficacy.

& Lamborn, 1992). That's in contrast to "busy work," as students call tasks they consider trivial, meaningless, or useless. Authentic work is more likely to engage students and promote achievement because it leads to "socially valued outcomes," like a brochure informing community residents of public health resources or tenth graders tutoring struggling readers in the third grade (Wehlage et al. 1989). In part, authentic work engages students because of its connection with the "real world." In undertaking authentic tasks, students often work with others both in school and out to accomplish learning goals. They get quick, clear evidence of success or the need to revise what they're doing, and they believe that the tasks they are undertaking have value beyond the immediate classroom.

Classroom instruction that consists of "real life" cognitive activities rather than "artificial" activities will challenge even the most creative and resourceful of teachers. The challenge may be overwhelming in communities feeling the pressure of accountability through standardized testing. However, secondary teachers use "hands-on" activities to motivate their students. Science students in Eichinger's study (1997) preferred active, participatory, and student-centered instruction, such as labs and projects, over more traditional methods, such as textbooks, lectures, memorization, and worksheets. A middle school science teacher I observed creatively engaged his students in a moon explorer simulation program using robotic rovers to map the moon's surface. Such hands-on science curriculum with embedded literacy strategy instruction could increase reading comprehension, strategy use, and problem solving (Guthrie et al., 1998). History teachers, like Ms. Hawthorne, can also use role-playing of historical characters and events, projects whose outcomes are useful products, current events that connect with their students' lives, and artifacts from historical sites to make inferences about a community's agriculture and culture (Hootstein, 1995). Furthermore, cognitive apprenticeships, which are consistent with situated or authentic learning, are feasible in classrooms (Shuell, 1996). The Reading Apprenticeship program designed to help students become conversant with reading in a teacher's subject area and described in Chapter 9 exemplifies this form of authentic learning.

***Higher order thinking.*** Throughout her middle and high school years, I periodically asked my daughter about the best question she heard in school on a particular day. Most of the time she reported that no one asked a question, and teachers neither asked for questions nor provided time to hear them. On some occasions, she said her teachers told students to "listen up" and hold down their questions. Answers, presumably, would come through the day's lecture. In "Taking Students Seriously," Gamoran and Nystrand (1992) report that, in most of the 54 English classrooms they studied, teachers delivered information, defined learning as information recall, and played the role of examiner. There were few occasions of high-quality discourse in which teachers helped students explore their ideas and thoughts, interpret literature, or argue for their point of view, just the kinds of things these authors believe teachers must do if they are to "take students seriously as thinkers."

But what evidence do we have that challenging students to think will lead to deeper levels of student engagement? Newmann (1992) and his associates watched about 500 social studies classes and interviewed teachers, department chairs, and principals in 16 high schools. He found significant correlations between the level of engagement and both the levels of student thoughtfulness and students' sense of being challenged. The results convinced him that students are "more likely to try, to concentrate, and to be interested in academic study when they are challenged to think." If you wanted to imitate teachers in the most thoughtful classrooms in his study, you would identify student thinking as your highest priority and view the development of your students' thinking as more important than delivering subject area content because that is what Newmann found that teachers in those classrooms did. All the social studies teachers in one school that emphasized the development of thinking began classes by posing a central question to focus student inquiry and structured class discussion to answer that question. Strategies useful for promoting higher order and critical thinking in content area classrooms are presented in several chapters of this book, especially Chapter 7.

In spite of our knowing that higher order thinking and challenging students to understand concepts yields higher levels of engagement, there are barriers to conducting content area classrooms where promotion of thinking takes a high priority. Teachers may need collegial and administrative support to pursue thoughtful classrooms in schools (Tishman, Perkins, & Jay, 1995; Unrau, 1997).

**Classroom community.** The power of the classroom social climate to engage or disengage students should not be underestimated. A classroom community that nurtures inclusion, invites inquiry, and supports challenging learning can heighten students' motivation, perhaps even keep them in school. When Wehlage and his associates (1989) studied schools that had a successful track record with at-risk students, they found one common factor among all the schools: Social bonds connecting students to their school. When a student's sense of identity is affirmed in schools and classrooms, a climate for membership arises (Alderman, 1999). But social identification with a group does not mean hard work to achieve your learning goals will automatically follow. In fact, like Ms. Hawthorne, you may face just the opposite, a culture of anti-achievement or non-achievement. However, Brown (1993) urges teachers to cultivate a positive peer culture to enhance academic motivation by:

1. Becoming aware of peer group structures and value systems, including the risks to students of "acting White" or becoming a "home boy," without stereotyping students. Students may be concerned about the loss of their cultural and social identity if they adapt to the school's performance expectations.
2. Avoiding a grading or tracking system that labels winners and losers.
3. Enhancing the value of academic achievement.

There are other steps you can take to promote literacy engagement by building on students' need for social interaction and bonding in classrooms. These include developing variety in instructional methods, using cooperative learning, engaging students in meaning negotiation, and adopting the practices of culturally responsive teachers.

*Variety in instructional methods.*   Paris, Wasik, and Turner (1991) advocate "multidimensional" classrooms in which teachers provide students with meaningful literacy tasks, use a variety of instructional approaches, and make opportunities for success available to all. Task variety proved to be motivational in classrooms, offered students different forms of cognitive engagement, and required the application of different strategies for completion. Using different methods of instruction also afforded more students opportunities to participate, achieve, and gain recognition.

*Cooperative groups.*   Many cooperative learning techniques build classroom communities. These cooperative learning methods promote social bonding, improve inter-group relations, enhance motivation, and heighten achievement (Slavin, 1995). Specific strategies covered in Chapter 6 include Numbered Heads Together, Think-Pair-Share, Group Investigation, Group Reading Activity, and Jigsaw. When designing group activities, remember to build in both some form of group recognition or reward and individual accountability. Reciprocal teaching, though not originally designed as a cooperative learning activity, also promotes team building while helping students develop reading strategies like summarizing, predicting, and questioning.

*Reader response groups.*   Some teachers use the principles of cooperative learning (Slavin, 1995; Slavin, Madden, Karweit, Dolan, & Wasik, 1994) to design ***reader response groups*** in English classes. The teacher delegates authority to each group that in turn has to delegate authority to each group member. In mixed-ability groups, members share responsibilities for learning, get a group grade, and are individually accountable for their learning and contributions. Reading response groups can be structured so that each team reads a different book that the teacher selects based on each team's interests. If a teacher knew that several of her students were interested in history, she could put them in a cooperative team to read historical novels focused on a specific event, such as the American Civil War.

*Meaning negotiation.*   The student and teacher factors that influence a reader's focus of motivation and achievement also affect meaning negotiation of texts in classroom contexts. They build the foundation not only for the meanings that individual readers construct, but also for meanings negotiated between individuals during reader-based instruction in classroom contexts. In addition, the design and function of the classroom learning environment further affects motivation to engage in literacy events and learning (Marshall, 1992; Unrau & Ruddell, 1995). (I explain this classroom negotiation process in Chapter 2.) We can expect readers to engage with reading, interact in the classroom community, and participate in the meaning-negotiation process if they are motivated to read and to learn, if prior knowledge is activated, if tasks are personally relevant, and if they are encouraged to actively construct meanings. As mentioned, the teacher who incorporates features like these is considered to be mastery-goal oriented and is more likely to witness productive learning among students (Ames, 1992; Covington, 1992).

If you want to deepen your students' engagement and motivation, classroom community negotiation of meanings is important to develop. You can provide activities, like reader response logs, reading or dialogue journals, and whole-class discussions of text interpretations, that enable your students to shape and share meanings. The sharing of those meanings enables them to participate in the evolution of an interpretive community.

*Culture pluralism and inclusion.*   When building communities in multicultural classrooms, Ginsberg and Wlodkowski (2000) cite four interacting motivational elements that culturally responsive teachers and their students continually recreate:

1. *Establishing inclusion.* Teachers exercise principles and practices that create a climate in which teacher and students feel respected and connected.
2. *Developing a positive attitude.* Teachers apply principles and practices that contribute to a "favorable disposition toward learning."
3. *Enhancing meaning.* Teachers design instruction that results in both challenging and engaging learning.
4. *Engendering competence.* Teachers employ principles and practices that engage students in learning what they value.

Assessment and reward system.   What would an assessment and reward program for reading look like if we wanted it to promote motivation to read? Assessment takes a multitude of forms when it comes to reading in the content areas. Usually, reading itself isn't assessed separately from overall learning when teachers evaluate their students. Reading is folded in with many other kinds of learning activities that contributed to a student's performance on a test covering a unit in biology, government, or health. But, if a teacher really wanted to assess and reward reading, she could find a way to do it.

Rewards for reading and learning come in many forms. Grades are among the most often used and, based on the weight middle school students give to grades on the Motivation for Reading questionnaire (Baker & Wigfield, 1999), they are very powerful motivators. Of 10 clusters influencing motivation to read, no cluster was given more weight. However, teachers design other kinds of token systems besides grades to reward students for reading. Some programs have rewarded students with McDonalds' meals, pizza, money, and books (Gambrell & Marinak, 1997).

While working with a middle school in Los Angeles that started a Sustained Silent Reading program and was evaluating its impact on students, I surveyed over 1,600 students and found that just over 75% thought that getting a letter grade for SSR time would make them work harder at it. Ironically, SSR is intended to build **intrinsic motivation** by providing students with choice and time to read whatever they might enjoy, so teachers were quite reluctant to provide students with the grade incentives students apparently thought would get them to read more.

Although teachers frequently use **extrinsic incentives,** some educators have voiced concerns that students may be adversely affected by reward systems. They argue that students may be "punished by rewards" that undermine their inherent or intrinsic motivation to learn (Kohn, 1993). Some researchers have expressed the concern that, if students who simply enjoy reading are given pizza or money for doing it, their intrinsic motivation will diminish, especially when the rewards are withdrawn (Deci et al., 1991).

While some studies indicate that tangible incentives can undermine intrinsic motivation (Deci, 1971), other studies show that tangible incentives can enhance it (Lepper, Greene, & Nisbett, 1973). Incentives appear to be particularly potent when participants' levels of interest are initially low and the activity does not become attractive until some time has been put into it or some degree of mastery is attained. Gambrell and Marinak (1997) emphasize that, in general, findings point to the key roles played by the kind of incentive provided and the kind of reader to whom it's given. Giving rewards for a task that students are already intrinsically motivated to undertake, like McDonalds' coupons to good readers, may undermine inherent interest in the task. But important and relevant rewards given to weakly motivated readers may heighten their motivation to read. In time, these incentives can be withdrawn as students become more interested and competent in the activity (Stipek, 1993).

Extrinsic incentives in the form of direct praise or feedback to students about their reading have been found to enhance student performance. Upon review of 96 experimental studies, Cameron and Pierce (1994) found evidence that would support the following principles related to intrinsic motivation:

◆ Intrinsic motivation increases through verbal praise and positive feedback because they communicate information to the reader that is useful.
◆ Intrinsic motivation is not undermined through tangible incentives if they are given when students complete a task according to set standards.

Gambrell (1996; Gambrell & Marinak, 1997) points out the importance of a close link between the incentive and the behavior. Her "reward proximity hypothesis" states that, when incentives are linked to desired behavior, intrinsic motivation is enhanced. According to the hypothesis, if you wanted to build your students' intrinsic motivation to read, you would provide incentives clearly linked to reading behavior, such as books or more reading time.

Quite often both intrinsic and extrinsic incentives operate on students simultaneously. The magnitude of each type of motivation may differ, as occurs when a student's curiosity about the roots of our Civil War is more important than his getting a good grade on an essay that describes the evolution of the war. Not only does the magnitude of different kinds of motivation vary at any given time, magnitudes of motivation change over time. A student's motivation to get a passing grade on today's unit exam covering World War II may be overshadowed tomorrow by his desire for an A on a paper he wrote about the sacrifices and suffering that families endured during the conflict.

To implement an assessment program based on motivation principles, Mac Iver (1993) designed a system that encouraged a mastery-focused orientation which emphasized learning goals, that gave equal opportunities for students of differing abilities to succeed, and that required strategic efforts for success. The system consisted of setting a base score and then giving a student the goal of increasing his base score by several points. If the student met his specific goal, he would get improvement points. Students who raised their performance level received official recognition. Slavin (1980, 1995) developed a similar system called Individual Learning Expectations (ILE) that recognized students for their improvement. Slavin found that, in comparison to traditional grading, ILE significantly increased student achievement.

Autonomy support.    Several studies support the positive motivational effects of giving students some degree of ownership in their learning (Alderman, 1999). Degrees of freedom in classrooms range from originator to pawn (deCharms, 1984). To be an originator, the student feels she has the competence to exercise choice. But to be a pawn is to feel controlled by a higher decision-making power. While providing choice may be motivating, you have a curriculum to teach that's probably based on state standards. As Alderman (1999) points out, you can give students opportunities to exercise control over certain domains, but you need not give them unlimited control. You will set boundaries, expectations, and responsibilities. But, depending on the degree of maturity your students manifest, you can support their autonomy as they pursue learning goals. For those with low levels of maturity, you will need to use more structure, including goals, directions, frequent monitoring, and feedback with corrections. For those with high-maturity levels, you may not need to provide much guidance because students will come to you when they need help. Otherwise, they'll set their own goals and work toward their achievement independently (Ames & Ames, 1996).

Although the curriculum may not always allow teachers to let students read as their interests dictate, Atwell (1998) found in her reading workshop approach that her students read more if they were given ample choices of interesting books. Research provides abundant evidence of a strong correlation between choice and the development of intrinsic motivation (Deci & Ryan, 1985). As Gambrell and Marinak (1997) point out, opportunities for self-selection are incentives for literacy growth. In a survey of what makes students want to read in middle school classrooms, Ivey and Broaddus (2001) found that students were motivated by discovering good reading materials and having freedom of choice over which they could read. If a content area teacher wanted to foster a student's motivation, she would give her students some choice when opportunities arose to select books to read.

In summary, all of these student and teacher factors contribute to creating and sustaining a focus of motivation. Although I have suggested how they are interrelated, I have done little more than suggest. Guthrie and Wigfield (2000) emphasize that important connections occur among instructional factors, and that their interconnections form a coherence. For example, aligning your students' reading skills and textual connections with your autonomy support in a classroom community magnifies cohesion. With cohesiveness, you can facilitate engagement, content area reading, and conceptual learning.

## GUIDELINES FOR PROMOTING READING ENGAGEMENT

If we are to become more effective in developing reader motivation, we must carefully reflect on the nature of our students' reading and learning. This discussion of motivation to read highlighted the complex, interactive roles of both student and teacher factors. We first examined factors primarily under student control, including student identity, expectations and self-efficacy, goals and task values, reading skills and knowledge, and textual connections. We then explored more teacher-controlled factors, including teacher engagement, the instructional program, the classroom community, the assessment and reward system, and autonomy support. I then discussed how these student and teacher factors interact and, when aligned, can increase cohesiveness and motivational impact.

Given the spectrum of factors influencing the focus of motivation, you can rely on several guidelines or rules of thumb that facilitate the creation of an optimum learning environment to promote reading and learning engagement. You can apply these 10 rules of thumb in your classrooms to promote your students' motivation in the present and to cultivate literacy over time. Each of the 10 recommendations is directly connected with one of the 10 student and teacher factors contributing to students' motivation to read. A specific suggested practice follows each recommendation.

1. *Student Identity:* Know your students; provide for the exploration of student identity, its roots and its possibilities; devise activities and interactions that bolster reflection and self-discovery. (Remember Nancy Atwell's readers' workshops and Jeff Waid's student chronicles.)
2. *Expectations and Self-Efficacy:* Establish literacy expectations that are appropriate to each student's reading capacities and provide support for the attainment of those expectations; help students develop reading competencies and confidence in their ability to succeed at reading tasks. (Remember to assess students' reading and find a "best fit" between their abilities and texts assigned. Struggling readers may need scaffolding to make challenging texts accessible.)
3. *Goals and Task Values:* Encourage students to work toward task-oriented goals that foster a sense of mastery and competency and that students see as useful in relation to their future goals; help students recognize the task value inherent in reading and the acquisition of reading strategies. (Remember that students are likely to ask themselves, "What will I get out of doing this reading assignment?" If they have a sound answer to that question that connects to their goals and task values, they are more likely to engage with the reading assignment. If they don't have an answer, they may look to you for one.)
4. *Reading Skills and Knowledge:* Teach students about how they read and how they can improve their reading strategically; activate and extend students' background knowledge to facilitate meaning construction; formulate or select tasks

that are suitable to students' text-processing resources and that allow students to internalize knowledge and skills to become increasingly independent, self-regulating, and self-reliant readers. (Remember the dozens of literacy fostering strategies presented in this book and descriptions for their use in classrooms like yours.)

5. *Textual Connections:* Provide, whenever possible, texts that match students' topic interests and reading capacity; watch for situational interests arising from students' reading and nurture those interests; provide accessible texts that offer the chance for the experience of "flow"; develop students' awareness of stance and its effects on engagement and comprehension. (Remember that influential teachers, like those in "beating the odds" classrooms, engaged their students in discovery and extended core concepts, once mastered, to other domains, including the exploration of their students' life experiences.)

6. *Teacher Engagement:* Cultivate characteristics of "influential" teachers, such as a commitment to know your students and how they learn; become and remain engaged in discovering and promoting your students' capacities for reading and learning; model reflectivity and metacognitive processes for students; monitor and cultivate your own motivation to teach engagingly; contribute to a positive teacher culture; a teacher's level of engagement influences that of his or her students. (Remember that influential teachers adapt instruction to the individual motives, interests, and aptitudes of their students while maintaining high expectations for them.)

7. *Achievement-Related Instruction:* Design achievement-related tasks that are perceived as important and valuable to students, that involve "real world" issues, that integrate strategic learning, and that involve students in serious, higher order thinking. (Remember to encourage student-generated questions and to provide time to discuss them.)

8. *Classroom Community:* Create classroom and school communities that promote inclusion, invite inquiry, and support challenging learning; cultivate a positive peer culture; thoughtfully apply cooperative learning strategies; encourage meaning negotiation in the classroom; allow students to gain a sense of ownership and share authority in the selection and interpretation of texts; discover and use students' cultural legacies as resources for constructing an environment that reflects students' orientations while developing understanding and tolerance for pluralistic classrooms. (Remember Group Investigation and Jigsaw.)

9. *Assessment and Reward System:* Set up assessment procedures that not only reward performance goals in reading but also foster learning goals and mastery of knowledge from texts; praise effort related to reading. (Remember there are hundreds of ways to say "Well done.")

10. *Autonomy Support:* Design an environment that intentionally builds student self-worth and autonomy rather than one that unintentionally threatens them; develop an atmosphere in which students see the acquisition of knowledge, skills, and strategies as incremental and issuing from effort that becomes increasingly self-regulated. (Remember to provide choices for learning if and when possible. Self-selections are often incentives for growth.)

As you reflect on your own teaching, you can examine and apply these guidelines in your own classroom to build and maintain a learning environment that promotes engagement with reading and learning.

By enhancing our knowledge of the critical factors that influence a reader's instructional engagement, we gain important insights into teaching that can lead to gains in the reader's focus of motivation. Our understanding of these motivational factors enables us, as teachers, to create an instructional environment that encourages the reader to participate in active learning, share learning responsibility, and in turn experience an increase in reading motivation. The engaged, responsive, and reflective teacher contributes to the development of focused reader motivation through attention to these many factors that constitute motivation's direction and intensity.

---

## DOUBLE-ENTRY JOURNAL: After Reading

Go to the Double-Entry Journal for Chapter 10 on our Companion Website at www.prenhall.com/unrau to complete your journal entry.

Having read this chapter, review the goals and reasons you initially wrote down for reading it. What goals and reasons in your prereading DEJ fit the motivational factors identified and explained in this chapter? Are there additional motivational factors that were brought to mind by reading this chapter that you would now add to your prereading list? Were any factors on your initial list not mentioned in the chapter? When designing instruction to promote literacy in your content area, what three or four motivational factors would you consider most important? Why do you think those factors are more important than others reviewed in the chapter?

---

### ACTIVITY BOX 🌿 Ms. Hawthorne's Dilemma

Ms. Hawthorne was discontented with the social studies program she found when she came to Jefferson Middle School two years ago. During her first year, she discovered that some of her eighth-grade students did read and complete tasks she assigned, but too many did so halfheartedly, infrequently, or not at all. The curriculum seemed unresponsive, impersonal, and unengaging. She knew that she and they could do better. With the encouragement of a couple of colleagues, a new principal, and faculty at a local university, she decided to investigate what she might do to redesign her program so that more students would become engaged.

She began her action research by collecting as much information as she could about her students to discover what made them tick—not only as readers but also as people. To get to know individual students better, to understand their motivation and their reading strategies, Ms. Hawthorne decided to conduct a few tutorials once a week after school.

On the day she made her announcement about the possibility of a tutorial with her, several students responded. One student, Cynthia Sharp*, jumped at the opportunity.

At the beginning of the school year, Ms. Hawthorne got the impression that Cynthia was a slightly hyperactive "social butterfly." But, as she got to know Cynthia during the tutorial meetings, she discovered far more complexity. The enthusiasm that Cynthia expressed when Ms. Hawthorne offered tutorial help demonstrates some aspects of Cynthia's sense of self and her complex motivation to learn. At her initial tutoring session, Cynthia told Ms. Hawthorne that she had good memories about school. She said she liked it because she had lots of opportunities to socialize with her friends. Both her parents helped her with school work, her mother in reading and writing, her father in math. In earlier elementary grades, Cynthia was often on the honor role. Like her mother, Cynthia was thinking about becoming a nurse, but she also imagined herself being a story writer, a travel agent, a model, and a fashion designer. She was obviously exploring possibilities for herself.

Cynthia said her favorite subject was history, and she had a passion for books about "old fashion" family life and orphans. She told Ms. Hawthorne that she had lots of these stories in her head and would much rather write them than complete assignments. During their first meeting together, Cynthia told Ms. Hawthorne that two of her goals for the year were to improve her reading and to reduce the number of mistakes she made in her writing.

To get an idea of Cynthia's reading achievement, Ms. Hawthorne administered an individual reading inventory. She found that Cynthia had an independent reading level of fourth grade, an instructional level of fifth grade, and a frustration level of sixth grade. She also discovered that Cynthia, who said that she understood the text that she had read, was unable to answer many literal and interpretive level questions about that text. After the assessment, Cynthia complained to Ms. Hawthorne that the last paragraph on the test, one at the eighth-grade level, was unfair because there were words in it that she didn't recognize. During the assessment and later in the tutorial, Ms. Hawthorne found that Cynthia had difficulty comprehending what she read and connecting concepts to make meaning. Ms. Hawthorne also observed that Cynthia would give up easily with text she had difficulty understanding and would express boredom or self-defeat rather than increased effort.

Ms. Hawthorne was impressed with Cynthia's "zest for writing." She could construct concept maps or outlines and finish a five paragraph essay in one period. However, Ms. Hawthorne discovered that Cynthia would often misplace her essays before turning them in. Furthermore, Ms. Hawthorne thought that Cynthia's writing was rudimentary in content and structure. In an essay containing paragraphs with four or five simple sentences, she would just restate the assignment and discuss only the most obvious points, making for what Ms. Hawthorne described as "conceptually dull" writing. Furthermore, her essays contained many grammar and spelling errors, an aspect of her writing that Cynthia wanted to improve.

As the special tutoring progressed, Ms. Hawthorne discovered that Cynthia's self-projected image of an enthusiastic learner wasn't always consistent with Cynthia's behavior. While Cynthia first appeared earnest in seeking help for her literacy needs, Ms. Hawthorne began to think that she was seeking attention and trying to evade standard class work. Ms. Hawthorne also noticed that, while Cynthia wrote enthusiastically, she often did not complete reading assignments, and her written work rarely got turned in when it was due. Inconsistency and "irresponsibility" marked her performance. In short, while

Cynthia showed enthusiasm for improvement, she appeared to have problems with self-regulation in addressing school work.

Cynthia's portrait is similar to that of many middle and high school students who reveal a mosaic of selves, including images of the enthusiastic learner, the engaged reader, the fast problem solver, the school socialite, the irresponsible kid, and the budding historian. Cynthia has had opportunities that others in her school have missed, such as a mother and father she views as supportive, but she is beset with motivational problems that keep her from making the kinds of effort that would result in more positive success.

## Responding to Ms. Hawthorne's Dilemma:

If Cynthia were in your class, what steps would you take to help her progress in her academic development? Describe what you would do to enhance Cynthia's motivation and/or help her improve some aspect(s) of her school work. Explain what you would do along with your reasons for doing it.

*Both Cynthia and Ms. Hawthorne are composites. (I wish to thank teachers and graduate students at CSULA for fieldwork contributing to these portraits.)

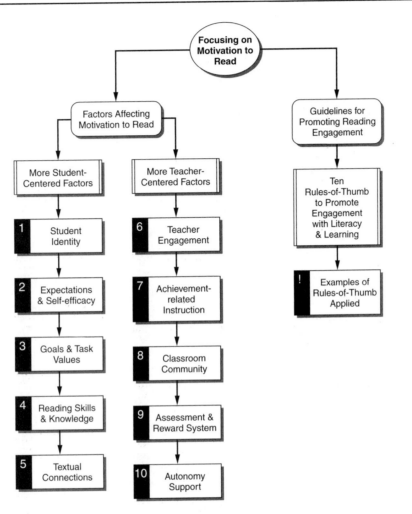

 For exercises to clarify your understanding of the chapter content, visit the self-assessments for Chapter 10 on our Companion Website at www.prenhall.com/unrau

# References

Alderman, M. K. (1999). *Motivation for achievement: Possibilities for teaching and learning*. Mahwah, NJ: Erlbaum.

Ames, C. (1992). Classrooms: Goals, structures, and student motivation. *Journal of Educational Psychology, 84*(3), 261–271.

Ames, C., & Archer, J. (1987). Mothers' beliefs about the role of ability and effort in school learning. *Journal of Educational Psychology, 79,* 409–414.

Ames, R., & Ames, C. (1996). Motivation and effective teaching. In J. L. Idol & B. F. Jones (Eds.), *Educational values and cognitive instruction: Implications for reformation* (pp. 247–261). Hillsdale, NJ: Erlbaum.

Atwell, N. (1998). *In the middle: New understandings about writing, reading, and learning* (2nd ed.). Portsmouth, NH: Boynton/Cook Publishers.

Baker, L., & Wigfield, A. (1999). Dimensions of children's motivation for reading and their relations to reading activity and reading achievement. *Reading Research Quarterly, 34,* 452–477.

Bandura, A. (1986). *Social foundations of thought and action*. Englewood Cliffs, NJ: Prentice Hall.

Brown, B. B. (1993). School culture, social politics, and the academic motivation of U.S. students. In T. M. Tomlinson (Ed.), *Motivating students to learn* (pp. 63–98). Berkeley, CA: McCutchan.

Cameron, J., & Pierce, W. D. (1994). Reinforcement, reward, and intrinsic motivation: A meta-analysis. *Review of Educational Research, 64,* 363–423.

Covington, M. (1992). *Making the grade: A self-worth perspective on motivation and school reform*. Cambridge: Cambridge University Press.

Csikszentmihalyi, M. (1990a). *Flow: The psychology of optimal experience*. New York: Harper & Row.

Csikszentmihalyi, M. (1990b). Literacy and intrinsic motivation. *Daedalus, 119*(2), 115–140.

deCharms, R. (1984). Motivational enhancement in educational settings. In R. E. Ames & C. Ames (Eds.), *Research on motivation in education* (pp. 275–310). Orlando, FL: Academic Press.

Deci, E. L. (1971). Effects of externally mediated rewards on intrinsic motivation. *Journal of Personality and Social Psychology, 18,* 105–115.

Deci, E. L., & Ryan, R. M. (1985). *Intrinsic motivation and self-determination in human behavior*. New York: Plenum.

Deci, E. L., Vallerand, R. M., Pelletier, L. G., & Ryan, R. M. (1991). Motivation and education: The self-determination perspective. *Educational Psychologist, 26,* 325–346.

Dweck, C. S., & Leggett, E. L. (1988). A social-cognitive approach to motivation and personality. *Psychological Review, 95,* 256–273.

Eichinger, J. (1997). Successful students' perceptions of secondary school science. *School Science and Mathematics, 97*(3), 122–131.

Elliot, A. J. (1997). Integrating the "classic" and "contemporary" approaches to achievement motivation: A hierarchical model of approach and avoidance achievement motivation. In M. L. Maehr & P. R. Pintrich (Eds.), *Advances in motivation and achievement* (Vol. 10, pp. 143–179). Greenwich, CT: JAI Press.

Erikson, E. (1968). *Identity: Youth and crisis*. New York: Norton.

Gambrell, L. B. (1996). Creating classroom cultures that foster reading motivation. *The Reading Teacher, 50,* 14–25.

Gambrell, L. B., & Marinak, B. A. (1997). Incentives and intrinsic motivation to read. In J. Guthrie & A. Wigfield (Eds.), *Reading engagement: Motivating readers through integrated instruction* (pp. 205–217). Newark, DE: International Reading Association.

Gamoran, A., & Nystrand, M. (1992). Taking students seriously. In F. M. Newmann (Ed.), *Student engagement and achievement in American secondary schools* (pp. 40–62). New York: Teachers College Press.

Garcia, T., & Pintrich, P. R. (1994). Regulating motivation and cognition in the classroom: The role of self-schemas and self-regulatory strategies. In D. H. Schunk & B. J. Zimmerman (Eds.), *Self-regulation of learning and performance: Issues and educational applications* (pp. 127–153). Hillsdale, NJ: Erlbaum.

Ginsberg, M. B., & Wlodkowski, R. J. (2000). *Creating highly motivating classrooms for all students: A schoolwide approach to powerful teaching with diverse learners.* San Francisco: Jossey-Bass.

Good, T., & Brophy, J. E. (2000). *Looking in classrooms* (2nd ed.). New York: Longman.

Guthrie, J. T., Van Meter, P., McCann, A. D., Anderson, E., & Alao, S. (1998). Does Concept-Oriented Reading Instruction increase strategy-use and conceptual learning from text? *Journal of Educational Psychology, 90*(2), 261–278.

Guthrie, J. T., & Wigfield, A. (2000). Engagement and motivation in reading. In M. L. Kamil, P. B. Mosenthal, P. D. Pearson, & R. Barr (Eds.), *Handbook of reading research* (Vol. III, pp. 403–422). Mahwah, NJ: Erlbaum.

Guthrie, J. T., Wigfield, A., & VonSecker, C. (2000). Effects of integrated instruction on motivation and strategy use in reading. *Journal of Educational Psychology, 92*(2), 331–340.

Hagen, A. S., & Weinstein, C. E. (1995). Achievement goals, self-regulated learning, and the role of classroom context. In P. R. Pintrich (Ed.), *Understanding self-regulated learning* (pp. 43–55). San Francisco: Jossey-Bass.

Heath, S. B., & McLaughlin, M. W. (1993). Building identities for inner-city youth. In S. B. Heath & M. W. McLaughlin (Eds.), *Identity and inner-city youth* (pp. 1–12). New York: Teachers College Press.

Hidi, S., & Harackiewicz, J. M. (2000). Motivating the academically unmotivated: A critical issue for the 21st century. *Review of Educational Research, 70*(2), 151–179.

Hootstein, H. (1995). Motivational strategies of middle school social studies teachers. *Social Education, 59,* 23–26.

Ivey, G., & Broaddus, K. (2001). "Just plain reading": A survey of what makes students want to read in middle school classrooms. *Reading Research Quarterly, 36*(4), 350–377.

Jago, C. (2000, Spring). Editor's column. *California English, 5,* 4.

Knowles, K. T. (1999). The effect of teacher engagement on student achievement and motivation. Dissertation Abstracts International, 60, 4A. (University Microfilms No. 0419–4209).

Kohn, A. (1993). *Punished by rewards: The trouble with gold stars, incentive plans, A's, praise, and other bribes.* Boston, MA: Houghton Mifflin.

Langer, J. A. (2001). Beating the odds: Teaching middle and high school students to read and write well. *American Educational Research Journal, 38*(4), 837–880.

Langer, J. A. (2000). Excellence in English in middle and high school: How teachers' professional lives support student achievement. *American Educational Research Journal, 37*(2), 397–439.

Lepper, M. R., Greene, D., & Nisbett, R. E. (1973). Undermining children's intrinsic interest with extrinsic reward. *Journal of Personality and Social Psychology, 28,* 124–137.

Louis, K. S., & Smith, B. (1992). Cultivating teacher engagement: Breaking the iron law of social class. In F. M. Newmann (Ed.), *Student engagement and achievement in American secondary schools* (pp. 119–152). New York: Teachers College Press.

Mac Iver, D. J. (1993). Effects of improvement-focused student recognition on young adolescents' performance in the classroom. In M. L. Maehr & P. R. Pintrich (Eds.), *Advances in motivation and achievement* (pp. 191–216). Greenwich, CT: JAI Press.

Markus, H., & Nurius, P. (1986). Possible selves. *American Psychologist, 41*(9), 954–969.

Marshall, H. (1992). Associate editor's introduction to centennial articles on classroom learning and motivation. *Journal of Educational Psychology, 84*(3), 259–260.

Meece, J. L. (1994). The role of motivation in self-regulated learning. In D. H. Schunk & B. J. Zimmerman (Eds.), *Self-regulation of learning and performance: Issues and educational applications* (pp. 25–44). Hillsdale, NJ: Erlbaum.

Meece, J. L., Wigfield, A., & Eccles, J. S. (1990). Predictors of math anxiety and its consequences for young adolescents' course enrollment intentions and performances in mathematics. *Journal of Educational Psychology, 82,* 60–70.

Midgley, C., Feldlaufer, H., and Eccles, J. (1989). Change in teacher efficacy and student self- and task-related beliefs in mathematics during the transition to junior high school. *Journal of Educational Psychology, 49,* 529–538.

Moyer, B. (1995). *The language of life.* New York: Doubleday.

Newmann, F. M. (1992). *Student engagement and achievement in American secondary schools.* New York: Teachers College Press.

Newmann, F. M., Wehlage, G. G., & Lamborn, S. D. (1992). The significance of sources of student engagement. In F. M. Newmann (Ed.), *Student engagement and achievement in American secondary schools* (pp. 11–39). New York: Teachers College Press.

Nicholls, J. G. (1984). Achievement motivation: Conception of ability, subjective experience, task choice, and performance. *Psychological Review, 91,* 328–346.

Paris, S. G., Wasik, B. A., & Turner, J. (1991). The development of strategic readers. In R. Barr, M. L. Kamil, P. B. Mosenthal, & P. D. Pearson (Eds.), *Handbook of reading research* (Vol. II). Mahwah, NJ: Erlbaum.

Pilgreen, J. L. (2000). *SSR handbook: How to organize and manage a sustained silent reading program.* Portsmouth, NH: Heinemann.

Pintrich, P. R. (2000a). The role of goal orientation in self-regulated learning. In M. Boekaerts, P. R. Pintrich, & M. Zeidner (Eds.), *The handbook of self-regulation* (pp. 451–502). San Diego, CA: Academic Press.

Pintrich, P. R. (2000b). Multiple goals, multiple pathways: The role of goal orientation in learning and achievement. *Journal of Educational Psychology, 92,* 544–555.

Rosenblatt, L. M. (1978). *The reader, the text, the poem: The transactional theory of the literary work.* Carbondale, IL: Southern Illinois University Press.

Rosenblatt, L. M. (1985). The transactional theory of the literary work: Implications for research. In C. R. Cooper (Ed.), *Researching response to literature and the teaching of literature* (pp. 33–53). Norwood, NJ: Ablex.

Ruddell, R. B. (1994). The development of children's comprehension and motivation during storybook discussion. In R. B. Ruddell, M. R. Ruddell, & H. Singer (Eds.), *Theoretical models and processes of reading* (4th ed., pp. 281–296). Newark, DE: International Reading Association.

Ruddell, R. B. (1995). Those influential literacy teachers: Meaning negotiators and motivation builders. *The Reading Teacher, 48*(6), 454–463.

Ruddell, R. B., Draheim, M., & Barnes, J. (1990). A comparative study of the teaching effectiveness of influential and non-influential teachers and reading comprehension development. In J. Zutell & S. McCormic (Eds.), *Literacy theory and research: Analyses from multiple paradigms* (pp. 153–162). Chicago, IL: National Reading Conference.

Ruddell, R. B., & Haggard, M. R. (1982). Influential teachers: Characteristics and classroom performance. In J. A. Niles & L. A. Harris (Eds.), *New inquiries in reading research and instruction,* 31st Yearbook of the National Reading Conference (pp. 227–231). Rochester, NY: National Reading Conference.

Ruddell, R. B., & Unrau, N. J. (1997). The role of responsive teaching in focusing reader intention and developing reader motivation. In J. T. Guthrie & A. Wigfield (Eds.), *Reading engagement: Motivating readers through integrated instruction* (pp. 102–125). Newark, DE: International Reading Association.

Schiefele, U. (1996). Topic interest, text representation, and quality of experience. *Contemporary Educational Psychology, 21,* 3–18.

Schunk, D. H. (1994). Self-regulation of self-efficacy and attributions in academic settings. In D. H. Schunk & B. J. Zimmerman (Eds.), *Self-regulation of learning and performance: Issues and educational applications* (pp. 75–99). Hillsdale, NJ: Erlbaum.

Schunk, D. H., & Zimmermann, B. J. (1997). Developing self-efficacious readers and writers: The role of social and self-regulatory processes. In J. T. Guthrie & A. Wigfield (Eds.), *Reading engagement: Motivating readers through integrated instruction* (pp. 34–50). Newark, DE: International Reading Association.

Sethi, S., Drake, M., Dialdin, D. A., & Lepper, M. R. (1995, April). *Developmental patterns of intrinsic and extrinsic motivation: A new look.* Paper presented at the annual meeting of the American Education Research Association, San Francisco.

Shuell, T. J. (1996). Teaching and learning in a classroom context. In D. C. Berliner & R. C. Calfee (Eds.), *Handbook of educational psychology* (pp. 726–764). New York: Simon & Schuster Macmillan.

Skinner, E. A., & Belmont, M. J. (1993). Motivation in the classroom: Reciprocal effects of teacher behavior and student engagement across the school year. *Journal of Educational Psychology, 85,* 571–581.

Slavin, R. E. (1980). Effects of Individual Learning Expectations on student achievement. *Journal of Educational Psychology, 72,* 520–524.

Slavin, R. E. (1995). *Cooperative learning* (2nd ed.). Boston, MA: Allyn & Bacon.

Slavin, R. E., Madden, N. A., Karweit, N. L., Dolan, L. J., & Wasik, B. A. (1994). Success for all: Getting reading right the first time. In E. H. Hiebert & B. M. Taylor (Eds.), *Getting reading right from the start,* pp. 125–147. Boston, MA: Allyn & Bacon.

Stipek, D. J. (1993). *Motivation to learn: From theory to practice* (2nd ed.). Boston, MA: Allyn & Bacon.

Tishman, S., Perkins, D. N., & Jay, E. (1995). *The thinking classroom: Learning and teaching in a culture of thinking.* Boston, MA: Allyn & Bacon.

Unrau, N. (1997). *Thoughtful teachers, thoughtful learners: A guide to helping adolescents think critically.* Scarborough, Ontario: Pippin Press.

Unrau, N. J., & Ruddell, R. B. (1995). Interpreting texts in classroom contexts. *Journal of Adolescent & Adult Literacy, 39,* 16–27.

Vigil, J. D. (1993). Gangs, social control, and ethnicity: Ways to redirect. In S. B. Heath & M. W. McLaughlin (Eds.), *Identity and inner-city youth* (pp. 94–119). New York: Teachers College Press.

Wehlage, G. G., Rutter, R. A., Smith, G. A., Lesko, N., & Fernandez, R. R. (1989). *Reducing the risk: Schools as communities of support.* Philadelphia: Falmer.

Wigfield, A. (1994). The role of children's achievement values in the self-regulation of their learning outcomes. In D. H. Schunk & B. J. Zimmerman (Eds.), *Self-regulation of learning and performance: Issues and educational applications* (101–124). Hillsdale, NJ: Erlbaum.

Wigfield, A., & Eccles, J. S. (1992). The development of achievement task values: A theoretical analysis. *Developmental Review, 12,* 265–310.

# 11

# DESIGNING LITERACY INTO ACADEMICALLY DIVERSE CONTENT AREA CLASSES: ALIGNING STANDARDS WITH STRATEGIES AND ASSESSMENTS

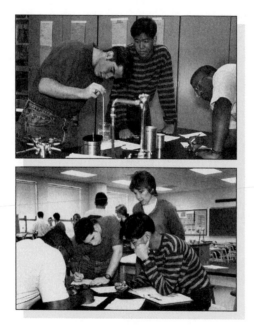

After reading Chapter 11, you should be able to answer the following questions:

1. What are content and performance standards and how can they shape instruction?
2. How can teachers design units and lessons that are responsive to the diversity of learners in classrooms?
3. What instructional models can teachers use to address content standards?
4. How can teachers integrate literacy strategies that will enable students to become better readers, writers, and learners?
5. How can students' progress toward meeting content standards be assessed?
6. How can teachers enhance students' learning by aligning standards with instructional strategies and appropriate assessment measures?

What impact has standards-based instruction had on teachers' practices? When putting together a unit of instruction in your content area, how would you deal with standards, literacy issues, student diversity, and assessment of student learning?

It's synthesis time. Much of what we covered in earlier chapters will be put together in this one. That includes your understanding of reading processes and classroom cultures, diagnosis of students, vocabulary instruction, comprehension and critical reading strategies, the uses of writing in your instructional program, strategies for struggling readings and English learners, and motivation to deepen engagement.

However, another major purpose for this chapter is to show you how to integrate literacy strategies, such as those presented in earlier chapters, into a standards-based instructional program so that your students learn not only content but also strategies. Your students can then transfer and apply those literacy and learning strategies to other texts and contexts, enabling them to become more effective learners.

I begin this chapter with a description of standards-based instruction, provide a brief history of its growth and impact on teachers, point out its effects on literacy instruction, explore teachers' responses to standards-based instruction, and explain how teachers cope with classroom diversity while implementing standards-based programs. To demonstrate how a teacher could put perspectives, procedures, and practices covered earlier in this book together, I describe the systematic planning and day-to-day teaching of an eighth-grade history teacher, Sally Peterson, who created a responsive standards-based unit on the Declaration of Independence.

## STANDARDS-BASED INSTRUCTIONAL PLANNING

### What Is Standards-Based Instruction?

When I began my teaching career in the mid-1960s, state standards and school accountability for achievement tied to those standards were nonexistent. What guided our secondary instructional programs then were local agreements, both school-wide and district-wide, about what should be taught in different content areas at progressive grade levels. Now, many states have extensive and detailed standards for every grade and, beginning with the sixth grade, for every content area. But what are standards and how can they shape your teaching?

Content standards.    Content or academic standards represent a high level of agreement among their drafters of the skills, knowledge, and abilities that all students should be able to master at each grade level. Content standards state the knowledge or skills that will be used as a foundation for judging learning at specific stages in students' education. A content standard for physical education could be that all students are to run the mile. Other examples of content standards for other content areas appear in Figure 11.1.

*Biology/Life Sciences (Grades 9 through 12)*

Cell Biology: The fundamental life processes of plants and animals depend on a variety of chemical reactions that occur in specialized areas of the organism's cells. As a basis for understanding this concept: a) Students know cells are enclosed within semi-permeable membranes that regulate their interaction with their surroundings. b) Students know enzymes are proteins that catalyze biochemical reactions without altering the reaction equilibrium and the activities of enzymes depend on the temperature, ionic conditions, and pH of the surroundings. . . . j) Students know how eukaryotic cells are given shape and internal organization by a cytoskeleton or cell wall or both. (California)

*Grade 8 Social Studies: TAAS II objectives and TEKS Student Expectations*

(TASS = Texas Assessment of Academic Skills; TEKS= Texas Essential Knowledge and Skills)

The student will demonstrate an understanding of issues and events in U.S. History.

(8.4)  History. The student understands the significant political and economic issues of the revolutionary era. The student is expected to:

   (A) analyze causes of the American Revolution, including mercantilism and British economic policies following the French and Indian War;

   (B) explain the roles played by significant individuals during the American Revolution, including Samuel Adams, . . . , King George III, Thomas Jefferson. . . .

   (C) explain the issues surrounding important events of the Revolution, including declaring independence. . . .

*English-Language Arts Content Standards (Ninth Grade and Tenth Grade)*

2.0 Reading Comprehension (Focus on Informational Materials). Students read and understand grade-level-appropriate material. They analyze the organizational patterns, arguments, and positions advanced. . . .

Structural Features of Informational Materials.

   2.1. Analyze the structure and format of functional workplace documents, including the graphics and headers, and explain how authors use the features to achieve their purposes. (California)

**FIGURE 11.1**   Examples of Content Standards from Various States.

*Performance standards.*   A performance standard is a level of achievement that students must attain to show they have mastered the articulated content standards. Performance standards define levels of competence at each grade level, and they indicate the degree to which a student has achieved the content standard. For example, the performance standard for running a mile is how quickly students are expected to run it. That performance standard could be expressed as a range from the maximum time allowed for "passing" the standard to Olympic records that students might strive to reach. Interim objectives or benchmarks could be set between maximum times allowed and world-class performance standards. As many educators have discovered, a standard for content is frequently much easier to articulate than deciding what makes up a level of acceptable mastery for the standard.

While many states now have content standards, fewer have articulated performance standards. However, most states have assessment programs that provide data on school and district performance. In some states, the assessment program does not directly assess their state's content standards although several states are currently working to align an assessment program with their state's standards.

Standards-based instruction.    Standards-based instruction is learning founded upon content standards and, if available, their accompanying performance standards. The evaluation of such instruction usually goes under the name "standards-based assessment," meaning that the assessment will be based on the content standards used to guide instruction. In Texas, for example, content standards are embodied in the Texas Essential Knowledge and Skills (TEKS). TEKS identify what each student should know and be able to do at each grade level and for each content area. Aligned with TEKS is the Texas Assessment of Academic Skills (TASS) which provides information about how each child and his district are performing. (See Figure 11.1, Grade 8 Social Studies: TAAS II Objectives and TEKS Student Expectations.) In some states, such as California, performance on standardized tests, mainly the Stanford 9, provides parents, schools, and districts with information about student performance. Performance in reading and math constitutes a significant portion of the Stanford 9. Furthermore, results on the Stanford 9 and the California Standards Test in English Language Arts contribute to each school's Academic Performance Index (API) which ranks each school on a 1 to 10 scale. A school's API for a given year is used to set growth rates (5% of the difference between a school's API and 800) for the subsequent year. Schools can receive financial awards if they exceed their growth rates.

   Some school districts require their new teachers to participate in "jump start" programs in standards-based instruction and assessment because these districts want to make sure their new faculty have detailed knowledge of standards and how to align them with instruction and assessment. After covering this chapter, you should have the knowledge needed to implement a standards-based curriculum with integrated literacy strategies in your classroom. You'll have been "jump-started."

## The Roots of Standards-Based Curriculum

Where did all the talk about standards in education originate? Some educators and educational commentators say they can find the origins of standards-based instruction back in the Goals 2000 program initiated by President George Bush (Senior) back in 1989. Then the commitment was to make American children first in the world in math and science by 2000. But, if we look at the international scores (PISA survey, 2002), we'll find that standardized tests indicate we're not there yet. In reality, the origins for standards-based instruction are much older than the Goals 2000 program. Purposes, objectives, and goals for instructional programs in schools and districts have been an integral part of local educational planning for many decades in America.

Locally controlled curriculum and assessment: Management by Objectives (MBO).    A few decades ago teachers in many districts and schools were required to explain their purposes with "behavioral objectives." These were statements that teachers would write to enable their administrators to evaluate teaching effectiveness in the classroom. They were related to management by objectives or MBO, a program popular in the business world during the late 1950s and 1960s and popular still in some quarters.

Managers applying MBO believe that, if they could get their business to base its operation on clearly stated, defined, and measurable objectives, the company would be more productive.

In schools, teachers learned how to apply Bloom's taxonomies of cognitive and affective objectives (Bloom et al., 1956). Bloom's taxonomy of cognitive objectives, which continues to influence instructional planning to this day, progresses from simple to complex or from lower to higher as follows:

1. Knowledge (recalling, remembering, reciting information).
2. Comprehension (interpreting, translating, understanding, inferring, summarizing, paraphrasing)
3. Application (solving problems, transfering knowledge from domain to domain, explaining)
4. Analysis (breaking down, separating parts, identifying main and supporting ideas)
5. Synthesis (create, recombine, writing, designing)
6. Evaluation (judging, assessing)

Lists of words to describe these cognitive objectives, as well as those for affective objectives, were distributed to teachers to help them formulate their teaching goals so that they could be measured. The "success" of a teacher's work could be clearly documented based on his or her behavioral objectives. The objectives described specific levels of performance that a teacher was trying to get students to attain.

Using principles from business and Bloom's theory of learning, teachers formulated their own classroom objectives and measured their instructional effectiveness based on them. Many state departments of education, school districts, and school administrators organized to train teachers how to write and measure their objectives. Further guidance came from Robert Mager's (1962) book *Preparing Instructional Objectives*. Objectives we were asked to generate were quite specific. For example, at the beginning of the school year, an English teacher would state on his teaching evaluation form that 85% of his tenth-grade students would be able to analyze a short story and state its theme by the end of the school year. A math teacher would assert that 95% of her Algebra I students could define slope and explain how to graph equations that expressed the slope of a line. In any case, near the end of the school year, teachers would have to gather data to demonstrate the degree to which their students had attained the "behavioral objectives" that teachers had stated at the beginning of the school year. Looking at the results would be an important part of the annual evaluation through which each teacher went.

But in the 1970s, 1980s, and most of the 1990s, teachers did not have state-wide standards that all students were expected to meet. Few, if any, states promulgated standards that could indictate whether or not students would make academic progress from grade to grade with their friends and classmates. Several states did present guidelines to schools for the development of curriculum, but those guidelines did not serve as measuring rods to gauge students' grade advancement. Teachers at that time tied their behavioral objectives to those that department chairs and members of departments formulated within their districts and schools. Control over academic achievement was held at the local level with individual teachers and groups empowered with the authority to construct appropriate academic expectations for their students.

The standard storyline: How standards became state-based.   One of the leaders of the standards-based "reform" movement in the United States, perhaps its driving force, was the chairman of IBM, Louis Gerstner. When in 1996 he convened the first education summit to focus on standards-based instruction and assessment in Palisades, New York, only 14 states had standards that outlined what students should know and be capable of doing in a particular subject at a particular grade level. But, by 1999, many state governors, state school superintendents, and business executives became committed to standards-based instructional and assessment programs (Steinberg, 1999). At the end of the decade, finding just one state without some form of standards-based program would have been extremely difficult. However, you might have had some luck if you'd traveled to Iowa where "local control" over the development of standards and teacher quality was still "valued" (J. Burger, Consultant, Iowa Dept. of Education, personal communication, December 15, 2001).

What prompted the rapid expansion of standards-based instruction?   Why did the states' commitment to standards-based instruction accelerate so rapidly? No single cause can explain the proliferation of the states' commitment to enter standards-based instruction. A myriad of causes drove its rapid spread across the states from the early 1990s to the end of the century. These causes include the following:

- *A Nation at Risk* (1983) alerted the public, business, and governments to the costs of neglecting education.
- The growth of economies worldwide meant more competition for America in a global market with accompanying concerns about loss of markets to competing countries, such as Japan, Korea, China, and Germany. Comparative educational data suggested that American schools were failing to produce students as competent as those graduating from schools abroad.
- The world of business needed employees emerging from the public school system with basic skills.
- The media frequently portrayed the nations' teachers as incompetent, failing to set high academic standards and to maintain schools where educational excellence had top priority—even over athletics and homecoming.
- Rise in public concerns about education came along with declining concerns about other domains that had previously preoccupied citizens and the media, such as the cold war (which dissolved), crime (which had subsided somewhat), and worries about the economy (which had been robust in the late 1990s).
- Some citizens believed that a standardized curriculum based on state-wide objectives would help to reduce what they perceived to be the erosion of a core curriculum that all students would be expected to know. With a standards-based instructional program, some citizens felt that all students would be held accountable for mastering a common body of knowledge about literature, history, mathematics, science, and so forth.
- Promotion resulting from seat-time was commonplace, often leaving students unaccountable for their learning.
- Real estate markets respond to the performance and quality of schools and schooling. Parents consult databases to compare regional performance on standardized state and national tests.
- Open for public scrutiny are state mandated annual tests, like those in Massachusetts, Texas, and California, that are used to assess educational progress.

- The results of tests nationally can be more easily accessed to compare performance across groups of students, teachers, schools, districts, and—quite importantly—across states.
- The business world and the general public wanted schools and the educational system supporting them to be more accountable. Increasing numbers of citizens believed that the outcomes of teaching should be measured and disseminated much like the outcomes of businesses and other enterprises.

The result of some or all of the above forces has been a decrease in "local" control over the articulation of objectives for instruction with an accompanying ascendancy of state-centered influence.

### Standards in the content areas.

In the mid-1990s, when I went to middle or high schools to talk about standards-based instruction, teachers and administrators were clearly confused about which standards they should use to guide their instructional programs. In 1997 a principal of a large, urban middle school asked a colleague and I to present guidelines to his teachers that would help them design standards-based instruction in all content areas. My colleague and I knew that teachers were troubled when asked to work with standards. Some teachers felt either ambivalent or even hostile about the intrusion of standards into their teaching. Furthermore, teachers got mixed and contradictory signals from administrators about which standards would guide their school's instructional program. Teachers' resentment and confusion was understandable.

I recall vividly one eighth-grade math teacher who had marshaled his frustration and directed it at his fellow teachers, his administrators, and us. He began by holding up four different sets of math standards. "Help me here, would you? I've got all these different standards for teaching math. Here's the standards from the National Council of the Teachers of Mathematics. Here are the district standards. Here's the old school guidelines. And here are the state standards. They're all different. Some in little ways, some in big ways. Bottom line: They say I should be teaching different topics to my eighth graders. I'm confused. Which one of these standards am I supposed to follow?" Although his confusion was well warranted, we suggested that the state standards should probably govern his standards-based instruction. However, we also pointed out that the confusion he experienced made complete sense to us because no clear voice spoke for one set of unrivaled standards at that point.

Soon after that, by the late 1990s, few teachers in most states doubted whose standards would guide standards-based instruction. Because the state gave the tests to assess individual school and district progress and because the test reflected many of (if not all) the state's standards, the state's standards became the unquestioned authority. At least for the time being. By the year 2000, at least in California, few teachers had any doubt about whose standards would be driving the curriculum. Yes, schools or districts might tinker with what the standards said when they put together a pamphlet or poster for teachers. But the state standards were clearly dominant. The tests confirmed their hegemony. And in many states, financial rewards flowing from the state followed improvement in school test scores.

Today, state standards are usually the ones that teachers across the country review and digest. Those standards provide teachers with information about what students should know and be able to do at each grade level and for each content domain. They are the maps that guide instruction in more and more classrooms.

In most states, departments of education initiate and guide the drafting and distribution of state standards in each content area for grades 6 through 12. Typically, teams of expert teachers, state education consultants, and university professors who are experts in their fields compile the standards. In drafting standards, committees take into account national standards that professional organizations, like the National Council of Teachers of English and International Reading Association or National Council of Teachers of Mathematics, develop.

These standards are often linked to publications explaining how teachers in their classrooms can teach students so that the standards are addressed. Frameworks for the realization of standards are frequently developed with many examples of instructional strategies that teachers can use (see Figure 11.1).

Standards are usually developed, distributed, and periodically revised in the following areas:

- English/Language Arts
- Mathematics
- History and Social Studies
- Science
- Health Education
- Physical Education
- Visual and Performing Arts

**Impact of standards-based instruction on learning and literacy.** What appear to be the costs and benefits to learning and reading performance attributable to standards-based instruction and accountability? From a critical perspective, much has been written to condemn standards, standardized testing, and accountability, especially with regard to its effects on the equal treatment of students in multicultural schools. A key message is that standardization not only damages teaching and learning but also equal treatment of races and social classes (McNeil, 2000). Many of these narratives are compelling and convincing. However, individual stories of dismay with standards-based instruction in specific schools may not generalize to the entire practice.

Positive standards-based stories have also emerged from individual schools and entire districts where accountability and testing programs have contributed to significant improvements in students' performance and learning (Skrla, 2001). In some instances, accountability has "smoked out" and made far more transparent patterns of weak performance, such as in reading. These patterns once recognized on the educational playing field could be addressed with added intensity and resources. For example, in Texas, a criterion-reference test (TAAS) sets a standard for all students. Scores are reported by school and district, and entities are held accountable for those scores. The scores, posted on a Web site (*www.tea.state.tx.us*), are also disaggregated and reported by racial group. With all that information available, concerned citizens and educators can see clearly what was formerly seen dimly.

Teachers and administrators can use knowledge of their students' performance in reading to target weaknesses and identify strengths. They can then plan literacy programs and reading instruction that address the weaknesses, implement new strategies and programs, and monitor their effects over time. Data from standards-based testing programs can promote the setting of higher performance expectations in reading and drive continuing student improvement. Many middle and high schools carefully review their performance in reading and discuss what next steps to take in order to prepare teachers to serve their students more effectively. Several studies document the positive outcome of interventions fomented by weak performance on tests and urged forward through monitoring results (Ragland, Asera, & Johnson, 1999; Reyes, Scribner, & Paredes Scribner, 1999; Schmoker, 1996, 2001).

With results of standards-based innovations emerging with greater frequency, with more states implementing standards-based programs, and with new federal educational programs stimulating state accountability in reading and math, the last chapter of standards-based instruction and accountability has yet to be written. Many studies have already demonstrated that the effects of standards-based instruction and accountability vary greatly from school to school. While some effects are pernicious, as in schools whose cultures become obsessively test-oriented, other effects indicate accountability can be potent and positive. Standards can promote school-wide clarity of purpose, focus on solutions, and collective effort.

## How Do Individual Teachers Respond to Standards?

With state standards and related assessment measures in place, what are teachers to do? When asked his viewpoint regarding the California state standards, Bill Gray, the chair of the English Department at Grossmont High School in La Mesa, California, said,

> The state assumes that ninth-graders are reading at a ninth-grade level, which isn't the case. We give many students a test when they enter high school, and so many of them aren't at grade level. The state and 'powers that be' are trying to raise the bar. That's fine, except a lot of students aren't capable of reading the curriculum. It's hard to elevate them when they need remediation. . . . We have created a reading class at the freshman level for low readers. We're talking to feeder middle schools in the district to find out who the low readers are. We're trying to teach standards on a cross-curriculum basis because math teachers tell us students can't read questions on the math test. ("Holding on to Creativity in the Face of Standards," 1999.)

Meanwhile Eileen Lavine, an eighth-grade social studies teacher at Parkway Middle School also in La Mesa, California, said,

> I'm making sure my eighth-grade social studies students are aware of what the standards are. In the past I had a personal agenda, focusing on what I thought was the most important and relevant information. Now I feel validated because the standards match up with what I have always taught. At my school, we are working in teams. My team is made up of one teacher each in English, math, social studies, and science. We get together once a week to talk about the curriculum and the kids. We work together to help the 'whole student' based on the standards. For example, if a child is a poor speller, teachers would try to improve his or her (spelling) skills in science and math classes through cross-curriculum, standards-based instruction. ("Holding on to Creativity in the Face of Standards," 1999.)

Some educators have been harsher critics of standards. In her book *One Size Fits Few,* Susan Ohanian (1999) argues that teachers must fight back against the march of the "Standardistos." She argues that they express a frightening confidence in asserting what every school child should know but that what they are creating is a "curriculum of death to children." While distant committees shape a "phantasmic pipe dream" of an essential curriculum for the workforce of tomorrow, nonstandard children can find no place in it. At its best, the agenda of the Standardistos is irrelevant to children's lives. At its worst, they poison the public's perception of what needs to happen in schools. "We must not allow the clamor of the Standardistos to drown out the voices of the children" (p. 13).

In contrast to Ohanian's belief that the teachers are the curriculum, standards-based reformers (Reeves, 1998) believe that only standards courageously applied will overcome the promotion of students from grade to grade based on seat time. Furthermore, they think standards-based instruction will lead to curricular reform and a high school diploma that is backed by a student's demonstration of proficiency. Fundamentally, standards-based instruction guided and supported by the states appears likely to prevail for years to come.

## How Can Teachers Teach to the Standards?

The main task and goal for all teachers in all content areas can be boiled down to six words: Align standards with instruction and assessment. Seasoned teachers in classrooms across the country have been faced with the challenge of adjusting their curricular and instructional program to requirements stated in their state's standards. For these seasoned teachers, I have digested these requirements into a few steps and procedures suggested by Susan Midori of California's Institute for Teaching (How to Cope with Standards, 1999):

1. Familiarize yourself with the standards for your content area and grade level.
2. Identify knowledge and skills for each standard you teach.
3. If there are more standards than teachable in the school year, prioritize and select those most important.
4. Select activities from your instructional resources that will enable you to teach and reach the standards.
5. As needed, create new teaching activities that will enable you to teach and reach the standards.
6. Collaborate with other teachers in your subject area that are below and above you. Confirm that your colleagues at lower levels are going to cover the standards they are expected to cover and inform those above your level that you will be covering the standards for your grade that you are expected to cover. If there are more standards than can be covered at a particular grade level, you will need to negotiate with colleagues above and below to confirm that all standards will eventually get covered so that students do not miss out on some aspect of their educational program.
7. Because many states have issued only content and not performance standards, you should create rubrics addressing the content standards.
8. After taking state-mandated tests that are supposed to measure students' performance, check with students to find out if the state tests included items that had not been covered or not covered sufficiently in class. Also check to see if topics covered in class were tested and if students felt they were well prepared for those items.

## How Sally Peterson Managed Standards, Diversity, Strategic Instruction in Literacy, and Assessment

After a first career in the film industry, Sally Peterson* discovered she wanted to work with adolescents and decided to become a teacher. At college, she had majored in history with a minor in psychology. In her sixth year of teaching, she became committed to working with middle school students. She loved her work and (usually) the kids she taught. Although she was committed to knowing her students well and to teaching them effectively, she found her fourth period a big challenge.

Sally's fourth period history class had 30 eighth graders. Five students with mild learning disabilities had been mainstreamed into her class. Five students in the class were in the academically gifted program. Two others were consistently on the honor role. Three of her "slackers" were grossly underachieving, but she thought she could reach and engage them. Two other students were so detached and disidentified with school that she knew they would probably soon stop coming to school physically as well as mentally. The other 13 she hoped wouldn't fall through the cracks. Having gotten the grade level equivalent reading scores for all her students, Sally knew that, on average, they were reading at about the fourth- or fifth-grade level, about three or four years below the level at which her history text was written. She also saw that the range of reading scores spread from a grade equivalent of 3.4 to over 10.8. Sally was a diagnostic teacher who wanted to engage each of her students so that each was optimally challenged to learn and grow.

Sally planned to put together a new unit for her American history class on the Declaration of Independence. She wanted to take into account the entire range of students she taught, including the range of students in her fourth period class. That meant she'd have to be prepared for teaching those students who were struggling readers and discouraged students as well as those who were quite advanced in reading proficiency and highly motivated.

When creating curriculum and planning instruction for classes with at-risk students, teachers like Sally Peterson need to keep several factors in mind while designing programs and lessons of high quality. According to Deshler, Ellis, and Lenz (1996), students' performance can improve if the following conditions are met:

- ◆ Teachers need to understand the nature of at-risk students' difficulties before making instructional decisions. That means that diagnostic teachers should figure out not only at-risk students' cognitive difficulties in learning but also the difficulties for those students that arise from their interactions with the school culture. What conflicts do these students encounter at school and how have they coped?
- ◆ At-risk adolescents ought to be included in the design and implementation of their instructional program. Many of these students can provide abundant information and insight about their interests, learning strategies, and academic strengths. Giving them an active role can heighten their engagement.
- ◆ Intensive strategy instruction improves the academic performance of at-risk students. Strategies should be taught and mastered through modeling, practice in a

---

*Sally Peterson is a composite of several teachers I have known who confronted the challenges of standards-based teaching in urban schools.

supportive environment, feedback on performance, and transfer training so that students see how a strategy that works in a familiar situation can apply to new situations in new settings.

  ♦ A majority of a student's teachers coordinate their instruction so that teachers not only share knowledge of the student but also teach strategies that are applied and reinforced in all classrooms.

Creating these conditions constitutes a major instructional challenge; however, their creation provides conditions for the success of at-risk students.

## Creating a Responsive Standards-Based Instructional Program

With these teaching challenges in mind, diagnostic teachers like Sally Peterson, who try to be responsive to the growing needs of each student, can take the following steps to create a standards-based instructional program that addresses their students' literacy development.

### STEP-BY-STEP: DESIGNING STANDARDS-BASED UNITS

**STEP 1.** Review and become familiar with the standards for your grade level and content area;

**STEP 2.** Identify the "big ideas" in your curriculum, ideas that link content-related information into networks or systems.

**STEP 3.** Gather information about your students, especially about their literacy levels, so that you know them and their various learning needs well enough to make informed instructional decisions.

**STEP 4.** Construct a unit "Planning Pyramid" to help you determine the content that **all** of your students should master, the content **most** should know, and the content that **some** will learn; in short, plan for differentiated instruction.

**STEP 5.** Create individual lessons with reference to your unit planning pyramid:

  5.1. Create lessons that weave together more than one standard or learning goal in a single task or activity.

  5.2. Integrate reading and/or writing strategies into lessons to facilitate learning or measure progress to mastery of the standards.

**STEP 6.** Develop criteria charts and rubrics for assessing learning progress as observed in outcomes; identify and confirm standards addressed in the criteria charts and rubrics.

**STEP 7.** Look at student work to determine student movement toward goals.

**STEP 8.** Enable students to identify and articulate in their own language their "next step" goals so that they know and own their personal instructional objectives.

**STEP 9.** Revisit lesson plans and re-teach to mastery as needed (see Figure 11.2).

In the following sections of this chapter, I'll expand on each of these steps in order to make clear what Sally did and what you can do to design standards-based units and lessons with integrated literacy.

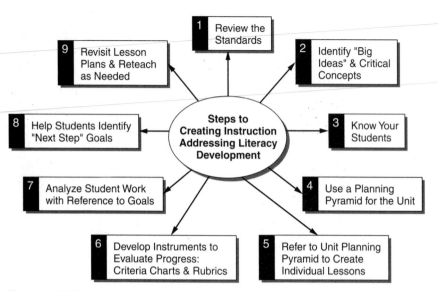

**FIGURE 11.2**    Creating Responsive Standards-Based Instruction.

**Step 1. Reviewing the standards.**    If your school, district, or state has content standards, you should familiarize yourself with the standards applicable to your field of instruction. I would also encourage your becoming familiar with one other domain: that of reading, literacy, or language arts, depending on what label a state has decided to use to cover literacy development through the grades. The reasons for attending to the reading or language arts standards are probably quite clear already. Your students will present a fairly wide range of literacy achievements, just like those in Sally Peterson's class. When you create your instructional program, you can refer to the literacy standards at your students' grade level. You can then weave these standards into the standards for your own content area.

If you are teaching in a middle school, you may be responsible for a combination of content areas, such as science and math or English and social studies. If that is the case, then you will need to acquaint yourself with the standards in those content domains that you teach. Although standards have been drafted for nearly every state, Sally Peterson teaches in California, and so California standards chart her instructional adventure.

In putting together a unit on the Declaration of Independence, Sally reviewed California state standards in both history and English for the eighth grade.

California state history and social science "analysis skills" describe specific "intellectual skills" that students in grades 6 through 8 should learn and apply. Among the "intellectual" or thinking skills relevant to this unit for eighth graders would be the following:

◆ Students explain how major events are related to one another in time.
◆ Students frame questions that can be answered by historical study and research.
◆ Students distinguish relevant from irrelevant information, essential from incidental information, and verifiable from unverifiable information in historical narratives and stories.
◆ Students assess the credibility of primary and secondary sources and draw sound conclusions from them.

◆ Students understand and distinguish cause, effect, sequence, and correlations in historical events, including the long- and short-term casual relations.

The Eighth Grade Content Standards for U.S. History and Geography specify the following relevant guidelines:

1. Students understand the major events preceding the founding of the nation and relate their significance to the development of American constitutional democracy.

The content standards also specify that students will "analyze the philosophy of government expressed in the Declaration of Independence, with an emphasis on government as a means of securing individual rights."

For California teachers of eighth-grade history, the History and Social Studies Framework lays out in even greater detail how the course of study should focus on events leading up to the founding of the nation and connect them with the development of our constitutional democracy. Entitled "Connecting with Past Learning: A New Nation," the unit in the framework is described as follows:

> This unit begins with an in-depth examination of the major events and ideas leading to the American War for Independence. Readings from the Declaration of Independence should be used to discuss these questions: What are "natural rights" and "natural laws"? What did Jefferson mean when he wrote that "all men are created equal" and "endowed by their Creator with certain unalienable rights"? What were the "Laws of Nature" and "Nature's God" to which Jefferson appealed?

These and additional guidelines provided Sally with directions that enabled her to address the state's content standards. While the framework need not be viewed as the sole means of addressing the standards in the state, it provides teachers, administrators, and assessment specialists with some clear expectations for what students ought to learn. The degree to which students do master the content standards and the fleshed out conceptual material in the framework could influence a school's performance on state-wide standardized testing and students' readiness to undertake subsequent study in high school history and social studies classes.

However, the English-Language Arts Content Standards also contained guidelines for instruction at the eighth-grade level that Sally could also address effectively in the unit on the Declaration of Independence. In fact, she saw that the unit provided a remarkable opportunity to help her students build vocabulary, reading comprehension, knowledge of text structure, and writing strategies.

According to the content standards, students in the eighth grade should "use word meanings within the appropriate context and show ability to verify those meanings by definition, restatement, example, comparison, or contrast." Many new and unfamiliar words with which Sally's students could become more familiar appear in the Declaration of Independence.

With respect to reading comprehension, students at the eighth-grade level are expected to "describe and connect the essential ideas, arguments, and perspectives of the text by using their knowledge of text structure, organization, and purpose." They should learn to analyze texts that use propositions and support patterns, as does the Declaration of Independence. They are also expected to "find similarities and differences between texts in the treatment, scope, or organization of ideas," and the Declaration provided a text structure that they could analyze to discover how Jefferson put his proposal and argument together.

With respect to writing, the content standards urge teachers to have their students write compositions with a controlling idea and a coherent thesis that leads to a clear and well-supported conclusion. The Declaration served as a model of those qualities. Using a prompt related to that document, students could compose a persuasive composition that included a well-defined thesis and presented detailed evidence, examples, and reasoning to support their arguments while differentiating between fact and opinion. By doing so, Sally's students worked toward a standard articulated for eighth-grade English-language arts.

Developing integrated units based on a state's content standards challenges even seasoned and knowledgeable teachers. If Sally were just beginning to teach history, she would probably feel overwhelmed. It takes a lot of work to identify relevant standards and learning goals, apply them to a unit, and discover materials in your field that will help your students meet the standards. Keep in mind, too, that in many states the extent to which students attain those standards will be assessed on annual standardized examinations. A school's scores not only in reading and math but also in specific knowledge domains, like the social studies or the sciences, are likely to be published. Furthermore, those published scores will show students' performance by grade level and, in many states, by ethnic group. Because addressing diversity in classrooms is quite challenging, Sally was fortunate to know strategies and procedures that she could use to cope with those challenges.

For teachers seeking a condensed, simplified procedure for unit planning, I've provided that in a Teacher Tip, Figure 11.3.

Step 2. Identifying the "big ideas" or critical concepts.   Early in Sally's second career as a teacher of history she discovered the tension between covering history and getting students to understand the history covered. Teaching for coverage and teaching for understanding are at war in nearly every teacher's mind in every content area. Sally learned that, as a history teacher, she would be in the middle of that battle between coverage and understanding throughout her career. Because history has produced more information than any teacher can hope to cover (and it won't stop!), she had to make decisions about what to teach and what to leave out. Besides, there were some concepts she wanted all her students to master and other information she considered less critical for all students to know.

Enter: Big ideas. These are the ideas that can link content-related information into networks or systems. Carnine (1994) developed the "Big Ideas Curriculum" to highlight the principles and concepts underlying content area domains. Mastery of these unifying concepts helps students overcome the problem of having bits and pieces of information, nothing but disconnected facts that fail to crystallize into any kind of holistic understanding. Without some unifying concepts, students have more trouble learning, remembering, and applying knowledge. If this reminds you of schema theory that offers an explanation of how ideas and information are organized in memory, you may be on to something. One of the merits of schemata was that they provide scaffolding that enables students to assimilate knowledge. If a student can activate a schema, it provides "slots" for incoming data, making both reading and learning more efficient and effective.

In their search for a unified social studies curriculum, Kinder and Bursuck (1991) identified some "big ideas" that help students understand major events in history, such as the ***problem-solution-effect model***. The model makes relationships between events and concepts easier for students to comprehend and remember. Many traditional history courses drive students nuts with dates and names that don't hang together in any meaningful way. However, individual events and historical actors make more sense to students if they fit a pattern, especially one that can be transferred to other domains of seemingly random information. An example of such a pattern is the problem-solution-effect model that students might apply when learning about the American Revolution.

The Declaration of Independence is a primary source document that Sally Peterson could teach to her students while using the "big idea" embodied in the problem-solution-effect model. The Declaration of Independence articulates a problem with substantial evidence, puts forth a solution, but leaves the effects rather ill-defined, mainly because history had to reveal how the solution would play out. Sally decided to use the problem-solution-effect pattern in history as a schema with "slots" to be filled with information gleaned from the Declaration of Independence and its surrounding historical context. She realized that she could return to that problem-solution-effect model to help her students understand many other situations in American history, from slavery in the nineteenth century to terrorism in the twenty-first.

**Step 3. Knowing students.**     Knowledge of students is essential and powerful. The first of five core propositions guiding the assessment of teachers pursuing certification by the National Board for Professional Teaching Standards is that "teachers are committed to students and their learning." Commitment to students and their learning is reflected in knowing who your students are and how they learn.

Earlier in this book, we explored the meaning of diagnostic teaching. We looked at the importance of knowing our students, their learning strengths, their interests, their readiness to learn. And, of course, we need to discover what impedes their learning, what leaves them cold.

As a diagnostic teacher, Sally not only watched what made her students flourish but also searched for the roots of her students' problems with learning in order to find ways to improve it. She was a close observer of her students, their thinking, and the artifacts that represented their learning. While teaching diagnostically, she was on the lookout for what worked and what needed to be modified to work for specific students. She observed the fit between the texts she expected her students to comprehend and her students' resources to comprehend them. If evidence of comprehension did not appear, she tried to discover the problem's origins, or she retaught concepts that she believed her students should master. She looked to see if her students' knowledge and strategies were sufficient for the tasks she gave them. If tasks were beyond her students' reach, then she modified her instruction to include strategies that made texts accessible. Her constant monitoring of her students' learning and her readiness to modify instruction to improve their learning revealed her commitment to students and their growth.

With knowledge of her students and their range of reading and writing skills, Sally could make instructional decisions that could move a student from a casual interest to a lifelong involvement. While some students came to her fired up and ready to consume every idea she had to give, others languished in her classrooms for reasons that were not always clear to her. On them her ideas often perished. Part of what she did as a diagnostic teacher was to discover the reasons for unproductive engagement and to watch for small sparks that might be fanned into a guiding flame.

If you have arrived at Sunday evening but have not yet created your standards-based, literacy integrated unit plan according to the nine-step method presented in these pages or if you have never done a unit plan like the one Sally Peterson has designed here and are stunned by the detail, there is hope. You can simplify. Important planning procedures and design elements may not contribute to the journey you plan for your students to meet their diverse needs, but you will have some idea where you're going. Leaving on an instructional trek without a map or compass can have unexpected consequences, sometimes delightful, too often disastrous.

If you need to simplify because this is one of your first excursions of this kind or you simply haven't had enough time to pack, you can compress some steps and eliminate others.

Step 1. In today's climate, disregarding your subject's content standards is likely to damage your students academically and trouble your colleagues. Then there's you. Best to confirm that content standards and local learning goals are guiding your instruction and its direction.

Step 2. Keep tabs on the "big ideas," but you may not have time to differentiate between them and the lesser ideas. Save that planning for another voyage.

Step 3. If you don't know your students yet, you can't use that knowledge to design units and lessons. However, you can commit yourself to discovering them daily.

Step 4. Use a Planning Pyramid when you have time to build a unit plan with it. However, you will still need a direction, and standards provide that. You can state your objectives based at least on the content standards that will guide your instruction and its evaluation. Integrating literacy strategies will help you teach and your students learn.

Step 5. In lieu of a Planning Pyramid, use the content standards and other learning goals to design individual lessons. Integrating literacy strategies will help you teach and your students learn. (That repetition isn't an error.)

Step 6. Criteria Charts using student input take time you may not have. You can develop rubrics independent of student input. Later, when you know your students better and have time, you can include them in the development of assessment tools.

Step 7. No reason you can't analyze your students' work. Carefully. What you discover will help you see if your students are on the trail you want them on. You may need to rethink your directions to get your students to the destinations you envisioned.

Step 8. No reason you can't help your students identify their next steps in pursuit of standards and learning goals. You should be able to ask them where they're going, and they should be able to give you (or anyone else who comes into your classroom) a pretty clear description in their own words of their destination.

Step 9. If your students haven't even begun the journey you planned or got hopelessly lost along the way, time has come to rethink the instructional venture you charted and what's gone wrong. If only a few strayed off course, some minor tweaking may be all that's needed. If all arrived safely, celebrate your success—and theirs.

FIGURE 11.3   Teacher Tip: Simplified Planning.

Students came into her classroom with an infinite assortment of hidden gifts and fleeting excitements that she tried to bring to light.

So in terms of capacities and degrees of engagement, Sally found her classroom filled with wide ranges. Given the same history text, some of her students read it completely on their own while others found mostly frustration that fed discontent unless she could offer strategic help for their learning. Some came into her classroom eager to absorb all she could give while others did all they could to squelch any possibility of knowledge being absorbed. That was part of the never-ending variety that made teaching an often delight-filled challenge for her.

Step 4. Planning Pyramid for units.   Having reviewed the standards applicable to her instruction in the content areas and having gathered information about her students' range of skills and resources, Sally was ready to climb the next, well, pyramid. A Planning Pyramid (Schumm, Vaughn, & Leavell, 1994) enables secondary teachers to decide what content they will teach after they have examined the standards they are expected to cover, the curriculum resources they have, and the educational needs of each student. Pyramid planning is based on a reality: Not all students can or will learn all the content presented to them. A **Planning Pyramid** enables you to graphically see the content you expect **all** of your students to master, the content you expect **some** of your students to gain, and the content you expect only a **few** of your students to learn (see Figure 11.4).

The base of Sally's pyramid contained information she believed all of her students needed to understand. Those broad, more abstract concepts or "big ideas" usually encompassed a great deal of detailed information about the specific content she planned to cover. What all students would gain was likely to be broader than the level above it. The next level up, what some students would gain, included facts and concepts about the "big ideas" in the level composing the pyramid's base. At the pyramid's pinnacle were the supplementary concepts and facts

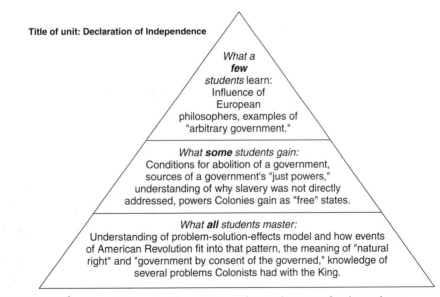

**Figure 11.4**  Pyramid Planning for a Unit on the Declaration of Independence.

that a few of her students would learn. This supplementary information, which was usually more complex, often required exceptional motivation on the part of students to acquire.

Although a Planning Pyramid segments concepts into categories, Sally did not tell students that she expected them to master a particular segment of her pyramid or all of it. That would establish overt expectations she had of individual students based on their ability and could contribute to self-fulfilling prophesies she did not want or intend to trigger (Good & Brophy, 2000). She believed that information from all levels should be equally available to all students. However, she knew that only a few students would be more eager and interested in mastering material in the upper levels of the pyramid.

When applying the Planning Pyramid to the development of the unit on the Declaration of Independence, Sally Peterson had to make decisions about concepts and information that her diverse classroom of students would understand.

She decided that *all* of her students should be able to answer the following questions after completing the unit:

1. How do the Declaration of Independence and events leading up to and following it fit into the problem-solution-effects model?
2. What are "natural rights" and which of these is held as "self-evident" in the Declaration of Independence?
3. What are several (at least six) problems the Colonists had with King George III?

She decided that *some* of her students should be able to answer the following questions after completing the unit:

1. When do people have the right to abolish a government that governs them?
2. What is the source for the just powers of governments?
3. Why didn't the Declaration directly address the problem of slavery in America?
4. What powers does the Declaration say the United Colonies will gain in their status as "free and independent states"?

She decided that a *few* of her students should be able to answer the following questions after completing the unit:

1. How did ideas from European philosophers influence the writing of the Declaration of Independence?
2. What are some examples of the King combining with others to establish "arbitrary government"?

A Planning Pyramid for organizing a unit on the Declaration of Independence (Figure 11.4) consists not only of the pyramid and its differentiated content instruction levels but also of other planning essentials:

1. Learning resources (books, demonstrations, videos, etc.)
2. Instructional Models (and reason for their use)
3. Literacy Strategies (and reason for their use)

In the sections following, we will explore the relevance of these three elements to planning for differentiated, standards-based instruction and the decisions Sally Peterson made about each.

*Learning resources.*   When engaged in long-term planning, as we would be in the development of a Planning Pyramid for units, Sally Peterson needed to account for the learning resources that would enable her to carry out the instruction suggested in the pyramid's sectors. These materials included the textbook commonly used for the course, demonstrations she was likely to give, videos she might show, and other instructional materials available to her. Some textbooks or anthologies provided limited access to additional information while others contained more resources than she could ever use and so required her thoughtful selection from them.

For the unit developed in this chapter, Sally had many resources to draw upon, including textbooks, videos, Web sites, and primary sources in the form of documents like the Declaration of Independence.

*Instructional models.*   Instructional models provide teachers with a framework and procedures used to teach concepts, academic content, and skills. They describe patterns of behavior that teachers apply to achieve their teaching objectives and learning goals. While an instructional model provided Sally with a broad framework that she could apply to help her achieve her aims, structured activities or plans in the form of strategies would help her along the way. Here we learn how Sally addressed instructional models. In the next section, we'll discover how she worked in literacy strategies.

Sally could choose from several instructional models depending on her instructional purposes. While educators have grouped instructional models into many different categories, Lasley, Matczynski, and Rowley (2002) organized them into the following four:

- ◆ Models that foster reasoning skills (such as inquiry),
- ◆ Models that foster reorganizing skills (such as concept formation),
- ◆ Models that foster remembering skills (such as direct instruction), and
- ◆ Models that foster relating skills (such as cooperative learning).

On closer inspection, most of the categories "leak," by which I mean models within a category flow into or overlap with other categories. For example, while cooperative learning certainly can foster relating skills, it can also promote reasoning, reorganization, and remembering. Furthermore, some instructional models, like lecturing, don't fit well into any of these categories. However, the categories do provide us with handy carrying cages for methods that often have a life of their own.

For this lesson on the Declaration of Independence, Sally decided that to facilitate concept formation her best bet for instructional success would be fostering reorganizing skills (or better yet, organizing skills). That was because she wanted to help students

1. organize information about the American revolution and the Declaration of Independence;
2. make connections between events, documents, and concepts; and
3. create and test hypotheses about how the data fit into a pattern, namely the problem-solution-effects model.

During the 1960s and 1970s, multitudes of history and social studies teachers learned concept formation as an instructional model from Hedda Taba (1971). They used it to help their students make observations, compare and contrast those observations, group similar data, form and label categories, and make conclusions based on the inter-connections observed.

To engage her students in the phases of concept formation using their knowledge of the American Revolution and the Declaration of Independence, she wanted them to:

1. Examine a set of data and/or documents. (Students would be evaluating the import of historical events and examining claims made in the Declaration of Independence.)
2. Create groupings of conceptually similar data. (Students group events, claims, and other data together.)
3. Provide concept labels for groups of data. (Having organized sets of events and claims together, students must label sections of the Declaration. Teachers may provide several labels that could be used as headings for sections of the document, including the labels "problem," "solution," and "effects.")
4. Expand categories they have created and labeled. (After students have reconstructed the Declaration from individual sentences and provided headings for sections of the document, students could add information under various categories that was not included in the original Declaration, such as what to do about the slavery issue in the 13 Colonies.)

To achieve closure and assessment for this activity, Sally emphasized the problem-solution-effects pattern posed in the Declaration and prepared students for that pattern's reappearance throughout their study of American history.

*Literacy strategies.*   With information about the reading levels and other literacy skills her students had, Sally made decisions about strategies that were likely to help her students gain literacy skills and strategies. When deciding which strategies to apply, she kept these questions in mind:

- Does the reading strategy target the problems my students have?
- Am I comfortable teaching the strategy or do I need some coaching?
- How will I discover if my students have learned the strategy and can apply it?

Once she answered those questions, she was ready to decide how to teach the strategy she wanted her students to know and use.

Sally thought this unit on the Declaration of Independence called for a set of literacy strategies. Taken as a package, those strategies prepared her students for their encounter with the document, activated their background knowledge related to it, addressed unfamiliar vocabulary, provided opportunity for repeated exposures to the text, and included a review that reinforced all students' understanding of the problem-solution-effects model. The strategies that she thought would enable these purposes to be achieved included the following:

1. Anticipation Guide
2. Journal Writing
3. Vocabulary Self-Collection Strategy (VSS)
4. Word Cards
5. Text Structure Identification
6. Reciprocal Teaching
7. Criteria Chart and/or Rubric Design
8. Cloze Procedure
9. Review Questions

Most of these strategies were described earlier in this text. Criteria Charts and Review Questions will be demonstrated in this section.

## Step 5. Create individual lessons with reference to a unit Planning Pyramid.

***5.1 Create lessons that weave together more than one standard or learning goal in a single task or activity.*** With the objective of weaving language arts strands into her history standards, Sally noted that the English-Language Arts Content Standards included vocabulary development, reading comprehension strategy instruction (including text structure and organization), and writing documents with a coherent thesis leading to a well-supported conclusion. These language arts standards complemented those of history and social studies, especially the ones calling for students to explain how historical events are connected to each other, to distinguish relevant from irrelevant information, to assess the credibility of sources, and to understand sequence and causal relations in historical events. Seeing how these strands from the language arts and social studies supported each other, Sally saw several opportunities to weave them together in her lessons on the Declaration of Independence.

***5.2 Integrate reading and/or writing strategies into lessons to facilitate learning or measure progress to mastery of the standards.*** Sally's daily lesson plans that she developed with reference to her Planning Pyramid and unit goals are presented below in summary form. After covering steps 6 through 9 in constructing a responsive standards-based instructional program, I will narrate what Sally did for each of the daily lesson plans outlined. There we will see what literacy enhancing strategies she used each day to help her students comprehend not only the surface but also the sub-surface meanings of the Declaration of Independence.

Day 1:    Activities: Anticipation Guide, Vocabulary Self-Collection Strategy, Journal Entry to Introduce Problem-Solution-Effects Model, Homework.

| Day 2: | Activities: Distribute Vocabulary List for Word Cards, Reconstructing the Declaration, Text Structure, Homework. |
| Day 3: | Reciprocal Teaching, Mini-lesson and Discussion, Homework. |
| Day 4: | Introduction of Writing Assignment, Development of Criteria Chart, Work in Class on Letter, Vocabulary Review and Quiz, Homework (Complete Letter to Newspaper). |
| Day 5: | Peer Response with Criteria Check-Sheet, "Next Steps" to Improve Letter in Student's Own Words, Prepare for Quiz on Concepts. |
| Day 6: | Revision of Persuasive Letter Submitted, Short-essay Test. |
| Day 7–9: | Begin New Unit. |
| Day 9–10: | Letter Returned with Teacher Assessment and Recommendation for Further Development. |

**Step 6. Develop criteria charts and rubrics to guide and assess progress.** Wanting to assess her students' learning with more than factual questions, Sally introduced a writing assignment on day four of her unit that would weave together several standards from both history and English. The assignment was as follows:

> Write a letter of persuasion to a Revolutionary Period newspaper in America or Britain explaining in your own words why you are convinced that the Colonies must separate from Great Britain. Your letter must include the following concepts and information: natural right, consent of the governed, exposition of several problems the Colonists had with the British, and benefits of the solution. One paragraph of the letter must contain an explanation of your understanding of the loyalist position and why you reject that position. The letter should be about 600 words.

Although Sally could have developed criteria for her own assignments, allowing her students to participate in creating criteria had several distinct advantages. First, all students got a clearer picture of what she expected them to do for an assignment. By going over each criterion that would be used to evaluate their performance, they knew more clearly how to perform. Second, if all her students participated in establishing criteria, they could not blame anyone else for judging their work by standards they knew nothing about. They "owned" the criteria applied to their work. Third, with all her students involved in setting criteria, the opportunities for each to succeed was enlarged, in part, because she gave each student more responsibility to contribute to the criteria that would be used to evaluate their work. Fourth, her students were more likely to focus on their learning than on their grades. However, she knew a price was to be paid for student participation in setting criteria. The process took time even though she thought the time was well invested.

*Developing Criteria T-Charts.* Gregory, Cameron, and Davies (1997) suggest introducing the process of developing criteria by using students' personal experiences, something all Sally's students knew and could draw upon. Sally had her students begin by exploring what makes a good friend. After brainstorming on paper for five minutes, her students met in small teams, shared their features, and agreed to a team list. Each team then contributed that list to a master list of features that a recorder wrote on the board. At that point, Sally and the class began to see what features fit into categories that she could help them label.

## STEP-BY-STEP: *Creating Criteria with Students (Gregory, Cameron, and Davies, 1997)*

**STEP 1. Brainstorming.** Because her assignment was to write a persuasive letter, she began criteria collection by distributing copies of a couple of model letters of persuasion from newspapers and asking her students to discuss what elements made these persuasive letters successful or effective. As they made observations, she recorded elements on the board. She contributed some of her own criteria to those that students identified because her students did not identify characteristics she knew were essential to excellent letters of persuasion, such as a clear statement of the writer's position and supporting evidence. She wanted to ensure that state content standards that were guiding her instruction were addressed in the criteria if students did not explicitly include them in their brainstorming. Furthermore, she wanted to include assessment criteria for key concepts, such as natural right, that were included in the prompt she gave them for the letter.

**STEP 2. Sort and Categorize.** With student participation, she reviewed the list of elements developed through brainstorming and grouped related elements together into categories. For example, while she was working on criteria for persuasive letters, all the elements related to the writer's position (or thesis) were grouped together as were elements related to clear written communication.

**STEP 3. Make and Post a Chart.** Making and posting a chart that included criteria for a persuasive letter and specific details of each category would remind her students of their goals. The categories used to evaluate the work went in the left-hand column while the more specific elements that made up each category went in the right-hand column (see Table 11.1).

**STEP 4. Add, Revise, and Refine.** Sally assumed that criteria for persuasive writing assignments would continuously be reviewed and evolve. After an assignment had been completed

**TABLE 11.1**  Criteria T-Chart for Letter of Persuasion

| Criteria | Details/Specifics |
|---|---|
| States a position. | Develops position consistently; Doesn't contradict position stated; Writer's voice reveals conviction. |
| Examples of problems with British. | Gives about 5 or 6 different examples. |
| Includes "natural right." | Defines concept in own words; Provides examples; Shows how it's related to Colonists' concerns. |
| Includes "consent of governed." | Explains in writers' own words; Explains why consent was critical to Colonists. |
| Includes "loyalist" position. | Explains loyalist stance; Gives reasons for rejecting. |
| Paragraphs have topic sentences. | No sentences that aren't relevant to topic of paragraph. |
| Well organized with transitions. | Ideas flow from paragraph to paragraph. |
| Variety of sentence structure. | No choppy, stiff sections. |
| Mechanics don't interfere with message. | Few spelling, grammar, or punctuation errors. |

and she returned it to her students with her evaluation based on the criteria, students could look at their own work and compare it with the criteria posted. New criteria might need to be added. Irrelevant criteria might need to be dropped. Criteria need to be reviewed and revised continually, especially for documents in other disciplines, like lab reports for science classes.

***From Criteria T-Charts to rubrics.***   Once Sally's students generated features for a criteria chart, she had but a short trip to rubrics. Papers would be scored from 4 (highest) to 1 (lowest) as follows:

4. The letter clearly addresses all parts of the writing task. It makes a clear, sustained claim that the Colonies should break with Great Britain and seek independence. It contains evidence in the form of at least five problems or "complaints" contained in the Declaration. It presents a consistent, solidly convincing argument for Colonists seeking independence from the homeland. It makes clear the meanings of "natural right" and "consent of the governed" and shows how those concepts were important to the Colonists. It develops and refutes the "loyalist" counter-argument. Organization, paragraph structure, sentence structure, grammar, punctuation, and spelling all contribute to a letter that clearly and convincingly communicates the writer's intent to seek independence from Britain.

3. The letter addresses most parts of the writing task. It claims that the Colonies should break with Great Britain and seek independence. It contains evidence in the form of at least three problems or "complaints" contained in the Declaration. It presents an argument for Colonists seeking independence from the homeland. It explains the meanings of "natural right" and "consent of the governed" and explains the importance of these concepts to the Colonists. It presents and refutes the "loyalist" counter-argument. Organization, paragraph structure, sentence structure, grammar, punctuation, and spelling all contribute to a letter that communicates the writer's intent to seek independence from Britain.

2. The letter addresses only some parts of the writing task. It claims that the Colonies should break with Great Britain and seek independence. It defends that position with at least one problem or "complaint" contained in the Declaration. It presents a weak argument for Colonists seeking independence from the homeland. It may not explain the meanings of "natural right" and "consent of the governed" or may not explain the importance of these concepts to the Colonists. It may not present or refute the "loyalist" counter-argument. Problems appear in the letter's organization, paragraph structure, sentence structure, grammar, punctuation, and/or spelling to an extent that they detract from the letter's intent.

1. The letter addresses only a few parts of the writing task. The letter makes no central claim about the Colonies breaking from Great Britain and seeking independence. The letter contains little or no evidence supporting the "facts" or "complaints" contained in the Declaration. The letter does not clarify the meanings of "natural right" and "consent of the governed" or show how those concepts were important to the Colonists. The letter does not develop or refute the "loyalist" counter-argument. The letter fails to develop a coherent or convincing argument for Colonists seeking independence from England. Organization, paragraph structure, sentence structure, grammar, punctuation, and spelling (singularly or in combination) detract significantly from the letter's message.

**Step 7. Analyze student work to evaluate proximity to goals.**   Sally used student writing to observe progress toward standards and learning goals, a process described in Chapter 8 on writing across the curriculum. She often examined her students' written work to generate next-step improvements. Following an analysis of her students' work, she could use her observations to guide her students' development in writing. Having a clear idea of what next steps would be beneficial to her students, a teacher like Sally could then help her students formulate in their own words what targets they should focus upon to move closer to mastery of articulated standards or learning goals.

Sally also belonged to a Critical Friends Group that met regularly to share and discuss student work. They followed certain protocols to look at student writing samples. With insights and support from those collaborating teachers, she made decisions about what next steps she could take to help her students improve their writing. (More on Critical Friends Groups will arrive in the next chapter.)

With support from her Critical Friends Group, Sally has been working on a research project of her own. In her classes, she is trying to discover the effectiveness of an innovative practice to help her students improve writing skills. She meets with her Critical Friends Group and a collaborating university professor to talk about her "teacher research" project and to get suggestions and insights from her colleagues. Sally has been exploring the effectiveness of using peer editing with criteria feedback sheets. Students working in pairs used structured response sheets to identify next steps toward improving the quality of papers before they are submitted to her for assessment.

Prior to class on day five, Sally identified students she planned to pair for peer response. For this day's peer response activity, she decided to pair what she considered a stronger writer with a weaker one. She recognized that some students were likely to get more guidance from the first round of response than others. However, by using a peer response format, she could give students an opportunity to become more familiar with the concepts she wanted them to learn and with criteria for successfully writing persuasive letters. Meanwhile, they could acquire tutoring skills.

However, without suggesting to students that she'd placed a stronger with a weaker writer, she simply paired them as she had planned and gave each student a sheet labeled "Criteria Feedback for Letter of Persuasion" (see Table 11.2). That assessment sheet, a modification of one suggested by Gregory, Cameron, and Davies (1997), included all the criteria the class and she agreed should be applied

**TABLE 11.2**   Criteria Feedback for Letter of Persuasion

| Criteria | Met | Not Yet | What's Needed Next |
|---|---|---|---|
| States a position | | | |
| Examples of problems with British | | | |
| Includes "natural right" | | | |
| Includes "consent of governed" | | | |
| Includes "loyalist" position | | | |
| Paragraphs have topic sentences | | | |
| Well organized with transitions | | | |
| Variety of sentence structure | | | |
| Mechanics don't interfere with message | | | |

to the letters along with three columns for evaluation and comments: Met, Not Yet, and What's Needed Next. After students read over their partner's paper, they checked off the appropriate category and, as they saw it, what steps in the paper's development should come next. Sally was finding that these structured responses during peer evaluation provided more students with more productive information to develop their papers further. As students read over their partner's papers, they could look up to see the criteria T-chart with the detail they filled in a day or two ago (see Table 11.1). The additional detail helped students communicate to their partners what needed to be improved to come closer to meeting the standards established.

### Step 8. Students identify and articulate "next-step" goals.

Sally believed her students needed to know clearly what had to be done next to improve the quality of their work. For Sally to know that they knew what should come next, she wanted her students to be able to put into their own words what they would have to do to improve their performance. She knew that with clear "next steps" both direction and desire for improvement would benefit.

After students completed assessment sheets for each other, Sally explained to the class that they should use these peer assessments and their own self-assessment to write out what next steps they would take to revise their letters. These "next step" goals she asked each student to write in their own words on the bottom of the "Criteria Feedback for Letter of Persuasion."

The range of "next step" goals was extensive. A few students had omitted concepts, such as "natural right," and needed to include those concepts in their papers along with examples. A couple of students had introduced the concept but hadn't explained it clearly or provided an illustration of it. Two or three students had left out the counter-argument to independence that a "loyalist" would make, and some that included it forgot to rebut it. Many students had problems with paragraph development, sentence structure, spelling, and punctuation. While individuals would work on their own "next step" goals, Sally also recognized that she could schedule some mini-lessons on topics, like paragraph structure, with which many students struggled.

Sally noticed that a couple of students were struggling to organize their entire letter and appeared to be confused about how to handle the concepts she wanted them to address. With these struggling writers, she held brief conferences as they formulated and wrote down their "next step" goals.

Sally thought to herself with satisfaction, "If someone ever wanted to come into my classroom to ask my kids what they were learning and what they needed to do to improve their performance, now would be the moment to walk through that door." Although no one walked in at that moment, she explained to her students that they should revise their persuasive letters with the assessments and their "next-step" goals in mind so that revised letters could be turned in to her the next day. She would share her sense of satisfaction with her Critical Friends Group the next time they met.

### Step 9. Revisit lesson plans and re-teach as needed.

This last phase in the process of implementing a standards-based instructional program implies that teachers not only reflect on their teaching practice but also embrace a mastery orientation for their students. Sally, as you might have guessed by now, is clearly both a diagnostic teacher and a reflective practitioner (Schon, 1983). She embodies in her practice the guiding images of reflective teaching which include an inquiry-orientation, an analytic approach to the effects of instruction on students, and a commitment to improving teaching and fostering continuous professional growth (Valli, 1992). Within the context of standards-based instruction, Sally provides her students with instruction designed to move them to higher ground. If they are unable to reach that higher ground on a first attempt, she's ready to provide the scaffolding they need to try again. She encourages collaboration not only between herself and her students but between student and student. As she moves forward, she monitors and assesses student progress, reflects upon that progress independently and with her colleagues, and looks for new ways to improve her instruction and her students' performance. Her design and execution of daily lessons for the Declaration of Independence unit show these characteristics of the reflective teacher.

## Sally Peterson's Lesson Sequence and Procedure

Day one.    Activities: Anticipation Guide, Vocabulary Self-Collection Strategy, Journal Entry to Introduce Problem-Solution-Effects Model, Homework.

The first day's lesson in the Declaration of Independence unit began with an Anticipation Guide (see Table 11.3). After students completed the Guide, Sally led them in a discussion based on their answers. As she talked with her students, she tried to discover their preconceived ideas and attitudes about the Declaration of Independence. Sally looked for possible conflicts between their beliefs and the content of the text that students would rectify as they became familiar with the document.

After completing the Anticipation Guide and discussion, Sally had students go into their cooperative learning groups to work on a Vocabulary Self-Collection Strategy (VSS). She asked teams of four to identify all unfamiliar words. She also asked the team to appoint a reporter and asked each team's reporter to provide four words to add to a list of unfamiliar words that she would write on the board. She explained to her students that she would use their list to compile a master list of vocabulary that students would be responsible for learning.

For the journal entry, Sally asked her students to take out their journal notebooks and describe a problem that they had experienced personally or read about or

TABLE 11–3    Anticipation Guide: True/False

|  | True | False |
|---|---|---|
| 1. The Declaration of Independence was written to warn Britain that war would break out in Boston on July 4, 1776. |  |  |
| 2. According to the Declaration, no truths are self-evident because evidence must be provided to prove a truth. |  |  |
| 3. According to the Declaration, the holding of slaves directly contradicts the claim that "all men are created equal." |  |  |
| 4. The Declaration includes a list of facts said to prove that the King of Great Britain pursued an absolute tyranny over the colonies. |  |  |
| 5. Among the facts listed is the claim that the King kept a standing army in the colonies without the consent of their legislatures. |  |  |

studied in school. When deciding which problem they should write about, she explained to them that it should be one that had a solution and effects that arose from that solution. She gave her students an example from her own experience that fit the pattern. She told her students that they'd have fifteen minutes to write about a problem, solution, and its effects. They could use about five minutes for each section.

After students completed their journal entries (she allowed a few more minutes for those needing more time), she asked them to find a partner and share the entry with that partner. After a few minutes, she asked for volunteers to share their entries with the whole class and worked toward showing students how the examples fit a problem-solution-effects pattern, as most did.

*Homework.*    Read the Declaration of Independence. Journal Entry: What was Jefferson's purpose in writing the document?

Day two.    Activities: Distribute Vocabulary List for Word Cards, Reconstructing the Declaration, Text Structure, Homework.

Sally compiled a list of vocabulary words based on the previous day's VSS activity and made a couple of additions. Preferring vocabulary and concepts important to understanding the document, Sally selected the following 15 terms: natural right, despotism, tyranny, formidable, appropriation, arbitrary, abdicate, perfidy, insurrection, petition for redress, unwarrantable jurisdiction, magnanimity, consanguinity, acquiesce, and rectitude. After distributing the list, she explained to her students that they should construct 3 × 5 word cards for each of these terms (see Figure 11.5). She showed students what the word card should contain: the term, its meaning, its part of speech, the original sentence where it occurred, a synonym, a keyword (if appropriate) to help them remember the word's meaning, and a situation in which they might use or apply the term. As an example, she put the term *rectitude* on the board and provided all the information about the word that she requested. Students

---

Word Card Format

Term: rectitude

Meaning: moral integrity; being correct in judgment or procedure

Part of Speech: noun

Original Sentence from Text: "We, therefore, the Representatives of the United States of America, . . . , appealing to the Supreme Judge of the World for the *rectitude* of our intentions, do, . . . , solemnly publish and declare, That these United Colonies are, and of Right ought to be Free and Independent States. . . ."

Synonym: rightness

Key word (if appropriate): Those who do not show themselves to be honest people are a wreck and make up a *Wreck*-titude, the very opposite of rectitude.

A situation in which you might use this term: A judge in a court might show *rectitude* during the prosecution of a defendant charged with treason and terrorist activity.

FIGURE 11.5   Word Card.

copied her sample from the board on the 3 × 5 cards she distributed. Then, after distributing dictionaries, she let her students practice with the word *acquiesce*. While they filled in required information on 3 × 5 cards, she walked around the room giving help as needed. After students completed a word card, she explained that their homework for the next day would be to complete cards for the remaining terms.

Sally then asked her students to group themselves into their cooperative learning teams which she had already established. She then explained that she would give each team a copy of the Declaration of Independence that she had cut into 10 sections. Without looking at the original document, the team was to put the sections of the text in their correct order and paste them together on paper she provided. All members of the team had to agree with the ordering of the fragments she asked them to reassemble.

Sally asked each team to look at the way the actual text of the Declaration was laid out and provide a description for it. Earlier in the year, Sally had taught her students about various text structures and how various patterns of ideas are organized in texts, including description, sequence, comparison-contrast, thesis-support, cause-effect, and problem-solution, as well as a review of story grammar (see Chapter 5). Confirming what Sally anticipated, many of the teams had trouble identifying the pattern. Some teams were close, and with guidance through questioning, Sally got them to identify the problem-solution structure into which much of the text fit. She agreed that other text patterns, such as cause-effect, could also be seen in the document, but that the problem-solution pattern appeared to fit best. In discussion, she had students summarize the problem Jefferson described, the solution proposed, and even to identify some of the effects that solution would have on the new United States.

**Day three.**   Reciprocal Teaching, Mini-Lesson and Discussion, Homework.

At the beginning of the class, Sally collected her students' word cards.

Sally had already taught her students the procedures for Reciprocal Teaching. Students knew that the strategies included summarizing, questioning, predicting, and clarifying. However, she knew that they would need a brief review before moving ahead, so she asked one of her cooperative learning teams to demonstrate reciprocal teaching using the first paragraph from the Declaration. She asked the team of four students to practice all four strategies that make up reciprocal teaching: summarizing (putting the gist of a passage into a student's own words), questioning (asking a "teacher-like" question about the passage for others in the team to answer), predicting (making a statement about where the text is likely to go next), and clarifying (identifying and explaining what a phrase or word means). She reminded the teams that, as they go through each section or sentence of the Declaration, they should rotate roles as summarizer, questioner, predictor, and clarifier. She then asked her class to move into their cooperative learning teams to apply reciprocal teaching to passages from the Declaration of Independence. Knowing that students might find large passages in the Declaration frustrating, she provided each student with a copy of the document marked with stop-points at shorter sections, even down to some difficult individual sentences, for the reciprocal teaching activity. While students engaged in the activity, she moved from team to team listening, monitoring, and assisting as needed.

After students used about half the period on reciprocal teaching, she returned to whole-class procedures for a mini-lesson on the concept of natural right. After a brief lecture on the "divine right" of monarchs in Europe, she drew her students into a discussion during which she addressed the following questions:

- ◆ What is natural right?
- ◆ What is the difference between "natural right" of citizens and "divine right" of monarchs?
- ◆ Are "life, liberty, and the pursuit of happiness" rights? If they are rights, who says so? If they are sanctioned and made possible by God, what happens to "natural rights" if no God exists?
- ◆ Do "natural rights" really exist in nature or did people invent them, sort of like they invented writing or the Constitution?
- ◆ How would a woman or a slave view the Declaration of Independence?

For the last of these questions, Sally had her students do a quickwrite for five minutes to think through the question. She then had them complete a Think-Pair-Share activity that gave students a chance to talk with a partner about what they wrote. Sally then conducted a whole-class discussion about what students wrote and said about the question during Think-Pair-Share time.

**Homework.** Journal Entry: Many colonists were also "loyalists," meaning they did not want to separate from Britain. Taking the position of a loyalist, write a 100 to 150 word position paper in which you defend your point of view toward independence. Also: prepare for vocabulary quiz on words and terms from the Declaration of Independence.

Day four. Introduction of Writing Assignment, Development of Criteria Chart, Work in Class on Letter, Vocabulary Review and Quiz, Homework (Complete Letter to Newspaper).

At the beginning of class, Sally had several students read their "loyalist" position statements. As students provided reasons and evidence for taking the loyalist position, Sally jotted them on the board as a set of reminders to students.

Sally then introduced the writing assignment described earlier that would weave together several of the standards from both history and English: A letter of persuasion to a Revolutionary Period newspaper in America or Britain explaining in their own words why they were convinced that the Colonies must separate from Great Britain.

The next part of Sally's lesson for the fourth day has already been described under phase 6 of planning for standards-based instruction: Developing Criteria Charts and Rubrics. Sally later transferred and transformed information collected from the Criteria T-Charts into rubrics that she later used to evaluate and score her students' persuasive letters. The original Criteria Charts she kept posted in her classroom along with the rubric she developed.

After she completed the Criteria Charts with her students, Sally had her students work independently on their persuasive letters while she went from student to student assisting as needed.

During the last 20 minutes of class, she asked her students to assemble in their co-operative learning teams and help each other prepare for a short vocabulary quiz. Teams were to help each other prepare, but each student would be held individually accountable for his or her performance on the quiz. However, each student's final score would reflect the weighted performance of the team on the quiz. Usually she used a ratio of about 3 to 1 when weighting individual and team performance for grades.

**Homework.** Complete Writing Assignment.

Day five.    Peer Response with Criteria Check-Sheet, "Next Steps" to Improve Letter in Student's Own Words, Prepare for Quiz on Concepts.

As previously described, Sally began class by distributing to her students a criteria feedback sheet that she had designed for assessing an early draft of a persuasive letter that they had written to a Revolutionary Period newspaper. Students working in pairs read each other's letters and completed the feedback sheets with recommendations for their partners. Each student then put into his or her own words what next steps he or she would take to meet the criteria established for the letter. During this process, Sally circulated among her students to help those pairs and individuals needing her guidance.

With time remaining, Sally reminded students that they would also have a quiz the next day on concepts and vocabulary related to the Declaration of Independence. To help them prepare for the quiz, she gave each student a set of review questions (see Figure 11.6) and asked them to assemble in their cooperative learning base teams. She explained to the class that she wanted all team members to feel confident about their ability to answer all the questions on the review sheet and to know the vocabulary words generated through the VSS process.

To help students master the review questions, Sally used Jigsaw. She established several "expert" teams whose task was to master answers to two specific questions on the review sheet. Each "expert" team had representatives from each base or home team in the class. As the expert teams gathered to address their questions, Sally visited each team to make sure its members understood how to answer the questions they were to master. When all of the expert teams reported to her that they understood how answer the questions and that each member of each expert team could explain those

---

How did the First Continental Congress and the battles of Lexington and Concord influence the colonies' relationship with the British?

What happened at the Second Continental Congress?

How did Paine's *Common Sense* influence attitudes in the colonies?

How did Europe's Enlightenment philosophers affect our Declaration of Independence?

What is "natural right"? What is the difference between "natural right" of citizens and "divine right" of monarchs?

Do "natural rights" really exist in nature or did people invent them, sort of like they invented writing or the Constitution?

How did conditions in the colonies contradict the notion of "government by consent of the governed"?

What kinds of problems did the colonists experience with British rule in the colonies?

How did the Declaration justify a break with Britain?

How do events of the Revolution fit into a problem-solution-effects pattern?

How would a woman or a slave view the Declaration of Independence?

---

FIGURE 11.6    Review Questions (a Sampler).

answers to their home team-mates, Sally asked everyone to return to their home team. Working with their home team, each "expert" then made sure all members of their home team could answer the questions on which they had become experts.

*Homework.*    Review for quiz on concepts and vocabulary related to Declaration of Independence.

Day six.    Revision of Persuasive Letter Submitted, Short Essay Test.
     Students turned in a revised copy of their letter of persuasion along with the first draft and the peer assessment sheet their partner completed for them. Sally explained that she would review all documents and return the letters in a few days. Students then had their short-essay test on concepts in the Declaration of Independence.

Day nine or ten.    Sally returned the letter with an evaluation based on the rubric and recommendation for the letter's further development.

---

DOUBLE-ENTRY JOURNAL: After Reading

Go to the Double-Entry Journal for Chapter 11 on our Companion Website at www.prenhall.com/unrau to complete your journal entry.

Review your response to the DEJ you wrote before reading this chapter. Having now read the chapter, how would you modify your approach to managing standards, literacy issues, student diversity, and assessment of student learning when planning instruction? What elements in your planning could you alter that you think might benefit your students' engagement and learning?

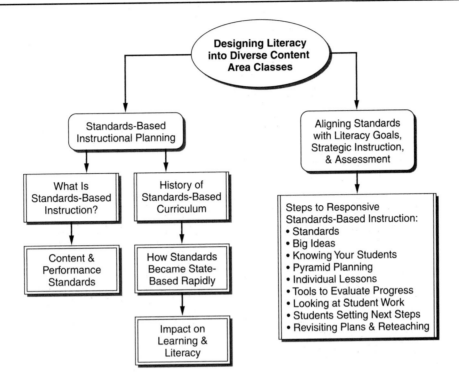

**Designing Literacy into Diverse Content Area Classes**

Standards-Based Instructional Planning

Aligning Standards with Literacy Goals, Strategic Instruction, & Assessment

What Is Standards-Based Instruction?

History of Standards-Based Curriculum

Content & Performance Standards

How Standards Became State-Based Rapidly

Impact on Learning & Literacy

Steps to Responsive Standards-Based Instruction:
- Standards
- Big Ideas
- Knowing Your Students
- Pyramid Planning
- Individual Lessons
- Tools to Evaluate Progress
- Looking at Student Work
- Students Setting Next Steps
- Revisiting Plans & Reteaching

Companion Website

For exercises to clarify your understanding of the chapter content, visit the self-assessments for Chapter 11 on our Companion Website at www.prenhall.com/unrau

413

# References

Bloom, B., Englehart, M., Furst, E., Hill, W., & Krathwohl, D. (1956). *Taxonomy of educational objectives: The classification of educational goals. Handbook I: Cognitive domain.* New York: Longmans Green.

Carnine, D. (1994). The BIG Accommodations Program. *Educational Leadership, 51,* 87–88.

Deshler, D. D., Ellis, E. S., & Lenz, B. K. (1996). *Teaching adolescents with learning disabilities: Strategies and methods.* Denver, CO: Love Publishing.

Ellis, A. K., & Fouts, J. T. (1997). *Research on educational innovations* (2nd ed.). Larchmont, NY: Eye on Education.

Good, T., & Brophy, J. E. (2000). *Looking in classrooms* (2nd ed.). New York: Longman.

Gregory, K., Cameron, C., & Davies, A. (1997). *Setting and using criteria.* Mervilli, British Columbia: Connections Publishing.

Holding on to creativity in the face of standards. (1999). *California Educator, 4*(3), 10–13.

How to cope with standards. (1999). *California Educator, 4*(3), 14–15.

Kinder, D., & Bursuck, W. (1991). The search for a unified social studies curriculum: Does history really repeat itself? *Journal of Learning Disabilities, 24*(5), 270–284.

Lasley, T. J., Matczynski, T. J., & Rowley, J. B. (2002). *Instructional models: Strategies for teaching in a diverse society.* Belmont, CA: Wadsworth.

Mager, R. (1962). *Preparing instructional objectives.* Palo Alto, CA: Fearon Publishers.

McNeil, L. M. (2000). *Contradictions of school reform: Educational costs of standardized testing.* New York: Routledge.

*A nation at risk: The imperative for educational reform.* (1983). Washington, DC: Government Printing Office.

Ohanian, S. (1999). *One size fits few: The folly of educational standards.* Portsmouth, NH: Heinemann.

PISA survey accents role of teacher. (2002, February/March). *Reading Today, 19*(4), p. 1, 6.

Ragland, M. A., Asera, R., & Johnson, J. F. (1999). *Urgency, responsibility, efficacy: Preliminary findings of a study of high performing Texas school districts.* Austin, TX: Charles A. Dana Center.

Reeves, D. B. (1998). *Making standards work: How to implement standards-based assessments in the classroom, school, and district.* Denver, CO: Center for Performance Assessment.

Reyes, P., Scribner, J. D., & Paredes Scribner, A. (1999). *Lessons from high performing Hispanic schools: Creating learning communities.* New York: Teachers College Press.

Schmoker, M. (1996). *Results: The key to continuous school improvement.* Alexandria, VA: Association for Supervision and Curriculum Development.

Schmoker, M. (2001). *The results fieldbook: Practical strategies from dramatically improved schools.* Alexandria, VA: Association for Supervision and Curriculum Development.

Schon, D. A. (1983). *The reflective practitioner.* New York: Basic Books.

Schumm, J. S., Vaughn, S., & Leavell, A. (1994). Planning pyramid: A framework for planning for diverse student needs during content area instruction. *The Reading Teacher, 47*(8), 608–615.

Skrla, L. (2001). Accountability, equity, complexity. *Educational Researcher, 30*(4), 15–21.

Steinberg, J. (1999, September 30). Educators Focus on "Pain" of Standards. *New York Times,* p. A20.

Taba, H. (1971). *Hilda Taba teaching strategies program.* Miami, FL: Institute for Staff Development.

Valli, L. (1992). *Reflective teacher education: Cases and critiques.* Albany, NY: State University of New York.

# 12

# TEACHER TO TEACHER: FOSTERING
# LITERACY AND REFLECTIVE PRACTICE

After reading Chapter 12, you should be able to answer the following questions:

1. As your career evolves, what kinds of reflective activities hold out the potential for enhancing professional development?
2. How do the professional lives of teachers in "beating the odds" schools support student achievement?
3. How do teams support literacy and learning across the curriculum?
4. How does technology serve as a resource for professional growth?
5. What kinds of services do professional organizations offer teachers in your content area?

DOUBLE-ENTRY JOURNAL: Before Reading

As your career evolves, how do you envision your teaching colleagues and other professionals in education helping you integrate literacy into your content area instruction and promoting reflection on your classroom instruction?

Now go to the Double-Entry Journal for Chapter 12 on our Companion Website at www.prenhall.com/unrau to fill out your journal entry.

## TEACHER ROLES IN SCHOOL LITERACY DEVELOPMENT

In this chapter, I want to give you some ideas about what teachers have done together, often in "tough" teaching situations, to help their students learn and achieve at unexpectedly high levels. But, keeping your career path in mind, I also want to give you professionally appropriate expectations for engaging students in literacy and learning growth. New or apprenticing teachers face different problems professionally from more seasoned teachers. So I want to give you a couple of case studies. They depict teachers at different stages in their readiness to engage students and the whole school culture in literacy development. In many schools, teams of teachers have collaborated to organize instruction, create learning communities, and to help themselves make professional progress. As they progress professionally, teachers often reflect on their work and that of their students. Because of the importance of developing a reflective practice, I'm going to present a range of vehicles that enable teachers to grow themselves and their careers, strategies that range from work with a master teacher or mentor to action research and National Board Certification. Along the way, there are many resources for career growth, including new technologies and long-standing professional organizations.

## A New Teacher Copes with Classroom Literacy Challenges

Jose Ricardo's first teaching assignment at Jefferson High School was U.S. History, a course primarily for eleventh graders.* From the time he was an elementary school kid, he had a love for history. He admired a couple of his high school teachers because of their interest in history, because they engaged him in research on several military battles, and because they talked with him about his other historical interests. After his sophomore year in college, Jose decided to major in history and become a teacher.

When Jose designed his first units for U.S. History, he relied heavily on the textbook that the Jefferson High School Social Studies Department had adopted about two years earlier. He thought it covered topics thoroughly and would appeal to his

---

*Jose Ricardo, Mrs. Takamori, and Alex Gerrard are pseudonyms, but their stories reflect actual events in real school settings.

students. Having become interested in cooperative learning during his teacher preparation program, he designed several activities that required students to read the book and work in cooperative teams. He planned to include some key words and concepts in his teaching and assumed his students were going to be able to read the text.

Signs of trouble with understanding concepts in the reading appeared during the first week of school. When he presented some of his discussion questions about chapter sections that students were assigned to read, few students responded. He mentioned to one of his new colleagues that carrying on a conversation with his students about historical issues was like "pulling teeth." His colleague smiled saying, "I mostly lecture."

Jose decided to give a few quizzes to see what students remembered from their readings. To answer the questions, students didn't have to make any significant inferences from what they read. They just had to remember content at the factual level. Nevertheless, Jose discovered that only one in four or five students passed the quizzes. Seventy-five to 80% of his students couldn't or didn't read what he'd assigned. Like his colleague, should he just lecture?

In a mild funk, Jose approached the chair of his department, Mrs. Takamori, with his dilemma. He explained to her that few of his students read his assignments, most failed his quizzes, and next to none would talk about what they'd read when he tried to get them into a discussion. His chair asked him if he'd evaluated students' reading ability before giving the reading assignment. He explained as politely as he could that he figured they could read the text he'd been asked to use to teach U.S. History. Mrs. Takamori asked if he'd had a course in content literacy during his teaching program at college. He said he had, but most of the social studies majors in the reading course said they didn't expect to use any of the ideas in the course. At least not for the first couple of years. They'd just lecture because that's what their professors did at the university and that's what they thought their high school students would expect. She asked if he lectured much. "I want them to discuss the readings with me," he said, "but they can't discuss what they haven't read. Maybe lecturing is the answer."

Mrs. Takamori asked Jose if he really thought that would be the best solution to the reading problem and if it would contribute to his students becoming lifelong learners. "Probably not," he said and added that he'd learned a few reading strategies, like Word Maps and Direct Reading–Thinking Activity (DR–TA), during his teacher preparation program but wasn't sure he could teach with them. She said she was familiar with DR–TA and several vocabulary development strategies and would coach him in their use if he wanted. Second period was her prep, and she could talk with him after school early the following week to review the strategies and set up a day for her to visit and observe his implementing them. She told him not to expect magic. A strategy wasn't a quick solution for years of reading problems, but it would be a start.

The first couple of times Jose tried DR–TA with his second period only a few students participated, just like before. But Mrs. Takamori encouraged him to keep trying. After the third or fourth time, a few more students responded to his guiding questions when they realized their predictions weren't going to lead to their being told they were wrong and feeling stupid. Some, he could see, were actually beginning to enjoy the process of guessing what would come next, discovering if they had made an accurate prediction, and quietly modifying their ideas as they read the text silently in class. Jose explained to students that, when they read their homework assignments, they should try to do on their own what they were doing together in class. "Try to form questions about headings and make predictions about where the story of history is going," he suggested to them.

Mrs. Takamori also made other recommendations to address his concern about the low participation in his history discussions. She suggested that, instead of asking his discussion questions in class without much think time, he give the questions to students along with the reading assignments and ask them to write responses to the questions in their journals. That way they'd have time to think about the questions.

She also suggested that, instead of only giving out questions to students, students should generate questions themselves based on their reading. She explained to him how to do ReQuest, a strategy he remembered from his training program. She also suggested that, from time to time, he have students review their reading when they got to class, write down a couple of questions on a 3 × 5 card, and turn the cards in to him for review while they wrote in their journals about his discussion questions. Then he could integrate questions they asked with some of his own during lecture/discussion time.

After a few weeks, Jose's students became somewhat more engaged in both reading and responding to his questions. He hadn't achieved the kind of learning climate he wanted, but he felt he was on his way. He was getting help, he was learning, and he was seeing some results. He was even tempted to acknowledge that the content literacy class he'd taken might have been more worthwhile than he originally thought.

## A Seasoned Teacher Confronts Reading and Changes School Culture

For eight years, Alex Gerrard* had taught eighth-grade social studies at Phoenix Middle School, a large Los Angeles school serving over 2,000 sixth, seventh, and eighth graders, mostly from homes where English was a second language. Alex faced frustration every time he assigned a reading from the history book for his class. According to readability formulas, the book was written at the eighth-grade level in reading difficulty, but for many of his students whose reading comprehension capacity was at the fourth-grade level or lower, it was very frustrating. Few of Alex's students read the assignments he gave. After facing years of frustration himself, he decided to make a bold move: Start a school-wide reading program.

Alex's plan was simple enough on the surface. One period of every day would be dedicated to teaching reading to each of the school's 2,200 students. They would be tested and placed at a level that would appropriately challenge their skills and move them forward. Fortunately, his principal supported his ambitious plan. So did the majority of the 100 or so teachers on the school's teaching staff.

Alex, a group of collaborating teachers, and his principal decided to use a direct instruction program that accommodated not only struggling readers who could not decode but also more successful readers who needed to develop more sophisticated reading comprehension and critical reading strategies. Every students' reading needs would be addressed at an appropriate level. Every teacher would have materials for their students and coaching support to help them teach the new program.

The first year was filled with struggles large and small. Scheduling was complex. Training teachers to implement the program required patience and perseverance. A few teachers resisted the program's structure because it seemed too rigid to them. Others had difficulties with implementing the program's essential components, including teaching to a level of mastery, correcting student errors, and maintaining a vigorous pace and point system.

---

*Jose Ricardo, Mrs. Takamori and Alex Gerrard are pseudonyms, but their stories reflect actual events in real school settings.

However, teachers at Phoenix began to see progress and, as time passed, students began to report that they could read better. Teachers in content area classes began to see that students who formerly could not read a text with any degree of fluency were becoming more fluent. That didn't mean, however, that they fully understood what they were reading. For many students, that would be the next step: to build vocabulary and improve comprehension.

At the end of the first year, many teachers reported that they felt profoundly satisfied with the progress they had seen students make in reading. Many students reported the same. Even standardized test scores used as part of the state's assessment program revealed significant growth in reading.

With that first year behind them and its sweet savor of success, the faculty at Phoenix decided not only to continue the program for a second year but to expand it so that the most delayed readers would have two periods of work on reading each day rather than one. Furthermore, teachers planned to set up a self-sustaining peer-coaching model to build or maintain their direct instruction skills.

Without this school-wide initiative driven by a determined social studies teacher, this school would not have been able to address the dire needs of its hundreds of struggling readers.

## REFLECTION ON PRACTICE

On some level, mirrors show us who we are. They may tell us far too little and maybe too much. They don't say where we've been or where we've headed. And they tell nothing about why. Teachers need mirrors, mirrors that give perspective, understanding, insights, even advice. These come from mirrors more complex than those on the walls. Fortunately they're available in many forms. Colleagues and mentors are mirrors. Video- and audiotapes are mirrors. Teachers can mirror their practice through written logs. They can look at their work in teams or through feedback in "Critical Friends Groups." They can mirror themselves in action research and in portfolios for National Board Certification. We'll look into each of these mirrors because each provides opportunities for professional growth and improved student learning. If Jose Ricardo and Alex Gerrard had not had mirrors to reflect on their teaching practice, the literacy problems they found in their classrooms and schools might not have been addressed.

## National Board for Professional Teaching Standards

"How do I most effectively teach what I know?" asked Melody in the midst of completing her portfolio entries for National Board Certification. That question arises repeatedly among candidates for National Board Certification because the process usually compels teachers to examine their teaching more closely than they ever had. While requiring intense reflection and self-examination, completing portfolio entries for certification has made teachers far more aware of what excellence in teaching can be and it has driven them to become better teachers (Unrau, in press).

The National Board for Professional Teaching Standards (NBPTS) was created in 1987 to retain, reward, and advance accomplished teachers through a voluntary system of "advanced" national certification. It does not replace state licensing, but it does establish advanced standards for experienced teachers. Across the nation, teachers pursuing certification can gauge their knowledge and skills in the classroom against peer-developed standards of advanced practice.

Five "Core Propositions" guide the development of the National Board's standards and assessment program. These five propositions about what teachers should know and be able to do include the following:

1. Teachers are committed to students and their learning.
2. Teachers know the subject they teach and how to teach those subjects to students.
3. Teachers are responsible for managing and monitoring student learning.
4. Teachers think systematically about their practice and learn from experience.
5. Teachers are members of learning communities.

These five propositions articulate the knowledge, skills, commitments, and dispositions that teachers must demonstrate to attain National Board Certification. They are reflected in the specific standards for each of over 20 fields that committees forge and that drive assessment.

The standards compel candidates to rethink their teaching. In a support group that I and a National Board Certified teacher (Myrna Estrada) coached, teachers pursuing certification rethought their curriculum, its coherence, its sequence, and the overall effectiveness of their instructional program (Unrau, in press). The standards forced candidates to "see things differently" in their classrooms. Candidates for certification in mathematics sought methods to engage their students in deeper levels of mathematical discourse while those pursuing certification in social sciences tried to engage students in the evaluation of evidence and deeper reasoning. They also discovered that they needed to deepen their knowledge of students and to develop a "wider net" of assessment instruments. Candidates learned about what to look for in their students' work that would inform subsequent instruction that would, in turn, improve student performance. As one candidate put it, "Often times we know which student is struggling, but we aren't forced to examine in detail how the student is thinking." In brief, the standards provided candidates with models of excellence in teaching and explicit directions for growth.

Teachers pursuing National Board Certification complete two forms of assessment: several portfolios based on classroom practice and a series of exercises at a computer-based testing center. Some of the classroom-based entries require videotaped episodes showing whole-class and small-group interactions between you and your students. Some entries also require that you submit student work that you've analyzed or that substantiates claims you've made about student performance. One entry asks that you explain and document your educational accomplishments beyond the classroom, engagements with parents, colleagues, and professional associations. All portfolios require extensive descriptive, analytic, and reflective writing.

At the assessment center, candidates for National Board Certification demonstrate command of content knowledge in their field. These exercises are administered by computer at locations across America and take about half a day.

If, for example, you sought the certificate in Adolescence and Young Adulthood/Science, which is for teachers of students ages 14 to 18+, you would be asked to demonstrate the following in your portfolios:

- How you help students make important conceptual connections in science during a sequence of instruction,
- How you use assessment to target important science understanding and to analyze and make sense of student performance,
- How you use inquiry strategies during different stages of scientific exploration to help students understand important ideas in science,
- How you use discussion strategies to facilitate student reasoning and understanding of an important concept in science,
- How you contribute to your professional community, and
- How you interact with your students' families.

Among the standards that guide these entries and their assessment is that of reflection, the concept that has guided the development of this chapter section because of its central importance to professional growth. According to that standard, "Accomplished science teachers constantly analyze, evaluate, and strengthen their practice in order to improve the quality of their students' learning experience."

National Board Certification is a series of classroom-based challenges that guide teachers toward deeper engagement with students, closer observation and analysis of their performance, and more extensive reflection on their practice. Teachers going through the process cannot avoid looking deeper into what they teach, why they teach it, how they teach it, who's getting it and who isn't, and what to do to teach it to more students better. The more knowledge, skills, and strategies teachers have to bring to bear on the tasks of teaching the more likely they may some day become National Board Certified teachers.

## Mentors

During the first weeks and months of a new teacher's career, a mentor can make all the difference. Jose Ricardo, the U.S. history teacher who found his way to his department chair, Mrs. Takamori, provides an example of mirroring and mentoring. She asked what he was doing, volunteered to observe his teaching, and offered several practical strategies to address reading problems he faced.

Many teacher preparation programs provide opportunities for mentoring. One built-in opportunity lies with student teaching when candidates teach in classrooms under the supervision of a master teacher. Although these relationships do not always produce magic, they often offer beginning teachers a model of instruction to observe and a compendium of teaching experience to draw upon for guidance. During debriefing after observing an apprenticing teacher, effective master teachers reflect what they observed and provide direction for instructional improvements.

In many teacher preparation programs, master teachers are encouraged to help beginning teachers integrate literacy assessment and literacy strategies into content area instruction because those features of student teaching are explicitly evaluated in student-teacher evaluation rubrics. Master teachers may look for evidence of candidates using formal or informal methods of assessing reading and writing proficiency, using strategies to promote literacy, and addressing the literacy needs of

English learners and struggling readers. Student teachers may also be expected to document their lesson's impact on students and show how those observations inform subsequent planning. They may be asked to demonstrate their capacity to reflect on student work and show how their analysis of it informs future instructional goals. Some programs expect that new teachers have internalized a capacity to refine their practice through self-reflection and self-examination, including participation in reflective practices, like maintaining a professional journal or teaching log.

## Teachers' Logs: A Technique for Self-Tuning

David Gorman (1998), a high school English teacher, kept a journal to assist him in his professional growth. A teacher's journal, he wrote, "can act as a master teacher who looks over a teacher's shoulder, questioning methods and discovering strengths and weaknesses." Gorman noted that keeping a journal helped him develop an ongoing reflective relationship with himself and his work. The journal enabled him to record classroom problems on paper, hold himself accountable, and begin to address them. One area of concern he selected to focus upon was the creation of a system of peer response, including peer editing.

Gorman reported that his teaching seemed to get better the day he started to "scribble" notes to himself. "The physical act of writing created concrete examples to focus my attention." His attention focused on the learning of at-risk students in his writing lab, all of whom were either Asian or Latino and most of whom lived in households where the family spoke a language other than English. These were clearly struggling writers.

To implement peer editing, Gorman began by asking students to write a letter to their principal in an effort to persuade her to bring a favored musical group to play on campus. He then had students exchange papers, adopt the role of school principal, and respond to the letter by deciding if they would or wouldn't be able to invite a group to perform and by explaining the grounds for their decision to support or deny an invitation. Gorman was pleased with students' engagement in their peer editing responses. "Students liked that I put them into the role of the principal," he wrote in his journal. "I think the importance of getting out of ourselves is vital for editing papers. . . . Each week, I have to come up with some unique response to create peer editing that is engaging."

Gorman discovered a strategy called "Ask Something" (Crowley, 1988) that required students to exchange papers in small groups and write questions on each other's paper about problems peer editors identified. Afterwards, the author got a chance to answer the question and revise the original paper. Gorman told his students that their grades would be affected by the quality of their answers to the questions that peer editors posed and the quality of their response to those questions in revisions of the paper. He noticed that most of his students addressed questions and confronted problems they were to correct. Gorman wrote:

> The benefit is when I read the revised essays, they actually respond to the students' essay problem questions, almost as though the peer pressure demands them to respond. All last year I had students whose revisions were just a recopying of the first draft with grammar and spelling errors corrected. With the peer edit questions, students are seriously considering the questions and responding to them. Last year, students had often bypassed my comments and it

affected their grades, and they still didn't care. But with the peer response, they are considering their writing and its effects on others.

Ultimately, Gorman attributed improvements in peer editing and in the quality of his students' writing to keeping a journal. Too much would have slipped out of his attention without focusing on what he'd decided to do and how his students responded to his instructional moves. For him, the journal was a "guide" and "guardian" that supported his taking "strategic risks" that created rewarding peer edit lessons.

Writing down his thoughts helped Gorman confront his instructional challenges and generate solutions that led to improved student performance. Just writing, however, would be insufficient. He had to act on self-reflections. Effective journal writing, as Gorman and many other teachers have found, can help teachers define their goals, shape strategies to achieve them, and continually assess their instructional performance. Summarizing his use of self-reflective writing to self-tune, Gorman wrote, "I will continue to use my journal for years to come as a tool for literacy development and learning."

## Collaborating in Critical Friends Groups to Build Learning Communities

In a profession that involved days or even weeks of isolation from peers, David Gorman (1998) found that his journals served as surrogate guides. However, teams serving a house of students or teams working to improve instruction can bridge that isolation and establish collaborative communities.

A recent movement among educators toward facilitated and guided group interactions promotes not only team collaboration but also the transformation of schools into communities of learning. A team of teachers with some training could become "critical friends" for each other while heightening the likelihood that their students' performance would improve (Costa & Kallick, 1993; Nave, 2000). Even though they don't belong to the same team or to any team, Critical Friends can come together in a school and still benefit their students' learning and their school's climate (McLaughlin & Talbert, 2001). By so doing, isolated teachers would be less like ships passing in the night and more like organized fleets formed for collaborative educational enterprises, such as the exploration of student work or the analysis of their own teaching. In effect, moving away from isolating individualism and toward collaborative learning communities for sharing work and building practice could re-culture middle and high school teaching.

A brief history of Critical Friends Groups.    During the 1990s, the National Coalition of Essential Schools and the Annenberg Institute for School Reform at Brown University created the National School Reform Faculty (NSRF). NSRF invited schools to bring together groups of faculty members to improve instruction and student achievement. These groups, called Critical Friends Groups (CFGs) and consisting of six to ten teachers, meet monthly with a coach primarily to examine student work and teacher practice. Sometimes the coach is a trusted observer or a CFG member selected for training at the Annenberg Institute. The coaches schedule and facilitate monthly meetings to analyze practice and promote instructional improvements (Nave, 2000).

During each meeting, the Critical Friends sit down with each other and their coach to discuss lesson plans, student work, or classroom observation notes. Having established an atmosphere of mutual trust, the group identifies strengths and weaknesses in the artifacts presented for discussion and gives suggestions to improve instruction and student performance. Art Costa and Bena Kallick (1993) compared the Critical Friends process to visiting the optometrist to have one's vision checked. Like a Critical Friend, the optometrist helps patients sharpen their focus by provided them with a variety of lenses. Which is clearer? 1 or 2? 2 or 3? Similarly, teachers working within Critical Friends Groups are given opportunities to see their teaching and the learning performance of their students more clearly.

CFG protocols.    Typically, CFGs use protocols to guide their conversation. A protocol is simply a set of guidelines that enable the CFG coach and its members to structure a discussion. The protocols are intended not only to build small group communication skills for collaborative work but also to nurture a more supportive and trusting culture. The structure created enables members of a CFG to ask questions that may challenge current practice and working assumptions about teaching and learning in a teacher's classroom. Protocols specify the amount of time allocated for certain activities during a meeting. These activities include

- a teacher presenting information about his instructional context,
- a description of the students whose work is to be explored,
- a focusing question to guide the group's inquiry,
- artifacts (such as examples of student work, a lesson plan, or a videotape of a classroom teaching episode),
- clarifying and probing questions that the facilitator or CFG members might ask, and
- feedback and reflection.

To cover these activities, each CFG session typically runs about an hour.

Scores of protocols have been designed to guide collaboration in CFGs while examining different kinds of teaching issues. While some protocols help teachers through peer observation to tune instruction and reach learning goals, others facilitate the exploration of teaching dilemmas (consultancies) or guide responses to professional texts. I've included examples of two protocols:

1. Learning from student work and
2. Learning from teacher work.

The sample protocols selected are intended to demonstrate how the protocol is conducted, what members are likely to gain from engaging in the process, and how it's likely to affect instruction.

*1. Learning from student work.*    In CFGs, analyzing student and teacher work has had the most impact on teachers' thinking and practice (Nave, 2000). In Chapter 8, I described the "ALTAS" protocol for looking at students' writing. That protocol was originally intended to be used in groups and applied to any content area, including math, science, and the social studies. Besides looking at students' written performance, teachers can look at students' problem-solving processes, their lab reports, or their videos of a simulated Supreme Court session.

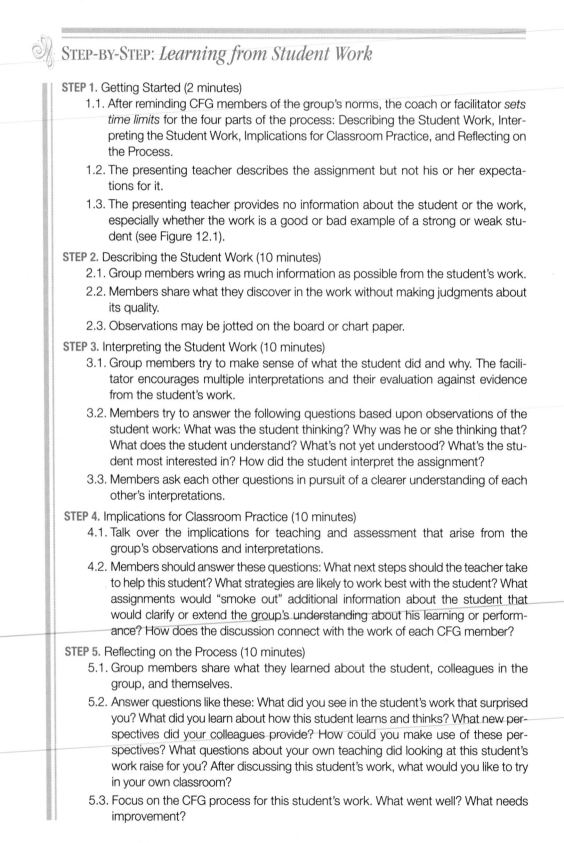

## STEP-BY-STEP: *Learning from Student Work*

**STEP 1.** Getting Started (2 minutes)

    1.1. After reminding CFG members of the group's norms, the coach or facilitator *sets time limits* for the four parts of the process: Describing the Student Work, Interpreting the Student Work, Implications for Classroom Practice, and Reflecting on the Process.

    1.2. The presenting teacher describes the assignment but not his or her expectations for it.

    1.3. The presenting teacher provides no information about the student or the work, especially whether the work is a good or bad example of a strong or weak student (see Figure 12.1).

**STEP 2.** Describing the Student Work (10 minutes)

    2.1. Group members wring as much information as possible from the student's work.

    2.2. Members share what they discover in the work without making judgments about its quality.

    2.3. Observations may be jotted on the board or chart paper.

**STEP 3.** Interpreting the Student Work (10 minutes)

    3.1. Group members try to make sense of what the student did and why. The facilitator encourages multiple interpretations and their evaluation against evidence from the student's work.

    3.2. Members try to answer the following questions based upon observations of the student work: What was the student thinking? Why was he or she thinking that? What does the student understand? What's not yet understood? What's the student most interested in? How did the student interpret the assignment?

    3.3. Members ask each other questions in pursuit of a clearer understanding of each other's interpretations.

**STEP 4.** Implications for Classroom Practice (10 minutes)

    4.1. Talk over the implications for teaching and assessment that arise from the group's observations and interpretations.

    4.2. Members should answer these questions: What next steps should the teacher take to help this student? What strategies are likely to work best with the student? What assignments would "smoke out" additional information about the student that would clarify or extend the group's understanding about his learning or performance? How does the discussion connect with the work of each CFG member?

**STEP 5.** Reflecting on the Process (10 minutes)

    5.1. Group members share what they learned about the student, colleagues in the group, and themselves.

    5.2. Answer questions like these: What did you see in the student's work that surprised you? What did you learn about how this student learns and thinks? What new perspectives did your colleagues provide? How could you make use of these perspectives? What questions about your own teaching did looking at this student's work raise for you? After discussing this student's work, what would you like to try in your own classroom?

    5.3. Focus on the CFG process for this student's work. What went well? What needs improvement?

As an example of the kind of student work used in a CFG protocol for learning from student work, I've included an assignment that Elliot Ibanez, a Biology teacher in a California high school, gave to his sheltered Biology class. The class had just finished a unit on ecology in which students studied the causes and effects of pollution on the environment. Elliot recognized that many students had strong feelings about the earth's condition and wanted them to express their understanding of global warming.

### Global Warming Assignment

For the past week we have covered the causes and effects pollution has had on our environment. In this assignment, you are to write a 1 1/2 to 2-page paper on global warming. Your paper should include the following:

- Explain global warming and the greenhouse effect
- Possible causes of global warming
- Effects of global warming
- Possible solutions

Spend time to research your paper and organize it in a presentable manner. Make sure to use scientific terms and avoid using irrelevant information. Watch out for language and sentence errors which hinder effective communication. I will use the scoring rubric on the other side of this sheet to grade your paper. You have a week to do this paper.

One of Elliot's "sheltered" English students wrote the following paper:

Global warming is really terrible because the world could get hot. Some plants could die. And it could also effect the greenhouse like if you have roses or a garden it could die. And this is a huge problem in the world because its going to increase, the carbon dioxide we are not going to have a lot of trees and the carbon dioxide (indecipherable word) get to us. And is our fault because we are polluting the air with smog and the ozone layer is getting holes. There's too much carbon dioxide in the atmosphere because of the cars, airplanes, boat and factories. And they are cutting our trees that doesn't help us in nothing because the trees is the ones that absorbe the carbon dioxide. And we are polluting the atmosphere with more carbon dioxide that make the earth hotter and more larger holes to ozone layer. The earth is like a green house . . .

After reading and analyzing a student's written response to Elliot's assignment (like that of the student above), members of the CFG would discuss what they found in the work without judging its quality. They then try to explain how the student interpreted the assignment and what the student was attempting to do when completing it. CFG members next explore the steps Elliot could take to help this student, including strategies likely to work best with the student and assignments likely to further the group's understanding of this student's learning. Following those recommendations, members reflect on their discussion to discover what new perspectives of his student's work Elliot gained, what questions arose about his teaching, and how he could act on both perspectives and questions.

FIGURE 12.1   Example of Assignment and Student Work for Learning from Student Work Protocol.

**2. Looking at teacher's work: best content literacy practices.** Many protocols have been designed for CFGs to examine the work of teachers, including their lesson plans, exams, and instructional episodes. Protocols normally apply to all content areas. However, the protocol provided here focuses on successful literacy practices that enhance learning.

---

## STEP-BY-STEP: *Best Content Literacy Practices*

The coach helps CFG members focus on features of a presenter's literacy instruction that contribute to its success. During analysis, members discover what makes the practice presented work well with students. A "best content literacy practice" is a strategy or process highly effective in promoting both content learning and literacy.

**STEP 1.** Identify a Success (5 minutes)
- 1.1. Each member writes out a short description of a "best content literacy practice" used or developed during the member's career.
- 1.2. Each member should be ready to explain what made the practice so different from others like it that were tried.

**STEP 2.** Presenters Describe the Success (5 minutes)
- 2.1. In groups of three, the first presenter tells the stories of his or her "best content literacy practice" along with elements contributing to its success.
- 2.2. Other members take notes.

**STEP 3.** Group Asks Clarifying Questions (3 minutes). Group members ask questions to fill in any gaps in understanding the strategy, process, or its outcome.

**STEP 4.** Group Asks Probing Questions (optional step). Because these questions are not intended to promote discussion, the presenter simply answers them. Sample stems include: Why do you think _____? What was different about _____? Why did you decide to _____? What were your assumptions about _____?

**STEP 5.** Group Reflects on the Success Story (8–10 minutes)
- 5.1. Group members discuss their understanding of what the presenter did.
- 5.2. They share their insights about what made the practice successful.
- 5.3. Those present silently take notes.

**STEP 6.** Presenter Reflects (5 minutes)
- 6.1. The presenter openly reflects upon the group's commentary about what contributed to the success of the practice.
- 6.2. Afterwards, the group discusses how they could apply what they learned to their own instruction.

**STEP 7.** Protocol Begins Again for the Next Group Member
- 7.1. Repeat steps 2 through 6 for each group member.
- 7.2. Focus on underlying principles or processes contributing to the success of the literacy practice.

---

**Research on CFGs.** Bill Nave (2000) conducted an evaluation of CFG programs and found three factors that contributed to members of CFGs feeling their work with colleagues was particularly satisfying. First, the work teachers did in CFGs wasn't done in a "one shot" workshop but through a continual, evolving process. Second, the focus was on their own teaching and their own students' learning. And third, the CFG process occurred within a small group of supportive and trusted colleagues all from the same school. These factors created a level of collaboration and trust that teachers rarely experienced in other professional development models.

But what impact can a school expect its CFGs to have? Nave (2000) identified four trends:

1. *Student skills improve.* In one school, for example, CFGs focused on student writing samples. As a result, student writing skills consistently improved.
2. *Teachers' thinking changes.* They become more aware of the connection between their planning (often done in response to looking at student work) and improvements in their students' performance.
3. *Teachers change their instructional practice.* Over time, teachers shift toward student-centered instruction and student-focused activities and away from "teaching as telling." As a result, students became more engaged in classroom work.
4. *The school culture changes.* Improving student performance by improving teacher skills became a deliberate school-wide commitment.

The results reported amount to more than a handful of small changes. These collaboratively sponsored and planned teacher groups can bring about significant alterations to many aspects of their schools, from the performance of students in their classrooms to the entire school culture.

## Teacher Research

What is teacher research? Teachers doing teacher research observe, analyze, and reflect upon their own classroom practice. Their inquiry entails immediate, constant, experience-near participation. They're like fish schooling inside the tank with all the other organisms. Unlike most fish, however, teachers can reflect on their practice, and they reflect for a purpose: to act on their findings and to improve instruction.

While gathering information about their teaching, they can use several methods of inquiry, both conventional and evolving. Conventional methods include standard experimental designs with agreed-upon procedures while evolving methods include memoirs and personal narratives that have no commonly accepted features to ensure validity and reliability.

Following an investigation of over 30 literacy-based, teacher-research studies, James Baumann and Ann Duffy-Hester (2000) identified general attributes of teacher research, processes used, methods applied, and means of reporting on classroom inquiry. As for general attributes, they found that all teacher researchers were reflective practitioners whose research was prompted by problems they faced and questions they posed within their classrooms. As for process, all teacher researchers learned from their students and were able to make more sense of their classroom through inquiry. Their selection of methods was based on practicality; the method adopted was the method that would get the research question addressed efficiently. With respect to reporting their findings, almost all teacher researchers used a narrative technique to describe what happened in their classrooms, often in the form of vignettes, and documented their findings with examples of student work or other artifacts.

Please recall David Gorman's problem of developing a peer editing system for students in his writing lab, his close observation of his students, his practical choice of a teacher's log to record and reflect upon his classroom practice, and his narrative method of relating what happened as he proceeded with various peer editing strategies. Yes, Gorman was doing teacher research.

Health education teacher integrates literacy.    Another student of mine, this one engaged in teacher research as a culminating activity for her Masters degree, faced the literacy problems of English learners in her health education class. Maria Sansui posed two questions to guide her inquiry:

1. Does the inclusion of reading and writing strategies enhance learning of content area subject matter?
2. Does the inclusion of reading and writing strategies improve students' reading level?

To answer these questions, Maria integrated a network of 13 content literacy strategies into her health education curriculum, including Directed Reading–Thinking Activity (DR–TA), K-W-L, Directed Inquiry Activity (DIA), Jigsaw, and graphic organizers. Over a two-month period, she also integrated other vocabulary, question-generation, and writing techniques to build literacy while students learned health education concepts. The health curriculum covered two units, one on first aid and safety and the other on drugs, alcohol, and tobacco.

To see if integrating literacy with health education curriculum would result in more learning and improved reading ability for ELs (English Learners) in comparison to a control class covering the same health education material but without integrated literacy strategies, Maria collaborated with one of her colleagues who also taught a section of "sheltered" health education.

Maria obtained pre- and post-test scores for each of the units taught from both her experimental class and the control class that her colleague taught. She also obtained pre- and post-intervention reading scores for both experimental and control groups by using a norm-referenced reading test.

Moreover, she developed case studies on six of her students to gain a closer look at what went on in their minds as they went through the two-month instructional program. Two of these students were above average in performance, two average, and two below average. Half were female, half male. One was Hispanic, one Korean, and two were Armenian. Maria developed questionnaires for these students, collected survey data from them, and conducted interviews with them.

On tests covering the first health education unit, Maria discovered that both her colleague's class and hers performed about equally. She speculated that, during the first month on instruction with the literacy strategies, many of her students were learning strategies that may have taken attention from their mastery of content concepts. On tests covering the second unit of instruction, Maria's students significantly outperformed her colleague's control group in gain scores. However, both Maria's class and that of her colleague showed similar growth on the standardized reading test. Maria speculated that, if she had run the experiment longer, her students may well have demonstrated significant improvement in reading as measured by norm-referenced tests. Perhaps the strategy instruction they received during the two-month program began to have effects only after students began to internalize and apply them so that they did not require extra attention while also learning content material.

Maria's case studies contributed to her making several observations that put the results of her teacher research into perspective. Case study students who read extensively at home, a feature she discovered as a result of doing the case studies, appeared to gain more reading skills as measured by the norm-referenced reading test. She acknowledged that variables such as pleasure reading at home may have influenced her inquiry's outcome.

While reflecting on her practice, Maria became part of a collaborative culture in her school and built a learning community in her classroom. She became far more familiar with the literacy work that other colleagues in her school were conducting, in part because she joined a Critical Friends Group at her high school that focused on literacy growth. In her classroom, she became more deeply aware of her students, their cultural heritages, their understanding of health education concepts, and their struggle to acquire literacy skills. She fostered literacy in her classroom and school cultures by integrating literacy enhancing strategies into her instructional program.

## TOWARD COLLABORATIVE CULTURES SERVING LITERACY AND LEARNING

Issues of student engagement and desire to gain literacy and learning skills are central to challenges teachers face nationwide. What kinds of teaching practices would address these challenges and contribute to increased success with nontraditional students that fill many of today's high school classrooms? Recall that collaborating teachers at Phoenix decided to use a direct instruction reading program that was structured and scripted, but there are many other solutions to the reading problems that students and faculties face.

The core of professional practice, what McLaughlin and Talbert (2001) call the "stuff" of teaching, can be represented in their classroom triangle of teacher, content, and student (see Figure 12.2).

**FIGURE 12.2**   The Core of Professional Practice.

In schools where non-traditional students experience success, McLaughlin and Talbert found the classroom triangle filled with the following dimensions of classroom practice:

1. students are active learners—not passive recipients,
2. content understanding is gained through the active construction of knowledge—not by sipping watered-down subject matter, and
3. teachers create and support student-centered learning communities—not all-too-familiar teacher-centered routines.

Innovations engaging both teachers and learners drive that pattern of successful teacher practice.

What McLaughlin and Talbert (2001) describe happening in schools they observed where non-traditional students experienced success is what Langer (2000) found happening in "beating the odds" classrooms. Langer identified a network of pedagogical principles that arose from research on "beating the odds" teachers who worked in classrooms and schools serving poor and low-performing students. However, students in those classrooms and schools demonstrated unusually high performance, beyond the performance of similar students in more typical classrooms and schools. At these "beating the odds" school sites, something exceptional was happening. Langer found learning situations among "beating the odds" classrooms that combined to enable teachers and students to prosper in rich learning communities. Teachers taught skills and knowledge through multiple forms of instruction, made connections across content to achieve coherence, emphasized strategies for thinking and doing, and organized classrooms to foster collaboration and share in the construction of knowledge. Their teaching integrated literacy strategies that students internalized and applied in multiple contexts.

New and apprenticing teachers seeking to adopt and implement "beating the odds" principles could use much of this book to achieve that aim. Research and practice presented in previous chapters form a knowledge base in reading, diagnostic tools, strategies to improve comprehension and critical thinking, group methods, writing procedures and practices, motivational techniques, and approaches to align standards with literacy instruction and assessment.

For new or apprenticing teachers to acquire all that information and integrate it with promising principles that seasoned teachers used to move their students to higher academic ground and higher levels of achievement is an admirable goal but one that will require, in most instances, some assistance. But is it that simple?

## Teacher Development and Engagement in "Beating the Odds" Schools

Here I want to return to that engagement crisis that I believe lies beneath many students' literacy and learning problems. Beyond individual teachers addressing meaningful engagement in classrooms, teachers need to work together to create learning communities to foster literacy growth and learning. Teachers passing each other as though they were ships in the dark of night need to reconsider their professional voyage. The problem of student engagement and motivation to gain literacy and learning skills that we reviewed in the first chapter lies not only with teacher's commitment to students and their learning but also to teachers' readiness to collaborate with each other.

Teachers that Langer (2000, 2001) studied who were in "beating the odds" classrooms and schools exemplified the pattern of practice that led to successful outcomes where meaningful academic work was more the norm than the exception. We've already reviewed in Chapter 1 what these teachers did in their classrooms (Langer, 2001). But what do they do to help each other achieve excellence at their school sites and in their classrooms? New and apprenticing teachers need substantial support in the form of teacher communities, mentors, and "Critical Friends." In schools where teachers shared progress in their careers in learning communities, teachers collaborated to help students achieve; had equal opportunities with colleagues, even those with more tenure, to teach courses at all levels; and felt rewarded intrinsically through seeing the success of all their students—not through perks that status or seniority yielded (McLaughlin & Talbert, 2001).

Langer (2000) identified six features that contributed to the success of schools and teachers in her "beating the odds" study (see Figure 12.3). In these schools, teachers:

1. *Coordinated efforts to improve achievement.* They identified needs at their school sites, investigated and developed improvement programs and strategies, and supported other teachers as they learned new practices and implemented them. As an example, Langer described the Dade County Comprehensive Reading Plan that emerged from collaborating teachers in the Miami and Dade County areas of southern Florida. After reviewing their students' needs, teachers in the Dade County area targeted reading and writing. Teachers arranged to convene 18 district reading specialists to participate in designing and implementing the plan. They focused on reciprocal teaching, tutorial programs, and "student-owned" strategies to foster independent reading. The Comprehensive Reading Plan included two hours of reading instruction daily plus half an hour of free reading. Content area teachers focused on applications of reading strategies, such as reciprocal teaching, in their content area courses. The overall plan included standards, strategies, and assessment tools to monitor the impact of the program. At individual schools in the district, reading specialists supported teachers' implementation of the program. Parents were given responsible roles, including training to tutor their children at school-sponsored tutoring sessions and at home.

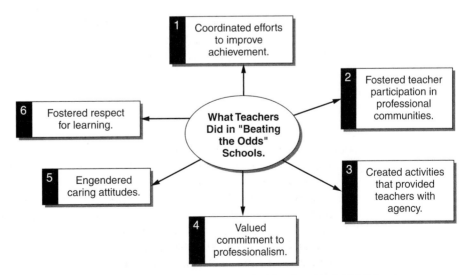

**FIGURE 12.3**   Features Contributing to Success in "Beating the Odds" Schools.

2. *Fostered teacher participation in professional communities.* Successful programs had teachers participating in multiple professional communities both within and beyond their schools. These collaborations ranged from interdisciplinary teams to work in professional organizations. One of the primary means for building professional communities within schools was through working teams that afforded an abundance of collaborative opportunities. At some schools in the study, these teams met daily while at other schools they met once a week during "common planning time."

3. *Created activities that provide teachers with agency.* Teachers had the power to bring about real change in their classrooms and school cultures. They developed curriculum, solved real instructional problems, and charted their own instructional directions, including significant work on cross-disciplinary teaching.

4. *Valued commitment to professionalism.* Teachers believed that they could help each other acquire and perfect skills to help students achieve. One teacher who had already implemented and become fluent in reciprocal teaching before her district developed their Comprehensive Reading Plan shared her knowledge of the strategy with the team developing the Plan and with other teachers through periodic workshops.

5. *Engendered caring attitudes.* These "beating the odds" teachers manifested care for both their students and their colleagues. During team meetings that ethos of care could be observed in the teachers' discussions about students whose problems they tried to address and solve before escalation. It could also be seen in the teachers' concerns about the curriculum and how students engaged with it. Student performance was closely monitored and informed discussions about the next instructional steps. This atmosphere of caring contributed to a unified sense of community.

6. *Fostered respect for learning.* These teachers loved learning themselves and served as models of lifelong learning for their colleagues and for their own students. They kept up with new developments in technology and established links to computer resources in schools and at home. During summer breaks, they participated in professional growth activities like the summer writing institutes sponsored by the National Writing Project.

These features of teachers' professional development and engagement spark their students' engagement and support their students' achievements. Few students can engage themselves in classrooms where disengaged teachers make insignificant investments in the learning lives of their students and colleagues (Louis & Smith, 1992).

We know the important contribution of collaboration to student achievement and to teachers' professional growth. But what could new and apprenticing teachers do collaboratively to address literacy concerns they encounter in classrooms and schools where they teach?

## TEAMING FOR LITERACY AND LEARNING ACROSS THE CONTENT AREAS

### The Team Model

Relationships between students and teachers matter most. They often form the reasons for students learning to read, discovering new interests, and finding pathways to a meaningful life. However, in many large schools, few opportunities for con-

structive relationships between engaged students and their teachers arise. Teams provide more opportunities to form meaningful relationships for learning and literacy development in classroom communities. Furthermore, they provide productive opportunities for teacher collaboration and the growth of teacher learning communities.

Knowledge about teams will help you understand why they are a central feature in the cultural life of many schools. If you are a new teacher joining a team, you will need time to learn the history of the team and how it functions. Usually, new teachers receive both formal and informal mentoring as they adjust to their roles. It's a good idea to take some time with other team members to learn about the team's work in the past, the team's long-term goals, the obstacles the team members have overcome, and the methods they have used to function effectively. What you learn from this chapter about teams and teaming is also intended to help you with the transition and adjustment to service on a school team.

Teams of two to four or even five teachers provide instruction to a common group of students. The teachers forming the team usually represent the core academic disciplines: English, social studies, math, and science. In some schools, teams include a special education teacher or a physical education teacher. No perfect model of teaming exists. Composition varies. However, well-functioning teams do share several common characteristics.

Research (Erb & Stevenson, 1999) on schools using teams has revealed several traits that contribute to their effectiveness:

♦ *Smaller is better.* The more students a team must serve, the less time teachers in that team have to work with each other and their students. Research shows that teams of 120 or fewer with a ratio of no more than 1:25 are linked to more substantial student learning. Partner teams with two or three teachers and 40 to 75 students provide advantages in communication, instruction, and community building.

♦ *Planning time is essential.*    Teachers in teams need time to discuss learning goals and learners. Schools often schedule common planning time (CPT) so teams can conduct their business. With adequate time to meet and discuss students and instruction, teachers in teams function more effectively and yield more benefits to students' performances. While some schools provide only one hour per week of CPT, others schedule as much as three or four hours.

♦ *Teachers collaborate in assessing their students' progress.*    Teams provide an exceptional opportunity for teachers to observe student growth. They can set goals, identify benchmarks, and watch each student's development. They can look at student work to discover how students respond to assignments and perform on assessment tasks. Through analysis and discussion of student work, teachers can also discover if their instruction needs to be modified so that students can master key concepts and skills.

♦ *Teachers design instruction.*    Teams usually decide how to achieve learning goals and reach standards for the students in their learning community. Teachers can discuss literacy issues, such as their students' reading performances, and integrate reading strategies into content area instruction during CPT. Opportunities for teachers to observe each other implement reading strategies and discuss those observations are also important. Protocols like those used in Critical Friends Groups can facilitate team development and teacher effectiveness.

While each of these features is important on its own, schools and teams combining them benefit more from their interaction.

Teams take time to develop and function efficiently. After spending a year in planning for the initial implementation, many schools take two or three years to implement a teaming program so that it runs effectively (Pounder, 1998). In schools with strong department identities, tensions between department expectations and team needs may arise and require negotiation for resolution. When making the transition to teams, teachers who have grown accustomed to working on their own need time to learn to work effectively with colleagues to develop skills of group planning and decision making. However, these impediments to teaming can be overcome so that the potential benefits of teaming to students' reading and learning can be realized.

## Turning to Teams in the Middle School

Team teaching has been around since the invention of the family. However, its place in our middle and high schools has received heightened attention during a recent round of school reform efforts. In 1989 the Carnegie Council on Adolescent Development published *Turning Points,* a set of well-researched guidelines for transforming the education of young adolescents. It urged middle schools to address the problem of students unprepared for what they were about to face in high school and in the workplace. *Turning Points* posed several principles to guide instruction in the middle grades. Four of those principles apply directly to our discussion of teams to facilitate literacy and content area instruction:

♦ Divide large middle schools into smaller communities for learning.
♦ Transmit a core of common knowledge to all students.

- Organize to ensure success for all students.
- Teachers and principals have the major responsibility and power to transform middle grade schools.

We'll explore these principles as we see how small is better, especially if we're pursuing student engagement, learning, and literacy growth. Although targeted primarily for middle schools, this blueprint for transforming middle schools and lessons learned from its implementation warrants the attention of all secondary level teachers. Several features found effective in the blueprint could transfer to and transform high schools. Some restructured high schools have already integrated them.

To counteract the impersonality of large institutions, authors of the report recommended that schools create smaller "houses" of not more than 500 students that would allow teams of teachers and students to form closer connections and learning communities. Through mastery of appropriate bodies of knowledge, students would learn to think critically. Teams of teachers would devise ways to reach curricular goals and standards through common planning time (CPT) during the school day. Working together, teams could discuss shared students, develop interdisciplinary themes, schedule classes, and select instructional methods and materials. With these team functions in mind, we should not lose sight of the potential for teams to learn reading strategies, to support strategy use in multiple content areas, and to assess students' application of those strategies.

After 10 years of middle school reform efforts based upon *Turning Points* principles, researchers have learned that schools implementing more of the report's recommended principles and practices with greater fidelity saw their students' performance increase significantly (Felner et al., 1997). In schools with low levels of implementation, students' performance drifted below state averages. Low-implementation schools, for example, institute teacher teams without providing adequate time for planning, curriculum integration, or examination of student work. Unfortunately, most of the academic conditions prevalent in middle schools at the beginning of the 1990s remain just as prevalent at the start of the twenty-first century (Lipsitz, Mizell, Jackson, & Austin, 1997). Changes have taken place least often in schools that need changing most: Urban schools where students demonstrate weak performance (Jackson & Davis, 2000). That means thousands of students head off to high school underprepared and unable to make a successful transition to new academic expectations.

In the original *Turning Points,* little was said about teaching reading to middle school students. A focus on reading came 10 years later with the Carnegie Corporation's publication of *Turning Points 2000* (Jackson & Davis, 2000). That report documented 10 years of work in over 200 schools implementing *Turning Points* principles as well as reforms in other middle schools that benefited young adolescents' education.

For all students to achieve success, they need to read, and researchers (Showers, Joyce, Scanlon, & Schnaubelt, 1998) have found that 30 percent of students leave the primary grades without basic reading skills. The percentage is significantly higher in many urban communities. During the late 1990s and into the twenty-first century, the average reading grade level equivalent for sixth graders in a large number of urban middle schools in the Los Angeles area hovered near the middle of the third grade on the Gates-MacGinitie reading test. In spite of efforts to limit "social promotion," many of these students move on to high schools where they will be expected to read high school–level texts with grade school–level skills. Under those conditions, thousands of students advanced from elementary school to middle school and from middle school to high school unable to read at basic levels or reading far below their grade level.

The authors of *Turning Points 2000* (Jackson & Davis, 2000) acknowledge that reading was often not a focus of instructional concern in middle schools because teachers, as well as parents, presumed that students had gotten a solid base for reading during their years in elementary school. Unfortunately, that assumption rested on misinformation about students' reading and their needs for lifelong literacy growth. Although most middle school teachers and middle school communities have not established themselves to serve students' literacy development and are usually not prepared to do so, ignoring students' struggles with reading in middle and high schools could no longer be condoned. With the acknowledgement of students' reading struggles, teacher teams can address those difficulties broadly through strategy instruction across the disciplines.

## Teams in the High School

Seeking more connections at Morton East High School in Illinois with more than 80% of its students from Hispanic backgrounds, Carla Jankowski (2002) designed a pilot program with five of her colleagues. Teams of five freshmen teachers who taught English, math, social studies, science, and some electives shared a common planning time and about 100 students in a "house." After several years, her school has 11 freshmen houses and many signs of an improved learning environment, including higher rates of attendance and graduation.

Each "house" at Morton East evolved its own culture and identity. Most houses extensively integrated English and social studies into a block of two back-to-back periods with 50 students. Even the newest houses share a coordinated classroom management scheme that provides behavioral guidelines to all students in a house.

Jankowski describes how her house and its four teachers evolved integrated, thematic units for the 100 students they shared. As she put it,

> Students researched famous artists and then portrayed them in a talk-show setting. They studied human genetics in biology (supplemented with lessons on probability in math), created personal family trees in art, and held a medical symposium where they took on the roles of geneticist, family physician, or therapist to inform parents about a variety of genetic diseases. We also combined the study of animals with the creation of fables. Students then designed and constructed their own animal masks so they could act out the fables in reader's theater.

Out of the experience of building these houses, Jankowski has drafted "House Keys," a manual for teachers to open the doors of collaborative teaching and surmount the challenges of team development. The connections teachers make with each other and their students breed supportive cultures with a strong curriculum.

## Disciplinary and/or Integrated Instruction

Team teachers have several instructional choices. During the same period of time each day, they can teach the same subject, say science, based on their interests and knowledge. They can teach a range of core content subjects but make no efforts to integrate knowledge bases associated with those subjects. Or they can integrate the knowledge associated with various subjects, like math and science or English and social studies or all four in well-planned units. In this last form of instruction, called integrated or interdisciplinary team instruction, students discover connections and relationships between "departmentalized" knowledge bases, often during extended class sessions created through "block" schedules that put two periods together.

Disciplinary curriculum.   State standards are discipline based and provide instructional objectives in math, science, history, and other content areas. The standards are usually organized by grade level with grade-appropriate knowledge and skills to be mastered in each discipline. Few will deny that the territory of a discipline, such as math or history, is vast and complex. Many educators believe that knowledge of one domain in a discipline like math or science is essential before exploring more complex domains. Without expert guidance, some students get lost in a discipline's mountains and forests. But teachers with a sound understanding of their subject area and how to teach it can guide their students through new terrain, even the territory where it's tough going. In short, from grades 6 to 12, a discipline's standards and a teacher's knowledge can guide instruction so that students learn how to travel, even in a less familiar country.

Furthermore, disciplines in colleges and universities have been housed in departments for hundreds of years. Middle and high schools mirror that organization by department. Cultures develop within those departments with teachers in a discipline sharing similar values and traditions, including traditions based on shared knowledge and approaches to instruction. Students get introduced to a discipline's domains of knowledge in widely agreed upon stages, such as biology before physics. Departments can also shape the overall culture and evolution of an entire school.

However, discipline-based instruction has been criticized for its lack of depth and its fragmentation of knowledge (Schmidt, McKnight, & Raizen, 1997). International studies have shown that American students do not have the degree of understanding or skills in math and science that students in other industrialized countries possess (Jackson & Davis, 2000). Furthermore, students immersed in one discipline's details may not see how knowledge and skills in that discipline have relevance or meaning to them. They get exposed to individual trees but fail to see how those trees have meaning in the larger territory or context of their lives. Shortcomings of discipline and standard's driven instruction has generated alternative approaches to instruction, at both middle and high school levels (Meier, 2000).

Integrated curriculum.   To develop depth of understanding within and between disciplines while reducing fragmentation of knowledge, several educators (Carnegie Council on Adolescent Development, 1989; Jackson & Davis, 2000; Jankowski, 2002) advocate integrated instruction. It offers teachers working in teams creative opportunities to address "big ideas" in order to deepen both students' understanding of concepts and their levels of engagement with learning. Discovering connections between disciplines often makes learning more interesting and meaningful.

When integrating instruction, teachers on a team first articulate the big ideas and rich questions upon which they would focus and rank the standards applicable to their discipline. Then, while keeping traditional instructional content and sequence in the background, teachers bring their list of big ideas, questions, and prioritized standards into a discussion to find overlapping concepts that cut across and integrate their separate disciplines. For example, the concept of "systems" emerged as a unifying idea among teachers during one team's discussion. When studying math, students could discover that the rules of algebra form a system. When studying science, students could investigate interacting systems, such as ecosystems. When studying social studies, students could analyze social, political, or economic systems to understand their elements and how they interact. Creative combinations and connections emerged. Grasping the concept of systems, their applicability across disciplines, and their interconnections heightened relevance and meaningfulness of learning for both students and teachers (Tomlinson, 1998).

## Teamwork to Address and Improve Literacy

One of the advantages of working on a team is that all teachers can focus attention on coordinating their students' curriculum and improving instructional strategies, including those that enhance literacy skills. While working in teams, teachers can integrate literacy strategies with content area coverage in any field, including social studies, science, and math.

All students served by a team of teachers could be assessed to discover their levels of reading and to identify any struggling readers who may need some form of reading intervention program. Some students may need an individual reading inventory (IRI) to identify their specific problems in reading. One teacher could perform that service for the "house."

Once the team understands the kinds of reading strengths and challenges their students bring to their classrooms, teachers can begin to integrate literacy strategies. In some schools, these strategies may be those that are to be used school-wide, as described earlier in this chapter. However, if no school-wide agreements exist, team members will need to select the strategies they believe are best for the literacy needs of their students. Team members will have to decide what kinds of professional development they may need to implement the strategies and how to proceed with integrating those strategies into all subjects taught. For example, if a team decides to use reciprocal teaching, then each team member will need to become comfortable using the strategy and integrating it with content instruction, whether that be social studies, English, science, or math.

Teams can also focus on the development of their students' writing skills. When students have completed written assignments, members of a team could meet to look carefully at their students' work. Protocols for that process can be found later in this chapter and in Chapter 8, which includes an explanation of how writing can promote learning and how teachers can use their students' written work to look deeper into their thinking and learning. That analysis is intended to inform teachers' decisions about what next instructional steps they should take to move their students closer to a team's learning goals.

Perhaps it is obvious already how potent a force teams in both middle and high schools can be. They not only provide teachers with opportunities to connect with each other but also with students on many levels. Among those opportunities for connection is that of delivering to the students powerful and pervasive reading strategies. Teams are a potent means of addressing problems in literacy and learning. If teams acquire reading strategies and implement them in all the content areas they teach, students can learn how strategies applied in one subject domain can be transferred for reading and learning in other domains.

## RESOURCES FOR COLLABORATION AND PROFESSIONAL GROWTH

## Technology and (New) Literacies

A Google search I ran on "literacy and technology" generated 877,000 sites. A search for "high school lesson plans" generated a mere 587,000. Although I didn't visit each of these sites, I did go to a few of them. One took me to a new *Journal of Literacy and Technology* where I could review the table of contents of the last issues and subscribe. Another revealed a Web site for a course called "Literacy and Technology" offered in a teacher preparation program in upstate New York. Most sites I visited offered lots of information, much useful, and often linked to further sources. Which is changing faster? Literacy or technology? Selecting a search engine has become an act of literacy.

Donald Leu, Jr. (2002), believes that electronic communication systems, such as the Internet, create new literacies at an accelerating pace. Searching the Web for sites related to literacy and technology produces such a vast array of information that it's hard to deny new literacies bursting on the screen. But what are these new literacies? Leu says they include "skills, strategies, insights necessary to successfully exploit the rapidly changing information and communication technologies that continuously emerge in our world." He says they change or emerge so fast we can't expect a more precise definition of them.

Some parents and educators feared that children would slip into solitude and isolation in classrooms where the computers worked as tools for literacy and learning (Schofield, 1997). However, they appear to promote interaction as students turn to each other sharing new Internet discoveries or seeking information about how to use the latest "new thing." Leu (2002) believes these new literacies are "highly social." Daily, we're becoming more networked into a global village than the media guru of the 1970s Marshall McLuhan ever dreamed. Want to see how the tundra's doing in northern Alaska? You can probably find a Web site with a camera looking out over the terrain. How about a look into the life of a sub-Saharan village? No problem.

Are all these new literacies moving us further and further from the traditional forms of literacy, reading and writing? On the contrary, those skills have become critical because reading provides fast access to worlds of electronic information and writing enables us to store and organize information. But both these forms of literacy are evolving as they interact with new technologies (Leu, 2002). Meanwhile what we write and how we read are being shaped by Internet forces ; -).

Leu (2002) believes we can safely make several conclusions about the new literacies emerging from our screens all over the world:

- The new literacies build on the previous literacies.
- Change is a defining element of the new literacies.
- The new literacies require new forms of strategic knowledge.
- The new literacies involve more critical reading of information and provide new definitions of multicultural education.
- The new literacies are, to a large extent, socially constructed.
- Interest and motivation provide special opportunities for supporting new literacies.

With the emergence of these new literacies, our role as teachers must be rewritten. We're going to have to learn new lines, new moves, and new routes to respond to new literacies. That's going to take a lot of collaboration with colleagues in our immediate school environment and with individuals or groups accessible through electronic means.

The electronic resources for developing literacy and enhancing learning in our classroom is rapidly approaching infinity. Shall I mention a few hundred thousand Web sites I happen to know of that could help you use technology to augment your teaching? Those noted below should at least get you started, no matter what your subject area.

## Professional Associations to Extend Collaborative Growth

Professional associations provide teachers with a knowledge base, research, publications, policies, conferences, colleagues, and other resources that promote career growth. These resources empower and extend collaborative efforts of individual teachers in each content area. Professional organizations are often instrumental in defining educational problems that arise in classrooms and schools, reviewing approaches to their solution, and formulating policies that resolve issues. As talk about standards moved toward written documents and state action, many professional organizations represented teachers' beliefs about what should be included in national and state content standards. With colleagues in one's field who share common concerns, educational issues that might never receive widespread, even national attention come into focus.

Many national educational organizations that represent teachers of specific disciplines also have state and local chapters. Teachers can work in concert locally and at the state level to address evolving educational concerns and to promote professional development. Conferences at the local and state level provide opportunities for new and experienced teachers to share ideas and to discover new teaching strategies. They are forums at which teachers can present their instructional innovations and teacher research. Teachers attending these conferences often find not only practical teaching ideas but inspiration to approach instructional and, what seem to be intractable, pedagogical problems in one's field of specialization.

Table 12.1 provides the names of professional organizations for all major content areas and their Web site addresses. These Web sites typically include access to an organization's mission statement, calendar of events, publications, online journals, membership information, national standards, standards-based lesson plans, chat rooms, and key links to content related Web sites.

**TABLE 12.1**   Professional Organizations and Web Site Addresses

| Content Area | Professional Organization | Web Site Address |
|---|---|---|
| English and the Language Arts | National Council of Teachers of English | www.ncte.org |
| | International Reading Association | www.reading.org |
| Foreign Languages | American Council on the Teaching of Foreign Languages | www.actfl.org |
| Economics | National Council on Economic Education | www.ncee.net |
| Mathematics | National Council of Teachers of Mathematics | www.nctm.org |
| Science | National Science Teachers Association | www.nsta.org |
| Social Studies | National Council for the Social Studies | www.ncss.org |
| Physical Education | National Association for Sport and Physical Education (NASPE) | www.aahperd.org |
| Health | Association for the Advancement of Health Education (AAHE) | www.aahperd.org |
| Music | National Association for Music Education | www.menc.org |
| Art | National Art Education Association | www.naea_reston.org |
| Vocational Education | National Association of Trade and Industrial Education (NATIE) | www.skillsusa.org/ |

## DOUBLE-ENTRY JOURNAL: AFTER READING

Go to the Double-Entry Journal for Chapter 12 on our Companion Website at www.prenhall.com/unrau to complete your journal entry.

Having read this chapter, how has your vision of collaboration with other teachers been altered or clarified with respect to integrating literacy into your teaching and promoting the development of a reflective teaching practice for professional growth? At this stage in your career, what specific steps do you see yourself taking in the future that would deepen your collaboration with learning communities, improve instructional programs, and promote the practice of colleagues in their classrooms?

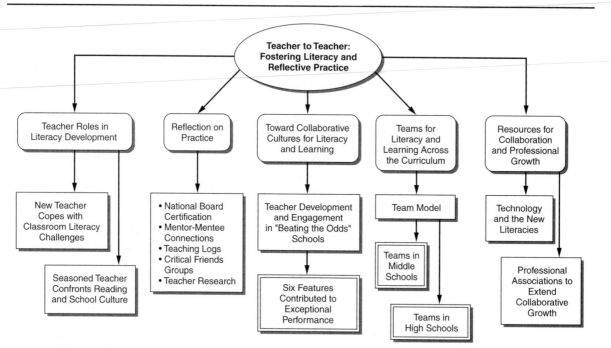

For exercises to clarify your understanding of the chapter content, visit the self-assessments for Chapter 12 on our Companion Website at www.prenhall.com/unrau

# References

Baumann, J., & Duffy-Hester, A. (2000). Making sense of classroom worlds: Methodology in teacher research. In M. Kamil, P. Mosenthal, P. D. Pearson, & R. Barr (Eds.), *Handbook of reading research* (Vol. 3, pp. 77–98). Mahwah, NJ: Erlbaum.

Carnegie Council on Adolescent Development. (1989). *Turning points: Preparing American youth for the 21st century.* The Report of the Task Force on Education of Young Adolescents. New York: Carnegie Corporation of New York.

Costa, A., & Kallick, B. (1993, October). Through the lens of a critical friend. *Educational Leadership, 51*(2), 49–51.

Crowley, P. (1988). Ask something. In C. Gilles, M. Bixby, P. Crowley, S. R. Crenshaw, M. Henrichs, F. E. Reynolds, & D. Pyle (Eds.), *Whole language strategies for secondary students* (p. 47). New York: Richard C. Owens.

Erb, T. O., & Stevenson, C. (1999). From faith to facts: *Turning Points* in action—What difference does teaming make? *Middle School Journal, 30*(3), 47–50.

Felner, R. D., Jackson, A. W., Kasak, D., Mulhall, P., Brand, S., & Flowers, N. (1997). The impact of school reform for the middle years: Longitudinal study of a network engaged in *Turning Points*–based comprehensive school transformation. *Phi Delta Kappan, 78,* 528–532, 541–550.

Gorman, D. (1998). Self-tuning teachers: Using reflective journals in writing classes. *Journal of Adolescent and Adult Literacy, 41*(6), 434–442.

Jackson, A. W., & Davis, G. A. (2000). *Turning points 2000: Educating adolescents in the 21st century.* New York: Teachers College Press.

Jankowski, C. G. (2002, March–April). Making the right connections in high school: Developing teaching teams to integrate the curriculum. *The Voice: A Newsletter of the National Writing Project, 7*(2), 18–19.

Langer, J. (2000). Excellence in English in middle and high school: How teachers' professional lives support student achievement. *American Educational Research Journal, 37*(2), 397–439.

Langer, J. (2001). Beating the odds: Teaching middle and high school students to read and write well. *American Educational Research Journal, 38*(4), 837–880.

Leu, D. J. (2002). The new literacies: Research on reading instruction with the Internet. In A. Farstrup & S. J. Samuels (Eds.), *What research has to say about reading instruction,* (3rd edition, pp. 310–336). Newark, DE: International Reading Association.

Lipsitz, J., Mizell, M. H., Jackson, A. W., & Austin, L. M. (1997). Speaking with one voice: A manifesto for middle-grades reform. *Phi Delta Kappan, 78,* 533–540.

Louis, K. S., & Smith, B. (1992). Cultivating teacher engagement: Breaking the iron law of social class. In F. Newmann (Ed.), *Student engagement and achievement in American secondary schools* (pp. 119–152). New York: Teachers College Press.

McLaughlin, M., & Talbert, J. E. (2001). *Professional communities and the work of high school teaching.* Chicago: University of Chicago Press.

Meier, D. (2000). *Will standards save public education?* Boston, MA: Beacon Press.

Nave, W. (2000). *Critical Friends Groups: Their impact on students, teachers, and schools.* Bloomington, IN: National School Reform Faculty Program.

Pilgreen, J. L. (2000). *SSR handbook: How to organize and manage a sustained silent reading program.* Portsmouth, NH: Heinemann.

Pounder, D. G. (1998). *Restructuring schools for collaboration: Promises and pitfalls.* Albany, NY: State University of New York Press.

Schmidt, W. H., McKnight, C. C., & Raizen, S. (1997). *A splintered vision: An investigation of U.S. science and mathematics education.* Dordrecht/Boston/London: Kluwer Academic Publishers.

Schofield, J. W. (1997). Computers and classroom social processes—A review of the literature. *Social Science Computer Review, 15,* 27–39.

Showers, B., Joyce, B., Scanlon, M., & Schnaubelt, C. (1998). A second chance to learn to read. *Educational Leadership, 55*(6), 27–30.

Tomlinson, C. A. (1998). For integration and differentiation choose concepts over topics. *Middle School Journal, 30*(2), 3–8.

Unrau, N. (2003). Lessons learned from MA candidates pursuing National Board Certification. *Issues in Teacher Education, 12*(1), 45–67.

# NAME INDEX

# SUBJECT INDEX